# The Pope Speaks to the
# American Church

# The Pope Speaks to the American Church

John Paul II's Homilies, Speeches,
and Letters to Catholics in
the United States

## Pope John Paul II

Foreword by Bernard Cardinal Law

Prepared by the Cambridge Center for
the Study of Faith and Culture

HarperSanFrancisco
*A Division of* HarperCollins*Publishers*

**The Cambridge Center for the Study of Faith and Culture**

The Cambridge Center for the Study of Faith and Culture, established by Bernard Cardinal Law, is a unique, freestanding Catholic research center.

Its mission is to provide a legitimate, autonomous, intellectual and respected voice for Catholic thought anchored in living Catholic tradition and engaged in interdisciplinary research and articulation of contemporary faith and culture issues.

**Library of Congress Cataloging-in-Publication Data**

John Paul II, Pope.
    The Pope speaks to the American church : John Paul II's homilies, speeches, and letters to Catholics in the United States / John Paul II ; foreword by Bernard Law ; prepared by the Cambridge Center for the Study of Faith and Culture.—1st ed.
      p.  cm.
    ISBN 0-06-064211-4 (alk. paper)
    1. John Paul II, Pope.—Journeys—United States. 2. Catholic Church—Church history—20th century. I. Cambridge Center for the Study of Faith and Culture (Cambridge, Mass.) II. Title.
BX1378.5.J5962 1992
252'.02—dc20                                91–55298
                                                CIP

94  95  96  HAD  10  9  8  7  6  5  4  3  2

This edition is printed on acid-free paper that meets the American National Standards Institute Z39.48 Standard.

# Contents

v

## 1981 and 1984 Visits to Alaska

## 1987 Apostolic Visit

MIAMI
September 10, 1987

## PART II: *AD LIMINA* ADDRESSES TO THE BISHOPS OF THE UNITED STATES

### 1978

## PART III: LETTERS TO THE BISHOPS OF THE UNITED STATES

# Acknowledgments

This volume has been prepared by the Cambridge Center for the Study of Faith and Culture, with the authorization of His Eminence Bernard Cardinal Law. It was directed and completed by Monsignor Richard Malone and Father Stephen DiGiovanni with the assistance of Clair Coleman, Dorothy Smith, Sean Tarrant, Michael Madden, William Mulvey, Sister Madonna Murphy, CSC, and the pastor and staff of Our Lady Help of Christians Parish in Newton, Massachusetts.

Special thanks goes to the Knights of Columbus for their initial generosity and support of the original project completed in 1989.

# Foreword

It is always helpful to see ourselves as others see us. Alexis de Toqueville remains part of a student's standard fare in the study of U. S. history. In focusing on the intersection of faith and culture in the United States, the observations and comments of the Holy Father have a unique importance. The Cambridge Center for the Study of Faith and Culture has rendered a special service by bringing together into one volume the talks of the Holy Father covering two visits to the United States, 1979 and 1987, and two visits with Bishops from the United States, 1983 and 1988. A helpful index has been provided, which unifies the themes separately treated. The words of the Holy Father both strengthen us in the faith and challenge us in the task of evangelizing the culture. Gratitude is due to the Knights of Columbus, who were helpful in the development of this project.

*Bernard Cardinal Law*

# Introduction

This one volume brings together the Holy Father's abundant communications with Catholics and with all persons of good will. This is a unique record, certainly worthy of study and reflection in parishes, religious education classes, courses of spirituality, seminaries and sessions for the formation of those interested in serving the Church.

These texts apply the major points of the Pope's teaching to the circumstances of Catholic life in the United States. They also apply to political life. The Pope, as a former professor of ethics, is an expert at commenting on the moral dimensions of national and world social issues.

John Paul II has made two visits to the United States. During the first, in the fall of 1979, he built his pastoral dialogue with the local Church around a programmatic address to the General Assembly of the United Nations in New York City. During this discourse he stressed the primacy of spiritual and moral values, respect for the inalienable rights of individuals and communities of peoples and the Church's activity aimed at a just and lasting peace based on respect for the dignity of the human person. He stated clearly that "only the safeguarding of this real completeness of rights for every human being without discrimination can ensure peace at its very roots" (Address to the United Nations). The Pope set this vision in a more explicit Christocentric vision that evening in his homily at a Mass celebrated in Yankee Stadium.

Complementing his exhortation of the United Nations, in which he urged that assembly to persevere in its identity, the Pope delivered an address to priests in Philadelphia on October 4, 1979, and to the bishops of the United States in Chicago the following day, exhorting them to persevere in their God-given identity.

Since this happened to be the Pope's first visit, he unveiled his pastoral program for Catholics in the United States in these major talks and in other shorter talks along the way. I single out his talks to the youth and to The Catholic University, subjects of great obvious personal interest to this former student of the University of Crakow and professor of the University of Lublin.

Since Pope John Paul II's visit coincided with Pro-Life Day in 1979, his last address during that trip was a rousing talk on marriage, family and human life, given on the Capital Mall on the evening of October 7, 1979.

John Paul's second visit in 1987 was intended to cover the parts of the United States he had not yet seen during his first visit—the South, Louisiana, Texas, the Southwest, California and Detroit.

This time the element of dialogue was built into the Pope's visit. This was an important element in the meeting in Miami with the priests, in Los Angeles with the bishops, in San Antonio with the Hispanic communities and in San Francisco with the laity. The Holy Father deals with themes of great importance for these sectors of the Church. One definitely feels that the Pope is acquainted with the United States, and he deals with a broad spectrum of Christian social and personal issues from the point of view of a father who is located at the heart of a universal family and who revels in the pluralism of that family. This gives him the advantage of a broader perspective in which to appreciate our strengths and to catch our blind spots.

The third section of this book brings to the reader the sets of instructions that mark the visits of the American bishops to Rome. The bishops are accountable to the Pope and to the heads of the offices who work with the Pope, so they meet with them at regular five-year intervals. The bishops prepare a written report on the state of their Dioceses during the five years preceding the meeting. They then travel to Rome for an oral discussion of these reports. The technical term for these visits is *ad limina,* that is, a visit to the thresholds (*limina*) of the tombs of the Apostles Peter and Paul, upon whom our Church was founded by Christ, and to the present-day Successor of Peter, the Bishop of Rome. The American bishops made formal visits in 1983 and in 1988. During these visits the Holy Father renewed his interest in particular points of pastoral life. The richness of Catholic life embraces this interaction between the Pope and the bishops.

In using this book, the reader will note that the Holy Father offers a consistent vision of Christian and human life. While we applaud his campaign for human rights and his attention to the oppressed in our society, we cannot ignore the fact that the teaching on sexual ethics and the protection of innocent human life at all stages flows from the same vision of the infinite dignity of the human person, fruit of a special act of love on God's part, redeemed by God's Son, Jesus Christ, endowed with a conscience and freedom of choice, and destined for eternal happiness with God.

It is John Paul's religious faith that inspires both aspects of the Holy Father's vision. In this practical American application we have the unique chance to see how the Pope articulates this vision in the face of the challenges to faith that come from our American way of life. The Holy Father never tires of calling our attention to Christ as the source of this Christian personalism. Through the sending of his Son as a human being into the world, God gave human life the dimension that he intended it to have from its first creation. Our happiness is found in taking up this key to the mystery of the human person to unlock the mystery of our current personal and social enigmas.

—*Monsignor Richard Malone*

Part I

---

# Apostolic Visits to the United States

# 1979 Apostolic Visit

## October 1 to October 8

### OCTOBER 1, 1979

### 1. ARRIVAL IN BOSTON

*Praised be Jesus Christ!*

It is a great joy for me to be in the United States of America, to begin my pastoral visit to the Catholic Church in this land, and at the same time to greet all the American people, of every race, color and creed.

#### Gratitude to President Carter and to the Bishops

I am grateful for the cordial welcome given me on behalf of President Carter, whom I thank most sincerely for his invitation to the United States. I am looking forward to meeting the president after my visit to the United Nations.

My thanks go also to the Cardinal Archbishop of Boston, who in this historic city offers me the first hospitality of this country. I am grateful to the Episcopal Conference and to all the individual Bishops who have so kindly asked me to come. My only regret is that I cannot accept all the invitations extended to me by religious and civil officials, by individuals, families and groups.

#### Comes with Sentiments of Friendship and Esteem

From so many quarters—Catholics, Protestants and Jews—America has opened her heart to me. And on my part I come to you—America—with sentiments of friendship, reverence and esteem. I come as one who already knows you and loves you, as one who wishes you to fulfill completely your noble destiny of service to the world. Once again I can now admire firsthand the beauty of this vast land stretching between two oceans; once again I am experiencing the warm hospitality of the American people.

### Greetings to All Americans

Although it is not possible for me to enter into every home, to greet personally every man and woman, to caress every child in whose eyes is reflected the innocence of love—still, I feel close to all of you, and you are all in my prayers.

Permit me to express my sentiments in the lyrics of your own song:

"America! America! God shed his grace on thee, And crown thy good with brotherhood, From sea to shining sea."

And may the peace of the Lord be with you always—America!

## 2. IN HOLY CROSS CATHEDRAL

Dear Cardinal Medeiros, dear Brothers and Sisters in Christ,

### Joy to Meet with the Catholic Community of Boston

On the first day of my pastoral visit to the United States of America, it is a great joy for me to come to this city of Boston, and in this Cathedral, and later tonight on the Common, to be able to meet with the Catholic community. It is the first time in history that a Successor of Peter is received in your midst. On this wonderful occasion I wish to render homage to the Most Holy Trinity, in whose name I have come. And I make my own the greeting of the Apostle Paul to the Corinthians: "To you who have been consecrated in Christ Jesus and called to be a holy people, and to all those who, wherever they may be, call on the name of our Lord Jesus Christ, their Lord and ours. Grace and peace from God our Father and the Lord Jesus Christ" (1 Cor. 1:2–3).

My cordial thanks go to you, Cardinal Medeiros, Archbishop of Boston, for your welcome today. In your Cathedral Church, I am happy to renew to you the expression of my deep esteem and friendship. Warm greetings also to the Auxiliary Bishops and to all the clergy, both diocesan and religious: you who are my brother priests in virtue of the Sacrament of Holy Orders. Through your priesthood, you are also God's gift to the Christian community. Because you are servants of the gospel, you will always be close to the people and their problems. Because you share in the Priesthood of Christ, your presence in the world shall always be marked by Christ's zeal, for he set you apart so that you might build up his Body, the Church (see Eph. 4:12).

I wish to extend a special blessing to you Religious, both Religious brothers and sisters, who have consecrated your lives to Jesus Christ. May you always find joy in his love. And to all of you, the laity of this Diocese, who are united with the cardinal and the clergy in a common mission, I open my heart in love and trust. You are the workers for evangelization in the realities of daily life, and you give witness to the love of Christ in the service that you give to all your fellow men and women, beginning with your own families.

## Remain United in Jesus Christ and in His Church

To all I want to say how happy I am to be in your midst. I pray for each one of you, asking you to remain always united in Jesus Christ and his Church, so that together we may "display to the world our unity in proclaiming the mystery of Christ, in revealing the divine dimension and also the human dimension of the Redemption, and in struggling with unwearying perseverance for the dignity that each human being has reached and can continually reach in Christ" (*Redemptor Hominis,* 11).

May this Cathedral, dedicated to the Holy Cross of Jesus, always be a reminder of our calling to greatness, for through the mystery of the Incarnation and of the redeeming Sacrifice of Jesus on the Cross we share in "the unsearchable riches of Christ" (Eph. 3:8).

From this Cathedral I send my greeting to all the people of this city of Boston: to those in particular who are, in one way or another, burdened by suffering; to the sick and the bedridden; to those whom society seems to have left by the wayside, and those who have lost faith in God and in their fellow human beings. To all I have come with a message of hope and peace—the hope and peace of Jesus Christ, for whom every human being is of immense value and dignity, and in whom are found all the treasures of justice and love.

## Greetings to the Community of Boston

In the city of Boston I am greeting a community that through the many upheavals of history has always been able to change and yet to remain true to itself— a community where people of all backgrounds, creeds, races and convictions have provided workable solutions to problems and have created a home where all people can be respected in their human dignity. For the honor of all the citizens of Boston, who have inherited a tradition of fraternal love and concern, may I recall what one of the founders of this city told his fellow settlers as they were aboard a ship en route to their new home in America: "We must love one another with a pure heart fervently, we must bear one another's burdens." These simple words explain so much of the meaning of life—our life as brothers and sisters in our Lord Jesus Christ.

May God's peace descend on this city of Boston and bring joy to every conscience and joy to every heart!

## 3. HOMILY ON THE BOSTON COMMON

Dear Brothers and Sisters, dear Young People of America,

1. Earlier today, I set foot on the soil of the United States of America. In the name of Christ I begin a pastoral journey that will take me to several of your cities. At the beginning of this year, I had the occasion to greet this continent and its people from a place where Christopher Columbus landed; today I stand at this gateway to the United States, and again I greet all of America. For its people, wherever they are, have a special place in the love of the Pope.

### As Successor of Peter and Pilgrim of Faith

I come to the United States of America as Successor of Peter and as a pilgrim of faith. It gives me great joy to be able to make this visit. And so my esteem and affection go out to all the people of this land. I greet all Americans without distinction; I want to meet you and tell you all—men and women of all creeds and ethnic origins, children and youth, fathers and mothers, the sick and the elderly—that God loves you, that he has given you a dignity as human beings that is beyond compare. I want to tell everyone that the Pope is your friend and a servant of your humanity. On this first day of my visit, I wish to express my esteem and love for America itself, for the experience that began two centuries ago and that carries the name "United States of America"; for the past achievements of this land and for its dedication to a more just and human future; for the generosity with which this country has offered shelter, freedom and a chance for betterment to all who have come to its shores; and for the human solidarity that impels you to collaborate with all other nations so that freedom may be safeguarded and full human advancement made possible. I greet you, America the beautiful!

### Comes to Address the United Nations

2. I am here because I wanted to respond to the invitation which the secretary-general of the United Nations Organization first addressed to me. Tomorrow I shall have the honor, as guest of the United Nations, to go to this supreme international forum of nations, and to deliver an address to the General Assembly: to make a plea to the whole world for justice and peace—a plea in defense of the unique dignity of every human being. I feel highly honored by the invitation of the United Nations secretary-general. At the same time I am conscious of the greatness and importance of the challenge that this invitation brings with it. I have been convinced from the very first that this invitation by the United Nations should be accepted by me *as Bishop of Rome and Pastor of the universal Church* of Christ. And so I express my deep gratitude also to the Hierarchy of the Church in the United States, who joined in the initiative of the United Nations. I have received many invitations from individual Dioceses and from different regions of this country, as well as from Canada. I deeply

regret that I am unable to accept all the invitations; I would willingly make a pastoral visit everywhere, if it were possible. My pilgrimage to Ireland on the occasion of the centenary of the Shrine of Our Lady at Knock constituted a fitting introduction to my visit with you. I sincerely hope that my whole visit in the United States will be seen in the light of the Second Vatican Council's *Constitution on the Church in the Modern World*.

And tonight I am deeply pleased to be with you on Boston Common. In you I greet the city of Boston and all its people, as well as the commonwealth of Massachusetts and all its civil authorities. With special warmth, I greet here Cardinal Medeiros and the whole Archdiocese of Boston. A special remembrance links me with the city, for three years ago, at the invitation of its Divinity School, I had the opportunity to speak at the University of Harvard. As I recall this memorable event, I wish to express once again my gratitude to the authorities of Harvard and to the dean of the Divinity School for that exceptionally valuable opportunity.

## A Special Word to Young People

3. During my first visit in the United States as Pope, on the eve of my visit to the United Nations Organization, I now wish to speak a special word to young people that are gathered here.

Tonight, in a very special way, I hold out my hands to the youth of America. In Mexico City and Guadalajara I met the youth of Latin America. In Warsaw and Cracow I met the youth of Poland. In Rome I meet frequently groups of young people from Italy and from all over the world. Yesterday I met the youth of Ireland in Galway. And now with great joy I meet you. For me, each one of these meetings is a new discovery. Again and again I find in young people the joy and enthusiasm of life, a searching for truth and for the deeper meaning of the existence that unfolds before them in all its attraction and potential.

## Recalls Jesus' Conversation with a Young Man

4. Tonight I want to repeat what I keep telling youth: you are the future of the world, and "the day of tomorrow belongs to you." I want to remind you of the encounters that Jesus himself had with the youth of his day. The Gospels preserve for us a striking account of a conversation Jesus had with a young man. We read there that the young man put to Christ one of the fundamental questions that youth everywhere ask: "What must I do . . . ?" (Mk. 10:17), and he received a precise and penetrating answer: "Then, Jesus looked at him with love and told him . . . Come and follow me" (Mk. 10:21). But see what happens: the young man, who had shown such interest in the fundamental question, "went away sad, for he had many possessions" (Mk. 10:22). Yes, he went away, and—as can be deduced from the context—he refused to accept the call of Christ.

### In Your Openness to Truth, Goodness and Beauty
### You Can Find Yourselves and Meet Jesus

This deeply penetrating event, in its concise eloquence, expresses a great lesson in a few words: it touches upon substantial problems and basic questions that have in no way lost their relevance. Everywhere young people are asking important questions—questions on the meaning of life, on the right way to live, on the true scale of values: "What must I do . . . ?" "What must I do to share in everlasting life?" This questioning bears witness to your thoughts, your consciences, your hearts and wills. This questioning tells the world that you, young people, carry within yourselves a special openness with regard to what is good and what is true. This openness is, in a sense, a "revelation" of the human spirit. And in this openness to truth, to goodness and to beauty, each one of you can find yourself; indeed, in this openness you can all experience in some measure what the young man in the Gospel experienced: "Jesus looked at him with love" (Mk. 10:21).

### Heed the Call of Christ

5. To each one of you I say therefore: heed the call of Christ when you hear him saying to you: "Follow me!" Walk in my path! Stand by my side! Remain in my love! There is a choice to be made: a choice for Christ and his way of life, and his commandment of love.

The message of love that Christ brought is always important, always relevant. It is not difficult to see how today's world, despite its beauty and grandeur, despite the conquests of science and technology, despite the refined and abundant material goods that it offers, is yearning for more truth, for more love, for more joy. And all of this is found in Christ and in his way of life.

### Reveal the True Meaning of Life
### in the Option of Love, Not Escape

Do I then make a mistake when I tell you, Catholic youth, that it is part of your task in the world and the Church to reveal the true meaning of life where hatred, neglect or selfishness threaten to take over the world? Faced with problems and disappointments, many people will try to escape from their responsibility: escape in selfishness, escape in sexual pleasure, escape in drugs, escape in violence, escape in indifference and cynical attitudes. But today, I propose to you the option of love, which is the opposite of escape. If you really accept that love from Christ, it will lead you to God. Perhaps in the priesthood or religious life; perhaps in some special service to your brothers and sisters: especially to the needy, the poor, the lonely, the abandoned, those whose rights have been trampled upon, or those whose basic needs have not been provided for. Whatever you make of your life, let it be something that reflects the love of Christ. The whole People of God will be all the richer because of the diversity of your commitments. In whatever you do, remember that Christ is calling you, in one way or another, to the service of love: the love of God and of your neighbor.

### Possessions Become Obstacles to Love

6. And now coming back to the story of the young man in the Gospels, we see that he heard the call—"Follow me"—but that he "went away sad, for he had many possessions."

The sadness of the young man makes us reflect. We could be tempted to think that many possessions, many of the goods of this world, can bring happiness. We see instead in the case of the young man in the Gospel that his many possessions had become an obstacle to accepting the call of Jesus to follow him. He was not ready to say *yes* to Jesus and *no* to self, to say *yes* to love and *no* to escape.

### Love Demands Effort, Commitment to God's Will, Discipline

Real love is demanding. I would fail in my mission if I did not clearly tell you so. For it was Jesus—our Jesus himself—who said: "You are my friends if you do what I command you" (Jn. 15:14). Love demands effort and a personal commitment to the will of God. It means discipline and sacrifice, but it also means joy and human fulfillment.

### Answer Christ's Call, Resist Temptations and Fads

Dear young people: Do not be afraid of honest effort and honest work; do not be afraid of the truth. With Christ's help, and through prayer, you can answer his call, resisting temptations and fads, and every form of mass manipulation. Open your hearts to the Christ of the Gospels—to his love and his truth and his joy. Do not go away sad!

### Pope's Mission Is to Tell Everyone to Follow Christ

And, as a last word to all of you who listen to me tonight, I would say this: the reason for my mission, for my journey through the United States, is to tell you, to tell everyone—young and old alike—to say to everyone in the name of Christ: "Come and follow me!"

Follow Christ! You who are married: share your love and your burdens with each other; respect the human dignity of your spouse; accept joyfully the life that God gives through you; make your marriage stable and secure for your children's sake.

Follow Christ! You who are single or who are preparing for marriage. Follow Christ! You who are young or old. Follow Christ! You who are sick or aging; who are suffering or in pain. You who feel the need for healing, the need for love, the need for a friend—follow Christ!

To all of you I extend—in the name of Christ—the call, the invitation, the plea: "Come and follow me." This is why I have come to America, and why I have come to Boston tonight: to call you to Christ—to call all of you and each of you to live in his love, today and forever. Amen!

## OCTOBER 2, 1979

## 4. ARRIVAL AT LA GUARDIA AIRPORT

Mr. Secretary-General, Ladies and Gentlemen,

### Gratitude for Invitation to the U.N.

I reply with deep gratitude to the greetings of the secretary-general of the United Nations Organization. I have looked forward to this moment since the day he extended to me, immediately after the beginning of my pontificate, the invitation to address the Thirty-fourth General Assembly. Your kind initiative, that honors me greatly, was thus at the basis of the journey that has taken me first to Ireland and that I shall continue in the United States of America.

Your organization has a special significance for the whole world, for in it the needs and the aspirations of all the people of our planet come together. The supreme international forum that it is brings together the efforts and the determination of all men and women of good will, who have resolved to honor the pledge that the founders of the United Nations made thirty-four years ago and inscribed in the first article of the charter: to work together to harmonize the actions of the nations in the attainment of international peace and security, to develop friendly relations among nations, to achieve international cooperation, and to promote respect for human rights and for fundamental freedoms for all, without distinction as to race, sex, language or religion.

### Expresses Esteem for Role of the U.N.

The very first day after the solemn beginning of my ministry as Supreme Pastor of the Catholic Church, in addressing the representatives of the states and the international organizations, I took the opportunity to express my esteem for the important role of the international organizations, and of the United Nations in particular. Here I wish to state again how greatly I value your institution. For as I stated on that other occasion, "You are the first to be convinced that there can be no true human progress or lasting peace without the courageous, loyal and disinterested pursuit of growing cooperation and unity among peoples" (October 23, 1978).

### Basis of Common Service: Dignity of Human Person

Yes, the conviction that unites us in this common service of humanity is that, at the basis of all efforts, there must be "the dignity and worth of the human person"

(Charter, Preamble). It is likewise the human person—every individual—who must make the aims of your organization come true in the concrete realities of friendly relations, of tolerance, of freedom and harmony for all. Decisions and resolutions can be adopted by the representatives of the nations, but their true embodiment will have to be brought about by the people.

Through you, then, Mr. Secretary-General and distinguished ladies and gentlemen, at the beginning of my visit to the United Nations, I greet all the men, women and children of the countries that are represented at the United Nations. May the hopes that they place in the efforts and in the solidarity that link us all never be disappointed. May they experience in the achievements of the United Nations the fact that there is only one world, and that it is the home of all.

Thank you, and may God sustain you in your high ideals.

## 5. ADDRESS TO THE THIRTY-FOURTH GENERAL ASSEMBLY OF THE UNITED NATIONS ORGANIZATION

Mr. President,

1. I desire to express my gratitude to the General Assembly of the United Nations, which I am permitted today to participate in and to address. My thanks go in the first place to the secretary-general of the United Nations Organization, Dr. Kurt Waldheim. Last autumn, soon after my election to the Chair of Saint Peter, he invited me to make this visit, and he renewed his invitation in the course of our meeting in Rome last May. From the first moment I felt greatly honored and deeply obliged. And today, before this distinguished assembly, I also thank you, Mr. President, who have so kindly welcomed me and invited me to speak.

### Special Bond of Cooperation Links Apostolic See and U.N.

2. *The formal reason for my intervention* today is, without any question, the special bond of cooperation that links the Apostolic See with the United Nations Organization, as is shown by the presence of the Holy See's Permanent Observer to this organization. The existence of this bond, which is held in high esteem by the Holy See, rests on the sovereignty with which the Apostolic See has been endowed for many centuries. The territorial extent of that sovereignty is limited to the small state of Vatican City, but the sovereignty itself is warranted by the need of the papacy to exercise its mission in full freedom, and to be able to deal with any interlocutor, whether a government or an international organization, without dependence on other sovereignties. Of course the nature and aims of the spiritual mission of the Apostolic See and the Church make their participation in the tasks and activities of the United Nations Organization very different from that of the states, which are communities in the political and temporal sense.

## The Apostolic See Has Expressed Agreement with the
## Significance of This Historical Forum

3. Besides attaching great importance to its collaboration with the United Nations Organization, *the Apostolic See has always, since the foundation of your organization, expressed its esteem and its agreement* with the historic significance of this supreme forum for the international life of humanity today. It also never ceases to support your organization's functions and initiatives, which are aimed at peaceful coexistence and collaboration between nations. There are many proofs of this. In the more than thirty years of the existence of the United Nations Organization, it has received much attention in papal messages and encyclicals, in documents of the Catholic Episcopate, and likewise in the Second Vatican Council. Pope John XXIII and Pope Paul VI looked with confidence on your important institution as an eloquent and promising sign of our times. He who is now addressing you has, since the first months of his pontificate, several times expressed the same confidence and conviction as his predecessors.

## This Confidence Is Rooted in the Religious and
## Moral Character of the Church's Mission

4. This confidence and conviction on the part of the Apostolic See is the result, as I have said, not of merely political reasons but of the religious and moral character of *the mission of the Roman Catholic Church.* As a universal community embracing faithful belonging to almost all countries and continents, nations, peoples, races, languages and cultures, the Church is deeply interested in the existence and activity of *the organization* whose very name tells us that it *unites and associates* nations and states. It unites and associates: it does not divide and oppose. It seeks out the ways for understanding and peaceful collaboration, and endeavors with the means at its disposal and the methods in its power to exclude war, division and mutual destruction within the great family of humanity today.

## The U.N. Respects the Moral and
## Religious Dimension of Human Problems

5. This is the real reason, *the essential reason,* for my presence among you, and I wish to thank this distinguished assembly for giving consideration to this reason, which can make my presence among you in some way useful. It is certainly a highly significant fact that among the representatives of the states, whose raison d'être is the sovereignty of powers linked with territory and people, there is also today the representative of the Apostolic See of the Catholic Church. This Church is the Church of Jesus Christ, who declared before the tribunal of the Roman judge Pilate that he was a king, but with a kingdom not of this world (see Jn. 18:36–37). When he was then asked about the reason for the existence of his kingdom among men, he explained: "For this I was born, and for this I have come into the world, to witness to

the truth" (Jn. 18:37). Here, *before the representatives of the states,* I wish not only to thank you but also to offer my special *congratulations,* since the invitation extended to the Pope to speak in your assembly shows that *the United Nations Organization accepts and respects* the religious and moral dimension of those human problems that the Church attends to, in view of the message of truth and love that it is her duty to bring to the world. The questions that concern your functions and receive your attention—as is indicated by the vast organic complex of institutions and activities that are part of or collaborate with the United Nations, especially in the fields of culture, health, food, labor and the peaceful uses of nuclear energy—certainly make it essential for us *to meet in the name of man in his wholeness,* in all the fullness and manifold riches of his spiritual and material existence, as I have stated in my encyclical *Redemptor Hominis,* the first of my pontificate.

### Service to the Human Person Justifies Political Action

6. Now, availing myself of the solemn occasion of my meeting with the representatives of the nations of the earth, I wish above all to send my greetings to all the men and women living on this planet. To every man and every woman, without exception whatever. Every human being living on earth is a member of a civil society, of a nation, many of them represented here. Each one of you, distinguished ladies and gentlemen, represents a particular state, system and political structure, but what you represent above all are *individual human beings;* you are all *representatives of men and women, of practically all the people of the world,* individual men and women, communities and peoples who are living the present phase of their own history and who are also part of the history of humanity as a whole, each of them a subject endowed with dignity as a human person, with his or her own culture, experiences and aspirations, tensions and sufferings, and legitimate expectations. This relationship is what provides the reason for *all political activity,* whether national or international, for in the final analysis this activity comes *from man,* is exercised *by man* and *for man.* And if political activity is cut off from this fundamental relationship and finality, if it becomes in a way its own end, it loses much of its reason to exist. Even more, it can also give rise to a specific alienation; it can become extraneous to man; it can come to contradict humanity itself. In reality, what justifies the existence of any political activity is service to man, concerned and responsible attention to the essential problems and duties of his earthly existence in its social dimension and significance, on which also the good of each person depends.

### The Progress of Humanity Is Measured by the Primacy Given to Spiritual Values and by Progress of Moral Life

7. I ask you, ladies and gentlemen, to excuse me for speaking of questions that are certainly self-evident for you. But it does not seem pointless to speak of them, since the most frequent pitfall for human activities is the possibility of losing sight, while performing them, of *the clearest truths, the most elementary principles.*

I would like to express the wish that, in view of its universal character, the United Nations Organization will never cease to be the forum, *the high tribune, from which all man's problems are appraised in truth and justice.* It was in the name of this inspiration, it was through this historic stimulus, that on June 26, 1945, toward the end of the terrible Second World War, the Charter of the United Nations was signed, and on the following October 24 your organization began its life. Soon after, on December 10, 1948, came its fundamental document, the *Universal Declaration of Human Rights,* the rights of the human being in his universal value. This document is a milestone on the long and difficult path of the human race. The progress of humanity must be measured not only by *the progress of science and technology,* which shows man's uniqueness with regard to nature, but also and chiefly by *the primacy given to spiritual values* and by *the progress of moral life.* In this field is manifested the full dominion of reason, through truth, in the behavior of the individual and of society, and also the control of reason over nature; and thus human conscience quietly triumphs, as was expressed in the ancient saying: *Genus humanum arte et ratione vivit.*

It was when technology was being directed in its one-sided progress toward goals of war, hegemony and conquest, so that man might kill man and nation destroy nation by depriving it of its liberty and the right to exist—and I still have before my mind the image of the Second World War in Europe, which began forty years ago on September 1, 1939, with the invasion of Poland and ended on May 9, 1945—it was precisely then that the United Nations Organization arose. And three years later the document appeared which, as I have said, must be considered a real milestone on the path of the moral progress of humanity—the *Universal Declaration of Human Rights.* The governments and states of the world have understood that, if they are not to attack and destroy each other, *they must unite.* The real way, the fundamental *way to this is through each human being,* through the definition and recognition of and respect for the inalienable rights of individuals and of the communities of peoples.

## Memory of Extermination Camps: A Warning Sign

8. Today, forty years after the outbreak of the Second World War, I wish to recall the whole of the experience by individuals and nations that were sustained by a generation that is largely still alive. I had occasion not long ago to reflect again on some of those experiences, in one of the places that are most distressing and overflowing with contempt for man and his fundamental rights—the extermination camp of *Oświęcim* (Auschwitz), which I visited during my pilgrimage to Poland last June. This infamous place is unfortunately only one of the many scattered over the continent of Europe. But the memory of even one should be *a warning sign* on the path of humanity today, in order that *every kind of concentration* camp anywhere on earth may once and for all *be done away with.* And everything that recalls those horrible experiences should also disappear for ever from the lives of nations and states, everything that is a continuation of those experiences under different forms, namely, the various kinds of torture and oppression, either physical or moral, carried out under

any system, in any land; this phenomenon is all the more distressing if it occurs under the pretext of internal "security" or the need to preserve an apparent peace.

## The Universal Declaration of Human Rights

9. You will forgive me, ladies and gentlemen, for evoking this memory. But I would be untrue to the history of this century, I would be dishonest with regard to the great cause of man, which we all wish to serve, if I should keep silent, I who come from the country on whose living body *Oświęcim* was at one time constructed. But my purpose in evoking this memory is above all to show what painful experiences and sufferings by millions of people gave rise to the Universal Declaration of Human Rights, which has been placed as the basic inspiration and *cornerstone* of the United Nations Organization. This declaration was paid for by millions of our brothers and sisters at the cost of their suffering and sacrifice, brought about by the brutalization that darkened and made insensitive the human consciences of their oppressors and of those who carried out a real genocide. This price cannot have been paid in vain! The Universal Declaration of Human Rights—with its train of many declarations and conventions on highly important aspects of human rights, in favor of children, of women, of equality between races, and especially the two international covenants on economic, social and cultural rights and on civil and political rights—must remain the basic value in the United Nations Organization with which the consciences of its members must be confronted and from which they must draw continual inspiration. If the truths and principles contained in this document were to be forgotten or ignored and were thus to lose the genuine self-evidence that distinguished them at the time they were brought painfully to birth, then the noble purpose of the United Nations Organization could be faced with the threat of a new destruction. This is what would happen if the simple yet powerful eloquence of the Universal Declaration of Human Rights were decisively subjugated by what is wrongly called political interest, but often really means no more than one-sided gain and advantage to the detriment of others, or a thirst for power regardless of the needs of others—everything which by its nature is opposed to the spirit of the declaration. "Political interest" understood in this sense, if you will pardon me, ladies and gentlemen, dishonors the noble and difficult mission of your service for the good of your countries and of all humanity.

## The Catholic Church Preaches, Prays and Educates for Peace

10. Fourteen years ago my great predecessor *Pope Paul VI* spoke from this podium. He spoke memorable words, which I desire to repeat today: "No more war, war never again! Never one against the other," or even "one above the other," but always, on every occasion, "with each other."

Paul VI was a tireless servant of the cause of peace. I wish to follow him with all my strength and continue his service. The Catholic Church in every place on earth proclaims a message of peace, prays for peace, *educates for peace*. This purpose is also shared by the representatives and followers of other churches and communities and of other religions of the world, and they have pledged themselves to it. In union with efforts by all people of good will, this work is certainly bearing fruit. Nevertheless, we are continually troubled by the armed conflicts that break out from time to time. How grateful we are to the Lord when a direct intervention succeeds in avoiding such a conflict, as in the case of the tension that last year threatened Argentina and Chile.

### Hopes for Solution to Mideast Crises

It is my fervent hope that a solution also to the Middle East crises may draw nearer. While being prepared to recognize the value of any concrete step or attempt made to settle the conflict, I want to recall that it would have no value if it did not truly represent the "first stone" of a general overall peace in the area, a peace that, being necessarily based on equitable recognition of the rights of all, cannot fail to include the consideration and just settlement of the Palestinian question. Connected with this question is that of the tranquillity, independence and territorial integrity of Lebanon within the formula that has made it an example of peaceful and mutually fruitful coexistence between distinct communities, a formula that I hope will, in the common interest, be maintained, with the adjustments required by the developments of the situation. I also hope for a special statute that, under international guarantees—as my predecessor Paul VI indicated—would respect the particular nature of Jerusalem, a heritage sacred to the veneration of millions of believers of the three great monotheistic religions, Judaism, Christianity and Islam.

We are troubled also by reports of development of weaponry exceeding in quality and size the means of war and destruction ever known before. In this field also we applaud the decisions and agreements aimed at reducing the arms race. Nevertheless, the life of humanity today is seriously endangered by the threat of destruction and by the risk arising even from accepting certain "tranquilizing" reports. And the resistance to actual concrete proposals of real disarmament, such as those called for by this assembly in a special session last year, shows that together with the will for peace that all profess and that most desire there is also in existence—perhaps in latent or conditional form but nonetheless real—the contrary and the negation of this will. The continual *preparations for war* demonstrated by the production of ever more numerous, powerful and sophisticated weapons in various countries show that there is a desire to be ready for war, and *being ready* means *being able to start it;* it also means taking the risk that sometime, somewhere, somehow, someone can set in motion the terrible mechanism of general destruction.

### The Spirit of War Springs Up
### Where Human Rights Are Violated

11. It is therefore necessary to make a continuing and even more energetic effort to do away with the very possibility of provoking war, and to make such catastrophes

impossible by influencing the attitudes and convictions, the very intentions and aspirations of governments and peoples. This duty, kept constantly in mind by the United Nations Organization and each of its institutions, must also be a duty for every society, every regime, every government. This task is certainly served by initiatives aimed at international cooperation for the fostering of development. As Paul VI said at the end of his encyclical *Populorum Progressio,* "If the new name for peace is development, who would not wish to labor for it with all his powers?" However, this task must also be served by constant reflection and activity aimed at *discovering the very roots of hatred,* destructiveness and contempt—the roots of everything that produces the temptation to war, not so much in the hearts of the nations as in the inner determination of the systems that decide the history of whole societies. In this titanic labor of building up the peaceful future of our planet, the United Nations Organization has undoubtedly a key function and guiding role, for which it must refer to the just ideals contained in the Universal Declaration of Human Rights. For this declaration has struck a real blow against the many deep roots of war, since the spirit of war, in its basic primordial meaning, *springs up and grows to maturity wherever the inalienable rights of man are violated.*

This is a new and deeply relevant vision of the cause of peace, one that goes deeper and is more radical. It is a vision that sees the genesis, and in a sense the substance, of war in the more complex forms emanating from injustice viewed in all its various aspects: this injustice first attacks human rights and thereby destroys the organic unity of the social order, and it then affects the whole system of international relations. Within the Church's doctrine, the encyclical *Pacem in Terris* by John XXIII provides in synthetic form a view of this matter that is very close to the ideological foundation of the United Nations Organization. This must therefore form the basis to which one must loyally and perseveringly adhere in order to establish true "peace on earth."

## Peace Is Greater than Private Interests

12. By applying this criterion we must diligently examine *which principal tensions* in connection with the inalienable rights of man can weaken the construction of this peace which we all desire so ardently and which is the essential goal of the efforts of the United Nations Organization. It is not easy, but it must be done. Anyone who undertakes it must take up a totally objective position and be guided by sincerity, readiness to acknowledge one's prejudices and mistakes and readiness even to renounce one's own particular interests, including political interests. Peace is something greater and more important than any of these interests. It is by sacrificing these interests for the sake of peace that we serve them best. After all, in whose "political interest" can it ever be to have another war?

Every analysis must necessarily start from the premise that—although each person lives in a particular concrete social and historical context—every human being is endowed with a dignity that must never be lessened, impaired or destroyed but must instead be respected and safeguarded if peace is really to be built up.

## Basic Human Rights Concern Man's Essential Needs

13. In a movement that one hopes will be progressive and continuous, the Universal Declaration of Human Rights and the other international and national juridical instruments are endeavoring to create general awareness of the dignity of the human being and to define at least some of the inalienable rights of man. Permit me to enumerate some of the most important human rights that are universally recognized: the right to life, liberty and security of person; the right to food, clothing, housing, sufficient health care, rest and leisure; the right to freedom of expression, education and culture; the right to freedom of thought, conscience and religion, and the right to manifest one's religion either individually or in community, in public or in private; the right to choose a state of life, to found a family and to enjoy all conditions necessary for family life; the right to property and work, to adequate working conditions and a just wage; the right of assembly and association; the right to freedom of movement, to internal and external migration; the right to nationality and residence; the right to political participation; and the right to participate in the free choice of the political system of the people to which one belongs. All these human rights taken together are in keeping with the substance of the dignity of the human being, understood in his entirety, not as reduced to one dimension only. These rights concern the satisfaction of man's essential needs, the exercise of his freedoms and his relationship with others; but always and everywhere they concern man, they concern man's full human dimension.

## Spiritual Values Are Preeminent

14. Man lives at the same time both in the world of material values and in that of spiritual values. For the individual living and hoping man, his needs, freedoms and relationship with others never concern one sphere of values alone, but belong to both. Material and spiritual realities may be viewed separately in order to understand better that in the concrete human being they are inseparable, and to see that any threat to human rights, whether in the field of material realities or in that of spiritual realities, is equally dangerous for peace, since in every instance it concerns man in his entirety. Permit me, distinguished ladies and gentlemen, to recall a constant rule of the history of humanity, a rule that is implicitly contained in all that I have already stated with regard to integral development and human rights. The rule is based on the relationship between spiritual values and material or economic values. In this relationship, it is the spiritual values that are preeminent, both on account of the nature of these values and also for reasons concerning the good of man. The preeminence of the values of the spirit defines the proper sense of earthly material goods and the way to use them. This preeminence is therefore at the basis of a just peace. It is also a contributing factor to ensuring that material development, technical development and the development of civilization are at the service of what constitutes man. This means enabling man to have full access to truth, to moral development,

and to the complete possibility of enjoying the goods of culture which he has inherited, and of increasing them by his own creativity. It is easy to see that material goods do not have unlimited capacity for satisfying the needs of man: they are not in themselves easily distributed and, in relationship between those who possess and enjoy them and those who are without them, they give rise to tension, dissension and division that will often even turn into open conflict. Spiritual goods, on the other hand, are open to unlimited enjoyment by many at the same time, without diminution of the goods themselves. Indeed, the more people share in such goods, the more they are enjoyed and drawn upon, the more then do those goods show their indestructible and immortal worth. This truth is confirmed, for example, by the works of creativity—I mean by the works of thought, poetry, music, and the figurative arts, fruits of man's spirit.

### Material Gain but Diminished Sensitivity to the Spiritual

15. A critical analysis of our modern civilization shows that in the last hundred years it has contributed as never before to the development of material goods, but that it has also given rise, both in theory and still more in practice, to a series of attitudes in which *sensitivity to the spiritual dimension of human existence is diminished* to a greater or lesser extent, as a result of certain premises which reduce the meaning of human life chiefly to the many different material and economic factors—I mean to the demands of production, the market, consumption, the accumulation of riches or of the growing bureaucracy with which an attempt is made to regulate these very processes. Is this not the result of having subordinated man to one single conception and sphere of values?

### Subordination of the Human Person to Material Goods Leads to War

16. What is the link between these reflections and the cause of peace and war? Since, as I have already stated, material goods by their very nature provoke conditionings and divisions, the struggle to obtain these goods becomes *inevitable in the history of humanity*. If we cultivate this one-sided subordination of man to material goods alone, we shall be incapable of *overcoming this state of need*. We shall be able to attenuate it and avoid it in particular cases, but we shall not succeed in eliminating it systematically and radically, unless we emphasize more and pay greater honor, before everyone's eyes, in the sight of every society, to *the second dimension of the goods of man*: the dimension that does not divide people but puts them into communication with each other, associates them and unites them.

I consider that the famous opening words of the Charter of the United Nations, in which "the peoples of the United Nations, determined to save succeeding generations from the scourge of war," solemnly reaffirmed "faith in fundamental human rights, in the dignity and worth of the human person, in the equal rights of men and women and of nations large and small," are meant to stress this dimension.

Indeed, the fight against incipient wars cannot be carried out on a merely superficial level, by treating the symptoms. It must be done in a radical way, by attacking the causes. The reason I have called attention to the dimension constituted by spiritual realities is my concern for the cause of peace, peace which is built up by men and women uniting around what is most fully and profoundly human, around what raises them above the world about them and determines their indestructible grandeur—indestructible in spite of the death to which everyone on earth is subject. I would like to add that *the Catholic Church* and, I think I can say, the whole of Christianity sees in this very domain *its own particular task*. The Second Vatican Council helped to establish what the Christian faith has in common with the various non-Christian religions in this aspiration. The Church is therefore grateful to all who show respect and good will with regard to this mission of hers and do not impede it or make it difficult. An analysis of the history of mankind, especially at its present stage, shows how important is the duty of revealing more fully the range of the goods that are linked with the spiritual dimension of human existence. It shows how important this task is for building peace and how serious is any threat to human rights. Any violation of them, even in a "peace situation," is a form of warfare against humanity.

It seems that in the modern world there are two main threats. Both concern human rights in the field of international relations and human rights within the individual states or societies.

## Unjust Distribution of Material Goods

17. The first of these systematic threats against human rights is linked in an overall sense with the distribution of material goods. This distribution is frequently unjust both within individual societies and on the planet as a whole. Everyone knows that these goods are given to man not only as nature's bounty: they are enjoyed by him chiefly as the fruit of his many activities, ranging from the simplest manual and physical labor to the most complicated forms of industrial production, and to the highly qualified and specialized research and study. Various forms of *inequality in the possession of material goods,* and in the enjoyment of them, can often be explained by different historical and cultural causes and circumstances. But, while these circumstances can diminish the moral responsibility of people today, they do not prevent the situations of inequality from being marked by injustice and social injury.

People must become aware that economic tensions within countries and in the relationship between states and even between entire continents contain within themselves substantial elements that restrict or violate human rights. Such elements are the exploitation of labor and many other abuses that affect the dignity of the human person. It follows that the fundamental criterion for comparing social, economic and political systems is not, *and cannot be,* the criterion of hegemony and imperialism; it can be, and indeed it must be, *the humanistic criterion,* namely the measure in which each system is really capable of reducing, restraining and eliminating as far as possible the various forms of exploitation of man and of ensuring for him, through work, not only the just distribution of the indispensable material goods, but also a participation, in keeping with his dignity, in the whole process of production and in the social life that grows up around that process. Let us not forget that, although man depends on the resources of the material world for his life, he cannot be their slave, but he must be their master. The words of the book of Genesis, "Fill the earth and subdue it" (Gn. 1:28), are in a sense a primary and essential directive in the field of economy and labor policy.

18. Humanity as a whole, and the individual nations, have certainly made remarkable progress in this field during the last hundred years. But it is a field in which there is never any lack of systematic threats and violations of human rights. Disturbing factors are frequently present in the form of the *frightful disparities* between excessively rich individuals and groups on the one hand, and on the other hand *the majority* made up of the poor or indeed of *the destitute,* who lack food and opportunities for work and education and are in great numbers condemned to hunger and disease. And concern is also caused at times by the radical separation of work from property, by man's indifference to the production enterprise to which he is linked only by a work obligation, without feeling that he is working for a good that will be his or for himself.

It is no secret that the abyss separating the minority of the excessively rich from the multitude of the destitute is a very grave symptom in the life of any society. This must also be said with even greater insistence with regard to the abyss separating countries and regions of the earth. Surely the only way to overcome this serious disparity between areas of satiety and areas of hunger and depression is through coordinated cooperation by all countries. This requires above all else a unity inspired by an authentic perspective of peace. Everything will depend on whether these differences and contrasts in the sphere of the "possession" of goods will be systematically reduced through truly effective means, on whether the belts of hunger, malnutrition, destitution, underdevelopment, disease and illiteracy will disappear from the economic map of the earth, and on whether peaceful cooperation will avoid imposing conditions of exploitation and economic or political dependence, which would only be a form of neocolonialism.

### Injustice in the Field of the Spirit

19. I would now like to draw attention to a *second systematic threat* to man in his inalienable rights in the modern world, a threat which constitutes no less a danger than the first to the cause of peace. I refer to the various forms of injustice in the field of the spirit.

Man can indeed be wounded in his inner relationship with truth, in his conscience, in his most personal belief, in his view of the world, in his religious faith and in the sphere of what are known as civil liberties. Decisive for these last is equality of rights without discrimination on grounds of origin, race, sex, nationality, religion, political convictions and the like. Equality of rights means the exclusion of the various forms of privilege for some and discrimination against others, whether they are people born in the same country or people from different backgrounds of history, nationality, race and ideology. For centuries the thrust of civilization has been in one direction: that of giving the life of individual political societies a form in which there can be *fully safeguarded the objective rights of the spirit, of human conscience and of human creativity, including man's relationship with God.* Yet in spite of this we still see in this field recurring threats and violations, often with no possibility of appealing to a higher authority or of obtaining an effective remedy.

Besides the acceptance of legal formulas safeguarding the principle of the freedom of the human spirit, such as freedom of thought and expression, religious freedom and freedom of conscience, structures of social life often exist in which the practical exercise of these freedoms condemns man, in fact if not formally, to become a second-class or third-class citizen, to see compromised his chances of social advancement, his professional career or his access to certain posts of responsibility, and to lose even the possibility of educating his children freely. It is a question of the highest importance that in internal social life, as well as in international life, *all human beings* in every nation and country *should be able to enjoy effectively their full rights under any political regime or system.*

Only the safeguarding of this real completeness of rights for every human being without discrimination can ensure peace at its very roots.

## Church Teaches Respect for the Rights of Conscience

20. With regard to religious freedom, which I, as Pope, am bound to have particularly at heart, precisely with a view to safeguarding peace, I would like to repeat here, as a contribution to respect for man's spiritual dimension, some principles contained in the Second Vatican Council's Declaration *Dignitatis Humanae:* "In accordance with their dignity, all human beings, because they are persons, that is, beings endowed with reason and free will and therefore bearing personal responsibility, are both impelled by their nature and bound by a moral obligation to seek the truth, especially religious truth. They are also bound to adhere to the truth once they come to know it and to direct their whole lives in accordance with its demands" (*Dignitatis Humanae,* 2).

"The practice of religion of its very nature consists primarily of those voluntary and free internal acts by which a human being directly sets his course towards God. No merely human power can either command or prohibit acts of this kind. But man's social nature itself requires that he give external expression to his internal acts of religion, that he communicate with others in religious matters and that he profess his religion in community" (*Dignitatis Humanae,* 3).

These words touch the very substance of the question. They also show how even the confrontation between *the religious view of the world and the agnostic or even atheistic view,* which is one of the "signs of the times" of the present age, could preserve honest and respectful human dimensions without violating the essential rights of conscience of any man or woman living on earth.

Respect for the dignity of the human person would seem to demand that, when the exact tenor of the exercise of religious freedom is being discussed or determined with a view to national laws or international conventions, the institutions that are by their nature at the service of religion should also be brought in. If this participation is omitted, there is a danger of imposing, in so intimate a field of man's life, rules or restrictions that are opposed to his true religious needs.

## Concern for the Child Is Fundamental

21. The United Nations Organization has proclaimed *1979 the Year of the Child.* In the presence of the representatives of so many nations of the world gathered here, I wish to express the joy that we all find in children, the springtime of life, the anticipation of the future history of each of our present earthly homelands. No country on earth, no political system can think of its own future otherwise than through the image of these new generations that will receive from their parents the manifold heritage of values, duties and aspirations of the nation to which they belong and of the whole human family. Concern for the child, even before birth, from the first moment of conception and then throughout the years of infancy and youth, is the primary and fundamental test of the relationship of one human being to another.

And so what better wish can I express for every nation and the whole of mankind, and for all the children of the world, than *a better future* in which respect for human rights will become a complete reality throughout the third millennium, which is drawing near.

22. But in this perspective we must ask ourselves whether there will continue to accumulate over the heads of this new generation of children the threat of common extermination for which the means are in the hands of the modern states, especially the major world powers. *Are the children to receive the arms race from us* as a necessary inheritance? How are we to explain this unbridled race?

The ancients said: *Si vis pacem, para bellum.* But can our age still really believe that the breathtaking spiral of armaments is at the service of world peace? In alleging the threat of a potential enemy, is it really not rather the intention to keep for oneself a means of threat, in order to get the upper hand with the aid of one's own arsenal of destruction? Here too it is the human dimension of peace that tends to vanish *in favor of ever new possible forms of imperialism.*

It must be our solemn wish here for our children, for the children of all the nations on earth, that this point will never be reached. And for that reason I do not cease to pray to God each day so that in his mercy he may save us from so terrible a day.

23. At the close of this address, I wish to express once more before all the high representatives of the states who are present a word of esteem and deep love for all the peoples, all the nations of the earth, for all human communities. Each one has its

own history and culture. I hope that they will live and grow in the freedom and truth of their own history. For that is the measure of the common good of each one of them. I hope that each person will *live and grow strong with the moral force of the community* that forms its members as citizens. I hope that the state authorities, while respecting the just rights of each citizen, will enjoy the confidence of all for the common good. I hope that all the nations, even the smallest, even those that do not yet enjoy full sovereignty, and those that have been forcibly robbed of it, will meet in full equality with the others in the United Nations Organization. I hope that the United Nations will ever remain the supreme forum of peace and justice, the authentic seat of freedom of peoples and individuals in their longing for a better future.

## 6. ADDRESS TO REPRESENTATIVES OF INTERGOVERNMENTAL AND NONGOVERNMENTAL ORGANIZATIONS TO THE UNITED NATIONS HEADQUARTERS

Ladies and Gentlemen,

It gives me great pleasure to extend my greetings to the representatives of the intergovernmental and nongovernmental organizations who are present here, and to thank you for your cordial welcome.

### Unity in Action

Your presence at the center of the United Nations' activities is a consequence of the growing awareness that the problems of today's world can only be solved when all forces are joined together and directed toward the same common aim. The problems that the human family faces today may seem overwhelming. I for my part am convinced that there is immense potential with which to face them. History tells us that the human race is capable of reacting and of changing direction every time it perceives clearly the warning that it is on the wrong course. You are privileged to witness in this building how the representatives of the nations endeavor to chart a common course in order that life on this planet will be lived in peace, order, justice and progress for all. But you are also aware that every individual must work toward the same end. It is individual actions put together which bring about today and tomorrow the total impact which is either beneficial or harmful for humanity.

The various programs and organizations that exist within the framework of the United Nations Organization, as well as the specialized agencies and other intergovernmental bodies, are an important part of that total effort. In the area of its own specialization—be it food, agriculture, trade, environment, development, science, culture, education, health, disaster relief or the problems of children and refugees—each one of these organizations makes a unique contribution not only to providing for people's wants but also to fostering respect for human dignity and the cause of world peace.

No organization, however, not even the United Nations or any of its specialized agencies, can alone solve the global problems which are constantly brought to its attention, if its concerns are not shared by all the people. It is then the privileged task of the nongovernmental organizations to help bring these concerns into the communities and the homes of the people, and to bring back to the established agencies the priorities and aspirations of the people, so that all the solutions and projects which are envisaged may be truly geared to the needs of the human person.

The delegates who drafted the Charter of the United Nations had a vision of united and cooperating governments, but behind the nations they saw also the individual, and they wanted every human being to be free and to enjoy his or her fundamental rights. This fundamental inspiration must be preserved.

I wish to express my best wishes to all of you here who work together to bring the benefits of concerted action to all parts of the world. My cordial greeting goes to the representatives of the various Protestant, Jewish and Moslem associations, and in a particular way to the representatives of the international Catholic organizations. May your dedication and your moral sense never become blunted by difficulties; may you never lose sight of the ultimate aim of your efforts: to create a world where every human person can live in dignity and loving harmony as a child of God.


## 7. ADDRESS TO THE JOURNALISTS

My dear Friends of the communications media,

It would hardly be possible for me to depart from the United Nations without saying "thank you" from my heart to those who have reported not only this day's events but all the activities of this worthy organization. In this international assembly, you can truly be instruments of peace by being messengers of truth.


### Servants of Truth

You are indeed servants of truth; you are its tireless transmitters, diffusers, defenders. You are dedicated communicators, promoting unity among all nations by sharing truth among all peoples.

If your reporting does not always command the attention you would desire, or if it does not always conclude with the success that you would wish, do not grow discouraged. Be faithful to the truth and to its transmission, for truth endures; truth will not go away. Truth will not pass or change.

And I say to you—take it as my parting word to you—that the service of truth, the service of humanity through the medium of the truth—is something worthy of your best years, your finest talents, your most dedicated efforts. As transmitters of truth, you are instruments of understanding among people and of peace among nations.

May God bless your labors for truth with the fruit of peace. This is my prayer for you, for your families and for those whom you serve as messengers of truth, and as instruments of peace.

## 8. ADDRESS TO THE MEMBERS OF THE STAFF OF THE UNITED NATIONS HEADQUARTERS

Ladies and Gentlemen, dear Friends,

It is with great pleasure that I take this opportunity to greet all the members of the staff of the United Nations headquarters in New York and to reiterate before you my firm belief in the extraordinary value and importance of the role and activities of this international institution, of all its agencies and programs.

### Servants of Unity

When you accepted to serve here, either in study or research, in administrative tasks or in planning, in secretarial or logistical activities, you did so because you believed that your work, often hidden and unnoticed in the complexity of this operation, would constitute a valuable contribution to the aims and objectives of the organization. And rightly so. For the first time in the history of humanity, there exists the possibility for all peoples, through their representatives, to meet constantly with each other in order to exchange views; to confer on and to seek peaceful solutions, effective solutions to the conflicts and problems that are causing suffering in all parts of the world to large numbers of men, women and children. You are part of this great and universal endeavor. You provide the necessary services, information and help that are indispensable for the success of this exciting adventure—you guarantee continuity of action and implementation. Each one of you is a servant of the unity, peace and brotherhood of all men.

Your task is no less important than that of the representatives of the nations of the world, provided you are motivated by the great ideal of world peace and fraternal collaboration between all peoples: what counts is the spirit with which you perform your tasks. Peace and harmony among the nations, the progress of all humanity, the possibility for all men and women to live in dignity and happiness depend on you, on each one of you, and on the tasks that you perform here.

### The Carvers of Stone

The builders of the pyramids in Egypt and Mexico, of the temples in Asia, of the cathedrals in Europe were not only the architects who laid out the designs, or those who provided financing, but also, and in no small way, the carvers of the stones, many of whom never had the satisfaction of contemplating in its entirety the beauty of the masterpiece that their hands helped create. And yet they were producing a work of art that would be the object of admiration for generations to come.

You are in so many ways the carvers of the stones. Even a lifetime of dedicated service will not always enable you to see the finished monument of universal peace, of fraternal collaboration and of harmony between peoples. Sometimes you will catch a glimpse of it, in a particularly successful achievement, in a problem solved, in the smile of a happy and healthy child, in a conflict avoided, in a reconciliation of minds and hearts achieved. More often, you will experience only the monotony of your daily labors, or the frustrations of bureaucratic entanglements. But know that your work is great and that history will judge your achievements with favor.

### Have Confidence in Your Ideals

The challenges that the world community will face in the coming years and decades will not diminish. The rapidly changing pace of world events, the tremendous steps forward of science and technology will increase both the potential for development and the complexity of the problems. Be prepared, be capable, but above all have confidence in the ideal you serve.

Look upon your contribution not only in terms of increased industrial production, of enhanced efficiency, of eliminated suffering. Above all look upon it in terms of growing dignity for every human being, of increased possibility for every person to advance to the fullest measure of spiritual, cultural and human completion. Your calling as international servants takes its value from the objectives pursued by the international organizations. These aims transcend the mere material or intellectual spheres; they reach out into the moral and spiritual fields. Through your work, you are able to extend your love to the entire human family, to every person who has received the wondrous gift of life, so that all may live together in peace and harmony, in a just and peaceful world, where all their basic needs—physical, moral and spiritual—may be fulfilled.

You have in the visitor who stands before you someone who admires what you do and who believes in the value of your task.

Thank you for your welcome. I send my heartfelt greetings also to your families. I especially hope that you may experience a deep and never-fading joy in the work that you perform for the benefit of all men, women and children on this earth.

### 9. ADDRESS UPON DEPARTURE FROM THE UNITED NATIONS ORGANIZATION

Mr. Secretary-General,

As I am about to conclude my all-too-brief visit at the world headquarters of the United Nations, I wish to express my heartfelt thanks to all who were instrumental in making this visit possible.

My thanks go first of all to you, Mr. Secretary-General, for your kind invitation, which I considered not only a great honor but also an obligation, since it allowed me by my presence here to attest publicly and solemnly to the commitment of the Holy See to collaborate, to the extent consonant with its own mission, with this worthy organization.

My gratitude goes also to the distinguished president of the Thirty-fourth General Assembly, who honored me in inviting me to address this unique forum of the delegates of nearly all the nations of the world. By proclaiming the incomparable dignity of every human being and by manifesting my firm belief in the unity and solidarity of all nations, I have been permitted to affirm once again a basic tenet of my encyclical letter: "After all, peace comes down to respect for man's inviolable rights" (*Redemptor Hominis,* 17).

May I also thank all the distinguished delegates of the nations represented here, as well as the whole staff of the United Nations, for the friendly reception which they have given to the representatives of the Holy See, particularly to our permanent observer, Archbishop Giovanni Cheli.

## Basis for Peace: Fatherhood of God and Brotherhood of Man

The message which I wish to leave with you is a message of certitude and hope: the certitude that peace is possible when it is based on the recognition of the fatherhood of God and the brotherhood of all men; the hope that the sense of moral responsibility which every person must assume will make it possible to create a better world in freedom, in justice and in love.

As one whose ministry is void of meaning except insofar as he is the faithful Vicar of Christ on earth, I now take leave of you with the words of the one whom I represent, of Jesus Christ himself: "Peace I leave with you, my peace I give to you" (Jn. 14:27). My constant prayer for all of you is this: that there may be peace in justice and in love. May the praying voice of all those who believe in God—Christians and non-Christians alike—bring it about that the moral resources present in the hearts of men and women of good will be united for the common good, and call down from heaven that peace which human efforts alone cannot effect.

May God bless the United Nations.

## 10. ADDRESS IN SAINT PATRICK'S CATHEDRAL

Dear Cardinal Cooke, dear Brothers and Sisters in Christ,

I consider it a special grace to come back to New York—to be back in Saint Patrick's during the Cathedral's centenary year.

## To Confirm You in Your Faith

Six months ago I wrote a letter to Cardinal Cooke, stating that it was "my earnest hope that the local ecclesial community, symbolized by this glorious edifice in stone (see 1 Pt. 2:5), may be renewed in the faith of Peter and Paul—in the faith of our Lord Jesus Christ—and that each one of you will find fresh vigor for authentic Christian living." And this is my hope for all of you today. This is why I am here: to confirm you in your holy, Catholic and apostolic faith; to invoke upon you the joy and strength that will sustain you in Christian living.

On this occasion I send my greetings to all the people of New York. In a special way my heart is with the poor, with those who suffer, with those who are alone and abandoned in the midst of this teeming metropolis.

## To Direct Human Hearts to God

I pray for the success of the apostolate in this Archdiocese: may the spires of Saint Patrick's Cathedral always reflect the thrust with which the Church fulfills her fundamental function in every age: "to direct man's gaze, to point [to] the awareness and experience of the whole of humanity towards the mystery of God, to help all men and women to be familiar with the profundity of Redemption taking place in Christ Jesus" (*Redemptor Hominis*, 10).

This too is included in the symbolism of Saint Patrick's; this is the mission of the Church in New York—the expression of her vital and distinctive service to humanity: to direct hearts to God, to keep alive hope in the world. And so we repeat with Saint Paul: "This explains why we work and struggle as we do; our hopes are fixed on the living God" (1 Tm. 4:10).

## 11. ADDRESS IN THE PARISH OF
## SAINT CHARLES BORROMEO IN HARLEM

Dear Friends, dear Brothers and Sisters in Christ,

"This is the day the Lord has made; let us be glad and rejoice in it" (Ps. 118:24).

I greet you in the joy and peace of our Lord Jesus Christ. I welcome this opportunity to be with you and to speak to you, and through you to extend my greetings to all black Americans.

At Cardinal Cooke's suggestion, I was happy to include in my plans a visit to the Parish of Saint Charles Borromeo in Harlem, and to its black community, which for half a century has nurtured here the cultural, social and religious roots of black people. I have greatly looked forward to being here this evening.

## Joy Is the Keynote of the Christian Message

I come to you as a servant of Jesus Christ, and I want to speak to you about him. Christ came to bring joy: joy to children, joy to parents, joy to families and to friends, joy to workers and to scholars, joy to the sick and to the elderly, joy to all humanity. In a true sense, joy is the keynote of the Christian message and the recurring motif of the Gospels. Recall the first words of the angel to Mary: "Rejoice, O full of grace, the Lord is with you"(Lk. 1:28). And at the birth of Jesus, the angels announced to the shepherds: "Listen, I bring you news of great joy, joy to be shared by all people" (Lk. 2:10). Years later as Jesus entered Jerusalem riding on a colt, "the whole group of disciples joyfully began to praise God at the top of their voices. 'Blessed is the King who comes in the name of the Lord!'" (Lk. 19:37–38). We are told that some Pharisees in the crowd complained, saying: "Master, stop your disciples." But Jesus answered: "I tell you, if they were silent, the very stones would cry out" (Lk. 19:39–40).

Are not those words of Jesus still true today? If we are silent about the joy that comes from knowing Jesus, the very stones of our cities will cry out! For we are an Easter people and "Alleluia" is our song. With Saint Paul I exhort you: "Rejoice in the Lord always, I say it again, rejoice" (Phil. 4:4).

Rejoice because Jesus has come into the world!

Rejoice because Jesus has died on the Cross!

Rejoice because he rose again from the dead!

Rejoice because in baptism, he washed away our sins!

Rejoice because Jesus has come to set us free!

And rejoice because he is the master of our life!

But how many people have never known this joy? They feed on emptiness and tread the paths of despair. "They walk in darkness and the shadow of death" (Lk. 1:79). And we need not look to the far ends of the earth for them. They live in our neighborhoods, they walk down our streets, they may even be members of our own families. They live without true joy because they live without hope. They live without hope because they have never heard, really heard, the Good News of Jesus Christ, because they have never met a brother or a sister who touched their lives with the love of Jesus and lifted them up from their misery.

We must go to them therefore as messengers of hope. We must bring to them the witness of true joy. We must pledge to them our commitment to work for a just society and city where they feel respected and loved.

And so I encourage you, be men and women of deep and abiding faith.

Be heralds of hope. Be messengers of joy. Be true workers for justice. Let the Good News of Christ radiate from your hearts, and the peace he alone gives remain forever in your souls.

My dear brothers and sisters in the black community: Rejoice. Alleluia!

## 12. GREETING TO THE SPANISH-SPEAKING PEOPLE OF THE SOUTH BRONX

Dear Brothers and Sisters and Friends,

### The Suffering Persons of the Inner City Deserve Special Attention on the Part of the Pope

One of the visits to which I attribute great importance, and to which I would like to be able to devote more time, is precisely the one that I am now making to the South Bronx, in this immense city of New York, where many immigrants of different colors, races and peoples live, among them the numerous Spanish-speaking community, you to whom I am now addressing myself.

I come here because I know of the difficult conditions of your existence, because I know that your lives are marked by pain. For this reason you deserve special attention on the part of the Pope.

My presence in this place is meant to be a sign of gratitude and an encouragement for what the Church has done and is continuing to do through her parishes, schools, health centers, institutes for assisting youth and the aging, on behalf of so many who experience inner anxiety and material deprivation.

### The Church Is a Flame of Hope in the Inner Cities: Working to Preserve Human Dignity

I would wish that this flame of hope—sometimes one of the least hopes—should not only not go out, but that it might increase in strength, so that all who live in the area and the city may succeed in being able to live with dignity and serenity, as individual human beings, as families, as sons and daughters of God.

Brothers and sisters and friends, do not give in to despair, but work together, take the steps possible for you in the task of increasing your dignity, unite your efforts toward the goals of human and moral advancement. And do not forget that God has your lives in his care, goes with you, calls you to better things, calls you to overcome.

But since help from outside is also necessary, I make an insistent call to the leaders, to those who can do it, that they should give their generous collaboration in such a praiseworthy and urgent task.

Please God that the house-building project—and other necessary projects—may soon become a beautiful reality, so that each person and each family may find suitable housing in which to live in peace beneath the gaze of God.

Friends: I greet you and all those dear to you, I bless you and I encourage you not to grow faint as you travel the right road.

## 13. HOMILY AT YANKEE STADIUM

1. "Peace be with you!"

### Jesus Is Peace and Justice

These were the first words that Jesus spoke to his Apostles after his Resurrection. With these words the Risen Christ restored peace to their hearts, at a time when they were still in a state of shock after the first terrible experience of Good Friday. Tonight, in the name of our Lord Jesus Christ, in the power of his Spirit, in the midst of a world that is anxious about its own existence, I repeat these words to you, for they are words of life: "Peace be with you!"

Jesus does not merely give us peace. He gives us *his* Peace accompanied by *his* Justice. He *is* Peace and Justice. He becomes *our* Peace and *our* Justice.

What does this mean? It means that Jesus Christ—the Son of God made man, the perfect man—perfects, restores and manifests in himself the unsurpassable dignity that God wishes to give to man from the beginning. He is the one who realizes in himself what man has the vocation to be: the one who is fully reconciled with the Father, fully one in himself, fully devoted to others. Jesus Christ is living Peace and living Justice.

Jesus Christ makes us sharers in what he is. Through his Incarnation, the Son of God in a certain manner united himself with every human being. In our inmost being he has re-created us; in our inmost being he has reconciled us with God, reconciled us with ourselves, reconciled us with our brothers and sisters: he is *our* Peace.

### We Are Beneficiaries of the Life of God

2. What unfathomable riches we bear within us, and in our Christian communities! We are bearers of the Justice and Peace of God! We are not primarily painstaking builders of a justice and peace that are merely human, always wearing out and always fragile. We are primarily the humble beneficiaries of the very life of God, who is Justice and Peace in the bond of Charity. During Mass, when the priest greets us with these words, "the peace of the Lord be with you always," let us think primarily of this Peace which is God's gift: Jesus Christ is our Peace. And when, before Communion, the priest invites us to give one another a sign of peace, let us think primarily of the fact that we are invited to exchange with one another the Peace of Christ, who dwells within us, who invites us to share in his Body and Blood, for our joy and for the service of all humanity.

For God's Justice and Peace cry out to bear fruit in human works of justice and peace, in all the spheres of actual life. When we Christians make Jesus Christ the center of our feelings and thoughts, we do not turn away from people and their needs. On the contrary, we are caught up in the eternal movement of God's love that comes to meet us; we are caught up in the movement of the Son, who came among us, who became one of us; we are caught up in the movement of the Holy Spirit, who visits the poor, calms fevered hearts, binds up wounded hearts, warms cold hearts, and gives us the fullness of his gifts. The reason why man is the primary and fundamental way for the Church is that the Church walks in the footsteps of Jesus: it is Jesus who has shown her this road. This road passes in an unchangeable way through the mystery of the Incarnation and Redemption; it leads from Christ to man. The Church looks at the world through the very eyes of Christ; Jesus is the principle of her solicitude for man (see *Redemptor Hominis,* 13–18).

### Urgent Priorities

3. The task is immense. And it is an enthralling one. I have just emphasized various aspects of it before the General Assembly of the United Nations, and I shall touch upon others during my apostolic journey across your country. Today, let me just dwell on the spirit and nature of the Church's contribution to the cause of justice and peace, and let me also mention certain urgent priorities which your service to humanity ought to concentrate upon today.

Social thinking and social practice inspired by the Gospel must always be marked by a special sensitivity toward those who are most in distress, those who are extremely poor, those suffering from all the physical, mental and moral ills that afflict humanity, including hunger, neglect, unemployment and despair. There are many poor people of this sort around the world. There are many in your own midst. On many occasions, your nation has gained a well-deserved reputation for generosity, both public and private. Be faithful to that tradition, in keeping with your vast possibilities and present responsibilities. The network of charitable works of each kind that the Church has succeeded in creating here is a valuable means for effectively mobilizing generous undertakings aimed at relieving the situations of distress that continually arise both at home and elsewhere in the world. Make an effort to ensure that this form of aid keeps its irreplaceable character as a fraternal and personal encounter with those who are in distress; if necessary, reestablish this very character against all the elements that work in the opposite direction. Let this sort of aid be respectful of the freedom and dignity of those being helped, and let it be a means of forming the conscience of the givers.

### Seek Out Structures That Foster Poverty

4. But this is not enough. Within the framework of your national institutions and in cooperation with all your compatriots, you will also want to seek out the structural reasons which foster or cause the different forms of poverty in the world and in your own country, so that you can apply the proper remedies. You will not allow yourselves to be intimidated or discouraged by oversimplified explanations, which are more ideological than scientific—explanations which try to account for a complex evil by some single cause. But neither will you recoil before the reforms— even profound ones—of attitudes and structures that may prove necessary in order

to re-create over and over again the conditions needed by the disadvantaged if they are to have a fresh chance in the hard struggle of life. The poor of the United States and of the world are your brothers and sisters in Christ. You must never be content to leave them just the crumbs from the feast. You must take of your substance, and not just of your abundance, in order to help them. And you must treat them like guests at your family table.

### Lay People Put Convictions into Practice

5. Catholics of the United States, while developing your own legitimate institutions, you also participate in the nation's affairs within the framework of institutions and organizations springing from the nation's common history and from your common concern. This you do hand in hand with your fellow citizens of every creed and confession. Unity among you in all such endeavors is essential, under the leadership of your Bishops, for deepening, proclaiming and effectively promoting the truth about man, his dignity and his inalienable rights, the truth such as the Church receives it in Revelation and such as she ceaselessly develops it in her social teaching in the light of the Gospel. These shared convictions, however, are not a ready-made model for society (see *Octogesima Adveniens,* 42). It is principally the task of lay people to put them into practice in concrete projects, to define priorities and to develop models that are suitable for promoting man's real good. The Second Vatican Council's Pastoral Constitution *Gaudium et Spes* tells us that "lay people should seek from priests light and spiritual strength. Let the lay people not imagine that their pastors are always such experts that to every problem which arises, however complicated, they can readily give a concrete solution, or even that such is their mission. Rather, enlightened by Christian wisdom and giving close attention to the teaching authority of the Church, let the lay people assume their own distinctive role" (*Gaudium et Spes,* 43).

### Greater Solidarity

6. In order to bring this undertaking to a successful conclusion, fresh spiritual and moral energy drawn from the inexhaustible divine source is needed. This energy does not develop easily. The life-style of many of the members of our rich and permissive societies is easy, and so is the life-style of increasing groups inside the poorer countries. As I said last year to the Plenary Assembly of the Pontifical Commission Justice and Peace, "Christians will want to be in the vanguard in favoring ways of life that decisively break with a frenzy of consumerism, exhausting and joyless" (November 11, 1978). It is not a question of slowing down progress, for there is no human progress when everything conspires to give free rein to the instincts of self-interest, sex and power. We must find a simple way of living. For it is not right that the standard of living of the rich countries should seek to maintain itself by draining off a great part of the reserves of energy and raw materials that are meant to serve the whole of humanity. For readiness to create a greater and more equitable solidarity between peoples is the first condition for peace. Catholics of the United States, and

all you citizens of the United States, you have such a tradition of spiritual generosity, industry, simplicity and sacrifice that you cannot fail to heed this call today for a new enthusiasm and a fresh determination. It is in the joyful simplicity of a life inspired by the Gospel and the Gospel's spirit of fraternal sharing that you will find the best remedy for sour criticism, paralyzing doubt and the temptation to make money the principal means and indeed the very measure of human advancement.

## Christ Condemns Selfish Use of Possessions

7. On various occasions, I have referred to the Gospel parable of the rich man and Lazarus. "Once there was a rich man who dressed in purple and linen and feasted splendidly every day. At his gate lay a beggar named Lazarus who was covered with sores. Lazarus longed to eat the scraps that fell from the rich man's table" (Lk. 16:19ff). Both the rich man and the beggar died, and judgment was rendered on their conduct. And the Scripture tells us that Lazarus found consolation, but that the rich man found torment. Was the rich man condemned because he had riches, because he abounded in earthly possessions, because he "dressed in purple and linen and feasted splendidly every day"? No, I would say that it was not for this reason. The rich man was condemned because he did not pay attention to the other man. Because he failed to take notice of Lazarus, the person who sat at his door and who longed to eat the scraps from his table. Nowhere does Christ condemn the mere possession of earthly goods as such. Instead, he pronounces very harsh words against those who use their possessions in a selfish way, without paying attention to the needs of others. The Sermon on the Mount begins with the words: "Blessed are the poor in spirit." And at the end of the account of the Last Judgment as found in Saint Matthew's Gospel, Jesus speaks the words that we all know so well: "I was hungry and you gave me no food, I was thirsty and you gave me no drink. I was away from home and you gave me no welcome, naked and you gave me no clothing. I was ill and in prison and you did not come and comfort me" (Mt. 25:42–43).

The parable of the rich man and Lazarus must always be present in our memory; it must form our conscience. Christ demands openness to our brothers and sisters in need—openness from the rich, the affluent, the economically advanced; openness to the poor, the underdeveloped and the disadvantaged. Christ demands an openness that is more than benign attention, more than token actions or half-hearted efforts that leave the poor as destitute as before or even more so.

All of humanity must think of the parable of the rich man and the beggar. Humanity must translate it into contemporary terms, in terms of economy and politics, in terms of all human rights, in terms of relations between the "First," "Second" and "Third World." We cannot stand idly by when thousands of human beings are dying of hunger. Nor can we remain indifferent when the rights of the human spirit are trampled upon, when violence is done to the human conscience in matters of truth, religion and cultural creativity.

We cannot stand idly by, enjoying our own riches and freedom, if, in any place, the Lazarus of the twentieth century stands at our doors. In the light of the parable of Christ, riches and freedom mean a special responsibility. Riches and freedom create a special obligation. And so, in the name of the solidarity that binds us all together in a common humanity, I again proclaim the dignity of every human person: the rich man and Lazarus are both human beings, both of them equally redeemed by Christ, at a great price, the price of "the precious blood of Christ" (1 Pt. 1:19).

## The Church Brings Christ to All

8. Brothers and sisters in Christ, with deep conviction and affection I repeat to you the words that I addressed to the world when I took up my apostolic ministry in the service of all men and women: "Do not be afraid. Open wide the doors for Christ. To his saving power open the boundaries of states, economic and political systems, the vast fields of culture, civilization and development. Do not be afraid. Christ knows what is in man. He alone knows it" (October 22, 1978).

As I said to you at the beginning, Christ is our Justice and our Peace, and all our works of justice and peace draw from this source the irreplaceable energy and light for the great task before us. As we resolutely commit ourselves to the service of all the needs of individuals and of peoples—for Christ urges us to do so—we shall nevertheless remind ourselves that the Church's mission is not limited to this witness to social fruitfulness of the Gospel. Along this road that leads the Church to man, she does not offer, in the matter of justice and peace, only the earthly fruits of the Gospel; she brings to man—to every human person—their very source; Jesus Christ himself, our Justice and our Peace.

## OCTOBER 3, 1979

## 14. MORNING PRAYER AT SAINT PATRICK'S CATHEDRAL

Dear Brothers and Sisters,

Saint Paul asks: "Who will separate us from the love of Christ?"

## United by Prayer into a Powerful Community

As long as we remain what we are this morning—a community of prayer united in Christ, an ecclesial community of praise and worship of the Father—we shall understand and experience the answer: that no one—nothing at all—will ever separate us from the love of Christ. For us today, the Church's Morning Prayer is a joyful, communal celebration of God's love in Christ.

The value of the Liturgy of the Hours is enormous. Through it, all the faithful, but especially the clergy and Religious, fulfill a role of prime importance: Christ's prayer goes on in the world. The Holy Spirit himself intercedes for God's people (see Rom. 8:27). The Christian community, with praise and thanksgiving, glorifies the wisdom, the power, the providence and the salvation of our God.

In this prayer of praise we lift up our hearts to the Father of our Lord Jesus Christ, bringing with us the anguish and hopes, the joys and sorrows of all our brothers and sisters in the world.

And our prayer becomes likewise a school of sensitivity, making us aware of how much our destinies are linked together in the human family. Our prayer becomes a school of love—a special kind of Christian consecrated love, by which we love the world, but with the heart of Christ.

Through this prayer of Christ to which we give voice, our day is sanctified, our activities transformed, our actions made holy. We pray the same psalms that Jesus prayed and come into personal contact with him—the person to whom all Scripture points, the goal to which all history is directed.

In our celebration of the word of God, the mystery of Christ opens up before us and envelops us. And through union with our Head, Jesus Christ, we become ever more increasingly one with all the members of his Body.

As never before, it becomes possible for us to reach out and embrace the world, but to embrace it with Christ: with authentic generosity, with pure and effective love, in service, in healing and in reconciliation.

The efficacy of our prayer renders special honor to the Father, because it is made always through Christ and for the glory of his name: "We ask this through our Lord Jesus Christ, your Son, who lives and reigns with you and the Holy Spirit, one God, for ever and ever."

As a community of prayer and praise, with the Liturgy of the Hours among the highest priorities of our day—each day—we can be sure that nothing will separate us from the love of God that is in Christ Jesus our Lord.

## 15. ADDRESS TO HIGH SCHOOL STUDENTS
## IN MADISON SQUARE GARDEN

Dear Young People,

I am happy to be with you in Madison Square Garden. Today this is a garden of life, where young people are alive: alive with hope and love, alive with the life of Christ. And it is in the name of Christ that I greet each one of you today.

### The Church Wants to Communicate Christ

I have been told that most of you come from Catholic high schools. For this reason I would like to say something about Catholic education, to tell you why the Church considers it so important and expends so much energy in order to provide you and millions of other young people with a Catholic education. The answer can be summarized in one word, in one person: Jesus Christ. The Church wants to communicate Christ to you.

## Educated to Reflect Christ

1. This is what education is all about, this is the meaning of life: to know Christ. To know Christ as a friend: as someone who cares about you and the person next to you, and all the people here and everywhere—no matter what language they speak, or what clothes they wear, or what color their skin is.

And so the purpose of Catholic education is to communicate Christ to you, so that your attitude toward others will be that of Christ. You are approaching that stage in your life when you must take personal responsibility for your own destiny. Soon you will be making major decisions which will affect the whole course of your life. If these decisions reflect Christ's attitude, then your education will be a success.

We have to learn to meet challenges and even crises in the light of Christ's Cross and Resurrection. Part of our Catholic education is to learn to see the needs of others, to have the courage to practice what we believe in. With the support of a Catholic education we try to meet every circumstance of life with the attitude of Christ. Yes, the Church wants to communicate Christ to you so that you will come to full maturity in him who is the perfect human being, and, at the same time, the Son of God.

## Christ Is the Fullness of Humanity

2. Dear young people: You and I and all of us together make up the Church, and we are convinced that only in Christ do we find real love and the fullness of life.

And so I invite you today to look to Christ.

When you wonder about the mystery of yourself, look to Christ who gives you the meaning of life.

When you wonder what it means to be a mature person, look to Christ who is the fullness of humanity.

And when you wonder about your role in the future of the world and of the United States, look to Christ. Only in Christ will you fulfill your potential as an American citizen and as a citizen of the world community.

## The Church and World Need You

3. With the aid of your Catholic education, you have received the greatest of gifts: the knowledge of Christ. Of this gift Saint Paul wrote: "I believe nothing can happen that will outweigh the supreme advantage of knowing Christ Jesus my Lord. For him I have accepted the loss of everything and I look on everything as so much rubbish if only I can have Christ and be given a place in him" (Phil. 3:8–9).

Be always grateful to God for this gift of knowing Christ. Be grateful also to your parents and to the community of the Church for making possible, through many sacrifices, your Catholic education. People have placed a lot of hope in you, and they now look forward to your collaboration in giving witness to Christ, and in transmitting the Gospel to others. The Church needs you. The world needs you, because it needs Christ, and you belong to Christ. And so I ask you to accept your responsibility in the Church, the responsibility of your Catholic education: to help—by your words, and, above all, by the example of your lives—to spread the Gospel. You do this by praying, and by being just and truthful and pure.

Dear young people: by a real Christian life, by the practice of your religion, you are called to give witness to your faith. And because actions speak louder than words, you are called to proclaim, by the conduct of your daily lives, that you really do believe that Jesus Christ is Lord!

## 16. ADDRESS AT BATTERY PARK

Dear Friends,

### Statue of Liberty: Symbol of Freedom

1. My visit to your city would not have been complete without coming to Battery Park, without seeing Ellis Island and the Statue of Liberty in the distance. Every nation has its historical symbols. They may be shrines or statues or documents; but their significance lies in the truths they represent to the citizens of a nation and in the image they convey to other nations. Such a symbol in the United States is the Statue of Liberty. This is an impressive symbol of what the United States has stood for from the very beginning of its history; this is a symbol of freedom. It reflects the immigrant history of the United States, for it was freedom that millions of human beings were looking for on these shores. And it was freedom that the young republic offered in compassion. On this spot, I wish to pay homage to this noble trait of America and its people: its desire to be free, its determination to preserve freedom, and its willingness to share this freedom with others. May the ideal of liberty, of freedom, remain a moving force for your nation and for all the nations in the world today!

2. It greatly honors your country and its citizens that on this foundation of liberty you have built a nation where the dignity of every human person is to be respected, where a religious sense and a strong family structure are fostered, where duty and honest work are held in high esteem, where generosity and hospitality are no idle words, and where the right to religious liberty is deeply rooted in your history.

Yesterday, before the General Assembly of the United Nations, I made a plea for peace and justice based on the full respect of all the fundamental rights of the human person. I also spoke of religious freedom, because it regards a person's relationship to God and because it is related in a special way to other human rights. It is closely allied with the right to freedom of conscience. If conscience is not secure in society, then the security of all other rights is threatened.

Liberty, in all its aspects, must be based on truth. I want to repeat here the words of Jesus, "the truth will make you free" (Jn. 8:32). It is then my wish that your sense of freedom may always go hand in hand with a profound sense of truth and honesty about yourselves and about the realities of your society. Past achievements can never be an acceptable substitute for present responsibilities toward the common good of the society you live in and toward your fellow citizens. Just as the desire for freedom is a universal aspiration in the world today, so is the quest for justice. No institution or organization can credibly stand for freedom today if it does not also support the quest for justice, for both are essential demands of the human spirit.

### Freedom Must Support Human Life

3. It will always remain one of the glorious achievements of this nation that, when people looked toward America, they received together with freedom also a chance for their own advancement. This tradition must be honored also today. The freedom that was gained must be ratified each day by the firm rejection of whatever wounds, weakens or dishonors human life. And so I appeal to all who love freedom and justice to give a chance to all in need, to the poor and the powerless. Break open the hopeless cycles of poverty and ignorance that are still the lot of too many of our brothers and sisters; the hopeless cycles of prejudices that linger on despite enormous progress toward effective equality in education and employment; the cycles of despair in which are imprisoned all those who lack decent food, shelter or employment; the cycles of underdevelopment that are the consequence of international mechanisms that subordinate human existence to the domination of partially conceived economic progress; and finally the inhuman cycles of war that spring from the violation of man's fundamental rights and produce still graver violations of them.

Freedom in justice will bring a new dawn of hope for the present generation as it has done before: for the homeless, for the unemployed, for the aging, for the sick and the handicapped, for the migrants and the undocumented workers, for all who hunger for human dignity in this land and in the world.

### Ethnic Variety and Freedom

4. With sentiments of admiration and with confidence in your potential for true human greatness, I wish to greet in you the rich variety of your nation, where people of different ethnic origins and creeds can live, work and prosper together in freedom and mutual respect. I greet and I thank for their cordial welcome all those who have joined me here, businessmen and laborers, scholars and managers, social workers and civil servants, old and young. I greet you with respect, esteem and love. My warm greetings go to each and every group: to my fellow Catholics, to the members of the different Christian Churches with whom I am united in the faith of Jesus Christ.

And I address a special word of greeting to the leaders of the Jewish community, whose presence here honors me greatly. A few months ago, I met with an international group of Jewish representatives in Rome. On that occasion, recalling the initiatives undertaken following the Second Vatican Council under my predecessor Paul VI, I stated that "our two communities are connected and closely related at the very level of their respective religious identities," and that on this basis "we recognize with utmost clarity that the path along which we should proceed is one of fraternal dialogue and fruitful collaboration" (*L'Osservatore Romano,* March 12–13, 1979). I am glad to ascertain that this same path has been followed here in the United States by large sections of both communities and their respective authorities and representative bodies. Several common programs of study, mutual knowledge, a common determination to reject all forms of anti-Semitism and discrimination, and various forms of collaboration for the human advancement inspired by our common biblical heritage have created deep and permanent links between Jews and Catholics. As one who in my homeland has shared the suffering of your brethren, I greet you with the word taken from the Hebrew language: Shalom! Peace be with you.

And to everyone here I offer the expression of my respect, my esteem and my fraternal love. May God bless all of you! May God bless New York!

## 17. ADDRESS AT SHEA STADIUM

Dear Friends in New York,

### A City Must Have a Soul!

It gives me great joy to have the opportunity to come and greet you on my way to La Guardia Airport at the end of my visit to the Archdiocese and to the metropolis of New York.

Thank you for your warm welcome. In you I wish to greet once again all the people of New York, Long Island, New Jersey and Connecticut, Brooklyn: all your parishes, hospitals, schools, and organizations, your sick and aged. And with special affection I greet the young people and the children.

From Rome I bring you a message of faith and love. "May the peace of Christ reign in your hearts!" (Col. 3:15). Make peace the desire of your heart, for if you love peace, you will love all humanity, without distinction of race, color or creed.

### Be Responsible for Your City

My greeting is also an invitation to all of you to feel personally responsible for the well-being and the community spirit of your city. A visitor to New York is always impressed by the special character of this metropolis: skyscrapers, endless streets, large residential areas, housing blocks, and above all the millions of people who live here or who look here for the work that will sustain them and their family.

### Love Must Be the Hallmark of Your Lives

Large concentrations of people create special problems and special needs. The personal effort and loyal collaboration of everybody are needed to find the right solutions, so that all men, women and children can live in dignity and develop to the full their potential without having to suffer for lack of education, housing, employment and cultural opportunities. Above all, a city needs a soul if it is to become a true home for human beings. You, the people, must give it this soul. And how do you do this? By loving each other. Love for each other must be the hallmark of your lives. In the Gospel Jesus Christ tells us: "You shall love your neighbor as yourself" (Mt. 22:39). This commandment of the Lord must be your inspiration in forming true human relationships among yourselves, so that nobody will ever feel alone or unwanted, or much less, rejected, despised or hated. Jesus himself will give you the power of fraternal love. And every neighborhood, every block, every street will become a true community because you will want it so, and Jesus will help you to bring it about.

Keep Jesus Christ in your hearts, and you will recognize his face in every human being. You will want to help him out in all his needs: the needs of your brothers and sisters. This is the way we prepare ourselves to meet Jesus, when he will come again, on the last day, as the Judge of the living and the dead, and he will say to us: "Come, you have my Father's blessing! Inherit the kingdom prepared for you from the creation of the world. For I was hungry and you gave me food, I was thirsty and you gave me drink. I was a stranger and you welcomed me, naked and you clothed me. I was ill and you comforted me, in prison and you came to visit me . . . I assure you as often as you did it for one of my least brethren, you did it for *me*" (Mt. 25:34–35, 39).

## To the Hispanic Community

I now wish to address a very cordial welcome to each and every member of the Spanish-speaking colony, coming from various countries, here in this stadium.

In you, I see and I wish to greet, with great affection, the whole of the numerous Hispanic community living in New York and many other places in the United States.

I wish to assure you that I am well aware of the place that you occupy in American society, and that I follow with lively interest your accomplishments, aspirations and difficulties within the social fabric of this nation, which is your homeland of adoption or the land that welcomes you. For this reason, from the very moment that I accepted the invitation to visit this country, I thought of you, who are an integral and specific part of this society, a very considerable part of the Church in this vast nation.

## The Spiritual Life Bolsters Human Life and Dignity

I wish to exhort you, as Catholics, always to maintain very clearly your Christian identity, with a constant reference to the value of your faith, values that must enlighten the legitimate quest for a worthy material position for yourselves and your families.

Since you are generally immersed in the environment of heavily populated cities and in a social climate where sometimes technology and material values take first place, make an effort to provide a spiritual contribution to your life and your neighborhood. Keep close to God in your lives, to the God who calls you to be ever more worthy of your condition as human beings with an eternal vocation, to the God who invites you to solidarity and to collaboration in building up an ever more human, just and fraternal world.

I pray for you, for your families and friends, above all for your children, for the sick and suffering, and to all of you I give my Blessing. May God be with you always! Good-bye, and God bless you.

## 18. VISIT IN THE CATHEDRAL OF SAINTS PETER AND PAUL

Dear Brothers and Sisters in Christ,

I give thanks to the Lord for permitting me to come back to this city of Philadelphia, to this state of Pennsylvania. I have very happy memories of being here before as your guest, and I remember especially the Eucharistic Congress and bicentennial celebration in 1976 that I attended as Archbishop of Cracow. Today, by the grace of God, I come here as Successor of Peter to bring you a message of love and to strengthen you in your faith. In your kind welcome I feel that you want to honor in me Christ, whom I represent and who lives in all of us—all of us who through the Holy Spirit form one community, one communion in faith and love. I feel moreover that I am truly among friends, and I feel very much at home in your midst.

In a very particular way I wish to thank you, Cardinal Krol, Archbishop of Philadelphia, for the invitation you extended to me to come here and celebrate the Eucharist together with you and your people. A heartfelt greeting also goes to the clergy, Religious and laity of this local Church. I have come as your brother in Christ, bringing with me the same message that the Lord Jesus himself brought to the villages and cities in the Holy Land: Let us praise the Lord our God and Father, and let us love one another!

### The Cathedral Symbolizes You

It gives me great pleasure to meet you here in the Cathedral of Philadelphia, for it has a deep meaning for me. Above all, it means *you*: the living Church of Christ, here and now, alive in faith, united in the love of Jesus Christ.

This Cathedral recalls the memory of Saint John Neumann, once Bishop of this See, and now and forever a saint of the universal Church. In this edifice, his message and his example of holiness must continually be transmitted to every new generation of young people. And if we listen carefully today we can hear Saint John Neumann speaking to all of us in the words of the Letter to the Hebrews: "Remember your leaders who spoke the word of God to you; consider how their lives ended, and imitate their faith. Jesus Christ is the same yesterday, today and forever" (Heb. 13:8).

Finally, this Cathedral links you to the great Apostles of Rome, Peter and Paul. They, in turn, continue to give you their testimony to Christ, to proclaim to you Christ's divinity, to acknowledge him before the world. Here today in Philadelphia, the confession of Peter becomes for all of us a personal act of faith, and this act of faith we make together, as we say to Jesus: "You are the Christ, the Son of the living God" (Mt. 16:16). And with Saint Paul, each one of us is called to say in the depths of our hearts and before the world: "I still live my human life, but it is a life of faith in the Son of God, who loved me and gave himself for me" (Gal. 2:20).

This Cathedral is also linked in religion to the heritage of this historic city. Every service to morality and spirituality is a service to the civilization of man; it is a contribution to human happiness and to true well-being.

And so from this Cathedral I offer my greetings to the whole city of Philadelphia, the civil authorities and all the people. As the city of brotherly love, as the first capital of the United States of America, you are a symbol of freedom and fraternal relations. My greeting is also a prayer.

May the common dedication and the united efforts of all your citizens—Catholics, Protestants and Jews alike—succeed in making your inner city and suburbs places where people are no strangers to each other, where every man, woman and child feels respected; where nobody feels abandoned, rejected or alone.

Asking for your prayerful support for my visit of friendship and pastoral concern, I extend my blessing to all of you, to those present here today, to your dear ones at home, to the aged and the sick, and in a very special way to all the young people and the children.

God bless Philadelphia!

## 19. HOMILY FOR MASS CELEBRATED AT LOGAN CIRCLE

Dear Brothers and Sisters of the Church in Philadelphia,

### Gathered as One Community of Grace

1. It is a great joy for me to celebrate the Eucharist with you today. All of us are gathered together as one community, one people in the grace and peace of God our Father and of the Lord Jesus Christ; we are gathered in the fellowship of the Holy Spirit. We have come together to proclaim the Gospel in all its power, for the Eucharistic Sacrifice is the summit and enactment of our proclamation: Christ has died, Christ is risen, Christ will come again!

From this altar of Sacrifice, there arises a hymn of praise and thanksgiving to God through Jesus Christ. We who belong to Christ are all part of this hymn, this Sacrifice of praise. The Sacrifice of Calvary is renewed on this altar, and it becomes our offering too—an offering for the benefit of the living and the dead, an offering for the universal Church.

Assembled in the charity of Christ, we are all one in his Sacrifice: the Cardinal Archbishop who is called to lead this Church in the path of truth and love; his

Auxiliary Bishops and the diocesan and religious clergy, who share with the Bishops in the preaching of the word; men and women Religious, who through the consecration of their lives show the world what it means to be faithful to the message of the Beatitudes; fathers and mothers, with their great mission of building up the Church in love; every category of the laity, with their particular task in the Church's mission of evangelization and salvation. This Sacrifice offered today in Philadelphia is the expression of our praying community. In union with Jesus Christ we make intercession for the universal Church, for the well-being of all our fellow men and women, and today, in particular, for the preservation of all the human and Christian values that are the heritage of this land, this country and this very city.

### Inalienable Rights

2. Philadelphia is the city of the Declaration of Independence, that remarkable document containing a solemn attestation of the equality of all human beings, endowed by their Creator with certain inalienable rights: life, liberty and the pursuit of happiness, expressing a "firm reliance on the protection of divine Providence." These are the sound moral principles formulated by your founding fathers and enshrined forever in your history. In the human and civil values that are contained in the spirit of this declaration there are easily recognized strong connections with basic religious and Christian values. A sense of religion itself is part of this heritage. The Liberty Bell, which I visited on another occasion, proudly bears the words of the Bible: "Proclaim liberty throughout the land" (Lv. 25:10). This tradition poses for all future generations of America a noble challenge: "One Nation under God, indivisible, with liberty and justice for all."

### Human and Christian Values

3. As citizens, you must strive to preserve these human values, to understand them better and to define their consequences for the whole community and as a worthy contribution to the world. As Christians, you must strengthen these human values and complement them by confronting them with the Gospel message, so that you may discover their deeper meaning, and thus assume more fully your duties and obligations toward your fellow human beings, with whom you are bound in a common destiny. In a way, for us who know Jesus Christ, human and Christian values are but two aspects of the same reality: the reality of man, redeemed by Christ and called to the fullness of eternal life.

In my first encyclical letter, I stated this important truth: "Christ, the Redeemer of the world, is the one who penetrated in a unique unrepeatable way into the mystery of man and entered his 'heart.' Rightly therefore does the Second Vatican Council teach: 'The truth is that only in the mystery of the Incarnate Word does the mystery of man take on light. For Adam, the first man, was a type of him who was to come (Rom. 5:14), Christ the Lord. Christ, the new Adam, in the very revelation of the mystery of the Father and his love, fully reveals man to himself and brings to light his most high calling.'" It is then in Jesus Christ that every man, woman and child is called to find the answer to the questions regarding the values that will inspire his or her personal and social relations.

## Human Dignity Must Be Protected

4. How then can a Christian, inspired and guided by the mystery of the Incarnation and Redemption of Christ, strengthen his or her own values and those that are embodied in the heritage of this nation? The answer to that question, in order to be complete, would have to be long. Let me, however, just touch upon a few important points. These values are strengthened when power and authority are exercised in full respect for all the fundamental rights of the human person, whose dignity is the dignity of one created in the image and likeness of God (see Gn. 1:26); when freedom is accepted not as an absolute and in itself, but as a gift that enables self-giving and service; when the family is protected and strengthened, when its unity is preserved, and when its role as the basic cell of society is recognized and honored. Human-Christian values are fostered when every effort is made so that no child anywhere in the world faces death because of lack of food, or faces a diminished intellectual and physical potential for want of sufficient nourishment, or has to bear all through life the scars of deprivation. Human-Christian values triumph when any system is reformed that authorizes the exploitation of any human being; when upright service and honesty in public servants is promoted; when the dispensing of justice is fair and the same for all; when responsible use is made of the material and energy resources of the world—resources that are meant for the benefit of all; when the environment is preserved intact for the future generations. Human-Christian values triumph by subjecting political and economic considerations to human dignity, by making them serve the cause of man—every person created by God, every brother and sister redeemed by Christ.

## Freedom Concerns Man's Relationship with Himself

5. I have mentioned the Declaration of Independence and the Liberty Bell, two monuments that exemplify the spirit of freedom on which this country was founded. Your attachment to liberty, to freedom, is part of your heritage. When the Liberty Bell rang for the first time in 1776, it was to announce the freedom of your nation, the beginning of the pursuit of a common destiny independent of any outside coercion. This principle of freedom is paramount in the political and social order, in relationship between the government and the people, and between individual and individual. However, man's life is also lived in another order of reality: in the order of his relationship to what is objectively true and morally good. Freedom thus acquires a deeper meaning when it is referred to the human person. It concerns in the first place the relation of man to himself. Every human person, endowed with reason, is

free when he is the master of his own actions, when he is capable of choosing that good which is in conformity with reason, and therefore with his own human dignity.

Freedom can never tolerate an offense against the rights of others, and one of the fundamental rights of man is the right to worship God. In the *Declaration on Religious Freedom,* the Second Vatican Council stated that the "demand for freedom in human society chiefly regards the quest for the values proper to the human spirit. It regards, in the first place, the free exercise of religion in society. . . . Religious freedom, which men demand as necessary to fulfill their duty to worship God, has to do with immunity from coercion in civil society. Therefore it leaves untouched traditional Catholic teaching on the moral duty of men and societies toward the true religion and toward the one Church of Christ" (*Dignitatis Humanae,* 1).

## Authentic Relationships

6. Christ himself linked freedom with the knowledge of truth: "You will know the truth and the truth will make you free" (Jn. 8:32). In my first encyclical I wrote in this regard: "These words contain both a fundamental requirement and a warning: the requirement of an honest relationship with regard to truth as a condition for authentic freedom, and the warning to avoid every kind of illusory freedom, every superficial unilateral freedom, every freedom that fails to enter into the whole truth about man and the world" (*Redemptor Hominis,* 12).

Freedom can therefore never be construed without relation to the truth as revealed by Jesus Christ and proposed by his Church, nor can it be seen as a pretext for moral anarchy, for every moral order must remain linked to truth. Saint Peter, in his first letter, says: "Live as free men, but do not use your freedom for malice" (1 Pt. 2:16). No freedom can exist when it goes against man in what he is, or against man in his relationship to others and to God.

This is especially relevant when one considers the domain of human sexuality. Here, as in any other field, there can be no true freedom without respect for the truth regarding the nature of human sexuality and marriage. In today's society, we see so many disturbing tendencies and so much laxity regarding the Christian view on sexuality that have all one thing in common: recourse to the concept of freedom to justify any behavior that is no longer consonant with the true moral order and teaching of the Church. Moral norms do not militate against the freedom of the person or the couple; on the contrary, they exist precisely for that freedom, since they are given to ensure the right use of freedom. Whoever refuses to accept these norms and to act accordingly, whoever seeks to liberate himself or herself from these norms, is not truly free. Free indeed is the person who models his or her behavior in a responsible way according to the exigencies of the objective good. What I have said here regards the whole of conjugal morality, but it applies as well to the priests with regard to the obligations of celibacy. The cohesion of freedom and ethics has also its consequences for the pursuit of the common good in society and for the national independence which the Liberty Bell announced two centuries ago.

## Fidelity to the Gospel

7. Divine law is the sole standard of human liberty and is given to us in the Gospel of Christ, the Gospel of Redemption. But fidelity to this Gospel of Redemption will never be possible without the action of the Holy Spirit. It is the Holy Spirit who guards the life-giving message entrusted to the Church. It is the Holy Spirit who ensures the faithful transmission of the Gospel into the lives of all of us. It is by the action of the Holy Spirit that the Church is built up day after day into a kingdom: a kingdom of truth and life, a kingdom of holiness and grace, a universal kingdom of justice, love and peace.

Today, therefore, we come before the Father to offer him the petitions and desires of our hearts, to offer him praise and thanksgiving. We do this from the city of Philadelphia for the universal Church and for the world. We do this as "members of the household of God" (Eph. 2:19) in union with the Sacrifice of Christ Jesus, our cornerstone, for the glory of the Most Holy Trinity. Amen.

## 20. AT THE SEMINARY OF SAINT CHARLES, OVERBROOK

Beloved Brothers and Sons in Christ,

One of the things I wanted most to do during my visit to the United States has now arrived. I wanted to visit a seminary and meet the seminarians; and through you I would like to communicate to all seminarians how much you mean to me, and how much you mean for the future of the Church—for the future of the mission given to us by Christ.

You hold a special place in my thoughts and prayers. In your lives there is great promise for the future of evangelization. And you give us hope that the authentic renewal of the Church which was begun by the Second Vatican Council will be brought to fruition. But in order for this to happen, you must receive a solid and well-rounded preparation in the seminary. This personal conviction about the importance of seminaries prompted me to write these words in my *Holy Thursday Letter to the Bishops of the Church*: "The full reconstitution of the life of the seminaries throughout the Church will be the best proof of the achievement of the renewal to which the Council directed the Church."

## God's Word and Discipline

1. If seminaries are to fulfill their mission in the Church, two activities in the overall program of the seminary are crucially important: the teaching of God's word, and discipline.

The intellectual formation of the priest, which is so vital for the times in which we live, embraces a number of the human sciences as well as the various sacred sciences. These all have an important place in your preparation for the priesthood.

But the first priority for seminaries today is the teaching of God's word in all its purity and integrity, with all its demands and in all its power. This was clearly affirmed by my beloved predecessor Paul VI, when he stated that Sacred Scripture is "a perpetual source of spiritual life, the chief instrument for handing down Christian doctrine, and the center of all theological study" (*Apostolic Constitution Missale Romanum,* April 3, 1969). Therefore, if you, the seminarians of this generation, are to be adequately prepared to take on the heritage and challenge of the Second Vatican Council, you will need to be well trained in the word of God.

Secondly, the seminary must provide a sound discipline to prepare for a life of consecrated service in the image of Christ. Its purpose was well defined by the Second Vatican Council: "The discipline required by seminary life should not be regarded merely as a strong support of community life and of charity. For it is a necessary part of the whole training program designed to provide self-mastery, to foster solid maturity of personality, and to develop other traits of character which are extremely serviceable for the ordered and productive activity of the Church" (*Optatum Totius,* 11).

When discipline is properly exercised, it can create an atmosphere of recollection which enables the seminarian to develop interiorly those attitudes which are so desirable in a priest, such as joyful obedience, generosity and self-sacrifice. In the different forms of community life that are appropriate for the seminary, you will learn the art of dialogue: the capacity to listen to others and to discover the richness of their personality, and the ability to give of yourself. Seminary discipline will reinforce rather than diminish your freedom, for it will help develop in you those traits and attitudes of mind and heart which God has given you, and which enrich your humanity and help you to serve more effectively his people. Discipline will also assist you in ratifying day after day in your hearts the obedience you owe to Christ and his Church.

## Human Dignity Requires Fidelity

2. I want to remind you of the importance of fidelity. Before you can be ordained, you are called by Christ to make a free and irrevocable commitment to be faithful to him and to his Church. Human dignity requires that you maintain this commitment, that you keep your promise to Christ no matter what difficulties you may encounter, and no matter what temptations you may be exposed to. The seriousness of this irrevocable commitment places a special obligation upon the rector and faculty of the seminary—and in a particular way on the spiritual director—to help you to evaluate your own suitability for Ordination. It is then the responsibility of the Bishop to judge whether you should be called to the priesthood.

It is important that one's commitment be made with full awareness and personal freedom. And so during these years in the seminary, take time to reflect on the serious obligations and the difficulties which are part of the priest's life. Consider whether Christ is calling you to the celibate life. You can make a responsible decision for celibacy only after you have reached the firm conviction that Christ is indeed offering you this gift, which is intended for the good of the Church and for the service of others (see *Letter to Priests,* 9).

To understand what it means to be faithful, we must look to Christ, the "faithful witness" (Rv. 1:5), the Son who "learned to obey through what he suffered" (Heb. 5:8); to Jesus who said: "My aim is to do not my own will, but the will of him who sent me" (Jn. 5:30). We look to Jesus not only to see and contemplate his fidelity to the Father despite all opposition (see Heb. 23:39ff) but also to learn from him the means he employed in order to be faithful: especially prayer and abandonment to God's will (see Lk. 22:39 ff).

## Word of God

3. My brothers and sons in Christ, keep in mind the priorities of the priesthood to which you aspire: namely, prayer and the ministry of the word (Acts 6:4): "It is prayer that shows the essential style of the priest; without prayer this style becomes deformed. Prayer helps us always to find the light that has led us since the beginning of our priestly vocation, and which never ceases to lead us. . . . Prayer enables us to be converted continually, to remain in a state of continuous reaching out to God, which is essential if we wish to lead others to him. Prayer helps us to believe, to hope and to love" (*Letter to Priests,* 10).

It is my hope that during your years in the seminary you will develop an ever greater hunger for the word of God (see Am. 8:11). Meditate on this word daily and study it continually, so that your whole life may become a proclamation of Christ, the Word made flesh (see Jn. 1:14). In this word of God are the beginning and end of all ministry, the purpose of all pastoral activity, the rejuvenating source for faithful perseverance and the one thing which can give meaning and unity to the varied activities of a priest.

## Limits of Human Wisdom

4. "Let the message of Christ, in all its richness, find a home with you" (Col. 3:16). In the knowledge of Christ you have the key to the Gospel. In the knowledge of Christ you have an understanding of the needs of the world. Since he became one with us in all things but sin, your union with Jesus of Nazareth could never and will never be an obstacle to understanding and responding to the needs of the world. And finally, in the knowledge of Christ, you will not only discover and come to understand the limitations of human wisdom and of human solutions to the needs of humanity, but you will also experience the power of Jesus, and the value of human reason and human endeavor when they are taken up in the strength of Jesus, when they are redeemed in Christ.

May our Blessed Mother Mary protect you today and always.

5. May I also take this opportunity to greet the lay people who are present today at Saint Charles Seminary. Your presence here is a sign of your esteem for the ministerial priesthood, as well as being a reminder of that close cooperation between laity and priests which is needed if the mission of Christ is to be fulfilled in our time. I

am happy that you are present and I am grateful for all that you do for the Church in Philadelphia. In particular I ask you to pray for these young men, and for all seminarians, that they may persevere in their calling. Please pray for all priests and for the success of their ministry among God's people. And please pray for the Lord of the harvest to send more laborers into his vineyard, the Church.

## OCTOBER 4, 1979

## 21. AT THE TOMB OF SAINT JOHN NEUMANN, IN THE CHURCH OF SAINT PETER

Dear Brothers and Sisters in Christ,

### Essential: We Are Loved by Christ

I have come to Saint Peter's Church to pray at the tomb of Saint John Neumann, a zealous missionary, a dedicated pastor, a faithful son of Saint Alphonsus in the Congregation of the Most Holy Redeemer, and the fourth Bishop of Philadelphia.

As I stand in this Church, I am reminded of the one thing which motivated Saint John Neumann throughout his life: his love for Christ. His own prayers show us this love; for from the time he was a child he used to say: "Jesus, for you I want to live; for you I want to die; I want to be all yours in life; I want to be all yours in death" (Nicola Ferrante, *S. Giovanni Neumann, CSSR, Pioniere del Vangelo,* p. 25). And at the first Mass he celebrated as a priest, he prayed in these words: "Lord, give me holiness."

My brothers and sisters in Christ: this is the lesson we learn from the life of Saint John Neumann, and the message which I leave with you today: what really matters in life is that we are loved by Christ, and that we love him in return. In comparison to the love of Jesus, everything else is secondary. And without the love of Jesus, everything else is useless.

May Mary, our Mother of Perpetual Help, intercede for us; may Saint John Neumann pray for us; and with the help of their prayers may we persevere in faith, be joyful in hope and be strengthened in our love for Jesus Christ, our Redeemer and Lord.

## 22. GREETING TO THE SPANISH-SPEAKING PEOPLE AT SAINT PETER'S CHURCH

Dear Spanish-speaking Brothers and Sisters,

### Saint John Neumann: An Example of the Immigrant's Catholic Faith

I greet you with joy and I thank you for your enthusiastic presence here, in the Church of Saint Peter, which houses the remains of Saint John Neumann, the first American man to be canonized a saint.

You, members of the Spanish-speaking community, have gathered in great numbers in this place, you who arrived in this country as immigrants, or who were born here of immigrant ancestors, but who preserve the Christian faith as the greatest treasure of your tradition.

Saint John Neumann too was an immigrant, and he experienced many of the difficulties that you yourselves have encountered: the difficulties of language, of a different culture, of social adaptation.

### Fidelity to the Gospel Leads to the Catholic Church

Everyone knows about your efforts and perseverance in preserving your own religious heritage, which is also at the same time placed at the service of the whole national community, so that it may be a witness of unity within a pluralism of religion, culture and social living.

In their fidelity to the saving message of Jesus Christ, your ecclesial communities will find the proper path for experiencing membership in the universal Church and for taking care of this world.

May devotion to Mary our Mother, and your communion with the Vicar of Christ, continue to be, as in the past, the power that fosters and increases your Christian faith.

To all of you here present, to those who have not been able to come, in particular to the sick and the aged, who are spiritually united with this meeting, with all my heart I impart my special Apostolic Blessing.

## 23. IN THE UKRAINIAN CATHEDRAL OF THE IMMACULATE CONCEPTION

*Praised be Jesus Christ!*

### Paternal Greetings

With this Christian greeting I address you, dear brothers and sisters, in your native Ukrainian language before beginning to speak to you in English.

In the first place I greet all the members of the Hierarchy here present, both of the metropolitan area of Philadelphia as well as that of Pittsburgh.

I greet all the dear priests and Religious men and women.

I cordially salute all you, dear faithful of the Ukrainian metropolitan area of Philadelphia, who are gathered here in this temple of the Most Holy Mother of God, to honor in my person the successor of Saint Peter in the See of Rome, the Vicar of Christ on earth.

On all of you, dear brothers and sisters, I invoke copious graces from almighty God, through the intercession of the Immaculate Virgin Mary, to whom your cathedral is dedicated.

I bless you all from the bottom of my heart. Praised be Jesus Christ!

Dear Brothers and Sisters,

## You Are Part of Christ's Household

"Now in Christ Jesus . . . you are citizens like all the saints, and part of God's household. You are part of a building that has the apostles and prophets for its foundations, and Christ Jesus himself for its main cornerstone" (Eph. 2:13, 19–20). With these words the Apostle Paul reminded the Ephesians of the tremendous blessing they had received in becoming members of the Church. And those words are still true today. You are part of the household of God. You, members of the Ukrainian tradition, are part of a building that has the apostles and prophets for its foundations, and Christ Jesus himself for its main cornerstone. This has all occurred according to the providential plan of God.

Several years ago, my beloved predecessor, Paul VI, gave a stone from the tomb of Saint Peter to be included in the construction of this beautiful Cathedral dedicated to Mary Immaculate. Pope Paul VI intended this gift to be a visible symbol of the love and esteem of the Apostolic See of Rome for the Ukrainian Church. At the same time, this stone was meant to serve as a sign of the fidelity of the Ukrainian Church to the See of Peter. In this profound symbolic gesture, Paul VI was reaffirming the teaching of the Apostle Paul in the letter to the Ephesians.

Today, as successor to Paul VI in the Chair of Saint Peter, I come to visit you in this magnificent new Cathedral. I am happy for this opportunity. I welcome the occasion to assure you, as universal pastor of the Church, that all who have inherited the Ukrainian tradition have an important and distinguished part to fulfill in the Catholic Church.

## Esteem for Ukrainian People and Their Traditions

As history testifies, the Church developed a number of rites and traditions as in the course of time she spread from Jerusalem to the nations and took flesh in the language, culture and human traditions of the individual peoples who accepted the Gospel with open hearts. These various rites and traditions, far from being a sign of deviation, infidelity or disunity, were in fact unfailing proof of the presence of the Holy Spirit who continually renews and enriches the Church, the kingdom of Christ already present in mystery (see *Lumen Gentium*, 3).

The various traditions within the Church give expression to the multitude of ways the Gospel can take root and flower in the lives of God's people. They are living evidence of the richness of the Church. Each one, while united to all the others in the "same faith, the same sacraments and the same government" (*Orientalium Ecclesiarum*, 2), is nevertheless manifested in its own liturgy, ecclesiastical discipline and spiritual patrimony. Each tradition combined particular artistic expressions and unique spiritual insights with an unparalleled lived experience of being faithful to Christ. It was in view of these considerations that the Second Vatican Council declared: "History, tradition, and numerous ecclesiastical institutions clearly manifest how much the universal Church is indebted to the Eastern Churches. Thus this sacred Synod not only honors this ecclesiastical and spiritual heritage with merited esteem and rightful praise, but also unhesitatingly looks upon it as the heritage of Christ's universal Church" (*Orientalium Ecclesiarum*, 5).

For many years, I have highly esteemed the Ukrainian people. I have known of the many sufferings and injustices you have endured. These have been and continue to be matters of great concern to me. I am also mindful of the struggles of the Ukrainian Catholic Church, throughout its history, to remain faithful to the Gospel and to be in union with the Successor of Saint Peter. I cannot forget the countless Ukrainian martyrs, in ancient and more recent times, most of whose names are unknown, who gave their lives rather than abandon their faith. I mention these in order to show my profound esteem for the Ukrainian Church and its proved fidelity in suffering.

I also wish to mention those things which you have preserved as your special spiritual patrimony: the Slavonic liturgical language, the ecclesiastical music and the numerous forms of piety which have developed over the centuries and continue to nourish your lives. Your appreciation of these treasures of the Ukrainian tradition is demonstrated by the way that you have maintained your attachment with the Ukrainian Church and have continued to live the faith according to its unique tradition.

My brothers and sisters in Christ, I want to recall in your presence the words Jesus prayed on the vigil of his death upon the Cross: "Father . . . that they may be one" (Jn. 17:11). We must never forget this prayer; in fact, we must continually search for still better ways to safeguard and strengthen the bonds of union which unite us in the one Catholic Church.

Remember the words of Saint Paul: "you form part of a building that has the apostles and prophets for its foundations, and Christ Jesus himself for its main cornerstone" (Eph. 2:20). The unity of this spiritual building, which is the Church, is preserved by fidelity to the cornerstone, who is Christ, and to the teaching of the apostles preserved and explained in the tradition of the Church. A real unity of doctrine binds us as one.

## Unity Depends on Mutual Charity

Catholic unity also entails a recognition of the Successor of Saint Peter and his ministry of strengthening and preserving intact the communion of the universal Church, while safeguarding the existence of legitimate individual traditions within it. The Ukrainian Church, as well as the other Eastern Churches, has a right and duty, in accordance with the teaching of the Council (see *Orientalium Ecclesiarum*, 5), to preserve its own ecclesiastical and spiritual patrimony. It is precisely because these individual traditions are also intended for the enrichment of the universal Church that the Apostolic See of Rome takes great care to protect and foster each one. In turn, the ecclesial communities that follow these traditions are called to adhere with love and respect to certain particular forms of discipline which my predecessors and I, in fulfilling our pastoral responsibility to the universal Church, have judged necessary for the well-being of the whole body of Christ.

To a great extent, our Catholic unity depends on mutual charity. Let us remember that the unity of the Church originated on the Cross of Christ, which broke down the barriers of sin and division and reconciled us with God and with one another. Jesus foretold this unifying act when he said: "and I, if I be lifted up from the earth, will draw all men to myself" (Jn. 12:32). If we continue to imitate the love of Jesus, our Savior, on the Cross, and if we persevere in love for one another, then we shall preserve the bonds of unity in the Church and witness the fulfillment of Jesus' prayer: "Father . . . that they may be one" (Jn. 17:11).

As for the future, I entrust you to the protection of Mary Immaculate, the Mother of God, the Mother of the Church. I know that you honor her with great devotion. This magnificent Cathedral dedicated to the Immaculate Conception bears eloquent witness to your filial love. And for centuries, our Blessed Mother has been the strength of your people throughout their sufferings, and her loving intercession has been a cause of their joy.

Continue to entrust yourselves to her protection.

Continue to be faithful to her son, our Lord Jesus Christ, the Redeemer of the world.

And may the grace of our Lord Jesus Christ be with you all.

## 24. HOMILY TO PRIESTS

Dear Brother Priests,

### Conformity with the Gospel

1. As we celebrate this Mass, which brings together the presidents or chairmen of the Priests' Senates, or Councils, of all the Dioceses of the United States, the theme that suggests itself to our reflection is a vital one: the priesthood itself and its central importance to the task of the Church. In the encyclical letter *Redemptor Hominis*, I described this task in these words: "The Church's fundamental function in every age and particularly in ours is to direct man's gaze, to point the awareness and experience of the whole of humanity towards the mystery of God, to help men to be familiar with the profundity of the Redemption taking place in Christ Jesus" (*Redemptor Hominis*, 10).

Priests' Senates are a new structure in the Church, called for by the Second Vatican Council and recent Church legislation. This new structure gives a concrete expression to the unity of Bishop and priests in the service of shepherding the flock of Christ, and it assists the Bishop in his distinctive role of governing the Diocese, by guaranteeing for him the counsel of representative advisers from among the presbyterium. Our concelebration of today's Eucharist is intended to be a mark of affirmation for the good that has been achieved by your Priests' Senates during these past years, as well as an encouragement to pursue with enthusiasm and determination this important aim, which is "to bring the life and activity of the People of God into greater conformity with the Gospel" (see *Ecclesiae Sanctae*, 16:1). Most of all, however, I want this Mass to be the special occasion on which I can speak through you to all my brother priests throughout this nation about our priesthood. With great love I repeat the words that I wrote to you on Holy Thursday: "For you I am a Bishop, with you I am a priest."

Our priestly vocation is given by the Lord Jesus himself. *It is a call which is personal and individual:* we are called by name as was Jeremiah. It is a call to service: we are sent out to preach the Good News, to "give God's flock a shepherd's care." It is a call to communion of purpose and of action: to be one priesthood with Jesus and with one another, just as Jesus and his Father are one—a unity so beautifully symbolized in this concelebrated Mass.

Priesthood is not merely a task which has been assigned; it is a vocation, a call to be heard again and again. To hear this call and to respond generously to what this call entails is a task for each priest, but it is also a responsibility for the Senates of Priests. This responsibility means *deepening our understanding of the priesthood as Christ instituted it, as he wanted it to be and to remain, and as the Church faithfully explains it and transmits it.* Fidelity to the call to the priesthood means building up this priesthood with God's people by a life of service *according to apostolic priorities:* concentration "on prayer and the ministry of the word" (Acts 6:4).

In the Gospel of Saint Mark the priestly call of the Twelve Apostles is like a bud whose flowering displays a whole theology of priesthood. In the midst of Jesus' ministry, we read that "he went up the mountain and summoned the men he himself had decided on, who came and joined him. He named twelve as his companions whom he would send to preach the good news. . . . " The passage then lists the names of the Twelve (Mk. 3:13–14). Here we see three significant aspects of the call given by Jesus: he called his first priests individually and by *name;* he called them for the service of his word, *to preach the Gospel;* and he made them his own *companions,* drawing them into that unity of life and action which he shares with his Father in the very life of the Trinity.

## Total Surrender to Christ's Call

2. Let us explore these three dimensions of our priesthood by reflecting on today's Scripture readings. For it is in the tradition of the prophetic call that the Gospel places the priestly vocation of the Twelve Apostles by Jesus. When the priest reflects on Jeremiah's call to be prophet, he is both reassured and disturbed. "Have no fear . . . because I am with you to deliver you," says the Lord to the one whom he calls, "for look, I place *my* words in your mouth." Who would not take heart at hearing such divine assurance? Yet when we consider *why* such reassurance is needed, do we not see in ourselves that same reluctance we find in Jeremiah's reply? Like him, at times, our concept of this ministry is too earthbound; we lack confidence in him who calls us. We also become too attached to our own vision of ministry, thinking that it depends too much on our own talents and abilities, and at times

forgetting that it is God who calls us, as he called Jeremiah from the womb. Nor is it our work or our ability that is primary: we are called to speak the words of God and not our own; to minister the sacraments he has given to his Church; and to call people to a love which he first made possible.

Hence *the surrender to God's call can be made with utmost confidence* and without reservation. Our surrender to God's will must be total—the "yes" given once for all which has as its pattern the "yes" spoken by Jesus himself. As Saint Paul tells us: "As God keeps his word, I declare that my word to you is not 'yes' one minute and 'no' the next. Jesus Christ . . . was not alternately 'yes' and 'no'; he was never anything but 'yes'" (2 Cor. 4:7). But this gift is not primarily for the priest himself; it is rather a gift of God for the whole Church and for her mission to the world. Priesthood is an abiding sacramental sign which shows that the love of the Good Shepherd for his flock will never be absent. In my letter to you priests last Holy Thursday, I developed this aspect of the priesthood as God's gift: our priesthood, I said, "constitutes a special *ministerium,* that is to say 'service', in relation to the community of believers. It does not however take its origin from that community, as though it were the community that 'called' or 'delegated.' The sacramental priesthood is truly a gift for this community and comes from Christ himself, from the fullness of his priesthood" (Letter, 5). In this gift-giving to his people, it is the divine giver who takes the initiative; it is he who calls the ones "he himself had decided on."

Hence when we reflect on the intimacy between the Lord and his prophet, his priest—an intimacy arising as a result of the call which he has initiated—we can better understand certain characteristics of the priesthood and realize their appropriateness for the Church's mission today as well as in times past:

a) Priesthood is forever—*tu es sacerdos in aeternum*—we do not return the gift once given. It cannot be that God who gave the impulse to say "yes" now wishes to hear "no."

b) Nor should it surprise the world that the call of God through the Church continues to offer us a celibate ministry of love and service after the example of our Lord Jesus Christ. God's call has indeed stirred us to the depths of our being. And after centuries of experience, the Church knows how deeply fitting it is that priests should give this concrete response in their lives to express the totality of the yes they have spoken to the Lord who calls them by name to his service.

c) The fact that there is a personal individual call to the priesthood given by the Lord to "the men he himself had decided on" is in accord with the prophetic tradition. It should help us too to understand that the Church's traditional decision to call men to the priesthood, and not to call women, is not a statement about human rights, nor an exclusion of women from holiness and mission in the Church. Rather this decision expresses the conviction of the Church about this particular dimension of the gift of priesthood by which God has chosen to shepherd his flock.

## Priesthood: A Shepherd's Care

3. Dear brothers: "God's flock is in your midst; give it a shepherd's care." How close to the essence of our understanding of priesthood is the role of shepherd;

throughout the history of salvation it is a recurring image of God's care for his people. And *only in the role of Jesus, the Good Shepherd, can our pastoral ministry as priests be understood.* Recall how, in the call of the Twelve, Jesus summoned them to be his companions precisely in order to "send them out to preach the good news." Priesthood is mission and service; it is being "sent out" from Jesus to "give his flock a shepherd's care." It means pointing the awareness of humanity to the mystery of God, to the profundity of Redemption taking place in Christ Jesus. Priestly ministry is missionary in its very core: it means being sent out for others, like Christ sent from his Father for the sake of the Gospel, sent to evangelize. In the words of Paul VI, "evangelizing means bringing the Good News into all the strata of humanity . . . and making it new" (*Evangelii Nuntiandi,* 18). At the foundation and center of its dynamism, evangelization contains a clear proclamation that salvation is in Jesus Christ the Son of God. It is his mystery that we proclaim to the world. And the effectiveness of our proclamation, and hence the very success of our priesthood, depends on our fidelity to the Magisterium, through which the Church guards "the rich deposit of faith with the help of the Holy Spirit who dwells within us" (2 Tm. 1:14).

As a pattern for every ministry and apostolate in the Church, priestly ministry is never to be conceived in terms of an acquisition; insofar as it is a gift, it is a gift to be proclaimed and shared with others. Do we not see this clearly in Jesus' teaching when the mother of James and John asked that her sons sit on his right hand and his left in his kingdom? "You know how those who exercise authority among the Gentiles lord it over them; their great ones make their importance felt. It cannot be like that with you. Anyone who aspires to greatness must serve the rest, and whoever wants to rank among you must serve the needs of all. Such is the case with the Son of Man who has come, not to be served by others, but to serve, to give his own life as a ransom for the many" (Mt. 20:25–28).

Just as Jesus was most perfectly a "man-for-others" in giving himself up totally on the Cross, so the priest is most of all servant and "man-for-others" when he acts *in persona Christi* in the Eucharist, leading the Church in that celebration in which this Sacrifice of the Cross is renewed. For in the Church's daily Eucharistic worship the "Good News" that the Apostles were sent out to proclaim is preached in its fullness; the work of our Redemption is reenacted.

How perfectly the Fathers at the Second Vatican Council captured this fundamental truth in their *Decree on Priestly Life and Ministry:* "The other sacraments, as every ministry of the Church and every work of the apostolate, are linked with the holy Eucharist and are directed towards it. . . . Hence the Eucharist shows itself to be source and the summit of all evangelization" (*Presbyterorum Ordinis,* 5). *In the celebration of the Eucharist, we priests are at the very heart of our ministry of service,* of "giving God's flock a shepherd's care." All our pastoral endeavors are incomplete until our people are led to the full and active participation in the Eucharistic Sacrifice.

### Companions of Jesus Through Prayer, Unity, Fraternity

4. Let us recall how Jesus named twelve of his *companions. The call to priestly service includes an invitation to special intimacy with Christ.* The lived experience of

priests in every generation has led them to discover in their own lives and ministry the absolute centrality of their personal union with Jesus, of being his companions. No one can effectively bring the good news of Jesus to others unless he himself has first been his constant companion through personal prayer, unless he has learned from Jesus the mystery to be proclaimed.

This union with Jesus, modeled on his oneness with his Father, has a further intrinsic dimension, as his own prayer at the Last Supper reveals: "that they may be one, Father, even as we are one" (Jn. 17:11). His priesthood is one, and this unity must be actual and effective among his chosen companions. Hence unity among priests, lived out in fraternity and friendship, becomes a demand and an integral part of the life of a priest.

*Unity among priests* is not a unity or fraternity that is directed toward itself. *It is for the sake of the Gospel,* to symbolize, in the living out of the priesthood, the essential direction to which the Gospel calls all people: to the union of love with him and one another. And this union alone can guarantee peace and justice and dignity to every human being. Surely this is the underlying sense of the prayer of Jesus when he continues: "I pray also for those who believe in me through their word, that all may be one as you, Father, are in me, and I in you" (Jn. 17:20–21). Indeed, how will the world come to believe that the Father has sent Jesus unless people can see in visible ways that those who believe in Jesus have heard his commandment to "love one another"? And how will believers receive a witness that such love is a concrete possibility unless they find it in the example of the unity of their priestly ministers, of those whom Jesus himself forms into one priesthood as his own companions?

My brother priests: have we not here touched upon the heart of the matter— our zeal for the service of the people. This concelebrated Mass, which so beautifully symbolizes the unity of our priesthood, gives to the whole world the witness of the unity for which Jesus prayed to his Father on our behalf. But it must not become a merely transient manifestation, which would render fruitless the prayer of Jesus. Every Eucharist renews this prayer for our unity: "Lord, remember your Church throughout the world; make us grow in love, together with John Paul our Pope, . . . our bishop, and all the clergy."

Your Priests' Senates, as new structures in the Church, provide a wonderful opportunity to give visible witness to the one priesthood you share with your Bishops and with one another, and to demonstrate what must be at the heart of the renewal of every structure in the Church: the unity for which Jesus himself prayed.

## Understand Priesthood in Its Ecclesial Aspects

At the beginning of this homily, I charged you with the task of taking responsibility for your priesthood, a task for each one of you personally, a charge to be shared with all the priests, and especially to be a concern for your Priests' Councils. The faith of the whole Church needs to have clearly in focus the proper understanding of the priesthood and of its place in the mission of the Church. So the Church depends on you to deepen ever more this understanding, and to put it into practice in your lives and ministry: in other words, to share the gift of your priesthood with the

Church by renewing the response you have already made to Christ's invitation—"come, follow me"—by giving yourselves as totally as he did.

At times we hear the words, "Pray for priests." And today I address these words as an appeal, as a plea, to all the faithful of the Church in the United States. Pray for priests, so that each and every one of them will repeatedly say *yes* to the call he has received, remain constant in preaching the Gospel message, and be faithful forever as the companion of our Lord Jesus Christ.

Dear Brother Priests: as we renew the Paschal Mystery and stand as disciples at the foot of the Cross with Mary the Mother of Jesus, let us entrust ourselves to her. In her love we shall find strength for our weakness and joy for our hearts.

## 25. SAINT PATRICK'S CHURCH

Dear Brothers and Sisters,

It gives me great pleasure to be here today with you, in the heartland of America, in this lovely Saint Patrick's Church at the Irish Settlement. My pastoral journey through the United States would have seemed incomplete without a visit, although short, to a rural community like this. Let me share with you some thoughts that this particular setting brings to mind, and that are prompted by my meeting with the families who make up this rural parish.

### Proclaim Christ

To proclaim Jesus Christ and his Gospel is the fundamental task which the Church has received from her Founder, and which she has taken up ever since the dawn of the first Pentecost. The early Christians were faithful to this mission which the Lord Jesus gave them through his Apostles: "They devoted themselves to the apostles' teaching and fellowship, to the breaking of the bread and the prayer" (Acts 2:42). This is what every community of believers must do: proclaim Christ and his Gospel in fellowship and apostolic faith, in prayer and in the celebration of the Eucharist.

How many Catholic parishes have been started like yours in the early beginnings of the settlement of this region: a small, unpretentious church at the center of a group of family farms, a place and a symbol of prayer and fellowship, the heart of a real Christian community where people know each other personally, share each other's problems and give witness together to the love of Jesus Christ!

On your farms you are close to God's nature; in your work on the land you follow the rhythm of the seasons; and in your hearts you feel close to each other as children of a common Father and as brothers and sisters in Christ. How privileged you are, that in such a setting you can worship God together, celebrate your spiritual unity and help to carry each other's burdens. The 1974 Synod of Bishops in Rome and Paul VI in his Apostolic Exhortation *Evangelii Nuntiandi* have devoted considerable attention to the small communities where a more human dimension is achieved than is possible in a big city or in a sprawling metropolis. Let your small community be a true place of Christian living and evangelization, not isolating yourselves from the Diocese or from the universal Church, knowing that a community with a human face must also reflect the face of Christ.

### Your Local Community: Part of the Universal Church

Feel grateful to God for the blessings he gives you, not least for the blessing of belonging to this rural parish community. May our heavenly Father bless you, each and every one of you. May the simplicity of your life-style and the closeness of your community be the fertile ground for a growing commitment to Jesus Christ, Son of God and Savior of the world.

I for my part thank the Lord for the opportunity he gave me to come and visit you, and as Vicar of Christ to represent him in your midst. Thank you also for your warm welcome and for offering me your hospitality as I prepare for my encounter with the larger group of people at the Living Farms.

My gratitude goes in a special way to the Bishop of Des Moines for his cordial invitation. He pointed out many reasons why a visit to Des Moines would be so meaningful: a city that is one of the major agricultural centers of this country; the headquarters also of the dynamic and deserving Catholic Rural Life Conference, whose history is so closely linked to the name of a pastor and a friend of the rural people, Monsignor Luigi Ligutti; a region distinguished by community involvement and family-centered activity, a Diocese that is involved, together with all the Catholic Bishops of the heartland, in a major effort to build community.

My greetings and best wishes go also to the whole state of Iowa, to the civil authorities and to all the people who have so generously extended to me a hospitality marked by kindness.

May God bless you through the intercession of Mary, the Mother of Jesus and the Mother of his Church.

## 26. HOMILY AT LIVING HISTORY FARMS

Dear Brothers and Sisters in Christ,

Here in the heartland of America, in the middle of the bountiful fields at harvest time, I come to celebrate the Eucharist. As I stand in your presence in this period of autumn harvest, those words which are repeated whenever people gather for the Eucharist seem to be so appropriate: "Blessed are you, Lord, God of all creation, through your goodness we have this bread to offer, which earth has given and human hands have made."

As one who has always been close to nature, let me speak to you today about the land, the earth and that "which earth has given and human hands have made."

## The Land: God's Gift; Man's Responsibility

1. The land is God's gift entrusted to people from the very beginning. It is God's gift, given by a loving Creator as a means of sustaining the life which he had created. But the land is not only God's gift; it is also man's responsibility. Man, himself created from the dust of the earth (see Gn. 3:7), was made its master (see Gn. 1:26). In order to bring forth fruit, the land would depend upon the genius and skillfulness, the sweat and the toil of the people to whom God would entrust it. Thus the food which would sustain life on earth is willed by God to be both that "which earth has given and human hands have made."

To all of you who are farmers and all who are associated with agricultural production I want to say this: the Church highly esteems your work. Christ himself showed his esteem for agricultural life when he described God his Father as the "vinedresser" (Jn. 15:1). You cooperate with the Creator, the "vinedresser," in sustaining and nurturing life. You fulfill the command of God given at the very beginning: "Fill the earth and subdue it" (Gn. 1:28). Here in the heartland of America, the valleys and hills have been blanketed with grain, the herds and the flocks have multiplied many times over. By hard work you have become masters of the earth and you have subdued it. By reason of the abundant fruitfulness which modern agricultural advances have made possible, you support the lives of millions who themselves do not work on the land, but who live because of what you produce. Mindful of this, I make my own the words of my beloved predecessor Paul VI: "It is the dignity of those who work on the land and of all those engaged in different levels of research and action in the field of agricultural development which must be unceasingly proclaimed and promoted" (Address to the World Food Conference, November 9, 1974, no. 4).

What then are the attitudes that should pervade man's relationship to the land? As always we must look for the answer beginning with Jesus, for, as Saint Paul says: "In your minds you must be the same as Christ Jesus" (Phil. 2:5). In the life of Jesus, we see a real closeness to the land. In his teaching, he referred to the "birds of the air" (Mt. 6:26), the "lilies of the field" (Mt. 7:17). He talked about the farmer who went out to sow the seed (Mt. 13:4ff); and he referred to his heavenly father as the "vinedresser" (Jn. 5:1) and to himself as the "good shepherd" (Jn. 10:14). This closeness to nature, this spontaneous awareness of creation as a gift from God, as well as the blessing of a close-knit family—characteristics of farm life in every age, including our own—these were part of the life of Jesus. Therefore, I invite you to let your attitudes always be the same as those of Christ Jesus.

2. Three attitudes in particular are appropriate for rural life. In the first place, gratitude. Recall the first words of Jesus in the Gospel we have just heard, words of gratitude to his heavenly father: "Father, Lord of heaven and earth, to you I offer praise." Let this be your attitude as well. Every day the farmer is reminded of how

much he depends upon God. From the heavens come the rain, the wind and the sunshine. They occur without the farmer's command or control. The farmer prepares the soil, plants the seed, and cultivates the crop. But God makes it grow; he alone is the source of life. Even the natural disasters, such as hailstorms and drought, tornadoes or floods, remind the farmer of his dependence upon God. Surely it was this awareness that prompted the early pilgrims to America to establish the feast which you call "Thanksgiving." After every harvest, whatever it may have been that year, with humility and thankfulness the farmer makes his own the prayer of Jesus: "Father, Lord of heaven and earth, to you I offer praise."

Secondly, the land must be conserved with care since it is intended to be fruitful for generation upon generation. You who live in the heartland of America have been entrusted with some of the earth's best land: the soil so rich in minerals, the climate so favorable for producing bountiful crops, with fresh water and unpolluted air available all around you. You are stewards of some of the most important resources God has given to the world. Therefore conserve the land well, so that your children's children and generations after them will inherit an even richer land than was entrusted to you. But also remember what the heart of your vocation is. While it is true here that farming today provides an economic livelihood for the farmer, still it will always be more than an enterprise of profit-making. In farming, you cooperate with the Creator in the very sustenance of life on earth.

In the third place, I want to speak about generosity, a generosity which arises from the fact that "God destined the earth and all it contains for all men and all peoples so that all created things would be shared fairly by all mankind under the guidance of justice tempered by charity" (*Gaudium et Spes,* 69). You who are farmers today are stewards of a gift from God which was intended for the good of all humanity. You have the potential to provide food for the millions who have nothing to eat and thus help to rid the world of famine. To you I direct the same question asked by Paul VI five years ago: "if the potential of nature is immense, if that of the mastery of the human genius over the universe seems almost unlimited, what is it that is too often missing . . . except that generosity, that anxiety which is stimulated by the sight of the sufferings and the miseries of the poor, that deep conviction that the whole family suffers when one of its members is in distress?" (*Address to the World Food Conference,* November 9, 1974, no. 9).

Recall the time when Jesus saw the hungry crowd gathered on the hillside. What was his response? He did not content himself with expressing his compassion. He gave his disciples the command: "Give them something to eat yourselves" (Mt. 14:16). Did he not intend those same words for us today, for us who live at the closing of the twentieth century, for us who have the means available to feed the hungry of the world? Let us respond generously to his command by sharing the fruit of our labor, by contributing to others the knowledge we have gained, by being the promoters of rural development everywhere and by defending the right to work of the rural population, since every person has a right to useful employment.

## Christ the Living Bread

3. Farmers everywhere provide bread for all humanity, but it is Christ alone who is the bread of life. He alone satisfies the deepest hunger of humanity. As Saint Augustine said: "Our hearts are restless until they rest in you" (*Confessions* I,1). While we are mindful of the physical hunger of millions of our brothers and sisters on all continents, at this Eucharist we are reminded that the deepest hunger lies in the human soul. To all who acknowledge this hunger within them Jesus says: "Come to me, all you who are weary and find life burdensome, and I will refresh you." My brothers and sisters in Christ: let us listen to these words with all our heart. They are directed to every one of us. To all who till the soil, to all who benefit from the fruit of their labors, to every man and woman on earth, Jesus says: "Come to me . . . and I will refresh you." Even if all the physical hunger of the world were satisfied, even if everyone who is hungry were fed by his or her own labor or by the generosity of others, the deepest hunger of man would still exist.

We are reminded in the letter of Saint Paul to the Galatians: "All that matters is that one is created anew." Only Christ can create one anew; and this new creation finds its beginning only in his Cross and Resurrection. In Christ alone all creation is restored to its proper order. Therefore, I say: Come, all of you, to Christ. He is the bread of life. Come to Christ and you will never be hungry again.

Bring with you to Christ the products of your hands, the fruit of the land, that "which earth has given and human hands have made." At this altar these gifts will be transformed into the Eucharist of the Lord.

Bring with you your efforts to make the land fruitful, your labor and your weariness. At this altar, because of the Life, Death and Resurrection of Christ, all human activity is sanctified, lifted up and fulfilled.

Bring with you the poor, the sick, the exiled and the hungry; bring all who are weary and find life burdensome. At this altar they will be refreshed, for his yoke is easy and his burden light.

Above all, bring your families and dedicate them anew to Christ, so that they may continue to be the working, living and loving community where nature is revered, where burdens are shared and where the Lord is praised in gratitude.

## 27. VISIT IN HOLY NAME CATHEDRAL

Dear Brothers and Sisters in Christ,

From Philadelphia to Des Moines, from Des Moines to Chicago! In one day I have seen a great part of your spacious land, and I have thanked God for the faith and the achievements of its people. This evening brings me to Chicago, to Holy Name Cathedral. I am grateful to the Lord for the joy of this encounter.

My special gratitude goes to you, Cardinal Cody, my Brother for many years in the College of Bishops, the Pastor of this great See of Chicago. I thank you for your kind invitation and for all you have done to prepare for my coming. A greeting of esteem and love goes also to all the priests, both diocesan and religious, who share so particularly and intimately in the responsibility of bringing the message of salvation to all the people. I am likewise looking forward to meeting people from all categories in the Church: deacons and seminarians, religious brothers and women religious, husbands and wives, mothers and fathers, the single, the widowed, the young and the children: so that we can celebrate together our ecclesial unity in Christ.

## Cathedral: Sign of Local Unity

It is with a special joy that I greet all of you who are present here in Holy Name Cathedral, to which, by God's grace, I return once more. Here there is symbolized and actuated the unity of this Archdiocese, this local Church—rich in history and in fidelity, rich in generosity to the Gospel, rich in the faith of millions of men, women and children who over the decades have found holiness and justice in our Lord Jesus Christ.

And today I wish to celebrate with you the great mystery expressed in the title of your Cathedral: the Holy Name of Jesus, Son of God and Son of Mary.

I have come to you to speak of salvation in Jesus Christ. I have come to proclaim it anew: to proclaim this message to you with you and for you—and for all the people. As Successor of the Apostle Peter speaking in the Holy Spirit, I too proclaim: "There is salvation in no one else, for there is no other name under heaven given by which we must be saved" (Acts 4:12).

It is in the name of Jesus that I come to you. Our service to the needy of the world is exercised in the name of Jesus. Repentance and the forgiveness of sins are preached in his name (see Lk. 24:27). And through faith, all of us have "life in his name" (Jn 20:31).

In this name—in the holy name of Jesus—there is help for the living, consolation for the dying and joy and hope for the whole world.

Brothers and sisters in the Church of Chicago: let us do everything "in the name of the Lord Jesus" (Col. 3:12).

May the words which I address to you on my arrival here—coming from him who is called to be servant of the servants of God—be for all of Chicago, the authorities and the people, an expression of my fraternal solidarity. How greatly I would like to meet each one of you personally, to visit you in your homes, to walk your streets so that I may better understand the richness of your personalities and the depth of your aspirations. May my words to you be an encouragement for all those who strive to bring to your community a sense of brotherhood, dignity and unity. For in coming here I want to show my respect—beyond the limit of the Catholic faith, even beyond all religion—for man, for the humanity that is in every human being. The Christ, whom I unworthily represent, taught me to do this. I must obey his command of fraternal love. And I do it with great joy.

May God uplift humanity in this great City of Chicago!

## 28. TO RELIGIOUS BROTHERS

Brothers in Christ,

### Christ Called to Follow Him More Closely

1. "I thank my God whenever I think of you; and every time I pray for you, I pray with joy, remembering how you have helped to spread the Good News from the day you first heard it right up to the present" (Phil. 1:3–5). These words of Saint Paul express my feelings this evening. It is good to be with you. And I am grateful to God for your presence in the Church and for your collaboration in proclaiming the Good News. Brothers, Christ is the purpose and the measure of our lives. In the knowledge of Christ, your vocation took its origin; and in his love, your life is sustained. For he has called you to follow him more closely in a life consecrated through the gift of the evangelical counsels. You follow him in sacrifice and willing generosity. You follow him in joy, "singing gratefully to God from your hearts in psalms, hymns, and inspired songs" (Col. 3:16). And you follow him in fidelity, even considering it an honor to suffer humiliation for the sake of his name (see Acts 5:42).

Your religious consecration is essentially an act of love. It is an imitation of Christ who gave himself to his Father for the salvation of the world. In Christ, the love of his Father and his love for mankind are united. And so it is with you. Your religious consecration has not only deepened your baptismal gift of union with the Trinity, but it has also called you to greater service of the people of God. You are united more closely to the person of Christ, and you share more fully in his mission for the salvation of the world.

It is about your share in the mission of Christ that I wish to speak this evening.

### Spiritual Freedom

2. Let me begin by reminding you of the personal qualities needed to share effectively with Christ in his mission. In the first place, you must be interiorly free, spiritually free. The freedom of which I speak is a paradox to many; it is even misunderstood by some who are members of the Church. Nevertheless, it is the fundamental human freedom, and it was won for us by Christ on the Cross. As Saint Paul said, "We were still helpless when at his appointed moment Christ died for sinful men" (Rom. 5:6).

This spiritual freedom which you received in Baptism you have sought to increase and strengthen through your willing acceptance of the call to follow Jesus more closely in poverty, chastity and obedience. No matter what others may contend or the world may believe, your promises to observe the evangelical counsels have not shackled your freedom: you are not less free because you are obedient; and you are not less loving because of your celibacy. On the contrary. The faithful practice of the evangelical counsels accentuates your human dignity, liberates the human heart and causes your spirit to burn with undivided love for Christ and for his brothers and sisters in the world (see *Perfectae Caritatis,* 1,12).

But this freedom of an undivided heart (see 1 Cor. 7:32–35) must be maintained by continual vigilance and fervent prayer. If you unite yourselves continually to Christ in prayer, you will always be free and ever more eager to share in his mission.

### Strength in the Eucharist

3. Secondly, you must center your life around the Eucharist. While you share in many ways in the Passion, Death and Resurrection of Christ, it is especially in the Eucharist where this is celebrated and made effective. At the Eucharist, your spirit is renewed, your mind and heart are refreshed and you will find the strength to live day by day for him who is the Redeemer of the world.

### Listen to God's Word

4. Thirdly, be dedicated to God's word. Remember the words of Jesus: "My mother and my brothers are those who hear the word of God and put it into practice" (Lk. 8:21). If you sincerely listen to God's word, and humbly but persistently try to put it into practice, like the seed sown in fertile soil, his word will bear fruit in your life.

### Fraternal Life and Charity

5. The fourth and final element which makes effective your sharing in Christ's mission is fraternal life. Your life lived in religious community is the first concrete expression of love of neighbor. It is there that the first demands of self-sacrifice and generous service are exercised in order to build up the fraternal community. This love which unites you as brothers in community becomes in turn the force which supports you in your mission for the Church.

### Original Charism

6. Brothers in Christ, today the universal Church honors Saint Francis of Assisi. As I think of this great saint, I am reminded of his delight in God's creation, his childlike simplicity, his poetic marriage to "Lady Poverty," his missionary zeal and his desire to share fully in the Cross of Christ. What a splendid heritage he has handed on to those among you who are Franciscans, and to all of us.

7. Similarly, God has raised up many other men and women outstanding in holiness. These too he destined to found religious families which, each in a distinctive way, would play an important role in the mission of the Church. The key to the effectiveness of every one of these religious institutes has been their faithfulness to the original charism God had begun in their founder or foundress for the enrichment of the Church. For this reason, I repeat the words of Paul VI: "Be faithful to the spirit of your founders, to their evangelical intentions and to the example of their holiness. . . . It is precisely here that the dynamism proper to each religious family finds

its origin" (*Evangelica Testificatio,* 11–12). And this remains a secure basis for judging what specific ecclesial activities each institute, and every individual member, should undertake in order to fulfill the mission of Christ.

### Goal: Community of the Trinity

8. Never forget the specific and ultimate aim of all apostolic service: to lead men and women of our day to communion with the Most Holy Trinity. In the present age, mankind is increasingly tempted to seek security in possessions, knowledge and power. By the witness of your life consecrated to Christ in poverty, chastity and obedience, you challenge this false security. You are a living reminder that Christ alone is "the way, the truth and the life" (Jn. 14:6).

9. Religious brothers today are involved in a wide range of activities: teaching in Catholic schools, spreading God's word in missionary activity, responding to a variety of human needs by both your witness and your actions, and serving by prayer and sacrifice. As you go forward in your particular service, keep in mind the advice of Saint Paul: "Whatever you do, work at it with your whole being. Do it for the Lord rather than for men" (Col. 3:23). For the measure of your effectiveness will be the degree of your love for Jesus Christ.

### Our Service Must Conform to the Gospel

10. Finally, every form of apostolic service, of either an individual or a community, must be in accord with the Gospel as it is put forward by the Magisterium. For all Christian service is aimed at spreading the Gospel; and all Christian service incorporates gospel values. Therefore be men of God's word: men whose hearts burn within them when they hear the word proclaimed (see Lk. 24:32); who shape every action according to its demands; and who desire to see the Good News proclaimed to the ends of the earth.

Brothers, your presence in the Church and your collaboration in promoting the Gospel are an encouragement and joy to me in my role as Pastor of the whole Church. May God give each of you long life. May he call many others to follow Christ in the religious life. And may the Virgin Mary, Mother of the Church and model of consecrated life, obtain for you the joy and consolation of Christ, her son.

### OCTOBER 5, 1979

### 29. ADDRESS AT PROVIDENCE OF GOD CHURCH

Dear Brothers and Sisters, dear Friends in Christ,

Thank you for your welcome!

I am happy to greet and bless those groups which the Campaign for Human Development has assisted and whose representatives are here today.

This Campaign has been a witness to the Church's living presence in the world among the most needy, and to her commitment to continuing the mission of Christ, who was sent "to bring glad tidings to the poor, to proclaim liberty to the captives, . . . and release to the prisoners" (Lk. 4:18–19).

I commend the Bishops of the United States for their wisdom and compassion in establishing the Campaign for Human Development ten years ago; and I thank the whole Catholic community for the generous support given to this initiative during all these years.

Nearly fifteen hundred groups and organizations, I have been told, have received campaign funding. The efforts aimed at establishing self-help projects deserve praise and encouragement, for in this way an effective contribution is made to removing the causes and not merely the evil effects of injustice. The projects assisted by the campaign have helped to create a more human and just social order, and they enable many people to achieve an increased measure of rightful self-reliance. They remain in the life of the Church a witness to the love and concern of our Lord Jesus Christ.

May God give you strength, courage and wisdom to continue this work for justice. God bless you all.

Dear Spanish-speaking Brothers and Sisters,

### Live in Fraternal Peace

I am very happy to be here among you in the course of my journey, a short but full one, through this large and beautiful country.

My visit is primarily a pastoral one. It is intended as an invitation to brotherly coexistence and to the peaceful development of good relations between men and peoples, an invitation to seek in Christ the source and the energy in order that God's call to us as men and as Christians may be realized in our lives.

I greatly trust in your prayers, especially in those of children, of old and sick people, and of all those who, through their physical or moral suffering, are closer to Christ, our Savior and Redeemer.

I greet you all with affection and give you my most cordial blessing.

## 30. MASS FOR THE POLISH COMMUNITY

Dear Brothers and Sisters,

### Catholic Poles: Signs of God's Love in America

In a while we shall be offering to God bread and wine. I shall accept those gifts from your hands to offer them to the heavenly Father. We do so during every Holy Mass. But although we do it each time in the same way, the offering *nevertheless each time* has another content, it sounds a different voice on our lips and reveals different secrets of our hearts. Today it speaks in a very special way.

By accepting *your offertory gifts* and placing them on this altar, I would like to express through them all the contributions that the sons and daughters of our first homeland, Poland, have made to the history and to the life of their second homeland across the ocean: all their toil, efforts, struggles and sufferings; all the fruits of their minds, hearts and hands; all the achievements of the individuals, families and communities. But also all the failures, pains and disappointments; all the nostalgia for their homes, when forced by great poverty they went across the ocean; all the price of love they had to part with in order to look here anew for multiplied family, social and all human threads.

I wish to include in this Eucharistic Sacrifice all *the pastoral care of the Church,* all the work done by the clergy and by this Seminary which has prepared priests through many years; the work of men and especially women Religious, who had followed their fellow countrymen from Poland. And also the activities of various organizations that proved the strength of spirit, the initiative and abilities, and above all the readiness to serve a good cause—a common one, though divided by the ocean between the new and the old homeland.

I have mentioned already here so many things, and I am aware that I have not yet listed them all. And that is why I ask you all, and each one of you: *complete the missing items.* I would like to place on this altar an offering of everything that you—the American Polonia—have represented from the very beginning, from the time of Kosciuszko and Pulaski throughout the generations, and of everything you represent today.

I wish to offer to God this Holy Sacrifice as a Bishop of Rome and as a Pope who is as well a son of the same nation that you came from.

In this way *I wish to fulfill a special obligation:* the obligation of my heart and the obligation of history. May our Lady of Jasna Góra be with us in her maternal way during this Holy Sacrifice, as well as the Patron Saints of our country, whose devotion you have brought over to this land.

May this extraordinary offering of bread and wine, this unique Eucharistic Sacrifice in the story of the American Polonia reunite you in great love and great work. May it enable Jesus Christ to proceed in building your faith and your hope.

## 31. QUIGLEY SOUTH SEMINARY, GREETING TO THE SICK AND HANDICAPPED

Dear Brothers and Sisters,

I have desired to address a heartfelt greeting to all the sick, bedridden and handicapped in the name of the Lord Jesus, who was himself "a man of suffering, accustomed to infirmity" (Is. 53:3).

### God Loves You

I would like to greet you, one by one, to bless you all individually, and to speak to you—to each one of you individually—about Jesus Christ, the one who took upon himself all human suffering so that he could bring salvation to the whole world. God loves you as his privileged children. For two reasons you are in a very special way my brothers and sisters: because of the love of Christ that binds us together, and particularly because you share so profoundly in the Mystery of the Cross and the Redemption of Jesus.

Thank you for the suffering you bear in your bodies and your hearts. Thank you for your example of acceptance, of patience and of "union with the suffering Christ for the sake of his body, the Church" (Col. 1:24).

## 32. MEETING WITH THE BISHOPS OF THE UNITED STATES OF AMERICA

Dear Brothers in our Lord Jesus Christ,

### Thank You for Your Partnership

1. May I tell you very simply how grateful I am to you for your invitation to come to the United States. It is an immense joy for me to make this pastoral visit, and in particular, to be here with you today.

On this occasion I thank you not only for your invitation, not only for everything you have done to prepare for my visit, but also for your partnership in the Gospel from the time of my election as Pope. I thank you for your service to God's holy people, for your fidelity to Christ our Lord, and for your unity with my predecessors and with me in the Church and in the College of Bishops.

I wish at this time to render public homage to a long tradition of fidelity to the Apostolic See on the part of the American Hierarchy. During the course of two centuries, this tradition has edified your people, authenticated your apostolate, and enriched the universal Church.

Moreover, in your presence today, I wish to acknowledge with deep appreciation the fidelity of your faithful and the renowned vitality that they have shown in Christian life. This vitality has been manifested not only in the sacramental practice of communities but also in abundant fruits of the Holy Spirit. With great zeal your people have endeavored to build up the Kingdom of God by means of the Catholic school and through all catechetical efforts. An evident concern for others has been a real part of American Catholicism, and today I thank the American Catholics for their generosity. Their support has benefited the Dioceses of the United States, and a widespread network of charitable works and self-help projects, including those sponsored by Catholic Relief Services and the Campaign for Human Development. Moreover, the help given to the missions by the Church in the United States remains a lasting contribution to the cause of Christ's Gospel. Because your faithful have been very generous to the Apostolic See, my predecessors have been assisted in meeting the burdens of their office; and thus, in the exercise of their worldwide mission of charity, they have been able to extend help to those in need, thereby showing the concern of the universal Church for all humanity. For me then this is *an hour of solemn gratitude*.

2. But even more, this is *an hour of ecclesial communion* and fraternal love. I come to you as a brother Bishop: one who, like yourselves, has known the hopes and challenges of a local church; one who has worked within the structures of a Diocese, who has collaborated within the framework of an Episcopal Conference; one who has known the exhilarating experience of collegiality in an Ecumenical Council as exercised by Bishops together with him who both presided over this collegial assembly and was recognized by it as *totius Ecclesiae Pastor*—invested with "full, supreme and universal power over the Church" (see *Lumen Gentium,* 22). I come to you as one who has been personally edified and enriched by participation in the Synod of Bishops; one who was supported and assisted by the fraternal interest and self-giving of American Bishops who traveled to Poland in order to express solidarity with the Church in my country. I come as one who found deep spiritual consolation for my pastoral activity in the encouragement of the Roman Pontiffs with whom, and under whom, I served God's people, and in particular in the encouragement of Paul VI, whom I looked upon not only as Head of the College of Bishops, but also as my own spiritual father. And today, under the sign of collegiality and because of a mysterious design of God's providence, I, your brother in Jesus, now come to you as Successor of Peter in the See of Rome, and therefore as Pastor of the whole Church.

### Leadership and the Beatitudes

Because of my personal pastoral responsibility, and because of our common pastoral responsibility for the people of God in the United States, I desire to strengthen you in your ministry of faith as local pastors, and to support you in your individual and joint pastoral activities by encouraging you to stand fast in the holiness and truth of our Lord Jesus Christ. And in you I desire to honor Jesus Christ, the Shepherd and Bishop of our souls (see 1 Pt. 2:25).

Because we have been called to be shepherds of the flock, we realize that we must present ourselves as humble servants of the Gospel. Our leadership will be effective only to the extent that our own discipleship is genuine—to the extent that the Beatitudes have become the inspiration of our lives, to the extent that our people really find in us the kindness, simplicity of life and universal charity that they expect.

We who, by divine mandate, must proclaim the duties of the Christian law, and who must call our people to constant conversion and renewal, know that Saint Paul's invitation applies above all to ourselves: "You must put on the new man created in God's image, whose justice and holiness are born of truth" (Eph. 4:24).

### First Priority: Holiness

3. *The holiness of personal conversion* is indeed the condition for our fruitful ministry as Bishops of the Church. It is our union with Jesus Christ that determines the credibility of our witness to the Gospel and the supernatural effectiveness of our activity. We can convincingly proclaim "the unsearchable riches of Christ" (Eph. 3:8)

only if we maintain fidelity to the love and friendship of Jesus, only if we continue to live in the faith of the Son of God.

God has given a great gift to the American Hierarchy in recent years: the canonization of John Neumann. An American Bishop is officially held up by the Catholic Church to be an exemplary servant of the Gospel and shepherd of God's people, above all because of his great love of Christ. On the occasion of the canonization, Paul VI asked: "What is the meaning of this extraordinary event, the meaning of this canonization?" And he answered, saying: "It is the celebration of holiness." And this holiness of Saint John Neumann was expressed in brotherly love, in pastoral charity, and in zealous service by one who was the Bishop of a Diocese and an authentic disciple of Christ.

During the canonization, Paul VI went on to say: "Our ceremony today is indeed the celebration of holiness. At the same time, it is a prophetic anticipation—for the Church, for the United States, for the world—of a renewal of love: love for God, love for neighbor." As Bishops, we are called to exercise in the Church this prophetic role of love and, therefore, of holiness.

Guided by the Holy Spirit, we must all be deeply convinced that holiness is the first priority in our lives and in our ministry. In this context, as Bishops we see the immense value of prayer: the liturgical prayer of the Church, our prayer together, our prayer alone. In recent times many of you have found that the practice of making spiritual retreats together with your brother Bishops is indeed a help to that holiness born of truth. May God sustain you in this initiative: so that each of you, and all of you together, may fulfill your role as a sign of holiness offered to God's people on their pilgrimage to the Father. May you yourselves, like Saint John Neumann, also be a prophetic anticipation of holiness. The people need to have Bishops whom they can look upon as leaders in the quest for holiness—Bishops who are trying to anticipate prophetically in their own lives the attainment of the goal to which they are leading the faithful.

### Holiness of Truth

4. Saint Paul points out *the relationship of justice and holiness to truth* (see Eph. 4:24). Jesus himself, in his priestly prayer, asks his Father to consecrate his disciples by means of truth; and he adds: "Your word is truth"—*Sermo tuus veritas est* (Jn. 17:14). And he goes on to say that he consecrates himself for the sake of the disciples, so that they themselves may be consecrated in truth. Jesus consecrated himself so that the disciples might be consecrated, set apart by the communication of what he was: the Truth. Jesus tells his Father: "I gave them your word"—"Your word is truth" (Jn. 17:14,17).

The holy word of God, which is truth, is communicated by Jesus to his Church, but only after he had implanted in his Church, through the power of the Holy Spirit, a special charism to guard and transmit intact the word of God.

With great wisdom, John XXIII convoked the Second Vatican Council. Reading the signs of the times, he knew that what was needed was a Council of a pastoral nature, a Council that would reflect the great pastoral care of Jesus Christ the Good Shepherd for his people. But he knew that a pastoral Council—to be genuinely effective—would need a strong doctrinal basis. And precisely for this reason, precisely because the word of God is the only basis for every pastoral initiative, John XXIII on the opening day of the Council—October 11, 1962—made the following statement: "*The greatest concern of the Ecumenical Council is this: that the sacred deposit of Christian doctrine should be more effectively guarded and taught.*"

This explains Pope John's inspiration; this is what the new Pentecost was to be: this is why the Bishops of the Church—in the greatest manifestation of collegiality in the history of the world—were called together: "so that the sacred deposit of Christian doctrine should be more effectively guarded and taught."

In our time, Jesus was consecrating anew his disciples by truth; and he was doing it by means of an Ecumenical Council; he was transmitting by the power of the Holy Spirit his Father's word to new generations. And what John XXIII considered to be the aim of the Council I consider as the aim of this post-conciliar period.

For this reason, in my first meeting last November with American Bishops on their *ad Limina* visit I stated: "This then is my own deepest hope today for the pastors of the Church in America, as well as for all the pastors of the Universal Church: that the sacred deposit of Christian doctrine should be more effectively guarded and taught." In the word of God is the salvation of the world. By means of the proclamation of the word of God, the Lord continues in his Church and through his Church to consecrate his disciples, communicating to them the truth that he himself is.

For this reason the Vatican Council emphasized the Bishop's role of announcing the full truth of the Gospel and proclaiming "the whole mystery of Christ" (*Christus Dominus,* 12). This teaching was constantly repeated by Paul VI for the edification of the universal Church. It was explicitly proclaimed by John Paul I on the very day he died, and I too have frequently reaffirmed it in my own pontificate. And I am sure that my successors and your successors will hold this teaching until Christ comes again in glory.

### American Bishop's Affirmation

5. Among the papers that were left to me by Paul VI there is a letter written to him by a Bishop, on the occasion of the latter's appointment to the episcopacy. It is a beautiful letter; and in the form of a resolution it includes *a clear affirmation of the Bishop's role* of guarding and teaching the deposit of Christian doctrine, of proclaiming the whole mystery of Christ. Because of the splendid insights that this letter offers, I would like to share part of it with you.

As he pledged himself to be loyal in obedience to Paul VI and to his successors, the Bishop wrote: "I am resolved:

—"To be faithful and constant in proclaiming the Gospel of Christ.

—"To maintain the content of faith, entire and uncorrupted, as handed down by the Apostles and professed by the Church at all times and places."

And then with equal insight, this Bishop went on to tell Paul VI that, with the help of Almighty God, he was determined

—"To build up the Church as the Body of Christ, and to remain united to it by your link, with the Order of Bishops, under the Successor of Saint Peter the Apostle.

—"To show kindness and compassion in the name of the Lord to the poor and to strangers and to all who are in need.

—"To seek out the sheep who stray and to gather them into the fold of the Lord.

—"To pray without ceasing for the people of God, to carry out the highest duties of the priesthood in such a way as to afford no grounds for reproof."

This then is the edifying witness of a Bishop, an American Bishop, to the episcopal ministry of holiness and truth. These words are a credit to him and a credit to all of you.

A challenge for our age—and for every age in the Church—is to bring the message of the Gospel to the very core of our people's lives—so that they may have the full truth of their humanity, their Redemption and their adoption in Jesus Christ—that they may be enriched with "the justice and holiness of truth."

## The Charity of Christ and Truth

6. In the exercise of your ministry of truth as Bishops of the United States, *you have, through statements and pastoral letters, collectively offered the word of God to your people,* showing its relevance to daily life, pointing to the power it has to uplift and heal, and at the same time upholding its inherent demands. Three years ago you did this in a very special way through your pastoral letter, so beautifully entitled "To Live in Christ Jesus." This letter, in which you offered your people the service of truth, contains a number of points to which I wish to allude today. With compassion, understanding and love, you transmitted a message that is linked to Revelation and to the mystery of faith. And so with great pastoral charity you spoke of God's love, of humanity and of sin—and of the meaning of Redemption and of life in Christ. You spoke of the word of Christ as it affects individuals, the family, the community and nations. You spoke of justice and peace, of charity, of truth and friendship. And you spoke of some special questions affecting the moral life of Christians: the moral life in both its individual and social aspects.

## You Spoke Clearly; I Ratify *Humanae Vitae*

You spoke explicitly of the Church's duty to be faithful to the mission entrusted to her. And precisely for this reason you spoke of certain issues that needed a clear reaffirmation, because Catholic teaching in their regard had been challenged, denied, or in practice violated. You repeatedly proclaimed human rights and human dignity and the incomparable worth of people of every racial and ethnic origin, declaring that "racial antagonism and discrimination are among the most persistent and destructive evils of our nation." You forcefully rejected the oppression of the weak, the manipulation of the vulnerable, the waste of goods and resources, the ceaseless preparations for war, unjust social structures and policies and all crimes by and against individuals and against creation.

With the candor of the Gospels, the compassion of pastors and the charity of Christ, you faced the question of the indissolubility of marriage, rightly stating: "The covenant between a man and a woman joined in Christian marriage is as indissoluble and irrevocable as God's love for his people and Christ's love for his Church."

In exalting the beauty of marriage you rightly spoke against both the ideology of contraception and contraceptive acts, as did the encyclical *Humanae Vitae*. And I myself today with the same conviction of Paul VI ratify the teaching of this encyclical, which was put forth by my predecessor "by virtue of the mandate entrusted to us by Christ" (AAS, 60, 1968, p. 485).

In portraying the sexual union between husband and wife as a special expression of their covenanted love, you rightly stated: "Sexual intercourse is a moral and human good only within marriage, outside marriage it is wrong."

As "men with the message of truth and the power of God" (2 Cor. 6:7), as authentic teachers of God's law and as compassionate pastors you also rightly stated: "Homosexual activity . . . as distinguished from homosexual orientation, is morally wrong." In the clarity of this truth, you exemplified the real charity of Christ; you did not betray those people who, because of homosexuality, are confronted with difficult moral problems, as would have happened if, in the name of understanding and compassion, or for any other reason, you had held out false hope to any brother or sister. Rather, by your witness to the truth of humanity in God's plan, you effectively manifested fraternal love, upholding the true dignity, the true human dignity, of those who look to Christ's Church for the guidance which comes from the light of God's word.

You also gave witness to the truth, thereby serving all humanity, when, echoing the teaching of the Council—"From the moment of conception life must be guarded with the greatest care" (*Gaudium et Spes,* 51)—you reaffirmed the right to life and the inviolability of every human life, including the life of unborn children. You clearly said: "To destroy these innocent unborn children is an unspeakable crime. . . . Their right to life must be recognized and fully protected by the law."

And just as you defended the unborn in the truth of their being, so also you clearly spoke up for the aged, asserting: "Euthanasia or mercy killing . . . is a grave moral evil. . . . Such killing is incompatible with respect for human dignity and reverence for life."

And in your pastoral interest for your people in all their needs—including housing, education, health care, employment and the administration of justice—you gave further witness to the fact that all aspects of human life are sacred. You were, in effect, proclaiming that the Church will never abandon man, nor his temporal needs, as she leads humanity to salvation and eternal life. And because the Church's greatest act of fidelity to humanity and her "fundamental functions in every age and particularly in ours is to direct man's gaze, to point the awareness and experience of the whole of humanity toward the mystery of God" (*Redemptor Hominis,* 10)—because of this you rightly alluded to the dimension of eternal life. It is indeed in this proclamation of eternal life that we hold up a great motive of hope for our people, against the onslaughts of materialism, against rampant secularism and against moral permissiveness.

### Pastoral Responsibility

7. A sense of pastoral responsibility has also been genuinely expressed *by individual Bishops* in their ministry as local pastors. To the great credit of their authors I would cite but two recent examples of pastoral letters issued in the United States. Both are examples of responsible pastoral initiatives. One of them deals with the issue of racism and vigorously denounces it. The other refers to homosexuality and deals with the issue, as should be done, with clarity and great pastoral charity, thus rendering a real service to truth and to those who are seeking this liberating truth.

Brothers in Christ: as we proclaim the truth in love, it is not possible for us to avoid all criticism; nor is it possible to please everyone. And so we are humbly convinced that God is with us in our ministry of truth, and that he "did not give us a spirit of timidity but a spirit of power and love and self-control" (2 Tm. 1:7).

One of the greatest rights of the faithful is to receive the word of God in its purity and integrity as guaranteed by the Magisterium of the universal Church: the Authentic Magisterium of the Bishops of the Catholic Church teaching in union with the Pope. Dear brothers: we can be assured that the Holy Spirit is assisting us in our teaching if we remain absolutely faithful to the universal Magisterium.

In this regard I wish to add an extremely important point which I recently emphasized in speaking to a group of Bishops making their *ad Limina* visit: "In the community of the faithful—which must always maintain Catholic unity with the Bishops and the Apostolic See—there are great insights of faith. The Holy Spirit is active in enlightening the minds of the faithful with his truth, and in inflaming their hearts with his love. But these insights of faith and this *sensus fidelium* are not independent of the Magisterium of the Church, which is an instrument of the same Holy Spirit and is assisted by him. It is only when the faithful have been nourished by the word of God, faithfully transmitted in its purity and integrity, that their own charisms are fully operative and fruitful. Once the word of God is faithfully proclaimed to the community and is accepted, it brings forth fruits of justice and holiness of life in abundance. But the dynamism of the community in understanding and living the word of God depends on its receiving intact the *depositum fidei;* and for this precise purpose a special apostolic and pastoral charism has been given to the Church. It is one and the same Spirit of truth who directs the hearts of the faithful and who guarantees the Magisterium of the pastors of the flock" (Address to Indian Bishops, May 31, 1979).

## Unity of Faith and Truth

8. *One of the greatest truths of which we are the humble custodians is the doctrine of the Church's unity*—that unity which is tarnished on the human face of the Church by every form of sin, but which subsists indestructibly in the Catholic Church (see *Lumen Gentium*, 8; *Unitatis Redintegratio*, 2, 3). A consciousness of sin calls us incessantly to conversion. The will of Christ impels us to work earnestly and perseveringly for unity with all our Christian brethren, being mindful that the unity we seek is one of perfect faith, a unity in truth and love. We must pray and study together, knowing however that intercommunion between divided Christians is not the answer to Christ's appeal for perfect unity. And with God's help we will continue to work humbly and resolutely to remove the real divisions that still exist, and thus to restore that full unity in faith which is the condition for sharing in the Eucharist (see Address of May 4, 1979). The commitment of the Ecumenical Council belongs to each of us; as does the Testament of Paul VI, who writing on ecumenism stated: "Let the work of drawing near to our separated brethren go on, with much understanding, with great love; but without deviating from the true Catholic doctrine."

## Safeguard the Sacrament of Reconciliation

9. As Bishops who are servants of truth, we are also called to be *servants of unity, in the communion of the Church.*

In *the communion of holiness* we ourselves are called, as I mentioned above, to conversion, so that we may preach with convincing power the message of Jesus: "Reform your lives and believe in the Gospel." We have a special role to play in safeguarding the Sacrament of Reconciliation, so that, in fidelity to a divine precept, we and our people may experience in our innermost being that "grace has far surpassed sin" (Rom. 5:20). I, too, ratify the prophetic call of Paul VI, who urged the Bishops to help their priests to "deeply understand how closely they collaborate through the Sacrament of Penance with the Savior in the work of conversion" (Address of April 20, 1978). In this regard I confirm again the Norms of *Sacramentum Paenitentiae,* which so wisely emphasize the ecclesial dimension of the Sacrament of Penance and indicate the precise limits of General Absolution, just as Paul VI did in his *ad Limina* address to the American Bishops.

Conversion by its very nature is the condition for that union with God which reaches its greatest expression in the Eucharist. Our union with Christ in the Eucharist presupposes, in turn, that our hearts are set on conversion, that they are pure. This is indeed an important part of our preaching to the people. In my encyclical I endeavored to express it in these words: "The Christ who calls to the Eucharistic banquet is always the same Christ who exhorts us to penance and repeats his 'Repent.' Without this constant and ever-renewed endeavor for conversion, partaking of the Eucharist would lack its full redeeming effectiveness" (*Redemptor Hominis*, 20). In the face of a widespread phenomenon of our time, namely, that many of our people who are among the great numbers who receive Communion make little use of Confession, we must emphasize Christ's basic call to conversion. We must also stress that the personal encounter with the forgiving Jesus in the Sacrament of Reconciliation is a divine means which keeps alive in our hearts and in our communities a consciousness of sin in its perennial and tragic reality, and which actually brings forth, by the action of Jesus and the power of his Spirit, fruits of conversion in justice and holiness of life. By this Sacrament we are renewed in fervor, strengthened in our resolves and buoyed up by divine encouragement.

## People Look for Reverence in Liturgy

10. As chosen leaders in *a community of praise and prayer,* it is our special joy to offer the Eucharist and to give people a sense of their vocation as an Easter people, with the "alleluia" as their song. And let us always recall that the validity of all liturgical development and the effectiveness of every liturgical sign presupposes the great principle that the Catholic liturgy is theocentric, and that it is above all "the worship of divine majesty" (see *Sacrosanctum Concilium,* 33), in union with Jesus Christ. Our people have a supernatural sense whereby they look for reverence in all liturgy, especially in what touches the mystery of the Eucharist. With deep faith our people understand that the Eucharist—in the Mass and outside the Mass—is the Body and Blood of Jesus Christ, and therefore deserves the worship that is given to the living God and to him alone.

As ministers of *a community of service,* it is our privilege to proclaim the truth of Christ's union with his members in his Body, the Church. Hence we commend all service rendered in his name and to his brethren (see Mt. 25:45).

In *a community of witness and evangelization* may our testimony be clear and without reproach. In this regard the Catholic press and the other means of social communication are called to fulfill a special role of great dignity at the service of truth and charity. The Church's aim in employing and sponsoring these media is linked to her mission of evangelization and of service to humanity; through the media the Church hopes to promote ever more effectively the uplifting message of the Gospel.

11. And each individual Church over which you preside and which you serve is *a community founded on the word of God and acting in the truth of this word.* It is in fidelity to the communion of the universal Church that our local unity is authenticated and made stable. In *the communion of the universal Church* local Churches find their own identity and enrichment ever more clearly. But all of this requires that the individual Churches should maintain complete openness toward the universal Church.

And this is the mystery that we celebrate today in proclaiming the holiness and truth and unity of the episcopal ministry.

Brothers: this ministry of ours makes us accountable to Christ and to his Church. Jesus Christ, the chief Shepherd (1 Pt. 5:4), loves us and sustains us. It is he who transmits his Father's word and consecrates us in truth, so that each of us may say in turn of our people: "For them I consecrate myself for their sake now, that they may be consecrated in truth" (Jn. 17:19).

## Pray for Vocations

Let us pray for and devote special energy to promoting and maintaining vocations to the sacred priesthood, so that the pastoral care of the priestly ministry may be ensured for future generations. I ask you to call upon parents and families, upon priests, Religious and laity to unite in fulfilling this vital responsibility of the entire community. And to the young people themselves let us hold up the full challenge of following Christ and of embracing his invitation with full generosity.

As we ourselves pursue every day the justice and holiness born of truth, let us look to Mary, Mother of Jesus, Queen of Apostles, and Cause of our Joy. May Saint Frances Xavier Cabrini, Saint Elizabeth Ann Seton and Saint John Neumann pray for you, and for all the people whom you are called to serve in holiness and truth and in the unity of Christ and his Church.

Dear brothers: "Grace be with all who love our Lord Jesus Christ with unfailing love" (Eph. 6:24).

# 33. ADDRESS TO THE SEMINARIANS

Dear Seminarians,

I extend a special greeting to all of you who are present here today. I want you to know that you have a special place in my thoughts and prayers.

## Faith Makes the Essential Difference

Dear sons in Christ: be strong in your faith—faith in Christ, and in his Church, faith in all that the Father has revealed and accomplished through his Son and in the Holy Spirit.

During your years in the minor seminary, you have the privilege of studying and deepening your understanding of the faith. Since baptism you have lived the faith, aided by your parents, your brothers and sisters, and the whole Christian community. And yet today I call upon you to live by faith even more profoundly. For it is faith in God which makes the essential difference in your lives and in the life of every priest.

Be faithful to your daily prayers; they will keep your faith alive and vibrant.

Study the faith diligently so that your knowledge and love of Christ will continually increase.

And nourish your faith each day at Mass, for in the Eucharist we have the source and greatest expression of our faith.

God bless you.

## 34. HOMILY AT GRANT PARK

Laudetur Iesus Christus!

My Brothers and Sisters in Jesus Christ,

### Reflect on Evangelization

1. The readings of today's celebration place us immediately before the deep mystery of our calling as Christians.

Before Jesus was taken up to heaven, he gathered his disciples around him, and he explained to them once more the meaning of his mission of salvation: "Thus it is written," he said, "that the Messiah must suffer and rise from the dead on the third day. In his name, penance for the remission of sins is to be preached to all nations" (Lk. 24:46–47). At the moment that he took leave of his Apostles he commanded them, and through them the whole Church, each one of us: to go out and bring the message of Redemption to all nations. Saint Paul expresses this forcefully in his second letter to the Corinthians: "He has entrusted the message of reconciliation to us. This makes us ambassadors of Christ, God as it were appealing through us" (2 Cor. 5:19–20).

Once again, the Lord places us fully in the mystery of humanity, a humanity that is in need of salvation. And God has willed that the salvation of humanity should take place through the humanity of Christ, who for our sake died and was raised up (see 2 Cor. 5:15), and who also entrusted his redeeming mission to us. Yes, we are truly "ambassadors for Christ" and workers for evangelization.

In the Apostolic Exhortation *Evangelii Nuntiandi,* which he wrote at the request of the Third General Assembly of the Synod of Bishops, my predecessor in the See of Saint Peter, Paul VI, invited the whole People of God to meditate on their basic duty of evangelization. He invited each one of us to examine in what way we might be true witnesses to the message of Redemption, in what way we might communicate to others the Good News that we have received from Jesus through his Church.

### Unity of the Church Is Necessary

2. There are certain conditions that are necessary if we are to share in the evangelizing mission of the Church. This afternoon, I wish to stress one of these conditions in particular. I am speaking about the unity of the Church, our unity in Jesus Christ. Let me repeat what Paul VI said about this unity: "The Lord's spiritual testament tells us that unity among his followers is not only the proof that we are his, but also the proof that he is sent by the Father. It is a test of credibility of Christians and of Christ himself. . . . Yes, the destiny of evangelization is certainly bound up with the witness of unity given by the Church" (*Evangelii Nuntiandi,* 77).

I am prompted to choose this particular aspect of evangelization by looking at the thousands of people whom I see gathered around me today. When I lift up my eyes, I see in you the People of God, united to sing the praises of the Lord and to celebrate his Eucharist. I see also the whole people of America, one nation formed of many people: *E pluribus unum*.

## Your Nation in Unity

3. In the first two centuries of your history as a nation, you have traveled a long road, always in search of a better future, in search of stable employment, in search of a homestead. You have traveled "from sea to shining sea" to find your identity, to discover each other along the way, and to find your own place in this immense country.

Your ancestors came from many different countries across the oceans to meet here with the people of different communities that were already established here. In every generation, the process has been repeated: new groups arrive, each one with a different history, to settle here and become part of something new. The same process still goes on when families move from the south to the north, from the east to the west. Each time they come with their own past to a new town or a new city, to become part of a new community. The pattern repeats itself over and over: *E pluribus unum*— the many form a new unity.

## Out of Various Cultures: A Rich Nation

4. Yes, something new was created every time. You brought with you a different culture and you contributed your own distinctive richness to the whole; you had different skills and you put them to work, complementing each other, to create industry, agriculture and business; each group carried with it different human values and shared them with the others for the enrichment of your nation. *E pluribus unum*: you became a new entity, a new people, the true nature of which cannot be adequately explained as a mere putting together of various communities.

And so, looking at you, I see people who have thrown their destinies together and now write a common history. Different as you are, you have come to accept each other, at times imperfectly and even to the point of subjecting each other to various forms of discrimination: at times only after a long period of misunderstanding and rejection; even now still growing in understanding and appreciation of each other's differences. In expressing gratitude for the many blessings you have received, you also become aware of the duty you have toward the less favored in your own midst and in the rest of the world—a duty of sharing, of loving, of serving. As a people, you recognize God as the source of your many blessings, and you are open to his love and his law.

This is America in her ideal and her resolution: "one nation, under God, indivisible, with liberty and justice for all." This is the way America was conceived; this is what she was called to be. And for all this, we offer thanks to the Lord.

## Mystery of Unity

5. But there is another reality that I see when I look at you. It is even deeper and more demanding than the common history and union which you built from the richness of your different cultural and ethnic heritages—those heritages that you now rightly want to know and to preserve. History does not exhaust itself in material progress, in technological conquest or in cultural achievement only. Coming together around the altar of sacrifice to break the Bread of the Holy Eucharist with the Successor of Peter, you testify to this even deeper reality: to your unity as members of the People of God.

"We, though many, are one body in Christ" (Rom. 12:5). The Church too is composed of many members and enriched by the diversity of those who make up the one community of faith and baptism, the one Body of Christ. What brings us together and makes us one is our faith—the one apostolic faith. We are all one, because we have accepted Jesus Christ as the Son of God, the Redeemer of the human race, the sole Mediator between God and man. By the Sacrament of Baptism we have been truly incorporated into the crucified and glorified Christ, and through the action of the Holy Spirit we have become living members of his one body. Christ gave us the wonderful Sacrament of the Eucharist, by which the unity of the Church is both expressed and continually brought about and perfected.

## Members of One Body

6. "One Lord, one faith, one baptism" (Eph. 4:5); thus we are all bound together, as the People of God, the Body of Christ, in a unity that transcends the diversity of our origin, culture, education and personality—in a unity that does not exclude a rich diversity in ministries and services. With Saint Paul we proclaim: "Just as each of us has one body with many members, and not all the members have the same function, so too we, though many, are one body in Christ, and individually members one of another" (Rom. 12:4–5).

If then the Church, the one Body of Christ, is to be a forcefully discernible sign of the Gospel message, all her members must show forth, in the words of Paul VI, that "harmony and consistency of doctrine, life and worship which marked the first days of her existence" (*Apostolic Exhortation on Reconciliation within the Church,* 2), when Christians "devoted themselves to the apostles' teaching and fellowship, to the breaking of bread and the prayers" (Acts 2:42).

Our unity in faith must be complete, lest we fail to give witness to the Gospel, lest we cease to be evangelizing. No local ecclesial community therefore can cut itself off from the treasure of the faith as proclaimed by the Church's teaching office, for it is to this teaching office of the Church, to this Magisterium that the deposit of faith has been especially entrusted by Christ. With Paul VI, I attest to the great truth: "While being translated into all expressions, the content of the faith must be neither impaired nor mutilated. While being clothed with the outward forms proper to each people . . . it must remain the content of the Catholic faith just exactly as the ecclesial Magisterium has received it and transmits it" (*Evangelii Nuntiandi, 65*).

### Love Gives Rise to Dialogue

7. Finally, and above all, the mission of evangelization that is mine and yours must be carried out through a constant unselfish witnessing to the unity of love. Love is the force that opens hearts to the word of Jesus and to his Redemption: love is the only basis for human relationships that respects in one another the dignity of the children of God created in his image and saved by the death and Resurrection of Jesus; love is the only driving force that impels us to share with our brothers and sisters all that we are and have.

Love is the power that gives rise to dialogue, in which we listen to each other and learn from each other. Love gives rise, above all, to the dialogue of prayer in which we listen to God's word, which is alive in the Holy Bible and alive in the life of the Church. Let love then build the bridge across our differences and at times our contrasting positions. Let love for each other and love for truth be the answer to polarization, when factions are formed because of differing views in matters that relate to faith or to the priorities for action. No one in the ecclesial community should ever feel alienated or unloved, even when tensions arise in the course of the common efforts to bring the fruits of the Gospel to society around us. Our unity as Christians, as Catholics, must always be a unity of love in Jesus Christ our Lord.

In a few moments, we shall celebrate our unity by renewing the Sacrifice of Christ. Each one will bring a different gift to be presented in union with the offering of Jesus: dedication to the betterment of society; efforts to console those who suffer; the desire to give witness for justice; the resolve to work for peace and brotherhood; the joy of a united family; or suffering in body or mind. Different gifts, yes, but all united in the one great gift of Christ's love for his Father and for us—everything united in the unity of Christ and his Sacrifice.

And in the strength and power, in the joy and peace of this sacred unity, we pledge ourselves anew—as one people—to fulfill the command of our Lord Jesus Christ: Go and teach all people my Gospel. By word and example give witness to my name. And, behold, I am with you always, until the end of the world.

## 35. CHICAGO SYMPHONY ORCHESTRA CONCERT

I am indeed honored by the splendid performance of the Chicago Symphony Orchestra.

I thank you for the opportunity to express my profound admiration for the artistic beauty which you have shared with me tonight. Please accept my deep gratitude.

And I am honored to be able, on this occasion, to join my voice to that of my predecessor Paul VI, who through the eloquent testimony of a long pontificate, showed himself to be the friend of artists. With all the intensity of his noble soul, he convincingly attested to the Church's esteem for the role of art. With consummate skill himself, he led the Catholic Church to a new level of dialogue with the artists of the world. It was his fond hope that all art and beauty would lift the gaze of man toward God, pointing the way to uncreated beauty.

For the honor of Paul VI, in my own name, and on behalf of the Church, I reiterate my respect and admiration for your uplifting contribution to humanity, for your artistic creation that exalts what is human and reaches what is religious and divine.

In the cultural and spiritual encounter of this evening, I extend my respectful greetings to all the artists of this land, extolling the role they are called to play, with prodigious capacity, for the advancement of true culture in the United States and in the whole world.

## OCTOBER 6, 1979

## 36. ARRIVAL AT ANDREWS AIR FORCE BASE

Mr. Vice President,

Dear Friends,

Dear Brothers and Sisters in Christ,

### Thanks to President Carter and the Episcopal Conference

I wish to express my sincere thanks for the gracious words of welcome that have been extended to me on my arrival at the nation's capital, the last stage of my first apostolic journey to the United States. I wish to say once more how grateful I am for the invitation of the Episcopal Conference and of President Carter to come and visit the United States.

I extend a cordial greeting to all those who have come to welcome me here: to you, Mr. Vice President, and to the other civil authorities, in whom I greet the whole American people and in a particular way all the citizens of the State of Maryland. A fraternal greeting to you, Cardinal Baum, Pastor of the Archdiocese of Washington, and through you to all the clergy, Religious and laity of the Catholic community. I am most happy to greet at the same time the president, officers and staff of the National Conference of Catholic Bishops that has its headquarters in this city, as well as all those who in the United States Catholic Conference provide all the indispensable services to the whole Catholic community of this country. To all my brother Bishops, a greeting and a blessing from the Bishop of Rome in the See of Saint Peter, for you and your Diocese.

I am looking forward to meeting the leaders of this young and flourishing country—in the first place, the president of the United States. I shall also be honored to visit the headquarters of the Organization of American States to bring to this deserving body a message of peace for all the peoples they represent.

It will give me a special pleasure, during these last days of my visit and pilgrimage, to come into contact with the Catholic community of this area, and to learn about their pastoral efforts, programs and activities.

May the blessings of Almighty God descend in abundance on all the people of this nation's capital.

## 37. CATHEDRAL OF SAINT MATTHEW

Mary says to us today: "I am the servant of the Lord. Let it be done to me as you say" (Lk. 1:38).

### Mary Believed

And with those words, she expresses what was the fundamental attitude of her life: her faith! Mary believed! She trusted in God's promises and was faithful to his will. When the angel Gabriel announced that she was chosen to be the Mother of the Most High, she gave her "Fiat" most humbly and with full freedom: "Let it be done to me as you say."

Perhaps the best description of Mary and, at the same time, the greatest tribute to her, was the greeting of her cousin Elizabeth: "Blessed is she who trusted that God's words to her would be fulfilled" (Lk. 1:45). For it was that continual trust in the providence of God which most characterized her faith.

All her earthly life was a "pilgrimage of faith" (see *Lumen Gentium, 58*). For like us she walked in shadows and hoped for things unseen. She knew the contradictions of our earthly life. She was promised that her son would be given David's throne, but at his birth, there was no room even at the inn. Mary still believed. The angel said her child would be called the Son of God; but she would see him slandered, betrayed and condemned, and left to die as a thief on the Cross. Even yet, Mary trusted that "God's words to her would be fulfilled" (Lk. 1:45), and that "nothing was impossible with God" (Lk. 1:37).

This woman of faith, Mary of Nazareth, the Mother of God, has been given to us as a model in our pilgrimage of faith. From Mary we learn to surrender to God's will in all things. From Mary we learn to trust even when all hope seems gone. From Mary we learn to love Christ, her Son and the Son of God. For Mary is not only the Mother of God, she is Mother of the Church as well. In every stage of the march through history, the Church has benefited from the prayer and protection of the Virgin Mary. Holy Scripture and the experience of the faithful see the Mother of God as the one who in a very special way is united with the Church at the most difficult moments in her history, when attacks on the Church become most threatening. Precisely in periods when Christ, and therefore his Church, provokes premeditated contradiction, Mary appears particularly close to the Church, because for her the Church is always her beloved Christ.

I therefore exhort you in Christ Jesus, to continue to look to Mary as the model of the Church, as the best example of the discipleship of Christ. Learn from her to be always faithful, to trust that God's word to you will be fulfilled, and that nothing is impossible with God. Turn to Mary frequently in your prayer "for never was it known that anyone who fled to her protection, implored her help or sought her intercession was left unaided."

As a great sign that has appeared in the heavens, Mary guides and sustains us on our pilgrim way, urging us on to "the victory that overcomes the world, our faith" (1 Jn. 5:5).

### 38. TO THE PRESIDENT, CONGRESS, CABINET, SUPREME COURT AND WHITE HOUSE STAFF

Mr. President,

#### Gratitude for Welcome

I wish to express my most sincere thanks for your kind words of welcome to the White House. It is indeed a great honor for me to meet with the president of the United States during a visit of which the aims are spiritual and religious in nature. May I convey at the same time to you, and through you to all your fellow Americans, my profound respect for all the federal and state authorities of this nation and for its beloved people. In the course of the last few days, I have had the opportunity to see some of your cities and rural areas; my only regret is that the time is too short to bring my greetings personally to all parts of this country, but I want to assure you that my esteem and affection go out to every man, woman and child without distinction.

Divine Providence in its own designs has called me from my native Poland to be the Successor of Peter in the See of Rome and the leader of the Catholic Church. It gives me great joy to be the first Pope in history to come to the capital of this nation, and I thank Almighty God for this blessing.

In accepting your courteous invitation, Mr. President, I have also hoped that our meeting today would serve the cause of world peace, international understanding and the promotion of full respect for human rights everywhere.

Mr. Speaker and Honorable Members of Congress,

Distinguished Members of the Cabinet and of the Judiciary,

Ladies and Gentlemen,

Your presence here honors me greatly, and I deeply appreciate the expression of respect which you thus extend to me. My gratitude goes to each one of you personally for your kind welcome, and to all I wish to say how profoundly I esteem your mission as stewards of the common good of all the people of America.

### Dignity of the Human Person

I come from a nation with a long tradition of deep Christian faith and with a national history marked by many upheavals; for more than a hundred years Poland was even erased from the political map of Europe. But it is also a country marked by a deep veneration for those values without which no society can prosper: love of freedom, cultural creativity, and the conviction that common endeavors for the good of society must be guided by a true moral sense. My own spiritual and religious mission impels me to be the messenger of peace and brotherhood, and to witness to the true greatness of every human person. This greatness derives from the love of God, who created us in his own likeness and gave us an eternal destiny. It is in this dignity of the human person that I see the meaning of history and that I find the principle that gives sense to the role which every human being has to assume for his or her own advancement and for the well-being of the society to which he or she belongs. It is with these sentiments that I greet in you the whole American people, a people that bases its concept of life on spiritual and moral values, on a deep religious sense, on respect for duty and on generosity in the service of humanity—noble traits which are embodied in a particular way in the nation's capital, with its monuments dedicated to such outstanding national figures as George Washington, Abraham Lincoln and Thomas Jefferson.

I greet the American people in their elected representatives, all of you who serve in Congress to chart, through legislation, the path that will lead every citizen of this country toward the fullest development of his or her potential, and the nation as a whole toward assuming its share of the responsibility for building a world of true freedom and justice. I greet America in all who are vested with authority, which can only be seen as an opportunity for serving your fellow citizens in the overall development of their true humanity and in the full and unimpeded enjoyment of all their fundamental rights. I salute the people of this land also in the members of the judiciary, who are servants of humanity in the application of justice, and who thus hold in their hands the awesome power of profoundly affecting, by their decisions, the lives of every individual.

For all of you I pray to Almighty God that he may grant you the gift of wisdom in your decisions, prudence in your words and actions, and compassion in the exercise of the authority that is yours, so that in your noble office you will always render true service to the people.

God bless America!

## 39. THE WHITE HOUSE ADDRESS AFTER MEETING WITH THE PRESIDENT OF THE UNITED STATES

Mr. President,

I am honored to have had, at your kind invitation, the opportunity for a meeting with you; for by your office as president of the United States of America you represent before the world the whole American nation, and you hold the immense responsibility of leading this nation in the path of justice and peace. I thank you publicly for this meeting and I thank all those who have contributed to its success. I wish also to reiterate here my deep gratitude for the warm welcome and the many kindnesses which I have received from the American people on my pastoral journey through your beautiful land.

## Authority Is Based on Solicitude

Mr. President, in responding to the kind words which you have addressed to me, I take the liberty of beginning with the passage from the Prophet Micah that you quoted at your inauguration: "You have been told, O man, what is good, and what the Lord requires of you: only to do right and to love goodness, and to walk humbly with your God" (Mi. 6:8). In recalling these words, I wish to greet you and all the authorities in the individual states and in the nation who are committed to the good of the citizens. There is indeed no other way to put oneself at the service of the whole human person except by seeking the good of every man and woman in all their commitments and activities. Authority in the political community is based on the objective ethical principle that the basic duty of power is the solicitude of the common good of society and that it serves the inviolable rights of the human person. The individuals, families, and various groups which compose the civic community are aware that by themselves they are unable to realize their human potential to the full, and therefore they recognize in a wider community the necessary condition for the ever better attainment of the common good.

I wish to commend those in public authority and all the people of the United States for having given, from the very beginning of the existence of the nation, a special place to some of the most important concerns of the common good. Three years ago, during the bicentennial celebration, which I was fortunate to participate in as the Archbishop of Cracow, it was obvious to everyone that concern for what is human and spiritual is one of the basic principles governing the life of this community. It is superfluous to add that respect for the freedom and the dignity of every individual, whatever his origin, race, sex or creed, has been a cherished tenet of the civil creed of America, and that it has been backed up by courageous decisions and actions.

Mr. President,

Ladies and Gentlemen,

## Commitment to Arms Limitation

I know and appreciate this country's efforts for arms limitation, especially of nuclear weapons. Everyone is aware of the terrible risk that the stockpiling of such weapons brings upon humanity. Since it is one of the greatest nations on earth, the United States plays a particularly important part in the quest for greater security in the world and for closer international collaboration. With all my heart I hope that there will be no relaxing of its efforts both to reduce the risk of a fatal and disastrous worldwide conflagration and to secure a prudent and progressive reduction of the destructive capacity of military arsenals. At the same time, by reason of its special position, may the United States succeed in influencing the other nations to join in a continuing commitment for disarmament. Without wholeheartedly accepting such a commitment, how can any nation effectively serve humanity, whose deepest desire is true peace?

Attachment to human values and to ethical concerns, which have been a hall-mark of the American people, must be situated, especially in the present context of the growing interdependence of peoples across the globe, within the framework of the view that the common good of society embraces not just the individual nation to which one belongs but the citizens of the whole world. I would encourage every action for the reinforcement of peace in the world, a peace based on liberty and justice, on charity and truth. The present-day relationship between peoples and be-tween nations demands the establishment of greater international cooperation also in the economic field. The more powerful a nation is, the greater becomes its interna-tional responsibility, the greater also must be its commitment to the betterment of the lot of those whose very humanity is constantly being threatened by want and need. It is my fervent hope that all the powerful nations in the world will deepen their awareness of the principle of human solidarity within the one great human family. America, which in the past decades has demonstrated goodness and generosity in providing food for the hungry of the world, will, I am sure, be able to match this generosity with an equally convincing contribution to the establishing of a world order that will create the necessary economic and trade conditions for a more just relationship between all the nations of the world, in respect for their dignity and their own personality. Since people are suffering under international inequality, there can be no question of giving up the pursuit of international solidarity, even if it involves a notable change in the attitudes and life-styles of those blessed with a larger share of the world's goods.

Mr. President,

Ladies and Gentlemen,

### Church and State Safeguard Dignity of the Human Person

In touching upon the common good, which embodies the aspiration of all hu-man beings to the full development of their capacities and the proper protection of their rights, I have dealt with areas where the Church that I represent and the polit-ical community that is the state share a common concern: the safeguarding of the dignity of the human person, and the search for justice and peace. In their own proper spheres, the political community and the Church are mutually independent and self-governing. Yet, by a different title, each serves the personal and social voca-tion of the same human beings.

For her part, the Catholic Church will continue her efforts to cooperate in promoting justice, peace and dignity through the commitment of her leaders and the members of her communities, and through her incessant proclamation that all human beings are created to the image and likeness of God, and that they are brothers and sisters, children of one heavenly Father.

May Almighty God bless and sustain America in her quest for the fullness of liberty, justice and peace.

## 40. TO THE ORGANIZATION OF AMERICAN STATES

Mr. President,

Mr. Secretary-General,

Ladies and Gentlemen,

### The Holy See Follows Events in the Americas with Great Interest and Special Attention

1. It is indeed a pleasure for me to have this opportunity to greet all the distinguished representatives of the different member nations of the Organization of American States. My sincere gratitude goes to you, Mr. President, for the cordial words of welcome you have extended to me. I thank also the secretary-general for his thoughtful invitation to come and visit the headquarters of the oldest of the regional international organizations. It is fitting that, after my visit to the United Nations Organization, the Organization of American States should be the first one among the many intergovernmental organizations and agencies to which I am privileged to address a message of peace and friendship.

### The Gospel and Christianity Have Entered Deeply into the Betterment of Peoples

The Holy See follows with great interest, and may I say, with special attention, the events and developments that touch upon the well-being of the peoples of the Americas. It felt therefore greatly honored by the invitation to send its own permanent observer to this institution—an invitation extended last year by a unanimous decision of the General Assembly. The Holy See sees in regional organizations such as yours intermediary structures that promote a greater internal diversity and vitality in a given area within the global community of nations. The fact that the American continent is provided with an organization concerned with ensuring more continuity for the dialogue between governments, with promoting peace, with advancing full development in solidarity, and with protecting man, his dignity and his rights is a factor contributing to the health of the whole human family. The Gospel and Christianity have entered deeply into your history and your cultures. I would like to call on this common tradition in order to present to you some reflections, in full respect for your personal convictions and your own competence, in order to bring to your endeavors an original contribution in a spirit of service.

### The Arms Race Works Against Peace and the Betterment of Peoples

2. Peace is a most precious blessing that you seek to preserve for your peoples. You are in agreement with me that it is not by accumulating arms that this peace can be ensured in a stable way. Apart from the fact that such accumulation increases in practice the danger of having recourse to arms to settle disputes that may arise, it takes away considerable material and human resources from the great peaceful tasks of development that are so urgent. It can also tempt some to think that the order built on arms is sufficient to ensure internal peace in the single countries.

I solemnly call on you to do everything in your power to restrain the arms race on this continent. There are no differences between your countries that cannot be peacefully overcome. What a relief it would be to your peoples, what new opportunities it would provide for their economic, social and cultural progress, and how contagious an example it would give the world, if the difficult enterprise of disarmament were here to find a realistic and resolute solution!

3. The painful experience of the history of my own country, Poland, has shown me how important national sovereignty is when it is served by a state worthy of the name and free in its decisions; how important it is for the protection not only of a people's legitimate material interests but also of its culture and its soul. Your organization is an organization of states, founded on respect for the full national sovereignty of each, on equal participation in common tasks, and on solidarity between your peoples. The legitimate demand by the states to participate on a basis of equality in the organization's common decisions must be matched by the will to promote within each country an ever more effective participation by the citizens in the responsibility and decisions of the nation through ways that take into account particular traditions, difficulties and historical experiences.

### There Is Never Any Justifiable Cause for Any Attack on the Inviolable Dignity of the Human Person and on the Authentic Rights that Protect This Dignity. Social Organizations Are at the Service of Man and Not Vice Versa.

4. However, while such difficulties and experiences can at times call for exceptional measures and a certain period of maturation in preparation for new advances in shared responsibility, they never, never justify any attack on the inviolable dignity of the human person and on the authentic rights that protect this dignity. If certain ideologies and certain ways of interpreting legitimate concern for national security were to result in subjugating to the state man and his rights and dignity, they would

to that extent cease to be human and would be unable to claim without gross deception any Christian reference. In the Church's thinking it is a fundamental principle that social organization is at the service of man, not vice versa. That holds good also for the highest levels of society, where the power of coercion is wielded and where abuses, when they occur, are particularly serious. Besides, a security in which the peoples no longer feel involved, because it no longer protects them in their very humanity, is only a sham; as it grows more and more rigid, it will show symptoms of increasing weakness and rapidly approaching ruin.

Without undue interference, your organization can, by the spirit with which it tackles all the problems in its competence, do much throughout the continent to advance a concept of the state and its sovereignty that is truly human and that is therefore the basis for the legitimacy of the states and of their acknowledged prerogatives for the service of man.

## The Human Person Is of Prime Importance
## Within All Societies

5. Man! Man is the decisive criterion that dictates and directs all your undertakings, the living value for whose service new initiatives are unceasingly demanded. The words that are most filled with meaning for man—words such as justice, peace, development, solidarity, human rights—are sometimes belittled as a result of systematic suspicion or party and sectarian ideological censure. They then lose their power to mobilize and attract. They will recover it only if respect for the human person and commitment to the human person are explicitly brought back to the center of all considerations. When we speak of the right to life, to physical and moral integrity, to nourishment, to housing, to education, to health care, to employment, to shared responsibility in the life of the nation, we speak of the human person. It is this human person whom faith makes us recognize as created in the image of God and destined for an eternal goal. It is this human person that is often threatened and hungry, without decent housing and employment, without access to the cultural heritage of his or her people or of humanity, and without a voice to make his or her distress heard. The great cause of full development in solidarity must be given new life by those who in one degree or another enjoy these blessings, for the service of all those— and there are many of them still on your continent—who are deprived of them to a sometimes dramatic extent.

## All That You Do for the Human Person Will Halt Violence
## and the Threats of Subversion and Destabilization

6. The challenge of development deserves your full attention. In this field too, what you achieve can be an example for humanity. The problems of rural and urban areas, of industry and agriculture, and of the environment are to a large extent a common task. The energetic pursuit of these will help to spread throughout the continent a sentiment of universal fraternity that extends beyond borders and regimes.

Without any disregard for the responsibilities of sovereign states, you discover that it is a logical requirement for you to deal with problems, such as unemployment, migration and trade, as common concerns whose continental dimension increasingly demands more organic solutions on a continental scale. All that you do for the human person will halt violence and the threats of subversion and destabilization. For by accepting courageous revisions demanded by "this single fundamental point of view, namely, the welfare of man—or, let us say, of the person in the community—which must, as a fundamental factor in the common good, constitute the essential criterion for all programs, systems and regimes" (*Redemptor Hominis,* 17), you direct the energies of your peoples toward the peaceful satisfaction of their aspirations.

### The Church Will Help by Advancing the Human Person and His or Her Dignity and Rights. They Serve the Earthly City, Its Cohesion and Its Lawful Authorities

7. The Holy See will always be happy to make its own disinterested contribution to this work. The local Churches in the Americas will do the same within the framework of their various responsibilities. By advancing the human person and his or her dignity and rights, they serve the earthly city, its cohesion and its lawful authorities. The full religious freedom that they ask for is in order to serve, not in order to oppose the legitimate autonomy of civil society and of its own means of action. The more all citizens are able to exercise habitually their freedoms in the life of the nation, the more readily will the Christian communities be able to dedicate themselves to the central task of evangelization, namely the preaching of the Gospel of Jesus Christ, the source of life, strength, justice and peace.

With fervent prayers for prosperity and concord, I invoke upon this important assembly, upon the representatives of all the member states and their families, upon all the beloved peoples of the Americas, the choicest favors and blessings of Almighty God.

My visit here in the Hall of the Americas, before this noble assembly dedicated to inter-American collaboration, expresses at the same time a wish and a prayer. My wish is that, in all the nations of this continent, no man, woman or child may ever feel abandoned by the constituted authorities, to whom they are ready to accord their full confidence to the extent that those authorities seek the good of all. My prayer is that Almighty God may grant his light to the peoples and the governments, that they may always discover new means of collaboration for building up a fraternal and just society.

One last word before I leave you—with great regret—after this first brief visit to your esteemed organization. When I visited Mexico, at the beginning of the year, I was amazed at the enthusiasm, spontaneity and joy of living of its people. I am convinced that you will succeed in preserving the rich human and cultural heritage of all your peoples, and thus maintain the indispensable basis for true progress, which is constituted, always and everywhere, by respect for the supreme dignity of man.

## 41. GREETING TO THE PEOPLE OUTSIDE THE ORGANIZATION OF AMERICAN STATES BUILDING

Dear Friends,

### Materialism Is Not the Answer; Do Not Lose Sight of the Things That Really Matter, the Things of the Spirit. God Gives Meaning to Our Lives

Thank you for coming here to greet me. To all of you: peace and joy!

Every time I have the opportunity to meet with a group of people, it gives me great happiness, for in you I see my brothers and sisters, children of the same God, who is our Father, and who has created us with a unique beauty and richness: the great beauty of being free human beings, capable of knowing truth, of offering love and understanding to each other, and of joining hands to make the world a better place to live in.

I have met many people during the last few days, many different people: in Ireland, at the United Nations, in the cities and rural areas of America, at this great Organization of American States. I have enjoyed being with them, but above all I have rejoiced in seeing how strongly every one believes in the possibility of bringing peace and well-being to all men, women and children in the world. So I would like to encourage you also in your dedication to truth and to justice, without which real peace can never exist.

One of the temptations of the modern world is a growing materialism in the outlook of people and of society itself. Many people have been deceived in this regard; they have been led to think that money, pleasure, comfort or self-indulgence can be substitutes for spiritual values.

So I invite all of you not to lose sight of the things that really matter, the things of the spirit; and let us remember, above all, that it is God who gives meaning to our lives.

To all of you, young and old, I say: do not let the material things of life rob you of the things that really count: God's love for you, and your love for one another.

God bless you!

Dear Spanish-speaking Friends,

### Let Each Person Feel Respected and Loved in His or Her Dignity as a Human Person

I have just visited the headquarters of the Organization of American States and I have met the representatives of this area, bringing them a message of peace, of friendship, of encouragement and of collaboration on the part of the Church.

The Pope's interest in this regional international organization is intended to indicate his interest also in each one of your countries and in each one of yourselves, both as family groups and as individuals.

The greeting I gave the representative of the American states now goes to you with all my heart. I also pray God to grant that you may always be able to look to this organization with eyes of hope, as a place that will echo your lawful expectations directed to goals of greater human and Christian dignity.

I know very well that throughout my journey in the United States I have been meeting many groups of the Hispanic community spread among the great crowds and big cities. Let no one feel that he or she has been forgotten by the Pope. Let each person feel respected and loved in his or her dignity as a human being with his or her own cultural and personal values, as well as for being a Christian and a child of God.

I exhort you and your friends and all the Spanish-speaking people to have solidarity of sentiment, and I encourage you to maintain your human and Christian values with valor and constancy.

Finally, I assure you of my remembrance as a friend and of my affectionate Blessing.

## 42. TO THE DIPLOMATIC CORPS

Your Excellencies, Ladies and Gentlemen,

### The Holy See and the Diplomatic Corps
### Stand Together in the Cause of Service to Humanity

It pleases me greatly that, in the midst of a program that is at the same time demanding and enjoyable, the opportunity has been offered to me to meet tonight with the distinguished members of the diplomatic corps in this city of Washington.

I thank you most cordially for the honor you bestow upon me by your presence, an honor given not only to my person but to the leader of the Catholic Church. I also see in your courteous gesture an encouragement for the activity of the Catholic Church and of the Holy See in the service of humanity.

In this cause of service to humanity the diplomatic corps and the Holy See stand together, each one in its own sphere, each one faithfully pursuing its own mission, but united in the great cause of understanding and solidarity among peoples and nations.

Yours is a noble task. Despite unavoidable difficulties, setbacks and failures, diplomacy retains its importance as one of the roads that must be traveled in the search for peace and progress for all mankind. "Diplomacy," in the words of my predecessor Paul VI, "is the art of making peace" (Address to the Diplomatic Corps, Rome, 12 January 1974). The efforts of diplomats, whether in a bilateral or in a multilateral setting, do not always succeed in establishing or maintaining peace, but they must always be encouraged, today as in the past, so that new initiatives will be born, new paths tried with the patience and tenacity that are the eminent qualities of the deserving diplomat. As one who speaks in the name of Christ, who called himself "the way, the truth, and the life" (Jn. 14:6), I would also like to make a plea for the fostering of other qualities that are indispensable if today's diplomacy is to justify the hopes that are placed in it: the ever deeper insertion of the supreme values of the moral and spiritual order into the aims of peoples and into the methods used in pursuit of these aims.

### Truth Is First among Ethical Imperatives in the Relations among Nations and Peoples

First among the ethical imperatives that must preside over the relations among nations and peoples is *truth*. As the theme for the Thirteenth World Day of Peace (January 1, 1980), I have chosen "Truth, the power of peace." I am confident that the governments and the nations which you represent will, as they have so admirably done in the past, associate themselves once again with this lofty aim: to instill truth into all relationships, be they political or economic, bilateral or multinational.

All too often, falsehood is met in personal as well as in collective life, and thus suspicion arises where truth is called for, and the ensuing reluctance to enter into dialogue makes any collaboration or understanding almost impossible. Bringing truth into all relations is to work for peace, for it will make it possible to apply to the problems of the world the solutions that are in conformity with reason and with justice—in a word, with the truth about man.

### True and Lasting Peace Is Based on Truth and Defends the Dignity of the Human Person

And this brings me to the second point I would like to make. If it is to be true and lasting, peace must be truly *human*. The desire for peace is universal. It is embedded in the hearts of all human beings, and it cannot be achieved unless the human person is placed at the center of every effort to bring about unity and brotherhood among nations.

### The Fundamental Duty of Power Is Solicitude for the Common Good

Your mission as diplomats is based on the mandate you receive from those who hold responsibility for the well-being of your nations. The power you partake of cannot be separated from the objective demands of the moral order or from the destiny of every human being. May I repeat here what I stated in my first encyclical letter: "the fundamental duty of power is solicitude for the common good of society; this is what gives power its fundamental rights. Precisely in the name of these premises of the objective ethical order, the rights of power can only be understood on the basis of respect for the objective and inviolable rights of man. The common good that authority in the state serves is brought to full realization only when all the citizens are sure of their rights. The lack of this leads to the dissolution of society, opposition by citizens to authority, or a situation of oppression, intimidation, violence and terrorism, of which many examples have been provided by the totalitarianisms of this century. Thus the principle of human rights is of profound concern to the area of social justice and is the measure by which it can be tested in the life of the political bodies" (*Redemptor Hominis,* 17). These considerations assume their full relevance also in the area of your immediate concern, the quest for international peace, for justice among nations and for cooperation in solidarity by all peoples. The success of today's diplomacy will, in the final analysis, be the victory of the truth about man.

I invoke from Almighty God abundant blessings upon your mission, which requires you to foster the interests of your own nation and to place it in the context of universal peace; upon you personally—who are in such a distinguished way artisans of peace; upon your spouses and families, who support and encourage you; and finally upon all who count on your dedicated service to see their own human dignity respected and enhanced. May God's peace be always in your hearts.

## OCTOBER 7, 1979

## 43. TO THE STUDENTS OF THE CATHOLIC UNIVERSITY

Dear Students of The Catholic University,

### Religious Values Are Essential

My first greeting on arriving at this campus is for you! To all of you I offer the peace and joy of our Lord Jesus Christ! I am told that you have held an all-night prayer vigil to ask God's blessing on my visit. Thank you most cordially for such a wonderful expression of communion with me, and for such a beautiful gift. I would like to talk to you at length: I would like to listen to you and know what you think about yourselves and the world. But the time I have been given is so short.

One thing you have told me already: by choosing to welcome me with the offering of your prayers, you have demonstrated that you understand what is most important in your lives—your contact with God, your searching for the meaning of life by listening to Christ as he speaks to you in the Scriptures. I am pleased to know that reflection on spiritual and religious values is part of your desire to live fully this time of your lives. Materialistic concerns and one-sided values are never sufficient to fill the heart and mind of a human person. A life reduced to the sole dimension of possessions, of consumer goods, of temporal concerns will never let you discover and enjoy the full richness of your humanity. It is only in God—in Jesus, God made man—that you will fully understand what you are. He will unveil to you the true greatness of yourselves: that you are redeemed by him who said about himself: "If the son frees you, you will be free indeed" (Jn. 14:6). He put all human life in the dimension of truth and of authentic love. True knowledge and true freedom are in

Jesus. Make Jesus always part of your hunger for truth and justice, and part of your dedication to the well-being of your fellow human beings.

Enjoy the privileges of your youth: the right to be dynamic, creative and spontaneous; the right to be full of hope and joy; the opportunity to explore the marvelous world of science and knowledge; and above all the chance to give of yourself to others in generous and joyful service.

I leave you now with this prayer: that the Lord Jesus will reveal himself to each one of you, that he will give you the strength to go out and profess that you are Christian, that he will show you that he alone can fill your hearts. Accept his freedom and embrace his truth, and be messengers of the certainty that you have been truly liberated through the Death and Resurrection of the Lord Jesus. This will be the new experience, the powerful experience, that will generate, through you, a more just society and a better world.

God bless you and may the joy of Jesus be always with you!

## 44. IN THE SHRINE

### A Woman's *Yes* That Pervades History

My first desire in this National Shrine of the Immaculate Conception is to direct my thoughts, to turn my heart to the woman of salvation history.

In the eternal design of God, this woman, Mary, was chosen to enter into the work of the Incarnation and Redemption. And this design of God was to be actuated through her free decision given in obedience to the divine will. Through her *yes*—a *yes* that pervades and is reflected in all history, she consented to be the Virgin Mother of our saving God, the handmaid of the Lord and, at the same time, the Mother of all the faithful who in the course of centuries would become the brothers and sisters of her Son.

Through her, the Sun of Justice was to rise in the world. Through her, the greater healer of humanity, the Reconciler of hearts and consciences—her Son, the God-man Jesus Christ—was to transform the human condition and, by his Death and Resurrection, uplift the entire human family.

As a great sign that appeared in the heavens in the fullness of time, the woman dominates all history as the Virgin Mother of the Son, and as the Spouse of the Holy Spirit—as the handmaid of humanity. And the woman becomes also—by association with her Son—the sign of contradiction to the world and, at the same time, the sign of hope whom all generations shall call blessed: the woman who conceived spiritually before she conceived physically; the woman who accepted the word of God; the woman who was inserted intimately and irrevocably into the mystery of the Church, exercising a spiritual Motherhood with regard to all people; the woman who is honored as Queen of Apostles, without herself being inserted into the hierarchical constitution of the Church. And yet this woman made all hierarchy possible, because she gave to the world the Shepherd and Bishop of our souls.

This woman, this Mary of the Gospel, who is not mentioned as being at the Last Supper, comes back again at the foot of the Cross, in order to consummate her contribution to salvation history. By her courageous act, she prefigures and anticipates the courage of all women throughout the ages who concur in bringing forth Christ in every generation. At Pentecost, the Virgin Mother once again comes forward to exercise her role in union with the Apostles, with and in and over the Church. Yet again she conceives of the Holy Spirit, to bring forth Jesus in the fullness of his Body, the Church—never to leave him, never to abandon him, but to continue to love and serve him through the ages.

This is the woman of history and destiny, who inspires us today: the woman who speaks to us of femininity, human dignity and love, and who is the greatest expression of total consecration to Jesus Christ, in whose name we are gathered today.

## 45. TO WOMEN RELIGIOUS

Dear Sisters,

May the grace, love and peace of God our Father and our Lord Jesus Christ be with you.

### Gratitude and Esteem for Women Religious

I welcome this opportunity to speak with you today. I am happy for this occasion because of my esteem for religious life, and my gratitude to women Religious for their invaluable contribution to the mission and very life of the Church.

I am especially pleased that we are gathered here in the National Shrine of the Immaculate Conception, for the Virgin Mary is the model of the Church, the Mother of the faithful and the perfect example of consecrated life.

### Ratified Baptismal Promises

1. On the day of our Baptism, we received the greatest gift God can bestow on any man or woman. No other honor, no other distinction will equal its value. For we were freed from sin and incorporated into Christ Jesus and his Body, the Church. That day and every day after, we were chosen "to live through love in his presence" (Eph. 1:4).

In the years that followed our Baptism, we grew in awareness—even wonder— of the mystery of Christ. By listening to the Beatitudes, by meditating on the Cross, conversing with Christ in prayer and receiving him in the Eucharist, we progressed toward the day, that particular moment of our life, when we solemnly ratified with full awareness and freedom our baptismal consecration. We affirmed our determination to live always in union with Christ, and to be, according to the gifts given us by the Holy Spirit, a generous and loving member of the People of God.

## Essence of Religious Consecration

2. Your religious consecration builds on this common foundation which all Christians share in the Body of Christ. Desiring to perfect and intensify what God had begun in your life by Baptism, and discerning that God was indeed offering you the gift of the evangelical counsels, you willed to follow Christ more closely, to conform your life more completely to that of Jesus Christ, in and through a distinctive religious community. This is the essence of religious consecration: to profess within and for the benefit of the Church, poverty, chastity and obedience in response to God's special invitation, in order to praise and serve God in greater freedom of heart (see 1 Cor. 7:34–35) and to have one's life more closely conformed to Christ in the manner of life chosen by him and his blessed Mother (see *Perfectae Caritatis*, 1; *Lumen Gentium*, 46).

## Faithfulness to Christ

3. Religious consecration not only deepens your personal commitment to Christ, but it also strengthens your relationship to his Spouse, the Church. Religious consecration is a distinctive manner of living in the Church, a particular way of fulfilling the life of faith and service begun in Baptism.

On her part, the Church assists you in your discernment of God's will. Having accepted and authenticated the charism of your various Institutes, she then unites your religious profession to the celebration of Christ's Paschal Mystery.

You are called by Jesus himself to verify and manifest in your lives and in your activities your deepened relationship with his Church. This bond of union with the Church must also be shown in the spirit and apostolic endeavors of every Religious Institute. For faithfulness to Christ, especially in religious life, can never be separated from faithfulness to the Church. This ecclesial dimension of the vocation of religious consecration has many important practical consequences for Institutes themselves and for each individual member. It implies, for example, a greater public witness to the Gospel, since you represent, in a special way as women Religious, the spousal relationship of the Church to Christ. The ecclesial dimension also requires, on the part of individual members as well as entire Institutes, a faithfulness to the original charism which God has given to his Church, through your founders and foundresses. It means that Institutes are called to continue to foster, in dynamic faithfulness, those corporate commitments which were related to the original charism, which were authenticated by the Church, and which still fulfill important needs of the People of God. A good example in this regard would be the Catholic School system, which has been invaluable for the Church in the United States, an excellent means not only for communicating the Gospel of Christ to the students, but also for permeating the entire community with Christ's truth and his love. It is one of the apostolates in which women Religious have made, and are still making, an incomparable contribution.

### Jesus: First in Mind and Heart

4. Dear sisters in Christ: Jesus must always be first in your lives. His person must be at the center of your activities—the activities of every day. No other person and no activity can take precedence over him. For your whole life has been consecrated to him. With Saint Paul you have to say: "All I want is to know Christ and the power of his Resurrection and to share his sufferings by reproducing the pattern of his death" (Phil. 3:10).

Christ remains primary in your life only when he enjoys the first place in your mind and heart. Thus you must continuously unite yourself to him in prayer. Without prayer, religious life has no meaning. It has lost contact with its source, it has emptied itself of substance, and it no longer can fulfill its goal. Without prayer there can be no joy, no hope, no peace. For prayer is what keeps us in touch with Christ. The incisive words written in *Evangelica Testificatio* cause us all to reflect: "Do not forget the witness of history: faithfulness to prayer or its abandonment is the test of the vitality or decadence of religious life" (*Evangelica Testificatio*, 42).

### Two Forces in Religious Life

5. Two dynamic forces are operative in religious life: your love for Jesus—and, in Jesus, for all who belong to him—and his love for you.

We cannot live without love. If we do not encounter love, if we do not experience it and make it our own, and if we do not participate intimately in it, our life is meaningless. Without love we remain incomprehensible to ourselves (see *Redemptor Hominis*, 10).

Thus every one of you needs a vibrant relationship of love to the Lord, a profound loving union with Christ, your spouse, a love like that expressed in the psalm: "God, you are my God whom I seek, for you my flesh pines and my soul thirsts like the earth, parched, lifeless and without water. Thus have I gazed toward you in the sanctuary to see your power and your glory" (Ps. 63:1–2).

Yet far more important than your love for Christ is Christ's love for you. You have been called by him, made a member of his Body, consecrated in a life of the evangelical counsels and destined by him to have a share in the mission that Christ has entrusted to the Church: his own mission of salvation. For this reason, you center your life in the Eucharist. In the Eucharist, you celebrate his Death and Resurrection and receive from him the Bread of eternal life. And it is in the Eucharist especially that you are united to the one who is the object of all your love. Here, with him, you find ever greater reason to love and serve his brothers and sisters. Here, with him—

with Christ—you find greater understanding and compassion for God's people. And here you find the strength to persevere in your commitment to selfless service.

## Public Witness to Inner Conversion

6. Your service in the Church is then an extension of Christ, to whom you have dedicated your life. For it is not yourself that you put forward, but Christ Jesus as Lord. Like John the Baptist, you know that for Christ to increase, you must decrease. And so your life must be characterized by a complete availability: a readiness to serve as the needs of the Church require, a readiness to give public witness to the Christ whom you love.

The need for this public witness becomes a constant call to inner conversion, to justice and holiness of life on the part of each Religious. It also becomes an invitation to each Institute to reflect on the purity of its corporate ecclesial witness. And it is for this reason that in my address last November to the International Union of Superiors General I mentioned that it is not unimportant that your consecration to God should be manifested in the permanent exterior sign of a simple and suitable religious garb. This is not only my personal conviction, but also the desire of the Church, often expressed by so many of the faithful.

As daughters of the Church—a title cherished by so many of your great saints—you are called to a generous and loving adherence to the authentic Magisterium of the Church, which is a solid guarantee of the fruitfulness of all your apostolates and an indispensable condition for the proper interpretation of the "signs of the times."

## Contemplative Communities

7. The contemplative life occupies today and for ever a place of great honor in the Church. The prayer of contemplation was found in the life of Jesus himself, and has been a part of religious life in every age. I take this opportunity therefore—as I did in Rome, in Mexico, in Poland and in Ireland—to encourage again all who are members of contemplative communities. Know that you will always fulfill an important place in the Church, in her mission of salvation, in her service to the whole community of the People of God. Continue faithfully, confidently and prayerfully, in the rich tradition that has been handed down to you.

In closing, I remind you, with sentiments of admiration and love, that the aim of religious life is to render praise and glory to the Most High Trinity, and, through your consecration, to help humanity enter into fullness of life in the Father, and in the Son and in the Holy Spirit. In all your planning and in all your activities, try also to keep this aim before you. There is no greater service you can give; there is no greater fulfillment you can receive. Dear sisters: today and forever: Praised be Jesus Christ!

## 46. IN THE NATIONAL SHRINE
## OF THE IMMACULATE CONCEPTION

### Common Love for Mary

This Shrine speaks to us with the voice of all America, with the voice of all the sons and daughters of America, who have come here from the various countries of the Old World. When they came, they brought with them in their hearts the same love for the Mother of God that was a characteristic of their ancestors and of themselves in their native lands. These people, speaking different languages, coming from different backgrounds of history and tradition in their own countries, came together around the heart of a Mother whom they all had in common. While their faith in Christ made all of them aware of being the one People of God, this awareness became all the more vivid through the presence of the Mother in the work of Christ and the Church.

Today, as I thank you, Mother, for this presence of yours in the midst of the men and women of this land—a presence which has lasted two hundred years—giving a new form to their social and civic lives in the United States, I commend them all to your Immaculate Heart.

With gratitude and joy I recall that you have been honored as Patroness of the United States, under the title of your Immaculate Conception, since the days of the Sixth Provincial Council of Baltimore in 1846.

I commend to you, Mother of Christ, and I entrust to you the Catholic Church: the Bishops, priests, deacons, individual Religious and Religious Institutes, the seminarians, vocations and the apostolate of the laity in its various aspects.

In a special way, I entrust to you the well-being of the Christian families of this country, the innocence of children, the future of the young, the vocation of single men and women. I ask you to communicate to all the women of the United States a deep sharing in the joy that you experienced in your closeness to Jesus Christ, your Son. I ask you to preserve all of them in freedom from sin and evil, like the freedom which was yours in a unique way from that moment of supreme liberation in your Immaculate Conception.

I entrust to you the great work of ecumenism here, in this land, in which those who confess Christ belong to different Churches and communions. I do this in order that the words of Christ's prayer may be fulfilled: "That they may be one." I entrust to you the consciences of men and women and the voice of public opinion, in order that they may not be opposed to the law of God but follow it as the fount of truth and good.

I add to this, Mother, the great cause of justice and peace in the modern world, in order that the force and energy of love may prevail over hatred and destructiveness, and in order that the children of light may not lack concern for the welfare of the whole human family.

Mother, I commend and entrust to you all that goes to make up earthly progress, asking that it should not be one-sided, but that it should create conditions for the full spiritual advancement of individuals, families, communities and nations. I commend to you the poor, the suffering, the sick and the handicapped, the aging and the dying. I ask you to reconcile those in sin, to heal those in pain and to uplift those who have lost their hope and joy. Show to those who struggle in doubt the light of Christ your Son.

Bishops of the Church in the United States have chosen your Immaculate Conception as the mystery to hold the patronage over the people of God in this land. May the hope contained in this mystery overcome sin and be shared by all the sons and daughters of America, and also by the whole human family. At a time when the struggle between good and evil, between evangelical love and the prince of darkness and father of lies is growing more acute, may the light of your Immaculate Conception show to all the way to grace and to salvation. Amen.

## 47. AT THE CATHOLIC UNIVERSITY: PRESIDENTS OF CATHOLIC COLLEGES AND UNIVERSITIES

Dear Brothers and Sisters in Christ,

### Faithful Adherence to Christ

1. Our meeting today gives me great pleasure, and I thank you sincerely for your cordial welcome. My own association with the university world, and more particularly with the Pontifical Theological Faculty of Cracow and The Catholic University of Lublin, makes our encounter all the more gratifying for me. I cannot but feel at home with you. The sincere expressions with which the chancellor and the president of The Catholic University of America have confirmed, in the name of all of you, the faithful adherence to Christ and the generous commitment to the service of truth and charity of your Catholic associations and institutions of higher learning are appreciated.

Ninety-two years ago Cardinal Gibbons and the American Bishops requested the foundation of The Catholic University of America, as a university "destined to provide the Church with worthy ministers for the salvation of souls and the propagation of religion and to give the republic most worthy citizens." It seems appropriate to me on this occasion to address myself not only to this great institution, so irrevocably linked to the Bishops of the United States, who have founded it and who generously support it, but also to all the Catholic universities, colleges, and academies of postsecondary learning in your land, those with formal and sometimes juridical links with the Holy See, as well as all those that are "Catholic."

### Greetings to Faculties, Parents

2. Before doing so, though, allow me first to mention the Ecclesiastical Faculties, three of which are established here at The Catholic University of America. I greet

these Faculties and all who dedicate their best talents in them. I offer my prayers for the prosperous development and the unfailing fidelity and success of these Faculties. In the Apostolic Constitution *Sapientia Christiana,* I have dealt directly with these institutions in order to provide guidance and to ensure that they fulfill their role in meeting the needs of the Christian community in today's rapidly changing circumstances.

I also wish to address a word of praise and admiration to the men and women, especially priests and Religious, who dedicate themselves to all forms of campus ministry. Their sacrifices and efforts to bring the true message of Christ to the university world, whether secular or Catholic, cannot go unnoticed.

The Church also greatly appreciates the work and witness of those of her sons and daughters whose vocation places them in non-Catholic universities in your country. I am sure that their Christian hope and Catholic patrimony bring an enriching and irreplaceable dimension to the world of higher studies.

A special word of gratitude and appreciation also goes to the parents and students who, sometimes at the price of great personal and financial sacrifice, look toward the Catholic universities and colleges for the training that unites faith and science, culture and the Gospel values.

To all engaged in administration, teaching or study in Catholic colleges and universities I would apply the words of Daniel: "They who are learned shall shine like the brightness of the firmament and those that instruct many in justice as stars for all eternity" (Dn. 12:3). Sacrifice and generosity have accomplished heroic results in the foundation and development of these institutions. Despite immense financial strain, enrollment problems and other obstacles, divine Providence and the commitment of the whole People of God have allowed us to see these Catholic institutions flourish and advance.

### Three Goals

3. I would repeat here before you what I told the professors and students of the Catholic universities in Mexico when I indicated three aims that are to be pursued. A Catholic university or college must make a specific contribution to the Church and to society through high-quality scientific research, in-depth study of problems and a just sense of history, together with the concern to show the full meaning of the human person regenerated in Christ, thus favoring the complete development of the person. Furthermore, the Catholic university or college must train young men and women of outstanding knowledge who, having made a personal synthesis between faith and culture, will be both capable and willing to assume tasks in the service of the community and of society in general, and to bear witness to their faith before the world. And finally, to be what it ought to be, a Catholic college or university must set up, among its faculty and students, a real community which bears witness to a living and operative Christianity, a community where sincere commitment to scientific research and study goes together with a deep commitment to authentic Christian living.

This is your identity. This is your vocation. Every university or college is qualified by a specific mode of being. Yours is the qualification of being Catholic, of affirming God, his revelation and the Catholic Church as the guardian and interpreter of that revelation. The term "Catholic" will never be a mere label, either added or dropped according to the pressures of varying factors.

## Surrender to Objectivity

4. As one who for long years has been a university professor, I will never tire of insisting on the eminent role of the university, which is to instruct but also to be a place of scientific research. In both these fields, its activity is closely related to the deepest and noblest aspiration of the human person: the desire to come to the knowledge of truth. No university can deserve the rightful esteem of the world of learning unless it applies the highest standards of scientific research, constantly updating its methods and working instruments, and unless it excels in seriousness, and therefore, in freedom of investigation. Truth and science are not gratuitous conquests, but the result of a surrender to objectivity and of the exploration of all aspects of nature and man. Whenever man himself becomes the object of investigation, no single method, or combination of methods, can fail to take into account, beyond any purely natural approach, the full nature of man. Because he is bound by the total truth on man, the Christian will, in his research and in his teaching, reject any partial vision of human reality, but he will let himself be enlightened by his faith in the creation of God and the Redemption of Christ.

The relationship to truth explains therefore the historical bond between the university and the Church. Because she herself finds her origin and her growth in the words of Christ, which are the liberating truth (see Jn. 8:32), the Church has always tried to stand by the institutions that serve, and cannot but serve the knowledge of truth. The Church can rightfully boast of being in a sense the mother of universities. The names of Bologna, Padua, Prague and Paris shine in the earliest history of intellectual endeavor and human progress. The continuity of the historic tradition in this field has come down to our day.

## Culture Steeped in the Gospel

5. An undiminished dedication to intellectual honesty and academic excellence are seen, in a Catholic university, in the perspective of the Church's mission of evangelization and service. This is why the Church asks these institutions, your institutions, to set out, without equivocation, your Catholic nature. This is what I have desired to emphasize in my Apostolic Constitution *Sapientia Christiana,* where I stated: "Indeed, the Church's mission of spreading the Gospel not only demands that the Good News be preached ever more widely and to ever greater numbers of men and women, but that the very power of the Gospel should permeate thought patterns, standards of judgment, and the norms of behavior; in a word, it is necessary that the whole of human culture be steeped in the Gospel. The cultural atmosphere in which

a human being lives has a great influence upon his or her way of thinking and, thus, of acting. Therefore, a division between faith and culture is more than a small impediment to evangelization, while a culture penetrated with the Christian spirit is an instrument that favors the spreading of the Good News" (*Sapientia Christiana,* I). The goals of Catholic higher education go beyond education for production, professional competence, technological and scientific competence; they aim at the ultimate destiny of the human person, at the full justice and holiness born of truth (see Eph. 4:24).

### A Special Word to Theologians

6. If then your universities and colleges are institutionally committed to the Christian message, and if they are part of the Catholic community of evangelization, it follows that they have an essential relationship to the hierarchy of the Church. And here I want to say a special word of gratitude, encouragement and guidance for the theologians. The Church needs her theologians, particularly in this time and age so profoundly marked by deep changes in all areas of life and society. The Bishops of the Church, to whom the Lord has entrusted the keeping of the unity of the faith and the preaching of the message—individual Bishops for their Dioceses, and Bishops collegially, with the Successor of Peter, for the universal Church—we all need your work, your dedication and the fruits of your reflection. We desire to listen to you and we are eager to receive the valued assistance of your responsible scholarship.

But true theological scholarship, and by the same token theological teaching, cannot exist and be fruitful without seeking its inspiration and its source in the word of God as contained in Sacred Scripture and in the Sacred Tradition of the Church, as interpreted by the authentic Magisterium throughout history (see *Dei Verbum,* 10). True academic freedom must be seen in relation to the finality of the academic enterprise, which looks to the total truth of the human person. The theologian's contribution will be enriching for the Church only if it takes into account the proper function of the Bishops and the rights of the faithful. It devolves upon the Bishops of the Church to safeguard the Christian authenticity and unity of faith and moral teaching, in accordance with the injunction of the Apostle Paul: "Proclaim the message and, welcome or unwelcome, insist on it. Refute falsehood, correct error, call to obedience" (2 Tm. 4:2). It is the right of the faithful not to be troubled by theories and hypotheses that they are not expert in judging or that are easily simplified or manipulated by public opinion for ends that are alien to the truth. On the day of his death, John Paul I stated: "Among the rights of the faithful, one of the greatest is the right to receive God's word in all its entirety and purity" (September 28, 1979). It behooves the theologian to be free, but with the freedom that is openness to the truth and the light that comes from faith and from fidelity to the Church.

In concluding I express to you once more my joy in being with you today. I remain very close to your work and your concerns. May the intercession of Mary, Seat of Wisdom, sustain you always in your irreplaceable service of humanity and the Church. God bless you.

## 48. ECUMENICAL MEETING AT TRINITY COLLEGE

Dearly Beloved in Christ,

### Service for Christian Unity

1. I am grateful to the providence of God that permits me on my visit to the United States of America to have this meeting with other religious leaders, and to be able to join with you in prayer for the unity of all Christians.

It is indeed fitting that our meeting should occur just a short time before the observance of the fifteenth anniversary of the Second Vatican Council's Decree of Ecumenism, *Unitatis Redintegratio.* Since the inception of my pontificate, almost a year ago, I have endeavored to devote myself to the service of Christian unity; for, as I stated in my first encyclical, it is certain "that in the present historical situation of Christianity and of the world the only possibility we see of fulfilling the Church's universal mission, with regard to ecumenical questions, is that of seeking sincerely, perseveringly, humbly and also courageously the ways of drawing closer and of union" (*Redemptor Hominis,* 6). On a previous occasion, I said that the problem of division within Christianity is "binding in a special way on the Bishop of the ancient Church of Rome, founded on the preaching and the testimonies of the martyrdom of Saints Peter and Paul" (General Audience, January 17, 1979). And today I wish to reiterate before you the same conviction.

### A United Confession

2. With great satisfaction and joy I welcome the opportunity to embrace you, in the charity of Christ, as beloved Christian brethren and fellow disciples of the Lord Jesus. It is a privilege to be able, in your presence and together with you, to give expression to the testimony of John, that "Jesus Christ is the Son of God" (1 Jn. 4:15), and to proclaim that "there is one Mediator between God and men, the man Christ Jesus" (1 Tm. 2:5).

In the united confession of faith in the divinity of Jesus Christ, we feel great love for each other and great hope for all humanity. We experience immense gratitude to the Father, who has sent his Son to be our Savior, "the expiation for our sins, and not for ours only but for the sins of the whole world" (1 Jn. 2:2).

By divine grace we are united in esteem and love for Sacred Scripture, which we recognize as the inspired word of God. And it is precisely in this word of God that we learn how much he wants us to be fully one in him and in his Father. Jesus prays that his followers may be one "so that the world may believe" (Jn. 17:21). That the credibility of evangelization should, by God's plan, depend on the unity of his followers is a subject of inexhaustible meditation for all of us.

### Ecumenical Initiatives

3. I wish to pay homage here to the many splendid ecumenical initiatives that have been realized in this country through the action of the Holy Spirit. In the last

fifteen years there has been a positive response to ecumenism by the Bishops of the United States. Through their committee for ecumenical and interreligious affairs, they have established a fraternal relationship with other Churches and ecclesial communities—a relationship which, I pray, will continue to deepen in the coming years.

Conversations are in progress with our brothers from the East, the Orthodox. Here I wish to note that this relationship has been strong in the United States and that soon a theological dialogue will begin on a worldwide basis in an attempt to resolve those difficulties which hinder full unity. There are also American dialogues with the Anglicans, the Lutherans, the Reformed Church, the Methodists and the Disciples of Christ—all having a counterpart on the international level. A fraternal exchange exists likewise between the Southern Baptists and American theologians.

My gratitude goes to all who collaborate in the matter of joint theological investigation, the aim of which is always the full evangelical and Christian dimension of truth. It is to be hoped that, through such investigation, persons who are well prepared by a solid grounding in their own traditions will contribute to a deepening of the full historical and doctrinal understanding of the issues.

The particular climate and traditions of the United States have been conducive to joint witness in the defense of the rights of the human person, in the pursuit of goals of social justice and peace, and in questions of public morality. These areas of concern must continue to benefit from creative ecumenical action, as must the fostering of esteem for the sacredness of marriage and the support of healthy family life as a major contribution to the well-being of the nation. In this context, recognition must be given to the deep division which still exists over moral and ethical matters. The moral life and the life of faith are so deeply united that it is impossible to divide them.

## Faithfulness to the Holy Spirit

4. Much has been accomplished, but there is still much to be done. We must go forward, however, with a spirit of hope. Even the very desire for the complete unity in faith—which is lacking between us, and which must be achieved before we can lovingly celebrate the Eucharist together in truth—is itself a gift of the Holy Spirit, for which we offer humble praise to God. We are confident that through our common prayer the Lord Jesus will lead us, at a moment dependent on the sovereign action of his Holy Spirit, to the fullness of ecclesial unity.

Faithfulness to the Holy Spirit calls for interior conversion and fervent prayer. In the words of the Second Vatican Council: "This change of heart and holiness of life, along with public and private prayer for the unity of Christians, should be regarded as the soul of the whole ecumenical movement" (Unitatis Redintegratio, 8). It is important that every individual Christian search his or her heart to see what may obstruct the attainment of full union among Christians. And let us all pray that the genuine need for the patience to await God's hour will never occasion complacency in the status quo of division of faith. By divine grace may the need for patience never become a substitute for the definitive and generous response which God asks be given to his invitation to perfect unity in Christ.

And so, as we are gathered here to celebrate the love of God that is poured out in our hearts by the Holy Spirit, let us be conscious of the call to show supreme fidelity to the will of Christ. Let us together perseveringly ask the Holy Spirit to remove all division from our faith, to give us that perfect unity in truth and love for which Christ prayed, for which Christ died: "to gather together in unity the scattered children of God" (Jn. 11:52).

I offer my respectful greeting of grace and peace to those whom you represent, to each of your respective congregations, to all who long for the coming of "our great God and Savior Jesus Christ" (Ti. 2:14).

## 49. TO JOURNALISTS

My dear Friends of the communications media,

### The Pope: Herald of Peace

Here we are together again at the end of another journey—a journey which this time has brought me to Ireland, to the United Nations and to the United States of America. The purpose of this journey was to permit the Pope to exercise his function as a herald of peace, in the name of Christ, who was referred to as the Prince of Peace. This message of peace was announced especially in those places and before those audiences where the problem of war and peace is perceived with particular sensitivity and where there exist the conditions of understanding, of good will and of the means necessary to building peace and cooperation among all nations and among all peoples.

The word "peace" is a synthesis. It has many components. I have touched on several of these during this journey, and you have diligently reported on these reflections. You have commented on them; you have interpreted them; you have performed the service of stimulating people to think about how they might contribute to a firmer foundation for peace, for cooperation and for justice among all persons.

Now we find ourselves at the moment of parting, in this capital city of one of the most powerful nations in the world. The power of this country, I believe, comes not from material wealth but from a richness of spirit.

### Religious Foundation of U.S.A.

In fact, the name of this city and of the tall monument which dominates it recalls the spirit of George Washington, the first president of the nation, who—with Thomas Jefferson, for whom an imposing memorial also exists here, and with other enlightened individuals—established this country on a foundation which was not only human but also profoundly religious.

As a consequence, the Catholic Church has been able to flourish here. The millions of faithful who belong to the Church testify to that fact, as they exercise the rights and duties which flow from their faith with full freedom. The great National Shrine of the Immaculate Conception in this city testifies to that fact. The existence in this capital city of two Catholic universities—Georgetown and The Catholic University of America—testifies to that fact. I have observed that the people of the United States of America proudly and gratefully pledge allegiance to their republic as "one nation under God."

This one nation is made up of many members—members of all races, of all religions, of all conditions of life—so that it is a type of microcosm of the world community and accurately reflects the motto *E pluribus unum.* As this country courageously abolished the plague of slavery under the presidency of Abraham Lincoln, may it never stop striving for the effective good of all the inhabitants of this one nation and for the unity which reflects its national motto. For this reason, the United States of America gives to all cause to reflect on a spirit which, if well applied, can bring beneficial results for peace in the world community.

I sincerely hope that all of you have profited from this journey, and that you have had the opportunity to reflect anew on the values which have come from Christianity to the civilization of this new continent. Most of all, however, we can draw hope for a peaceful world community from the example of persons of all races, of all nationalities and of all religions living together in peace and in unity.

As we prepare to part, my dear friends, I am consoled by the fact that you will continue to inform and to form world public opinion with a profound consciousness of your responsibility and with the realization that so many persons depend on you.

Finally, I say good-bye to you and to America. I thank you again, and with all my heart I ask God to bless you and your families.

## 50. TO THE KNIGHTS OF COLUMBUS

Dear Knights of Columbus,

### Gratitude for Your Love and Respect

It gives me great pleasure to be with you on the occasion of my pastoral visit to the United States. I thank you most sincerely for the respect and love which you have manifested toward me as Successor of Peter, Bishop of Rome and Pastor of the universal Church.

In the person of the Supreme Knight and the Members of the Supreme Board, I greet all the Knights of Columbus: the more than 1,300,000 Catholic laymen all over the world, who display a spirit of profound attachment to their Christian faith and of loyalty to the Apostolic See.

### Your Work of Evangelizing

Many times in the past, and again today, you have given expression to your solidarity with the mission of the Pope. I see in your support a further proof—if further proof were ever necessary—of your awareness that the Knights of Columbus highly value their vocation to be part of the evangelization effort of the Church. I am happy to recall here what my revered predecessor, Paul VI, said about this task in his Apostolic Exhortation *Evangelii Nuntiandi,* as he emphasized the specific role of the laity: "Their own field of evangelizing activity is the vast and complicated world of politics, society and economics, but also the world of culture, of the sciences and the arts, of international life, of the mass media. It also includes other realities which are open to evangelization, such as human love, the family, the education of children and adolescents, professional work and suffering" (no. 70).

These words of one who never ceased to encourage you clearly indicate the road which your association must travel. I am aware of the many efforts you make to promote the use of mass media for the spreading of the Gospel and for the wider diffusion of my own messages. May the Lord reward you, and through your efforts bring forth abundant fruits of evangelization in the Church. May your dedicated activity in turn help you to realize in yourselves those interior attitudes without which no one can truly evangelize: trust in the power of the Holy Spirit, true holiness of life, deep concern for the truth, and an ever-increasing love for God's children.

May the Lord's blessing be upon you, upon your families and upon all the Knights of Columbus.

## 51. HOMILY ON CAPITOL MALL

Dear Brothers and Sisters in Jesus Christ,

### Let the Children Come to Me

1. In his dialogue with his listeners, Jesus was faced one day with an attempt by some Pharisees to get him to endorse their current views regarding the nature of marriage. Jesus answered by reaffirming the teaching of Scripture: "At the beginning of creation God made them male and female; for this reason a man shall leave his father and mother and the two shall become one. They are no longer two but one in flesh. Therefore let no man separate what God has joined" (Mk. 10:6–9).

The Gospel according to Mark immediately adds the description of a scene with which we are all familiar. This scene shows Jesus becoming indignant when he noticed how his own disciples tried to prevent the people from bringing their children closer to him, and so he said: "Let the children come to me and do not hinder them. It is to just such as these that the kingdom of God belongs. . . . Then he embraced them and blessed them, placing his hands on them" (Mk. 10:14–16). In proposing these readings, today's liturgy invites all of us to reflect on the nature of marriage, on the family, and on the value of life—three themes that are so closely interconnected.

## Family and Human Life

2. I shall all the more gladly lead you in reflecting on the word of God as proposed by the Church today, because all over the world the Bishops are discussing marriage and family life as they are lived in all Dioceses and nations. The Bishops are doing this in preparation for the next World Synod of Bishops, which has as its theme: "The Role of the Christian Family in the Contemporary World." Your own Bishops have designated next year as a year of study, planning and pastoral renewal with regard to the family. For a variety of reasons there is a renewed interest throughout the world in marriage, in family life and in the value of all human life.

This very Sunday marks the beginning of the annual Respect Life Program, through which the Church in the United States intends to reiterate its conviction regarding the inviolability of human life in all stages. Let us then, all together, renew our esteem for the value of human life, remembering also that, through Christ, all human life has been redeemed.

## All Human Life Is Sacred

3. I do not hesitate to proclaim before you and before the world that all human life—from the moment of conception through all subsequent stages—is sacred, because human life is created in the image and likeness of God. Nothing surpasses the greatness or dignity of a human person. Human life is not just an idea or an abstraction; human life is the concrete reality of a being that lives, that acts, that grows and develops; human life is the concrete reality of a being that is capable of love, and of service to humanity.

Let me repeat what I told the people during my recent pilgrimage to my homeland: "If a person's right to life is violated at the moment in which he is first conceived in his mother's womb, an indirect blow is struck also at the whole of the moral order, which serves to ensure the inviolable goods of man. Among those goods, life occupies the first place. The Church defends the right to life, not only in regard to the majesty of the Creator, who is the First Giver of this life, but also in respect of the essential good of the human person" (June 8, 1979).

## A Gift from God

4. Human life is precious because it is the gift of a God whose love is infinite; and when God gives life, it is for ever. Life is also precious because it is the expression and the fruit of love. This is why life should spring up within the setting of marriage, and why marriage and the parents' love for one another should be marked by generosity in self-giving. The great danger for family life, in the midst of any society whose idols are pleasure, comfort and independence, lies in the fact that people close their

hearts and become selfish. The fear of making permanent commitments can change the mutual love of husband and wife into two loves of self—two loves existing side by side, until they end in separation.

In the Sacrament of Marriage, a man and a woman—who at Baptism became members of Christ and hence have the duty of manifesting Christ's attitudes in their lives—are assured of the help they need to develop their love in a faithful and indissoluble union, and to respond with generosity to the gift of parenthood. As the Second Vatican Council declared: Through this Sacrament, Christ himself becomes present in the life of the married couple and accompanies them, so that they may love each other and their children, just as Christ loved his Church by giving himself up for her (see *Gaudium et Spes,* 48; see Eph. 5:25).

## Open to Life

5. In order that Christian marriage may favor the total good and development of the married couple, it must be inspired by the Gospel, and thus be open to new life—new life to be given and accepted generously. The couple is also called to create a family atmosphere in which children can be happy and lead full and worthy human and Christian lives.

To maintain a joyful family requires much from both the parents and the children. Each member of the family has to become, in a special way, the servant of the others and share their burdens (see Gal. 6:2; Phil. 2:2). Each one must show concern not only for his or her own life but also for the lives of the other members of the family: their needs, their hopes, their ideals. Decisions about the number of children and the sacrifices to be made for them must not be taken only with a view to adding to comfort and preserving a peaceful existence. Reflecting upon this matter before God, with the graces drawn from the Sacrament, and guided by the teaching of the Church, parents will remind themselves that it is certainly less serious to deny their children certain comforts or material advantages than to deprive them of the presence of brothers and sisters, who could help them to grow in humanity and to realize the beauty of life at all its ages and in all its variety.

If parents fully realized the demands and the opportunities that this great sacrament brings, they could not fail to join in Mary's hymn to the author of life—to God—who has made them his chosen fellow workers.

## We Will Stand Up in Defense

6. All human beings ought to value every person for his or her uniqueness as a creature of God, called to be a brother or sister of Christ by reason of the Incarnation and the universal Redemption. For us, the sacredness of human life is based on these premises. And it is on these same premises that there is based our celebration of life—all human life. This explains our efforts to defend human life against every influence or action that threatens or weakens it, as well as our endeavors to make every life more human in all its aspects.

And so, we will stand up every time that human life is threatened. When the sacredness of life before birth is attacked, we will stand up and proclaim that no one ever has the authority to destroy unborn life. When a child is described as a burden or is looked upon only as a means to satisfy an emotional need, we will stand up and insist that every child is a unique and unrepeatable gift of God, with the right to a loving and united family. When the institution of marriage is abandoned to human selfishness or reduced to a temporary, conditional arrangement that can easily be terminated, we will stand up and affirm the indissolubility of the marriage bond. When the value of the family is threatened because of social and economic pressures, we will stand up and reaffirm that the family is "necessary not only for the private good of every person, but also for the common good of every society, nation and state" (General Audience, January 3, 1979). When freedom is used to dominate the weak, to squander natural resources and energy, and to deny basic necessities to people, we will stand up and reaffirm the demands of justice and social love. When the sick, the aged or the dying are abandoned in loneliness, we will stand up and proclaim that they are worthy of love, care and respect.

I make my own the words which Paul VI spoke last year to the American Bishops: "We are convinced, moreover, that all efforts made to safeguard human rights actually benefit life itself. Everything aimed at banishing discrimination—in law or in fact—which is based on race, origin, color, culture, sex or religion (see *Octogesima Adveniens,* 16) is a service to life. When the rights of minorities are fostered, when the mentally or physically handicapped are assisted, when those on the margin of society are given a voice—in all these instances the dignity of life, and the sacredness of human life are furthered. . . . In particular, every contribution made to better the moral climate of society, to oppose permissiveness and hedonism, and all assistance to the family, which is the source of new life, effectively uphold the values of life" (May 26, 1978).

### The Care of Human Life

7. Much remains to be done to support those whose lives are wounded and to restore hope to those who are afraid of life. Courage is needed to resist pressures and false slogans, to proclaim the supreme dignity of all life, and to demand that society itself give it its protection. A distinguished American, Thomas Jefferson, once stated: "The care of human life and happiness and not their destruction is the just and only legitimate object of good government" (March 31, 1809). I wish therefore to praise all members of the Catholic Church and other Christian Churches, all men and women of the Judeo-Christian heritage, as well as all people of good will who unite in common dedication for the defense of life in its fullness and for the promotion of all human rights.

Our celebration of life forms part of the celebration of the Eucharist. Our Lord and Savior, through his Death and Resurrection, has become for us "the bread of life" and the pledge of eternal life. In him we find the courage, perseverance and inventiveness which we need in order to promote and defend life within our families and throughout the world.

Dear brothers and sisters: we are confident that Mary, the Mother of God and the Mother of Life, will give us her help so that our way of living will always reflect our admiration and gratitude for God's gift of love that is life. We know that she will help us to use every day that is given to us as an opportunity to defend the life of the unborn and to render more human the lives of all our fellow human beings, wherever they may be.

And through the intercession of Our Lady of the Rosary, whose feast we celebrate today, may we come one day to the fullness of eternal life in Christ Jesus our Lord. Amen.

## 52. DEPARTURE FOR ROME

Mr. Vice President,

My dear Friends in America, and my Brothers and Sisters in the
faith of our Lord Jesus Christ,

### Gratitude to All

As I leave this capital city of Washington, I wish to express my gratitude to the president of the United States and to all the religious and civil authorities of this country.

My thoughts turn likewise to all the American people: to all Catholics, Protestants and Jews, and to all men and women of good will; to people of every ethnic origin, and in particular to the descendants of the first inhabitants of this land, the American Indians; to all of you whom I have greeted personally; those who have been close to me through the providential media of press, radio and television; those who have opened their hearts to me in so many ways. Your hospitality has been warm and filled with love, and I am grateful for all your kindnesses.

I believe strongly in the message of hope that I have held up to you, in the justice and love and truth that I have extolled, and in the peace that I have asked the Lord to give to all of you.

And now I must leave the United States and return to Rome. But all of you will constantly be remembered in my prayers, which I look upon as the best expression of my loyalty and friendship.

Today, therefore, my final prayer is this: that God will bless America, so that she may increasingly become—and truly be—and long remain—"One Nation, *under God,* indivisible, with liberty and justice for all."

God bless America!

God bless America!

## OCTOBER 8, 1979

## 53. ARRIVAL AT AIRPORT, ROME

### The Church Desires That Peace Which Springs from the True Idea of Man, from Respect for Man's Rights and the Accomplishment of His Duties, an Idea That Is Based Chiefly upon Justice

As I set foot once more on the beloved soil of Italy, after the unforgettable emotions of more than a week of liturgical celebrations, meetings and talks, I am filled with sentiments of deep gratitude and joy before the Lord, who in his provident goodness has once more enabled me to meet personally so many brothers and sisters, sons and daughters, and so many representatives and people in authority, men and women of good will.

My brief stay in Ireland enabled me to get to know that country more closely, and to admire its ancient traditions of faith, which witness to its attachment to the Apostolic See, and to appreciate its precious moral values. I am happy to have accepted the Irish Bishops' invitation to celebrate with all the faithful the centenary of the apparition of Our Lady at Knock. In this way I was enabled to express my filial gratitude to Mary, who in every land offers clear and tangible signs of her motherly care and loving help, which we have invoked especially for peace and reconciliation in that beloved island.

I then went to the General Assembly of the United Nations, where the peoples of the world are represented and as it were come together. This meeting is a continuation of the visit fourteen years ago, as part and symbol of his persevering peace mission, by my unforgettable predecessor Paul VI. I too, willingly accepting the invitation of the secretary-general, wished to assure the United Nations that the Church is close to those who work for peace, and wished to inspire and support their efforts, through the sole desire to serve humanity. In fact, the Church desires that peace which springs from the true idea of man, from respect for man's rights and the accomplishment of his duties, an idea that is based chiefly upon justice. The Church will never cease to urge people to think about the future destiny of society and the world, with an outlook that is ever renewed and converted.

Thirdly, in response to the desire expressed by the president of the United States and the worthy members of the American Episcopate, I spent some days in their great country. It is a country that certainly has an eminent part to play, and a grave responsibility—precisely by reason of the high level of well-being and technical and social progress that it has attained—in the building up of a world that is just and worthy of man. My visit was mainly an ecclesial contact with the faithful and their pastors, to refresh their spirits and increase their courage to think and to live not in man's way but in God's way.

The devoted and enthusiastic welcome given me by all the people of the United States has left me with a desire for an ever more direct and intimate contact with my dear sons and daughters in that country.

As I conclude these brief remarks, I wish to express in the first place to the president of the Council of Ministers my lively and profound thanks for the noble and cordial words with which he has welcomed me back to Italy. With deep respect I also extend my thanks to the Cardinals, the representatives of the state and the Italian government, the members of the diplomatic corps, led by their worthy dean, the members of the Roman Curia and all those who have given me this festive welcome and made the moment of my return even more pleasant by their affectionate presence.

I also feel the pleasant duty to express my satisfaction and gratitude to the directors of the airlines, to the pilots and crews of the various aircraft, and to all who have worked with generous devotion for the complete success of my journey.

Once more I offer to Christ the Lord, the Prince of Peace, aspirations and resolves for peaceful coexistence, fraternal collaboration and human and Christian solidarity of the peoples of the earth, and together with my Apostolic Blessing I invoke the divine outpouring of grace and mercy upon all of you here present, and upon the beloved sons and daughters of the City of Rome and of all humanity.

# 1981 and 1984 Visits
# to Alaska

FEBRUARY 26, 1981

## 1. MEETING WITH THE CLERGY
## AND WITH MEN AND WOMEN RELIGIOUS,
## HOLY FAMILY CATHEDRAL, ANCHORAGE

### The Church Lives an Authentic Life
### When She Professes and Proclaims Mercy

Dear Brothers and Sisters in Christ,

1. "I thank God whenever I think of you; and every time I pray for all of you, I pray with joy, remembering how you have helped to spread the Good News" (Phil. 1:3–4).

These words of Saint Paul express the sentiments of my heart as I greet you today here in Anchorage. Indeed, I pray with joy whenever I think of my brother priests and my brothers and sisters in religious life. *I thank God for your dedication to Christ, your presence in the Church and your collaboration in her mission.* And I thank God for your prayers, in which you unite with the whole body of Christ in praising the name of the Most Holy Trinity and in asking God's mercy for his people.

2. In writing my last encyclical my thoughts often turned to you who in a particular way share with me the *mission of proclaiming the mercy of God to the present generation.* Every evening we pray in the Liturgy of the Hours the words of Mary: "His mercy is from age to age on those who fear him" (Lk. 1:50). It is this truth of salvation, the truth about the mercy of God, which we must proclaim to our generation, to the men and women of our age who seem to be moving away from the mystery of God's mercy. Thus I wrote in the encyclical, "The Church lives an authentic life when she professes and proclaims mercy—the most stupendous

attribute of the Creator and of the Redeemer—and when she brings people close to the sources of the Saviour's mercy, of which she is the trustee and dispenser" (*Dives in Misericordia,* 13).

### The Priesthood and Religious Life Are of Vital Importance in the Mission of Proclaiming God's Mercy

3. My brothers and sisters in Christ, never doubt the vital importance of your presence in the Church, the vital importance of religious life and the ministerial priesthood in the mission of proclaiming the mercy of God. Through your daily lives, which are often accompanied by the sign of the Cross, and through your faithful service and persevering hope, you show your deep faith in *God's merciful love,* and you bear witness to that *love which is more powerful than evil, and stronger than death.*

Have confidence therefore in the one who called you to this life. Have confidence in God "whose power, working in us, can do infinitely more than we can ask or imagine; glory be to him from generation to generation in the Church and in Christ Jesus for ever and ever. Amen" (Eph. 3:20–21).

## 2. HOMILY AT MASS, DELANEY PARK STRIP, ANCHORAGE

Dear Brothers and Sisters,

> Sing to the Lord a new song;
> Sing to the Lord, all the earth!
> Declare his glory among the nations,
> His marvelous works among all peoples!

### God's Presence Is Felt in the Manifold Handiwork of His Creation in Alaska

1. The joyful sentiments that moved the heart of the Psalmist to praise the Lord in these words are the same sentiments that well up within us as we gather here in Anchorage to celebrate this Mass of the Holy Spirit. What better way could we express praise to God than *in that Spirit, who is the vital principle of the Church's life?* What more fitting song could be sung than one that tells of the Holy Spirit's inspiration and guidance in proclaiming the Gospel of Christ to the world? What else gives so much cause for rejoicing as the indwelling of the Spirit that is for us a pledge, a foretaste, a guarantee of the glory that awaits us in heaven?

2. Being here in Alaska, so richly endowed with the beauties of nature, at once so rugged and yet so splendid, *we sense the presence of God's Spirit in the manifold handiwork of creation.* And not only do we feel this presence in inanimate nature and

in the order of plants and animals, but all the more so in the precious gift of life which God has breathed into each one of his sons and daughters.

### Each Human Person Is the Image of God, Called to Unity in Faith by the Holy Spirit.

Having fashioned man and woman in his own image, God remains with each individual on the pilgrimage of this earthly life, inviting, calling, prompting through his Spirit an acceptance of the salvation offered in Christ.

As I look out over this gathering here, I see the evidence of the Holy Spirit's call of faith in Alaska. Here *many peoples of diverse backgrounds and cultures are drawn into one community of faith.* Here native Alaskans—Eskimos, Aleuts and Indians—join together with people from all parts of the United States to form one ecclesial community. Here in recent years Hispanics have come in increasing numbers to join in the united fellowship of the Church. In acknowledging this activity of the Spirit, are we not impelled to make a joyful song to the Lord? Do not our hearts overflow in speaking of all the wonderful blessings that the Spirit has infused into the Church?

3. But there is another reason for giving thanks to the Holy Spirit in this hour. Having now completed a pastoral journey during these past eleven days that took me to Pakistan, the Philippines, Guam, Japan and now here in Alaska, I wish to express profound gratitude to the Holy Spirit for his guidance and protection throughout this visit. In the name of the Most Holy Trinity, I began my journey as a pilgrim of faith, responding to the charge that Jesus gave to Peter: "Strengthen your brothers" (Lk. 22:32). It was to fulfill this responsibility, which through the working of the Holy Spirit had been entrusted to me, that I undertook this journey, and I hope that with the assistance of the same Holy Spirit these efforts will be a source of encouragement for the Bishops and for all my brothers and sisters in the faith.

### The Response of Faith— Our Acknowledgement of God as Father

4. We may well ask: how does the Spirit move human hearts to respond to the revelation of the Lord's glory? Jesus tells us in the Gospel today that the mysteries of faith are hidden from the learned and clever of this world and made known instead to mere children. The response of faith is always a childlike response—one that acknowledges God as Father.

Jesus himself teaches us this lesson when he accepts his life's mission, not seeking to do his own will but rather the will of the one who sent him (cf. Jn. 5:30). Conceived by the power of the Holy Spirit, Jesus is the bearer of the Spirit in every situation of his public ministry. When he has fulfilled the will of his Father in his Passion, Death and Resurrection, Jesus sends the Holy Spirit upon his disciples in order to continue and to bring to completion the Father's universal plan of salvation.

It is well for us to reflect for a few moments on what is implied in *the Sonship of Christ,* in which we share through the Holy Spirit. In this respect, our second reading from Saint Paul's Letter to the Romans is of great benefit.

## We Share an Intimate Relationship
## with God Our Father

The Apostle describes the status of a son as being distinct from the condition of a slave. There is a different relationship—one of intimacy, and this intimacy is indicated in the name by which the Father is known and addressed. Saint Paul tells us that those who are born of water and the Holy Spirit speak to the Divine Father in the very words which Jesus used in the intimacy of his prayer in Gethsemane: "Abba, Father" (cf. Rom. 8:16). Our sonship in Christ, then, involves a relationship that is closer and more personal than that of a child to the parent who has generated life. On the part of the Father there is a love "which not only creates the good but also grants participation in the very life of God: Father, Son and Holy Spirit" (*Dives in Misericordia,* 7).While the slave had an obligation to a master, the son is free and can thus return the very love by which he has been loved.

## Prayer Strengthens Our Union in Love

As children of God, our love, given and sustained in the Holy Spirit, invites us over and over again into a deeper intimacy with the Father. And how willing and enthusiastic should be our response! This invitation is perceived in prayer—which is not just a duty to be performed but also a means of strengthening our union in love. This activity of prayer in the Church is never limited to certain groups or particular individuals. It is a privilege and duty for all. Nor should prayer be limited to participation in the liturgical prayer of the Church; it should also reflect the constant search of individuals deepening their union in Christ.

In this context we can recognize the wisdom of Paul VI, who observed that it is through prayer that Christians attain the first fruit of the Spirit, which is joy: "The Holy Spirit raises up therein a filial prayer that springs from the depths of the soul and is expressed in praise, thanksgiving, reparation, and supplication. Then we can experience joy which is properly spiritual, the joy which is a fruit of the Holy Spirit. It consists in the human spirit's finding repose and deep satisfaction in possession of the Triune God, known by faith and loved with the charity that comes from him" (*Gaudete in Domino,* III).

## Persecution, Opposition and Misunderstanding
## Belong to Our Cross for the Faith

The presence of this joy, however, does not exclude the possibility of suffering. Saint Paul readily points this out when he says that *a share in Christ's sonship means to share also in his suffering.* For to glory in Christ is to glory in his Cross (cf. Gal.

6:14). If we seek to deepen our relationship with the Father in the Holy Spirit, then we should not be surprised to find that we are misunderstood, opposed or even persecuted for our beliefs.

5. Nine days ago I beatified Lorenzo Ruiz and his companions in the Philippines. These holy men and women knew well the meaning of Christ's words: "If they persecuted me, they will persecute you" (Jn. 15:20). But despite the opposition they encountered, they trusted in the guidance of the Holy Spirit to sustain them in the face of suffering.

Such faith has also marked the history of *the missionaries in these Alaskan territories*. They too met the Cross in the form of physical limitations, disappointments and opposition in their efforts to spread the faith. Often their endeavors seemed to bear little results in their own lifetime, but the seeds were planted for the witness of a faith that is in evidence today.

Dear brothers and sisters, let us learn the wisdom of the children of God to trust and hope in the abiding presence of the Holy Spirit in the Church. May we never be confounded by the suffering that may come into our lives, but seek rather to transform it in the light of the Cross of our Savior Jesus Christ. May our confidence always be in the Holy Spirit in order to discover in each new situation an opportunity to extend Christ's redemptive love.

6. *The present generation brings with it new challenges and new opportunities for the Church in Alaska.* The Gospel needs to be proclaimed anew every day, and the fire of faith needs to be fanned into flame. The Church needs someone to preach, to teach and administer the sacraments of Christ's love. I do not hesitate to ask the youth of Alaska to respond to this challenge. Among your numbers, the Holy Spirit is surely sowing seeds of priestly and religious vocations. Do not stifle that call, but give yourselves generously to the service of Christ's Gospel.

At the same time, the Holy Spirit has spoken through the Second Vatican Council of a need for increased involvement of the laity in the apostolate of the Church. In the varying circumstances of their lives, lay persons are called to participate in the Church's mission. In their families and in their daily occupations, in works of mercy and charity, in catechesis and the cause of justice, lay men and women must build up the Church and help consecrate the world. Each member of the Church has a special charism that the Spirit of God has given for the good of the Church. Each gift must be used to benefit the entire Body of Christ.

### The Holy Spirit, Present in the Church at Pentecost, Remains with the Church Today

7. My dear friends in Christ, let us never cease praising *the Holy Spirit,* who is the inexhaustible source of our life in Christ. He was present to the Church on the first Pentecost. He remains with the Church today and for ever. Let us be confident in his strengthening power and learn to be ever docile in following his ways. Let us be increasingly sensitive to his influence on our actions and always ready to pray for his divine assistance:

Come, Holy Spirit, fill the hearts of your faithful
And enkindle in them the fire of your love.
Send forth your Spirit and they shall be created
and you will renew the face of the earth. Amen.

## 3. DEPARTURE FROM
## ANCHORAGE INTERNATIONAL AIRPORT

Dear Friends,

### United in Faith and in the Eucharist
### with Catholics Around the World

1. I am happy that, on my return to Rome from my pastoral visit to the Philippines, Guam and Japan, I have been able to stop here in Anchorage. It has been a joy to spend these few hours in your midst, to meet the people of Alaska and above all to celebrate the Eucharist with my brothers and sisters of the Catholic faith.

2. At this time I want to thank you for the kind reception and warm hospitality which you have extended to me, and I am grateful to all those who generously assisted in the planning and organization of this day. Permit me also to add a special word of gratitude to President Reagan, who has sent a personal delegation to meet me here in Anchorage.

3. Before continuing my journey, may I take this occasion to extend my greetings to all the citizens of the United States of America. This brief stop in Alaska and the cordial welcome accorded to me here brings to mind my previous pastoral visit to your country, the memory of which I still hold dear. I pray that God will bless you and your families.

And now as I leave Alaska to complete the last part of this pastoral journey which has taken me around the world, my thoughts turn to God and to his praises expressed in the words of the Psalmist: "O Lord, our Lord, how glorious is Your Name over all the earth" (Ps. 8:2).

## MAY 2, 1984

## 1. ADDRESS ON ARRIVAL AT FAIRBANKS AIRPORT

### Even When I Am Miles Away I Hold the People of
### Alaska and Those of the Whole of the United States
### Close to Me in My Heart

Praised be Jesus Christ! Mr. President, dear people of Alaska, esteemed citizens of America, it gives me great pleasure to visit Alaska once again—and from this northern state to send a greeting of special warmth and affection to all the citizens of the United States of America. As you know, today I have begun a pastoral journey that will take me to Korea, Papua, New Guinea, the Solomon Islands and Thailand. And I am delighted that this pilgrimage enables me to stop here in Fairbanks and to be among you.

I am deeply honored by the presence of President Reagan, who himself is just returning from an important trip to China. Mr. President, I thank you for your kind welcome on my arrival, and I wish to reaffirm through you my friendship and esteem for all the citizens of your great nation.

My thanks go as well to Bishop Whelan for his much appreciated invitation to the Diocese of Fairbanks. I also extend my good wishes to Bishop Kaniecki. And I pray that the Lord will grant him many joyful years of service to the Church.

I would also offer a word of greeting to the Cardinal and Bishops of the United States' Episcopal Conference, who have shown their paternal union with me by coming here on this happy occasion.

When I arrived on my first visit to your beautiful state, dear people of Alaska—and it is beautiful, your state—I remember being welcomed by a lovely little child, Molly Marie, who reached out and handed me a bouquet of forget-me-nots, your state flower. Shortly afterward, that little girl was called home to her heavenly Father, but her loving gesture is not forgotten, and her memory is held in blessing.

I found in what she did at that time a living truth about the people of the vast Alaskan territory, that in your thoughts and in your prayers you remember the Pope today. I'm here in person to give you the assurance that I have not forgotten you. Even when I am miles away I hold the people of Alaska and those of the whole of the United States close to me in my heart.

I do not forget you, for we are linked by bonds of friendship, of faith and of love. In some ways, Alaska can be considered today as a crossroads of the world. President Reagan is returning from visiting the beloved people of China even as I am making my way to a neighboring area in the Far East.

## Within Alaska Is a Wonderful Ethnic Diversity Which Provides the Context in Which Each Person, Each Family, Each Ethnic Group Is Challenged to Live in Harmony and Concord One with the Other

The city of Fairbanks reminds us also of another direction, for it is called "the heart of the golden North." Here in this vast state, sixty-five languages are spoken, and people of many diverse backgrounds find a common home with the Aleuts, Eskimos and Indians. This wonderful diversity provides the context in which each person, each family, each ethnic group is challenged to live in harmony and concord one with the other.

To achieve this aim requires a constant openness to each other on the part of each individual and group—an openness of heart, a readiness to accept differences and an ability to listen to each other's viewpoint without prejudice. Openness to others, by its very nature, excludes selfishness in any form. It is expressed in a dialogue that is honest and frank, one that is based on mutual respect. Openness to others begins in the heart. As I stated at the beginning of this year in my message for the World Day of Peace—if men and women hope to transform society, they must begin by changing their own hearts first. Only with a new heart can one discover, rediscover clearsightedness and impartiality with freedom of spirit, the sense of justice with respect to the rights of man, the sense of equity with global solidarity between the rich and poor, mutual trust and fraternal love.

Here in Fairbanks, you have the opportunity to rediscover such values and express them in your harmonious relationship with your neighbor, which reflects the stupendous harmony of nature which pervades this region. May God grant you the strength to express this harmony in your own lives, in your relationships with others. May he give you the courage to share generously and selflessly the blessings that you yourself have received in abundance. God bless America!

## 2. HOMILY DURING A PARALITURGICAL SERVICE
## AT FAIRBANKS AIRPORT

### Through His Suffering and Death
### Christ Fashioned the Church

Dear Brothers and Sisters in our Lord Jesus Christ,

Peace be with you!

I greet you with the very words that we have just heard the Risen Christ address to his disciples in the Gospel of Saint John. I use this expression not only to emphasize the wonderful joy that is ours in this Easter season, but also in remembrance of Christ's promise: "Where two or three are gathered in my name, there am I in the midst of them" (Mt. 18:20). Since we have come together in the name of Christ, Christ is here in our midst.

My dear brothers and sisters, do we not have a feeling of overwhelming happiness, a deep calm, in knowing that Jesus—our Risen Savior, our Paschal Sacrifice, the Light of the World—this Jesus is dwelling in our hearts and offering us his peace? I must tell you how good it is for me to be united with you today in the peace of the Risen Christ.

Observing the joy of the disciples when they see the Lord, we notice from the Gospel passage that there is something different about him. The doors are closed and yet he enters. He bears the marks of death and yet he lives. The Gospel narratives of both Saint John and Saint Luke are at pains to tell us that after the Resurrection the body of Jesus is different. He has entered into the stage of his risen and glorious life.

In Saint John's Gospel this is the second appearance of Jesus to the disciples assembled as a group. After the first appearance, their exhilaration at seeing Jesus was so great that, when they met Thomas afterward, they could not resist exclaiming: "We have seen the Lord!" But Thomas would not accept their witness: "I will never believe it without probing the nail-prints in his hands, without putting my finger in the nailmarks and my hand into his side." Perhaps it is easy for us to judge Thomas too harshly for his disbelief. After all, do we not often use the expression, "seeing is believing?" Does not our age tend to believe only what can be proved by the senses? Does not modern man remain incredulous of what he cannot see or touch or hear?

Jesus understands Thomas and the reasons for his doubts. When he meets Thomas, Jesus immediately says to him: "Take your finger and examine my hands. Put your hand into my side. Do not persist in your unbelief, but believe." So over-whelmed is Thomas by the Lord's gentleness, compassion and patience that he can barely utter in humble recognition: "My Lord and my God!" Yes, this truly was the Lord, transformed by the Resurrection, and fully alive.

### By God's Will the Church Becomes
### the Sacrament of Christ on Earth

The side of Christ into which Thomas placed his hand is the very same that had been pierced by the soldier's spear and from which "came out blood and water." And with the flowing of that "blood and water" the Church is born from the side of Christ. Thus, through his suffering and death, Christ fashions the Church from his own side in order that his risen presence may be manifested to the world. By God's will, the Church becomes the sacrament or sign of Christ on earth. As the Body of Christ, she becomes the point of encounter between God and humanity: between the Creator and creatures, between the Redeemer and the redeemed. And as Thomas was invited to "see and believe" by experiencing the risen presence of Christ in his glorified body, so too are all people invited to "see and believe" by experiencing the same risen presence of Christ in his Mystical Body, the Church.

In our first reading today from the Acts of the Apostles, which tells us what happened in the house of the Roman centurion Cornelius, we see that the message of faith is communicated through the Church: Peter was not preaching on his own initiative alone. The Scripture tells us that Cornelius had been directed by an angel to send for Peter, and Peter had gone there on instructions from the Holy Spirit. In addition, while Peter was preaching on the meaning of the events of Jesus' Life, Death and Resurrection, "the Holy Spirit fell on all who heard the word." By his preaching, Peter was involved in a profoundly ecclesial activity. And so is everyone who evan-gelizes, for one can authentically proclaim the Gospel of Christ only in the name of the Church and in union with the Church.

### Each Believer Exercises Not a Personal Mission Initiated by
### Himself but the Mission of the Church, Initiated by Christ

My predecessor Paul VI made reference to this truth in his Apostolic Exhorta-tion *Evangelii Nuntiandi*: "When the most obscure preacher, catechist or pastor in the most distant land preaches the Gospel, gathers his little community together or ad-ministers a Sacrament, even alone, he is carrying out an ecclesial act, and his action is certainly attached to the evangelizing activity of the whole Church by institutional relationships, but also by profound invisible links in the order of grace. This presupposes that he acts not in virtue of a mission which he attributes to himself or by a personal inspiration, but in union with the mission of the Church and in her name."

How aptly this description applies to the Church in Alaska and particularly in the Diocese of Fairbanks, where the population is scattered over 409,000 square miles. In reading the history of the missionary activity in this vast area, might we not ask whether the first missionaries would have dared to penetrate the interior of Alaska unless they had been fired by a profound love for Christ's Church and utterly convinced of the Church's duty to proclaim the Gospel to all people? The early missionary efforts of the Oblates and Mary Immaculate and the continuing labors of the Society of Jesus are well known. The missionaries stand out in this history as the true heroes of the faith, whose courage and zeal made possible the building up of the Church in this land.

Today the work of preaching and teaching the Gospel in the name of the Church is zealously continued by Religious and diocesan priests, by deacons, by women Religious, Religious brothers and catechists. Many of them undertake great personal sacrifices, often traveling long distances to bring the word of God with its message of hope and love to their brothers and sisters.

These missionary efforts still today come under the pastoral care of the Sacred Congregation of the Propagation of the Faith and are assisted by the Pontifical Missionary Societies. Specifically, this means that evangelization in this Diocese, and in so many others like it throughout the world, is supported by the interest and solidarity of others. In this regard the Catholics of North America have exercised a special role in sustaining and promoting the missionary efforts of the Holy See. They are owed an immense debt of gratitude. And today, standing on this missionary soil of America, I wish to express my heartfelt thanks to the Church throughout the United States for everything it has done for the cause of spreading the light of Christ's Gospel.

Dear brothers and sisters: let us beseech the Lord, who calls laborers into his harvest, to grant that many young people will dedicate their lives to the missionary work of the Church. May these young people respond generously to the Lord's call to the priesthood and religious life. And thus may the presence of the Risen Christ continue to be revealed in his Church, and "the good news of peace proclaimed through Jesus Christ who is the Lord of all" (Acts 9:36).

Dear brothers and sisters in Alaska: May the peace of the Risen Jesus be with you always!

# 1987 Apostolic Visit

## September 10 to September 20

### SEPTEMBER 10, 1987

### 1. ARRIVAL AT MIAMI AIRPORT

Mr. President,

Dear Friends,

Dear People of America,

1. It is a great joy for me once again to be in your country, and I thank you for your *warm welcome*. I am deeply grateful to you all.

#### Special Thanks to the President, to the Bishops' Conference

I express my special thanks to *the president of the United States,* who honors me by his presence here today. I thank *the Bishops' Conference* and *all the individual Bishops* who have invited me to their Dioceses, and who have done so much to prepare for my visit.

#### Greeting to the People of This Land

My cordial greetings and good wishes go to *all the people of this land.* I thank you for opening your hearts to me and for supporting me by your prayers. I assure you of my own prayers.

### I Come to Proclaim the Gospel to All Who Choose to Listen

2. To everyone I repeat on this occasion what I said on that memorable day in 1979 when I arrived in Boston: "On my part I come to you—America—with sentiments of friendship, reverence and esteem. I come as one who already knows you and loves you, as one who wishes you to fulfill completely your noble destiny of service to the world" (October 1, 1979).

Today, like then, I come *to proclaim the Gospel of Jesus Christ* to all those who freely choose to listen to me; to tell again the story of God's love in the world; to spell out once more the message of human dignity, with its inalienable human rights and its inevitable human duties.

### I Come as a Pilgrim of Justice, as a Pastor, as a Friend

3. Like so many before me coming to America and to this very city of Miami, I come as *a pilgrim:* a pilgrim in the cause of justice and peace and human solidarity—striving to build up the one human family.

I come here as *a pastor*—the pastor of the Catholic Church, to speak and pray with the Catholic people. The theme of my visit, "Unity in the Work of Service," affords me the welcome opportunity to enter into ever deeper communion with them in our common service to the Lord. It also enables me to experience ever more keenly with them their hopes and joys, their anxieties and griefs.

I come as *a friend*—a friend of America and of all Americans: Catholics, Orthodox, Protestants and Jews, people of every religion, and all men and women of good will. I come as a friend of the poor and the sick and the dying; those who are struggling with the problems of each day; those who are rising and falling and stumbling on the journey of life; those who are seeking and discovering, and those not yet finding, the deep meaning of "life, liberty and the pursuit of happiness."

### I Come to Join You as You Celebrate
### the Bicentennial of the Constitution

4. And finally I come *to join you as you celebrate the bicentennial* of that great document, the Constitution of the United States of America. I willingly join you in your prayer of thanksgiving to God for the providential way in which the Constitution has served the people of this nation for two centuries: for the union it has formed, the justice it has established, the tranquillity and peace it has ensured, the general welfare it has promoted and the blessings of liberty it has secured.

### I Ask God to Inspire You to Continue to Share with So Many

I join you also in asking God to inspire you—as Americans who have received so much in freedom and prosperity and human enrichment—to continue to share all this with so many brothers and sisters throughout the other countries of the world who are still waiting and hoping to live according to standards worthy of the children of God.

With great enthusiasm I look forward to being with you in the days ahead. Meanwhile, my prayer for all of you, dear people of America, is this:

The Lord bless you and keep you!
The Lord let his face shine upon you, and be gracious to you!
The Lord look upon you kindly and give you peace. (Nm. 6:24–26)

God bless America!


## 2. ADDRESS AT SAINT MARY'S CATHEDRAL


Dear Archbishop McCarthy and my other brother Bishops,

Dear Brothers and Sisters,

Dear Friends,

1. It is a great joy for me to begin my pastoral visit here in Miami, in this Cathedral of Saint Mary. This Church represents *a long history of faith and dedicated Christian life and witness* on the part of countless clergy, Religious and laity in this city and in the state of Florida.

### I Commend You for the Jubilee Year of Reconciliation and for the Archdiocesan Synod

In coming among you, I wish to commend you for the Jubilee Year of Reconciliation that you have observed in preparation for my visit, and for the Archdiocesan Synod that you are holding. These events are meant to be of *lasting spiritual value* for all of you of the Archdiocese, so that your Christian witness in everyday life may be ever more fruitful in the society of which you are a part. I also commend you for meeting the challenges of a rapidly expanding local Church. Over the years, you have welcomed hundreds of thousands of refugees of different languages and cultures, fleeing religious or political oppression. You have struggled along with them and for them to build *a united community in Christ*. I urge all of you—the clergy, Religious and laity of Miami, in communion with your Archbishop and with me—to continue seeking ways to deepen our ecclesial unity in the one Body of Christ.

### I Commend You for Building a United Communion and for Using All the Sources of Unity, Especially Prayer

This unity is expressed in many ways. It is unity in preaching the Gospel, professing the Creed, celebrating the liturgy and participating in the Sacraments, especially the Holy Eucharist. It is unity in going forward as a missionary Church to evangelize the world. But our very presence in this house of God reminds us of another source of unity. I am referring to *the personal prayer of each and every one of us,* whether offered here in a moment of silence or amid the many settings in which our daily life unfolds. "The spiritual life," as the Second Vatican Council reminds us, "is not confined to participation in the liturgy. The Christian is certainly called to pray with others, but he must also enter into his room to pray to the Father in secret; indeed, according to the teaching of the Apostle Paul, he should pray without ceasing" (*Sacrosanctum Concilium,* 12).

### The Focus in Prayer Is on Our Heavenly Father, His Name, Will and Kingdom

2. People always have a great interest in prayer. Like the Apostles, they want *to know how to pray.* The response that Jesus gives is one known to all of us: it is the "Our Father," in which he reveals in a few simple words all the essentials of prayer. The focus is not primarily on ourselves, but on the heavenly Father to whom we commit our lives in faith and trust. Our first concern must be his name, his Kingdom, his will. Only then do we ask for our daily bread, for forgiveness and for deliverance from trials yet to come.

### Our Relationship to God Is One of Dependence; God Widens Our Hearts So We May Receive

The *"Our Father"* teaches us that our relationship to God is one of dependence. We are his adopted sons and daughters through Christ. All that we are and all that we have comes from him and is destined to return to him. The "Our Father" also presents prayer to us as an expression of our desires. Beset as we are by human weakness, we naturally ask God for many things. Many times we may be tempted to think that he does not hear or answer us. But as Saint Augustine wisely reminds us, God already knows what we desire even before we ask. He says that prayer is for our benefit, because in praying we "exercise" our desires so that we will grasp what God is preparing to give us. It is an opportunity for us to "widen our hearts" (see *Letter to Proba,* Epistle 30).

### God Listens with a Love Far Greater and a Knowledge Far Deeper than Our Own

In other words, God is always listening to us and answering us—but from the perspective of *a love far greater and a knowledge far deeper* than our own. When it appears that he is not fulfilling our desires by granting the things we ask, however unselfish and noble they may be, in reality he is purifying those desires of ours for the sake of a higher good that often surpasses our understanding in this life. The challenge is to "widen our hearts" by hallowing his name, by seeking his Kingdom, and by accepting his will. Like Christ in the Garden of Gethsemane, we may some-times pray either for ourselves or others, "Father, you have the power to do all things. Take this cup away!" But also like Christ we must add, "Not my will but your will be done" (see Mt. 26:39, 42; Mk. 14:36; Lk. 22:42).

### The Act of Praying Opens Us Up to God and Neighbor in Action

The act of praying is also meant to open us up to God and our neighbor, not only in words but also in action. That is why Christian spirituality, following Jesus himself (see Mt. 6), associates prayer with *fasting and almsgiving*. A life of self-denial and charity is a sign of conversion to God's way of thinking, to his way of love. By humbling ourselves through penance, we open ourselves to God. By giving in charity, over and above the demands of justice, we open ourselves to our neighbor. Saint Peter Chrysologus gives witness to this tradition when he says: "Prayer, fasting, and mercy . . . give life to one another. What prayer knocks for upon a door, fasting successfully begs and mercy receives. For, fasting is the soul of prayer; and mercy is the life of fasting. . . . Fasting does not germinate unless watered by mercy" (Sermon 43).

### Prayer Furthers the Church's Redemptive Mission

3. Dear brothers and sisters: we must never underestimate the power of prayer to further the Church's redemptive mission and to bring good where there is evil. As I mentioned earlier, we must be united in prayer. We pray not just for ourselves and our loved ones, but also for the needs of *the universal Church and of all mankind:* for the missions and for priestly and religious vocations, for the conversion of sinners and the salvation of all, for the sick and the dying. As members of *the Communion of Saints,* our prayer also embraces the souls of those in Purgatory who, in the loving mercy of God, can still find after death the purification they need to enter into the happiness of heaven. Prayer also makes us realize that sometimes our own troubles and desires are small compared to the needs and to the sufferings of so many of our brothers and sisters throughout the world. There is the spiritual suffering of those who have lost their way in life because of sin or a lack of faith in God. There is the material suffering of millions of people who lack food, clothing, shelter, medicine and education; of those who are deprived of the most fundamental human rights; of those who are exiles or refugees because of war and oppression. I know that Miami is no stranger to this kind of suffering. We must act to alleviate it, but we must also pray not only for those who suffer, but also for those who inflict suffering.

### Pray That I May Have the Courage to Proclaim the Gospel as I Should

Dear brothers and sisters: as Pastor of the whole Church I have benefited from the prayers of millions of the faithful throughout the world, and today I express my gratitude to you for the prayers you offer for me, and I ask you to continue. Indeed, with Saint Paul I say: "Pray for me that God may put his word on my lips, that I may courageously make known the mystery of the Gospel. . . . Pray that I may have courage to proclaim it as I ought" (Eph. 6:19). And at this moment I am praying in a special way for all of you who make up the household of the faith in this Archdiocese. We are called today and always *to remain united in prayer:* for the glory of the Father, and of the Son, and of the Holy Spirit. Amen.

## 3. MEETING WITH PRIESTS FROM THROUGHOUT THE UNITED STATES

Dear Brother Priests,

### In Communion of Faith, Hope and Love

1. Coming here today, I wish to open my heart to you and to *celebrate with you the priesthood* that we all share. "*Vobis sum Episcopus, vobiscum sacerdos.*" I am convinced that there is no better way to start than *to direct our thoughts and our hearts to that Shepherd whom we all know*—the Good Shepherd, the one High Priest, our Lord and Savior Jesus Christ.

My heart is full of gratitude and praise as I *express my love for the priesthood,* the beautiful vocation, the wonderful vocation in which we participate not because we are worthy, but because Christ has loved us, loves us and has entrusted to us this particular ministry of service. *And I thank God for you, my brother priests.* In the words of Saint Paul, "I thank God . . . whenever I remember you in my prayers—as indeed I do constantly night and day" (2 Tm. 1:3).

*I am also grateful to you my brother priests* for your welcome of fraternal love, expressed personally and through Father McNulty as your representative. I address my words to all of you present here and to all the priests in the United States. To all of you I express my gratitude for your ministry, for your perseverance, for your faith and love, for the fact that you are striving to live the priesthood, close to the people, in truth—the truth of being ministers of Christ the Good Shepherd.

As priests, *we all hold a "treasure in earthen vessels"* (2 Cor. 4:7). Through no merit of our own, and with all our human weaknesses, we have been called to proclaim God's word, to celebrate the sacred mysteries, especially the Eucharist, to care for the People of God, and to continue the Lord's ministry of reconciliation. In this way, we are servants both of the Lord and of his people, being ourselves constantly called to conversion, constantly invited to "walk in newness of life" (Rom. 6:4).

### I Have Come to Confirm Your Faith

I have come to the United States, my brother priests, in order to confirm you in your faith, according to the will of Christ (Lk. 22:32). I have come to you because I want all distances to be bridged, so that, together, we may grow and become ever more truly *a communion of faith, hope and love.* I affirm you in the good gifts you have received and in the generous response you have made to the Lord and his people, and I encourage you to become more and more like Jesus Christ, the Eternal High Priest, the Good Shepherd.

Saint Paul reminds us, as he reminded Timothy, to be fearless in serving Christ: "The Spirit God has given us is no cowardly spirit, but rather one that makes us strong, loving and wise. Therefore, *never be ashamed of your testimony to our Lord* . . . but with the strength which comes from God bear your share of the hardship which the Gospel entails" (2 Tm. 1:7–8). We know that proclaiming the Gospel and living out our ministry very definitely entail hardship. It would be wrong to reduce priestly life to this one dimension of suffering, but it would also be wrong not to recognize this dimension or to resent it when we encounter it. We are not exempt from the human condition, nor can we ever escape that *emptying of self,* after the example of Jesus, who "was himself tested through what he suffered" (Heb. 2:18).

### Priestly Fulfillment Depends on Our Relationship to Christ and on Our Service to the Church

2. It is important that we find satisfaction in our ministry, and that we be clear about the nature of the satisfaction which we can expect. The physical and emotional health of priests is an important factor in their overall human and priestly well-being, and it is necessary to provide for these. I commend your Bishops and you yourselves for giving particular attention to these matters in recent years. Yet the fulfillment that comes from our ministry does not, in the final analysis, consist in physical or psychological well-being; nor can it ever consist in material comfort and security. *Our fulfillment depends on our relationship with Christ and on the service that we offer to his Body, the Church.* Each of us is most truly himself when he is "for others."

### The Priesthood: Instrument of God's Mercy and Truth

3. And just here, of course, arises a problem for us in our ministry. So much is asked of us by so many different people, and so often it seems that our response is inadequate to their needs. Sometimes this is due to our own human limitations. We can then be tempted to indulge in excessive self-criticism, forgetting that *God can use our weakness as easily as our strength* in order to accomplish his will.

It is a great credit to you, my brothers, that *you are striving to be merciful and gentle and forgiving like the Good Shepherd* whom you know and imitate and love, and to whom you have pledged your fidelity. No other path is possible. Sometimes, however, what is asked of you in the name of compassion may not be in accord with the full truth of God, whose eternal law of love can never contradict the fact that he is always "rich in mercy" (Eph. 2:4). True mercy takes into account God's plan for humanity, and this plan—marked by the sign of the Cross—was revealed by a merciful High Priest, who is able "to sympathize with our weakness, . . . one who was tempted in every way that we are, yet never sinned" (Heb. 4:15). If on the other hand, what is claimed to be a gesture of mercy goes contrary to the demands of God's word, it can never be truly compassionate or beneficial to our brothers and sisters in need. Jesus, who was himself the perfect expression of the Father's love, was also conscious of being "a sign of contradiction" (Lk. 2:34). The Apostle John tells us that, at a certain point in the Lord's ministry, "many of his disciples broke away and would not remain in his company any longer" (Jn. 6:66).

And today there are indeed *many sensitive issues* which priests must deal with in their daily ministry. I know from listening to many priests and many Bishops that there are different approaches to such issues. What is seen in one way by some of our brothers is evaluated differently by others. Yes, we all have questions that arise from the exercise of our priesthood, *questions which require* us to seek continually *the light and wisdom that comes only from the Holy Spirit.*

### The Holy Spirit Guides the Church to the Fullness of Truth Through the Charism of the Magisterium

In this regard, however, it is important for us to realize that the same Holy Spirit from whom come all the different and wonderful charisms, and who dwells in the hearts of all the faithful, has placed in the Church the specific charism of the Magisterium, through which *he guides the whole community to the fullness of truth*. Through the action of the Holy Spirit the promise of Christ is constantly being fulfilled: "Know that *I am with you always*, until the end of the world" (Mt. 28:20). We know that through the Second Vatican Council the Church has clearly and collegially expressed her teaching on many of the sensitive issues and that much of this teaching has subsequently been reiterated in the different sessions of the Synod of Bishops. By its nature therefore this teaching of the Church is normative for the life of the Church and for all pastoral service. The forthcoming Synod, after extensive consultation and fervent prayer, will consider at length and take a pastoral position on other important issues in the life of the Church.

I am very much aware that *your fidelity to Christ's will for his Church and your pastoral sensitivity demand great sacrifice and generosity of spirit.* As I told the Bishops of the United States just a few weeks after I was elected Pope, "Like yourselves, I learned as a Bishop to understand firsthand the ministry of priests, the problems affecting their lives, the splendid efforts they are making, the sacrifices that are an integral part of their service to God's people. Like yourselves, I am fully aware of how much Christ depends on his priests in order to fulfill in time his mission of redemption" (November 9, 1978).

### An Invitation to Trust in God

4. In expressing the conviction that Christ needs his priests and wills to associate them with himself in his mission of salvation, we must also emphasize the consequence of this: *the need for new vocations to the priesthood*. It is truly necessary for the whole Church to work and pray for this intention. As Father McNulty stated so

well, we priests must personally invite generous young men to give their lives in the service of the Lord; they must truly be attracted by the joy that we project in our own lives and ministry.

### The Power of Christ: Essential for Vocations

There is still one more factor to be considered in evaluating the future of vocations, and it is *the power of Christ, of Christ's Paschal Mystery*. As the Church of Christ, we are all called to profess his power before the world; to proclaim that he is able, in virtue of his Death and Resurrection, to draw young people to himself, in this generation as in the past; to declare that he is strong enough to attract young men even today to a life of self-sacrifice, pure love and total dedication to the priesthood. As we profess this truth, as we proclaim with faith the power of the Lord of the harvest, we have a right to expect that he will grant the prayers that he himself has commanded to be offered. *The present hour calls for great trust* in him who has overcome the world.

### Priests, Proclaiming and Living the Word of God, Call All to Renewal

5. The authentic renewal of the Church initiated by the Second Vatican Council has been a great gift of God to his people. Through the action of the Holy Spirit an immense amount of good has been done. We must continue to pray and work that the Holy Spirit will bring his design to fulfillment in us. In this regard *priests have an indispensable role to play in the renewed life of the Church*.

Each day the Church is being renewed by grace as she seeks a deeper and more penetrating understanding of the word of God, as she strives to worship more authentically in spirit and in truth, and as she recognizes and develops the gifts of all her members. These dimensions of renewal require those enduring tasks of priests which give their ministry its unique character: namely, *the ministry of word and Sacrament, the tending of the flock of Christ.*

True renewal presupposes the clear, faithful and effective *proclamation of the word of God*. The Second Vatican Council indicated that this is *the priest's first task* (*Presbyterorum Ordinis*, 4). Those who preach must do so with dynamic fidelity. This means being ever faithful to what has been handed on in tradition and Scripture, as taught by the living pastoral authority of the Church, and making every effort to present the Gospel as effectively as possible in its application to new circumstances of life. As often as the word is truly proclaimed, Christ's work of redemption continues. But what is proclaimed must first be lived.

### Authentic Renewal Depends upon the Church's Life of Worship . . .

Renewal in Christ's grace and life greatly depends on the development of *the Church's life of worship*. Because we priests preside at the liturgy, we must come to know and appreciate the rites of the Church through study and prayer. We are called to lead celebrations which are both faithful to the Church's discipline and legitimately adapted, according to her norms, for the good of our people.

### . . . As Well as upon the Priests Tending the Flock of Christ

Genuine renewal also depends upon the way in which the priests exercise their *task of tending the flock of Christ,* especially as they encourage the faithful to use their gifts in the apostolate and in various special forms of service. The Church's *commitment to evangelization,* to proclaiming the word of God, to calling people to holiness of life, cannot be sustained without the tireless efforts and selfless support of priests. In the matter of inviting people, as Jesus did, to conversion—the total conversion of the Gospel—*the example of priests* is extremely important for the authenticity of the Church's life.

### Renewal Through the Sacrament of Penance

This is particularly true in *our own use of the Sacrament of Penance,* through which we are repeatedly converted to the Lord. On this condition rests the full supernatural effectiveness of our "ministry of reconciliation" (2 Cor. 5:18) and of our whole priestly lives. The experience of the Church teaches us that "the priest's celebration of the Eucharist and administration of the other Sacraments, his pastoral zeal, his relationship with the faithful, his communion with his brother priests, his collaboration with his Bishop, his life of prayer—in a word, the whole of his priestly existence, suffers an inexorable decline if by negligence or for some other reason he fails to receive the Sacrament of Penance at regular intervals and in a spirit of genuine faith and devotion. If a priest were no longer to go to confession or properly confess his sins, his *priestly being* and his *priestly action* would feel its effects very soon, and this would also be noticed by the community of which he was the pastor" (*Reconciliatio et Paenitentia,* 31).

### The Priest: Another Christ

People expect us to be men of faith and prayer. People look to us for *Christ's truth* and the teaching of his Church. They ask to see *Christ's love* incarnate in our lives. All this reminds us of a very basic truth, that the priest is "another Christ." In a sense, we priests are Christ to all those to whom we minister. This is true of all aspects of our priestly work. But it is particularly true in *the Eucharistic Sacrifice*—from which our priestly identity flows and in which it is expressed most clearly and effectively. This truth has special relevance also for our service as *ministers of the Sacrament of Reconciliation,* through which we render a unique service to the cause of conversion and peace, and to the advancement of God's Kingdom on earth. At this point I would like to repeat those words which I have already addressed to priests of the Church: "Praise then to this silent army of our brothers who have served well and serve each day the cause of reconciliation through the ministry of sacramental Penance" (*Reconciliatio et Paenitentia,* 29).

### Priests and Laity:
### When United in Faith They Challenge the World

In her *mission to the world,* the Church is renewed as she calls humanity to respond to God's commandment of love, and as she upholds and promotes the values of the Gospel as they affect public life. In doing this she becomes a prophetic voice on matters of truth and justice, mercy and peace. In these tasks involving the world, the leadership of priestly ministry has been and continues to be decisive. Priests who *encourage and support* the laity help them to exercise their own mission to bring the values of the Gospel into public life. Thus, priests and lay people working together can challenge society itself to defend life, to defend all human rights, to protect family life, to work for greater social justice, to promote peace.

### Spiritual Renewal of Priests

6. One of the notable experiences of priests in the United States in the years since the Council has been a *renewal of their spiritual lives.* Many priests have sought this renewal in groups of fraternal support, through spiritual direction, retreats and other commendable endeavors. These priests have found their ministry revitalized by a rediscovery of the importance of personal prayer. As you continue to discover Christ both in your prayer and in your ministry, you will experience more deeply that he—the Good Shepherd—is *the very center of your life, the very meaning of your priesthood.*

### Prayer Is Essential to the Pastoral Life

My brothers: in speaking to you about *prayer,* I am not telling you what you do not know or urging you to do something that you do not practice. Prayer has been part of your daily lives since your seminary years and even earlier. But *perseverance in prayer,* as you know, is difficult. Dryness of spirit, external distraction, the tempting rationalization that we could be spending our time more usefully—these things are familiar to anyone who is trying to pray. Inevitably, at one time or another, these elements assail the prayer life of a priest.

For us priests, prayer is neither a luxury nor an option to be taken up or put aside as seems convenient. *Prayer is essential to the pastoral life.* Through prayer we grow in sensitivity to the Spirit of God at work in the Church and in ourselves. And we are made more aware of others, becoming more "attentive to their needs, to their lives and destiny" (*Holy Thursday Letter to Priests,* 1987, no. 11). Indeed, through prayer we come to love deeply those whom Jesus has entrusted to our ministry. Of special importance for our lives and our ministry is the *great prayer of praise*—the Liturgy of the Hours—which the Church enjoins on us and which we pray in her name and in the name of our Lord Jesus Christ.

## Fraternal Support in the Priesthood

7. In recent years, priests have often told me of the need they feel for *support in their ministry*. The challenges of priestly service today are indeed great, and the demands on our time and energy seem to increase every day. In such circumstances how easily we can give in to temptations to discouragement! But, dear brothers, at these times it is more important than ever that we heed the advice of the Letter to the Hebrews: "*Let us keep our eyes fixed on Jesus,* who inspires and perfects our faith. For the sake of the joy which lay before him he endured the Cross, heedless of its shame. . . . Remember how he endured the opposition of sinners; hence do not grow despondent or abandon the struggle" (Heb. 12:2–4).

The encouragement and support that we find *in one another* is a great gift of God's love—a characteristic of Christ's priesthood. The increase of mutual support among brother priests through prayer and sharing is a most encouraging sign. The same can be said, on a different level, for the development of presbyteral councils committed to the solidarity of priests with one another and with their Bishop in the mission of the universal Church.

## The Priest: Pastoral Artist

As priests we also need *examples of priestly ministry,* "artists" of pastoral work who both inspire us and intercede for us—priests like Philip Neri, Vincent de Paul, John Vianney, John Bosco, Maximilian Kolbe. And we can also reflect upon the priestly lives of men whom we have known personally, exemplary priests who inspire us because they have lived the one priestly ministry of Jesus Christ with deep generosity and love.

To persevere in our pastoral ministry we need above all that "one thing only" which Jesus tells us is "required" (see Lk. 10:42). We need to know the Shepherd very well. We need *a deep personal relationship with Christ*—the source and supreme model of our priesthood—a relationship that requires union in prayer. Our love for Christ, rekindled frequently in prayer—especially prayer before the Blessed Sacrament—is at the foundation of our commitment to celibacy. This love also makes it possible for us, as servants of God's Kingdom, *to love our people freely and chastely and deeply.*

## Gratitude to Priests

8. My brothers: sharing in the one priesthood of Christ, we share the same joys and sorrows. What a joy it is for me to be with you today. I thank you again for the gift of yourselves to Christ and his Church, and I want you to know that I am close to you in your efforts to serve the Lord and his people. You have my gratitude, my prayers, my support and my love. And as I conclude, I express the hope that each of us will always experience the joy of which the Psalmist speaks: "Behold, *how good it is,* and how pleasant, *where brethren dwell at one!*" (Ps. 132 [133]: 1).

### Catholic Unity Is Essential to Priestly Ministry

Dear brother priests: *Catholic unity is our vocation.* As priests in America you are called to live this Catholic unity in the particular Churches—the Dioceses—to which you belong. But all these particular Churches are never more completely themselves, never more faithful to their identity, than when they are living to the full the communion of faith and love of the universal Church. *At the summit of your priestly ministry is this mystery of ecclesial unity,* and you are called to live it in sacrifice and love, in union with Mary the Mother of Jesus.

The protection and tender human love of our Blessed Mother is a great support to all of us priests. Her prayers assist us, her example challenges us, her closeness consoles us. In her presence we experience the joy and hope that we need so much. Is this not the day and the hour, dear brother priests, to turn to her, as we must have done on our ordination day, and *to entrust to her anew ourselves, our people and our sacred ministry?* Why? For the glory of the Father, and of the Son and of the Holy Spirit.

Dear priests of America, dear brothers: "My love to all of you in Christ Jesus" (1 Cor. 16:24).


## 4. MEETING WITH THE PRESIDENT AND MRS. REAGAN


Mr. President,

1. I am grateful for the great courtesy that you extend to me by coming personally to meet me in this city of Miami. Thank you for this gesture of kindness.

On my part I cordially greet you as the elected chief executive of the United States of America. In addressing you I express *my own deep respect for the constitutional structure of this democracy,* which you are called to "preserve, protect and defend." In addressing you, Mr. President, I greet once again *all the American people,* with their history, their achievements and their great possibilities of serving humanity.


### Thank Americans for Their Generosity to Millions in Need

I willingly pay honor to the United States for what she has accomplished for her own people, for all those whom she has embraced in a cultural creativity and welcomed into an indivisible national unity, according to her own motto: *E pluribus unum. I thank America* and all Americans—those of past generations and those of the present—for their generosity to millions of their fellow human beings in need throughout the world. Also today, I wish *to extol* the blessings and gifts that America has received from God and cultivated, and which have become *the true values of the whole American experiment* in the past two centuries.

### The Celebration of the Constitution Should Stress the Moral and Spiritual Values That Influenced the Founders

2. For all of you this is a special hour in your history: the celebration of *the bicentennial of your Constitution*. It is a time to recognize the meaning of that document and to reflect on important aspects of the constitutionalism that produced it. It is a time to recall the original American political faith with its appeal to the sovereignty of God. To celebrate the origin of the United States is *to stress those moral and spiritual principles, those ethical concerns that influenced your founding fathers* and have been incorporated into the experience of America.

Eleven years ago, when your country was celebrating *another great document,* the Declaration of Independence, my predecessor Paul VI spoke to American congressmen in Rome. His statement is still pertinent today: "At every turn," he said, "your Bicentennial speaks to you of moral principles, religious convictions, inalienable rights given by the Creator." And he added: "We earnestly hope that . . . this commemoration of your Bicentennial will constitute a rededication to those sound moral principles formulated by your founding fathers and enshrined forever in your history" (Address of April 26, 1976).

### Freedom Was Directed Toward Forming a Well-Ordered Society to Safeguard All Human Rights

3. *Among the many admirable values of this nation* there is one that stands out in particular. It is *freedom*. The concept of freedom is part of the very fabric of this nation as a political community of free people. Freedom is a great gift, a great blessing of God.

From the beginning of America, freedom was directed to forming a well-ordered society and to promoting its peaceful life. Freedom was channeled to the fullness of human life, to the preservation of human dignity and to the safeguarding of all human rights. *An experience in ordered freedom is truly a cherished part of the history of this land.*

### The Freedom to Live the Truth of Who We Are Before God

This is the freedom that America is called to live and guard and to transmit. She is called to exercise it in such a way that it will also benefit the cause of freedom in other nations and among other peoples. The only true freedom, the only freedom that can truly satisfy is the freedom to do what we ought as human beings created by God according to his plan. It is *the freedom to live the truth of what we are and who we are* before God, the truth of our identity as children of God, as brothers and sisters in a common humanity. That is why Jesus Christ linked truth and freedom together, stating solemnly: "You will know the truth and the truth will set you free" (Jn. 8:32). All people are called to recognize the liberating truth of the sovereignty of God over them both as individuals and as nations.

### The Effort to Guard the Gift of Freedom
### Must Include the Pursuit of Truth

4. The effort to guard and perfect the gift of freedom must also include the relentless pursuit of truth. In speaking to Americans on another occasion about *the relationship between freedom and truth,* I said that "as a people you have *a shared responsibility for preserving freedom and for purifying it.* Like so many other things of great value, freedom is fragile. Saint Peter recognized this when he told the Christians never to use their freedom 'as a pretext for evil' (1 Pt. 2:16). Any distortion of truth or dissemination of non-truth is an offense against freedom; any manipulation of public opinion, any abuse of authority or power, or, on the other hand, just the omission of vigilance, endangers the heritage of a free people. But even more important, every contribution to promoting truth in charity consolidates freedom and builds up peace. When shared responsibility for freedom is truly accepted by all, a great new force is set at work for the service of humanity" (Address of June 21, 1980).

### Service to Humanity Has Always Had Pride of Place
### Along with a Sense of Responsibility

5. *Service to humanity has always been a special part of the vocation of America* and is still relevant today. In continuity with what I said to the president of the United States in 1979 I would now repeat: "Attachment to human values and to ethical concerns, which have been a hallmark of the American people, must be situated, especially in the present context of the growing interdependence of peoples across the globe, within the framework of the view that the common good of society embraces not just the individual nation to which one belongs but the citizens of the whole world. . . . The present-day relationships between peoples and between nations demand the establishment of greater international cooperation also in the economic field. The more powerful a nation is, the greater becomes its international responsibility, the greater also must be its commitment to the betterment of the lot of those whose very humanity is constantly being threatened by want and need. . . . America, which in the past decades has demonstrated goodness and generosity in providing food for the hungry of the world, will, I am sure, be able to match this generosity with an equally convincing contribution to the establishing of a world order that will create the necessary economic and trade conditions for a more just relationship between all the nations of the world, in respect for their dignity and their own personality" (Address at the White House, October 6, 1979).

### A New Birth of Freedom Is Necessary—
### to Exercise Responsibility,
### Meet the Challenge of Service, to Live by Truth

6. Linked to service, freedom is indeed a great gift of God to this nation. *America needs freedom to be herself and to fulfill her mission in the world.* At a difficult moment

in the history of this country, a great American, Abraham Lincoln, spoke of a special need at that time: "that this nation under God shall have a new birth of freedom." *A new birth of freedom is repeatedly necessary:* freedom to exercise responsibility and generosity; freedom to meet the challenge of serving humanity, the freedom necessary to fulfill human destiny, the freedom to live by truth, to defend it against whatever distorts and manipulates it, the freedom to observe God's law—which is the supreme standard of all human liberty—the freedom to live as children of God, secure and happy: *the freedom to be America* in that constitutional democracy which was conceived to be "One Nation under God, indivisible, with liberty and justice for all."

## SEPTEMBER 11, 1987

## 5. MEETING WITH JEWISH LEADERSHIP

Dear Friends,

Representatives of so many Jewish organizations assembled here from across the United States, my dear Jewish Brothers and Sisters,

### Words of Gratitude

1. I am grateful to you for your kind words of greeting. I am indeed pleased to be with you, especially at this time when *the United States tour of the Vatican Judaica Collection begins.* The wonderful material, including illuminated Bibles and prayer books, demonstrates but a small part of the immense spiritual resources of Jewish tradition across the centuries and up to the present time—spiritual resources often used in fruitful cooperation with Christian artists.

### A Common Belief

It is fitting at the beginning of our meeting *to emphasize our faith in the One God,* who chose Abraham, Isaac and Jacob, and made with them a Covenant of eternal love, which was never revoked (see Gn. 27:13; Rom. 11:29). It was rather confirmed by the gift of the *Torah* to Moses, opened by the Prophets to the hope of eternal redemption and to the universal commitment for justice and peace. The Jewish people, the Church and all believers in the *Merciful God*—who is invoked in the Jewish prayers as *'Av Ha-Rakhamîm*—can find in this fundamental Covenant with the Patriarchs *a very substantial starting point for our dialogue and our common witness in the world.*

It is also fitting *to recall God's promise to Abraham and the spiritual fraternity which it established:* "in your descendants all the nations shall find blessing—all this because you obeyed my command" (Gn. 22:18). This spiritual fraternity, linked to obedience to God, requires *a great mutual respect* in humility and confidence. An objective consideration of our relations during the centuries must take into account this great need.

## Jews and Catholics in America:
## Cooperation in the Experiment of Religious Freedom

2. It is indeed worthy of note that the United States was founded by people who came to these shores often as religious refugees. They aspired to being treated justly and to being accorded hospitality according to the word of God, as we read in Leviticus: "You shall treat the alien who resides with you no differently than the natives born among you; have the same love for him as for yourself; for you too were once aliens in the land of Egypt. I, the Lord, am your God" (Lv. 19:34). Among these millions of immigrants there was a large number of Catholics and Jews. The same *basic religious principles* of freedom and justice, of equality and moral solidarity, affirmed in the *Torah* as well as in the *Gospel,* were in fact reflected in the high human ideals and in the protection of universal rights found in the United States. These in turn exercised a strong positive influence on the history of Europe and other parts of the world. But the paths of the immigrants in their new land were not always easy. Sadly enough, prejudice and discrimination were also known in the New World as well as in the Old. Nevertheless, together, Jews and Catholics have contributed to the success of the American experiment in religious freedom, and, in this unique context, have given to the world a *vigorous form of interreligious dialogue* between our two ancient traditions. For those engaged in this dialogue, so important to the Church and to the Jewish people, I pray: May God bless you and make you strong for his service!

## Despite Differences, Reconciliation

3. At the same time, our common heritage, task and hope do not eliminate *our distinctive identities.* Because of her specific Christian witness, "The Church must preach Jesus Christ to the World" (*1974 "Guidelines,"* I). In so doing we proclaim that "Christ is our peace" (Eph. 2:14). As the Apostle Paul said: "All this is from God, who through Christ reconciled us to himself and gave us the ministry of reconciliation" (2 Cor. 5:18). At the same time, we recognize and appreciate the spiritual treasures of the Jewish people and their religious witness to God. A fraternal theological dialogue will try to understand, in the light of the mystery of Redemption, how differences in faith should not cause enmity but open up the way of *"reconciliation,"* so that in the end "God may be all in all" (1 Cor. 15:28).

In this regard I am pleased that the National Conference of Catholic Bishops and the Synagogue Council of America are initiating a consultation between Jewish leaders and Bishops which should carry forward a dialogue on issues of the greatest interest to the two faith communities.

4. Considering history in the light of the principles of faith in God, we must also reflect on the catastrophic event of the *Shoah,* that ruthless and inhuman attempt to exterminate the Jewish people in Europe, an attempt that resulted in millions of

victims—including women and children, the elderly and the sick—*exterminated only because they were Jews.*

### Through Suffering, the Church and the Jewish People Share a Common Bond

Considering this mystery of the suffering of Israel's children, their witness of hope, of faith and of humanity under dehumanizing outrages, the Church experiences ever more deeply her *common bond with the Jewish people* and with their treasure of spiritual riches in the past and in the present.

### Pius XI and Pius XII Condemned Nazism and Anti-Semitism

It is also fitting to recall the strong, unequivocal efforts of the Popes *against anti-Semitism* and Nazism at the height of the persecution against the Jews. Back in 1938, Pius XI declared that "anti-Semitism cannot be admitted" (September 6, 1938), and he declared the total opposition between Christianity and Nazism by stating that the Nazi cross is an "enemy of the Cross of Christ" (*Christmas Allocution, 1938*). And I am convinced that history will reveal ever more clearly and convincingly how deeply Pius XII felt the tragedy of the Jewish people, and how hard and effectively he worked to assist them during the Second World War.

### U.S. Bishops Denounced Atrocities

Speaking in the name of humanity and Christian principles, the Bishops' Conference of the United States denounced the atrocities with a clear statement: "Since the murderous assault on Poland, utterly devoid of every semblance of humanity, there has been a premeditated and systematic extermination of the people of this nation. The same satanic technique is being applied to many other peoples. We feel a deep sense of revulsion against the cruel indignities heaped upon the Jews in conquered countries and upon defenseless peoples not of our faith" (November 14, 1942).

We also remember many others, who, at risk of their own lives, helped persecuted Jews, and are honored by the Jews with the title of *Tzaddiqê 'ummôt ha-'olâm* (Righteous of the Nations).

5. The terrible tragedy of your people has led many *Jewish thinkers* to reflect on the human condition with acute insights. Their vision of man and the roots of this vision in the teachings of the Bible, which we share in our common heritage of the Hebrew Scriptures, offer Jewish and Catholic scholars much useful material for reflection and dialogue. And I am thinking here above all of the contribution of Martin Buber and Emmanuel Levinas.

### *Shoah* Leads Catholics and Jews to Collaborative Study

In order to understand even more deeply *the meaning of the Shoah* and *the historical roots of anti-Semitism* that are related to it, *joint collaboration and studies by*

Catholics and Jews on the *Shoah* should be continued. Such studies have already taken place through many conferences in your country, such as the National Workshops on Christian-Jewish Relations.

The religious and historical implications of the *Shoah* for Christians and Jews will now be taken up formally by the International Catholic-Jewish Liaison Committee, meeting later this year in the United States for the first time. And as was affirmed in the important and very cordial meeting I had with Jewish leaders in Castelgandolfo on September 1, a Catholic document on the *Shoah* and anti-Semitism will be forthcoming, resulting from such serious studies.

### Holocaust: Never Again!

Similarly, it is to be hoped that common educational programs on our historical and religious relations, which are well developed in your country, will truly promote mutual respect and teach future generations about *the Holocaust* so that never again will such a horror be possible. Never again!

When meeting the leaders of the Polish Jewish community in Warsaw, in June of this year, I underscored the fact that through the terrible experience of the *Shoah,* your people have become "a loud warning voice for all of humanity, for all nations, for all the powers of this world, for every system and every individual . . . a saving warning" (Address of June 14, 1987).

### Correct Catholic Teaching and Preaching
### on Jews and Judaism

6. It is also desirable that *in every Diocese Catholics should implement, under the direction of the Bishops,* the statement of the Second Vatican Council and the subsequent instructions issued by the Holy See regarding the correct way to preach and teach about Jews and Judaism. I know that a great many efforts in this direction have already been made by Catholics, and I wish to express *my gratitude* to all those who have worked so diligently for this aim.

### Jewish Right to a Homeland

7. Necessary for any sincere dialogue is the intention of each partner to allow others *to define themselves "in the light of their own religious experience"* (1974 "Guidelines," Introduction). In fidelity to this affirmation, Catholics recognize among the elements of the Jewish experience that Jews have a religious attachment to the land, which finds its roots in biblical tradition.

After the tragic extermination of the *Shoah,* the Jewish people began a new period in their history. They have a *right to a homeland,* as does any civil nation, according to international law. "For the Jewish people who live in the State of Israel and who preserve in that land such precious testimonies to their history and their faith, we must ask for the desired security and the due tranquillity that is the prerogative of every nation and condition of life and of progress for every society" (*Redemptionis Anno,* April 20, 1984).

### Palestinian Right to a Homeland

What has been said about the right to a homeland also applies to the Palestinian people, so many of whom remain homeless and refugees. While all concerned must honestly reflect on the past—Muslims no less than Jews and Christians—it is time to forge those solutions which will lead to *a just, complete and lasting peace in that area.* For peace I earnestly pray.

### Partners in Dialogue; Fellow Believers; Children of Abraham

8. Finally, as I thank you once again for the warmth of your greeting to me, *I give praise and thanks to the Lord for this fraternal meeting,* for the gift of dialogue between our peoples, and for the new and deeper understanding between us. As our long relationship moves toward its third millennium, it is our great privilege in this generation to be witnesses to this progress.

It is my sincere hope that, as partners in dialogue, as fellow believers in the God who revealed himself, as the children of Abraham, we will strive to render *a common service to humanity,* which is so much needed in this our day. We are called to collaborate in service and to unite in a common cause wherever a brother or sister is unattended, forgotten, neglected or suffering in any way; wherever human rights are endangered or human dignity offended; wherever the rights of God are violated or ignored.

With the Psalmist, I now repeat:

I will hear what God proclaims;
the Lord—for he proclaims peace
To his people, and to his faithful ones,
and to those who put in him their hope. (Ps. 85:9)

To all of you, dear friends, dear brothers and sisters; to all of you dear Jewish people of America: with great hope I wish you the peace of the Lord: *Shalom! Shalom!* God bless you on this Sabbath and in this year: *Shabbath Shalom! Shanah Tovah we-Hatimah Tovah!*

## 6. HOMILY AT MASS CELEBRATED AT TAMIAMI PARK

*Let the peoples praise you, O God;*
Let all the peoples praise you.
Que todos los pueblos te alaben. (Ps. 66/67:6)

Dear Brothers and Sisters in Christ,

## Give Glory to the Father Through Jesus

1. The psalm of today's liturgy urges all the peoples and nations of the earth to give glory to God. In the exultant spirit of this exhortation I find myself on American soil, joined with all of you here in Miami, to express and praise the glory of God *through the Sacrifice of Jesus Christ, in the Eucharist.* There is no better way to express God's glory than this Sacrament. *There is no other prayer* which more profoundly unites earth with heaven, or the creature with the Creator, than the Eucharist. There is *no other sacrifice* in which everything that exists, and particularly man, is able to become a gift for the one who has so generously lavished him with gifts.

Dear brothers and sisters in Christ, all of you assembled here today in southern Florida and all the people of this land, *you the great nation of the United States:* give glory to God together with me—the Bishop of Rome, the Successor of Saint Peter, who is beginning here in Miami his act of papal service. May *God's blessing be upon us!* May the holy fear of God reach the ends of the earth! (see Ps. 66–67:8).

## More than Fifty Years Before the Pilgrims at Plymouth, the Resurrection Was Recalled in Florida

2. I am very pleased to be with you in *Florida,* this beautiful land of the sun. I warmly greet you, my brothers and sisters of the Catholic faith, and I extend cordial greetings to those of you who are not members of the Church but are here as welcome friends. I thank you all for coming. I also acknowledge among you the presence of so many ethnic groups, including Cubans, Haitians, Nicaraguans, others from Central America and the Caribbean, together with all the rest who make up the community of the Church. I embrace you all in the love of Christ.

The Church of Florida has a rich and varied history, extending more than four and a half centuries. Ponce de Leon discovered this land at Easter time in 1513 and gave it the Spanish name for Easter, *Pascua Florida.* Hence the very name of your state recalls the central mystery of our Christian faith, the Resurrection of our Lord and Savior Jesus Christ. The first settlement and the first parish of North America were established here in the early 1560s, more than fifty years before the Pilgrim Fathers landed at Plymouth Rock.

## Diverse Cultures and Languages

While Floridians can rightly be proud of their *illustrious history,* they can also boast of *contemporary dynamism and expansion.* Today, Miami is emerging as an international city of ever-increasing influence. It is a gateway, *a crossroads of diverse cultures and languages,* a center of communication, travel and commerce, a bridge connecting early and modern American history.

This land of fascinating nature, this home of so many different peoples, this place of tourists and haven of senior citizens, this center of the scientific achievements of Cape Canaveral, this state which is Florida, has also been *a land of rapid growth in building up the Body of Christ.* An indication of this remarkable recent growth is the fact that within just twenty-nine years the Catholic Church in Florida has grown from one Diocese to seven. It is indeed a joy for me to be in the midst of this dynamic Church in Florida, a Church which proclaims by word and deed *the Good News of the Easter mystery.*

## God, the Creator of All Good Things, Shows Us the Way to Salvation

3. *Who is the God whose glory we desire to proclaim by means of the Eucharist?*

*He is the God who shows us the way of salvation.* Thus the Psalmist, who urges all the nations of the earth to praise the glory of God, at the same time exclaims: "May your ways be known upon earth; among all nations your salvation" (Ps. 67:3). Our God shows us the way. He is not the God of intellectual abstraction, but *the God of the Covenant, the God of salvation, the Good Shepherd.*

## Christ, the Good Shepherd, Leads Us to Unity in the Father

Christ, the Son of the living God, speaks to us this very day in the Gospel, using *this word,* so simple yet so eloquent and rich: *Shepherd!* "I am the Good Shepherd," he says. "I know my sheep and my sheep know me in the same way that the Father knows me and I know the Father" (Jn. 10:14–15). In another passage of the Gospel, Christ says to us: "No one knows the Son but the Father, and no one knows the Father but the Son—and anyone to whom the Son wishes to reveal him" (Mt. 11:27). *The Son, Jesus Christ,* is the Shepherd precisely *because he reveals the Father to us.* He is the Good Shepherd. And the Father is our Shepherd through the Son, through Christ. And in his Son the Father wants us to have eternal life.

## The Father Gives Us Life Through His Son

4. Jesus goes on to tell us, in words that speak eloquently of his deep love for us: *"The Good Shepherd lays down his life for the sheep"* (Jn. 10:11).

Who is this God whose truth we desire to confess by means of the Eucharist? *He is the Father* who in Christ gives life to us whom he created in his own image and likeness. This *life in God is salvation.* It is liberation from death. It is Redemption from our sins. And this God is *Christ,* the Son who is of one substance with the Father, who became man for us and for our salvation, Christ the Good Shepherd who *has given his very own life for the sheep.*

## Our New Life in God Begins in the Eucharist

*The Eucharist* proclaims this truth about God. The Sacrament of the Body and Blood of Christ is offered as a redemptive Sacrifice for the sins of the world. It is the Sacrament of the Death and Resurrection of Christ, *in which our new life in God begins.*

## Love Desires What Is Good for All

*This God is Love*. The Good Shepherd expresses this truth about God. More than the truth, he expresses the very *reality of God as Love*. Love desires what is good. It desires salvation. It is "gentle and patient," and it "will have no end" (see 1 Cor. 13:4–8). It will not rest *before it has nourished and given life to all* in the great sheepfold, before it has embraced all. For this reason Jesus says: "I have other sheep that do not belong to this fold. I must lead them, too, and they shall hear my voice. There shall be one flock then, one shepherd" (Jn 10:6).

## Christ: Head and Shepherd Leading to Unity in the One Body, the Church

5. We draw *the image of the flock,* and the sheepfold, from the text of John's Gospel. At the same time, the reading from the Letter to the Ephesians that we have heard in today's liturgy enables us to see this image with the eyes of Paul the Apostle. For him *the flock* is *"the body"* of which the head is Christ. And thus it is the Body of Christ. In this context it is not difficult to find the likeness between the Head and the Shepherd.

## Christ Is the Source of Life for All

At the same time, however, the entire image acquires a new meaning and a new expression. *The Shepherd leads* the flock to the springs of life. *As Head, Christ is the source of life for all* those who make up his Body. Thus all of us, who as one single flock follow Christ the Good Shepherd, are at the same time called "to build up the body of Christ" (Eph. 4:12).

## Personal and Communal Dimensions of the Church

According to the Letter to the Ephesians, this "building up" has two dimensions: *a personal dimension and a community dimension*. Each person must attain that form of perfection which is Christ come to full stature (see Eph. 4:13). At the same time, we must all come *to maturity "together" in the community of the Church*. As the whole People of God we move toward this fullness in Christ.

## A Great Diversity of Vocations with a Goal of Unity in Christ

Christ gives the Church *a rich variety of charisms* for the purpose of deepening our communion as his Body. He bestows on the Church *a great diversity of vocations,* not just for the well-being of each person but for the good of all. As Saint Paul says of Jesus, "It is he who gave apostles, prophets, evangelists, pastors and teachers in roles of service for the faithful *to build up the body of Christ, till we become one* in faith and in the knowledge of God's Son" (Eph. 4:11–13).

## The Church in Miami: Unity in Diversity

6. The Church in the United States, and in a particular way the Church in Miami, experiences *this mystery of unity in diversity* in a very real sense. Yours is a community of compassion, which over and over again has echoed the message inscribed on the Statue of Liberty: "Give me your tired, your poor, your huddled masses yearning to breathe free." The civic community and the Church in southern Florida have time after time opened their arms to immigrants and refugees. These people were strangers and you welcomed them. And be sure that as often as you did it for them, you did it for Christ (see Mt. 25:31–46).

## The Church's Concern for Immigrants

I take this occasion to assure you of the Church's particular concern for those who leave their native countries in suffering and desperation. The frequent repetition of this experience is one of the saddest phenomena of our century. Yet it has often been accompanied by hope and heroism and new life. Here in Miami, I know, there are many who in the face of distress have been *faithful to the Gospel and the law of God.* Like others who have remained faithful to Christ and his Church in time of oppression, you must guard and protect your Catholic faith as you now live your lives in freedom.

## Fidelity to Christ in a Complex and Industrialized Society

Fidelity to religious practice requires great personal effort in a complex and industrialized society. It takes maturity of faith and strong conviction to take up the cross each day and follow in the footsteps of Christ. In today's second reading we hear Saint Paul's encouragement: "Let us, then, be children no longer, tossed here and there, carried about by every wind of doctrine that originates in human trickery and skill in proposing error. Rather, let us *profess the truth in love* and *grow to the full maturity of Christ* the head" (Eph. 4:14–15).

As I gaze at this great city with its many peoples and cultures, I pray that you will all *help one another with your gifts.* Stay in touch with your own roots, your cultures and your traditions; pass on your heritage to your children; and at the same time, place all these gifts at the service of the whole community. Above all, "Make every effort to preserve the unity which has the Spirit as its origin and peace as its binding force" (Eph. 4:3).

## Despite Progress, There Is Much That Opposes Truth

7. The work of building up the Body of Christ rests upon all of us in the Church. Certainly there is a vital need today for *evangelization.* And it takes a variety of forms. There are many ways to serve the Gospel. Despite scientific and technological progress, which truly reflects a form of human cooperation in the creative work of God,

faith is challenged and even directly opposed by ideologies and life-styles which acknowledge neither God nor the moral law.

## Evil in Our Society

*Basic human and Christian values are challenged* by crime, violence and terrorism. Honesty and justice in *business and public life* are often violated. Throughout the world, great sums are spent on armaments while millions of poor people struggle for the basic necessities of life. Alcohol and drug abuse take a heavy toll on *individuals* and on *society*. The commercial exploitation of sex through pornography offends human dignity and endangers the future of *young people*. *Family life* is subjected to powerful pressures as fornication, adultery, divorce and contraception are wrongly regarded as acceptable by many. The unborn are cruelly killed and the lives of the elderly are in serious danger from a mentality that would open the door wide to euthanasia.

## Grace Is More Powerful than Sin

In the face of all this, however, faithful Christians must not be discouraged, nor can they conform to the spirit of the world. Instead, they are called upon to acknowledge the supremacy of God and his law, to raise their voices and join their efforts on behalf of moral values, to offer society the example of their own upright conduct, and to help those in need. Christians are called to act with the serene conviction that *grace is more powerful than sin* because of *the victory of Christ's Cross*.

## Reconciliation: Central to Renewal

An important part of the mission of evangelization is the task of *reconciliation*. God "has reconciled us to himself through Christ and has given us the ministry of reconciliation" (2 Cor. 5:18). For this reason, I am happy that in preparation for my visit to the United States you have made specific efforts to promote reconciliation—reconciliation with God, among yourselves and between different races and cultures. In this context too I remind you of Christ's promise in today's Gospel, namely, that when all of us truly listen to his voice, "there shall be *one flock* then, *one shepherd*" (Jn. 10:16).

## The God of Grace

8. Deeply conscious of the truth as it is presented to us in this liturgy by the word of God, let us exclaim once again *with the Psalmist:* "God be gracious to us and bless us, *may the light of your face shine upon us*" (Ps. 66–67:2).

*Who is this God* to whom our prayer is addressed? Who is this God whom our community proclaims and to whom our hearts speak? Let us listen once again to the words of the prophet Zephaniah: "Fear not, O Zion, be not discouraged! *The Lord, your God, is in your midst, a mighty savior*" (Zep. 3:16–17).

## The Mighty One!

It is he whom we invoke here, in this land, which in so many ways manifests the strengths and achievements of humanity, of human genius, of intellect, of knowledge and of science, of technology and progress.

Who is this God? Once again let us repeat: the Mighty One!
. He alone is the Mighty One!
He who *is!* (see Ex. 3:14)
He in whom "we live and move and have our being!" (Acts 17:28)
"The Alpha and the Omega!" (Rv. 1:8)
*He alone is the Mighty One! Because he alone is Love.*

## God Is Love: Only Love Saves

Here in this land, in this culture of the most advanced progress and affluence, is not the human person at times *insecure and confused* about the ultimate meaning of existence—the ultimate meaning of life? Is not the human person at times very far from Love?

Yet *only Love saves*, and God is Love!

O God of love, O God who saves, "may the light of your face shine upon us!" (Ps. 67:2) Amen.

## 7. ADDRESS AT SAINT PETER'S CHURCH

Dear Bishop Unterkoefler,

Dear Brothers and Sisters in Christ,

"You are the Messiah, the Son of the living God." (Mt. 16:16)

### One Faith Professed in Unity with Peter

1. These words, which are recorded in the Gospel of Saint Matthew, were spoken by Simon Peter, the first Bishop of Rome. They are full of meaning for every one who believes in Christ, but they have special meaning for us who are gathered here today in this *Church of Saint Peter in Columbia,* which the Successor of Peter is privileged to visit.

It is a great joy for me to come to the *Diocese of Charleston.* I thank you for receiving me with such warmth and fraternal love. Your famous "southern hospitality" makes me feel at home.

As you know, I have come to Columbia to take part in ecumenical dialogue with national leaders of other Christian Churches and ecclesial communities, and to join with a large gathering of our brothers and sisters in an ecumenical prayer service. Our Lord prayed "that all may be one" (Jn. 17:21). We all want to do our part to make this unity come about.

### Peter's Faith Is That of the Church of Jesus Christ

2. *"You are the Messiah, the Son of the living God."*
These words of Peter express *the heart of our faith,* for they reveal the mystery of Christ; they reveal Christ as the Son of the living God, the eternal Word who became man and was born of the Virgin Mary.

### Faith in Christ Is a Gift

*Peter* was the first of the Apostles, *the first disciple* to make a public declaration of his faith in Jesus the Messiah. The words of Peter's profession of faith were words spoken with real personal conviction; and yet, these words did not find their ultimate origin in him. As Jesus told him: "Blest are you, Simon son of Jonah! No mere man has revealed this to you, but my heavenly Father" (Mt. 16:17). *Faith in Christ is a gift.* It is not a human achievement. Only God the Father can draw us to Jesus, only he can give us the grace to know Jesus, to accept him as the eternal Son of God, and to profess our faith in him.

### The Person of Jesus: Center of the Church's Life

3. From that day in the neighborhood of Caesarea Philippi, Peter's life was radically changed. And not only his life! The other Apostles, the other disciples as well, were granted the gift of faith and they too became witnesses of the words and deeds of Jesus. A whole new era began in the history of the world, in the history of salvation. And so it has continued down through the ages. People of all centuries, people from all countries have, like Peter, come to know Jesus, to accept him as God's Son—one in being with the Father—to profess their faith in him, and to make his holy Gospel the basis of their Christian lives. *The person of Jesus Christ and his word are forever the center of the Church's life.*

### Faith in Jesus Is Accompanied by the Cross

4. But the wonderful gift of faith is not separate from the Cross. Belief in Christ is not free from difficulties. It is not without cost. In fact, *our faith in Jesus Christ is often put to the test.* Peter came to know this only too well. And therefore he writes: "You may for a time have to suffer the distress of many trials; but this is *so that your faith,* which is more precious than the passing splendor of fire-tried gold, *may by its genuineness lead to praise, glory, and honor* when Jesus Christ appears" (1 Pt. 1:6–7).

### Lord, to Whom Shall We Go?

The Master spoke of the mystery of the Eucharist, when "many of his disciples broke away and would not remain in his company any longer. Jesus then said to the Twelve, 'Do you want to leave me too?' Simon Peter answered him, 'Lord, to whom shall we go? You have the words of eternal life. We have come to believe; we are convinced that you are God's holy one'" (Jn. 6:66–69).

When our faith is tested, when we are tempted to doubt and turn away, we can find courage and renewed hope in these words of Peter: *"Lord, to whom shall we go? You have the words of eternal life."* Christ gives us the strength to live according to our faith, and to meet all the challenges against it. *From Christ, we must learn the way to overcome those sad divisions which still exist today among Christians.* We must be eager to be fully one in faith and love.

### A Long History of Ecumenical Initiative and a Search for Unity

5. I know that you share this *ecumenical conviction* with me. Indeed, Catholics in South Carolina have long felt the need for ecumenical dialogue and collaboration. First of all, because you are a distinct minority, less than 3 percent of the population. Moreover, the Catholic Church here has *a long tradition of ecumenical initiative.* Your first Bishop, *John England,* accepted the invitations of other Christians to preach in their churches and to explain the teachings of our faith. And, with the passage of the years, you have never lost this ecumenical spirit.

In more recent times in particular, you have joined with other Christian believers to promote justice and truth, to further mutual understanding and collaboration. This cooperation has been particularly striking in regard to efforts to improve racial relations among citizens of your state. I commend you in these deserving endeavors, so worthwhile and so important.

At the same time, you must never cease to strive for *personal holiness and conversion of heart.* For, as the Second Vatican Council has said, "This change of heart and holiness of life, along with public and private prayer for the unity of Christians, should be regarded as the soul of the whole ecumenical movement" (*Unitatis Redintegratio,* 8).

### The Pope Admires You and Your Efforts to Preserve Your Faith in Jesus Christ

6. Dear friends in Christ, representatives of all the Catholics of the Diocese of Charleston: I thank you for coming to greet me. I wish to assure you of my esteem for all of you who make up this local Church, spread out across this entire state of South Carolina. Know that the Pope admires all the efforts you and your forebears have made to preserve your faith in Jesus Christ, to live this faith, and to transmit it to your children.

And now I ask you to take home with you those other words ascribed to Peter—words which explain so well what it means to believe in Christ, the Son of the living God. He wrote: *"Although you have never seen him, you love him,* and without seeing *you now believe in him,* and rejoice with inexpressible joy touched with glory because you are achieving *faith's goal, your salvation"* (1 Pt. 1:8—9).

Dear Catholic people of this Diocese of Charleston: never forget that faith in Jesus Christ brings you to salvation and to eternal life!


## 8. GREETING AT THE UNIVERSITY OF SOUTH CAROLINA


Dear Dr. Holderman, dear Friends,

### A Christian's Solemn Duty
### Is to Work for the Unity of All Christians

1. Thank you for your thoughtful words of greeting and for the cordial welcome which you have extended to me. I am most grateful. For many months I have looked forward to my visit to South Carolina. It is a great joy for me finally to be here.

At the same time, I come to this state in response to *a solemn duty.* Indeed, is it not the duty of every follower of Christ to work for the unity of all Christians? To desire anything else would be not only a scandal, but a betrayal—a betrayal of the Lord who himself prayed that his disciples would be one, and who died on the Cross in order *"to gather into one* all the dispersed children of God" (Jn. 11:52). I pray that the ecumenical initiative which we are undertaking today will be pleasing in God's sight and bring us all closer to the full union of faith and love in our Savior.


### Human Knowledge at the Service of Humanity

2. It is a pleasure for me to come to the campus of this major university. As you know, I myself have had a long and happy association with *the university world* in my homeland. I know how important universities are for *the advancement of research and for the development of knowledge and culture.* I offer all of you my personal encouragement for the educational program which you carry out here in Columbia and for the contribution that you are making to the future of society. To place human knowledge at the service of humanity is a great task.


### Students Prepare to Make Their Own Contribution to Society

I wish to add a special word of greeting and support *for the students* of the University of South Carolina. Before you lies *the wonderful world of knowledge and the immense challenge of truth.* Here you can come to much greater understanding of yourself and of the universe. You can delve into the wealth of literature handed down from the past. You can explore the vast fields of the sciences and the arts. You can engage in research and future planning. Here in this center of higher education you must prepare yourselves to make your own contribution to society.

My special hope for you is this: that you will always have a *great love for truth*— the truth about God, the truth about man and the truth about the world. I pray that through truth you will serve humanity and experience real freedom. In the words of Jesus Christ, "You will know the truth and the truth will set you free" (Jn. 8:32).

May God, the source of life and truth, bless all of you at the University of South Carolina.

## 9. MEETING WITH ECUMENICAL LEADERSHIP

Dear Friends, dear Brothers and Sisters,

### We Are Committed to Treading the Path to Unity Opened by the Holy Spirit

1. I praise "the God and Father of our Lord Jesus Christ who has bestowed on us in Christ every spiritual blessing in the heavens!" (Eph. 1:3) In particular I give thanks to him today for granting me the opportunity of this meeting with you, representatives of Christian Churches and ecclesial communities in the United States. I believe that our meeting is important not only in itself, for the reflections and Christian experience that we share with each other, but also as an outspoken testimony on our part that *we are definitively committed* to treading the path which the Holy Spirit has opened before us: the path of repentance for our divisions and of working and praying for that perfect unity which the Lord himself wishes for his followers.

I am grateful to you for your presence, and for the statement with which you have wished to open this meeting. And in the wider perspective, I wish *to thank you for the ecumenical contacts and collaboration* in which you so willingly engage here in the United States with the National Conference of Bishops and the Catholic Dioceses. Indeed, I am grateful for all the earnest ecumenical activity carried out in this country.

### *Koinonia:* Unity of the Baptized

2. In recent decades, especially under the impulse of the Second Vatican Council, the Catholic Church has placed renewed emphasis on the term "communion" (*koinonia*) as an especially appropriate way of describing the profound divine and human reality of the Church, the Body of Christ, *the unity of the baptized in the Father, the Son, and the Holy Spirit.* Our communion is primarily with the Triune God, but it intimately unites us among ourselves.

## The Church Is Endowed with Gifts, Ministries and Charisms
## Which Serve Ecclesial Life

This communion is increased in us as we share in the gifts with which Christ has endowed his Church. Some of these are eminently spiritual in nature, such as the life of grace, faith, hope and charity and other interior gifts of the Holy Spirit (see *Unitatis Redintegratio,* 3). In addition, there are exterior gifts, which include the word of God in Sacred Scripture, Baptism and the other Sacraments, as well as the ministries and charisms which serve ecclesial life.

## We Recognize the Presence of Christ's Gifts

Although we are not yet in agreement as to how each of our Churches and ecclesial communities relates to the fullness of life and mission which flow from God's redemptive act through the Cross and Resurrection of Jesus Christ, it is no small achievement of the ecumenical movement that after centuries of mistrust, we humbly and sincerely *recognize in each other's communities the presence and fruitfulness of Christ's gifts at work.* For this divine action in the lives of all of us we offer thanks to God.

## A Spiritual Yearning in America and in the World

3. I wish to note in particular the reference made in the opening statement to the sense of spiritual yearning among Christians in this country, a yearning which in part manifests itself in an increasing interest in the life of prayer, in spirituality and in ecumenism. In a word, it is *a yearning for deeper insights into our Christian identity* and, consequently, for *a renewal of our ecclesial life.* This important phenomenon can be found to a greater or lesser degree in all ecclesial communities, not only in the United States but throughout the world. Surely it is a sign of the action of the Holy Spirit in the People of God. As leaders in our respective Communions, we have the awesome task and privilege of collaborating to ensure that this grace will not be received by us in vain (see 2 Cor. 6:1).

## Purification and Renewal of Catholic Life

From the Catholic perspective, a primary factor relating to ecumenical involvement with other Christian bodies has been, from the outset, *the purification and renewal of Catholic life itself.* The Second Vatican Council's Decree on Ecumenism indicated, "In ecumenical work, Catholics must assuredly be concerned for their separated brethren, praying for them, keeping them informed about the Church, making the first approaches toward them. But their primary duty is to make an honest and careful appraisal of whatever needs to be renewed and achieved in the Catholic household itself" (*Unitatis Redintegratio,* 4).

## A Call to Holiness and to Greater Love

It is not difficult to see how the internal renewal and purification of the ecclesial life of all of us is essential to any progress we may make toward unity. *For Christ's call to unity is at the same time a call to holiness and a call to greater love.* It is a call for us to render our witness more authentic. Only by becoming more faithful disciples of Jesus Christ can we hope to travel the path of unity under the guidance of the Holy Spirit and in the strength of his grace. Only by fully accepting Jesus Christ as the Lord of our lives can we empty ourselves of any negative thinking about each other.

## Prayer and Conversion of Heart Are Essential to Unity

It is important for all of us to realize how much conversion of heart depends on prayer, and how much prayer contributes to unity. The Second Vatican Council spoke about a *"spiritual ecumenism,"* which it described as "the soul of the whole ecumenical movement," and which it identified as "a change of heart and holiness of life, coupled with public and private prayer for the unity of Christians" (*Unitatis Redintegratio*, 8).

## Common Christian Service and Study

4. In speaking of the priority of internal renewal and prayer in the ecumenical task, I do not intend in any way to minimize other important factors such as our *common Christian service* to those in need or our *common study* carried out in theological dialogues.

In the case of *dialogues*, the results reached in them thus far merit the most serious consideration and gratitude from all of us. They tend to increase mutual understanding in ways that have already greatly changed our relationship for the better. Our meeting here today is itself a testimony of this.

## Common Study Reveals the Sources of Our Common Faith

Further, these dialogues continue to uncover the deep sources of our common faith and the extent to which that faith, even while we remain apart, is truly shared by our Churches and ecclesial communities. In doing so, such exchanges help us *to face our remaining differences in a more intelligible context.* It is the task of dialogue to face these differences and to work toward the time when it will be possible for Christians to confess together the one faith and to celebrate the one Eucharist.

On the international level, the response of the Catholic Church to the document *Baptism, Eucharist and Ministry,* which has now been sent to the Commission on Faith and Order, is an effort to contribute to this process directed toward confessing the one faith together. I am convinced that the Lord will give us the light and strength to pursue this course together for the glory of his name.

## Our Common Efforts Lead Not Just to Common Study, but to Actual Unity and Communion

Indispensable as the work of dialogue is, and even though the act of dialogue itself begins to improve relations between us, our ultimate purpose goes beyond the statements and reports of ecumenical commissions. Those statements must be properly evaluated by our respective Churches and ecclesial communities in order to determine the level of ecclesial communion that actually exists, so that it may be *properly reflected in the lifestream of ecclesial life.* We must greatly rejoice in discovering the extent to which we are already united, while we respectfully and serenely acknowledge the factors that still divide us.

## How May We Collaborate?

5. In regard to *our common service and collaboration,* the statement you have presented puts before all of us important questions. How may we collaborate to promote justice, exercise compassion, search for peace, bring the witness of the Gospel to unbelievers, and manifest our *koinonia?* These issues challenge all of us. Together we must seek to discover the concrete ways in which we may respond in common.

## Ecumenism Is Not a Matter of Power or of Human Tactics; It Is a Service in Love and Humble Submission to God

You rightly designate these questions as "points of conversation" among us. As an initial approach, an introduction to our conversation, I would like to make the following brief remarks. First, we are all convinced that the deepest lessons a Christian can learn in this life are learned at the foot of the Cross. When our Churches and ecclesial communities address one another and the whole human family, we must do so *from the foot of the Cross of Jesus Christ,* the wellspring of wisdom and the source of our witness. From the Cross we learn the qualities required in our ecumenical search for unity. "For it is from newness of attitudes (see Eph. 4:23), from self-denial and unstinted love that yearnings for unity take their rise and grow toward maturity" (*Unitatis Redintegratio,* 7). Ecumenism is not a matter of power and human "tactics." *It is a service of truth in love and humble submission to God.*

## We Collaborate for the Sake of Christ

Similarly, our collaboration in the important areas you list is not a matter of measured calculation. We do not collaborate simply for the sake of efficiency, or for reasons of mere strategy, or for advantage and influence. *We collaborate for the sake of Christ,* who urges us to be one in him and in the Father, so that the world may believe (see Jn. 17:21).

## Breaking Down Barriers of Misunderstanding
## in Order to Bring About Unity

6. The ecumenical community has now welcomed me twice to this country. I in turn have had the joyful opportunity of welcoming many of you to Rome, the City of the Apostles and Martyrs, Peter and Paul. I believe that these and other cordial meetings have the effect, with God's grace, of breaking down the barriers of misunderstanding that have plagued us for centuries. How often we read in the Scriptures of encounters being occasions of grace, either encounters of the Lord with his disciples or encounters of the disciples with others to whom they are bringing the word. I believe that in meetings such as these, where two or three or more of us are gathered in his name, *Christ is here in our midst,* asking from each of us a greater depth of commitment to service in his name, and therefore, a greater degree of unity among ourselves.

## We Pray That the Father May Be Glorified
## in the Fulfillment of Christ's Prayer: Unity

I join my prayer to yours that the Christian communities of the United States may continue *to meet with each other, to work with each other, and to pray with each other,* so that the Father will be glorified in the fulfillment of Christ's prayer:

*That their unity may be complete.*
So shall the world know that you sent me,
and that you loved them as you loved me.
(Jn. 17:23)

So be it.

## 10. ADDRESS AT THE ECUMENICAL PRAYER SERVICE

Praised be Jesus Christ!

Dear Brothers and Sisters,

## Side by Side, to Confess Jesus Christ

1. I greet each one of you in our Lord and Savior Jesus Christ. It is indeed the "Lord of both the dead and the living" (Rom. 14:9) who has brought us together in this holy assembly of Christian people, a joy-filled gathering of different Ecclesial Communions: Orthodox, Anglicans, Methodists, Baptists, Lutherans, Presbyterians, members of the United Church of Christ and of other Reformed Churches, Disciples of Christ, members of the Peace Churches, Pentecostals, members of the Polish National Catholic Church and Catholics.

We stand, side by side, *to confess Jesus Christ,* "the one mediator between God and man" (1 Tm. 2:5), for "at Jesus' name every knee must bend in the heavens on the earth and under the earth, and every tongue proclaim to the glory of God the Father: Jesus Christ is Lord" (Phil 2:10)!

## A Pilgrim People United in Baptism

We have come here to pray, and in doing so we are following the example of all the saints from the beginning, especially the Apostles, who in awaiting the Holy Spirit "devoted themselves to prayer, together with the women and Mary the Mother of Jesus, and with his brethren" (Acts 1:14). Together we are renewing our common faith in the eternal Redemption which we have obtained through the Cross of Jesus Christ (see Heb. 9:12), and our hope that, just as Jesus rose from the dead, so too we shall rise to eternal life (see Phil. 3:11). In fact, through our *Baptism in the name of the Father and of the Son and of the Holy Spirit,* we have been buried with Christ "so that, just as Christ was raised from the dead by the glory of the Father, we too might live a new life" (Rom. 6:4). Living a new life in the Spirit, we are *a pilgrim people,* pressing forward amid the persecutions of the world and the consolations of God, announcing the death of the Lord until he comes (see 1 Cor. 11:26; *Lumen Gentium,* 8).

## Sons and Daughters of the One Father

Brothers and sisters: we are divided in many ways in our faith and discipleship. But we are here together today as sons and daughters of *the one Father,* calling upon *the one Lord Jesus Christ,* in the love which *the same Holy Spirit* pours forth into our hearts. Let us give thanks to God and let us rejoice in this fellowship! And let us commit ourselves further to the great task which Jesus himself urges upon us: to go forward along the path of Christian reconciliation and unity "without obstructing the ways of divine Providence and without prejudging the future inspiration of the Holy Spirit" (*Unitatis Redintegratio,* 24).

## The Scriptures Are Dear to All of Us

2. In this service of Christian witness we have listened together to the word of God given to us in the Holy Scriptures. *The Scriptures are dear to all of us. They are one of the greatest treasures we share.* In the Sacred Scriptures and in the deeds of divine mercy which they narrate, God our Father, out of the abundance of his love, speaks to us as his children and lives among us. The Bible is holy because in its inspired and unalterable words the voice of the Holy Spirit lives and is heard among us, sounding again and again in the Church from age to age and from generation to generation (see *Dei Verbum,* 21).

### Marriage and the Family Are Sacred Realities

3. Today this stadium has resounded with passages from Holy Scripture bearing on the reality of *the family*. We have heard the plea and promise made by the young widow, Ruth: "wherever you go I will go, wherever you lodge I will lodge, your people shall be my people, and your God my God. Wherever you die I will die and there be buried" (Ru. 1:16–17). To hear these words is to be moved with a deep feeling for the *strength of family ties:* stronger than the fear of hardships to be faced; stronger than the fear of exile in an unfamiliar land; stronger than the fear of possible rejection. The bond that unites a family is not only a matter of natural kinship or of shared life and experience. It is essentially a holy and religious bond. *Marriage and the family are sacred realities.*

## Christian Marriage:
## Symbol of God's Union with His People, the Church

The sacredness of Christian marriage consists in the fact that in God's plan the marriage covenant between a man and a woman becomes *the image and symbol of the Covenant which unites God to his people* (see Hos. 2:21; Jer. 3:6–13; Is. 54:5–10). It is the sign of Christ's love for his Church (see Eph. 5:32). Because God's love is faithful and irrevocable, so those who have been married "in Christ" are called to remain faithful to each other forever.

Did not Jesus himself say to us: "What therefore God has joined together, let no man put asunder" (see Mt. 19:6)?

### Perseverance in Union of Love

Contemporary society has a special need of the witness of couples who persevere in their union, as an eloquent, even if sometimes suffering, "sign" in our human condition of the steadfastness of God's love. Day after day *Christian married couples are called to open their hearts ever more to the Holy Spirit, whose power never fails,* and who enables them to love each other as Christ has loved us. And, as Saint Paul writes to the Galatians, "the fruit of the Spirit is love, joy, peace, patient endurance, kindness, generosity, faith, mildness and chastity" (Gal. 5:22–23). All of this constitutes the rule of life and the program of personal development of Christian couples. And each Christian community has a great responsibility to sustain couples in their love.

### Christian Families: A Communion of Persons in Love

4. From such love Christian families are born. In them *children are welcomed as a splendid gift of God's goodness,* and they are educated in the essential values of human life, learning above all that "man is more precious for what he is than for what he has" (see *Gaudium et Spes,* 35). The entire family endeavors to practice respect for the

dignity of every individual and to offer disinterested service to those in need (see *Familiaris Consortio,* 37).

## The Church and Families:
### Representations of the Love of the Trinity

Christian families exist to form *a communion of persons in love.* As such, the Church and the family are, each in its own way, living representations in human history of the eternal loving communion of the Three Persons of the Most Holy Trinity. In fact, the family is called the Church in miniature, "the domestic church," a particular expression of the Church through the human experience of love and common life (see *Familiaris Consortio,* 49). Like the Church, the family ought to be a place where the Gospel is transmitted and *from which the Gospel radiates to other families and to the whole of society.*

## The Family Is Threatened and Shaken
### by Sins Against Love and Against Life

5. In America and throughout the world, *the family is being shaken* to its roots. The consequences for individuals and society in personal and collective instability and unhappiness are incalculable. Yet it is heartening to know that in the face of this extraordinary challenge many Christians are committing themselves to the defense and support of family life. In recent years the Catholic Church, especially on the occasion of the 1980 Synod of the world's Bishops, has been involved in an extensive reflection on the role of the Christian family in the modern world. This is a field in which there must be the maximum collaboration among all who confess Jesus Christ.

### Destruction of the Family Threatens the Unity of Generations

So often the pressures of modern living separate husbands and wives from one another, threatening their lifelong *interdependence in love and fidelity.* Can we also not be concerned about the impact of cultural pressures upon *relations between the generations,* upon parental authority and the transmission of sacred values? Our Christian conscience should be deeply concerned about the way in which *sins against love and against life* are often presented as examples of "progress" and emancipation. Most often, are they not but the age-old forms of selfishness dressed up in a new language and presented in a new cultural framework?

### False Notion of Individual Freedom

6. Many of these problems are the result of *a false notion of individual freedom at work in our culture,* as if one could be free only when rejecting every objective norm

of conduct, refusing to assume responsibility, or even refusing to put curbs on instincts and passions! Instead, *true freedom* implies that we are capable of choosing a good, without constraint. This is the truly human way of proceeding in the choices—big and small—which life puts before us. The fact that we are also able to choose *not* to act as we see we should is a necessary condition of our moral freedom. But in that case we must account for the good that we fail to do and for the evil that we commit. This sense of moral accountability needs to be reawakened if society is to survive as a civilization of justice and solidarity.

## We Are Free and Responsible Beings Seeking Truth, the Root and Rule of Freedom

It is true that our freedom is weakened and conditioned in many ways, not least as a consequence of the mysterious and dramatic history of mankind's original rebellion against the Creator's will, as indicated in the opening pages of the Book of Genesis. But *we remain free and responsible beings* who have been redeemed by Jesus Christ, and we must *educate our freedom* to recognize and choose what is right and good, and to reject what does not conform to the original truth concerning our nature and our destiny as God's creatures. *Truth*—beginning with the truth of our Redemption through the Cross and Resurrection of Jesus Christ—*is the root and rule of freedom, the foundation and measure of all liberating action* (see *Instruction on Christian Freedom and Liberation*, 3).

## The Duty to Choose Well; the Duty to Choose Truth

7. It would be a great tragedy for the entire human family if the United States, which prides itself on its consecration to freedom, were to lose sight of the true meaning of that noble word. America: you cannot insist on the right to choose, without also insisting *on the duty to choose well, the duty to choose the truth*. Already there is much breakdown and pain in your own society because fundamental values, essential to the well-being of individuals, families and the entire nation, are being emptied of their real content.

## Recognizing the Primacy of Moral Values

And yet, at the same time, throughout this land there is *a great stirring,* an awareness of *the urgent need to recapture the ultimate meaning of life and its fundamental values.* Surely by now we must be convinced that only by recognizing the primacy of moral values can we use the immense possibilities offered by science and material progress to bring about the true advancement of the human person in truth, freedom and dignity. As Christians, our specific contribution *is to bring the wisdom of God's word to bear on the problems of modern living,* in such a way that modern culture will be led to a more profoundly restored covenant with divine Wisdom itself (see *Familiaris Consortio,* 8). As we heard proclaimed in the Gospel reading, Jesus indicates that the supreme norm of our behavior and our relationships, including our relationship with him, is always obedience to the will of the Creator: "Whoever does the will of my heavenly Father is brother and sister and mother to me" (Mt. 12:50).

## The Well-Being of Society and of the Church
## Depends upon the Strength of Families

8. Brothers and sisters: to the extent that God grants us to *grow in Christian unity, let us work together to offer strength and support to families,* on whom the well-being of society depends, and on whom our Churches and ecclesial communities depend. May the families of America live with grateful hearts, giving thanks to the Lord for his blessings, praying for one another, bearing one another's burdens, welcoming one another as Christ has welcomed them.

My prayer for all of you at the end of this second day of my visit echoes the words of Paul to the Thessalonians: "May the God of peace make you perfect in holiness. . . . May the grace of our Lord Jesus Christ be with you" (1 Thes. 5:23, 28).

## SEPTEMBER 12, 1987

## 11. ADDRESS AT SAINT LOUIS CATHEDRAL

"The grace of the Lord Jesus Christ, and the love of God, and the fellowship of the Holy Spirit be with you all!" (2 Cor. 13:14)

Dear Archbishop Hannan,

Dear Brothers and Sisters,

### Christ: The Very Center of Our Lives

1. From this Cathedral of Saint Louis I am happy to greet, in the name of the Most Holy Trinity, the whole Church in New Orleans—all those who make up her membership, all those who work together to fulfill her mission. In particular today I greet all of you, dear priests and Religious of Louisiana. Here in this mother Church of the Archdiocese, *I give thanks and praise to the living God* for your lives of dedicated service to Christ and his Church.

This temple of God, this house of prayer and gate of heaven, stands as the *central point of the city of New Orleans,* and from this place all distances are measured. Here Christ dwells in your midst, present in word and Sacrament, making this a place of grace and blessing for all the People of God. Here God the Father is adored in spirit and truth (see Jn. 4:23); and here the Holy Spirit is always at work in the hearts of the faithful, preparing them for the glory of the heavenly Jerusalem.

And just as this Cathedral of Saint Louis is the focal point of the city of New Orleans, *so too Christ is the very center of your lives.* Christ is for you "the beginning and the end" (Rv. 21:6); he is for you "the way, and the truth, and the life" (Jn. 14:6). So closely are you identified with Christ that each of you can say, as did Saint Paul: "The life I live now is not my own; Christ is living in me. I still live my human life, but it is a life of faith in the Son of God, who loved me and gave himself for me" (Gal. 2:20). And together with Saint Paul you must proclaim: "Nothing will be able to separate us from the love of God that comes to us in Christ Jesus, our Lord" (Rom. 8:39).

### Debt of Gratitude to Priests and Religious

The Church in Louisiana owes a great debt of gratitude to the many priests and Religious who have labored here from the beginning. That tradition of heroic dedication in proclaiming the Gospel of Christ by word and deed continues today in the service that you render to the People of God. Always remember that the supernatural effectiveness of your service within the Church is linked to *the witness of your life lived in union with Christ.* You are therefore called to conform your lives more and more to the person and message of Jesus Christ. And never forget that the precise goal of all apostolic service is to lead all people to communion with the Most Holy Trinity.

### The Goal of the Apostolate:
### Communion with the Most Holy Trinity

2. Our lives as Christians find their origin and destiny in *the mystery of the Most Holy Trinity,* the fundamental mystery of our Christian faith. The one God whom we worship is a unity of Three Divine Persons, "equal in majesty, undivided in splendor, yet one Lord, one God, ever to be adored" (Preface of the Most Holy Trinity). The Father and the Son and the Holy Spirit exist in an eternal communion of life and love with one another. In the Church we are privileged *to participate now and forever in the communion of life and love,* which is the mystery of God, One in Three.

The Second Vatican Council teaches that "it is from the mission of the Son and the mission of the Holy Spirit that the Church takes her origin, in accordance with the decree of God the Father." Thus as members of the Church we benefit from *the mission of the Son* and *the mission of the Holy Spirit* which flow from "that fountain of love or charity within God the Father." It is from the Father, "who is 'origin without origin,' that the Son is begotten and the Holy Spirit proceeds through the Son" (*Ad Gentes,* 2).

In revealing to us the mystery of the Father, *the Son carries out the Father's will and brings about our salvation.* And in describing the mission of the Holy Spirit, the Council says: "When the work which the Father had given the Son to do on earth (see Jn. 17:4) was accomplished, the Holy Spirit was sent on the day of Pentecost in order that he might forever sanctify the Church, and thus all believers would have access to the Father through Christ in the one Spirit (see Eph. 2:18)" (*Lumen Gentium,* 4).

### Only the Son Has Revealed the Trinity

3. In Saint John's Gospel we read: "No one has ever seen God. It is God the only Son, ever at the Father's side who revealed him" (Jn. 1:18). Although the Old Testament contained elements that prepared us for the revelation of Jesus, it did not unveil this profound mystery of God: the mystery of the Father, the intimate life of God, the communion of the Three Divine Persons. *Only the Son of God made man bears witness to the truth about the Trinity; only he reveals it.*

The truth about the divine Sonship of Jesus and the Trinitarian mystery of the Father and the Son and the Holy Spirit are alluded to at the time of the Annunciation, as well as during the baptism of Jesus in the Jordan. Moreover, during his public ministry Jesus speaks about his Father and the Holy Spirit. In the Gospel of John we find many affirmations by Jesus about the intimate union that he shares with the Father. But it is during his discourse *at the Last Supper* that *Jesus discloses in a definitive way the truth about the Holy Spirit* and the relationship which the Spirit has with the Father and the Son.

We can say that throughout his teaching Jesus "has opened up vistas closed to human reason" (*Gaudium et Spes,* 24) concerning the life of the One God in the Trinity of Divine Persons. When he had completed his Messianic mission and he was taking leave of his Apostles on the day of his Ascension, Jesus announced to them: "Go, therefore, and make disciples of all nations. Baptize them in the name of the Father, and of the Son, and of the Holy Spirit" (Mt. 28:19). Thus with these last words *Jesus solemnly entrusts to them the supreme truth of the undivided Unity of the Most Holy Trinity.*

### God—Father, Son and Holy Spirit—Loves His People

4. Dear brothers and sisters: your life of service dedicated to Christ and his Church bears witness *to the reality of God's love for his people.* You joyfully proclaim the Good News of faith, that "God is love" (1 Jn. 4:8). In Jesus' conversation with Nicodemus we hear those words: "Yes, God so loved the world that he gave his only Son, that whoever believes in him may not die but may have eternal life" (Jn. 3:16). The Father so loved the world that he sent us his only Son, and through his Son he sent the Holy Spirit. Today and each day of our lives we celebrate the love of God the Father for each of us—the love revealed in the Word made flesh and in the gift of the Holy Spirit. Moreover, we proclaim that God sent his only Son into the world *not to condemn the world,* but that the world might be saved through him. Yes, we proclaim to the world *God's everlasting love.*

May the prayers of the Blessed Virgin Mary, Our Lady of Prompt Succor and Mother of Divine Love, help you and the whole Church in New Orleans and throughout Louisiana to bear witness to the merciful love of the Father, and the Son, and the Holy Spirit.

## 12. MEETING WITH BLACK CATHOLIC LEADERSHIP

Dear Brothers and Sisters in Christ,

### The Church Responds to Christ's Command
### to Proclaim the Good News to All

1. "Go into the whole world and *proclaim the Good News* to all creation" (Mk. 16:15). With these words, our Lord Jesus Christ directed the Church to speak his own message of life to the whole human family. The Apostles first responded to the Savior's call and traveled throughout the known world, sharing with every one who would listen what they had seen and heard (see 1 Jn. 1:3), speaking about God's Kingdom and about reconciliation in Christ.

Today, almost two thousand years later, the Church still seeks to respond generously to Christ's command. The world we must serve today is much bigger, and the people who long to hear the word of life are numerous indeed. While the words of the Lord remain true, "The harvest is good but laborers are scarce" (Mt. 9:37), still we rejoice that the Holy Spirit has enriched the Church with many hands for the harvest. There are worthy laborers in every corner of the earth, people of every culture, who are eager *to live the Gospel and to proclaim it by word and example.*

### To Embrace the Saving and Uplifting Gospel of Christ

I am especially happy to meet with you who make up the black Catholic leadership in the United States. Your great concern, both as blacks and as Catholics, is—and must always be—that all your black brothers and sisters throughout America may hear and embrace the saving and uplifting Gospel of Jesus Christ. I willingly join my voice to those of the Bishops of your country who are encouraging you *to give priority to the great task of evangelization,* to be missionaries of Christ's love and truth within your own black community. To all the members of the black community throughout the United States, I send my greetings of respect and esteem.

### College of Bishops:
### A Sign of Unity and Universality of the Church

2. My dear brother Bishops, who share with me the burdens and joy of the episcopacy: I am pleased that the universality of the Gospel and the cultural diversity of your nation are increasingly mirrored in the composition of the American hierarchy. While your apostolic ministry draws you to serve all the faithful of your respective Dioceses—and in collegial unity the whole Body of Christ—it is fitting for many reasons that your own black brothers and sisters should have a special right to your pastoral love and service. United with the Successor of Peter *in the College of Bishops, you are a sign of the unity and universality of the Church* and of her mission. As Bishops, we are entrusted with the task of preserving in its integrity the Good News of salvation and of presenting it as effectively as possible to our people, so that they may all discover in Jesus Christ "the way, and the truth, and the life" (Jn. 14:6).

## Priests: Transmit the Teaching of Faith
## and Celebrate the Sacred Mysteries

Our brothers *in the priesthood,* ministering in the person of Christ and in union with us, transmit the teaching of the faith and celebrate the sacred mysteries of salvation. How fruitful it is for the mission of the Church in America when so many priests from different racial and ethnic groups proclaim together Christ's liberating Gospel and thus bear witness to the fact that it rightfully belongs to everyone.

## Deacons: Heralds of the Gospel
## and Servant Ministers of Christ

The Church in the United States is distinguished by its large number of *deacons,* among whom are several hundred from the black Catholic community. As heralds of the Gospel and servant ministers of Christ, dear brothers, you complete the threefold ministry of the Sacrament of Orders. In the Church you are called to the service of the word, of the Eucharist and of charity. Your generous response is a clear indication of the growing maturity of the black Catholic community, a maturity emphasized by the black Bishops of your country in their pastoral letter "What We Have Seen and Heard."

## The Holy Spirit Breaks the Shackles of Every Form of Slavery

Even in those days—by the grace of God now long past—when your people struggled under the terrible burden of slavery, brave spirits within the community embraced the evangelical counsels and dedicated themselves to *the religious life.* Thus they bore eloquent witness to the power of the Holy Spirit accomplishing the work of spiritual freedom even in the moment of physical oppression. Black Religious today offer a comparable witness to the Church and society, proclaiming God's Kingdom to a world shackled by consumerism, mindless pleasure-seeking and irresponsible individualism—shackles of the spirit which are *even more destructive than the chains of physical slavery.*

I am close to the whole black community in the great mission and responsibility of encouraging more and more young Americans of their race to respond to the Lord's invitation to religious life and the priesthood. I urge you to be faithful to prayer and to do all you can to ensure that those who are called will find the support and the assistance which they need in order to pursue these vocations and to persevere in them.

## The Christian Life and Witness of Lay People

3. The Church's work of evangelization finds entry into the human community in a special way through the lives of *lay people.* As my predecessor Paul VI pointed out, the laity's "own field of evangelizing activity is the vast and complicated world of

politics, society and economics, but also the world of culture, of the sciences and the arts, of international life, of the mass media" (*Evangelii Nuntiandi*, 70). By fulfilling worthily the broad range of their temporal involvement, lay men and women bear witness in a unique way to *the universal call to holiness*. The witness of their faithful lives speaks an uplifting message to the world.

## The Pope's Love and Esteem for the Black Community

I express *my deep love and esteem for the black Catholic community in the United States*. Its vitality is a sign of hope for society. Composed as you are of many lifelong Catholics, and many who have more recently embraced the faith, together with a growing immigrant community, you reflect the Church's ability to bring together a diversity of people united in faith, hope and love, sharing a communion with Christ in the Holy Spirit. I urge you to keep alive and active *your rich cultural gifts*. Always profess proudly before the whole Church and the whole world *your love for God's word;* it is a special blessing which you must forever treasure as a part of your heritage. Help us all to remember that *authentic freedom* comes from accepting the truth and from living one's life in accordance with it—and the full truth is found only in Christ Jesus. Continue to inspire us by your desire to forgive—as Jesus forgave—and by your *desire to be reconciled* with all the people of this nation, even those who would unjustly deny you the full exercise of your human rights.

## Rediscover the Spirit of Family Life

4. I am sure that you share with me a special concern for that most basic human community, *the family*. Your faithful Christian families are a source of comfort in the face of the extraordinary pressures affecting society. Today, you must *rediscover the spirit of family life* which refuses to be destroyed in the face of even the most oppressive forces. Surely that spirit can be found in exploring your spiritual and cultural heritage. The inspiration you draw from the great men and women of your past will then allow your young people to see the value of a strong family life. Know that the Pope stands united with the black community as it rises to embrace its full dignity and lofty destiny.

## The Family: Domestic Church

The family is *the first setting of evangelization,* the place where the Good News of Christ is first received, and then, in simple yet profound ways, handed on from generation to generation. At the same time, families in our time vitally depend upon the Church to defend their rights and to teach the obligations and responsibilities which lead to the fullness of joy and life. Thus, I urge all of you, especially the clergy and the Religious, to work for the promotion of family values within the local community. And I remind those responsible for making and administering laws and public policies that social problems are never solved, but only worsened, by positions which weaken or destroy the family.

## Because the Black Community in America Suffers, the Church Cannot Be Silent

5. Even in this wealthy nation, committed by its founding fathers to the dignity and equality of all persons, the black community suffers a disproportionate share of economic deprivation. Far too many of your young people receive less than an equal opportunity for a quality education and for gainful employment. The Church must continue to join her efforts with the efforts of others who are working to correct all imbalances and disorders of a social nature. Indeed, *the Church can never remain silent in the face of injustice,* wherever it is clearly present.

## The Nonviolent Witness of the Black Community Is a Monument of Honor

In the most difficult hours of your struggle for civil rights amidst discrimination and oppression, God himself guided your steps along the way of peace. Before the witness of history *the response of nonviolence stands, in the memory of this nation, as a monument of honor to the black community* of the United States. Today, as we recall those who with Christian vision opted for nonviolence as the only truly effective approach for ensuring and safeguarding human dignity, we cannot but think of the Reverend Dr. Martin Luther King, Jr., and of the providential role he played in contributing to the rightful human betterment of black Americans and therefore to the improvement of American society itself.

## Christ's Paschal Mystery Liberates History and Individual Lives

My dear brothers and sisters of the black community: it is the hour to give thanks to God for his liberating action in your history and in your lives. This liberating action *is a sign and expression of Christ's Paschal Mystery,* which in every age is effective in helping God's people to pass from bondage into their glorious vocation of full Christian freedom. And as you offer your prayer of thanksgiving, you must not fail to concern yourselves with the plight of your brothers and sisters in other places throughout the world. *Black Americans must offer their own special solidarity of Christian love to all people who bear the heavy burden of oppression,* whatever its physical or moral nature.

## The Church's Contribution to the Black Community

6. The Catholic Church has made a profound contribution to the lives of many members of the black community in this land through the gift of education received

in *Catholic schools*. Because of the splendid commitment of Dioceses and parishes, many of you here today have joined us at the table of unity and faith as a result of evangelization carried out in these institutions. Catholic schools have a special place in the work of spreading the Gospel of Christ. They are a great gift from God. Keep your Catholic schools strong and active. Their uncompromising *Catholic identity and Catholic witness* at every level must continue to enrich the black communities of this nation.

### The Media: A Tool of Evangelization

7. In addition to the schools, other means of evangelization should also be given priority. Among these *the means of social communication* deserve special attention. The mass media are also a great gift of God's Providence and should be fully utilized in the service of the Gospel of our Lord Jesus Christ. They can be of immense service to millions of black people who long to hear the Good News of salvation proclaimed in ways that speak to their own heritage and traditions.

### The Church Is Truly Catholic

While remaining faithful to her doctrine and discipline, *the Church esteems and honors all cultures;* she respects them in all her evangelizing efforts among the various peoples. At the first Pentecost, those present heard the Apostles speaking in their own languages (see Acts 2:4ff). With the guidance of the Holy Spirit, we try in every age to bring the Gospel convincingly and understandably to people of all races, languages and cultures. It is important to realize that there is no black Church, no white Church, no American Church; but there is and must be, in the one Church of Jesus Christ, a home for blacks, whites, Americans, every culture and race. What I said on another occasion, I willingly repeat: "The Church is catholic . . . because she is able to present in every human context the revealed truth, preserved by her intact in its divine content, in such a way as to bring it into contact with the lofty thoughts and just expectations of every individual and every people" (*Slavorum Apostoli,* 18).

### The Church Needs the Cultural Heritage
### of the Black Community

Dear brothers and sisters: *your black cultural heritage enriches the Church* and makes her witness of universality more complete. In a real way *the Church needs you, just as you need the Church,* for you are part of the Church and the Church is part of you. As you continue to place this heritage at the service of the whole Church for the spread of the Gospel, the Holy Spirit himself will continue through you his work of evangelization. With a joyful and a hopeful heart, I entrust you and the whole black community to the loving care of Mary, Mother of our Savior. May she, who both listened to the word and believed in it, guide your lives and those of future genera-tions of black Catholics within the one People of God, the one Mystical Body of

Christ. Through her intercession may grace be to all of you "who love our Lord Jesus Christ with unfailing love" (Eph. 6:23).

## 13. MEETING WITH LEADERSHIP IN CATHOLIC ELEMENTARY, SECONDARY AND RELIGIOUS EDUCATION

Dear Brothers and Sisters,

### A Day of Prayerful Celebration of Catholic Education in the United States

1. I thank all of you for your warm welcome and I praise our Lord and Savior Jesus Christ who gives me this opportunity to meet with you, *the representatives of Catholic elementary and secondary schools and leaders in religious education.* My first word to you is one of esteem and encouragement: I wish to assure you that I fully appreciate the extraordinary importance of your commitment to Catholic education. I commend you for your concern for the vitality and Catholic identity of the educational centers in which you work, throughout the length and breadth of the United States. I encourage you to continue to fulfill *your special role within the Church and within society* in a spirit of generous responsibility, intelligent creativity and the pursuit of excellence.

### Religious Freedom Has Allowed Growth of Catholic Schools

2. It is fitting that we should be meeting in this historic city, itself the meeting point of several rich cultures, where the Capuchin Fathers and the Ursuline Sisters founded schools at the very dawn of your emergence as a nation. You are preparing to observe *the two hundredth anniversary of the signing of the Constitution of the United States.* There is no doubt that the guarantee of religious freedom enshrined in the Bill of Rights has helped make possible the marvelous growth of Catholic education in this country.

Over the years much has been attempted and much has been achieved by Catholics in the United States to make available for their children the best education possible. Much has been done in the specific area of bringing the wealth of our Catholic faith to children and adults in the home, in schools, and through religious education programs. The presence of the Church in the field of education is wonderfully manifested in the vast and dynamic network of schools and educational programs extending from preschool through the adult years. *The entire ecclesial community*—Bishops, priests, Religious, the laity—the Church in all her parts, *is called to value ever more deeply the importance of this task and mission, and to continue to give it full and enthusiastic support.*

## Men and Women Religious:
## Witnesses to the Gospel in Catholic Education

3. In the beginning and for a long time afterward, women and men Religious bore the chief organizational and teaching responsibilities in Catholic education in this country. As pioneers they met that challenge splendidly and they continue to meet it today. The Church and, I am certain, the nation will forever feel a debt of gratitude toward them. The importance of *the presence of committed Religious, and of religious communities, in the educational apostolate has not diminished with time*. It is my heartfelt prayer that the Lord will continue to call many young people to the religious life, and that their witness to the Gospel will remain a central element in Catholic education.

## Lay Teachers: Full Partners in Catholic Education

4. In recent years, thousands of *lay people* have come forward as administrators and teachers in the Church's schools and educational programs. By accepting and developing the legacy of Catholic thought and educational experience which they have inherited, they take their place as *full partners in the Church's mission* of educating the whole person and of transmitting the Good News of salvation in Jesus Christ to successive generations of young Americans. Even if they do not "teach religion," their service in a Catholic school or educational program is part of the Church's unceasing endeavor to lead all to "profess the truth in love and grow to the full maturity of Christ the head" (Eph. 4:15).

I am aware that not all questions relating to the organization, financing and administration of Catholic schools in an increasingly complex society have been resolved to the satisfaction of all. We hope that such matters will be settled with justice and fairness for all. In this regard it is important to proceed in a proper perspective. For a Catholic educator, the Church should not be looked upon merely as an employer. The Church is the Body of Christ, carrying on the mission of the Redeemer throughout history. It is our privilege to share in that mission, to which we are called by the grace of God and in which we are engaged together.

## Parents: First and Foremost Educators

5. Permit me, brothers and sisters, to mention briefly something that is of special concern to the Church. I refer to *the rights and duties of parents in the education of their children*. The Second Vatican Council clearly enunciated the Church's position: "Since parents have conferred life on their children, they have a most solemn obligation to educate their offspring. Hence, parents must be acknowledged as the first and foremost educators of their children" (*Gravissimum Educationis*, 3). In comparison with the educational role of all others their role is primary; it is also *irreplaceable and inalienable*. It would be wrong for anyone to attempt to usurp that unique responsibility (see *Familiaris Consortio*, 36). Nor should parents in any way be penalized for choosing for their children an education according to their beliefs.

## Catholic Educators Cooperate with Parents

Parents need to ensure that their own homes are places where spiritual and moral values are lived. They are right to insist that their children's faith be respected and fostered. As educators you correctly see your role as cooperating with parents in their primary responsibility. Your efforts to involve them in the whole educational process are commendable. This is an area in which pastors and other priests can be especially supportive. To these I wish to say: try to make every effort to ensure that religious education programs and, where possible, parish schools are *an important part of your ministry;* support and encourage teachers, administrators and parents in their work. Few efforts are more important for the present and future well-being of the Church and of the nation than efforts expended in the work of education.

## Quality Catholic Education for the Poor

6. *Catholic schools* in the United States have always enjoyed *a reputation for academic excellence and community service.* Very often they serve large numbers of poor children and young people, and are attentive to the needs of minority groups. I heartily encourage you to continue to provide quality Catholic education for the poor of all races and national backgrounds, even at the cost of great sacrifice. We cannot doubt that such is part of God's call to the Church in the United States. It is a responsibility that is deeply inscribed in the history of Catholic education in this country.

## Catholic Schools Form Communities in Gospel Values

On another occasion, speaking to the Bishops of the United States, I mentioned that the Catholic school "has contributed immensely to the spreading of God's word and has enabled the faithful 'to relate human affairs and activities with religious values in a single living synthesis' (*Sapientia Christiana,* 1). In the community formed by the Catholic school, the power of the Gospel has been brought to bear on thought patterns, standards of judgment and norms of behavior. As an institution the Catholic school has to be judged extremely favorably if we apply the sound criterion: 'You will know them by their deeds' (Mt. 7:16), and again, 'You can tell a tree by its fruit' (Mt. 7:20)" (Address of October 28, 1983).

## Heroic Sacrifices for Catholic Education

At this point I cannot fail to praise the *financial sacrifices of American Catholics* as well as the substantial contributions of individual benefactors, foundations, organizations and businesses to Catholic education in the United States. The heroic sacrifices of generations of Catholic parents in building up and supporting parochial and diocesan schools must never be forgotten. Rising costs may call for new approaches, new forms of partnership and sharing, new uses of financial resources. But I am sure that all concerned will face the challenge of Catholic schools with courage and dedication, and not doubt the value of the sacrifices to be made.

## Catholic Education Teaches the Dignity of the Human Person

7. But there is another challenge facing all those who are concerned with Catholic education. It is the pressing challenge of clearly identifying *the aims of Catholic education* and applying proper methods in Catholic elementary and secondary education and religious education programs. It is the challenge of fully understanding the educational enterprise, of properly evaluating its content, and *of transmitting the full truth concerning the human person,* created in God's image and called to life in Christ through the Holy Spirit.

## Essential Criterion: Fidelity to Church Teaching

The *content of the individual courses* in Catholic education is important both in religious teaching and in all the other subjects that go to make up the total instruction of human persons and to prepare them for their life's work and their eternal destiny. It is fitting that teachers should be constantly challenged by *high professional standards in preparing and teaching their courses.* In regard to the content of religion courses, the essential criterion is fidelity to the teaching of the Church.

## Educators Form the Character of Students

Educators are likewise in a splendid position to inculcate into young people *right ethical attitudes.* These include attitudes toward material things and their proper use. The whole life-style of students will reflect the attitudes that they form during their years of formal education.

In these tasks you will find guidance in many documents of the Church. Your own Bishops, applying the universal teaching of the Church, have helped point the way for you, notably in their pastoral letter *To Teach As Jesus Did,* and in The National Catechetical Directory. I would also remind you of the Holy See's documents on *The Catholic School* and *Lay Catholics in Schools: Witnesses to Faith.* There we are reminded that it is the school's task to cultivate in students the intellectual, creative and aesthetic faculties of the individual; to develop in students the ability to make correct use of their judgment, will and affectivity; to promote in them a sense of values; to encourage just attitudes and prudent behavior; to introduce them to the cultural patrimony handed down from previous generations; to prepare them for their working lives, and to encourage the friendly interchange among students of diverse cultures and backgrounds that will lead to mutual understanding and love.

## Ultimate Goal of Catholic Education:
## Salvation in Jesus Christ

8. *The ultimate goal of all Catholic education is salvation in Jesus Christ.* Catholic educators effectively work for the coming of Christ's Kingdom; this work includes transmitting clearly and in full the message of salvation, which elicits the response of faith. In faith we know God, and the hidden purpose of his will (see Eph. 1:9). In

faith we truly come to know ourselves. *By sharing our faith we communicate a complete vision of the whole of reality and a commitment to truth and goodness.* This vision and this commitment draw the strands of life into a purposeful pattern. By enriching your students' lives with the fullness of Christ's message and by inviting them to accept with all their hearts Christ's work, which is the Church, you promote most effectively their integral human development and you help them to build a community of faith, hope and love.

This Christian message is the more urgent for those young ones who come from broken homes and who, often with only one parent to encourage them, must draw support and direction from their teachers in school.

## Creative Methodology and Catholic Truth

In your apostolate of helping to bring Christ's message into the lives of your students, the whole Church supports you and stands with you. The Synod of Bishops, in particular, has recognized the importance of your task and the difficulties you face. For these reasons it has called for concerted efforts to compose a universal catechism. This project will not eliminate the great challenge of a need for creativity in methodology, nor will it minimize the continued need for the inculturation of the Gospel, but it will assist all the local Churches in effectively presenting in its integrity the content of Catholic teaching. In the Church in America, an important part of the truly *glorious chapter of Catholic education* has been the transmitting of Christ's message through *religious education programs* designed for children and young people outside Catholic schools. For this too I give thanks to God, recalling all those who throughout the history of this nation have so generously collaborated in this "work of faith and labor of love" (1 Thes. 1:30).

## Build Community

9. *Community is at the heart of all Catholic education,* not simply as a concept to be taught, but as a reality to be lived. In its deepest Christian sense, community is a sharing in the life of the Blessed Trinity. Your students will learn to understand and appreciate the value of community *as they experience love, trust and loyalty in your schools and educational programs,* and as they learn to treat all persons as brothers and sisters created by God and redeemed by Christ. Help them to grasp this sense of community by active participation in the life of the parish and the Diocese and especially by receiving the Sacraments of Penance and the Eucharist. The Second Vatican Council explicitly includes learning to adore God in spirit and in truth among the aims of all Christian education (see *Gravissimum Educationis,* 2).

A sense of community implies *openness to the wider community.* Often, today, Catholic education takes place in changing neighborhoods; it requires respect for cultural diversity, love for those of different ethnic backgrounds, service to those in need, without discrimination. Help your students to see themselves as members of the universal Church and the world community. Help them to understand the implications of justice and mercy. Foster in your students *a social consciousness* which will move them to meet the needs of their neighbors, and to discern and seek to remove the sources of injustice in society. No human anxiety or sorrow should leave the disciples of Jesus Christ indifferent.

### Holiness: A Gift Offered to All

10. The world needs more than just social reformers. It needs saints. Holiness is not the privilege of a few; it is a gift offered to all. *The call to holiness is addressed also to you and to your students.* To doubt this is to misjudge Christ's intentions: for "each of us has received God's favor in the measure in which Christ bestowed it" (Eph. 4:7).

Brothers and sisters: take Jesus Christ the Teacher as the model of your service, as your guide and source of strength. He himself has told us: *"You address me as 'Teacher' and 'Lord,' and fittingly enough, for that is what I am"* (Jn. 13:13). He taught in word and deed, and his teaching cannot be separated from his life and being. In the apostolic exhortation on catechesis I stated: "The whole of Christ's life was a continual teaching: his silences, his miracles, his gestures, his prayer, his love for people, his special affection for the little and the poor, his acceptance of the total sacrifice on the Cross for the Redemption of the world, and his Resurrection. . . . Hence for Christians the crucifix is one of the most sublime and popular images of Christ the Teacher" (*Catechesi Tradendae,* 9).

### Openness to God

11. Dear friends: Jesus shares with you his teaching ministry. Only in close communion with him can you respond adequately. This is my hope, this is my prayer: *that you will be totally open to Christ.* That he will give you an ever greater love for your students and an ever stronger commitment to your vocation as Catholic educators. If you continue to be faithful to the ministry today, as you have been in the past, you will be doing much in shaping a peaceful, just and hope-filled world for the future. *Yours is a great gift to the Church, a great gift to your nation.*

### 14. YOUTH RALLY

### PART I

Dear Young People of New Orleans,

Dear Young People of America,

### You Are Partners in the Mission of the Church

1. Listening to what you are telling me by your presence and through your representatives, I know that you are *very much conscious of having a special mission in this world,* of being partners in the mission of the Church.

I also know that in fulfilling your mission you are willing to give, you are willing to share and you are willing to serve. And you are willing to do all this, *together,* not alone! In this you are like Jesus: Jesus *gave* and he *served* and he was never alone. He tells us: "The one who sent me is with me. He has not left me alone" (Jn. 8:29).

### Let No One Deceive You in Any Way

Yes, dear young people, I too want *to speak about your mission,* the reason for your life on earth, *the truth of your lives.* It is extremely vital for you to have a clear idea of your mission, to avoid being confused or deceived. In speaking to the Christians of his time, Saint Paul explicitly urged them: "Let no one deceive you in any way" (2 Thes. 2:3). And today I say the same to you, young people of America: "Let no one deceive you in any way"—about your mission, about the truth, about where you are going. *Let no one deceive you about the truth of your lives.*

### The Opposite of Deception Is Truth: Jesus Christ

2. But what is the opposite of deception? Where can you turn to find answers that satisfy, answers that will last? The opposite of deception is truth—the person who *tells* the truth, the person who *is* the truth. Yes, *the opposite of deception is Jesus Christ,* who tells us: "I am the way, and *the truth,* and the life" (Jn. 14:6). Jesus Christ is the Son of God. He reveals the truth of God. But he is also man. He shares in our humanity and came into the world to teach us about ourselves, to help us discover ourselves.

### No One Is Free While Living Under the
### Power of Error or the Deceit of Sin

You young people are proud to live in a free country and you should be grateful to God for *your freedom.* But even though you can come and go as you like, and do what you want, you are not really free if you are living under the power of error or falsehood, or deceit, or sin. Only Jesus Christ can make you fully free through his truth. And that is why he added: "If the Son frees you, you will really be free" (Jn. 8:32,36). Dear young people: the whole message of Jesus in the Gospels and through his Church helps you to discover who you really are, to discover all the dimensions of your lives.

### God Loves Us and Has a Plan for Us

3. Each of us is *an individual,* a person, a creature of God, one of his children, someone very special whom God loves and for whom Christ died. This identity of ours determines the way we must live, the way we must act, the way we must view our mission in the world. We come from God, we depend on God, *God has a plan for*

*us*—a plan for our lives, for our bodies, for our souls, for our future. This plan for us is extremely important, so important that God became man to explain it to us.

## We Are Individuals Called to Community in Christ

In God's plan we are individuals—yes—but we are also part of a *community*. The Second Vatican Council emphasized the fact that God did not call us to share his life merely as unrelated individuals. Rather he wanted to mold us into a people as his sons and daughters (see *Ad Gentes,* 2). This aspect of our being a community, of our sharing God's life as a people, is part of our identity—who we are, what we are, where we are going.

## Freedom Brings with It Responsibility

Right away we can see that as persons we have responsibilities and that *these responsibilities are part of our freedom.* The Vatican Council went so far as to say that "man is defined first of all by his responsibilities toward his brothers and sisters and toward history" (*Gaudium et Spes,* 55).

To understand ourselves as members of a community, as individuals linked together to make up the People of God, *as persons with responsibility for others is a* great insight—an insight that is necessary for fulfilling our mission properly.

## There Is No Room for Self

4. As Christians you have these insights, and Christ today wants to reinforce them in you. You speak about "being partners," of sharing and serving and working together. And all of this is linked to God's plan, according to which we are brothers and sisters in Christ—brothers and sisters who belong to the People of God and who are made to live in community, to think about others, to help others. Dear young people of America: in the Church there are many different gifts. There is room for many different cultures and ways of doing things. *But there is no room in the Church for selfishness.* There is no room in the world for selfishness. It destroys the meaning of life; it destroys the meaning of love; it reduces the human person to a subhuman level.

## Solidarity Between All the Young People of the World

When we speak about the need of being open to others, of taking into account the community, of fulfilling our responsibilities to all our brothers and sisters, we are actually talking about the whole world. Your mission as young people today is to *the whole world.* In what sense? You can never forget the interdependence of human beings wherever they are. When Jesus tells us to love our neighbor he does not set a geographical limit. What is needed today is a solidarity between all the young people of the world—a solidarity especially with the poor and all those in need. You young people must change society *by your lives* of justice and fraternal love. It is not just a question of your own country, but of the whole world. This is certainly your mission, dear young people. You are partners with each other, partners with the whole Church, *partners with Christ.*

## To Change the World in Jesus' Name

5. In order, however, to accomplish this great work, to be in a condition to change the world in the name of Jesus, you yourselves must actually be living according to your own identity, *according to God's plan for your lives.* Once again it is the word of Jesus that directs your lives and tells you what that plan is. You remember how much Jesus insisted on the commandment of love, how much he insisted on living according to certain norms, called the Beatitudes: "Blessed are the meek . . . Blessed are the merciful . . . Blessed are the clean of heart . . . Blessed are the peacemakers." All of this is part of the plan.

Believe no one who contradicts Christ. When Saint Paul says, "Let no one deceive you," he is in effect saying: Do not believe anyone who contradicts Jesus or his message, which is transmitted to you by the Church. Jesus speaks to you young people and tells you the value of meekness, mercy and humility. Other voices in the world will immediately shout out: "weakness!" In the Gospel Jesus emphasizes the value of honesty, uprightness, justice and fairness. But when you practice these virtues, you are liable to be accused of being "naive." Jesus and his Church hold up to you God's plan for human love, telling you that sex is a great gift of God that is reserved for marriage. At this point the voices of the world will try to deceive you, with powerful slogans, claiming that you are "unrealistic," "out of it," "backward," even "reactionary." But the message of Jesus is clear: purity means true love and it is the total opposite of selfishness and escape.

## The Purpose of Freedom: To Say "Yes" to God

6. Jesus' message applies to all the areas of life. He reveals to us the truth of our lives and all aspects of this truth. Jesus tells us that *the purpose of our freedom is to say "yes" to God's plan for our lives.* What makes our "yes" so important is that we say it freely; we are able to say "no." Jesus teaches us that we are accountable to God, that we must follow our consciences, but that our consciences must be formed according to God's plan for our lives. In all our relationships to other people and to the world, Jesus teaches us what we must do, how we must live in order not to be deceived, in order to walk in truth. And today, dear young people, I proclaim to you again Jesus Christ: *the way* and the truth and the life—your way, *your truth* and your life.

*What is in accord with the truth of Jesus is fulfillment, joy and peace,* even if it means effort and discipline. What is not in accord with his truth means disorder, and when done deliberately it means sin. Deliberate or not, it eventually means unhappiness and frustration.

## The Supreme Theft: Robbing One of Hope

7. It is with the truth of Jesus, dear young people, that you must face the great questions in your lives, as well as the practical problems. The world will try to deceive you about many things that matter: about your faith, about pleasure and material things, about the dangers of drugs. And at one stage or another the false voices of the world will try to exploit your human weakness by telling you that life has no meaning at all for you. *The supreme theft in your lives would be if they succeeded in robbing you of hope.* They will try but not succeed if you hold fast to Jesus and his truth.

## Invincible in Hope

*The truth* of Jesus *is capable of reinforcing all your energies.* It will unify your lives and consolidate your sense of mission. You may still be vulnerable to attack from the pressures of the world, from the forces of evil, from the power of the devil. *But you will be invincible in hope:* "in Christ Jesus our hope" (1 Tm. 1:1).

## The Church's Response to the Culture of Death and Deceit: The Truth of Jesus

Dear young people: *the word of Jesus and his truth* and his promises of fulfillment and life *are the Church's response* to the culture of death, to the onslaughts of doubt and to the cancer of despair.

Let me just add two practical thoughts from the Second Vatican Council. The Council tells us that we must avoid thinking that we have at hand the solutions to all the *particular* problems of life. But at the same time the Church knows that *she possesses the light* in which the solutions to the problems of humanity *can be discovered* (see *Gaudium et Spes*, 12, 33). What is this light? What can it be? Only *the truth of Jesus Christ!*

## PART II

Dear Young People,

## Communion with God in Prayer

8. I would like to add something else to what I have already said to you. I would like to speak to you briefly about *prayer,* about communion with God, a communion that is deeply personal between ourselves and God.

In prayer we express to God our feelings, our thoughts, our sentiments. We wish to love and to be loved, to be understood and to understand. Only God loves us perfectly, with an everlasting love. In prayer, we open our hearts and our minds to this God of love. And it is prayer that makes us one with the Lord. Through prayer we come to share more deeply in God's life and in his love.

## Jesus: Active Ministry and Deep Prayer

9. One of the most striking things about Jesus was *his habit of prayer*. In the midst of an active public ministry, we find him going away by himself to be alone in silence and communion with his Father in heaven. On the Sabbath, he made it a practice to go to the synagogue and pray with others in common. When he was together with his disciples, or when he was by himself, he prayed to the Father, whom he dearly loved.

Saint Mark's Gospel describes an evening in Capernaum when Jesus cured many who were sick and expelled many demons. After giving us this description of Christ's generous care for others, Saint Mark adds: "Rising early the next morning, he went off to a lonely place in the desert; there *he was absorbed in prayer*" (Mk. 1:35).

And Saint Luke informs us that, before Jesus selected the Twelve to be his Apostles, *"he went out to the mountain to pray, spending the night in communion with God"* (Lk. 6:12). In fact, it seems that it was his example of prayer that *prompted his disciples to want to pray:* "One day he was praying in a certain place," Luke tells us, and "when he had finished, one of his disciples asked him, 'Lord, teach us to pray'" (Lk. 11:1). That was the occasion when Jesus taught them the prayer we call the "Lord's Prayer," or the "Our Father."

## Prayer Is the Key to Your Life in Christ

10. If you really wish to follow Christ, if you want your love for him to grow and last, then you must be *faithful to prayer*. It is *the key to the vitality of your life in Christ*. Without prayer, your faith and love will die. If you are constant in daily prayer and in the Sunday celebration of Mass, your love for Jesus will increase. And your heart will know deep joy and peace, such as the world could never give.

But many young people tell me that they do not know *how to pray,* or they wonder if they are praying in a way that is correct. Here again, you must look to the example of Christ. How did Jesus himself pray?

First of all, we know that his prayer is marked by a spirit of joy and praise. *"Jesus rejoiced in the Holy Spirit* and said: 'I offer you praise, O Father, Lord of heaven and earth'" (Lk. 10:21). In addition, he entrusted to the Church at the Last Supper the celebration of the Eucharist, which remains for all ages the most perfect means of offering to the Father glory and thanksgiving and praise.

Yet, there were also times of suffering when, in great pain and struggle, Jesus poured out his heart to God, seeking to find in his Father both comfort and support. For example, in the Garden of Gethsemane, when the inner struggle became even more difficult, then, *"in his anguish he prayed with all the greater intensity,* and his sweat became like drops of blood falling to the ground" (Lk. 22:44). "He prayed with all the greater intensity"—what an example for us when we find life difficult, when we face a painful decision or when we struggle with temptation. At times like these, Jesus prayed with all the greater intensity. We must do the same!

## Never Cease to Pray

When it is difficult therefore to pray, the *most important thing* is *not to stop praying,* not to give up the effort. At these times, *turn to the Bible* and to *the Church's liturgy.* Meditate on the life and teachings of Jesus as recorded in the Gospels. Ponder the wisdom and counsel of the Apostles and the challenging messages of the Prophets. Try to make your own the beautiful prayers of the Psalms. You will find in the inspired word of God the spiritual food you need. Above all, your soul will be refreshed when you take part wholeheartedly with the community in the celebration of the Eucharist, the Church's greatest prayer.

## To Know and to Do the Will of Jesus

11. Do you recall the story of Jesus and his Mother Mary at the wedding feast of Cana? At a certain point in the feast, when they have run out of wine, Mary tells those waiting on table, *"Do whatever he tells you"* (Jn. 2:5). When the waiters follow Mary's advice, Jesus rewards their faith and changes water into wine, a wine that far surpasses the quality of what had been served before. And Mary's advice still holds true today. For the true success of our lives consists *in knowing and doing the will of Jesus,* in doing whatever Jesus tells us. When you pray, you must realize that prayer is not just asking God for something or seeking special help, even though prayers of petition are true ways of praying. But prayer should also be characterized by *thanksgiving and praise,* by *adoration and attentive listening,* by *asking God's pardon* and forgiveness. If you follow Jesus' advice, and pray to God constantly, then you will learn to pray well. God himself will teach you.

## Prayer: Looking Away from Oneself to God

Prayer can truly change your life. For it turns your attention away from yourself and directs your mind and your heart toward the Lord. If we look only at ourselves, with our own limitations and sins, we quickly give way to sadness and discouragement. But if we keep *our eyes fixed on the Lord,* then our hearts are filled with hope, our minds are washed in the light of truth, and we come to know the fullness of the Gospel with all its promise and life.

## The Holy Spirit Inflames Our Hearts
## with Enthusiasm for God and Love of Neighbor

12. Prayer also helps us *to be open to the Holy Spirit,* the Spirit of truth and love, the Spirit who was given to the Church so that she could fulfill her mission in the world. It is the Holy Spirit who gives us the strength to resist evil and do good, to do our part in building up the Kingdom of God.

It is significant that the symbol of the Holy Spirit on Pentecost was *tongues of fire.* In fact, fire is often the symbol that the Bible uses to speak of the action of God in our lives. For the Holy Spirit truly inflames our hearts, engendering in them enthusiasm for the works of God. And when we pray, the Holy Spirit stirs up within us love of God and love of our neighbor.

### The World Cannot Offer Lasting Joy or Peace

*The Holy Spirit brings us joy and peace.* The modern technological world can offer us many pleasures, many comforts of life. It can even offer us temporary escapes from life. But what the world can never offer is lasting joy and peace. And these are the gifts that I ask for you, so that you may be strong in hope and persevering in love. But *the condition for all of this is prayer,* which means contact with Christ, communion with God.

Dear young people: my message to you is not new. I have given it before and, with God's grace, I will give it again. And so, as long as the memory of this visit lasts, may it be recorded that I, John Paul II, came to America *to call you to Christ, to invite you to pray!*

### 15. HOMILY AT NEW ORLEANS MASS

"My Lord, be patient with me and I will pay you back in full." (Mt. 18:26; see v. 29)

Dear Brothers and Sisters in Christ,

### All Are Debtors to God: Forgiven and Forgiving

1. This plea is heard twice in the *Gospel parable.* The first time it is made by the servant who owes his master ten thousand talents—an astonishingly high sum according to the value of money in New Testament times. Shortly afterward the plea is repeated by another servant of the same master. He too is in debt, not to his master, but to his fellow servant. And his debt is only a tiny fraction of the debt that his fellow servant had forgiven.

The point of the parable is the fact that the servant with the greatest debt receives understanding from the master to whom he owes much money. The Gospel tells us that "the master let the official go and wrote off the debt" (Mt. 18:27). Yet that same servant would not listen to the plea of his fellow servant who owed him money. He had *no pity* on him, but "had him put in jail until he paid back what he owed" (Mt. 18:30).

Jesus often used parables like this one in his teaching; they are *a special method of proclaiming the Good News.* They enable the listener to grasp more easily the "Divine Reality" which Jesus came to reveal. In today's parable, we sense almost immediately that it is a prelude to the words which Jesus commands us to use when we pray to our heavenly Father: *"forgive us our debts, as we forgive our debtors"* (Mt. 6:12).

These words from the "Our Father" also have something very important to teach us. If we want God to hear us when we plead like the servant—"Have patience with me"—then we must be equally willing to listen to our neighbor when he pleads: "Give me time and I will pay you back in full." Otherwise we cannot expect pardon from God, but punishment instead. In the parable the servant is punished because, though a debtor himself, he is intolerant as a creditor toward his fellow servant.

Christ is very clear: when we ourselves are without sympathy or mercy, when we are guided by *"blind" justice* alone, then we cannot count on the mercy of that "Great Creditor" who is God—God, before whom we are all debtors.

### God's Justice Is Merciful

2. In the parable, we find two different standards or ways of measuring: *God's standard and man's standard.* The divine standard is one in which justice is totally permeated by *merciful love.* The human standard is inclined to stop at justice alone— justice which is without mercy, and which in a sense is "blind" with regard to man.

### Man's Justice Is Often Vengeful

Indeed, human justice is often governed by *hatred and revenge,* as the first reading from the Book of Sirach reminds us. It reads—and the words of the Old Testament are strong—"Should a man nourish anger against his fellow and expect healing from the Lord? . . . If he who is but flesh cherishes wrath, who will forgive his sins? . . . Remember your last days, set enmity aside. . . . Think of the commandments, hate not your neighbor. . . . Should a man refuse mercy to his fellows, yet seek pardon for his own sins?" (Sir. 28:3,5–7,4).

The exhortations in the Book of Sirach and in the Gospel both move in the same direction. The human way of measuring—the measure of justice alone—which is often "blind" or "blinded" by hatred—*must accept God's standard.* Otherwise, justice by itself easily becomes injustice, as we see expressed in the Latin saying: *summum ius, summa iniuria.* The rigorous application of the law can sometimes be the height of injustice.

As I said in my encyclical letter on the Mercy of God: "In every sphere of interpersonal relationships justice must, so to speak, be *'corrected'* to a considerable extent by that love which, as Saint Paul proclaims, 'is patient and kind' or, in other words, possesses the characteristics of that merciful love which is so much of the essence of the Gospel and Christianity" (*Dives in Misericordia,* 14).

### The Gospel's Radical Command: Merciful Love

3. Merciful love is also the basis of the Lord's answer to Peter's question: "When my brother wrongs me, how often must I forgive him? Seven times?" "No," Jesus replied, "not seven times; I say, *seventy times seven times*" (Mt. 18:21–22). In the symbolic language of the Bible, this means that we must be able to forgive everyone

every time. Surely this is one of the most difficult and *radical* commands of the Gospel. Yet how much suffering and anguish, how much futility, destruction and violence would be avoided if only we put into practice in all our human relationships the Lord's answer to Peter.

## Merciful Love Is Essential in Marriage and in Families

Merciful love is absolutely necessary, in particular, *for people who are close* to one another: for husbands and wives, parents and children, and among friends (see *Dives in Misericordia,* 14). At a time when family life is under such great stress, when a high number of divorces and broken homes are a sad fact of life, we must ask ourselves whether human relationships are being based, as they should be, on the merciful love and forgiveness revealed by God in Jesus Christ. We must examine our own heart and see how willing we are to forgive and to accept forgiveness in this world as well as in the next.

## Without Merciful Love There Is Brokenness and Suffering

No relationship as intense and close as marriage and the family can survive without forgiveness "seventy times seven times." If couples cannot forgive with the tenderness and sensitivity that mercy brings, then they will inevitably begin to see their relationship only in terms of justice, of what is mine and what is yours— emotionally, spiritually and materially—and in terms of real or perceived injustices. This can lead to *estrangement and divorce,* and often develops into a bitter dispute about property and, more tragically, about children. The plight of the children alone should make us realize that the refusal to forgive is not in keeping with the true nature of marriage as God established it and as he wants it to be lived. No doubt some people will object that Christ's teaching about the indissolubility of marriage, as it is upheld by the Church, is lacking in compassion. But what must be seen is the ineffectiveness of divorce, and its ready availability in modern society, to bring mercy and forgiveness and healing to so many couples and their children, in whose troubled lives there remain a brokenness and a suffering that will not go away. The words of the merciful Christ, who fully understands the human heart, remain forever: "What therefore God has joined together, let no man put asunder" (Mt. 19:6).

## The Goal of Forgiveness Is Not Contrary to Justice

At the same time, merciful love and forgiveness are never meant to cancel out *a person's right to justice,* even in marriage. In the encyclical to which I referred a moment ago I said that "properly understood, justice constitutes . . . the goal of forgiveness. In no passage of the Gospel message does forgiveness or mercy . . . mean indulgence toward evil, scandals, injury or insult. . . . Reparation for evil and scandal, compensation for injury, and satisfaction for insult are conditions for forgiveness" (*Dives in Misericordia,* 14). All forgiveness requires repentant love.

## Mercy Instead of "Blind" Justice of Financial Mechanism

This also applies in the wider context of *social, political, cultural and economic* life within and among nations and peoples. May we not hope for what Pope Paul VI described as the "civilization of love" instead of "an eye for an eye and a tooth for a tooth" attitude which ravages the face of the earth and scars the family of mankind? As I have said, this love, based on the forgiveness which Jesus described to Peter, does not mean that the objective demands of justice, which people legitimately seek, are thereby canceled out. Sometimes those demands, however, are very complex.

A case with special urgency today is *the international debt question.* As you know, many developing countries are heavily in debt to industrialized nations, and for a variety of reasons are finding it harder and harder to repay their loans. "Blind" justice alone cannot solve this problem in an ethical way that promotes the human good of all parties. Merciful love calls for mutual understanding and a recognition of human priorities and needs, above and beyond the "blind" justice of financial mechanisms. We must arrive at solutions that truly reflect both complete justice and mercy (see *At the Service of the Human Community: An Ethical Approach to the International Debt Question,* Pontifical Commission, *Iustitia et Pax,* 1986).

## To Do Justice—But Also to Love

The nature of the Church's concern in these matters is reflected in the pastoral message on the American economy issued by the Bishops of the United States. They say: "We write . . . as heirs of the biblical prophets who summon us 'to do justice, to love kindness and to walk humbly with our God' (Mi. 6:8). . . . We speak as moral teachers, not economic technicians. We seek . . . to lift up the human and ethical dimensions of economic life" (nos. 4, 7). *To do justice, yes—but also to love.* This is at the heart of Christ's message. It is the only way to reach that "civilization of love" that ensures peace for ourselves and for the world.

## Debtors for Creation and for Redemption

4. "Forgive us . . . as we forgive."

The Eucharist which we are celebrating and in which we are taking part is linked to the deepest truth of these words. Each time we participate in the Eucharist, we must *translate,* as it were, the parable of today's Gospel into the reality of that Sacrament which is the "great mystery of faith." When we gather together, we must be aware of how much we are *debtors to God the Creator, God the Redeemer.* Debtors— first for our Creation, and then for our Redemption. The Psalmist exclaims:

Bless the Lord, O my soul;
and all my being, bless his holy name.
Bless . . . and forget not all his benefits.
(Ps. 102/103:1–2)

This exhortation is directed to each one of us, and at the same time to the whole community of believers. Forget not . . . the gift of God. Forget not . . . that you have received his bounty: *in Creation*—that is to say, in your existence and in all that is in and around you; *in Redemption*—in that grace of adoption as sons and daughters of God in Christ, at the price of his Cross.

### We Who Are Forgiven Must Give the Gift of Forgiveness

When we receive a gift we are a debtor. Indeed we are more than a debtor because it is not possible to repay a gift adequately. And yet we must try. *We must give a gift in return for a gift.* God's generous gift must be repaid by our gift. And our gift, reflecting as it does our great limitations, must aim at imitating the divine generosity, the divine standard of giving. In Christ our gift must be transformed, so as to unite us with God. The Eucharist is the Sacrament of such a *transformation.* Christ himself makes us "an everlasting gift to the Father." Truly this is the great mystery of faith and love.

### New Orleans: A Home to Racial and Cultural Diversity

5. "Forgive us our debts, as we forgive our debtors."

With these words from the prayer taught to us by the Son of God, I address all those gathered here in *New Orleans* in the spirit of the Gospel, all those who make up the Eucharistic assemblies of the local Churches of this region. I greet you as the proud heirs of *a rich and diverse cultural history,* as people who can therefore appreciate the need for merciful love among individuals and groups. Here we have represented the cultures of France and other European nations, of black people, Hispanics and more recently Vietnamese. Today this region continues to be the home of various races and cultures now united in one nation, the United States.

### You Are the Recipients of Numerous Gifts

All of those races and cultures have enriched the life of your local Church within the distinctively French heritage that men like Robert Cavelier, Sieur de la Salle, and Jean Baptiste Le Moyne, Sieur de Bienville, conferred upon this land centuries ago. You are also a people who have only to look about you to see the many *wonderful gifts* conferred by the mighty Mississippi River and its fertile delta, and by the riches of the sea. All this comes to you as a gift from God. By wise stewardship and the responsible use of these resources, you can find dignity in your work as you seek to provide for yourselves and your families. May you continue to work in harmony for the good of the society you belong to, always keeping in mind the words of Christ's prayer: "Forgive us our debts, as we forgive our debtors."

### Your Genius and Industry Are Gifts from God

*Modern man* easily forgets the proportion, or rather, the lack of proportion between what he has received and what he is obliged to give. He has grown so much in his own eyes, and is so sure that everything is the work of his own genius and of his own "industry," that he no longer sees the One who is the Alpha and the Omega, the Beginning and the End, the One who is the First Source of all that is, as well as its Final End, the One in whom all that exists finds its proper meaning.

## You Have Received Gifts from God, Now Repay Him with Gifts to His Image

Modern man easily *forgets that he has received a great gift.* Yet, at the base of all that he is and of all that the world is, there is the gift—the free gift of Love. As man loses this awareness, he also *forgets the debt* and the fact that he is a debtor. He loses his *consciousness of sin.* Many people today, especially those caught up in a civilization of affluence and pleasure, live as though sin did not exist and as if God did not exist.

For this reason we need to listen with special attention to the Letter to the Romans: "None of us lives as his own master and none of us dies as his own master. While we live we are responsible to the Lord, and when we die we die as his servants. Both in life and in death we are the Lord's. That is why Christ died and came to life again, that he might be Lord of both the dead and the living" (Rom. 14:7–9). We must *listen carefully* to these words of Saint Paul and *remember* them well:

"My Lord, *be patient with me* and I will pay you back in full."

"Love is patient; love is kind. . . . Love does not rejoice in what is wrong but rejoices with the truth. . . . Love never fails" (1 Cor. 13:4, 6, 8). Yes, love is supreme! Amen.

## 16. MEETING WITH LEADERSHIP OF CATHOLIC HIGHER EDUCATION

Dear Friends,

Dear Leaders in Catholic Higher Education,

### God's Good Blessing of Catholic Education

1. At the end of this day dedicated to *the prayerful celebration of Catholic education in the United States,* I greet you and all those whom you represent, with esteem and with affection in our Lord Jesus Christ. I thank the Association of Catholic Colleges and Universities for having arranged this meeting. I express my gratitude to Dr. Norman Francis and to all at Xavier University for their hospitality at this Institution, which, in so many ways, serves the cause of Catholic higher education.

I will bless the Lord at all times;
his praise shall be ever in my mouth.
Glorify the Lord with me,
*let us together extol his name.*
(Ps. 34:2,4)

Yes, let us join in *thanking God* for the many good things that he, the Father of Wisdom, has accomplished through Catholic colleges and universities. In doing so, let us be thankful for the special strengths of your schools—for their Catholic identity, for their service of truth, and for their role in helping to make the Church's presence felt in the world of culture and science. And let us be *thankful above all for the men and women committed to this mission,* those of the past and those of today, who have made and are making Catholic higher education the great reality that it is.

### Catholic Education in the United States: Without Parallel

2. The United States is unique in its *network of more than 235 colleges and universities* which identify themselves as Catholic. The number and diversity of your institutions are in fact without parallel; they exercise an influence not only within the United States but also throughout the universal Church, and they bear a responsibility for her good.

### Bicentennial of Catholic Higher Education in the United States

Two years from now you will celebrate the two hundredth anniversary of the founding by John Carroll of Georgetown University, the first Catholic university in the United States. After Georgetown, through the leadership of religious congregations and far-seeing Bishops, and with the generous support of the Catholic people, other colleges and universities have been established in different parts of this vast country. For two centuries these institutions have contributed much to *the emergence of a Catholic laity,* which today is intimately and extensively involved in industry, government, the professions, arts and all forms of public and private endeavor—all those activities that constitute the characteristic dynamism and vitality of this land.

### Catholic Identity Depends upon Explicit Profession of Catholicity

Amidst changing circumstances, Catholic universities and colleges are challenged to retain *a lively sense of their Catholic identity* and to fulfill their specific *responsibilities to the Church and to society.* It is precisely in doing so that they make their distinctive contribution to the wider field of higher education.

The Catholic identity of your institutions is a complex and vitally important matter. This identity depends upon *the explicit profession of Catholicity* on the part of the university as an institution, and also upon *the personal conviction and sense of mission* on the part of its professors and administrators.

### Synthesis of Faith and Culture

3. During my pastoral visit to this country in 1979, I spoke of various elements that contribute to the mission of Catholic higher education. It is useful once again to stress the importance of *research into questions vital for the Church and society*—a

research carried out "with a just sense of history, together with the concern to show the full meaning of the human person regenerated in Christ"; to emphasize the need for *educating men and women of outstanding knowledge* who, "having made a personal synthesis between faith and culture, will be both capable and willing to assume tasks in the service of the community and of society in general, and to bear witness to their faith before the world"; and finally, to pursue the establishment *of a living community of faith,* "where sincere commitment to scientific research and study goes together with a deep commitment to authentic Christian living" (Address at Catholic University, Washington, D.C., October 7, 1979, no. 3).

### Catholic Faith and Love of Learning
### Have a Close Relationship

4. To appreciate fully the value of your heritage, we need to recall the origins of Catholic university life. The university as we know it began in close association with the Church. This was no accident. *Faith and love of learning have a close relationship.* For the Fathers of the Church and the thinkers and academics of the Middle Ages, the search for truth was associated with the search for God. According to Catholic teaching—as expressed also in the First Vatican Council—the mind is capable not only of searching for the truth but also of grasping it, however imperfectly.

Religious *faith itself calls for intellectual inquiry;* and the confidence that there can be no contradiction between faith and reason is a distinctive feature of the Catholic humanistic tradition, as it existed in the past and as it exists in our own day.

### Catholic Higher Education Is Called
### to Exercise a Share in the Work of Truth

Catholic higher education is called to exercise, through the grace of God, an extraordinary "share in the work of truth" (3 Jn. 8). The Catholic university is dedicated to the service of the truth, as is every university. In its research and teaching, however, it proceeds from the vision and perspective of faith and is thus enriched in a specific way.

### Intimate Relationship Between the Catholic University
### and the Church's Teaching Office

From this point of view one sees that there is an intimate relationship between the Catholic university and the teaching office of the Church. The Bishops of the Church, as *Doctores et Magistri Fidei,* should be seen not as external agents but as participants in the life of the Catholic university in its privileged role as protagonist *in the encounter between faith and science and between revealed truth and culture.*

### The Catholic University Addresses Modern Issues
### from a Faith Perspective

Modern culture reflects many tensions and contradictions. We live in an age of great technological triumphs but also of great human anxieties. Too often, today, the individual's vision of reality is fragmented. At times experience is mediated by forces over which people have no control; sometimes there is not even an awareness of these forces. The temptation grows to relativize moral principles and to privilege process over truth. This has grave consequences for the moral life as well as for the intellectual life of individuals and of society. The Catholic university must address all these issues from the perspective of faith and out of its rich heritage.

### Pluralism: Directed to the Fullness of Truth

5. Modern culture is marked by a pluralism of attitudes, points of view and insights. This situation rightly requires mutual understanding; it means that society and groups within society must respect those who have a different outlook from their own. But *pluralism* does not exist for its own sake; it *is directed to the fullness of truth*. In the academic context, the respect for persons which pluralism rightly envisions does not justify the view that ultimate questions about human life and destiny have no final answers or that all beliefs are of equal value, provided that none is asserted as absolutely true and normative. Truth is not served in this way.

### The Gospel Must Challenge the Assumptions and Accomplishments of Every Age

It is true of course that the culture of every age contains certain ambiguities, which reflect the inner tensions of the human heart, the struggle between good and evil. Hence the Gospel, in its continuing encounter with culture, must always *challenge the accomplishments and assumptions of the age* (see Rom. 12:2). Since, in our day, the implications of this ambiguity are often so destructive to the community, so hostile to human dignity, it is crucial that *the Gospel should purify culture, uplift it and orient it to the service of what is authentically human*. Humanity's very survival may depend on it. And here, as leaders in Catholic education in the United States, you have an extremely important contribution to make.

### Fidelity to the Word of God

Today there exists an increasingly evident need for philosophical reflection concerning the truth about the human person. A metaphysical approach is needed as an antidote to intellectual and moral relativism. But what is required even more is *fidelity to the word of God,* to ensure that human progress takes into account the entire revealed truth of the eternal act of love in which the universe and especially the human person acquire ultimate meaning. The more one seeks to unravel the mystery of the human person, the more open one becomes to the mystery of transcendence. The more deeply one penetrates the divine mystery, the more one discovers the true greatness and dignity of human beings.

## The Data of Theology Are the Data
## of God's Revelation Entrusted to the Church

6. In your institutions, which are privileged settings for the encounter between faith and culture, *theological science has a special role* and deserves a prominent place in the curriculum of studies and in the allocation of research resources. But theology, as the Church understands it, is much more than an academic discipline. Its data are the data of God's Revelation entrusted to the Church. The deeper understanding of the mystery of Christ, the understanding which theological reflection seeks, is ultimately *a gift of the Holy Spirit given for the common good of the whole Church*. Theology is truly a search to understand ever more clearly the heritage of faith preserved, transmitted and made explicit by the Church's teaching office. And theological instruction serves the community of faith by helping new generations to understand and to integrate into their lives the truth of God, which is so vital to the fundamental issues of the modern world.

## Authentic Theology Exists Only in an Ecclesial Context

7. *Theology is at the service of the whole ecclesial community.* The work of theology involves an interaction among the various members of the community of faith. The Bishops, united with the Pope, have the mission of authentically teaching the message of Christ; as Pastors, they are called to sustain the unity in faith and Christian living of the entire People of God. In this they need the assistance of Catholic theologians, who perform an inestimable service to the Church. But theologians also need the charism entrusted by Christ to the Bishops and, in the first place, to the Bishop of Rome. The fruits of their work, in order to enrich the life-stream of the ecclesial community, must ultimately be tested and validated by the Magisterium. In effect, therefore, *the ecclesial context of Catholic theology gives it a special character and value, even when theology exists in an academic setting.*

## Unity in the Work of Service

Here, the words of Saint Paul concerning the spiritual gifts should be a source of light and harmony for us all: "There are different gifts but the same Spirit; there are different ministries but the same Lord; there are different works but the same God who accomplishes all of them in everyone. To each person the manifestation of the Spirit is given for the common good" (1 Cor. 12:4–7). In the different offices and functions in the Church, it is not some power and dominion that is being divided up, but rather *the same service of the Body of Christ that is shared according to the vocation of each.* It is a question of *unity in the work of service.* In this spirit I wish to express cordial support for the humble, generous and patient work of theological research and education being carried out in your universities and colleges in accordance with the Church's mission to proclaim and teach the saving wisdom of God (see 1 Cor. 1:21).

### Religious and Moral Education
### and the Pastoral Care of Students

8. My own university experience impels me to mention another related matter of supreme importance in the Catholic college and university, namely, *the religious and moral education of students and their pastoral care.* I am confident that you too take this special service very seriously, and that you count it among your most pressing and most satisfying responsibilities. One cannot meet with college and university students anywhere in the world without hearing their questions and sensing their anxieties. In their hearts your students have many questions about faith, religious practice and holiness of life. Each one arrives on your campuses with a family background, a personal history and an acquired culture. They all want to be accepted, loved and supported by *a Christian educational community* which shows friendship and authentic spiritual commitment.

It is your *privilege to serve your students in faith and love;* to help them deepen their friendship with Christ; to make available to them the opportunities for prayer and liturgical celebration, including the possibility to know the forgiveness and love of Jesus Christ in the Sacrament of Penance and the Eucharist. You are able, as Catholic educators, to introduce your students to *a powerful experience of community* and to *a very serious involvement in social concerns that will enlarge their horizons,* challenge their life-styles and offer them authentic human fulfillment.

### The Gospel Call to the Service of Others

University students, for example, are in a splendid position to take to heart the Gospel invitation to go out of themselves, to reject introversion and to concentrate on the needs of others. Students with the opportunities of higher education can readily grasp *the relevance for today of Christ's parable of the rich man and Lazarus* (see Lk. 16:19ff), with all of its consequences for humanity. What is at stake is not only the rectitude of individual human hearts but also the whole social order as it touches the spheres of economy, politics and human rights and relations.

### Crumbs of Freedom, Truth and Bread
### Are Not Enough for the Disadvantaged

Here in the Catholic university centers of this nation, vivified by the inspiration of the Gospel, must be drawn up *the blueprints for the reform of attitudes and structures* that will influence the whole dynamic of peace and justice in the world, as it affects East and West, North and South. It is not enough to offer to the disadvantaged of the world crumbs of freedom, crumbs of truth and crumbs of bread. The Gospel calls for much more. The parable of the rich man and the poor man is directed to the conscience of humanity, and, today in particular, to the conscience of America. But that conscience often passes through the halls of academe, through nights of study and hours of prayer, finally to reach and embrace the whole prophetic message of the Gospel. "Keep your attention closely fixed on it," we are told in the Second Letter of

Peter, "as you would on a lamp shining in a dark place until the first streaks of dawn appear and the morning star rises in your hearts" (2 Pt. 1:19).

### Challenge of the Third Millennium: Preserve the Catholic Character of Catholic Universities and Colleges

9. Dear brothers and sisters: as leaders in Catholic university and college education, you have inherited a tradition of service and academic excellence, the cumulative effort of so many who have worked so hard and sacrificed so much for Catholic education in this country. Now there lies before you the wide horizon of the third century of the nation's constitutional existence, and the third century of Catholic institutions of higher learning serving the people of this land. The challenges that confront you are just as testing as those your forefathers faced in establishing the network of institutions over which you now preside. Undoubtedly, the greatest challenge is, and will remain, that of *preserving and strengthening the Catholic character of your colleges and universities*—that institutional commitment to the word of God as proclaimed by the Catholic Church. This commitment is both an expression of spiritual consistency and a specific contribution to the cultural dialogue proper to American life. As you strive to make the presence of the Church in the world of modern culture more luminous, may you listen once again to Christ's prayer to his Father for his disciples: *"Consecrate them by means of truth—'Your word is truth'"* (Jn. 17:17).

May the Holy Spirit, the Counselor and Spirit of Truth, who has enlivened and enlightened the Church of Christ from the beginning, give you great confidence in the Father's word, and sustain you in the service that you render to the truth through Catholic higher education in the United States of America.

### SEPTEMBER 13, 1987

### 17. HOMILY AT MASS CELEBRATED AT WESTOVER HILLS

My soul, give thanks to the Lord; all my being, bless his holy name
(Ps. 102/103:1)

Dear Brothers and Sisters,

Dear Friends, Citizens of San Antonio and of the State of Texas,

1. It gives me an immense joy to be with you on this Sunday morning and to invoke God's blessings upon this vast state and upon the whole Church in this region.

### The Name "Texas" Evokes a Rich Historical Development, Even the Memory of Massanet's Mass in 1691

Texas! The name immediately brings to mind the *rich history and cultural development* of this part of the United States. In this marvelous setting, overlooking the *city of San Antonio,* I cannot but reverently evoke the memory of the Franciscan Father Massanet who, on the feast of Saint Anthony of Padua, June 13, 1691, celebrated Mass along the banks of the San Antonio River for the members of an early Spanish expedition and a group of local Indian people.

### Gratitude to Representatives of the City and State, to the Archbishop, Bishops, Priests and Laity

Since then, people of many different origins have come here, so that today yours is *a multicultural society,* striving for the fullness of harmony and collaboration among all. I express my cordial gratitude to the representatives of the State of Texas and the city of San Antonio who have wished to be present at this moment of prayer. I also greet the members of the various Christian Communions who join us in praising the name of our Lord Jesus Christ. A special word of thanks to Archbishop Flores and to the Bishops, priests, deacons, Religious, and all the Catholic faithful of Texas. The peace of Christ be with you all!

### Sunday Is for Personal Thanksgiving, as God Rejoiced in His Creation on the Seventh Day

2. *Today is Sunday:* the Lord's Day. Today is like the "seventh day" about which the Book of Genesis says that "God rested from all the work he had undertaken" (Gn. 2:2). Having completed the work of creation, he "rested." God rejoiced in his work; he "looked at everything that he had made, and he found it very good" (Gn. 1:31). *"So God blessed the seventh day and made it holy"* (Gn. 2:3). On this day we are called to reflect more deeply on the mystery of creation, and therefore of our own lives. We are called to "rest" in God, the Creator of the universe. Our duty is to praise him: "My soul give thanks to the Lord . . . give thanks to the Lord *and never forget all his blessings"* (Ps. 102/103:1–2). This is a task for each human being. Only the human person, created in the image and likeness of God, is capable of raising a hymn of praise and thanksgiving to the Creator. The earth, with all its creatures, and the entire universe, call on man to be their voice. Only the human person is capable of releasing from the depths of his or her being that hymn of praise, proclaimed without words by all creation: "My soul, give thanks to the Lord; *all my being,* bless his holy name" (v. 1).

### "Both in Life and Death We Are the Lord's." Remember Our Immortal Destiny

3. What is the message of today's liturgy? To us gathered here in San Antonio, in the State of Texas, and taking part in the Eucharistic Sacrifice of our Lord and Savior Jesus Christ, Saint Paul addresses these words: *"None of us lives as his own master, and none of us dies as his own master.* While we live we are responsible to the Lord and when we die we die as his servants. Both in life and death *we are the Lord's"* (Rom. 14:7–8).

These words are *concise but filled with a moving message.* "We live" and "we die." We live in this material world that surrounds us, limited by the horizons of our earthly journey through time. We live in this world, *with the inevitable prospect of death,* right from the moment of conception and of birth. And yet, we must look beyond the material aspect of our earthly existence. Certainly bodily death is a necessary passage for us all; but it is also true that what from its very beginning has borne in itself the image and likeness of God cannot be completely given back to the corruptible matter of the universe. This is a fundamental truth and attitude of our Christian faith. In Saint Paul's terms: "While we live we are responsible to the Lord, and when we die we die as his servants." We live *for* the Lord, and our dying too is life in the Lord.

Today, on this Lord's Day, I wish to invite all those who are listening to my words not to forget our immortal destiny: life after death—the eternal happiness of heaven, or the awful possibility of eternal punishment, eternal separation from God, in what the Christian tradition has called hell (see Mt. 25:41; 22:13; 15:30). *There can be no truly Christian living without an openness to this transcendent dimension of our lives.* "Both in life and death we are the Lord's" (Rom. 14:8).

### Without Love, There Is No Life; Love Is the Victory over Sin and Death. The Source of This Victory Is Christ.

4. The Eucharist that we celebrate constantly confirms our living and dying "in the Lord": *"Dying you destroyed our death, rising you restored our life."* In fact, Saint Paul wrote: "we are the Lord's. That is why Christ died and came to life again, that he might be Lord of both the dead and the living" (Rom. 14:8–9). Yes, *Christ is the Lord!*

The Paschal Mystery has transformed our human existence, so that it is no longer under the dominion of death. In Jesus Christ, our Redeemer, "we live for the Lord" and "we die for the Lord." Through him and with him and in him, *we belong to God* in life and in death. We exist not only "for death" but "for God." For this reason, on this day "made by the Lord" (Ps. 118/119:24), the Church *all over the world* speaks her blessing from the very depths of the Paschal Mystery of Christ: "My soul, give thanks to the Lord; all my being bless his holy name. Give thanks . . . *and never forget all his blessings"* (Ps. 102/103:1–2).

*"Never forget!"* Today's reading from the Gospel according to Saint Matthew gives us an example of a man who has forgotten (see Mt. 18:21–35). He has forgotten the favors given by his Lord—and consequently he has shown himself to be cruel and heartless in regard to his fellow human being. In this way the liturgy *introduces us to the experience of sin* as it has developed from the beginning of the history of man alongside the experience of death.

We die in the physical body when all the energies of life are extinguished. *We die through sin when love dies in us. Outside of Love there is no Life.* If man opposes love and lives without love, death takes root in his soul and grows. For this reason Christ cries out: "I give you a new commandment: Love one another. Such as my love has been for you, so must your love be for each other" (Jn. 13:34). The cry for love is the cry for Life, for the victory of the soul over sin and death. The source of this victory is *the Cross of Jesus Christ: his Death and his Resurrection.*

## "It Is Above All in the Sacrament of Forgiveness and Reconciliation That the Power of the Redeeming Blood of Christ Is Made Effective in Our Personal Lives"

5. Again, in the Eucharist, our lives are touched by *Christ's own radical victory over sin—sin which is the death of the soul* and—ultimately—the reason for bodily death. "That is why Christ died and came to life again, that he might be Lord of the dead" (see Rom. 14:9)—that he might give life again to those who are dead in sin or because of sin.

And so, the Eucharist begins with *the penitential rite.* We confess our sins in order to obtain forgiveness through the Cross of Christ, and so receive a part in his Resurrection from the dead. But if our conscience reproaches us with *mortal sin,* our taking part in the Mass can be fully fruitful only if beforehand we receive absolution *in the Sacrament of Penance.*

The *ministry of reconciliation* is a fundamental part of the Church's life and mission. Without overlooking any of the many ways in which Christ's victory over sin becomes a reality in the life of the Church and of the world, it is important for me to emphasize that it is above all *in the Sacrament of Forgiveness and Reconciliation that the power of the redeeming blood of Christ is made effective in our personal lives.*

## Though Many Reasons Explain the Neglect of the Sacrament of Penance, the Church's Certainty of Christ's Offer of Forgiveness Has Not Wavered

6. In different parts of the world there is *a great neglect of the Sacrament of Penance.* This is sometimes linked to an obscuring of the religious and moral conscience, a loss of the sense of sin, or a lack of adequate instruction on the importance of this Sacrament in the life of Christ's Church. At times the neglect occurs because we fail to take seriously our lack of love and justice, and God's corresponding offer of reconciling mercy. Sometimes there is a hesitation or an unwillingness to accept maturely and responsibly the consequences of the objective truths of faith. For these reasons it is necessary to emphasize once again that "*with regard to the substance of the Sacrament* there has always remained firm and unchanged in the consciousness of the Church *the certainty* that, by the will of Christ, forgiveness is offered to each individual by means of sacramental absolution given by the ministers of Penance" (*Reconciliatio et Paenitentia,* 30).

Again I ask all my brother Bishops and priests to do everything possible to make the administration of this Sacrament *a primary aspect* of their service to God's people. There can be no substitute for the means of grace which Christ himself has placed in our hands. The Second Vatican Council never intended that this Sacrament of Penance be less practiced; what the Council expressly asked for was that the faithful might more easily understand the sacramental signs and more eagerly and *frequently* have recourse to the Sacraments (see *Sacrosanctum Concilium,* 59). And just as sin deeply touches the individual conscience, so we understand why the absolution of sins must be individual and not collective, except in extraordinary circumstances as approved by the Church.

## Confession Is an Act of Honesty, an Act of Entrusting Ourselves to God's Mercy

I ask you, dear Catholic brothers and sisters, not to see Confession as a mere attempt at psychological liberation—however legitimate this too might be—but as a Sacrament, a liturgical act. *Confession* is an act of honesty and courage; *an act of entrusting ourselves,* beyond sin, *to the mercy of a loving and forgiving God.* It is an act of the prodigal son who returns to his Father and is welcomed by him with the kiss of peace. It is easy, therefore, to understand why "every confessional is a special and blessed place from which there is born new and uncontaminated a reconciled individual—a reconciled world!" (*Reconciliatio et Paenitentia,* 31, V; see III).

## The Use of the Sacrament of Penance Offers Immeasurable Potential for an Authentic Renewal

The potential for *an authentic and vibrant renewal of the whole Catholic Church* through the more faithful use of the Sacrament of Penance is immeasurable. It flows directly from the loving heart of God himself! This is a certainty of faith which I offer to each one of you and to the entire Church in the United States.

## Come Back to This Source of Grace

To those who have been far away from the Sacrament of Reconciliation and forgiving love I make this appeal: *come back to this source of grace; do not be afraid!* Christ himself is waiting for you. He will heal you, and you will be at peace with God!

## It Is a Mark of Greatness to Be Able to Confess a Mistake, to Beg Forgiveness, to Try Again in Christ

To all the young people of the Church, I extend a special invitation to receive Christ's forgiveness and his strength in the Sacrament of Penance. It is *a mark of greatness* to be able to say: I have made a mistake; I have sinned, Father; I have offended you, my God; I am sorry; I ask for pardon; I will try again, because I rely on your strength and I believe in your love.

And I know that the power of your Son's Paschal Mystery—the Death and Resurrection of our Lord Jesus Christ—*is greater than my weaknesses and all the sins of the world*. I will come and confess my sins and be healed, and I will live in your love!

## God's Mercy Obliges Us to Be Reconciled Among Ourselves, Especially at the Level of Cultures

7. In Jesus Christ the world has truly known the mystery of forgiveness, mercy and reconciliation, which is proclaimed by God's word this day. At the same time, God's inexhaustible mercy to us obliges us *to be reconciled among ourselves*. This makes practical demands on the Church in Texas and the Southwest of the United States. It means bringing *hope and love wherever there is division and alienation*.

## Your History Registers a Meeting of Cultures

Your history registers *a meeting of cultures,* indigenous and immigrant, sometimes marked by tensions and conflicts, yet *constantly moving toward reconciliation and harmony*. People of different races and languages, colors and customs, have come to this land to make it their home. Together with the indigenous peoples of these territories, there are the descendants of those who came from almost every country in Europe: from Spain and France, from Germany and Belgium, from Italy, Hungary and Czechoslovakia, from Ireland, England and Scotland. And even from my own native Poland—for it was to Texas, and *Panna Maria,* that the first Polish immigrants came to the United States. There are descendants of those who came in chains from Africa; those from Lebanon, the Philippines and Vietnam, and from every Latin American country, especially from Mexico.

## You Are a Laboratory Testing America's Commitment to Her Founding Moral Principles and Human Values

*This land is a crossroads,* standing at the border of two great nations, and experiencing both the enrichment and the complications which arise from this circumstance. You are thus a symbol and a kind of laboratory testing America's commitment to her founding moral principles and human values. These principles and values are now being reaffirmed by America, as she celebrates the bicentennial of her Constitution and speaks once more about justice and freedom, and about the acceptance of diversity within a fundamental unity—a unity arising from a shared vision of the dignity of every human person, and a shared responsibility for the welfare of all, especially of the needy and the persecuted.

## The Church Responds to the Movement of People Northward

8. Against this background one may speak of a current phenomenon here and elsewhere—*the movement of people northward,* not only from Mexico but from other

southern neighbors of the United States. On this matter also there is work of reconciliation to be done. Among you there are people of great courage and generosity who have been doing much on behalf of suffering brothers and sisters arriving from the south. They have sought to show compassion in the face of complex human, social and political realities. *Here* human needs, both spiritual and material, continue to call out to the Church with thousands of voices, and the whole Church must respond by the proclamation of God's word and by selfless deeds of service. Here too there is ample space for continuing and growing collaboration among members of the various Christian communions.

### The Hispanic Community Faces the Greatest Challenge

In all this, *the Hispanic community itself faces the greatest challenge.* Those of you of Hispanic descent—so numerous, so long present in this land, so well equipped to respond—are called to hear the word of Christ and take it to heart: "I give you a new commandment: love one another. Such as my love has been for you, so must your love be for each other" (Jn. 13:34). And Jesus specified that this love embraces the entire range of human needs from the least to the greatest: "I promise you that whoever gives a cup of cold water to one of these lowly ones . . . will not want for his reward" (Mt. 10:42). The Hispanic community also needs to respond to its own needs and to show generous and effective solidarity among its own members. I urge you to hold fast to your Christian faith and traditions, especially in defense of the family. And I pray that the Lord may provide many more vocations to the priesthood and to the religious life among your young people.

May you who have received so much from God hear the call to a renewal of your Christian life and to fidelity to the faith of your fathers. O may you respond in the spirit of Mary, the Virgin Mother whom the Church sees "maternally present and sharing in the many complicated problems which today beset the lives of individuals, families and nations . . . helping the Christian people in the constant struggle between good and evil, to ensure that it 'does not fall,' or if it has fallen, that it 'rises again'" (*Redemptoris Mater,* 52).

### Celebrating the Victory of Life over Death,
### We Journey Together in Hope

9. Today's liturgy helps us to reflect deeply *on life and death,* on the victory of life over death. On this earth, in the visible world of creation, *man exists "for death";* and yet, in Christ, he is called to communion with God, with *the living God who gives life.* He is called to this communion precisely through the death of Christ—the death which "gives life."

Today, all over the world, countless people—people of many countries and continents, languages and races, are sharing sacramentally in the death of Christ. *We, here in Texas, journey together with them* toward the fulfillment of the Paschal Mystery in life. We journey, conscious of being sinners, conscious of being mortal. But we journey on *in hope,* in union with the Sacrifice of Christ, through Eucharistic communion with him and *with love* for each other. *We live for the Lord! We die for the Lord! We belong to the Lord! Come, Lord Jesus!* (see Rv. 22:20). Amen.

## 18. THE ANGELUS

1. At the end of this Eucharistic celebration, I invite you to join me in praying the *Angelus.*

### With Mary Let Us Respond with Love to God's Love

Whenever we turn to *Mary* the Mother of God in prayer, we are reminded that she is *"full of grace."* This is how the Angel Gabriel greeted her at the time of the Annunciation: "Hail, full of grace, the Lord is with you" (Lk. 1:28). And indeed these words of the angel are true. Of all the people God has created, she alone was always free from sin. From the first moment of her existence she was in communion with the Father, and the Son, and the Holy Spirit. *Mary responded to this great gift of God* with openness and generosity: "Let it be done to me" she said, "according to your word" (Lk 1:38).

2. Like Mary, *we too have been given the gift of God's grace,* even though we have not received its fullness. Like Mary, we are called to respond, to be open to God's word, to be generous in saying yes to God. For us this means doing God's will, living according to his commandments, serving our neighbor, avoiding sin. In other words, *with Mary we must respond with love to God's love.*

Let us turn then to Mary whom we honor under many titles, but here today in San Antonio under her special title of *Our Lady of Guadalupe.*

## 19. MEETING WITH REPRESENTATIVES OF CATHOLIC CHARITIES

Dear Brothers and Sisters,

I am grateful for your presentation of the vast network of Christian love and human solidarity in which you are engaged. May the Lord sustain you in your zeal. "May mercy, peace and love be yours in ever greater measure" (Jude 1).

### Catholic Charities Makes the Loving Compassion of Our Lord Present to Human Needs

1. Catholic Charities is a title that speaks wonderfully well of the generous commitment of the Catholic people of the United States to the cause of human solidarity and Christian love. It gives me great joy to be among you, members of

Catholic Charities U.S.A., your associated agencies and your colleague organizations in social ministry. Through your efforts you help *to make the loving compassion of our Lord and Savior Jesus Christ present to human needs.*

### The Church Must Reflect in Her Life and Action
### God's Love for His Creatures

Jesus Christ was born poor, lived poor, and died poor. He loved the poor. In his kingdom the poor have a special place. The Church cannot be any different. She must be ever more fully aware of her fundamental duty to reflect in her life and action the very love with which God loves his creatures. For what is at stake is the mystery of God's love as explained in the First Letter of John: "We, for our part, love because *he first loved us*" (1 Jn. 4:19). *All service has its first moment in God.*

### In Scripture We Discover God's Burning Love of Justice
### and His Urgent Appeals for Service to the Needy

2. You carry on a tradition and you live out a teaching grounded in Sacred Scripture, proclaimed by the Church and relevant to every age. *Service to the needy* not only builds up social harmony, it *reveals God, our Father, the rescuer of the oppressed.* In the Old Testament it was God's love for his people that decreed a special concern for the stranger, the widow and the orphan. As God had treated his people, so were they to treat others. The year of jubilee and the sabbatical year restored economic balance: slaves were set free, land was returned to its original owners, debts were canceled (see Ex. 21ff.; Lv. 25). Justice and mercy alike were served. The Prophets repeatedly drew attention to the inner qualities of heart that must animate the exercise of justice and service: "Not as man sees does God see, because man sees the appearance but the Lord looks into the heart" (1 Sm. 16:7).

### What We Do for the Poor and Defenseless Is Done for Jesus

In the New Testament the mystery of God's love is further revealed: "God so loved the world that he gave his only Son" (Jn. 3:16). *Through the heart of Jesus the fullness of God's infinite mercy appeared in the world.* Marveling at the Incarnation of God's Son, Mary exclaims that through this child the lowly shall be lifted up, their hunger shall be satisfied, and God's mercy shall be extended to all (see Lk. 1:46–55). Years later, in announcing his own ministry, Jesus sums up his life's program in the words of Isaiah: "to bring glad tidings to the poor, to proclaim liberty to captives, recovery of sight to the blind and release to prisoners, to announce a year of favor from the Lord" (Lk. 4:18–19). Jesus identifies himself with the poor and the defenseless: what we do for them is done for him, the service we fail to render them is service denied to him (see Mt. 25:31–46).

## Gross Disparities of Wealth Today
## Reenact the Parable of the Rich Man and Lazarus

*Gross disparities of wealth* between nations, classes and persons *reenact the Gospel parable of the rich man and the poor man Lazarus.* And with the same dire consequences of which the Gospel speaks: "My child, replied Abraham, remember that you were well off in your lifetime, while Lazarus was in misery. Now he has found consolation here, but you have found torment" (Lk. 16:25). The warning is as valid today as it was two thousand years ago.

## The Second Vatican Council Reaffirmed the Church's
## Vocation to Love and Serve All Those Afflicted in Any Way

3. From the beginning the Church has worked to carry out this teaching in her ministry. It is not necessary here to trace the extremely varied history of Christian service. The Church has always sought to respond to the stranger, the widow and the orphan; she has founded countless schools, hospitals, hospices, child-care facilities and shelters. In our own times the Second Vatican Council has forcefully reaffirmed *the Church's vocation,* in fidelity to her Lord, *to love all those who are afflicted in any way:* to recognize in the poor and the suffering the likeness of her poor and suffering Founder; to do all she can to relieve their needs, striving to serve Christ in them (see *Lumen Gentium,* 8). Twenty years after the Council, the Christian community is more than ever aware that the poor, the hungry, the oppressed, the sick and the handicapped share in a special way in the Cross of Christ and therefore need the Church's ministry.

## Works of Mercy, Compassion and Justice Are Basic
## to the Life of the Church in the United States

*Works of mercy, justice and compassion are basic to the history of the Church in the United States.* The two American women who have been numbered among the saints, Frances Xavier Cabrini and Elizabeth Ann Seton, have been thus honored principally because of their work for their poorer brothers and sisters. The initiatives of Catholic charities in the United States go back to before the Declaration of Independence. Countless institutions and structures have been established to assist the orphan, the immigrant, the ethnic groups, all persons in need—of every race and creed. Countless Americans of all extractions have made the compassionate service of their fellow human beings the whole purpose and method of their lives. In particular, generations of Religious, women and men, have consumed themselves in selfless service, under the sign of love.

## Poverty Is Often a Matter of Material Deprivation;
## It Is also a Matter of Spiritual Impoverishment

4. The Church has always proclaimed a love of preference for the poor. Perhaps the language is new, but the reality is not. Nor has the Church taken a narrow view

of poverty and the poor. *Poverty*, certainly, is often a matter of *material deprivation.* But it is also a matter of *spiritual impoverishment, the lack of human liberties,* and the result of *any violation of human rights and human dignity.* There is a very special and pitiable form of poverty: *the poverty of selfishness,* the poverty of those who have and will not share, of those who could be rich by giving but choose to be poor by keeping everything they have. These people too need help.

### The Aim of Christian Solidarity Is to Defend and Promote the Dignity and Fundamental Rights of Every Person

The Christian view is that human beings are to be valued for what they are, not for what they have. In loving the poor and serving those in whatever need, the Church seeks above all to respect and heal their human dignity. *The aim of Christian solidarity and service is to defend and promote, in the name of Jesus Christ, the dignity and fundamental human rights of every person.* The Church "bears witness to the fact that this dignity cannot be destroyed, whatever the situation of poverty, scorn, rejection or powerlessness to which a human being has been reduced. She shows her solidarity with those who do not count in a society by which they are rejected spiritually and sometimes even physically. She is particularly drawn with maternal affection toward those children who, through human wickedness, will never be brought forth from the womb to the light of day, as also for the elderly, alone and abandoned. The special option for the poor, far from being a sign of particularism or sectarianism, manifests the universality of the Church's being and mission" (*Instruction on Christian Freedom and Liberation*, 68).

### In Her Love of Preference for the Poor, the Church Must Also Proclaim and Relieve Their Higher Needs of the Spirit

For "the poor in spirit" the Church has a very special love. She has inherited it from Christ, who called them "blest" (Mt. 5:3). On the one hand the Church knows, from the words of Christ, that despite all human efforts the poor will always be with us (see Mt. 26:11). On the other hand, in all her efforts to uplift the poor she knows and proclaims the ambivalence of possessions. Indeed, where the pursuit of wealth is treated as the supreme good, human beings become imprisoned in the hardening of their hearts and in the closing of their minds (see *Populorum Progressio,* 19). For this reason too, the Church, in the very act of serving the poor and relieving their sufferings, must also continue to proclaim and serve their higher needs, those of the spirit.

### Service to Those in Need Should Also Lead Them to the Dignity of Self-Reliance

5. Service to those in need must take the form of direct action to relieve their anxieties and to remove their burdens, and at the same time lead them to the dignity of self-reliance. In this respect I wish to express *the Church's immense gratitude to the*

*many Americans* who are working to help their fellow human beings, in all the different forms which relief and development take in today's world. And I solemnly thank the American people for the generous way in which they respond to the appeal for financial support for the many splendid programs of assistance carried out in their name. In the case of the many programs run by the Catholic Church, I wish to invite all who have responsibility for them to ensure that they will always be, and be seen to be, in full accord with Catholic principles of truth and justice.

### No Institution Can Replace the Human Heart

The organizational and institutional response to needs, whether in the Church or in society, is extremely necessary but it is not sufficient in itself. In this regard I would repeat a concern I mentioned in my Apostolic Letter on Human Suffering: "Institutions are very important and indispensable; nevertheless, *no institution can by itself replace the human heart, human compassion, human love or human initiative,* when it is a question of dealing with the sufferings of another. This refers to physical sufferings, but it is even more true when it is a question of the many kinds of moral suffering and when it is primarily the soul that is suffering" (*Salvifici Doloris,* 29).

### Do Not Reduce Human Beings to Mere Units of Social Planning and Action

Furthermore, in the necessary organizational and institutional response to needs, it is essential to avoid reducing human beings to mere units or categories of political or social planning and action. Such a process leads to new and other unjust forms of anonymity and alienation.

### Service to the Needy Involves Trying to Reform Structures of Oppression

6. Service to the poor also involves speaking up for them, and trying *to reform structures which cause or perpetuate their oppression.* As committed Catholics involved in helping to meet people's many concrete needs, you are still called to reflect on another dimension of a worldwide problem: *the relationship between rich societies and poor societies,* rich nations and poor nations. Your insights must be prayerfully joined to those of many other people to see what can be done as soon as possible to purify the social structures of all society in this regard.

### Social Injustice and Unjust Structures Exist Because Individuals Maintain or Tolerate Them, in "Social" Sin

In the final analysis, however, we must realize that social injustice and unjust social structures exist only because individuals and groups of individuals deliberately maintain or tolerate them. It is these *personal choices,* operating through structures, that breed and propagate situations of poverty, oppression and misery. For this reason, overcoming "social" sin and reforming the social order itself must begin with *the conversion of our hearts*. As the American Bishops have said: "The Gospel confers on each Christian the vocation to love God and neighbor in ways that bear fruit in the life of society. That vocation consists above all in a change of heart: a conversion expressed in praise of God and in concrete deeds of justice and service" (*Economic Justice for All: Catholic Social Teaching and the U.S. Economy,* 327).

### Mercy and Conversion Are Tools
### That Take into Account Redeemed Human Dignity

To many people, mercy and conversion may seem like poor tools for solving social problems. Some are tempted to accept ideologies that use force to carry out their programs and impose their vision. Such means sometimes produce what appear to be successes. But these successes are not real. Force and manipulation have nothing to do with true human development and the defense of human dignity. Catholic social teaching is totally different, not only as regards goals, but also as regards the means to be used. For the Christian, *putting right human ills must necessarily take into account the reality of Creation and Redemption.* It means *treating every human being as a unique child of God,* a brother or sister of Jesus Christ. The path of human solidarity is the path of service; and true service means selfless love, open to the needs of all, without distinction of persons, with the explicit purpose of reinforcing each person's sense of God-given dignity.

### Solidarity and Service Must Involve the Whole Community

7. *Solidarity and service are above all a duty of Christian love* which must involve the whole community. When we are tempted to congratulate ourselves on what we have done, we must bear soberly in mind the words of Jesus: "When you have done all you have been commanded to do, say, 'We are useless servants. We have done no more than our duty'" (Lk. 17:10). When we are faced with the vastness of this duty of love, with the boundless needs of the poor in America and throughout the world, when we are disappointed by slowness and setbacks in the reform of structures and in our own conversion, let us not lose heart, and let us not settle for what has already been accomplished. *Love can overcome great obstacles, and God's love can totally transform the world.*

### In Prayer and Liturgy the Church Is Confirmed
### in Her Solidarity with the Weak

As the Church tries to express Christian solidarity in generous service, she also wishes to draw attention to *the importance of worship and prayer and their relationship to service.* In looking to the example of Christ, the Church can never forget that all Christ's actions were accompanied by prayer. It is in prayer that the Church develops and evaluates her social consciousness and unceasingly discovers anew her vocation to serve the needy of the world, as Jesus did. Addressing a group of American Bishops during their last *ad Limina* visit, I spoke of this specifically Christian and ecclesial dimension of all social and charitable action: "Only a worshiping and praying Church can show herself sufficiently sensitive to the needs of the sick, the suffering, the lonely—especially in the great urban centers—and the poor everywhere. The Church as *a community of service* has first to feel the weight of the burden carried by so many individuals and families, and then strive to help alleviate these burdens. The discipleship that the Church discovers in prayer she expresses in deep interest for Christ's brethren in the modern world and for their many different needs. Her concern, manifested in various ways, embraces—among others—the areas of housing, education, health care, unemployment, the administration of justice, the special needs of the aged and the handicapped. In prayer, the Church is confirmed in her solidarity with the weak who are oppressed, the vulnerable who are manipulated, the children who are exploited, and everyone who is in any way discriminated against" (Address of December 3, 1983, no. 6).

### Catholic Charities Have Lent God
### Their Hands to Do His Work

8. *Catholic Charities and related organizations exist essentially to spread Christian love.* It is especially through charitable activities at the parish level that the entire Church in the United States joins in the tasks of mercy, justice and love. We have seen today how Catholic Charities and all its colleague associations have lent God their own flesh—their hands and feet and hearts—so that his work may be done in our world. For your long and persevering service—creative and courageous, and blind to distinctions of race or religion—you will certainly hear Jesus' words of gratitude: *"you did it for me"* (Mt. 25:40).

Gather, transform and serve! When done in the name of Jesus Christ, this is the spirit of Catholic Charities and of all who work in this cause, because it is the faithful following of the One who did "not come to be served but to serve" (Mk. 10:45). By working for a society which fosters the dignity of every human person, not only are you serving the poor, but you are renewing *the founding vision of this nation under God!* And may God reward you abundantly!

## 20. MEETING WITH SEMINARIANS AND RELIGIOUS IN FORMATION, SAN FERNANDO CATHEDRAL

Remove the sandals from your feet, for *the place where you stand is holy ground.* (Ex. 3:5)

## Moses' Mission Began in the Awareness of the Awesome Presence of Almighty God

1. These words of God marked the beginning of a new way of life for Moses. The place where he was standing was holy ground, for he was standing in *the awesome presence of Almighty God*. And on that holy ground, he heard a voice calling him to a special mission of service to the People of God. From that moment forward, Moses' life would be radically altered. He would henceforth place his life at the service of the God of Abraham, Isaac and Jacob. No longer would his life be his own. He would lead the Chosen People out of slavery in Egypt toward freedom in the Promised Land. In meeting God on holy ground, speaking with him there and hearing his summons to service, Moses came to a new understanding of himself and entered into a deeper commitment to God and his people. *The mission of Moses began under the sign of God's holiness.*

## You Have Heard the Voice of God Calling You to the Holy Ground of a Special Vocation in the Church

Dear brothers and sisters in the Lord: it is a deep joy for me to be with you today in this historic Cathedral of San Fernando, the oldest cathedral sanctuary in the United States. It is with great gratitude to God that I meet with you who are preparing to serve the Lord as priests and Religious, you who in a singular and remarkable way have, like Moses, heard the voice of God calling you to that "holy ground" of a special vocation in the Church. You have stood in the awesome presence of the Lord and heard him call you by name. And listening to his voice with prayerful discernment you have joyfully begun your formation for the priesthood or the religious life.

## A Vocation Begins with the Discovery of the Person of Christ

2. A vocation in the Church, from the human point of view, *begins with a discovery*, with finding the pearl of great price. You discover Jesus: his person, his message, his call. In the Gospel which we have heard today, we reflect on the call of Jesus to the first disciples. The first thing that Andrew did after meeting Jesus was to seek out his brother Simon and tell him: *"We have found the Messiah!"* Then Philip, in a similar way, sought out Nathanael and told him: *"We have found the one Moses spoke of in the Law—the prophets too—Jesus, son of Joseph, from Nazareth"* (see Jn. 1:35–51).

## A Dialogue in Prayer Ensues

After the initial discovery, a dialogue in prayer ensues, a dialogue between Jesus and the one called, *a dialogue which goes beyond words* and expresses itself in love.

*Questions* are an important part of this dialogue. For example, in the Gospel account of the call of the disciples, we are told that "when Jesus turned around and noticed them following him, he asked them, 'What are you looking for?' They said to him, 'Rabbi' [which means teacher], where do you stay?' 'Come and see,' he answered" (Jn. 1:38–39).

### The Dialogue Opens Up a Prayerful Process of Discernment

What begins as a discovery of Jesus moves to a greater understanding and commitment through *a prayerful process of questions and discernment.* In this process, our motives are purified. We come face to face with pointed questions such as "What are you looking for?" And we even find ourselves asking questions of Jesus, as Nathanael did: *"How do you know me?"* (Jn. 1:48). It is only when we have reflected candidly and honestly in the silence of our hearts that we begin to be convinced that the Lord is truly calling us.

### The Dialogue of Prayer Continues to Deepen
### Our Knowledge and Love of Christ

Yet, even then, the process of discernment is not over. Jesus says to us as he said to Nathanael: *"You will see much greater things than that"* (Jn. 1:50). Throughout our lives, after we have made a sacred and permanent commitment and after our active service of the Lord has begun, we still need the dialogue of prayer that will continually deepen our knowledge and love of our Lord Jesus Christ.

### You Stand in a Long Line of Generous Priests and Religious
### Who Have Served the Church in Texas or Elsewhere

Dear students for the priesthood and candidates for the Religious life: you stand in *a long line of people who have given themselves totally* for the sake of the Kingdom of God, and who have shared our Lord's Sacrifice and entered into his paschal victory. For generations many of the generous priests and Religious who have served the Church in Texas have come with immigrants from other lands, or as missionaries from other places. I wish to express my gratitude to God for the contribution which they have made to establishing the Church here. At the same time I praise the Lord of the harvest for all of you and for the number of native-born vocations, and I fervently pray that this increase continues.

### If Christ Is the Center of Your Lives,
### Then Your Generosity Will Know No Limits

Like all those who have gone before you, you will have trials. Your fidelity will be ensured only when you invoke the strength of the Lord, only when you rely on Christ's grace. But if Christ is the center of your lives, the one for whom you live and die, then your generous service to your brothers and sisters will know no limits. You will love those who are difficult to love, and you will *enrich the world with the Gospel* of Jesus Christ.

## Seminarians, You Need a Clear Understanding of Your Vocation

3. I would now like to speak *to the seminarians*. Dear brothers in Christ: as men preparing for priestly ordination, it is important for you to have *a clear understanding of the vocation* to which you feel called so that your promise of lifelong fidelity may be maturely made and faithfully kept.

Your life in the priesthood will closely join you with the Eucharist; you will be ministers of the mysteries of God; you will be expected to preach and teach in the name of the Church.

## The Eucharist Is the Principal Reason for the Priesthood

*The Eucharist is the principal reason for the ordained priesthood.* As I said in my 1980 Holy Thursday Letter: "Through our ordination . . . we priests are united in a singular and exceptional way to the Eucharist. In a certain way we derive *from* it and exist *for it*" (no. 2). No work we do as priests is so important. The celebration of the Eucharist is the way that we best serve our brothers and sisters in the world because it is the source and center of the dynamism of their Christian lives.

## Cultivate a Deep Love for the Eucharist, a Thorough Theological Grasp of the Mystery, and a Grasp of the Liturgical Norms

How crucial it is then, for our own happiness and for the sake of a fruitful ministry, that we *cultivate a deep love for the Eucharist*. During your seminary days, a thorough theological study of the nature of the Eucharistic mystery and an accurate knowledge of liturgical norms will prepare you well to foster the full, conscious and active participation of the community in the liturgy. The future priest is called to reflect and to profess with the Second Vatican Council that "the other sacraments, as well as every ministry of the Church and every work of the apostolate, are linked with the Holy Eucharist and are directed toward it. For the most Blessed Eucharist contains the Church's entire spiritual wealth, that is, Christ himself" (*Presbyterorum Ordinis,* 5).

## Foster a Deep Understanding of the Word of God as Lived and Proclaimed by the Church

The task of *preaching the Gospel* is of supreme importance in the priesthood. And since, as Saint Paul says, "faith comes through hearing, and what is heard is the word of Christ" (Rom. 10:17), seminary formation must aim at fostering *a deep understanding of the word of God* as it is lived and proclaimed by the Church. Always remember the words of the Prophet Jeremiah: "When I found your words, I devoured them; they became my joy and the happiness of my heart, because I bore your name, O Lord" (Jer. 15:16).

## Nourish in Mind and Heart
## an Internal Adherence to the Magisterium

In order for your preaching to bear fruit in the lives of those whom you will serve, you will have to nourish in your own mind and heart *a real internal adherence to the Magisterium* of the Church. For, as the Council reminded us, "the task of priests is not to teach their own wisdom but God's word, and to summon all people urgently to conversion and to holiness" (*Presbyterorum Ordinis,* 4).

## The Priest Is Set Apart So That He May Be Totally Dedicated

The priest needs to know the real living conditions of the people he serves, and he must live among them as a true brother in Christ. He can never be separated from the community. But there is a real sense in which, like the Apostle Paul, he is—in the very words of Scripture—*"set apart to proclaim the Gospel of God"* (Rom. 1:1). In his priestly identity he is commissioned for a special service—a unique service—to the Body of Christ. For this reason, the Second Vatican Council spoke in this way: "By their vocation and ordination, priests of the New Testament are indeed set apart in a certain sense within the midst of God's people. But this is so, not that they may be separated from this people or from any man, but that they may be totally dedicated to the work for which the Lord raised them up. They cannot be ministers of Christ unless they are witnesses and dispensers of a life other than this earthly one" (*Presbyterorum Ordinis,* 3).

## Celibacy Means the Gift of Yourself to God
## and a Greater Closeness to God's People

Each one of you is called to embrace freely a celibate life for the sake of Jesus and his Kingdom, in order to become a "man for others." If modeled on the generous divine and human love of Jesus for his Father and for every man, woman and child, your celibacy will mean an enhancement of your life, *a greater closeness to God's people,* an eagerness to give yourself without reserve. By embracing celibacy in the context of the priesthood, you are committing yourself to a deeper and more universal love. Above all, *celibacy means the gift of yourself to God.* It will be the response, in Christ and the Church, to the gifts of Creation and Redemption. It will be part of your sharing, at the deepest level of human freedom and generosity, in the Death and Resurrection of Jesus. Humanly speaking, this sacrifice is difficult because of our human weaknesses; without prayer it is impossible. It will also require discipline and effort and persevering love on your part. But in your gift of celibacy to Christ and his Church, even the world will be able to see the meaning of the Lord's grace and the power of his Paschal Mystery. This victory must always be visible in your joy.

## The Essential Difference Between
## the Ordained Priesthood and That of the Baptized
## Lies in the Special Mission of the Twelve

The Council stressed the *essential difference* between the ordained priesthood and the priesthood of all the baptized and prescribed a priestly formation in seminaries which is distinct from other forms of formation (see *Lumen Gentium*, 10; *Optatam Totius*, 4). At the heart of this essential difference is the truth that Jesus entrusted the Twelve with the authority to proclaim the Gospel, celebrate the Eucharist, forgive sins and provide for the pastoral care of the community. This authority is given for a truly specific purpose and through Ordination is shared by the successors of the Apostles and their collaborators in the ordained priesthood. It is given for *a particular ministry of service* to be carried out in imitation of the Son of Man who came to serve. The ministry of the ordained priest is essential to the life and development of the Church; it is an essential service to the rest of the Church. It is clear that those who are preparing for this specific ministry will have *special needs and requirements* that differ from those of the rest of the community.

## Priests Are to Encourage and Assist the Faithful
## by Being Faithful to Their Priestly Ministry

All the members of the Church are summoned to share in her mission by reason of their Baptism and Confirmation. Priests can best assist and encourage others in the service of the Gospel by being faithful themselves to their priestly ministry in the Church. "Hence, whether engaged in prayer and adoration, preaching the word, offering the Eucharistic Sacrifice, and ministering the other sacraments, or performing any of the works of the ministry for people, priests are contributing to the extension of God's glory as well as to the development of divine life in people" (*Presbyterorum Ordinis*, 2).

## To Those Preparing for Religious Life,
## Yours Is a Special Invitation

4. And now I turn to you, my brothers and sisters who are preparing for the *Religious life*. Yours too is a great and specific gift of God's love. To each of you, as to the first disciples, Jesus has said: *"Come and see"* (Jn. 1:39). There is no force or coercion on the part of Christ, but rather an invitation, extended simply and personally, to come and stay in his house, to be in his presence, and with him to praise his Father in the unity of the Holy Spirit.

### It Is a Gift of the Love of God
### That Strengthens the Bonds of Baptism

A Religious vocation is *a gift,* freely given and freely received. It is a profound expression of *the love of God* for you and, on your part, it requires in turn *a total love for Christ.* Thus, the whole life of a Religious is aimed at strengthening the bond of love which was first forged in the *Sacrament of Baptism.* You are called to do this in Religious consecration through the profession of the evangelical counsels of chastity, poverty and obedience (see can. 573 secs. 1–2).

During your years of preparation, the Church is eager that you receive a formation that will prepare you to live your Religious consecration in fidelity and joy, a formation that is both deeply human and Christian, a formation that will help you to accept ever more generously *the radical demands of the Gospel* and bear public witness to them. Your very life is meant to be a confident and convincing affirmation that Jesus is "the Way, and the Truth, and the Life" (Jn. 14:6).

### You Must Develop the Habit and Discipline of Prayer

What you must develop, first and foremost, is *the habit and discipline of prayer.* For who you *are* is more fundamental than any service you perform. In this regard, the Second Vatican Council said that Religious should "seek God before all things" and "combine contemplation with apostolic love" (*Perfectae Caritatis,* 5). This is no easy task, for prayer has many dimensions and forms. It is both personal and communal, liturgical and private. It deepens our union with God and fosters our apostolic love. A climate of silence is needed as well as a personal life-style that is simple and ready for sacrifice.

### The Eucharist Will Be the Meeting Point
### of Your Offering with Christ's Own Sacrifice

The liturgical life of the community greatly influences the personal prayer of all the members. The *Eucharist* will always be the source and summit of your life in Christ. It is the Sacrament through which *the worship of your whole existence is presented to God in union with Christ* (see can. 607, sec. 1). The Eucharist is the point where the offering of your chastity, poverty and obedience is made one with the Sacrifice of Christ.

### The Sacrament of Penance Is a Constant Call to Conversion

In your Religious consecration, *the Sacrament of Penance* is a constant reminder to you of the call of Jesus to conversion and newness of life. Precisely because you are called by your Religious profession to bear witness to the holiness of God, you must help the People of God *never to lose their sense of sin.* To be authentic in following Christ in the perfection of charity, you must be the first to recognize sin in your hearts, to repent and to glorify God's grace and mercy. Conversion is a lifelong process requiring repentant love. The Sacrament of Penance is the Sacrament in which our weakness meets God's holiness in the mercy of Christ.

## The Church Needs Your Collaboration, Talents, Availability, Work in Her Mission for the Kingdom

In a thousand ways the Church will call you into service in her mission for the Kingdom of God. She needs your talents, your availability to come and go according to the needs of the hour, which are often the needs of the poor. She needs your collaboration in the cause of faith and justice. *She needs your work* and everything that you can do for the Gospel. But above all, the Church needs what you are; *she needs you*: men and women consecrated to God, living in union with Christ, living in union with his Church, striving after the perfection of love. Why? *Because of the holiness of God!* Dear brothers and sisters: *What you do is important, but what you are is even more important*—more important for the world, more important for the Church, more important for Christ.

## In Mary We See the Meaning of the Evangelical Counsels

In Mary, the Mother of Christ and the Church, you will understand the identity of your own life. She showed throughout her life the meaning of the evangelical counsels, to which your Religious consecration is directed. Her words to the angel— "I am the servant of the Lord. Let it be done to me as you say" (Lk. 1:38)—show the obedient total surrender which our consecration to God requires and which your vows express.

## You Will Collaborate with the Laity and Help Them Realize the Call to Holiness

5. Of course, *the call to holiness* is a *universal call*. All members of the Church, without exception, are summoned by God to grow in personal sanctity and to share in the mission of the Church. A heightened awareness of this truth has been one of the fruits of the Second Vatican Council. And it has helped foster a clearer awareness of *the role of the laity* in building up the Kingdom, as well as a closer collaboration of the laity with the clergy and Religious. As persons preparing for the priesthood and Religious life, it will be your privilege to help explore still more effective forms of collaboration in the future. But even more importantly, you will be in a position to encourage the lay people to fulfill *that mission which is uniquely their own* in those situations and places in which the Church can be the salt of the earth only through them.

The Council spoke very clearly about their special mission. Among other things it stated: "The laity, by their very vocation, seek the Kingdom of God by engaging in temporal affairs and by ordering them according to the plan of God. They live in the world, that is, in each and in all of the secular professions and occupations. They live in the ordinary circumstances of family and social life, from which the very web of their existence is woven" (*Lumen Gentium*, 31). This activity of the laity constitutes a specific contribution to the Body of Christ. Yours is another charism, a different gift to be lived differently, so that, in true diversity, there may be real unity in the work of service.

### Special Gratitude to Those Responsible
### for the Formation of Candidates

6. On this occasion, I cannot fail to express my special gratitude and encouragement to those of you who are responsible for the formation of candidates for the priesthood and Religious life. Be assured that all your efforts, work and sacrifice are deeply appreciated by the Church and by me personally. Your task is a vital one for the future of the Church, and your contribution to the life of the People of God is a lasting one. Certainly it is crucial that you yourselves be steeped in sound doctrine, pastoral experience and holiness of life. Of great importance is your attitude of faith, and particularly your personal example of *filial love for the Church,* as well as *your loyal adherence to her authentic ordinary Magisterium* (see *Lumen Gentium,* 25). Saint Paul tells us: "Christ loved the Church. He gave himself up for her to make her holy" (Eph. 5:25–26). I pray that your own lives will be always animated by this kind of sacrificial love.

### A Word of Deep Appreciation to All Parents
### Who Sustain Their Children

I wish to add a word of deep appreciation to all those parents who sustain and encourage their children in the following of Christ. The prayerful support, understanding and love that you give them is of immense value.

### I Wish to Appeal to the Church for Vocations
### and for Prayer for This Purpose

7. At this time I wish to appeal to the Church in the United States for *vocations* to the priesthood and Religious life. The duty of fostering such vocations rests on the whole Christian community, and certainly families have traditionally made the greatest contribution. We must always remember too the impact on vocations that can be made by zealous priests and Religious, by their example of generous service, by the witness of their charity, their goodness and their joy. Above all, *the key to vocations is persevering prayer,* as Jesus himself commanded: "The harvest is good but laborers are scarce. Beg the harvest master to send out laborers to gather his harvest" (Mt. 9:37–38).

Dear brothers and sisters: you have come to know the Lord Jesus. You have *heard his voice, discovered his love* and *answered his call.* May he, the Lord Jesus, who has begun this good work in you bring it to completion for the glory of his Father and by the power of his Spirit. Remember always: "the place where you stand is holy ground" (Ex. 3:5).

And may the Blessed Virgin Mary help you by her prayers and by the example of her love.

## 21. ADDRESS TO THE SPANISH-SPEAKING COMMUNITY, 'OUR LADY OF GUADALUPE PLAZA'

Dear Brothers and Sisters in Christ,

### Joy over This Meeting with Members of the Hispanic Community

1. This is a moment of great joy for me. I have looked forward to this meeting with you, *members of the Hispanic community* of San Antonio, present here as representatives of all your Hispanic brothers and sisters in the United States. You are here too as *a parish community,* and through you therefore my words are addressed to every parish community throughout the United States.

### I Greet You with Love in Our Lord in This Square Dedicated to Our Lady of Guadalupe

I greet each one of you with love in our Lord and Redeemer Jesus Christ. I am particularly happy to speak to you in the beautiful Spanish language, in this square named in honor of Our Lady of Guadalupe. Our gathering here is a vivid reminder, in the current Marian Year, of *the special place of the Mother of the Redeemer in the mystery of Christ and of the Church.* It speaks to us of how dear our Blessed Mother has always been to you people of Hispanic culture and how important she continues to be today in your lives of faith and devotion. Marian shrines and places of pilgrimage are a kind of "geography" of faith by which we seek to meet the Mother of God in order to find a strengthening of our Christian life (see *Redemptoris Mater,* 28). Popular devotion to the Blessed Virgin Mary is rooted in sound doctrine, and authentic religious experience is appropriate and important in the lives of all Christ's followers.

### You Must Be Evangelizers in the Line of the Hispanic Heritage of the Southwest

2. *The Hispanic heritage of San Antonio and the Southwest is very important for the Church.* Spanish was the language of the first evangelizers of this continent, precisely in this region. The missions here in San Antonio and throughout the Southwest are visible signs of the many years of evangelization and service carried out by the first

missionaries. Their preaching of salvation in Jesus Christ was authenticated by their own integrity of life and by the spiritual and corporal works of mercy and love which they performed. Following their example, thousands of dedicated priests, Religious and lay people have labored to build up the Church here. Today it is your turn, in fidelity to the Gospel of Jesus Christ, to build your lives on the rock of your Christian faith. It is your turn to be evangelizers of each other and of all those whose faith is weak or who have not yet given themselves to the Lord. May you be no less zealous in evangelization and in Christian service than your forebears!

### The Parish Gathers for Instruction, Building Up
### a Living Community, the Eucharist and the Life of Prayer

3. Today I wish to speak to you about *your parish,* which is the place and community in which you nourish and express your Christian life. I wish to speak of the parish as *the family of families,* for parish life is especially related to the strengths and weaknesses and needs of the families that make it up. There are of course many things that could be said about parish life; today it is only possible for me to emphasize certain aspects.

It is useful to begin with a well-known passage from the New Testament which helps us to keep in mind just why the members of a Catholic parish come together in the name of Jesus. In the Acts of the Apostles we read about the early Christians: "They devoted themselves to the Apostles' instruction and the communal life, to the breaking of bread and prayers" (2:42). *Instruction in the faith of the Apostles, the building up of a living community, the Eucharist and the other sacraments, and the life of prayer*—these are essential factors of the life of every parish.

### Catechesis Has an Objective Content
### in and from the Universal Community of Faith

4. First, instruction or *catechesis.* Everyone needs to be instructed in the faith. Saint Paul summarizes it this way: "Everyone who calls on the name of the Lord will be saved. But how shall they call on him in whom they have not believed? And how can they believe unless they have heard of him? *And how can they hear unless there is someone to preach?*" (Rom. 10:13–14).

In a parish *the faith is proclaimed and transmitted* in many ways: through the liturgy, and especially the Eucharist with its appropriate homilies; through religious instruction in schools and catechetical programs; through adult religious education; through prayer groups and associations for pastoral activity; through the Catholic press.

There are two things that I wish to emphasize about transmitting the faith. *Catechesis has an objective content.* We cannot invent the faith as we go along. We must receive it *in* and *from* the universal community of faith, the Church to whom Christ himself has entrusted a teaching office under the guidance of the Spirit of Truth. Every catechist must sincerely and reverently be able to apply to himself or herself the words of Jesus: "My doctrine is not my own, it comes from him who sent me" (Jn. 7:16; see *Catechesi Tradendae*, 6). Likewise, *every baptized person,* precisely by reason of being baptized, has *the right to receive the authentic teaching of the Church* regarding doctrinal and moral aspects of Christian life (see can. 229; *Catechesi Tradendae*, 14).

### Family Catechesis Precedes, Accompanies and Enriches All Other Forms of Catechesis

The other point I wish to make about instruction in the faith is that *family catechesis precedes, accompanies and enriches all other forms of catechesis* (see *Catechesi Tradendae*, 68). This means that the parish, in considering its catechetical programs, should give particular attention to its families. But above all it means that the family itself is the first and most appropriate place for teaching the truths of the faith, the practice of Christian virtues and the essential values of human life.

### The Vitality of the Parish Depends on the Spiritual Vigor of Its Families

5. The second aspect of parish life that is contained in the text from the Acts of the Apostles concerns *the parish's task of building up a living community.* I have already said that every parish is *a family of families.* The vitality of a parish greatly depends on the spiritual vigor, commitment and involvement of its families. The family in fact is the basic unit of society and of the Church. It is "the domestic church." Families are those living cells which come together to form the very substance of parish life. Some are healthy and filled with the love of God, which is poured forth into our hearts through the Holy Spirit who has been given to us (see Rom. 5:5). In some there is little energy for the life of the Spirit. Some have broken down altogether. The priests and their collaborators in a parish must try to be very close to all families in their need for pastoral care, and to provide the support and spiritual nourishment they require.

### The Pastoral Care of Families Is an Urgent Service

The pastoral care of families is a vast and complex field of the Church's ministry, but it is a most urgent and pressing service. Each parish must be fully committed to it, especially in the face of so much breakdown and undermining of family life in society. I appeal to all priests—pastors, associates and all concerned—to the permanent deacons, and to the Religious and lay leaders to do everything possible, working together, *to serve the family* as effectively as possible. *This involves proclaiming the whole truth about marriage and family life:* the exclusive nature of conjugal love, the indissolubility of marriage, the Church's full teaching on the transmission of life and the respect due to human life from the moment of conception until natural death, the rights and duties of parents with regard to the education of their children, especially their religious and moral education, including proper sex education. *Parents and family members must, moreover, be helped and sustained in their struggle to live by the sacred truths of faith.* The Church must furnish families with the spiritual means of persevering in their sublime vocation and of growing in the special holiness to which Christ calls them.

## The Family Has Obligations to the Parish
## in Openness to Others

6. *Just as the parish is responsible for the family, so the family must be aware of its obligations to the parish,* which is the larger family. Today, Catholic couples and families must think especially of the service which they have a duty to render to other couples and families, especially those who experience problems. This apostolate of couple to couple and family to family can be carried out in many ways: prayer, good example, formal or informal instruction or counseling and material assistance of many sorts (see *Familiaris Consortio,* 71). I appeal to you, the Catholic families of the United States: *be true families*—united, reconciled and loving; and *be true Catholic families*—prayerful communities living the Catholic faith, open to the needs of others, taking part fully in the life of the parish and of the Church at large.

## Worthy Celebration of the Sacraments,
## Especially Marriage, Eucharist and Penance

7. Another fundamental aspect of parish life is *the worthy celebration of the Sacraments,* including sacramental marriage. This Sacrament forms *the stable basis of the whole Christian community.* Without it, Christ's design for human love is not fulfilled, his plan for the family is not followed. It is precisely because Christ established marriage as a Sacrament and willed it to be a sign of his own permanent and faithful love for the Church that the parish must explain to the faithful why all trial marriages, merely civil marriages, free unions, and divorces do not correspond to Christ's plan.

The sacramental life of the Church is centered above all upon the Eucharist, which celebrates and brings about the unity of the Christian community—unity with God and unity with one another. *In the Mass, the Sacrifice of the Cross is perpetuated* throughout the centuries until Christ comes again. *The Body and Blood of the Lord are given to us as our spiritual food.* The parish community has no greater task or privilege than to gather, like Christ's first disciples, for "the breaking of the bread" (Acts 2:42).

## Foster Public and Private Devotion to the Eucharist

I now repeat especially to all parishes the invitation already addressed to the whole Church: to promote and foster *public and private devotion to the Holy Eucharist also outside of Mass* (see *Inaestimabile Donum,* 20ff). For, in the words of the Second Vatican Council, "The most blessed Eucharist contains the Church's entire spiritual wealth, that is, Christ himself" (*Presbyterorum Ordinis,* 5).

### Promote a Deep Love of the Sacrament of Penance

The sacramental life of a parish extends also to the other Sacraments which mark the important moments of the life of individuals and families, and of the entire parochial community. I wish to mention in particular *the Sacrament of Penance* and the *important need for Catholics to confess their sins regularly.* In recent years, many have grown neglectful of this wonderful gift by which we obtain Christ's forgiveness of our sins. The state of the Sacrament of Penance in each parish and in each local Church is a good indicator of the authentic maturity of the faith of the priests and people. It is necessary that Catholic families instill in their members a deep love of this beautiful means of reconciliation with our heavenly Father, with the Church and with our neighbor. Parents, more by example than by words, should encourage their children to go to Confession regularly. Parishes need to encourage families to do this; they need to support them through proper catechesis. Needless to say, priests, who are the ministers of God's grace in this Sacrament, should make certain that the Sacrament is conveniently available in its authorized forms.

### The Life of Prayer Is an Area for Interaction
### Between the Parish and the Family

8. Finally, I refer briefly to *the life of prayer* as it manifests itself within the Christian community. This is an area in which the interaction between the family and the parish is especially clear and profound. *Prayer begins in the home.* The prayers that serve us well in life are often those learned at home when we were children. But prayer in the home also serves to introduce the children to the liturgical prayer of the whole Church; it helps all to apply the Church's prayer to everyday events and to the special moments of a family's experience (see *Familiaris Consortio,* 61).

### Encourage Family Prayer

Everyone involved in parish life should be concerned to encourage and support *family prayer* by every means available; and families themselves should be making efforts to engage in family prayer and to integrate that prayer into the prayer life of the wider ecclesial community.

### Pray for Vocations Among Hispanic Young People

I am happy to know that the number of Hispanic priests and men and women Religious is growing. But many more are needed. Young Hispanics: is Christ calling you? Hispanic families: are you willing to give your sons and daughters to the Church's service? *Do you ask the Lord to send laborers into his harvest?* Christ needs Hispanic laborers for the great harvest of the Hispanic community and the whole Church.

### Reach Out to Brothers and Sisters Who Have Drifted Away

9. And finally I wish to encourage all families and parishes not to be inward-looking, not to dwell on themselves. *Jesus commands us to serve our neighbor,* to reach out to those in need. And I ask you especially to reach out to those brothers and sisters in the faith who have drifted away because of indifference or who have been hurt in some way. I invite all you who are unsure about the Church or who doubt that you will be welcome *to come home to the family of families, to come home to your parish.* You belong there! It is your family in the Church, and the Church is the household of God, in which there are no strangers or aliens (see Eph. 2:19).

### Keep Mary Present in Your Family Prayers, in Your Family Life

We are gathered in front of a parish which is dedicated to *Our Lady of Guadalupe,* Mother of Jesus, Mother of the Church, Mother of the Americas, and in particular of Mexico. When Jesus died on the Cross, he entrusted his Mother to his Beloved Disciple, John. The Gospel tells us that from that moment the disciple took her into his home (see Jn. 19:27). What better way is there for you to celebrate this Marian Year than by taking Mary, the Mother of the Redeemer, into your homes! This means *imitating her faith and discipleship;* it means keeping her present in your family prayers, especially the family rosary; turning to her, asking her intercession for the grace of conversion and renewal; entrusting yourselves and your families to her maternal care.

May God bless each and every one of you.

May he bless every family and parish.

May the Blessed Virgin of Guadalupe love and protect the Hispanic people of the land.

*¡Viva la Virgen de Guadalupe!*

### SEPTEMBER 14, 1987

### 22. MESSAGE TO THE PEOPLE OF NEW MEXICO

Dear People of New Mexico,

### Cordial Greetings and Best Wishes, Especially to Native Americans

1. Although it has not been possible to include New Mexico in this pastoral visit to the United States, I am happy to have this occasion to extend to all of you my cordial good wishes. I wish to include in this greeting all the people of every cultural and religious tradition, particularly *the Native Americans.* The ancient Indian dwellings which still remain today speak eloquently of the richness of your unique heritage. May you always preserve and draw strength from the worthy traditions which have been handed down to you from the past.

### Greetings to Catholic Brothers and Sisters, Who Owe the Beginnings of Faith to the Spanish Missionaries

I offer a special greeting to my brothers and sisters of *the Catholic faith* who live in New Mexico. The first beginnings of the faith in this area go back to the time of the first Spanish missionaries who came from Mexico. The impact of the Gospel on your history and culture is clearly reflected in the names of your cities, such as Las Cruces, Santa Rosa and Socorro. Even your colorful mountains refer to Christ and the Saints, with names such as Sangre de Cristo, San Andreas and San Mateo. It seems very fitting, then, that the capital of your state and your Archdiocesan See should bear the name of *Santa Fe,* the holy faith. For indeed the Catholic faith has greatly influenced the history and culture of New Mexico.

### May Faith Shape Our Lives and Our Vision of the Future

2. My sentiments in your regard are captured by the words of Saint Paul, who said: "*We keep thanking God for all of you and we remember you in our prayers,* for we constantly are mindful before our God and Father of the way you are *proving your faith,* and *laboring in love,* and *showing constancy of hope in our Lord Jesus Christ*" (1 Thes. 1:2–3).

Our *identity* as Christians is rooted in *the gift of faith.* We have come to know and to believe in Christ. We are convinced that he is "the way, and the truth, and the life" (Jn. 14:6). And while we treasure this gift of faith, we know too that it must be guarded and developed, strengthened and shared. We must exercise our faith in love, putting it into practice in every aspect of our daily lives.

This precious gift shapes our whole vision of the future. For the deeper our love for Christ, the more confidently we trust in God's providential care for ourselves and those who are dear to us, and for the future of the world. As the Letter to the Hebrews says: "*Faith is confident assurance* concerning what we hope for, and conviction about things we do not see" (Heb. 11:1).

And so, dear brothers and sisters in the Lord: "Let us lay aside every encumbrance of sin which clings to us and persevere in running the race which lies ahead. *Let us keep our eyes fixed on Jesus, who inspires and perfects our faith*" (Heb. 12:1–2).

May the Lord strengthen each of you in faith, and fill you with love and joy. God bless New Mexico!

## 23. VISIT TO SAINT MARY'S BASILICA

Dear Friends,

1. With fraternal esteem, I extend to all of you—the people of *Phoenix and the American Southwest*—my greetings of joy and peace! You have welcomed me with open arms. I thank you for your most cordial hospitality.

## Special Greetings to Our *Spanish-Speaking* Brothers and Sisters

In particular today, I wish to greet our Spanish-speaking brothers and sisters. Your hospitality is a reminder of the great strength, vitality and generosity which the Hispanic community has brought to the United States. I ask you to grow ever closer to your Church and to enrich her with the profession and faithful practice of your faith—the faith of pioneers, missionaries and martyrs. Long live Our Lady of Guadalupe!

## Congratulations on Your Seventy-fifth Anniversary of Statehood and Give Thanks for So Many Blessings

2. By a happy act of providence, my visit to Arizona coincides with *the seventy-fifth anniversary of Arizona's statehood.* On this happy occasion, I offer to all of you my best wishes and congratulations.

Like all of America's Southwest, Arizona faces challenges of *amazing growth.* I am told that the motto of your state is *Ditat Deus,* "God enriches." And indeed you have all around you ample proof of this enrichment: in the majesty and beauty of your landscape, and especially in the diversity and giftedness of your people. Your state and the ever-growing number of its citizens have been greatly blessed and enriched by God. In the past forty years, in particular, you have experienced *remarkable progress and development.* And this brings with it increased obligations and responsibilities.

## Development Must Contribute to the Good of the Whole Person

3. My visit to Arizona also coincides with another anniversary. *Twenty years* have passed since Pope Paul VI published his important encyclical *Populorum Progressio,* which was a document of great insight on the topic of true human development as seen in the light of the Gospel of Jesus Christ. Although two decades have passed since the encyclical first appeared, its message remains today, as then, both challenging and prophetic.

A fundamental principle put forth by Pope Paul is that development, in order to be truly authentic, must *contribute to the good of the whole person* (see *Populorum Progressio,* 14). Thus, development can never be reduced to economic expansion alone or to values that are strictly temporal. What is at stake ultimately is the well-being of persons in all *the spiritual and physical dimensions* of their humanity, including the moral, social, cultural and economic aspects.

## Efforts Aimed at Promoting Development Need to Be Accompanied by a Search for Transcendent Humanism

Efforts aimed at promoting development need to be accompanied by the search for *a transcendent humanism,* a humanism which is oriented toward God. Your

Arizona state motto expresses well the reason for this: *God enriches.* Yes, God alone is the source of all that is good. God alone is the Creator of all things. As the Apostle Saint Paul once said, "It is he [God] who gives to all life and breath and everything else. . . . In him we live and move and have our being" (Acts. 17:25–28). In order to be genuine, development must aim at improving people's living conditions and at the same time promote a transcendent humanism which acknowledges the sovereignty of God.

## True Human Advancement Must Reach Out
## to Include More People in Its Influence

4. By its very nature, true human advancement is *necessarily outgoing;* it cannot be concentrated on itself. It must reach out to include more and more people in its influence. Any progress which would secure the betterment of a select few at the expense of the greater human family would be an erroneous and distorted progress. It would be an outrage against the demands of justice and an affront to the dignity of every human being.

## The Temptation to Avarice Is Part and Parcel
## of Our Common Conditions

In this regard, the following words of Pope Paul VI ring true: "Both for nations and for individuals, avarice is the most evident form of moral underdevelopment" (*Populorum Progressio,* 19). And that is why he insisted on the need for a *spirit of human solidarity* to accompany all efforts of development. The temptation toward avarice is certainly not restricted to any one nation or group of people. In fact, it is part and parcel of our common human condition, which stands in need of constant conversion. Yet does not the temptation present itself more forcefully to those who have received a larger share in the material goods of the earth?

## May Your Hearts Go Out to the Less Fortunate

The Second Vatican Council of the Catholic Church stated unequivocally: "Advanced nations have a very heavy obligation to help the developing peoples" (*Gaudium et Spes,* 86). These words apply with special relevance to the people of Arizona and of all the United States whom God has so richly blessed. As you look with gratitude upon the high standard of living that many of you enjoy, at least in comparison to the rest of the world, *may your hearts go out to the less fortunate.* May your hearts and hands be open to the poor, both within your own society and in developing nations of the world. Just as God enriches you, so may you be channels of enrichment for others.

### In Jesus' Own Humility and His Sharing of His Riches
### He Forged a Bond of Solidarity with Every Person

5. Those of us who are Christians draw inspiration to take up this task from the words and example of our *Lord Jesus Christ.* Although he is God, he humbled himself and assumed our humanity, becoming one like us in all things but sin (see Phil. 2:5–11; Heb. 4:15). Thus, he forged a bond of *unbreakable solidarity with every human being.* In him our humanity is sacred and forever linked with God.

In his public ministry we see how *Jesus came to serve and not to be served.* One of the signs of his mission was that he preached the Gospel to the poor (see Mt. 11:2–5), and he showed in daily life a special love for the poor and suffering. We are convinced, therefore, that if we follow the teaching and example of our beloved Lord, we shall find ourselves more closely united with one another, especially the needy, and we shall experience that transcendent dimension of life which can only be attained in union with God.

### The New Name for Peace Is Development

Dear Friends: I have spoken with you today about development because I am convinced, as was Pope Paul VI, that in our highly technological age *"the new name for peace is development"* (see *Populorum Progressio,* 87). If we wish then to promote the tranquillity of order in our world, we must be deeply committed to that authentic development which contributes to the good of every person everywhere, in all the dimensions of human life. For this reason *my appeal to America is for human solidarity throughout this land and far beyond its borders.* This is the culmination of true progress; this is the measure of true greatness; this is the condition of true and lasting peace for America and for the world!

God bless Arizona! God bless you all! *Ditat Deus!*

## 24. MEETING WITH CATHOLIC
## HEALTH CARE REPRESENTATIVES

### Jesus Continues His Healing Ministry Through You

Dear Brothers and Sisters,

Leaders in Catholic Health Care,

1. In the joy and peace of our Lord Jesus Christ I greet you and thank you for your warm welcome. This meeting gives us the opportunity to honor and give thanks to God for one of the most extensive and fundamental works of the Catholic Church in the United States—all that is embraced in the term "Catholic health care." I am pleased to be able to express to you who represent so many of your country's health care organizations *the esteem, support and solidarity of the whole Church.* In you, Jesus Christ continues his healing ministry, "curing the people of every disease and illness" (see Mt. 4:23).

## Witnesses to God's Kingdom

This is the high dignity to which you and your colleagues are called. This is your vocation, your commitment and the path of your specific witness to the presence of God's Kingdom in the world. Your health care ministry, pioneered and developed by congregations of women Religious and by congregations of Brothers, *is one of the most vital apostolates* of the ecclesial community and *one of the most significant services* which the Catholic Church offers to society in the name of Jesus Christ. I have been told that membership in the Catholic Health Association extends to 620 hospitals and 300 long-term care facilities: that Catholic hospital beds number 11 percent of the total number in the country; that Catholic institutions administer approximately 17 percent of the health care throughout the nation, and that they cared for nearly 46 million people last year. I am grateful to Sister Mary Eileen Wilhelm and to your president, Mr. Curley, for illustrating to us this immense network of Christian service.

## Compassion, Love and Mercy: Signs of God's Kingdom

2. Because of your dedication to caring for the sick and the poor, the aged and the dying, you know from your own daily experience how much illness and suffering are basic problems of human existence. When the sick flocked to Jesus during his earthly life, they recognized in him a friend whose deeply compassionate and loving heart responded to their needs. He restored physical and mental health to many. These cures, however, involved more than just healing sickness. They were also *prophetic signs of his own identity and of the coming of the Kingdom of God,* and they very often caused a new spiritual awakening in the one who had been healed.

## The Life and Prayer of the Church:
## A Source of Healing and Reconciliation

The power that went out from Jesus and cured people of his own time (see Lk. 6:19) has not lost its effect in the two-thousand-year history of the Church. *This power remains, in the life and prayer of the Church, a source of healing and reconciliation.* Ever active, this power confirms the identity of the Church today, authenticates her proclamation of the Kingdom of God, and stands as a sign of triumph over evil.

## Your Apostolate Penetrates and Transforms America

With all Catholic health care the immediate aim is to provide for the well-being of the body and mind of the human person, especially in sickness or old age. By his example, Christ teaches the Christian "to do good by his or her suffering and to do good to those who suffer" (*Salvifici Doloris,* 3). This latter aspect naturally absorbs the greater part of the energy and attention of health care ministry. Today in the United States, Catholic health care extends the mission of the Church in every state of the union, in major cities, small towns, rural areas, on the campuses of academic institutions, in remote outposts and in inner-city neighborhoods. By providing health care in all these places, especially to the poor, the neglected, the needy, the new-comer, *your apostolate penetrates and transforms the very fabric of American society*. And sometimes you yourselves, like those you serve, are called to bow, in humble and loving resignation, to the experience of sickness—or to other forms of pain and suffering.

### Witness to the Christian View of Suffering and the Meaning of Life and Death

3. *All concern for the sick and suffering is part of the Church's life and mission*. The Church has always understood herself to be charged by Christ with the care of the poor, the weak, the defenseless, the suffering and those who mourn. This means that, as you alleviate suffering and seek to heal, you also bear witness to the Christian view of suffering and to the meaning of life and death as taught by your Christian faith.

### Equal Health Care for All

In the complex world of modern health care in industrialized society, this wit-ness must be given in a variety of ways. First, it requires continual efforts *to ensure that everyone has access to health care*. I know that you have already examined this question in the report of your Task Force on Health Care of the Poor. In seeking to treat patients equally, *regardless of social and economic status,* you proclaim to your fellow citizens and to the world Christ's special love for the neglected and powerless. This particular challenge is a consequence of your Christian conviction, and it calls for great courage on the part of Catholic bodies and institutions operating in the field of health care. It is a great credit to your zeal and efficiency when, despite formidable costs, you still succeed in preventing the economic factor from being the determinant factor in human and Christian service.

### The Inalienable Dignity of Every Human Person Demands Quality Health Care

Similarly, the love with which Catholic health care is performed and its profes-sional excellence have the value of a sign testifying to the Christian view of the human person. *The inalienable dignity of every human being is, of course, fundamental to all Catholic health care*. All who come to you for help are worthy of respect and love, for all have been created in the image and likeness of God. All have been redeemed by Christ and, in their sufferings, bear his Cross. It is fitting that our meeting is taking place on the Feast of the Triumph of the Cross. Christ took upon himself the whole of human suffering and radically transformed it through the Paschal Mystery of his Passion, Death and Resurrection. *The Triumph of the Cross gives human suffering a new dimension, a redemptive value* (see *Salvifici Doloris*, 24). It is your privilege to bear constant witness to this profound truth in so many ways.

## Structural Changes Must Not Threaten
## the Spiritual Dimension of Catholic Health Care

The structural changes which have been taking place within Catholic health care in recent years have increased the challenge of *preserving and even strengthening the Catholic identity of the institutions and the spiritual quality of the services given.* The presence of dedicated women and men Religious in hospitals and nursing homes has ensured in the past, and continues to ensure in the present, that spiritual dimension so characteristic of Catholic health care centers. The reduced number of Religious and new forms of ownership and management should not lead to a loss of a spiritual atmosphere, or to a loss of a sense of vocation in caring for the sick. This is an area in which the Catholic laity, at all levels of health care, have an opportunity to manifest the depth of their faith and to play their own specific part in the Church's mission of evangelization and service.

## Catholic Health Care: Part of the Church's Mission

4. As I have said, Catholic health care must always be carried out within the framework of the Church's saving mission. This mission she has received from her divine Founder, and she has accomplished it down through the ages with the help of the Holy Spirit who guides her into the fullness of truth (see Jn. 16:13; *Lumen Gentium*, 4). *Your ministry therefore must also reflect the mission of the Church as the teacher of moral truth,* especially in regard to the new frontiers of scientific research and technological achievement. Here too you face great challenges and opportunities.

## The Church Defends the Dignity and
## Rights of the Human Person

Many times in recent years the Church has addressed issues related to the advances of biomedical technology. She does so not in order to discourage scientific progress or to judge harshly those who seek to extend the frontiers of human knowledge and skill, but in order to affirm the moral truths which must guide the application of this knowledge and skill. Ultimately, the purpose of the Church's teaching in this field is *to defend the innate dignity and fundamental rights of the human person.* In this regard the Church cannot fail to emphasize the need to safeguard the life and integrity of the human embryo and fetus.

## Human Life Is Sacred Because the Human Person Is Sacred

5. The human person is a unique composite—a unity of spirit and matter, soul and body, fashioned in the image of God and destined to live forever. Every human

life is sacred, because every human person is sacred. It is in the light of this fundamental truth that *the Church constantly proclaims and defends the dignity of human life
from the moment of conception to the moment of natural death.* It is also in the light of
this fundamental truth that we see the great evil of abortion and euthanasia.

## The Church's Cause:
## The Cause of Human Life and Human Dignity

Not long ago, in its *Instruction on Respect for Human Life in Its Origin and on the
Dignity of Procreation,* the Congregation for the Doctrine of the Faith once more dealt
with certain vital questions concerning the human person. Once more it defended
the sanctity of innocent human life from the moment of conception onward. Once
again it affirmed the sacred and inviolable character of the transmission of human
life by the procreative act within marriage. It explained that new technologies may
afford new means of procreation, but "what is technically possible is not for that very
reason morally admissible" (Introduction, 4). To place new human knowledge at the
service of the integral well-being of human persons does not inhibit true scientific
progress but liberates it. The Church encourages all genuine advances in knowledge,
but she also insists on the sacredness of human life at every stage and in every
condition. The cause she serves is *the cause of human life and dignity.*

## Forming Society's Moral Vision

6. In the exercise of your professional activities you have a magnificent opportunity, by your constant witness to moral truth, to contribute to *the formation of
society's moral vision.* As you give the best of yourselves in fulfilling your Christian
responsibilities, you will also be aware of the important contribution you must make
to building a society based on truth and justice. Your service to the sick enables you
with great credibility *to proclaim to the world the demands and values of the Gospel of
Jesus Christ,* and to foster hope and renewal of heart. In this respect, your concern
with the Catholic identity of your work and of your institutions is not only timely
and commendable, it is essential for the success of your ecclesial mission.

## Mutual Responsibility of the Institution and the Church

*You must always see yourselves and your work as part of the Church's life and mission.*
You are indeed a very special part of the People of God. You and your institutions
have precise responsibilities toward the ecclesial community, just as that community
has responsibilities toward you. It is important at every level—national, state and
local—that there be *close and harmonious links between you and the Bishops,* who
"preside in the place of God over the flock whose shepherds they are, as teachers of
doctrine, priests of sacred worship and officers of good order" (*Lumen Gentium,* 20).
They for their part wish to support you in your witness and service.

## Encouragement in the Apostolate of Health Care

7. I have come here today *to encourage you in your splendid work* and to confirm you in your vital apostolate. Dear brothers and sisters: for your dedication to meeting the health care needs of all people, especially the poor, I heartily congratulate you. You embody the legacy of those pioneering women and men Religious who selflessly responded to the health care needs of a young and rapidly expanding country by developing an extensive network of clinics, hospitals and nursing homes.

## A Compassionate Response in the AIDS Crisis

Today you are faced with new challenges, new needs. One of these is the present crisis of immense proportions which is that of AIDS and AIDS-Related Complex (ARC). Besides your professional contribution and your human sensitivities toward all affected by this disease, you are called to show the love and compassion of Christ and his Church. As you courageously affirm and implement your moral obligation and social responsibility to help those who suffer, *you are, individually and collectively, living out the parable of the Good Samaritan* (see Lk. 10:30–32).

## The Good Samaritan

The Good Samaritan of the parable showed compassion to the injured man. By taking him to the inn and giving of his own material means, he truly gave of himself. This action, a universal symbol of human concern, has become one of the essential elements of moral culture and civilization. How beautifully the Lord speaks of the Samaritan! He "was neighbor to the man who fell in with the robbers" (Lk. 10:36). To be "neighbor" *is to express love, solidarity and service,* and to exclude selfishness, discrimination and neglect. The message of the parable of the Good Samaritan echoes a reality connected with today's Feast of the Triumph of the Cross: "the kindness and love of God our Savior appeared . . . that we might be justified by his grace and become heirs, in hope, of eternal life" (Ti. 3:4–7). In the changing world of health care, it is up to you *to ensure that this "kindness and love of God our Savior" remains the heart and soul of Catholic health services.*

Through prayer and with God's help, may you persevere in your commitment, providing professional assistance and selfless personal care to those who need your services. I pray that your activities and your whole lives *will inspire and help all the people of America, working together, to make this society a place of full and absolute respect for the dignity of every person,* from the moment of conception to the moment of natural death.

And may God, in whom "we live and move and have our being" (Acts 17:28), sustain you by his grace. God bless you and your families and your contribution to America!

## 25. VISIT TO SAINTS SIMON AND JUDE CATHEDRAL

Dear Bishop O'Brien,

Dear Brothers and Sisters in Christ,

### Cathedral Celebrates Two Men of Courageous Faith
### Who Bore Witness to the Risen Savior

1. It is a joy for me to come to *the Cathedral of Saints Simon and Jude,* and to be with you who make up this local Church in Phoenix. This house of prayer and worship, this mother church of the Diocese, is named after two of the Twelve Apostles, two men of courageous faith who personally received from our Risen Savior the mandate to preach the Gospel to the ends of the earth. Jesus said to them and the rest of the Twelve: "*Go,* therefore, and *make disciples of all the nations.* Baptize them in the name of the Father, and of the Son, and of the Holy Spirit. Teach them to carry out everything I have commanded you" (Mt. 28:19–20).

Simon and Jude responded wholeheartedly to this summons and spent the rest of their lives seeking "to open up for all people a free and sure path to full participation in the mystery of Christ" (*Ad Gentes,* 5).

### Church Has Inherited the Same Mission of the Twelve and
### So Has the Mandate to Bring the Gospel to Everyone

The Church, built as she is on the foundation of the Apostles and Prophets (see Eph. 2:20), has inherited the same mission that Jesus first entrusted to the Twelve. *The Church is by her very nature missionary,* "for it is from the mission of the Son and the mission of the Holy Spirit that she takes her origin, in accordance with the decree of God the Father" (*Ad Gentes,* 2). She has the honor and privilege, and also the obligation, of bringing the Good News of salvation to all nations, to every person. As the Bishops of the United States stated last November in their Pastoral Statement on World Mission: "We are faithful to the nature of the Church to the degree that we love and sincerely promote her missionary activity" (*To the Ends of the Earth,* 2).

### The Church in Phoenix Stands on the Missionary Work
### of Fathers Kino and Garces

2. *The Church in Phoenix,* like every other local Church in the world, is *the fruit of evangelization.* The Gospel was first brought to Arizona three hundred years ago by the renowned Jesuit missionary, *Father Eusebio Kino,* also known as the "Apostle of Sonora and Arizona." At great personal sacrifice Father Kino worked tirelessly to establish missions throughout this area so that the Good News concerning our Lord Jesus Christ might take root among the people living here.

And the Gospel did take root, and numerous other missionaries came after Father Kino to continue the evangelizing effort. Perhaps the most zealous among these was the Franciscan *Francisco Garces*. With particular love for the Indian people, he sought to present the Gospel to them in a way adapted to their culture; at the same time he also encouraged them to live in harmony and peace among themselves. So completely was his life patterned on that of our Lord that he ended his labors here by shedding his blood for the Gospel.

The missionary efforts continued down through the years, and the Church became firmly established in Arizona. *The rich fruit of this evangelization* is clearly evident today in this quickly growing Diocese of Phoenix and in the expanding Dioceses of the surrounding area. The Gospel has truly taken root here and has brought forth fruit in abundance.

### The Work of Evangelization Is Not Over but Rests on Every Member of the Church

3. And yet the work of evangelization is *not over*. On earth it will never be over. Indeed, so much remains to be done. Let us not forget the words of the Second Vatican Council, which said that missionary activity is "a supremely great and sacred task of the Church" (*Ad Gentes*, 29). The duty of carrying forward this work rests on the whole Church and on every member of the Church.

### The Church Has Need of Many More Missionaries

The Church, at the close of the twentieth century, has *need of many more missionaries* with the zeal of Father Kino and Father Garces, persons of heroic faith like *Saint Isaac Jogues, Saint John Neumann* and *Saint Frances Cabrini*, who are willing to leave their own homeland to bring the message of salvation to people in other lands, especially to those who have never heard the word of God.

Who will meet this need? The Gospel message has still not been heard by two-thirds of the world's population. Who will respond to God's missionary call at the end of the twentieth century? Jesus says: "Whoever loves father or mother, son or daughter more than me is not *worthy of me*" (Mt. 10:37). We must be *worthy of Christ*.

### All Are Called to Do Their Part; Not Everyone Is Asked to Leave Home

Not everyone is asked to leave home and loved ones for this task, but *all are called* to bear the burden, to do their part. As the American Bishops have said so well, "Jesus' great commission to the first disciples is now addressed to us. . . . This mission to the peoples of all nations must involve all of us personally in our parishes and at the diocesan and universal levels of the Church" (*To the Ends of the Earth*, 3).

### Thank You for Your Support in Prayer,
### Material Help and Personnel

Missionaries in foreign countries deserve our prayerful support and material help. American Catholics have been especially generous in the past, a generosity and interest that show your genuine missionary spirit. The practice of "twinning" between American parishes and Dioceses and those of Africa and Asia has been of great benefit. With gratitude I commend you, and in the name of the universal Church I ask your continued help and prayers. Great assistance has been given to the missions by mission aid societies such as the Society for the Propagation of the Faith and the Association of the Holy Childhood. Nor can we ever forget the generous missionary work that has been carried out for decades by religious Institutes and Missionary Societies of the United States, and also by generous *Fidei Donum* priests and by lay missionaries. The reward of those who have sacrificed everything to spread the Gospel will be great in heaven.

### God Makes His Chosen Ones Perfect Through Suffering
### by Giving Them a Share in the Cross of Christ

4. Dear brothers and sisters: the Letter to the Hebrews tells us that God the Father considered it fitting to make Christ, our leader in the work of salvation, *"perfect through suffering"* (Heb. 2:10). In a similar way, he led the Apostles Simon and Jude through the suffering of martyrdom to perfection in eternity. In every age of the Church, God makes his chosen ones "perfect through suffering," bringing them to the fullness of life and happiness by giving them on earth a share in the Cross of Christ.

### Christian Love Does Not Exist for Us
### Without Effort, Discipline and Sacrifice

It is easy to understand that God's plan for us passes along the way of the Holy Cross, because it was so for Jesus and his Apostles. Brothers and sisters: never be surprised to find yourselves passing under the shadow of the Cross. *Christian life finds its whole meaning in love, but love does not exist for us without effort, discipline and sacrifice* in every aspect of our life. We are willing to give in proportion as we love, and when love is perfect the sacrifice is complete. God so loved the world that he gave his only Son, and the Son so loved us that he gave his life for our salvation.

### Triumph of the Cross Invites Us to Place Our Hope
### in the Crucified Savior

On this day when Catholics around the world celebrate the Triumph of the Cross, the Church invites us to look once again at the meaning of our Christian discipleship, to understand the sacrifices it involves, and *place all our hope in our Crucified and Risen Savior.*

O Triumphant Cross of Christ, inspire us to continue the task of evangelization!

O Glorious Cross of Christ, strengthen us to proclaim and live the Gospel of salvation!

O Victorious Cross of Christ, our only hope, lead us to the joy and peace of the Resurrection and eternal life! Amen.

## 26. MEETING WITH NATIVE AMERICANS

Dear Brothers and Sisters,

1. I have greatly looked forward to this visit with you, the original peoples of this vast country. *I greet you with love and respect.* And as I greet you, I wish to tell you how pleased I am to find among you one of your sons raised to the episcopacy, Bishop Pelotte. I thank you for inviting me to be with you and for sharing with me some aspects of your rich and ancient culture.

### I Traced in My Heart the History of Your Tribes and Nations

I have listened to your concerns and hopes. As your representatives spoke, I traced in my heart the history of your tribes and nations. I was able to see you as *the noble descendants of countless generations of inhabitants of this land,* whose ways were marked by great respect for the natural resources of land and river, of forest and plain and desert. Here your forefathers cherished and sought to pass on to each new generation their customs and traditions, their history and way of life. Here they worshiped the Creator and thanked him for his gifts. In contact with the forces of nature they learned the value of prayer, of silence and fasting, of patience and courage in the face of pain and disappointment.

### The Early Encounter Was Harsh and Painful but It Did Bring
### You the Gospel and the Equality of All Men and Women

2. *The early encounter between your traditional cultures and the European way of life was an event of such significance and change that it profoundly influences your collective life even today.* That encounter was a harsh and painful reality for your peoples. The cultural oppression, the injustices, the disruption of your life and of your traditional societies must be acknowledged.

At the same time, in order to be objective, history must record the deeply positive aspects of your peoples' encounter with the culture that came from Europe. Among these positive aspects I wish to recall the work of *the many missionaries who strenuously defended the rights of the original inhabitants of this land.* They established missions throughout this southwestern part of the United States. They worked to improve living conditions and set up educational systems, learning your languages in order to do so. Above all, they proclaimed the Good News of salvation in our Lord

Jesus Christ, an essential part of which is that all men and women are equally children of God and must be respected and loved as such. *This Gospel of Jesus Christ is today, and will remain forever, the greatest pride and possession of your people.*

### Fray Junípero Serra Was a Missionary Who Fought to Prevent Exploitation of Native Americans

3. One priest who deserves special mention among the missionaries is *the beloved Fray Junípero Serra,* who traveled throughout lower and upper California. He had frequent clashes with the civil authorities over the treatment of Indians. In 1773 he presented to the Viceroy in Mexico City a *Representación,* which is sometimes termed a "Bill of Rights" for Indians. The Church had long been convinced of the need to protect them from exploitation. Already in 1537, my predecessor *Pope Paul III proclaimed the dignity and rights of the native peoples of the Americas by insisting that they not be deprived of their freedom or the possession of their property (Pastorale Officium,* May 29, 1537: DS 1495). In Spain the Dominican priest, Francisco de Vitoria, became the staunch advocate of the rights of the Indians and formulated the basis for international law regarding the rights of peoples.

### We Are Called to Learn from the Mistakes of the Past to Work for Reconciliation

Unfortunately, not all the members of the Church lived up to their Christian responsibilities. But let us not dwell excessively on mistakes and wrongs, even as we commit ourselves to overcoming their present effects. Let us also be grateful to those who came to this land, faithful to the teachings of Jesus, witnesses of his new commandment of love. These men and women, with good hearts and good minds, shared knowledge and skills from their own cultures and shared their most precious heritage, the faith, as well. Now *we are called to learn from the mistakes of the past and we must work together for reconciliation and healing,* as brothers and sisters in Christ.

### I Encourage You to Keep Alive Your Cultures, Languages, Values and Customs

4. It is time to think of the present and of the future. Today, people are realizing more and more clearly that we all belong to the one human family and are meant to walk and work together in mutual respect, understanding, trust and love. Within this family *each people preserves and expresses its own identity and enriches others with its gifts of culture,* tradition, customs, stories, song, dance, art and skills.

From the very beginning, the Creator bestowed his gifts on each people. It is clear that stereotyping, prejudice, bigotry and racism demean the human dignity which comes from the hand of the Creator and which is seen in variety and diversity. I encourage you, as native people belonging to the different tribes and nations in the east, south, west and north, *to preserve and keep alive your cultures, your languages, the values and customs* which have served you well in the past and which provide a solid foundation for the future. Your customs that mark the various stages of life, your love for the extended family, your respect for the dignity and worth of every human being, from the unborn to the aged, and your stewardship and care of the earth: these things benefit not only yourselves but the entire human family.

### Your Gifts Can Be Expressed More Fully in the Christian Way of Life

Your gifts can also be expressed even more fully in the Christian way of life. *The Gospel of Jesus Christ is at home in every people. It enriches, uplifts and purifies every culture.* All of us together make up the People of God, the Body of Christ, the Church. We should all be grateful for the growing unity, presence, voice and leadership of Catholic Native Americans in the Church today.

### The Best-Known Witness of Christian Holiness Among the Native Peoples Is Kateri Tekakwitha

Jesus speaks of the word of God as the seed which falls on good ground and produces abundant fruit (see Mt. 13:4ff). The seed has long since been planted in the hearts of many of you. And it has already produced the fruits which show its transforming power—the fruits of holiness. *The best-known witness of Christian holiness among the native peoples of North America is Kateri Tekakwitha,* whom I had the privilege, seven years ago, of declaring "Blessed" and of holding up to the whole Church and the world as an outstanding example of Christian life. Even when she dedicated herself fully to Jesus Christ, to the point of taking the prophetic step of making a vow of perpetual virginity, *she always remained what she was, a true daughter of her people,* following her tribe in the hunting seasons and continuing her devotions in the environment most suited to her way of life, before a rough cross carved by herself in the forest. The Gospel of Jesus Christ, which is the great gift of God's love, is never in contrast with what is noble and pure in the life of any tribe or nation, since all good things are his gifts.

### The Gospel Does Not Destroy What Is Best; It Enriches from Within

5. I would like to repeat what I said at my meeting with native peoples at the Shrine of Saint Anne de Beaupre during my visit to Canada in 1984: "Your encounter with the Gospel has not only enriched you; it has enriched the Church. We are well aware that this has not taken place without its difficulties and, occasionally, its blunders. However, and you are experiencing this today, the Gospel does not destroy what is best in you. On the contrary, it enriches, as it were from within, the spiritual qualities and gifts that are distinctive of your cultures" (no. 3). The American Bishops' Statement on Native Americans rightly attests that our Catholic faith is capable of

thriving "within each culture, within each nation, within each race, while remaining the prisoner of none" (Statement of May 4, 1977).

## I Appeal to Local Churches in Their Outreach to Native Americans

Here too I wish to urge the local Churches to be truly "catholic" in their outreach to native peoples, and *to show respect and honor for their culture and all their worthy traditions.* From your ranks have come a Bishop, a number of priests, many permanent deacons, men and women Religious and lay leaders. To all of you who have an active part in the Church's ministry I wish to express my gratitude and support. But the Church has some special needs at this time. And for this reason *I directly appeal to you,* especially to you *young Native Americans, to discover if Jesus is calling you to the priesthood or to the religious life.* Hear him and follow him! He will never let you down! He will lead you, in the Church, to serve your own peoples and others in the best way possible, in love and apostolic generosity.

## I Call upon Native American Communities to Work Together

At the same time I call upon your native Catholic communities to *work together to share their faith and their gifts,* to work together on behalf of all your peoples. There is much to be done in solving common problems of unemployment, inadequate health care, alcoholism and chemical dependency. You have endured much over hundreds of years, and your difficulties are not yet at an end. Continue taking steps toward true human progress and toward reconciliation within your families and your communities, and among your tribes and nations.

## "I Came That They Might Have Life."

6. One day Jesus said: "The thief comes only to steal and slaughter and destroy. I came that they might have life and have it to the full" (Jn. 10).

## The Time Has Come to Have a New Life in Christ

*Surely, the time has come for the native peoples of America to have a new life in Jesus Christ*—the new life of adopted children of God, with all its consequences: A life in justice and full human dignity!

A life of pride in their own good traditions, and of fraternal solidarity among themselves and with all their brothers and sisters in America!

A deeper life in charity and grace, leading to the fullness of eternal life in heaven!

All consciences must be *challenged.* There are real injustices to be addressed and biased attitudes to be changed. But the greatest challenge is to you yourselves, as Native Americans. You must continue to grow in respect for your own inalienable human dignity, for the gifts of Creation and Redemption as they touch your lives and the lives of your peoples. You must unyieldingly pursue your spiritual and moral goals. You must *trust* in your own future.

As Catholic Native Americans, you are called to become *instruments of the healing power of Christ's love,* instruments of his peace. May the Church in your midst—your own community of faith and fellowship—truly bear witness to the new life that comes from the Cross and Resurrection of our Lord and Savior Jesus Christ!

## 27. HOMILY AT MASS CELEBRATED AT ARIZONA STATE UNIVERSITY

The Son of Man must be lifted up. (Jn. 3:14)

Dear Brothers and Sisters,

### Our Thoughts Go to the Victorious Cross of Our Savior

1. On this day when I have the joy of celebrating the Eucharist with you here in Phoenix, let our first thoughts be directed to *the victorious Cross* of our Savior, to the Son of Man who is lifted up! Let us adore and praise Christ, our Crucified and Risen Lord. To him, and to the Father and the Holy Spirit, be glory and thanksgiving now and forever!

### Phoenix Is a Symbol of Christ's Rising in Triumph Over Sin and Death

How good it is to join our voices in praise of God on this *feast of the Triumph of the Cross.* And how appropriate to celebrate the feast here in the city of *Phoenix,* which bears the name of an ancient symbol often depicted in Christian art to represent the meaning of the victorious Cross. The phoenix was a legendary bird that, after dying, rose again from its own ashes. Thus, it came to be a symbol of Christ who, after dying on the Cross, rose again in triumph over sin and death.

### The Cross Has Brought Forth Great Fruit Here

We can rightly say that, by divine providence, the Church in Phoenix has been called in a particular way to *live the mystery of the victory of the Cross.* Certainly, the Cross of Christ has marked the progress of evangelization in this area since its beginning: from the day, three hundred years ago, when Father *Eusebio Kino* first brought the Gospel to Arizona. The Good News of salvation has brought forth great fruit here in Phoenix, in Tucson and throughout this whole area. The Cross is indeed *the Tree of Life.*

2. *"The Son of Man must be lifted up"* (Jn. 3:14).

Today the Church makes special reference to these words of Christ as she celebrates the feast of the Triumph of the Cross. Beyond the particular historical circumstances that contributed to the introduction of this feast in the liturgical calendar, there remain these words that Christ spoke *to Nicodemus* during that conversation which took place at night: "The Son of Man must be lifted up."

### Nicodemus Came at Night to Find Answers

Nicodemus, as we know, was a man who loved God's word and who studied the word with great attention. Prompted by his hunger for the truth, by his eagerness to understand, Nicodemus came to Jesus at night to find answers to his questions and doubts. It is precisely to him, to Nicodemus, that Jesus speaks these words which still echo in a mysterious way: "The Son of Man must be lifted up, *that all who believe may have eternal life in him*" (Jn. 3:14–15).

### Christ Enlightened Nicodemus About the Cross by Referring to the Serpent in the Desert

Nicodemus could not have known at this point that these words contain, in a certain sense, the summary of the whole Paschal Mystery which would crown the messianic mission of Jesus of Nazareth. *When Jesus spoke of being "lifted up," he was thinking of the Cross on Calvary:* being lifted up *on* the Cross, being lifted up *by means of* the Cross. Nicodemus could not have guessed this at the time. And so Christ *referred to an event from the history of the Old Testament* which he knew about, namely, Moses lifting up the serpent in the desert.

### The Bronze Serpent Brought a Cure from Poisonous Serpents

3. It was an unusual event that took place *during Israel's journey from Egypt to the Promised Land.* This journey that lasted forty years was full of tests: *the people "tested" God with* their infidelity and lack of trust; in turn this provoked *many tests from the Lord* in order to purify Israel's faith and deepen it. Near Mount Hor a particular test took place, which was that of the *poisonous serpents.* These serpents "bit the people" with the result that many of them died (Nm. 21:6). *Then Moses,* ordered by the Lord, "*made a bronze serpent* and mounted it on a pole, and whenever anyone who had been bitten by a serpent looked at the bronze serpent, he recovered" (Nm. 21:9).

We might ask: why such a test? *The Lord had chosen Israel to be his own;* he had chosen this people, in order to initiate them gradually into his plan of salvation.

### Jesus Explains That the Bronze Serpent Was the Symbolic Figure of the Crucified One

4. Jesus of Nazareth explains the salvific designs of the God of the Covenant. *The bronze serpent* in the desert was *the symbolic figure of the Crucified One.* If someone

who had been bitten looked upon the serpent "lifted up" by Moses on a high pole, that person was saved. He remained alive, not because he had looked upon the serpent, but because *he had believed in the power of God* and his saving love. Thus when the Son of Man is lifted up on the Cross of Calvary, "all who believe will have eternal life in him" (see Jn. 3:15).

### The Analogy Lies in the Salvation from Spiritual Death That Came Through a Man

There exists then a profound *analogy between that figure and this reality,* between that sign of salvation and this reality of salvation contained in the Cross of Christ. The analogy becomes even more striking if we keep in mind that the salvation from physical death, caused by the poison of the serpents in the desert, came about through a serpent. *Salvation from spiritual death*—the death that is sin and that was caused by man—*came about through a man,* through the Son of Man "lifted up" on the Cross.

In this nighttime conversation, Jesus of Nazareth helps Nicodemus to discover the true sense of God's designs. While Jesus is speaking, *the fulfillment of these divine designs belongs to the future,* but at this point the future is not far away. Nicodemus himself will be a witness to this fulfillment. *He will be a witness* to the paschal events in Jerusalem. *He will be a witness* to the Cross, upon which the One who speaks with him this night—the Son of Man—will be lifted up.

### Jesus Prepares Nicodemus to Understand the Mystery of the Cross; Jesus Will Be Judged by the Sins of the World

5. Jesus goes on even further. The conversation becomes even deeper: *Why the Cross?* Why must the Son of Man be "lifted up" on the wood of the Cross? Because *"God so loved the world that he gave his only Son* that whoever believes in him may not die but may have eternal life" (Jn. 3:16). Yes, eternal life. This is the type of salvation that Jesus is speaking about: *eternal life in God.*

And then Jesus adds: "God did *not* send the Son into the world *to condemn the world,* but that the world might be saved through him" (Jn. 3:17). Many thought that the Messiah would be first of all *a severe judge* who would punish, "separating the wheat from the chaff" (see Mt. 3:12). If at one moment he will have to come as judge—at the end of the world—now "in the fullness of time" (see Gal. 4:4) *he comes to be judged himself by the sins of the world,* and therefore because of the sins of the world. And thus, Christ lifted up on the Cross becomes the Redeemer of the human race, the Redeemer of the world.

Jesus of Nazareth prepares Nicodemus, the eager student of the Scriptures, so that in time *he will understand the saving mystery contained in the Cross of Christ.* And we know that, in time, Nicodemus did understand, but not during that night.

## This Absolute Lowering, This Emptying,
## Is the Source of the Lifting Up of Humanity

6. *What, then, does this "being lifted up" mean?*

In the second reading of today's liturgy, taken from Saint Paul's Letter to the Philippians, *"being lifted up" means first of all "being brought low."* The Apostle writes about Christ, saying, "Though he was in the form of God, he did not deem equality with God something to be grasped at. Rather, he emptied himself and *took the form of a slave*, being born *in the likeness of men*" (Phil. 2:6–7). The God-man! God becoming man. God taking on our humanity: this is the first dimension of "being brought low," and at the same time it is a "lifting up." God is brought low, so that man may be lifted up. Why? *Because "God so loved the world."* Because he is love!

Then the Apostle writes: "[Christ] was known to be of human estate, and it was thus that *he humbled himself, obediently accepting death, death on a Cross*" (Phil. 2:7–8). This is *the second and the definitive dimension of being brought low.* It is the dimension of being emptied which confirms in the strongest way the truth of those words: "God so loved the world that he gave his only Son." He *gave. This emptying is itself the gift.* It is the greatest gift of the Father. It surpasses all other gifts. It is the source of every gift. In this absolute lowering, in this emptying, is the beginning and source of every "lifting up," *the source of the lifting up of humanity.*

## The Cross Lifted Up Was the Culmination of Humiliation
## but in the Eyes of God It Was Different

7. The Cross was "lifted up" on Golgotha. And Jesus was nailed to the Cross and was therefore lifted up with it. *To the human eye,* this was *the culmination of humiliation and disgrace.* But *in the eyes of God* it was different. It was different in the eternal designs of God.

The Apostle continues: "Because of this, God highly exalted him and bestowed on him the name above every other name, so that at Jesus' name every knee must bend in the heavens, on the earth, and under the earth, and every tongue proclaim to the glory of God the Father: *Jesus Christ is Lord*" (Phil. 2:9–11).

Christ *is* the Lord! This will be confirmed in the Resurrection, but it is *already* contained in the *Crucifixion.* Precisely in the Crucifixion.

## To Be Crucified Is to Be Disgraced,
## but Christ Becomes Lord of All in This Elevation

To be crucified, humanly speaking, is to be disgraced and humiliated. But from God's point of view it means being lifted up. Indeed, to be lifted up by means of the Cross. Christ is the Lord, and he becomes Lord of everything and everyone in this elevation by means of the Cross. It is in this way that we look upon the Cross, with the eyes of faith, *instructed by the word of God,* guided by the power of God.

Here then is the mystery of *the Triumph of the Cross.*

### This Mystery Reaches Us in a Particular Way in the Sacrament of the Anointing of the Sick

8. This mystery reaches us in a particular way and with a special power when the Church celebrates *the Sacrament of the Anointing of the Sick,* as she does this evening. By means of this Sacrament, and through all her pastoral service, the Church continues *to care for the sick and dying as Jesus did* during his earthly ministry. Through the laying on of hands by the priest, the anointing with oil and the prayers, our brothers and sisters are strengthened with the grace of the Holy Spirit. They are enabled to bear their sufferings with courage and thus to embrace the Cross and follow after Christ with stronger faith and hope.

### This Holy Anointing Brings Special Grace and Consolation to the Dying

This holy Anointing does not prevent physical death, nor does it promise a miraculous healing of the human body. But it does bring *special grace and consolation to those who are dying,* preparing them to meet our loving Savior with lively faith and love and with firm hope for eternal life. It also brings *comfort and strength to those who are not dying* but who are suffering from serious illness or advanced age. For these the Church seeks healing of both body and soul, praying that the whole person may be renewed by the power of the Holy Spirit.

### Every Celebration Proclaims the Church's Belief in the Victory of the Cross

Every time that the Church celebrates this Sacrament, she is *proclaiming her belief in the victory of the Cross.* It is as if she were repeating the words of Saint Paul: "I am certain that *neither death nor life,* neither angels nor principalities, neither the present nor the future, nor powers, neither height nor depth nor any other creature, *will be able to separate us from the love of God* that comes to us in Christ Jesus, our Lord" (Rom. 8:38–39).

### The Church Welcomes the People Who Came to Phoenix for Health Care

From the very early days until now, Phoenix has been a city to which people have come for health care, for relief of suffering, for new beginnings and fresh starts. Today as in the past, the Church welcomes such people, offering them love and understanding. She is grateful to the sick and elderly for the special mission which they fulfill in the Kingdom of our Savior. Your hospitality, which I myself have also received, reflects the beautiful saying in Spanish: *"mi casa, su casa."* I pray that you will always remain faithful to this tradition of Christian community and generous service.

### Suffering and Death Are Not the Last Word,
### It Is the Risen Christ

By such fidelity to your Christian heritage, through the Sacrament of the Anointing of the Sick, and in the celebration of the Holy Eucharist, you express your deep conviction that suffering and death are not the last words of life. The last word is the Word made flesh, *the Crucified and Risen Christ.*

9. The responsorial psalm of today's liturgy exhorts us:

*Hearken, my people, to my teaching;*
Incline your ears to the words of my mouth . . .
I will utter mysteries from of old. (Ps. 77/78:1–2)

It was exactly in this way that Christ revealed the mystery of salvation to Nicodemus, and to us. And to all people.

The words which follow, in that same psalm, also refer to us:

But *they flattered him* with their mouths
*and lied to him with their tongues,*
Though their hearts were not steadfast toward him,
nor were they faithful to his covenant. (Ps. 77/78:36–37)

And nevertheless:

While he slew them they sought him
and inquired after God again;
Remembering that *God was their rock*
and the Most High God, *their Redeemer.* (Ps. 77/78:34–35)

And this is how God continues among us, from one generation to the next, as our Rock, our Redeemer. This is *the mystery of the Triumph of the Cross, the rock of our salvation.*

Let us fix our gaze upon the Cross!

Let us be reborn from it!

Let us return to God!

May the humiliation of Christ—his being brought low by means of the Cross—serve once again to lift up humanity toward God.

*Sursum corda!* Lift up your hearts! Amen.


### SEPTEMBER 15, 1987

### 28. VISIT TO SAINT VIBIANA'S CATHEDRAL


Dear Archbishop Mahony,

Dear Cardinal Manning,

Dear Brothers and Sisters,

1. I greet you today *in the name of our Lord Jesus Christ.* Through his love and mercy we are gathered together in the Church to offer praise and thanksgiving to our

heavenly Father. Grace and peace be to all of you—the clergy, Religious and laity of this city named in honor of our Lady of the Angels. May she continue to assist you in praising God both now and forever with the angels, the patroness of this Cathedral—Saint Vibiana—and all the Saints.

## The Name of Jesus Unites Us
## in One Household of Faith and Love

I wish to join my voice to the chorus of praise offered to God in the name of Jesus in so many languages and by people of different races and ethnic origins in this great metropolis. It is his name above all that *unites us in one household* of faith, hope and love. It is the name of Jesus that transcends every division and heals every antagonism within the human family.

As the Successor of Peter, I come to you today in the name of Jesus. It cannot be otherwise, since every true minister of the Gospel preaches not himself or any message of human origin, but he *preaches Jesus Christ* as Lord (see 2 Cor. 4:5). To the fears, doubts and struggles of individuals and nations, the Church seeks to apply the healing power of that name which belongs to him who alone is the Word of God (see Rv. 19:13).

## The Name of Jesus Brings Salvation and Life

2. In a world filled with competing ideologies and so many false and empty promises, the name of Jesus Christ brings salvation and life. The Hebrew word *"Jesus" means "Savior,"* as the Angel said to Joseph in his dream: "You are to name him Jesus because he will save his people from their sins" (Mt. 1:21). At the very beginning of the Church's mission, Saint Peter proclaims that "there is no salvation in anyone else, for there is no other name in the whole world given to men by which they are to be saved" (Acts 4:12). This name is a source of life for those who believe (see Jn. 20:31); it delivers us from evil and leads us to the truth that alone can set us free (see Jn. 8:32).

## The Name of Jesus Is a Cry for Deliverance

The name of Jesus is therefore *a cry of deliverance* for all humanity. It has the power to comfort and heal the sick (see Acts 3:6; Jas. 5:14–15), to cast out demons (see Mk. 16:17; Lk. 10:17; Acts 16:18), and to work every kind of miracle (see Mt. 7:22; Acts 4:30). Most importantly it is in the name of Jesus and through his power that our sins are forgiven (see 1 Jn. 2:12).

## The Name of Jesus at the Heart of Worship
## Is the Motive of Charity

The *name of Jesus* is at the heart of Christian worship in this Cathedral and in every Church throughout the world: "Where two or three are gathered in my name, there am I in their midst" (Mt. 18:20). The name of Jesus is at the heart of all Christian prayer: "All you ask the Father in my name he will give you" (Jn. 15:16). It is a motivation for charity, because as Jesus himself explained, "Whoever gives you a cup of water to drink because you bear the name of Christ, will by no means lose his reward" (Mk. 9:41). It calls forth the gift of the Holy Spirit, "the Paraclete, whom the Father will send in my name" (Jn. 14:26).

## Christians, We Are Obliged to Speak and Act in the Name of Jesus

3. My dear brothers and sisters: we are called Christians, and therefore the name of Jesus Christ is also our name. At the baptismal font we received a "Christian name" which symbolizes our communion with Christ and his saints. Our identification with him is reflected in the rule of life which Saint Paul proposes in the Letter to the Colossians: "Whatever you do, whether in speech or in action, do it in the name of the Lord Jesus. Give thanks to God the Father through him" (Col. 3:17). We are obliged not only to give thanks, but also *to speak and act* in the name of Jesus, even at the risk of being ill-treated, persecuted, and hated "for the sake of the name," as Jesus foretold (Acts 5:41; see also Mk. 13:13, Lk. 21:12).

## In a Secularized World to Speak and Act in the Name of Jesus Can Bring Opposition

As citizens of the United States, you must give thanks to God for the religious liberty which you enjoy under your Constitution, now in its two hundredth year. However, freedom to follow your Catholic faith does not automatically mean that it will be easy to "speak and act" in the name of the Lord Jesus with a conscience formed by the word of God authentically interpreted by the Church's teaching (see *Dei Verbum,* 9ff). In a secularized world, to speak and act in the name of Jesus can bring *opposition and even ridicule.* It often means being out of step with majority opinion. Yet if we look at the New Testament, we find encouragement everywhere for perseverance in this testing of our faith. As the First Letter of Saint Peter tells us: "If anyone suffers for being a Christian . . . he ought not to be ashamed. He should rather glorify God in virtue of that name" (1 Pt. 4:6). And Jesus himself says, "In the world you will have trouble, but take courage, I have conquered the world" (Jn. 16:33).

## The Message of Jesus' Victory Is Important for Young People, for Parents, for Clergy and Religious

Is not this message extremely important for young people who are trying *to live a responsible moral life* in the face of a tide of popular culture and peer pressure that is indifferent, if not hostile, to Christian morality? And for their parents, who face daily pressures in the conduct of both their private and public life? And for the clergy and Religious, who may sometimes find it difficult to speak the full truth of the Church's teaching because it is a "hard saying" that many will not readily accept?

### In the Name of Jesus We Find the Strength
### to Proclaim and Live the Gospel

4. Dear brothers and sisters, the name of Jesus, like the Word of God that he is, is a two-edged sword (see Heb. 4:12). *It is a name that means salvation and life;* it is a name that means a struggle and a cross, just as it did for him. But it is also the name in which we find *strength to proclaim and live the truth of the Gospel:* not with arrogance, but with confident joy; not with self-righteousness, but with humble repentance before God; never with enmity, and always with charity.

### The Name of Jesus Is a Source of Hope

Dear people of this great Archdiocese of Los Angeles, with its many problems, its enormous challenges and its immense possibilities for good: *The name of Jesus is your life and your salvation.* It is your pride and joy, and the pride and joy of your families and your parishes. In this name you find strength for your weaknesses and energy for daily Christian living. In your struggle against evil and the Evil One, and in your striving for holiness, the name of Jesus is the source of your hope, because in the name of Jesus you are invincible!

Continue, then, dear Catholic people of Los Angeles, to invoke this holy name of Jesus in your joys and your sorrows; continue to teach this name to your children, so that they in turn can teach it to their children, until the Lord Jesus himself comes in glory to judge the living and the dead!

## 29. ADDRESS DURING A YOUTH TELECONFERENCE
## AT THE UNIVERSAL AMPHITHEATRE

Dear young Friends,

### Enjoy Your Company; You Bring Hope to the World

1. I think that you already know, without my saying it, how happy I am to be with you today. Wherever I travel around the world, I always make it a point to meet with young people. A few days ago I was with them in New Orleans, and today *I enjoy being with you.* From my early days as a young priest, I have spent many hours talking with students on university campuses or while hiking along lakes or in the mountains and hills. I have spent many evenings singing with young men and women like yourselves. Even now as Pope, during the summer months, various groups of young people come to Castelgandolfo for an evening and we sing and talk together.

As you probably know, I often say that you who are young bring *hope* to the world. The future of the world shines in your eyes. Even now, you are helping to shape the future of society. Since I have always placed high hopes in young people, I would like to speak to you today precisely *about hope.*

### People of Hope Are Those Who Believe God Created Them for a Purpose and That He Will Provide

2. *We cannot live without hope.* We have to have some purpose in life, some meaning to our existence. We have to aspire to something. Without hope, we begin to die. Why does it sometimes happen that a seemingly healthy person, successful in the eyes of the world, takes an overdose of sleeping pills and commits suicide? Why, on the other hand, do we see a seriously disabled person filled with great zest for life? Is it not because of hope? The one has lost all hope; in the other, hope is alive and overflowing. Clearly, then, hope does not stem from talents and gifts, or from physical health and success! It comes from something else. To be more precise, *hope comes from someone else,* someone beyond ourselves.

### Life Is More Important than Food and the Body, More than Clothing

Hope comes *from God,* from our belief in God. People of hope are those who believe God created them for a purpose and that he will provide for their needs. They believe that God loves them as a faithful Father. Do you remember the advice that Jesus gave his disciples when they seemed to be *fearful of the future?* He said: "Do not be concerned for your life, what you are to eat, or for your body, what you are to wear. *Life is more important* than food and the body more than clothing. Consider the ravens: they do not sow, they do not reap, they have neither cellar nor barn—yet God feeds them. *How much more important you are than the birds!"* (Lk. 12:22–24).

Yes, God knows all our needs. He is the foundation for our hope.

### Without Faith in God There Can Be No Hope, No Lasting Authentic Hope

3. But what about people who do not believe in God? This is indeed a serious problem, one of the greatest of our time—*atheism,* the fact that many of our contemporaries have no faith in God. When I visited Australia last year, I told a group of children: "The hardest thing about being Pope is to see that many people do not accept the love of Jesus, do not know who he really is and *how much he loves them.* . . . [Jesus] does not force people to accept his love. He offers it to them and leaves them free to say *yes* or *no.* It fills me with joy to see how many people know and love our Lord, how many say *yes* to him. But it saddens me to see that some people say *no"* (November 29, 1986). Without faith in God, there can be no hope,

no lasting, authentic hope. To stop believing in God is to start down a path that can lead only to emptiness and despair.

## We Do Not Lose Heart,
## Because Our Inner Being Is Renewed Each Day

But those who have the gift of faith live with confidence about things to come. They *look to the future with anticipation and joy,* even in the face of suffering and pain; and the future that they are ultimately looking toward is everlasting life with the Lord. This kind of hope was very prominent in the life of Saint Paul, who once wrote: "We are afflicted in every way possible, but we are not crushed; full of doubts, we never despair. We are persecuted but never abandoned; we are struck down but never destroyed. . . . *We do not lose heart,* because our inner being is renewed each day" (2 Cor. 4:8–9, 16). Only God can renew our inner self each day. Only God can give meaning to life, God who has drawn near to each of us in "Christ Jesus our hope" (1 Tm. 1:1).

## May You Have Strong Faith and Be Messengers of Hope

In the New Testament there are two letters ascribed to Saint Peter. In the first of these, he said: "Venerate the Lord, that is, Christ, in your hearts. Should anyone ask you *the reason for this hope of yours,* be ever ready to reply" (1 Pt. 3:15). Dear young friends, I pray that your faith in Christ will always be lively and strong. In this way, you will *always be ready to tell others the reason* for your hope; you will *be messengers of hope for the world.*

## Listen Carefully to God's Voice in Your Heart

4. I am often asked, especially by young people, *why I became a priest.* Maybe some of you would like to ask the same question. Let me try briefly to reply.

I must begin by saying that it is impossible to explain entirely. For it remains a mystery, even to myself. How does one explain the ways of God? Yet I know that, at a certain point in my life, I became convinced that Christ was saying to me what he had said to thousands before me: *"Come, follow me!"* There was a clear sense that *what I heard in my heart* was no human voice, nor was it just an idea of my own. Christ was calling me to serve him as a priest.

And you can probably tell, *I am deeply grateful* to God for my vocation to the priesthood. Nothing means more to me or gives me greater joy than *to celebrate Mass each day* and *to serve God's people* in the Church. That has been true ever since the day of my ordination as a priest. Nothing has ever changed it, not even becoming Pope.

Confiding this to you, I would like to invite each of you to listen carefully to God's voice in your heart. *Every human person is called to communion with God.* That is why the Lord made us, to know him and love him and serve him, and—in doing this—to find the secret to lasting joy.

### Church Needs Priests, Religious and Holy Lay People
### in Married and in the Single State

In the past the Church in the United States has been rich in vocations to the priesthood and religious life. And it could be especially true today. At the same time, the Church needs the Gospel witness of holy lay people, in married life and in the single state. Be assured that *the Lord knows each of you by name* and wishes to speak to your heart in a dialogue of love and salvation. *God continues to speak* to young people on the banks of *the Mississippi River* and on the slopes of the Rocky Mountains. God continues to speak in the cities on the *West Coast* of America and across the *rolling hills and plains.* God continues to speak to every human person.

Dear young people of America, *listen to his voice.* Do not be afraid. Open up your hearts to Christ. The deepest joy there is in life is the joy that comes from God and is found in Jesus Christ, the Son of God. He is the hope of the world. Jesus Christ is your hope and mine!

## 30. MEETING WITH COMMUNICATIONS SPECIALISTS

Ladies and Gentlemen of the Communications Industry,

Dear Friends,

1. I am very pleased to be here with you. I would like to be able to greet each one of you personally and to express my regard for you individually. Although this is not possible, I wish to express my sincere respect for *all the categories of the media* that you represent—the film industry, the music and recording industry, radio, electronic news, television and all those who inform the world through the written word—and for *the diverse functions* that you perform as workers, writers, editors, managers and executives. I greet you in the full range of your activities, from the very visible to the relatively hidden.

### You Represent One of the Most Important
### American Influences on the World Today

My visit to Los Angeles, and indeed to the United States, would seem incomplete without this meeting, since you represent *one of the most important American influences on the world today.* You do this in every area of social communications and contribute thereby to the development of a mass popular culture. Humanity is profoundly influenced by what you do. *Your activities affect communication itself:* supplying information, influencing public opinion, offering entertainment. The consequences of these activities are numerous and diverse. You help your fellow citizens to enjoy leisure, to appreciate art and to profit from culture. You often provide the stories they tell and the songs they sing. You give them news of current events, a vision of humanity and motives for hope. Yours is indeed a profound influence on society. Hundreds of millions of people see your films and television programs, listen to your voices, sing your songs and reflect your opinions. It is a fact that your smallest decisions can have global impact.

### Your Work Can Reveal What Is Noble and Uplifting or Appeal to What Is Debased in People

2. Your work can be *a force for great good or great evil.* You yourselves know the dangers as well as the splendid opportunities open to you. Communication products can be works of great beauty, revealing what is *noble and uplifting* in humanity and promoting what is just and fair and true. On the other hand, communications can appeal to and promote what is *debased* in people: dehumanized sex through pornography or through a casual attitude toward sex and human life; greed through materialism and consumerism or irresponsible individualism; anger and vengefulness through violence or self-righteousness. All the media of popular culture which you represent can build or destroy, uplift or cast down. You have untold possibilities for good, ominous possibilities for destruction. It is the difference between death and life—the death or life of the spirit. And it is a matter of choice. The challenge of Moses to the people of Israel is applicable to all of us today: "I set before you life and death. . . . Choose life" (Dt. 30:19).

### The Constitution Links in the First Amendment the Exercise of Religion and the Art of Human Expression

3. There is something of great interest for all of us in the Constitution of the United States. The same amendment that guarantees freedom of speech and freedom of the press also guarantees freedom of religious practice. *The link between the art of human expression and the exercise of religion is profound.* Social communications in fact provide an important first step in uniting human beings in mutual love, and this first step is also a step to God, "for God is love" (1 Jn. 4:8). *Religious practice* for its part fosters communication with God. But it also fosters human communication, since *human communication is part of that relationship of love for neighbor* that is mandated in both the Old and New Testaments.

It is easy to see why the Church has recognized and taught that people have a right to communicate. Linked to this right is *the right to information,* about which the Second Vatican Council speaks in these words: "Because of the progress of modern society and the increasing interdependence of its members, it is clear that information has become very useful and generally necessary. . . . There exists therefore in human society a right to information on the subjects that are of concern to people" (*Inter Mirifica,* 5).

## The Right to Information Demands That the Content
## of What Is Communicated Be True

In this way, then, the Church recognizes the need for freedom of speech and freedom of the press, just as does your Constitution. But she goes further. *Rights imply corresponding duties.* The proper exercise of the right to information demands that the content of what is communicated be true and—within the limits set by justice and charity—complete (see *Inter Mirifica*, 5). Your very profession invites you to reflect on this *obligation to truth and its completeness.* Included here is the obligation *to avoid any manipulation of truth for any reason.* This manipulation in fact takes place when certain issues are deliberately passed over in silence, in order that others may be unduly emphasized. It also occurs when information is altered or withheld so that society will be less able to resist the imposition of a given ideology.

## Truth and Completeness Apply to All Your Work

The obligation to truth and its completeness applies not only to the coverage of news, but to all your work. Truth and completeness should characterize the content of artistic expression and entertainment. You find a real meaning in your work when you exercise your role as collaborators of truth—*collaborators of truth in the service of justice, fairness and love.*

## You Have Marvelous Tools to Promote What Is Human
## and Direct It to the Work of People

4. Your industry not only speaks to people and for people; it makes communication possible among them. In this we see how your activities transcend the categories of both rights and duties and confer upon you *inestimable privileges.* Just before joining you this afternoon, I met with young people in several cities by using satellite links. For me this is just one example of how your industry can help foster communication and unite people in fraternal love. It is within your power to use technology to promote what is deeply human and to direct it to the work of peace. You have *marvelous tools* which others lack. They must be employed *in the service of people's right to communicate.*

## People Should Have the Opportunity
## to Participate in the Communication Process

In today's modern world there is always the danger of communication becoming exclusively one-way, depriving audiences of the opportunity *to participate in the communication process.* Should that happen with you, you would no longer be communicators in the full, human sense. The people themselves, the general public whom you serve, should not be excluded from having the opportunity for public dialogue.

In order to foster such a dialogue, you yourselves, as communicators, must listen as well as speak. You must seek to communicate with people, and not just speak to them. This involves learning about people's needs, being aware of their struggles and *presenting all forms of communications with the sensitivity that human dignity requires*— your human dignity and theirs. This applies especially to all audio-visual programs.

## Social Communications Must Support Human Dignity

5. *At the basis of all human rights is the dignity of the human person* created in the image and likeness of God (Gn. 1:27). A recognition of this human dignity is also a part of your civil tradition in the United States, and is expressed in the declaration of your nation's independence: all people are created equal in their human dignity and are endowed by their Creator with inalienable rights to life, liberty and the pursuit of happiness. All other rights too are rooted in human dignity, including the right to maintain one's privacy and not to be exploited in the intimacy of one's family.

The fundamental dignity of the human person is still more strongly *proclaimed by the Church*. She raises her voice on behalf of people everywhere, declaring the dignity of every human being, every man, woman and child. None is excluded because all bear the image of God. Physical and mental handicaps, spiritual weaknesses and human aberrations cannot obliterate the dignity of man. You will understand why the Church attaches such importance to this principle found on the first page of the Bible; it will later become the basis of the teaching of Jesus Christ as he says: "Always treat others as you would like them to treat you" (Mt. 7:12).

In particular, *social communications must support human dignity,* because the world is constantly tempted to forget it. Whether in news or in drama, whether in song or in story, you are challenged to respect what is human and to recognize what is good. Human beings must never be despised because of limitations, flaws, disorders or even sins. Twenty years ago, my predecessor Pope Paul VI, speaking to a gathering much like this one, told that creative community in Rome: "It is a fact that when, as writers and artists, you are able to reveal in the human condition, however lowly or sad it may be, a spark of goodness, at that very instant a glow of beauty pervades your whole work. We are not asking that you should play the part of moralists, but we are expressing confidence in your mysterious power of opening up the glorious regions of light that lie behind the mystery of human life" (Allocution of May 6, 1967).

## Is What You Communicate Consistent with the Full Measure of Human Dignity?

As you do precisely this—open up the glorious regions of light that lie behind the mystery of human life—you must ask yourselves *if what you communicate is consistent with the full measure of human dignity.* How do the weakest and the most defenseless in society appear in your words and images: the most severely handicapped, the very old, foreigners and the undocumented, the unattractive and the lonely, the sick and the infirm? Whom do you depict as having—or not having—human worth?

## Society Relies So Much on Your Good Will

6. Certainly your profession subjects you to *a great measure of accountability*—accountability to God, to the community and before the witness of history. And yet at times it seems that everything is left in your hands. Precisely because your responsibility is so great and your accountability to the community is not easily rendered juridically, society relies so much on your good will. In a sense the world is at your mercy. Errors in judgment, mistakes in evaluating the propriety and justice of what is transmitted, and wrong criteria in art can offend and wound consciences and human dignity. They can encroach on sacred fundamental rights. The *confidence* that the community has in you *honors you deeply and challenges you mightily*.

## Respect Your Own Dignity; Cultivate the Integrity Consonant with Your Own Human Dignity

7. I would encourage you in yet another way: *to respect also your own dignity*. All that I have said about the dignity of human beings applies to you.

*Daily cares oppress you* in ways different from those arising in other kinds of work. Your industry reflects the fast pace of the news and changing tastes. It deals with vast amounts of money that bring with them their own problems. It places you under extreme pressure to be successful, without telling you what "success" really is. Working constantly with images, you face the temptation of seeing them as reality. Seeking to satisfy the dreams of millions, you can become lost in a world of fantasy.

At this point, you must cultivate *the integrity consonant with your own human dignity*. You are more important than success, more valuable than any budget. Do not let your work drive you blindly; for if work enslaves you, you will soon enslave your art. Who you *are* and what you *do* are too important for that to happen. Do not let money be your sole concern, for it too is capable of enslaving art as well as souls. In your life there must also be room for your families and for leisure. You need time to rest and be re-created, for only in quiet can you absorb the peace of God.

## You Have a Great Part in Shaping the Culture of Many Nations

You yourselves are called to what is noble and lofty in human living, and you must study the highest expressions of the human spirit. You have *a great part in shaping the culture* of this nation and other nations. To you is entrusted an important portion of the vast heritage of the human race. In fulfilling your mission you must always be aware of *how your activities affect the world community,* how they serve the cause of universal solidarity.

## The Church Has Promoted the Arts
## for Centuries and Does So Today

8. *The Church* wishes you to know that she *is on your side*. For a long time she has been a patron and defender of the arts; she has promoted the media and been in the forefront of the use of new technology. The first book for the printing press of Johannes Gutenberg, the inventor of movable type, was the inspired word of God, the Bible. Vatican Radio was established under the direction of the inventor of radio, Guglielmo Marconi.

Today, too, the Church stands ready to help you by her encouragement and *to support you in all your worthy aims*. She offers you her challenge and her praise. I pray that you will welcome that help and never be afraid to accept it.

Ladies and gentlemen of the communications industry: I have set before you the broad outlines of *a choice for good within the framework of your profession*. I ask you to choose common good. It means honoring the dignity of every human being.

## You Are the Stewards of an Immense
## Spiritual Power to Enrich the Human Community

I am convinced that to a great extent we can share a common hope, rooted in *a vision of the human race harmoniously united through communication*. I am sure too that all of you, whether Christian or not, will permit me to allude to the great fascination that surrounds the mystery of the communicating word. For Christians, the communicating word is the explanation of all reality as expressed by Saint John: "In the beginning was the Word; the Word was in God's presence, and the Word was God" (Jn. 1:1). And for all those who hold the Judeo-Christian tradition, the nobility of communication is linked to the wisdom of God and expressed in his loving revelation. Thus the Book of Deuteronomy records God's communication to Israel: "You shall love the Lord your God with all your heart, and with all your soul, and with all your strength. Take to heart these words which I enjoin on you today" (Dt. 6:6).

Ladies and gentlemen: *as communicators of the human word, you are the stewards and administrators of an immense spiritual power* that belongs to the patrimony of mankind and is meant to enrich the whole of the human community. The challenge that opens up before you truly requires generosity, service and love. I am sure that you will strive to meet it. And, as you do, I pray that you will experience in your own lives a deep satisfaction and joy. And may the peace of God dwell in your hearts.

## 31. HOMILY AT MASS CELEBRATED IN THE
## LOS ANGELES COLISEUM

And you yourself shall be pierced with a sword. (Lk. 2:35)

Dear Brothers and Sisters of the Archdiocese of Los Angeles,
and of the Dioceses of Orange, San Diego, San Bernardino,
and Fresno,

## The Church Feels Very Deeply
## the Suffering of the Mother of Golgotha

1.The Church's meditation today focuses on the sufferings of Mary, the Mother standing at the foot of her Son's Cross. This *brings to completion* yesterday's feast of the Triumph of the Cross. Jesus had said, "Once I am lifted up, I will draw all men to myself" (Jn. 12:32). These words were fulfilled when he was "lifted up" *on the Cross.*

The Church, which constantly lives this mystery, feels very deeply the suffering of the Mother on Golgotha. The agony of the Son who in his terrible pain entrusts the whole world to his Father, that agony is united with the agony in the heart of the Mother there on Calvary. Today's Gospel reminds us that, when Jesus was only forty days old, *Simeon* had foretold this agony in the heart of the Mother when he said: "And you yourself shall be pierced with a sword" (Lk. 2:35).

## "Not As I Will, But As You Will"

The entire *mystery of obedience to the Father* is encompassed by the Son's agony: "he humbled himself, obediently accepting even death, death on a cross" (Phil. 2:8), as yesterday's liturgy proclaimed. And today we read in the Letter to the Hebrews: "In the days when he was in the flesh, [Christ] offered prayers and supplications with loud cries and tears to God, who was able to save him from death" (Heb. 5:7). These words have special application to the agony in the Garden of Gethsemane when he prayed: "My Father, if it is possible, let this cup pass me by" (Mt. 26:39–42). The author of the Letter to the Hebrews immediately adds that Christ "was heard because of his reverence" (Heb. 5:7). Yes, he was heard. He had said, "not as I will but as you will" (Mt. 26:39). And so it came to pass.

## "Son Though He Was, He Learned Obedience . . . "

The agony of Christ was, and still is, the mystery of his obedience to the Father. *At Gethsemane. On Calvary,* "Son though he was," the text continues, "he learned obedience from what he suffered" (Heb. 5:8). This includes Christ's obedience even unto death—the perfect sacrifice of Redemption. "And when perfected, he became the source of eternal salvation for all who obey him" (v. 9).

## Mary's Pilgrimage of Faith
## Is United with the Agony of Mary's Maternal Heart

2. As we celebrate Our Lady of Sorrows during this Marian Year, let us call to mind the teaching of the Second Vatican Council concerning the presence of Mary,

the Mother of God, in the mystery of Christ and of the Church. Let us recall in particular the following words: "The Blessed Virgin advanced in her *pilgrimage of faith,* and loyally persevered in her union with her Son unto the Cross, where she stood, in keeping with the divine plan" (*Lumen Gentium,* 58).

Mary's pilgrimage of faith! It is precisely at the foot of the Cross that this pilgrimage of faith, which began at the Annunciation, *reaches its high point,* its culmination. There it is united with the agony of Mary's maternal heart. "Suffering grievously with her only-begotten Son . . . she lovingly consented to the immolation of this Victim which she herself had brought forth" (*Lumen Gentium,* 58). At the same time, the agony of her maternal heart also represents a fulfillment of the words of Simeon: "And you yourself shall be pierced with a sword" (Lk. 2:35). Surely these prophetic words express the *"divine plan"* by which Mary is destined to stand at the foot of the Cross.

## The Sequence Presents Us with the Union of the Mother at the Foot of the Cross

3. Today's liturgy makes use of the ancient poetic text of the sequence which begins with the Latin words *Stabat Mater:*

> By the Cross of our salvation
> Mary stood in desolation
> While the Savior hung above.
> All her human powers failing,
> Sorrow's sword, at last prevailing,
> Stabs and breaks her heart of love. . . .
> Virgin Mary, full of sorrow,
> From your love I ask to borrow
> Love enough to share your pain.
> Make my heart to burn with fire,
> Make Christ's love my one desire,
> Who for love of me was slain.

The author of this sequence sought, in the most eloquent way humanly possible, to present the *"compassion" of the Mother* at the foot of the Cross. He was inspired by those words of Sacred Scripture about the sufferings of Mary which, though few and concise, are deeply moving.

## At the Foot of the Cross the "Great Things" Find Perfect Fulfillment

It is appropriate that *Mary's song of praise,* the Magnificat, should also find a place in our celebration: "My being proclaims the greatness of the Lord. . . . For he has looked upon his servant in her lowliness. . . . God who is mighty has done great things for me. . . . His mercy is from age to age. . . . Even as he promised our fathers, Abraham and his descendants forever" (Lk. 1:46–55).

Can we not suppose that these words, which reflect the fervor and exultation of the young mother's heart, still ring true at the foot of the Cross? That they still reveal her heart now that she finds herself in agony with her Son? Humanly speaking, it does not seem possible to us. However, within the fullness of divine truth, the words of the Magnificat actually *find their ultimate meaning* in the light of Christ's Paschal Mystery, from the Cross through the Resurrection.

It is precisely in this Paschal Mystery that the "great things" which God who is mighty has done for Mary find their *perfect fulfillment,* not only for her, but for all of us and for all of humanity. It is precisely at the foot of the Cross that the promise is fulfilled which God once made to Abraham and to his descendants, the people of the Old Covenant. It is also at the foot of the Cross that there is an overflow of *the mercy* shown to humanity from generation to generation by him whose name is holy.

Yes, at the foot of the Cross, the "humility of the Lord's servant"—the one upon whom "God has looked" (see Lk. 1:48)—reaches its full measure together with the absolute humiliation of the Son of God. But from that same spot *the "blessing" of Mary by "all ages to come"* also begins. There, at the foot of the Cross—to use the description of the prophet Isaiah in the first reading—the Virgin of Nazareth is fully "clothed with a robe of salvation" (see Is. 61:10): she whom already at the Annunciation the Archangel hailed as "full of grace" (Lk. 1:28); she who was redeemed in the most perfect manner; she who was conceived without stain in view of the merits of her Son. At the price of the Cross. In virtue of Christ's Paschal Mystery.

### All of Us Experience Suffering in Our Lives

4. Dear brothers and sisters of Los Angeles and Southern California: it is a joy for me to celebrate this liturgy today with you. California has been a symbol of hope and promise for millions of people who continue to come here to make a home for themselves and their families. Today the people of California play *a major role in shaping the culture of the United States,* which has such a profound influence on the rest of the world. Your state also leads in research and technology designed to improve the quality of human life and to transcend the limitations which impede human freedom and progress.

Yet amid the many blessings that you enjoy within this beautiful and prosperous state, I know that the mention of Mary as a Mother of sorrows and suffering still strikes a responsive chord in your hearts. This is because all of us, in some way, experience *sorrow and suffering in our lives.* No amount of economic, scientific or social progress can eradicate our vulnerability to sin and to death. On the contrary, progress creates new possibilities for evil as well as for good. Technology, for example, increases what we can do, but it cannot teach us the right thing to do. It increases our choices, but it is we who must choose between evil and good. Besides moral suffering, physical and emotional sufferings are part of every human life. The Gospel message is certainly no enemy of human progress or of the promotion of our temporal welfare, but neither does the Paschal Mystery allow us to run away from human sorrow and suffering.

## The Answer to Suffering Is Found Only Through the Obedience to God, Who So Loved the World

5. The message of the crucified Son and his Mother at the foot of the Cross is that the mysteries of suffering, love and Redemption are inseparably joined together. In bitterness and alienation from God and our fellow human beings we will never find the answer to the question—the "why?" of suffering. Calvary teaches us that we will find an answer only *through the "obedience"* mentioned in the Letter to the Hebrews. It is not obedience to a cruel or unjust god of our own making, but obedience to the God who "so loved the world that he gave his only Son" (Jn. 3:16). Jesus prayed: "not as I will, but as you will . . . your will be done" (Mt. 26:39, 42). And Mary began her pilgrimage of faith with the words, "I am the servant of the Lord. Let it be done to me as you say" (Lk. 1:38).

## Christ's Answer Is a Call to Take Part in His Own Work of Saving the World

Looking upon the suffering Son and Mother in the light of Scripture, we cannot equate their obedience with fatalism or passivity. Indeed, the Gospel is *the negation of passivity* in the face of suffering (*Salvifici Doloris,* 30). What we find is a loving act of self-giving on the part of Christ for the salvation of the world, and on the part of Mary as an active participant from the beginning in the saving mission of her Son. When we have striven to alleviate or overcome suffering, when like Christ we have prayed that "the cup pass us by" (see Mt. 26:39), and yet suffering remains, then we must walk "the royal road" of the Cross. As I mentioned before, Christ's answer to our question "why" is above all *a call, a vocation.* Christ does not give us an abstract answer, but rather he says, "Follow me!" He offers us the opportunity through suffering to take part in his own work of saving the world. And when we do take up our cross, then gradually the salvific meaning of suffering is revealed to us. It is then that in our sufferings we find inner peace and even spiritual joy (see *Salvifici Doloris,* 26).

## Suffering Has the Power to Transform from Within

The Letter to the Hebrews also speaks of being made perfect through suffering (see Heb. 5:8–10). This is because the purifying flames of trial and sorrow have the power *to transform us from within* by unleashing our love, teaching us compassion for others, and thus drawing us closer to Christ. Next to her Son, Mary is the most perfect example of this. It is precisely in being the Mother of Sorrows that she is a mother to each one of us and to all of us. The spiritual sword that pierces her heart opens up a river of compassion for all who suffer.

## From Mary Learn to Be a Compassionate Neighbor

6. My dear brothers and sisters: as we celebrate this Marian Year in preparation for the Third Millennium of Christianity, let us join the Mother of God in her pilgrimage of faith. Let us learn *the virtue of compassion* from her whose heart was pierced with a sword at the foot of the Cross. It is the virtue that prompted the Good Samaritan to stop beside the victim on the road, rather than to continue on or to cross over to the other side. Whether it be the case of the person next to us or of distant peoples and nations, we must be Good Samaritans to all those who suffer. We must be the compassionate "neighbor" of those in need, not only when it is emotionally rewarding or convenient, but also when it is demanding and inconvenient (see *Salvifici Doloris,* 28–30). Compassion is a virtue we cannot neglect in a world in which the human suffering of so many of our brothers and sisters is needlessly increased by oppression, deprivation and underdevelopment—by poverty, hunger and disease. Compassion is also called for in the face of the spiritual emptiness and aimlessness that people often experience amid material prosperity and comfort in developed countries such as your own. Compassion is a virtue that brings healing to those who bestow it, not only in this present life but in eternity: "Blessed are they who show mercy, mercy shall be theirs" (Mt. 5:7).

## Through the Faith of Mary, Let Us Fix Our Gaze on the Mystery of Christ

7. Through the faith of Mary, then, let us fix our gaze on *the mystery of Christ.* The mystery of the Son of Man, written in the earthly history of humanity, is at the same time the definitive manifestation of God in that history.

Simeon says: "This child is destined to be the downfall and the rise of many in Israel, a sign that will be opposed" (Lk. 2:34). How profound these words are! How far down these words reach into the history of man! Into the history of us all: Christ is destined for the ruin and the resurrection of many! Christ is a sign of contradiction! Is this not also true in our time? In our age?

*In our generation?*

And standing next to Christ is Mary. To her Simeon says: ". . . so that the thoughts of many hearts may be laid bare. And you yourself shall be pierced with a sword" (Lk. 2:35).

Today we ask for humility of heart and for a clear conscience:

before God
through Christ.

Yes, we ask that the thoughts of our hearts may be laid bare. We ask that our *consciences may be pure:*

before God
through the Cross of Christ
in the heart of Mary. Amen.

## SEPTEMBER 16, 1987

## 32. HOMILY DURING THE CELEBRATION
## OF MORNING PRAYER

God's flock is in your midst; give it a shepherd's care. *Watch over it willingly as God would have you do.* (1 Pt. 4:2)

Dear Brothers in our Lord Jesus Christ,

1. A very full day lies before us, *a day that the Lord has made.* It is good that we begin it by joining our voices in praise of the living God.

### "Be Generous" in Caring for the Flock

On this feast of Saints Cornelius and Cyprian, we have listened to the words of Peter as he appeals to his "fellow elders" to *be generous* in caring for the People of God, and to "*be examples* to the flock" (1 Pt. 4:3), the Church. These words of Peter are most appropriate for us as we begin this day together.

### Peter Is a Witness of the Suffering Christ

Peter describes himself as "*a witness* of Christ's sufferings and *a sharer* in the glory that is to be revealed" (1 Pt. 4:1). There is no doubt in Peter's mind about the witness he is called to bear. He is a witness of *the suffering Christ.* Perhaps he was mindful, however, of an earlier time in his life, precisely during the Passion itself, when out of fear for his own safety he had denied that he ever knew his Master. How far Peter has come from that day of sorrow and despair. For *love is more powerful than fear,* and the Lord is merciful and forgiving. The same Peter who denied his Master is now, in word and in deed, bearing witness with courage to the Crucified and Risen Christ.

### We Are Witnesses to His Cross and Resurrection

2. Our task as Bishops in the Church today is still centered on the person of Jesus Christ. We are witnesses to his Cross and Resurrection. Each of us has been consecrated by the Holy Spirit to be for our people a *living sign of Jesus Christ:*

— a living sign of *the praying Christ,* who himself took time during his public ministry to be alone with his Father in prayer;

— a living sign of *the compassionate Redeemer,* who healed the sick, forgave sinners and comforted the sorrowful;

— a living sign of *the love of our Savior,* a love which is stronger than sin and death;

— a living sign of *the fidelity of the Lord,* and therefore like Christ *a sign of contradiction.*

In the midst of our priests and among ourselves as Bishops, each of us is meant to be *a sign of Jesus' fraternal love*. And for our people we are called to be *a sign of the Good Shepherd, who came to serve* and not to be served.

"Be examples to the flock," Peter tells us. And we shall be precisely that to the extent that our lives are centered on the person of Jesus Christ.

"To him whose power now at work in us can do immeasurably more than we ask or imagine—*to him be glory in the Church* and in Christ Jesus through all generations, world without end. Amen!" (Eph. 3:20–21).

## 33. MEETING WITH THE AMERICAN BISHOPS

### PART I

Dear Brothers in our Lord Jesus Christ,

### Gratitude for Your Invitations and for the Preparation

1. Before beginning to respond to the context of our fraternal exchanges, I wish to express to you *my deep gratitude:* gratitude for your many invitations to make this pastoral visit, gratitude for your presence here today, and gratitude for the immense amount of preparation which this visit required. Over and above all this, I thank you for your daily toil, and *your partnership with me in the Gospel.* In a word, I thank you for "your work of faith and labor of love and steadfastness of hope in our Lord Jesus Christ" (1 Thes. 1:3).

### The Ecclesiology of *Communio* Is the Central and Fundamental Idea of the Council's Documents

Cardinal Bernardin has given us an introduction to *the extremely important reality of "communio,"* which is the best framework for our conversation. As Bishops, we can never tire of prayerfully reflecting on this subject. Since, as the Extraordinary Session of the Synod of Bishops in 1985 indicated, "the ecclesiology of communion is the central and fundamental idea of the Council's documents" (*Relatio Finalis,* C,1), it follows that we must return time and again to those same documents in order to be imbued with *the profound theological vision of the Church* which the Holy Spirit has placed before us, and which constitutes *the basis of all pastoral ministry* in the Church's pilgrimage through human history.

### Renewal of Catholic Life Will Come About in a Deeper Understanding of the Core Vision of the Church's Nature

*The program of our collegial ministry* cannot be other than to release into the lifestream of ecclesial life all the richness of the Church's self-understanding, which was given by the Holy Spirit to the community of faith in the celebration of the

Second Vatican Council. *The renewal of Catholic life* which the Council called for *is to be measured* not primarily in terms of external structures, but *in deeper and more effective implementation* of the core vision of her true nature and mission which the Council offered to the Church at the close of the second millennium of the Christian era. That renewal depends on the way the Council's fundamental insights are authentically received in each particular Church and in the universal Church.

### *Communio* Is a Sharing in the Life of the Trinity
### Through Sacramental Union with Christ and
### Through Participation in the Reality of the Church

At the heart of the Church's self-understanding is the notion of *communio:* primarily, *a sharing through grace in the life of the Father given us through Christ and in the Holy Spirit.* "God chose us in him"—in Christ—"before the world began, to be holy and blameless in his sight, to be full of love" (Eph. 1:4). This communion has its origin in a divine call, the eternal decree which predestined us to share the image of the Son (see Rom. 8:28–30). It is realized through sacramental union with Christ and through organic participation in all that constitutes the divine and human reality of the Church, the Body of Christ, which spans the centuries and is sent into the world to embrace all people without distinction.

### The Time Has Come to Give the
### "Vertical Dimension" Its Proper Place

2. It is clear that in the decades since the Council this *"vertical dimension"* of ecclesial communion has been less deeply experienced by many who, on the other hand, have a vivid sense of its *"horizontal dimension."* Unless, however, the entire Christian community has a keen awareness of the marvelous and utterly gratuitous outpouring of "the kindness and love of God our savior" which saved us "not because of any righteous deeds we had done, but because of his mercy" (Ti. 3:4–5), the whole ordering of the Church's life and the exercise of her mission of service to the human family will be radically weakened and never reach the level intended by the Council.

The ecclesial body is healthy in the measure in which Christ's grace, poured out through the Holy Spirit, is *accepted* by the members. Our pastoral efforts are fruitful, in the last analysis, when the People of God—we Bishops with the clergy, Religious and laity—are led to Christ, grow in faith, hope and charity, and become authentic witnesses of God's love in a world in need of transfiguration.

### There Can Only Be One Loyalty—
### to the Word of God Proclaimed in the Church

Cardinal Bernardin has stated very well that just as there is but one faith, one Lord, one baptism, so there can be *but one loyalty—to the word of God perennially proclaimed in the Church* entrusted to the Episcopal College with the Roman Pontiff as its visible head and perpetual source of unity. The word of God, which is the power of God leading all who believe to salvation (see Rom. 1:16; *Dei Verbum,* 17), is fully revealed in the Paschal Mystery of the Death and Resurrection of Jesus Christ. This Paschal Mystery brings about a salvation that is transcendent and eternal: "He died for us, that all of us . . . together might live with him" (1 Thes. 5:10). It is the Church's task, therefore, while she seeks in every way possible to increase her service to the human family in all its needs, *to preach Christ's call to conversion and to proclaim Redemption in his blood.*

## As a Communion of Particular Churches
## the Catholic Church Subsists in Each Particular Church

3. The "vertical dimension" of ecclesial communion is of profound significance in understanding *the relationship of the particular Churches to the universal Church.* It is important to avoid a merely sociological view of this relationship. "In and from such individual Churches there comes into being the one and only Catholic Church" (*Lumen Gentium,* 23), but this universal Church cannot be conceived as the sum of the particular Churches, or as a federation of particular Churches.

In the celebration of the Eucharist these principles come fully to the fore. For, as the Council document on the Liturgy specifies: "the principal manifestation of the Church consists in the full, active participation of all God's holy people in the same liturgical celebrations, especially in the same Eucharist, in one prayer, at one altar, at which the Bishop presides, surrounded by his presbyterate and by his ministers" (*Sacrosanctum Concilium,* 41). Wherever a community gathers around the altar under the ministry of a Bishop, there Christ is present and there, because of Christ, the one, holy, Catholic and apostolic Church gathers together (see *Lumen Gentium,* 26).

## The Particular Church Can Be Truly Complete
## Through Communion in Faith, Sacraments
## and Unity with the Whole Body of Christ

*The Catholic Church herself subsists in each particular Church,* which can be truly complete only through effective communion in faith, Sacraments and unity with the whole Body of Christ. Last November, in my letter to you during your meeting in Washington, I dealt at some length with this aspect of communion. At that time I wrote: "The very *mystery of the Church* impels us to recognize that the one, holy, Catholic and apostolic Church is present in each particular Church throughout the world. And since the Successor of Peter has been constituted for the whole Church as Pastor and as Vicar of Christ (see *Lumen Gentium,* 22), all the particular Churches—precisely because they are Catholic, precisely because they embody in themselves the mystery of the universal Church—are called to live in communion with him."

## As Pastors of Particular Churches
## in Which Subsists the Fullness of the Universal Church
## You Must Be in Communion with Peter

"*Our own relationship of ecclesial communion—collegialitas effectiva et affectiva*—is discovered in the same mystery of the Church. It is precisely because you are pastors of particular Churches in which there subsists the fullness of the universal Church that you are, and must always be, in full communion with the Successor of Peter. To recognize your ministry as 'vicars and delegates of Christ' for your particular Churches (see *Lumen Gentium,* 27) is to understand all the more clearly the ministry of the Chair of Peter, which 'presides over the whole assembly of charity, protects legitimate variety, and at the same time sees to it that differences do not hinder unity but rather contribute to it' (*Lumen Gentium,* 13)." (Letter of November 4, 1986).

## The Ministry of the Successor of Peter Belongs to the
## Essence of Each Particular Church from "Within"

4. In this perspective too, we must see *the ministry of the Successor of Peter* not only as a "global" service, reaching each particular Church from "outside" as it were, but *as belonging already to the essence of each particular Church from "within."* Precisely because this relationship of ecclesial communion—our *collegialitas effectiva et affectiva*—is such an intimate part of the structure of the Church's life, its exercise calls for each and every one of us to be completely one in mind and heart with the will of Christ regarding our different roles in the College of Bishops. The Council took pains not only to formulate these roles but also to place the exercise of authority in the Church in its proper perspective, which is precisely the perspective of *communio*. In this respect also the Council was—in the words of the Extraordinary Synod—"a legitimate and valid expression and interpretation of the deposit of faith as it is found in Sacred Scripture and in the living tradition of the Church" (*Relatio Finalis,* I, 2).

## We Must Continue to Proclaim Together
## Jesus Christ and His Gospel

As I also wrote to you last year, I have endeavored to fulfill my role as Successor of Peter in a spirit of fraternal solidarity with you. I wish only to be of service to all the Bishops of the world, and—in obedience to my specific responsibility at the service of the Church's unity and universality—to confirm them in their own collegial ministry. I have always been greatly encouraged in this task by your fraternal support and your partnership in the Gospel, for which I express to you again my profound gratitude. It is of great importance to the Church *that in the full power of the Church's communion we continue to proclaim together Jesus Christ and his Gospel.* In this way we ourselves live fully, as Successors of the Apostles, the mystery of ecclesial communion. At the same time, through our ministry we enable the faithful to enter ever more deeply into the Church's life of communion with the Most Holy Trinity.

## PART II

### To Proclaim a Body of Moral Teaching
### Is an Inseparable Part of the Church's Mission

5. Archbishop Quinn has spoken of the Church as a community that wishes to remain faithful to *the moral teaching of our Lord Jesus Christ*. To proclaim a body of moral teaching is in fact an inseparable part of the Church's mission in the world. From the beginning, the Church under the guidance of the Holy Spirit has striven to apply God's revelation in Christ to all the many aspects of our living in this world, knowing that we are called to "lead a life worthy of the Lord and pleasing to him in every way" (Col. 1:10).

### The Error That Dissent Is Compatible with Being a "Good Catholic" Challenges the Teaching Office of the Bishops

It is sometimes reported that a large number of Catholics today do not adhere to the teaching of the Church on a number of questions, notably sexual and conjugal morality, divorce and remarriage. Some are reported as not accepting the Church's clear position on abortion. It has also been noted that there is a tendency on the part of some Catholics to be selective in their adherence to the Church's moral teachings. It is sometimes claimed that dissent from the Magisterium is totally compatible with being a "good Catholic" and poses no obstacle to the reception of the Sacraments. This is a grave error that challenges the teaching office of the Bishops of the United States and elsewhere. I wish to encourage you in the love of Christ to address this situation courageously in your pastoral ministry, *relying on the power of God's truth* to attract assent *and on the grace of the Holy Spirit* which is given both to those who proclaim the message and to those to whom it is addressed.

### The Challenge of the Gospel
### Remains Inherent in the Christian Message

We must also constantly recall that the teaching of Christ's Church—like Christ himself—is a "sign of contradiction." It has never been easy to accept the Gospel teaching in its entirety, and it never will be. The Church is committed, both in faith and morals, to make her teaching as clear and understandable as possible, presenting it in all the attractiveness of divine truth. And yet *the challenge of the Gospel remains inherent in the Christian message* transmitted to each generation. Archbishop Quinn has made reference to a principle with extremely important consequences for every area of the Church's life: "The revelation of God par excellence is found in the Cross of Christ which makes God's folly wiser than human wisdom. Often human wisdom in a given age appears to have the last word. But the Cross brings a perspective that changes judgments radically." Yes, dear brothers, *the Cross—in the very act of revealing mercy, compassion and love—changes judgments radically.*

## In Faith Assent to the Word of God as Transmitted by the
## Church's Magisterium Is the Basic Attitude of the Believer

6. A number of other general points may be made. First, the Church is a community of faith. To accept faith is to give assent to the word of God as transmitted by the Church's authentic *Magisterium*. Such assent constitutes the basic attitude of the believer, and is an act of the will as well as of the mind. It would be altogether out of place to try to model this act of religion on attitudes drawn from secular culture.

## Theological Discussion Takes Place
## Within the Framework of Faith

Within the ecclesial community, *theological discussion takes place within the framework of faith*. Dissent from Church doctrine remains what it is: dissent; as such it may not be proposed or received on an equal footing with the Church's authentic teaching.

## Opinions at Variance with Church Teaching
## Cannot Be the Basis for Pastoral Practice

Moreover, as Bishops we must be especially responsive to our role as authentic teachers of the faith when opinions at variance with the Church's teaching are proposed *as a basis for pastoral practice*.

## The Title "Catholic Theologian" Expresses a Vocation and
## a Responsibility at the Service of the Community of Faith

I wish to support you as you continue to engage in fruitful dialogue with theologians regarding *the legitimate freedom of inquiry* which is their right. You rightly give them sincere encouragement in their difficult task, and assure them how much the Church needs and deeply appreciates their dedicated and constructive work. They, on their part, will recognize that the title "*Catholic* theologian" expresses a vocation and a responsibility at the service of the community of faith, and subject to the authority of the pastors of the Church. In particular, your dialogue will seek to show the unacceptability of dissent and confrontation as a policy and method in the area of Church teaching.

## Need for New Effort of Evangelization and Catechesis
## Directed to the Mind

7. Speaking on your behalf, Archbishop Quinn has shown full awareness of the seriousness of the challenge facing your teaching ministry. He has spoken of the dual task of *the conversion of the mind* and *the conversion of the heart*. The way to the heart very often passes through the mind, and throughout the length and breadth of the

Church there is need today for a new effort of evangelization and catechesis directed to the mind. Elsewhere I have mentioned the relationship between the Gospel and culture. Here I wish to underline the importance of the formation of the mind at every level of Catholic life.

### The Formation of the Mind Must Take Place at Every Level

Catholic children and young people need to be given *an effective opportunity to learn the truths of the faith,* in such a way that they become capable of formulating their Catholic identity in terms of doctrine and thought. *Here the Catholic press can make a magnificent contribution* to raising the general level of Catholic thought and culture. Seminaries, especially, have the responsibility of ensuring that future priests should acquire a high level of intellectual preparation and competence. Continuing education programs for priests, Religious and laity play an important part in stimulating a necessary and serious intellectual approach to the multitude of questions confronting faith in our contemporary world.

### Bishops Have the Duty and Right to Safeguard
### the Catholic Identity of Colleges and Universities

A crucial aspect of this "apostolate of the mind" concerns the *duty and right of Bishops to be present in an effective way in Catholic* colleges and universities and institutes of higher studies in order *to safeguard and promote their Catholic character,* especially in what affects the transmission of Catholic doctrine. It is a task which requires personal attention on the part of Bishops, since it is a specific responsibility stemming from their teaching office. It implies frequent contacts with teaching and administrative personnel, and calls for providing serious programs of pastoral care for students and others within the academic community. Much is already being done, and I take the opportunity to encourage you to seek ways of intensifying these apostolates.

### Consolidate Present and Future Generations
### in a Sound Understanding of Their Faith

One of the greatest services we Bishops can render to the Church is to consolidate present and future generations of Catholics in a sound and complete understanding of their faith. The ecclesial community will thus be wonderfully strengthened for all aspects of Christian moral living and for generous service. The intellectual approach that is needed, however, is one intimately linked to faith and prayer. *Our people must be aware of their dependence on Christ's grace* and of the great need to open themselves ever more to its action. Jesus himself wants us all to be convinced of his words: *"Apart from me you can do nothing"* (Jn. 15:5).

## PART III

8. The Synod to be held this coming month in Rome will undoubtedly deal in further detail with the many important points raised by Archbishop Weakland in his presentation on *the role of the laity.* These remarks, like my own, particularly concern the Catholic laity in the United States.

### Cause for Rejoicing and Gratitude
### in Having the Largest Number of Educated Faithful

It has been stated that "the Church in the United States of America can boast of having the largest number of educated faithful in the world." This statement has many implications. The situation which it describes *is cause for humble rejoicing and gratitude* because it represents a major achievement: the sustained educational effort by the Church in this country for many, many decades. At the same time the education of the faithful offers great promise and potential in the years ahead. For "it can be assumed they will continue to take a prominent role in U.S. society and culture in the future."

### Through Her Laity the Church Can Exercise
### Great Influence on the Culture

Primarily through her laity, the Church is in a position to exercise great influence upon *American culture.* This culture is *a human creation.* It is created through shared insight and communication. It is built by an exchange among the people of a particular society. And culture, while having a certain dynamic endurance, is always changing and developing as a way of life. Thus the American culture of today stands in continuity with your culture of fifty years ago. Yet it has changed; it has been greatly influenced by attitudes and currents of thought.

### Is American Culture Influenced by the Gospel?
### Does It Clearly Reflect Christian Inspiration?

But *how is the American culture evolving today?* Is this evolution being influenced by the Gospel? Does it clearly reflect Christian inspiration? Your music, your poetry and art, your drama, your painting and sculpture, the literature that you are producing—are all those things which reflect the soul of a nation being influenced by the spirit of Christ for the perfection of humanity?

### Are the Laity Bringing the Gospel to Bear
### on the World of Culture?

I realize these are difficult questions to answer, given the complexity and diversity of your culture. But they are relevant to any consideration of the role of the

Catholic laity, "the largest number of educated faithful in the world." And it is above all the laity, once they have themselves been inspired by the Gospel, who *bring the Gospel's uplifting and purifying influence to the world of culture,* to the whole realm of thought and artistic creativity, to the various professions and places of work, to family life and to society in general. As Bishops, with the task of leading the laity and of encouraging them to fulfill their ecclesial mission in the world, we must continue to support them as they endeavor to make their specific contribution to the evolution and development of culture and to its impact on society.

### We Bring a Priestly Service of Transforming the Laity So That They Can Change the World from Within

9. With reference to this question, and in such areas as politics, economics, mass media and international life, *the service we bring is primarily a priestly service:* the service of preaching and teaching the word of God with fidelity to the truth, and of drawing the laity ever more into the dialogue of salvation. We are charged to lead our people to holiness, especially through the grace of the Eucharist and the whole sacramental life. The service of our pastoral leadership, purified in personal prayer and penance, far from bearing an authoritarian style in any way, must listen and encourage, challenge and at times correct. Certainly, there is no question of condemning the technological world but rather of urging the laity to transform it from within so that it may receive the imprint of the Gospel.

### We Serve Them Best by Providing Them with a Comprehensive and Solid Program of Catechesis

10. We serve our laity best when we make every effort to provide for them, and in collaboration with them, *a comprehensive and solid program of catechesis* with the aim of "maturing the initial faith and of educating the true disciple of Christ by means of a deeper and more systematic knowledge of the person and the message of our Lord Jesus Christ" (*Catechesi Tradendae,* 19). Such a program will also assist them in developing that habit of discernment which can distinguish the spirit of the world from the Spirit of God, and which can distinguish authentic culture from elements that degrade human dignity. It can provide them a solid basis for growing in their knowledge and love of Jesus Christ through continual conversion and personal commitment to the demands of the Gospel.

### I Wish to Support You in All You Are Doing for Family Life

11. In speaking of the laity, I feel a particular desire to support you in all you are doing on behalf of *family life.* Archbishop Weakland has mentioned "the large number of divorces and the breakup of so many families" as a special pastoral problem. I know that all of us feel great sadness and deep pastoral concern for all those whose lives are affected in this way.

As you will recall, on the occasion of your *ad Limina* visits four years ago, I spoke at some length on the topic of *marriage*. Without repeating all that I said on that occasion, I wish to encourage you to continue in your many zealous and generous efforts to provide *pastoral care to families*. I also urge you in the face of all the trends which threaten the stability of marriage, the dignity of human love, and the dignity of human life, as well as its transmission, never to lose confidence and courage. Through the grace given us as pastors we must endeavor to present as effectively as possible the whole teaching of the Church, including the prophetic message contained in *Humanae Vitae* and in *Familiaris Consortio*.

### You Must Teach the Intrinsic Relationship Between the Unitive and Procreative Dimensions of the Marital Act

The faithful teaching of the intrinsic relationship between the unitive and procreative dimensions of the marriage act is of course only a part of our pastoral responsibility. With pastoral solicitude for couples, *Familiaris Consortio* pointed out that "the ecclesial community at the present time must take on the task of instilling conviction and offering practical help to those who wish to live out their parenthood in a truly responsible way. . . . This implies a broader, more decisive and more systematic effort to make the natural methods of regulating fertility known, respected and applied" (no. 35).

### You Should Promote Natural Family Planning

On the occasion of the last *ad Limina* visits I stated: "Those couples who choose the natural methods perceive the profound difference—both anthropological and moral—between contraception and natural family planning. Yet they may experience difficulties; indeed they often go through a certain conversion in becoming committed to the use of the natural methods, and they stand in need of competent instruction, encouragement and pastoral counseling and support. We must be sensitive to their struggles and have a feeling for the needs that they experience. We must encourage them to continue their efforts with generosity, confidence and hope. As Bishops we have the charism and the pastoral responsibility to make our people aware of *the unique influence that the grace of the Sacrament of Marriage has on every aspect of married life, including sexuality* (see *Familiaris Consortio*, 33). The teaching of Christ's Church is not only light and strength for God's people, but it uplifts their hearts in gladness and hope.

"Your Episcopal Conference has established a special program to expand and coordinate efforts in the various Dioceses. But the success of such an effort requires the abiding pastoral interest and support of each Bishop in his Diocese, and I am deeply grateful to you for what you do in this most important apostolate" (Address of September 24, 1983).

## I Am Grateful for Your Work in the Defense of Human Life,
## in Promoting Peace and Fostering Justice

12. My profound gratitude to you extends to the many other areas in which, with generous dedication, you have worked *for and with the laity*. These include your persevering efforts at *promoting peace, fostering justice* and *supporting the missions*. In the area of *the defense of human life,* you have worked with exceptional commitment and constancy. Already during the *ad Limina* visits of 1978, Paul VI drew attention to this activity of yours, assuring you of the appreciation of the Holy See. Because of their exceptional importance, I wish to quote at some length his words of strong support for you and make them my own:

"In the name of Jesus Christ, we thank you for your ministry at the service of life. We know that you have labored precisely in order that the words of the Good Shepherd would be fulfilled: 'that they may have life and have it to the full.' Under your leadership, so many of the Catholic people—priests, deacons, Religious and laity—have joined in numerous initiatives aimed at defending, healing and promoting human life.

"With the enlightenment of faith, the incentive of love and an awareness of your pastoral accountability, you have worked to oppose whatever wounds, weakens or dishonors human life. Your pastoral charity has found a consistent expression in so many ways—all related to the question of life, all aimed at protecting life in its multiple facets. You have endeavored to proclaim in practice that all aspects of human life are sacred.

"In this regard, *your efforts have been directed to the eradication of hunger, the elimination of subhuman living conditions, and the promotion of programs on behalf of the poor, the elderly and minorities. You have worked for the improvement of the social order itself*. At the same time, we know that you have held up to your people the goal to which God calls them: the life above, in Christ Jesus (see Phil. 3:14).

"Among your many activities at the service of life there is one which, especially at this juncture of history, deserves our firmest support: it is the continuing struggle against what the Second Vatican Council calls the 'abominable crime' of abortion (*Gaudium et Spes,* 51). Disregard for the sacred character of life in the womb weakens the very fabric of civilization; it prepares a mentality, and even a public attitude, that can lead to the acceptance of other practices that are against the fundamental rights of the individual. This mentality can, for example, completely undermine concern for those in want, manifesting itself in insensitivity to social needs; it can produce contempt for the elderly, to the point of advocating euthanasia; it can prepare the way for those forms of genetic engineering that go against life, the dangers of which are not yet fully known to the general public.

"It is therefore very encouraging to see the great service you render to humanity by constantly holding up to your people the value of human life. We are confident that, relying on the words of the Good Shepherd, who inspires your activity, you will continue to exercise leadership in this regard, sustaining the entire ecclesial community in their own vocation at the service of life.

"It is also a source of worldwide honor that, in your country, so many upright men and women of differing religious convictions are united in a profound respect for the laws of the Creator and Lord of life, and that, by every just means at their disposal, they are endeavoring, before the witness of history, to take a definitive stand for human life" (Address of May 26, 1978).

Nine years have passed since these words were spoken, and yet they are *still relevant today*—relevant in their prophetic vision, relevant in the needs they express, relevant in the defense of life.

### The Aim of the Church's Efforts on Behalf of Women Is to Promote Their Dignity

13. In his encyclical *Pacem in Terris*, Pope John XXIII placed the question of *the advancement of women* in the context of the characteristics of the present day, "the signs of the times." He made it clear that the cause in question was one of *human dignity*. This is indeed the aim of all the Church's efforts on behalf of women: to promote their human dignity. The Church proclaims *the personal dignity of women as women*—a dignity equal to that of men. This dignity must be affirmed in its ontological character, even before consideration is given to any of the special and exalted roles fulfilled by women as wives, mothers or consecrated women.

### Two Firm Principles Are the Basis of All Considerations— the Equal Dignity of Women and Their Feminine Humanity

There are many other aspects involved in the question of women's equal dignity and responsibility, which will undoubtedly be properly dealt with in the forthcoming Synod of Bishops. At the basis of all considerations are two firm principles: *the equal human dignity of women and their true feminine humanity*. On the basis of these two principles, *Familiaris Consortio* has already enunciated much of the Church's attitude toward women, which reflects the "sensitive respect of Jesus toward the women that he called to his following and his friendship" (no. 22). As I have stated and as Archbishop Weakland has pointed out, women are not called to the priesthood. Although the teaching of the Church on this point is quite clear, it in no way alters the fact that women *are indeed an essential part of the Gospel plan to spread the Good News of the Kingdom*. And the Church is irrevocably committed to this truth.

### PART IV

14. My interest in the question of *vocations* is well known to all of you. It is a recurring theme in my conversations with Bishops around the world. It is one of the subjects I frequently speak about in my meetings with young people. It is a crucial factor for the future of the Church as we draw near to the beginning of the third millennium. Therefore, I am very pleased that you have chosen this topic as one of those to be emphasized today.

Archbishop Pilarczyk has presented an "overview of the ministerial realities of the Church in this country," mentioning aspects that offer *much consolation* to you as Bishops and aspects which are cause for pastoral concern. He mentioned that it was important "to speak of some of the very positive implications of lay, religious and clerical vocations in America." In doing this, he rightly drew attention to the way that *the Holy Spirit is at work in your midst,* something that we must indeed be ever attentive to and grateful for. As *Lumen Gentium* reminds us, "The Spirit guides the Church into the fullness of truth (see Jn. 16:13) and gives her unity of fellowship and service. . . . By the power of the Gospel the Spirit makes the Church grow, perpetually renews her, and leads her to perfect union with her Spouse" (no. 4).

### Active Participation of the Laity
### in the Mission of the Church Is an Eloquent Sign
### of the Fruitfulness of the Second Vatican Council

It is indeed encouraging to note how *lay people,* in ever-increasing numbers, have become involved in the life of the Church, and how this has led to "a depth and variety of ministry far greater than ever before." Certainly, *the more active participation of the laity in the mission of the Church is an eloquent sign of the fruitfulness of the Second Vatican Council,* one for which we all give thanks. And I am confident that the forthcoming Synod of Bishops will give fresh impetus to this participation and solid direction for its continued growth and consolidation.

### The Ministry of the Priest
### and Lay Involvement Are Complementary

It is important for our people to see clearly that *the ministry of the ordained priest and the involvement of the laity in the Church's mission* are not at all opposed to one another. On the contrary, the *one complements the other.* Just as the priestly ministry is not an end in and of itself, but serves to awaken and unify the various charisms within the Church, so too the involvement of the laity does not replace the priesthood, but supports it, promotes it and offers it space for its own specific service.

At this time, I would like to make a few remarks about *vocations to the priesthood and to the religious life.*

### We Are Facing a Difficult Change in Society

The *insufficient number of seminarians and candidates for religious life is indeed a cause of pastoral concern* for all of us, for we know that their public witness to the Gospel and their specific roles in the Church are irreplaceable. In many parts of the world the Church is experiencing, as Archbishop Pilarczyk observed, that "society is becoming increasingly secular and therefore increasingly inhospitable to Christian belief." It is especially difficult today for young people to make the generous sacrifices entailed in accepting God's call. Yet it is possible for them to do so through grace and with the support of the community. And it is precisely in this situation that we are called to bear witness to the hope of the Church.

## Continue in Your Efforts
## to Promote Vocations in the New Situation

In our pastoral mission we must often evaluate a situation and decide on a course of action. We must do this with prudence and pastoral realism. At the same time, we know that today, as always, there are "prophets of doom." We must resist them in their pessimism, and *continue in our efforts to promote vocations to the priesthood and the religious life*.

### Prayer for Vocations Remains the Primary Way

*Prayer for vocations* remains the primary way to success, since Jesus himself left us the commandment: "Beg the harvest master to send out laborers to gather his harvest" (Mt. 9:38). I ask you therefore to encourage prayer for vocations among all the people, particularly among priests and Religious themselves, but also in families, where the first seeds of vocations are usually planted, and in schools and religious education programs. The prayers of the elderly and the sick have an efficacy that must not be forgotten.

### You Must Also Invite People

In addition to prayer, young people *must be invited*. It was Andrew who brought his brother Peter to the Lord. It was Philip who brought Nathanael. And how many of us and of our priests and Religious came to hear the Lord's call through the invitation of someone else? Your own presence among the youth is a blessing and an opportune time to extend this invitation to them and to ask young people themselves to pray for vocations.

### As We Proclaim with Faith the Power of the Lord of the
### Harvest, We Can Expect Him to Hear Our Prayers

Just last Thursday, speaking in Miami about vocations to the priesthood, I emphasized the basis of our hope: "There is still one more factor to be considered in evaluating the future of vocations, and it is *the power of Christ's Paschal Mystery*. As the Church of Christ, we are all called to profess his power before the world; to proclaim that he is able, in virtue of his Death and Resurrection, to draw young people to himself, in this generation as in the past; to declare that he is strong enough to attract young men even today to a life of self-sacrifice, pure love and total dedication to the priesthood. As we profess this truth, as we proclaim with faith the power of the Lord of the harvest, we have a right to expect that he will grant the prayers that he himself has commanded to be offered. The present hour calls for great trust in him who has overcome the world.

### Gratitude for Ensuring a Solid Formation for the Priesthood

15. I would like to thank you for all you are doing to ensure *a solid formation for the priesthood in the United States*. The apostolic visitation to the seminaries has been carried out with generous collaboration. And I am grateful for the letters many of you have sent me expressing your appreciation for this initiative and telling me of the many positive effects which have resulted from it.

At the same time, your pastoral interest and personal involvement in seminary training is something that can never end. It is too central a task and too important a priority in the life of the Church. The Church of tomorrow passes through the seminaries of today. With the passing of time, the pastoral responsibility will no longer be ours. But at present the responsibility *is* ours, and it is heavy. Its zealous fulfillment is a great act of love for the flock.

In particular, I ask you to be vigilant that *the dogmatic and moral teaching of the Church* is faithfully and clearly presented to the seminarians, and fully accepted and understood by them. On the opening day of the Second Vatican Council, October 11, 1962, John XXIII told his brother Bishops: "The greatest concern of the Ecumenical Council is this: *that the sacred deposit of Christian doctrine should be more effectively guarded and taught*." What Pope John expected of the Council is also a primary concern for priestly formation. We must ensure that our future priests have a solid grasp of the entirety of the Catholic faith; and then we must prepare them to present it in turn to others in ways that are intelligible and pastorally sound.

### Gratitude for Your Great Sense of Cooperation
### with the Commission on Religious Life

16. I cannot let this opportunity pass without expressing once again my gratitude for the great interest you have taken in the *religious life*. I am pleased to note, as Archbishop Pilarczyk has said, that there is "an increased understanding of and appreciation for religious life on the part of bishops and priests, thanks, in large part, to the pontifical commission" established in 1983.

In asking the commission to study *the problem of vocations,* I did so "with a view to encouraging a new growth and fresh move forward in this most important sector of the Church's life." The response which you have all made to this request has been most gratifying. And I know you will continue with this important effort. *The religious life is a precious gift from the Lord,* and we must continue to assure Religious of the love and esteem of the Church.

17. There are many other issues, dear brother Bishops, which come to mind as we reflect together in this extraordinary hour of ecclesial communion. All of them touch us in our role as Pastors and challenge our apostolic love and zeal.

## Make Every Effort to See That the Norms for
## General Absolution Are Observed

Because of its importance in the life of the Church, I spoke to the priests in Miami about *Confession* and our own need to receive the Sacrament regularly. I also expressed my gratitude for their generous ministry in making Confession available to the faithful. In this regard I would ask you as Bishops to make every effort to ensure that the important norms of the universal Church with regard to *the use of general absolution* are understood and observed in a spirit of faith. In this regard I would ask that the Post-Synodal Apostolic Exhortation *Reconciliatio et Paenitentia* continue to be the object of prayerful reflection.

## Give Special Encouragement to All Persons Striving to
## Live the Gospel Precept of Chastity

18. I wish to encourage you also in the pastoral care that you give to *homosexual persons*. This includes a clear explanation of the Church's teaching, which by its nature is unpopular. Nevertheless, your own pastoral experience confirms the fact that the truth, howsoever difficult to accept, brings grace and often leads to a deep inner conversion. No matter what problem individual Christians have, and no matter what degree of response to grace they make, they are always worthy of the Church's love and Christ's truth. All homosexual and other persons striving to fulfill the Gospel precept of chastity are worthy of special encouragement and esteem.

## Help Parents to Become Effective
## in Fulfilling the Task of Sex Education

19. From time to time the question of *sex education,* especially as regards programs being used in schools, becomes a matter of concern to Catholic parents. The principles governing this area have been succinctly but clearly enunciated in *Familiaris Consortio.* First among these principles is the need to recognize that sex education is *a basic right and duty of parents themselves.* They have to be helped to become increasingly more effective in fulfilling this task. Other educational agencies have an important role, but always in a subsidiary manner, with due subordination to the rights of parents.

Many parents will undoubtedly be heartened by the reference in the pastoral letter of the Bishops of California, *A Call to Compassion,* to an absolutely essential aspect of this whole question: "The recovery of the virtue of chastity"— they wrote— "may be one of the most urgent needs of contemporary society." We cannot doubt that the Catholic Church in the United States, as elsewhere, is called to make great efforts to assist parents in teaching their children the sublime value of self-giving love; young people need great support in living this fundamental aspect of their human and Christian vocation.

### Provide Adequate Care for the Military
### and Their Dependents

20. Among your many pastoral obligations is *the need to provide for the spiritual care of the military and their dependents*. This you do through the Military Ordinariate. The functioning of this extended Archdiocese requires the fraternal and sensitive collaboration of all the Bishops in permitting and encouraging priests to commit themselves to this worthy ministry. The Church is grateful to all the chaplains who generously serve God's people in this particular situation, with its special needs.

21. I wish at this time to offer you my encouragement as you seek to guide the Church of God in so many areas: as you seek to lead your people *in fulfilling their mission within the United States and well beyond her boundaries*. Everything you do to help your people to look outside themselves to *Christ in need* is a great ecclesial and apostolic service.

### Call to Holiness and Daily Conversion

My final word is about *our pastoral identity as Bishops of Jesus Christ and his Church*. The Second Vatican Council speaks to us those remarkable and inspiring words: "In the Bishops . . . our Lord Jesus Christ, the Supreme High Priest, is present in the midst of those who believe" (*Lumen Gentium,* 21). These words tell us so much about who we are and what we are about. They spell out our identity. And because of this identity we are called to *holiness* and to daily conversion. In speaking to you eight years ago in Chicago I stated: "*The holiness of personal conversion is indeed the condition* for our fruitful ministry as Bishops of the Church. It is our union with Jesus Christ that determines the credibility of our witness to the Gospel and the supernatural effectiveness of our activity" (Discourse of October 5, 1979). May God give us all this great gift of *union with Jesus* and allow us to live it *together* in strength and joy, *in the communion of the Church of God.*

### 34. MEETING WITH CHILDREN
### OF IMMACULATE CONCEPTION SCHOOL

Dear Students of Immaculate Conception School,

It is a real pleasure for me to visit your school today, together with your Archbishop and with Mrs. Reagan, the wife of the president of the United States. When I speak about visiting your school I mean visiting *you!*

### "Religion" Is Most Important

1. I consider *your school*—and all the other parochial schools in America—*to be very important* for your future and for the future of the Church and of your country.

In this school, you learn not only reading, writing and arithmetic, but also—and most important—*religion*. You learn about God, about God's Son, Jesus Christ, and about God's love. You learn that God made you to know him, to love him and to serve him in this life and to be happy with him forever in the next. You learn how much *God loves you* and how much he wants you to share that love with others, as Jesus taught us.

### You Learn to Love God and to See His Image in Parents, Teachers, Fellow Students

*You learn to love God,* and to see his image and *to love him* in your parents, your teachers, your fellow students and *in all God's children.* You learn to love your country and all the people in it, no matter who they are. And you learn to love the people outside the United States, those in other countries—both near and far away.

You learn how important it is, in order to be truly happy, *to follow God's commandments.* You learn how important it is therefore to be truthful, honest, kind and considerate, and to avoid cheating and fighting and lying. You learn to know the difference between good and bad influences, and how important it is to avoid those things—such as the use of drugs—which hurt yourselves and others and which give offense to God. Sometimes they can even destroy your lives and the lives of others. You have seen this happen around you.

### One of the Most Important Things You Can Learn Is to Pray

2. In short, in this school you learn how to live in a way that is *pleasing to God* and that will bring *happiness and peace to you,* your families and your community. You learn *skills* that help you to become a more complete person and a more conscientious citizen, and prepare you for your future. You learn how to be morally good and how to build a better society.

One of the most important things you can ever learn here is *to pray:* to speak to God, to express what is in your heart, to show your dependence on him, to thank him for the gift of life, for your families, and for everything you have received. Here you also learn how to pray as a community, at Mass, together with Christ and with each other.

### Catholic Schools Provide a Vision of Life's Purposes and a Gateway to Life's Opportunities

3. For many, many years, Catholic schools such as Immaculate Conception have been *an important part of education in the United States of America.* They have truly helped to form this nation. Catholic schools have educated the first Americans, the Native Americans; they have educated black Americans and white Americans and the children of immigrants *from every race and from every nation*—and indeed from many

*different religious denominations.* Catholic schools continue to provide not only a vision of life's purpose but a gateway to life's opportunities.

Students of Immaculate Conception School: you can be proud of your school. Make sure that your school can always be proud of you. *Your parents, your parish and your Archdiocese* have made great·efforts to give you this Catholic education. Do not let them down.

### "Treat Others the Way You Would Have Them Treat You"

4. Finally, dear boys and girls, I ask you to do me a favor: *to think frequently about these words of Jesus:* "Treat others the way you would have them treat you" (Mt. 7:12). The words that are important in life are not "me," but "others"; not "to get," but "to give" and "to serve"—*to give* and *to serve* the way Jesus did, with love and sacrifice *for others.*

May God bless you, and your teachers, and your families, and all *those who work and sacrifice* to make this school and every Catholic school a place that prepares students to lead a good Christian life and to be happy with God for ever in heaven.

### 35. MEETING WITH INTERRELIGIOUS LEADERS

Dear Brothers and Sisters,

Representatives of World Religions and Religious Leaders,

Dear Friends,

### I Wish to Thank You for This Meeting and the Japanese Community for Their Hospitality

It is a great joy for me to meet with you, the local representatives of great religions of the world, during the course of my pastoral visit. I wish to thank in particular the Japanese community of Los Angeles for their hospitality at this Center, which is a symbol of cultural diversity within the United States as well as a symbol of dialogue and interaction at the service of the common good. I understand that the Japanese community has been present in this area of Los Angeles for a century. May God continue to bless you with every good gift now and in the future. I also wish to extend *cordial greetings to all* religious leaders and to all people of good will who honor us with their presence today.

### We Must Use Every Opportunity to Show Love and Respect for One Another

It is my conviction that we must make use of every *opportunity to show love and respect* for one another in the spirit of *Nostra Aetate,* which, as the theme of our meeting affirms, is indeed alive twenty-two years after its promulgation among the documents of the Second Vatican Council. This declaration on the relation of the Catholic Church to non-Christian religions speaks of "that which people have in common and of those things which tend to promote fellowship among them" (*Nostra Aetate*, 1). This continues to be the basis of our efforts to develop a fruitful relationship among all the great religions of the world.

### The Church Is Committed to Proclaim the Gospel and to Dialogue with People of Other Religions

2. As I stated earlier this year, the Catholic Church remains firmly committed to the proclamation of the Gospel and to dialogue with people of other religions: *proclamation of the Gospel,* because as *Nostra Aetate* points out, the Church "must ever proclaim Christ, 'the way, the truth, and the life' (Jn. 14:6) in whom people find the fullness of religious life, and in whom God has reconciled all things to himself (see 2 Cor. 5:18–19)"; *dialogue and collaboration with the followers of other religions,* because of the spiritual and moral goods that we share (*Nostra Aetate,* 2). That dialogue "is a complex of human activities, all founded upon respect and esteem for people of different religions. It includes the daily living together in peace and mutual help, with each bearing witness to the values learned through the experience of faith. It means a readiness to cooperate with others for the betterment of humanity, and a commitment to search together for true peace. It means the encounter of theologians and other religious specialists to explore, with their counterparts from other religions, areas of convergence and divergence. Where circumstances permit, it means a sharing of spiritual experiences and insights. This sharing can take the form of coming together as brothers and sisters to pray to God in ways which safeguard the uniqueness of each religious tradition" (Address to the Members and Staff of the Secretariat for Non-Christians, April 28, 1987).

### I Have Promoted Proclamation and Dialogue in View of Fostering Greater Interreligious Understanding and Cooperation

Throughout my pontificate it has been my constant concern to fulfill this twofold task of proclamation and dialogue. On my pastoral visits around the world I have sought to encourage and strengthen the faith of the Catholic people and other Christians as well. At the same time I have been pleased to meet with leaders of all religions in the hope of promoting greater interreligious *understanding and cooperation* for the good of the human family. I was very gratified at the openness and good will with which the *World Day of Prayer for Peace in Assisi* last October was received, not only by the various Christian Churches and ecclesial communities but by the other religions of the world as well. I was also pleased that another World Day of Prayer subsequently took place in Japan at Mount Hiei.

## Humanity Must Draw from Its Deepest Sources in the Great Battle for Peace

3. What I said in Assisi also applies to our meeting today: "The fact that we have come here does not imply any intention of seeking a consensus among ourselves or of negotiating our faith convictions. Neither does it mean that religions can be reconciled at the level of a common commitment in an earthly project which would surpass them all. Nor is it a concession to relativism in religious beliefs, because every human being must sincerely follow his or her upright conscience with the intention of seeking and obeying the truth. Our meeting attests only—and this is its real significance for the people of our time—that in the great battle for peace, humanity, in its very diversity, must draw from its deepest and most vivifying sources where its conscience is formed and upon which is founded the moral action of all people" (Message to the Participants at the World Day of Prayer for Peace, Assisi, October 27, 1986).

## I Wish to Greet Each Community

It is in that spirit that I wish, through you, to greet each of your communities before saying something further about the concern for peace that we all share.

*To the Buddhist Community,* which reflects numerous Asian traditions as well as American: I wish respectfully to acknowledge your way of life, based upon compassion and loving kindness and upon a yearning for peace, prosperity and harmony for all beings. May all of us give witness to compassion and loving kindness in promoting the true good of humanity.

*To the Islamic Community:* I share your belief that mankind owes its existence to the One, Compassionate God who created heaven and earth. In a world in which God is denied or disobeyed, in a world that experiences so much suffering and is so much in need of God's mercy, let us then strive together to be courageous bearers of hope.

*To the Hindu Community:* I hold in esteem your concern for inner peace and for the peace of the world, based not on purely mechanistic or materialistic political considerations, but on self-purification, unselfishness, love and sympathy for all. May the minds of all people be imbued with such love and understanding.

*To the Jewish Community:* I repeat the Second Vatican Council's conviction that the Church "cannot forget that she received the revelation of the Old Testament through the people with whom God in his mercy established the Ancient Covenant. Nor can she forget that she draws sustenance from the root of that good olive tree onto which has been grafted the wild olive branches of the Gentiles (see Rom. 11:17–24)" (*Nostra Aetate,* 4). With you, I oppose every form of anti-Semitism. May we work for the day when all peoples and nations may enjoy security, harmony and peace.

## The Great Questions of Life Draw Us Together in a Common Concern for Man's Earthly Welfare, Especially Peace and Final Destiny

4. Dear brothers and sisters of these religions and of every religion: so many people today experience inner emptiness even amid material prosperity, because they overlook the *great questions of life:* "What is man? What is the meaning and purpose of life? What is goodness and what is sin? What gives rise to suffering and what purpose does it serve? What is the path to true happiness? What is death, judgment and retribution after death? What, finally, is that ultimate, ineffable mystery which embraces our existence, from which we take our origin and toward which we move?" (*Nostra Aetate,* 1).

These profoundly spiritual questions, which are shared to some degree by all religions, also draw us together in a *common concern* for man's earthly welfare, especially world peace. As I said at Assisi: "[World religions] share a common respect of and obedience to conscience, which teaches all of us to seek the truth, to love and serve all individuals and peoples, and therefore to make peace among individuals and among nations" (Message at the Conclusion of the World Day of Prayer for Peace, Assisi, October 27, 1986).

## Let Us Seek Peace Through Prayer, Penance, Constant Initiatives on Behalf of the Rights of Individuals and Nations

In the spirit of the kind words with which you addressed me earlier as an advocate of peace, let us continue *to seek peace for the human family:* through prayer, since peace transcends our human efforts; through penance, since we have not always been "peacemakers"; through prophetic witness, since old divisions and social evils need to be challenged; and through constant initiatives on behalf of the rights of individuals and nations, and on behalf of justice everywhere. The fragile gift of peace will survive only if there is a concerted effort on the part of all, to be concerned with the "glaring inequalities not merely in the enjoyment of possessions but even more in the exercise of power" (*Populorum Progressio,* 9). In this regard world leaders and international bodies have their special role to play. But universal sensitivity is also called for, particularly among the young.

I believe that the *Prayer of Saint Francis of Assisi,* universally recognized as a man of peace, touches the conscience of us all. It is that prayer that best expresses my sentiments in meeting with all of you today:

Lord, make me an instrument of your peace;
where there is hatred, let me sow love;
where there is injury, pardon;
where there is doubt, faith;
where there is despair, hope;
where there is darkness, light;
and where there is sadness, joy.

O Divine Master, grant that I may not so much seek to be consoled as to console; to be understood as to understand, to be loved as to love; for it is in giving that we receive, it is in pardoning that we are pardoned, and it is in dying that we are born to eternal life.

## 36. HOMILY AT MASS CELEBRATED IN DODGER STADIUM

The Lord has made his salvation known in the sight of the nations.
(Ps. 97/98:2)

Dear Brother Bishops,

Dear Brothers and Sisters in Christ,

People of this City of Our Lady of the Angels, once known as
El Pueblo de Nuestra Señora de los Angeles,

Citizens of this State of California,

### We Join Christ's Prayer for the Church in Every Time and Place for All of Us Gathered Here, for Everyone

1. Today, from this City of Los Angeles on the Pacific Coast, in which are gathered all the Bishops of the United States, we return together to *the Upper Room* in Jerusalem. We hear words from the prayer which Christ pronounced there. Surrounded by his Apostles, *Jesus prays for the Church of every time and place.* He says to the Father: "I do not pray for them alone. I pray also for those who will believe in me through their word" (Jn. 17:20). Christ, the one Eternal Priest of the new and everlasting Covenant, *prays for us,* for all of us gathered here, for everyone who lives here in Los Angeles on the West Coast of the United States of America, for everyone in the world. Yes, *every one of us is included in this priestly prayer of the Redeemer.*

### How Many Passed on This Word of Salvation in How Many Places!

2. Jesus says to the Father: "I pray also for *those who will believe in me through their word*" (Jn. 17:20). This is *the Church* of all ages that he is praying for. How many generations of disciples have already heard these words of Christ! How many Bishops, priests, men and women Religious, and how many parents and teachers in the course of the centuries *have passed on this word of salvation!* In how many places of the world, among how many peoples and nations, has this mystery of the Redemption continued to unfold and bear fruit! It is the word of salvation from which *the Church* has grown and *continues to grow.* This is true for the universal Church and for each local Church. It is true for the Church in Los Angeles, which is visited today by the Bishop of Rome, the Successor of Peter.

## Fray Junípero Serra and His Brothers
## Brought the Word to California

*In 1769 Father Junípero Serra and his Franciscan companions brought the word of God to California.* Leaving behind all that was familiar and dear to them, they freely chose to come to this area to preach the Good News of our Lord Jesus Christ. This initial effort of evangelization very quickly showed impressive results as thousands of Native Americans accepted the Gospel and were baptized. Soon, a whole series of missions was established all along *El Camino Real,* each of them bearing the name of a Saint or a mystery of the Christian faith: San Diego, San Bernardino, San Gabriel, San Buenaventura, Santa Barbara, San Fernando and all the rest.

## Mexican and Spanish Settlers Moved to California,
## Bringing Their Heritage of Faith

Within years of this first missionary effort, *immigrants began to settle in California.* Coming mostly from Mexico and Spain, these early settlers had *already* been *evangelized,* and thus they brought as part of their heritage the Catholic and apostolic faith. Little did they know at the time that, in God's providence, they were initiating a pattern which would characterize California for years to come.

## California Has Become a Haven for Immigrants
## of the Most Varied Ethnic Diversity

Subsequently, California has become *a haven for immigrants,* a new home for refugees and migrants, a place where people from every continent have come together to fashion a society of the *most varied ethnic diversity.* Many of these, like their earliest predecessors, have brought not only their specific cultural traditions but also the Christian faith. As a result, the Church in California, and particularly the Church in Los Angeles, is *truly Catholic in the fullest sense,* embracing peoples and cultures of the widest and richest variety.

## The One Risen Christ Is Living in Each Person
## Who Accepted God's Word and Is Baptized

Today, in the Church in Los Angeles, Christ is Anglo and Hispanic, Christ is Chinese and Black, Christ is Vietnamese and Irish, Christ is Korean and Italian, Christ is Japanese and Filipino, Christ is Native American, Croatian, Samoan and many other ethnic groups. In this local Church, the *one Risen Christ,* the one Lord and Savior, is living in each person who has accepted the word of God and been washed clean in the saving waters of Baptism. And *the Church, with all her different members, remains the one Body of Christ,* professing the same faith, united in hope and in love.

## The Unity in Diversity of the Inner Life of the Trinity
## Is the Real Model for the Church

3. *What does Jesus pray for in the Upper Room* the night before his Passion and Death? "*That all may be one as you,* Father, are in me, and I in you; I pray that they may be one in us, that the world may believe that you sent me" (Jn. 17:21). "One in us"—the mystery of the inscrutable divine Being, the mystery of the intimate life of God: the divine Unity and at the same time *the Trinity.* It is the divine "We" of the Father and the Son and the Holy Spirit. And even though it is not attainable in its absolute fullness, this most perfect Unity is the real *model for the Church.* According-ing to the teaching of the Second Vatican Council, "the Church shines forth as a people made one by the unity of the Father, the Son and the Holy Spirit" (*Lumen Gentium,* 4).

## This Is the Type of Unity of the Church's Communion

It is for this type of unity for the Church of all times that Christ prays in the Upper Room: "that they may be one, as we are one—*I living in them, you living in me*—that their unity may be complete. So shall the world know that you sent me, and that you loved them as you loved me" (Jn. 17:22–23). This is the unity of the Church's communion which is *born from the communion of Three Persons in the Most Holy Trinity.*

## Isaiah Foretold the Movement of People from the Entire
## World Toward the Light of Christ—a New Humanity

4. People of all times and places are called to this communion. This truth of revelation is first presented to us in today's liturgy, *through the image of the holy city of Jerusalem* found in the reading from the Prophet Isaiah, who writes: "Nations shall walk by your light, and kings by your shining radiance. Raise your eyes and look about; they all gather and come to you: your sons *come from afar,* and your daughters in the arms of their nurses" (Is. 60:3–5). Isaiah spoke these words in Jerusalem as he foresaw *a great light* which would descend upon the city: *This light is Christ.* The awesome movement toward Christ of people from all over the world begins as a result of the Gospel. Animated by the Holy Spirit, in the power of the Cross and Resurrec-tion of Christ, *this movement of people culminates in a new unity* of humanity. Thus, the words of Jesus come to pass: "and I—once I am lifted up from the earth—will draw all men to myself" (Jn. 12:32).

The Second Vatican Council gave prominence to this dimension of the unity of the Church, above all *in the teaching on the People of God.* "This People, while remain-ing one and unique, is to be spread throughout the whole world and must exist in all ages, so that the purpose of God's will may be fulfilled" (*Lumen Gentium,* 13).

### The Unity in Which We Are Constituted in Christ
### Is Called the Body of Christ

5. However, that *People is at the same time the Body of Christ*. The Body is yet another image, and in a certain sense another dimension, of the same truth of the unity that we all constitute in Christ under the action of the Holy Spirit. Accordingly, Saint Paul exhorts us: "Make every effort to preserve *the unity which has the Spirit as its origin* and peace as its binding force. There is but *one body* and *one Spirit,* just as there is but one hope given all of you by your call. There is *one Lord, one faith, one baptism;* one God and Father of all, who is over all, and works through all, and is in all" (Eph. 4:3–6). The unity for which Christ prayed in the Upper Room is realized in this way. It does not come from us, but *from God: from the Father, through the Son, in the Holy Spirit.*

### Communion—in the Trinity and in the Church—
### Is a Unity in Diversity

6. *This unity does not at all erase diversity.* On the contrary, *it develops it.* There is constantly "unity in diversity." Through the work of the one Lord, by means of the one faith and the one baptism, this diversity—a diversity of human persons, of individuals—tends toward unity, a unity which is *communion* in the likeness of God the Trinity.

### The Unity of the Body of Christ
### Gives Life and Serves Diversity

The unity of the Body of Christ gives life; at the same time, it *serves diversity* and develops it. This is the diversity of "everyone" and at the same time of "each one." It is the truth that we find in the letter to the Ephesians, where Paul writes: "*Each of us has received God's favor* in the measure in which Christ bestows it. . . . It is he who gave apostles, prophets, evangelists, pastors and teachers in roles of service for the faithful to build up the body of Christ" (Eph. 4:7, 11–12). As such then it is *the Holy Spirit* who is the source of both *the unity* and diversity in the Church: the unity because it finds its origin solely in the Spirit; the diversity since the Spirit bestows *the variety of gifts,* the variety of vocations and ministries found in the Church, which is the Body of Christ and at the same time the People of God.

### Cornelius and Cyprian Remind Us of the Unity
### of the Universal Church, Served by Peter's Successor,
### and the Diversity of Particular Churches

7. The saints whom we honor in today's liturgy, *Cornelius and Cyprian,* remind us of one concrete example of unity in diversity: *the unity of the universal Church,* which is served by the Successor of Saint Peter, and the diversity of the particular

Churches which help to build up the whole Body through the leadership of the local Bishops.

Pope Saint Cornelius was called to shepherd the universal Church in the middle of the third century, a time of religious persecution from without and a time of painful dissension within. His efforts to strengthen the Church's communion were greatly aided by the persuasive talents of the Bishop of Carthage, Saint Cyprian, who while caring for his own flock also promoted unity throughout North Africa. These two men of different backgrounds and temperaments were united *by a mutual love for the Church* and by their *zeal for the unity of the faith.* How appropriate that we should observe their feast on the day when the present Successor of Peter is meeting with the Bishops of the United States.

## The Unity of the Bishops Deeply Affects the Unity of the Members of the Church

The feast focuses our attention on a basic truth, namely, that *the unity of the members of the Church* is deeply affected by *the unity of the Bishops* among themselves and by their communion with the Successor of Peter.

The Second Vatican Council put it this way: "The Roman Pontiff, as the Successor of Peter, is the perpetual and visible source and foundation of the unity of the Bishops and of the multitude of the faithful. The individual Bishop, however, is the visible principle and foundation of unity in his particular Church, fashioned after the model of the universal Church. In and from such individual Churches there comes into being the one and only Catholic Church" (*Lumen Gentium,* 23).

## Evangelization Calls for a Proclamation That Uses the Symbols of the Local Culture Without Betraying the Essential Truth

8. The Church's concrete *methods of evangelization* and her efforts to promote peace and justice are shaped to a large extent by the fact that the Church is one and yet diverse. The Good News of Jesus must be proclaimed *in the language that particular people understand,* in *artistic symbols* that give meaning to their experience, in ways that correspond as far as possible to their own aspirations and needs, their manner of looking at life and the way in which they speak to God. At the same time, there must be *no betrayal of the essential truth* while the Gospel is being translated and the Church's teaching is being passed down.

The *ethnic universality of the Church* demands a keen sensitivity to authentic cultures and a real sense of what is required by the process of inculturation. In this regard, Pope Paul VI stated very accurately the task to be done: "The question is undoubtedly a delicate one. Evangelization loses much of its force and effectiveness if it does not take into consideration the actual people to whom it is addressed, if it does not use their language, their signs and symbols, if it does not answer the questions they ask, and if it does not have an impact on their concrete life. But on the other hand evangelization risks losing its power and disappearing altogether if one empties or adulterates its content under the pretext of translating it; if, in other words, one sacrifices this reality and destroys the unity without which there is no universality" (*Evangelii Nuntiandi,* 63).

### Evangelization Is Influenced by Pastoral Concern for the Plight of Refugees, Immigrants and the Poor

Closely aligned with the Church's evangelization is her *action on behalf of peace and justice,* and this too is deeply influenced by her pastoral concern for particular peoples, especially for refugees, immigrants and the poor. For over two hundred years, *the Church has welcomed* the waves of *new immigrants* to the shores of your country. It was the love and compassion of the Church that so many new arrivals first felt when they stepped onto the soil of this young nation. While that continuous pastoral care of the immigrant focused primarily on the East Coast in the early decades, that *pastoral outreach* now extends to virtually every major city in the country. Los Angeles—where this evening we celebrate the diversity of peoples who make up your country—has now become the new major point of entry for the latest waves of immigrants.

I commend you, my brother Bishops and all of those working closely with you, for your active collaboration in helping several million undocumented immigrants to become legal residents. This pastoral care of the immigrant in our own day reflects the love of Christ in the Gospels and the legitimate work of the Church in carrying on the challenge of the Lord, *"I was a stranger and you welcomed me"* (Mt. 25:35).

### Church's Challenge Is Preaching the Word in Cultures Which Tend to Exalt Utility, Productivity and Hedonism

9. The Church faces a particularly difficult task in her efforts to preach the word of God in all *cultures* in which the faithful are constantly challenged by *consumerism and a pleasure-seeking mentality,* where utility, productivity and hedonism are exalted while God and his law are forgotten. In these situations, where ideas and behavior directly contradict the truth about God and about humanity itself, the Church's witness must be *unpopular.* She must take a *clear* stand on the word of God and proclaim the whole Gospel message with great confidence in the Holy Spirit. In this effort, just as in all others, the Church shows herself to be *the Sacrament of salvation* for the whole human race, the people God has chosen to be his channel of peace and reconciliation in a world torn by division and sin.

### Faithfulness to the Truth Makes the Church the Sacrament of Salvation for the Whole Human Race, an Instrument Restoring the Unity of the Human Family

While the Church's unity is not her own achievement but a precious gift from the Lord, it is nonetheless her serious responsibility to be an instrument for *guarding and restoring unity* in the human family. She does this by being faithful to the truth and by directly opposing the devil, who is "the Father of lies." She does this by efforts to break down prejudice and ignorance as she fosters new understanding and trust. She also promotes unity by being a faithful channel of Christ's mercy and love.

### We Join Christ's Prayer for Unity in the City
### that Takes Its Name from the Angels,
### Who See the Face of God in the Beatific Vision

10. Today, with *the very prayer for unity said by Christ* in the Upper Room, we celebrate the liturgy of the Eucharist here, on the rim of the Pacific, in the city that takes its *name from the angels.* And with the Psalmist, we say: "Sing to the Lord a new song, for he has done wondrous deeds" (Ps. 97/98:1). Yes, God has done so many wondrous deeds that confirm his salvific action in our world—the "God and Father of all, who is over all, and works through all, and is in all" (Eph. 4:6). "The Lord has made his salvation known: . . . he has revealed his justice." He constantly remembers "his kindness and his faithfulness" (Ps. 97/98:2–3). *This is the way God is, the God of our faith,* the Father of our Lord Jesus Christ.

### We Draw Our Hope from the
### Same Prayer of Christ in the Upper Room

The angels in heaven see "the face of God" in the beatific vision of glory. All of us, people of this planet, *walk in faith* toward that same vision. And we walk *in hope.* We draw the strength of this hope from the same prayer of Christ in the Upper Room. Did not Christ say in the words addressed to the Father: "I have given them the glory you gave me that they may be one, as we are one—I living in them, you living in me" (Jn. 17:22–23)?

### We Are Called to Share in the Glory

"*The glory* . . . I gave to them." We are called in Christ *to share in the glory* that is part of the beatific vision of God.

Truly, "all the ends of the earth have seen the salvation by our God." For this reason, "Sing to the Lord a new song!" (Ps. 97/98:3,1). Amen.

### 37. ACT OF ENTRUSTING
### TO THE BLESSED VIRGIN MARY

1. I wish at this time to turn my thoughts once more to *the Woman of faith and of all salvation history:* Mary, the Mother of Jesus and Mother of his Church; Mary, the Patroness of the United States under the title of her Immaculate Conception.

I entrust to you, Virgin Mother of God, *all the faithful* of this land. I entrust them to you, not only as individual men and women in the nobility of their personhood, but as the Christian community, living corporately the life of your divine Son.

I entrust to you *my brother Bishops* in their great mission as servant pastors of God's people, in communion with the Successor of Peter. I entrust to you all *the priests,* who minister generously in the name of the Good Shepherd; all *the deacons* bearing witness to Christ's servanthood; all *women and men Religious* proclaiming by their lives the holiness of God; all *the laity* working in virtue of their Baptism and Confirmation to order all temporal affairs according to the plan of God.

I entrust to you *all the holy People of God*—the pilgrim People of God—called to be mindful of their Christian dignity, called to conversion, called to eternal life.

In particular I entrust to you *the families* of America, in their quest for holiness, in their struggle against sin, in their vocation to be vital cells in the Body of Christ. I ask you to bless all *husbands and wives,* all *fathers and mothers,* and to confirm them in their high vocation of human love and openness to life. I entrust to you *the children* of this generation, asking you to preserve them in innocence, to protect them from all harm and abuse, and to let them grow up in a world of peace and justice and fraternal love.

I entrust to you *all the women of the Church* and the cause of their true human advancement in the world and their ever-fuller participation in the life of the Church, according to the authentic plan of God. May they discover in you, O Mary, and in the freedom that was yours from that moment of supreme liberation in your Immaculate Conception the secret of living totally their femininity in fulfillment, progress and love.

I commend to your protection *the young people* that make up the future of the United States. I pray that in your Son Jesus Christ they may grasp the meaning of life, and come to understand deeply their call to serve their fellow human beings; that they may discover the profound fulfillment of chaste love, and the joy and strength that come from Christian hope.

I offer to your loving care *the elderly people* with all their sufferings and joys, and with their yet unfinished mission of service in your Church. I ask you to console and assist *the dying,* and to renew within the whole community a sense of the importance of human life at every stage, even when it is weak and defenseless.

I ask you to assist *the single people* with their special needs and special mission. Give them strength to live according to the Beatitudes and to serve with generosity and gladness.

2. I entrust to you all *those engaged in the great Christian struggle of life:* all those who, despite human weaknesses and repeated falls, are striving to live according to the word of God; all those who are confused about the truth and are tempted to call evil good and darkness light; all those who are yearning for truth and grasping for hope.

I ask you to show yourself once again as a Mother with that deep human concern which was yours at Cana of Galilee. Help *all those weighed down by the problems of life.* Console the suffering. Comfort the sad and dejected, those tormented in spirit, those without families, loved ones or friends.

Assist *the poor and those in need,* and those subjected to discrimination or other forms of injustice. Come to the help of the unemployed. Heal the sick. Aid the handicapped and disabled, so that they may live in a manner befitting their dignity as children of God. *Stir up the consciences of us all,* to respond to the needs of others, with justice, mercy and love.

3. Through your intercession I ask *that sinners may be reconciled,* and that the whole Church in America may become ever more attentive to Christ's call to conversion and to holiness of life.

I pray that all those baptized in Christ your Son will be strengthened in the great cause of Christian unity, according to his will.

I ask your prayers so *that citizens may work together to conquer evil with good,* oppose violence, reject war and its weapons, satisfy hunger, overcome hatred and remedy all forms of personal, social, national and international injustice.

I ask you *to strengthen the Catholic people* in truth and love, in their obedience to the commandments of God, and in their fidelity to the Sacraments.

Virgin Mother of God, Our Lady of the Angels: I entrust to you *the whole Church in America.* Help her to excel in sacrifice and service. Purify her love, renew her life, and convert her constantly to the Gospel of your Son. Lead her children with *all their Christian and non-Christian brethren* to eternal life, for the glory of your Son Jesus Christ, who lives and reigns with the Father in the unity of the Holy Spirit, for ever and ever. Amen.

## SEPTEMBER 17, 1987

## 38. HOMILY AT MASS CELEBRATED AT LAGUNA SECA

Be careful not to forget the Lord, your God. (Dt. 8:11)

Dear Brothers and Sisters of the Monterey Peninsula,

Brothers and Sisters of California and other areas of the United States,

### Words of Admonition Addressed to People Living in the Midst of Extraordinary Beauty of Land and Sea

1. Originally these words were addressed by Moses to the Israelite people as they were on the point of entering the promised land—a land with streams of water, with springs and fountains welling up in the hills and valleys, a land producing an abundance of every fruit and food, a land where the people would lack nothing (see Dt. 8:7–9). Today, these words are addressed to the People of God here in Monterey, in the State of California, against the background of an extraordinary beauty of land and sea, of snowcapped mountains and deep lakes, oak groves and forests of fir and pine, mighty redwoods, a land among the richest and most fruitful of the earth. Yes, today, these words are addressed to all of us gathered here: *"Be careful not to forget the Lord, your God."*

### Moses Knew the Heart's Tendency to Cry Out to the Lord in Time of Need but to Neglect Him in Time of Prosperity

2. These words, pronounced thousands of years ago, have still today a special meaning and relevance. Moses, the great teacher of his people, was concerned that in their future prosperity they might abandon God—the God who brought them out of the land of slavery and guided them through the desert with its parched ground, feeding them with manna along the way (see Dt. 8:15–16). Moses knew the tendency of the human heart to cry out to the Lord in time of need, but easily "to neglect his commandments and decrees and statutes" (see Dt. 8:11) in the time of well-being and prosperity. He knew that *God is easily forgotten.*

### Practical Atheism Can Be Accepted Where There Is an Abundance

In our own day are we not perhaps witnesses of the fact that often in rich societies, where there is an abundance of material well-being, permissiveness and moral relativism find easy acceptance? And where the moral order is undermined, God is forgotten and questions of ultimate responsibility are set aside. *In such situations a practical atheism pervades private and public living.*

From the moment of *original sin,* man has been inclined to see himself in the place of God. He often thinks, just as Moses warned he might: "It is my own power and the strength of my own hand that has obtained for me this wealth" (Dt. 8:17). He acts as if the One who is the source of all life and goodness were just not there. He ignores a fundamental truth about himself: *the fact that he is a creature;* that he has been created and owes everything to his creator, who is also his Redeemer.

### The Most Technically Developed Nations Are Tempted to Forget God and to Build a World for Themselves

In these closing years of the twentieth century, on the eve of the third millennium of the Christian era, a part of the human family—the most economically and technically developed part—is being specially tempted, perhaps as never before, to imitate the ancient model of all sin—the original rebellion that expressed itself saying: "I will not serve." *The temptation today is to try to build a world for oneself,* forgetting the Creator and his design and loving providence. But sooner or later we must come to grips with this: that *to forget God, to feign the death of God, is to promote the death of man* and of all civilization. It is to threaten the existence of individuals, communities and all society.

### God's Presence Permeates the Human Heart and the Whole of Created Reality

3. Today's readings from the New Testament are in contrast to such a position. They speak of *God's presence, which permeates the human heart and the whole of created*

*reality.* Jesus teaches that the reign of God is like the growth of the seed that a man scatters on the ground (see Mk. 4:26–29). Certainly, human activity is essential. Man "goes to bed and gets up every day." He plants. And "when the crop is ready he wields the sickle." Even the rich valleys of California would produce nothing without human ingenuity and toil. But the word of God says that "*the soil produces of itself* first the blade, then the ear, finally the ripe wheat in the ear" (v. 28). As if to say: the growth of the wheat and its maturing, which greatly depends on the fertility of the soil, comes from the nature and vitality of creation itself. Consequently, there is *another source of growth*: the One who is *above nature and above the man who cultivates the earth.*

### The Human Person Discovers the
### Action of God in His Creation

In a sense, the Creator *"hides himself"* in this life-giving process of nature. It is the human person, with the help of intellect and faith, who is called to "discover" and "unveil" the presence of God and his action in all of creation: *"So may your way be known upon earth; among all nations, your salvation"* (Ps. 67:3).

### Human Activity Must Be Finalized in
### Works of Justice, Love and Peace

If the parable of the seed indicates the growth of the Kingdom of God in the world, the words of Saint Paul in the second reading speak of how God's generous giving aims at drawing "good works" *from the human heart:* "God can multiply his favors among you . . . for good works." The whole of human activity must be finalized in works of justice, peace and love. All human work—including, in a very direct way, the noble work of agriculture in which many of you are engaged—is to be carried out at the service of man and for the glory of God.

### We Must Use the Land to Sustain
### Every Human Being in Life and Dignity

4. *The land is God's gift.* From the beginning, God has entrusted it to the whole human race as a means of sustaining the life of all those whom he creates in his own image and likeness. We must use the land to sustain every human being in life and dignity. Against the background of the immense beauty of this region and the fertility of its soil, let us proclaim together our gratitude for this gift, with the words of the responsorial psalm: *"the earth has yielded its fruit, the Lord our God has blessed us"* (Ps. 67:7).

As we read in Genesis, human beings earn their bread by the sweat of their brows (Gn. 3:17). We toil long hours and grow weary at our tasks. *Yet work is good for us.* "Through work man not only transforms nature, adapting it to his own needs, but he also achieves fulfillment as a human being and indeed in a sense becomes 'more a human being'" (*Laborem Exercens,* 9).

## Work Supports and Gives Stability to the Family

The value of work does not end with *the individual.* The full meaning of work can only be understood in relation to *the family* and society as well. Work supports and gives stability to the family. Within the family, moreover, children first learn the human and positive meaning of work and responsibility. In each community and in the nation as a whole, work has a fundamental social meaning. It can, moreover, either join people in the solidarity of a shared commitment or set them at odds through exaggerated competition, exploitation and social conflict. *Work is a key to the whole social question,* when that "question" is understood to be concerned with *making life more human* (see *Laborem Exercens,* 3).

## Agricultural Work Is a God-Given Mission, a Noble Task, a Contribution to Civilization

5. Agricultural work exemplifies all these principles—the potential of work for the fulfillment of the human person, the "family" dimension of work and social solidarity. *Agricultural work is*—as Pope John XXIII described it—*a vocation, a God-given mission, a noble task and a contribution to civilization* (see *Mater et Magistra,* 149). God has blessed the United States with some of the richest *farm land* in the world. The productivity of American agriculture is a major success story. Clearly, it is a history of hard and wearying work, of courage and enterprise, and it involves the interaction of many people: growers, workers, processors, distributors and finally consumers.

I know too that recently thousands of *American farmers* have been introduced to poverty and indebtedness. Many have lost their homes and their way of life. Your Bishops and the whole Church in your country are deeply concerned; and they are listening to the voices of so many farmers and farmworkers as they express their anxieties over the costs and the risks of farming, the difficult working conditions, the need for a just wage and decent housing, and the question of a fair price for products. On an even wider scale is heard *the voice of the poor,* who are bewildered in a land of plenty and still experience the pangs of hunger.

## At Every Level of the Agricultural Process the Dignity, Rights and Well-Being of People Must Be the Central Issue

6. All agree that the situation of the farming community in the United States and in other parts of the world is highly complex, and that simple remedies are not

at hand. The Church, on her part, while she can offer no specific technical solutions, does present a social teaching based on the primacy of the human person in every economic and social activity. At every level of the agricultural process, *the dignity, rights and well-being of people must be the central issue.* No one person in this process—grower, worker, packer, shipper, retailer or consumer—is greater than the other in the eyes of God.

Giving voice therefore to the sufferings of many, I appeal to all involved to work together to find appropriate solutions to all farm questions. This can only be done in a community marked by a sincere and effective *solidarity*—and, where still necessary, *reconciliation*—among all parties to the agricultural productive process.

And what of our responsibility to future generations? The earth will not continue to offer its harvest, except *with faithful stewardship.* We cannot say we love the land and then take steps to destroy it for use by future generations. I urge you to be sensitive to the many issues affecting the land and the whole environment and to unite with each other to seek the best solutions to these pressing problems.

## To Landowners, Growers, Respect the Just Claims of Those Who Work the Land

7. *Each one of us is called to fulfill his or her respective duties before God and before society.* Since the Church is constrained by her very nature to focus her attention most strongly on those least able to defend their own legitimate interests, I appeal to landowners, growers and others in positions of power to respect the just claims of their brothers and sisters who work the land. These claims include the right to share in decisions concerning their services and the right to free association with a view to social, cultural and economic advancement (see *Laborem Exercens,* 21). I also appeal to all workers to be mindful of their own obligations of justice and to make every effort to fulfill a worthy service to mankind.

## Welcome New Citizens into Your Society

New legislation in your country has made it possible for many people, especially migrant farmworkers, *to become citizens* rather than remain strangers among you. Many of these people have worked here with the same dream that your ancestors had when they first came. I ask you to welcome these new citizens into your society and to respect the human dignity of every man, woman and child.

Two hundred years after the Constitution confirmed the United States as a land of opportunity and freedom, it is right to hope that there may be a general and renewed *commitment to those policies needed to ensure that within these borders equity and justice will be preserved and fostered.* This is an ever-present requirement of America's historical destiny.

## Look Beyond Your Country
## to See the Greater Needs of the Poorer Nations

It is also important for America at this time *to look beyond herself* and all her own needs *to see the even greater needs of the poorer nations of the world.* Even as local communities mobilize to work ever more effectively for the integral human advancement of their own members, they must not forget their brothers and sisters elsewhere. We must be careful not to forget the Lord, but we must be careful also not to forget those whom he loves.

### See the Tourist Industry as a Form of Service and Solidarity

8. The hidden attributes of the Creator are reflected in the beauty of his creation. The beauty of the Monterey Peninsula attracts a great number of visitors; as a result, so many of you are involved in *the tourist industry.* I greet you and encourage you to see your specific work as a form of service and of solidarity with your fellow human beings.

Work—as we have seen—is an essential aspect of our human existence, but so also is the necessary rest and recreation which permits us to recover our energies and strengthen our spirit for the tasks of life. Many worthwhile values are involved in tourism: relaxation, the widening of one's culture and the possibility of using leisure time for spiritual pursuits. These include prayer and contemplation, and pilgrimages, which have always been a part of our Catholic heritage; they also include fostering human relationships within the family and among friends. Like other human activities, tourism can be a source of good or evil, a place of grace or sin. I invite all of you who are involved in tourism *to uphold the dignity of your work* and to be always willing *to bear joyful witness to your Christian faith.*

9. Dear brothers and sisters: it is *in the Eucharist* that the fruits of our work—and all that is noble in human affairs—become an offering of the greatest value in union with the Sacrifice of Jesus Christ, our Lord and Savior. In fostering what is authentically human through our work and through deeds of justice and love, we set upon the altar of the Lord those elements which will be transformed into Christ: "Blessed are you Lord, God, of all creation. Through your goodness we have this bread to offer, which earth has given and human hands have made. *It will become for us the bread of life.*"

I ask you to join with me *in praising the Most Holy Trinity* for the abundance of life and goodness with which you have been gifted: "The earth has yielded its fruit. God, our God, has blessed us" (Ps. 67:7). But may your abundance never lead you to forget the Lord or cease to acknowledge him as the source of your peace and well-being. Your prayer for yourselves and for all your brothers and sisters must always be an echo of the psalm:

May God have pity on us and bless us;
may he let his face shine on us. (Ps. 67:2)

For years to come may the Lord's face shine on this land, on the Church in Monterey, and on all America: "From sea to shining sea." Amen.

## 39. VISIT TO THE CARMEL MISSION BASILICA

Dear Bishop Shubsda,

Dear Brothers and Sisters,

### This Serene Place, Mission of San Carlos, Is the Spiritual Heart of California

1. I come today as a pilgrim to this Mission of San Carlos, which so powerfully evokes the heroic spirit and heroic deeds of Fray Junípero Serra and which enshrines his mortal remains. This serene and beautiful place is truly *the historical and spiritual heart of California*. All the missions of *El Camino Real* bear witness to the challenges and heroism of an earlier time, but not a time forgotten or without significance for the California of today and the Church of today.

### These Buildings and the Missionaries Recall the Decision to Proclaim the Gospel at the Dawn of a New Age

These buildings and the men who gave them life, especially their spiritual father, Junípero Serra, are reminders of an age of discovery and exploration. The missions are the result of a conscious moral decision made by people of faith in a situation that presented many human possibilities, both good and bad, with respect to the future of this land and its native peoples. It was a decision rooted in a love of God and neighbor. It was *a decision to proclaim the Gospel* of Jesus Christ at the dawn of a new age, which was extremely important for both the European settlers and Native Americans.

### Father Junípero Serra, Apostle of California, Understood the Richness of the Work of Evangelization

2. Very often, at crucial moments in human affairs, God raises up men and women whom he thrusts into roles of decisive importance for the future development of both society and the Church. Although their story unfolds within the ordinary circumstances of daily life, they become larger than life within the perspective of history. We rejoice all the more when their achievement is coupled with a holiness of life that can truly be called heroic. So it is with Junípero Serra, who in the providence of God was destined to be *the Apostle of California* and to have a permanent influence over the spiritual patrimony of this land and its people, whatever their religion might be. This apostolic awareness is captured in the words ascribed to him: "In California is my life and there, God willing, I hope to die." Through Christ's Paschal Mystery,

that death has become a seed in the soil of this state that continues to bear fruit "thirty—or sixty—or a hundred-fold" (Mt. 13:9).

Father Serra was a man *convinced of the Church's mission,* conferred upon her by Christ himself, to evangelize the world, to "make disciples of all the nations, baptizing them in the name of the Father and of the Son and of the Holy Spirit" (Mt. 28:19). The way in which he fulfilled that mission corresponds faithfully to the Church's vision of today of what evangelization means: "the Church evangelizes when she seeks to convert, solely through the divine power of the Message she proclaims, both the personal and collective consciences of people, the activities in which they engage, and the lives and concrete milieux which are theirs" (*Evangelii Nuntiandi,* 18).

### Junípero Serra Was Defender and Champion of Native Americans

He not only brought the Gospel to the Native Americans, but as one who lived the Gospel he also became their *defender and champion.* At the age of sixty he journeyed from Carmel to Mexico City to intervene with the Viceroy on their behalf—a journey which twice brought him close to death—and presented his now-famous *Representación* with its "bill of rights," which had as their aim the betterment of every phase of missionary activity in California, particularly the spiritual and physical well-being of its Native Americans.

### Father Serra Was Convinced That the Gospel Is Something of Immense Value

3. Father Serra and his fellow missionaries shared the conviction found everywhere in the New Testament that the Gospel is a matter of life and salvation. They believed that in offering to people Jesus Christ, they were doing *something of immense value,* importance and dignity. What other explanation can there be for the hardships that they freely and gladly endured, like Saint Paul and all the other great missionaries before them: difficult and dangerous travel, illness and isolation, an ascetical life-style, arduous labor, and also, like Saint Paul, that "concern for all the churches" (2 Cor. 11:28) which Junípero Serra, in particular, experienced as *presidente* of the California Missions in the face of every vicissitude, disappointment and opposition.

### We Are Called to Be Evangelizers: Single-Mindedness Should Mark Every State of Life

Dear brothers and sisters: like Father Serra and his Franciscan brethren, we too are *called to be evangelizers,* to share actively in the Church's mission of making disciples of all people. The way in which we fulfill that mission will be different from theirs. But their lives speak to us still because of their sure faith that the Gospel is true, and because of their passionate belief in the value of bringing that saving truth to others at great personal cost. Much to be envied are those who can give their lives for something greater than themselves in loving service to others. This, more than words or deeds alone, is what draws people to Christ.

This *single-mindedness* is not reserved for great missionaries in exotic places. It must be at the heart of each priest's ministry and the evangelical witness of every Religious. It is the key to their personal sense of well-being, happiness and fulfillment in what they are and what they do. This single-mindedness is also essential to the Christian witness of the Catholic laity. The covenant of love between two people in marriage and the successful sharing of faith with children require the effort of a lifetime. If couples cease believing in their marriage as a sacrament before God, or treat religion as anything less than a matter of salvation, then the Christian witness they might have given to the world is lost. Those who are unmarried must also be steadfast in fulfilling their duties in life if they are to bring Christ to the world in which they live.

### God's Power Shines Through Human Weakness

"In him who is the source of my strength I have strength for everything" (Phil. 4:13). These words of the great missionary, Saint Paul, remind us that *our strength is not our own*. Even in the martyrs and saints, as the liturgy reminds us, it is "God's power shining through our human weakness" (*Preface of Martyrs*). It is the strength that inspired Father Serra's motto: "always forward, never back." It is the strength that one senses in this place of prayer so filled with his presence. It is the strength that can make each one of us, dear brothers and sisters, missionaries of Jesus Christ, witnesses of his message, doers of his word.

### 40. VISIT TO MISSION DOLORES BASILICA

Dear Archbishop Quinn,

Dear Brothers and Sisters in Christ,

1. Thank you for your very kind welcome to *San Francisco*. It is a joy to be here with all of you. As I begin my pastoral visit to your historic city, I extend fraternal greetings to all the citizens of this metropolitan area. In the love of Christ I greet my brothers and sisters of the Catholic community. And in a special way I welcome this opportunity to be with you who are present in this *Basilica dedicated to Our Lady of Sorrows*. May the grace and peace of God our Father and our Lord Jesus Christ be with you all.

### Spirit of Saint Francis of Assisi, Whose Life Proclaims the Love of Christ and the Goodness of God

San Francisco! Both in name and by history you are linked to *the spirit of Saint Francis of Assisi*. And thus, as I come to your city on this pastoral visit, I think of all that Saint Francis means, not only to yourselves but to people all around the world. There is something about this man, who was born over eight hundred years ago in a little Italian town, that continues in our day to inspire people of vastly different cultures and religions.

Saint Francis was a man of peace and gentleness, a poet and lover of beauty. He was a man of poverty and simplicity, a man in tune with the birds and animals, enchanted by all of God's creation. Above all, Francis was a man of prayer whose whole life was shaped by *the love of Jesus Christ.* And he wished to live in a way that spoke in the clearest terms of the everlasting love of God.

As I come today, then, to the city of San Francisco, I come in the spirit of this saint *whose whole life proclaims the goodness and mercy of God.*

## God's Love for Us Is Freely Given, Unearned, and Embraces the Whole of Our Human Condition

2. Accordingly, I wish to speak to you about the all-embracing love of God. Saint John says: *"Love, then, consists in this:* not that we have loved God but *that he has loved us* and *has sent his Son as an offering for our sins"* (1 Jn. 4:10). God's love for us is freely given and unearned, surpassing all we could ever hope for or imagine. He does not love us because we have merited it or are worthy of it. God loves us, rather, because he is true to his own nature. As Saint John puts it, *"God is love,* and he who abides in love abides in God" (1 Jn. 4:16).

The greatest proof of God's love is shown in the fact that he loves us in our human condition, with our weaknesses and our needs. Nothing else can explain the mystery of the Cross. The Apostle Paul once wrote: "You can depend on this as worthy of full acceptance: that *Christ Jesus came into the world to save sinners.* Of these, I myself am the worst. But on that very account I was dealt with mercifully, so that in me, as an extreme case, Jesus Christ might display *all his patience,* and that I might become an example to those who would later have faith in him and gain everlasting life" (1 Tm. 1:15–16).

*The love of Christ is more powerful than sin and death.* Saint Paul explains that Christ came to forgive sin, and that his love is greater than any sin, stronger than all my personal sins or those of anyone else. This is the faith of the Church. This is the Good News of God's love that the Church proclaims throughout history, and that I proclaim to you today: God loves you with an everlasting love. He loves you in Christ Jesus, his Son.

## God's Fatherly Love Expressed in Parable of Prodigal Son

3. God's love has many aspects. In particular, *God loves us as our Father.* The parable of the prodigal son expresses this truth most vividly. You recall that moment, in the parable, when the son came to his senses, decided to return home and set off for his father's house. *"While he was still a long way off,* his father caught sight of him and was deeply moved. *He ran out to meet him,* threw his arms around his neck, and

kissed him" (Lk. 15:20). This is the fatherly love of God, a love always ready to forgive, eager to welcome us back.

## God's Fatherly Love, Strong, Faithful and Merciful
### Gives Us Hope for Conversion

God's love for us as our Father is a strong and faithful love, a love which is full of mercy, a love which *enables us to hope for the grace of conversion when we have sinned.* As I said in my encyclical on the Mercy of God: "The parable of the prodigal son expresses in a simple but profound way *the reality of conversion.* Conversion is the most concrete expression of the working of love and of the presence of mercy in the human world. . . . Mercy is manifested in its true and proper aspect when it restores to value, promotes and *draws good from all the forms of evil* existing in the world" (*Dives in Misericordia,* 6).

It is the reality of God's love for us as our father that explains why Jesus told us *when we pray* to address God as *"Abba, Father"* (see Lk. 11:2; Mt. 6:9).

## God's Love Is Experienced
### as the Compassionate Love of a Mother

4. It is also true to say that *God's love for us is like that of a mother.* In this regard, God asks us, through the Prophet Isaiah: "Can a mother forget her infant, be without *tenderness for the child of her womb?* Even should she forget, *I will never forget you*" (Is. 49:15). God's love is tender and merciful, patient and full of understanding. In the Scriptures, and also in the living memory of the Church, the love of God is indeed depicted and has been experienced as *the compassionate love of a mother.*

*Jesus himself* expressed a compassionate love when he wept over Jerusalem, and when he said: "O Jerusalem, Jerusalem . . . How often would I have gathered your children together *as a hen gathers* her brood under her wings" (Lk. 13:34).

## God's Surpassing Love Is Made Concrete
### in His Son Jesus Christ and in the Church

5. Dear friends in Christ: the love of God is so great that it goes *beyond the limits of human language,* beyond the grasp of artistic expression, beyond human under-standing. And yet it is *concretely embodied in God's Son, Jesus Christ,* and in his Body, the Church. Once again this evening, here in Mission Dolores Basilica, I repeat to all of you the ageless proclamation of the Gospel: God loves you!

### God's Love for Aids Sufferers Is Unconditional

God loves you all, without distinction, without limit. He loves those of you who are elderly, who feel the burden of the years. He loves those of you who are sick, those who are suffering from AIDS and from AIDS-Related Complex. He loves the relatives and friends of the sick and those who care for them. He loves us all with an unconditional and everlasting love.

In the spirit of Saint Francis, then, I urge you all to open your hearts to God's love, to respond by your prayers and by the deeds of your lives. Let go of your doubts and fears, and let the mercy of God draw you to his heart. *Open the doors of your hearts* to our God who is rich in mercy.

> See what love the Father has bestowed on us
> in letting us be called children of God!
> Yet that is what we are. (1 Jn. 3:1)

Yes, that is what we are today and forever: children of a loving God!

## 41. MEETING WITH MEN AND WOMEN RELIGIOUS

Dear Sisters and Brothers in Christ,

Dear Religious of the United States of America,

### Liturgical Prayer, the Voice of the Bride and of the Bridegroom

1. In their deepest spiritual significance, the Vespers that you have prayed together are *the voice of the Bride* addressing the Bridegroom. They are also *the voice of the Bridegroom,* "the very prayer which Christ himself, together with his body, addresses to the Father" (see *Sacrosanctum Concilium,* 84). With one and the same voice the Bride and the Bridegroom praise the Father in the unity of the Holy Spirit.

### Religious Life Bears Witness to the Presence of God in Human Life

In this liturgical song of praise you gave expression to "the real nature of the true Church"—"both human and divine, visible and yet invisibly endowed, eager to act and yet devoted to contemplation, present in the world and yet not at home in it" (*Sacrosanctum Concilium,* 2). It is precisely *the presence of God* in human life and human affairs that you proclaim through your religious consecration and the practice of the evangelical counsels. It is to the reality of *God's love in the world* that you bear witness by means of the many forms of your loving service to God's people.

### Meeting with Religious: High Point of Visit

2. Dear Religious sisters, and Religious priests and brothers: for me, this is one of the most important moments of my visit. Here, with all of you, men and women Religious of the United States, and in the spiritual presence of all the members of your congregations spread throughout this land or serving in other countries, *I give*

*heartfelt thanks to God for each and every one of you.* He who is mighty has done great things for you, holy is his name! (see Lk. 1:49).

## Gratitude for Manifold Forms of Generous Service

*I greet each one of you with love and gratitude.* I thank you for the warm welcome you have given me and I thank Sister Helen Garvey and Father Stephen Tutas, who have presented a picture of your dedicated lives. I rejoice because of your deep love of the Church and your generous service to God's people. Every place I have visited in this vast country bears the marks of the diligent labor and immense spiritual energies of Religious of both contemplative and active congregations in the Church. The extensive Catholic educational and health care systems, the highly developed network of social services in the Church—none of this would exist today, were it not for your highly motivated dedication and the dedication of those who have gone before you. The spiritual vigor of so many Catholic people testifies to the efforts of generations of Religious in this land. The history of the Church in this country is in large measure *your history at the service of God's people.*

As we remember your glorious past, let us be filled with hope that *your future* will be no less beneficial for the Church in the United States, and no less a prophetic witness of God's Kingdom to each new generation of Americans.

## Conciliar Renewal Consists in an Ever-Greater Fidelity to Jesus Christ and His Self-Giving

3. The single most extraordinary event that has affected the Church in every aspect of her life and mission during the second half of the twentieth century has been the Second Vatican Council. The Council called the whole Church to conversion, to "newness of life," to renewal—to *a renewal that consists essentially in an ever-increasing fidelity to Jesus Christ, her divine Founder.* As "men and women who more closely follow and more clearly demonstrate the Savior's self-giving" (*Lumen Gentium,* 42), it is only natural that Religious should have experienced the call to renewal in a radical way. Thousands of Religious in the United States have generously responded to this call, and continue to live it, with profound commitment. The results, the good fruits of this response, are evident in the Church: we see a Gospel-inspired spirituality, which has led to a deepening of personal and liturgical prayer; a clearer sense of the Church as a communion of faith and love in which the grace and responsibility entrusted to each member are to be respected and encouraged; a new appreciation of the legacy of your founders and foundresses, so that the specific charism of each congregation stands out more clearly; a heightened awareness of the urgent needs of the modern world where Religious, in close union with the Bishops and in close collaboration with the whole Church, seek to carry on the work of the Good Shepherd, the Good Samaritan and the Good Teacher.

## Overcome Polarization by Reaching Out to
## One Another in a Spirit of Love

It would be unrealistic to think that such a deep and overall process of renewal could take place without risks and errors, without undue impatience on the part of some and undue fears on the part of others. Whatever the tension and polarization occasioned by change, whatever the mistakes made in the past, I am sure that all of you are convinced that the time has come *to reach out once again to one another in a spirit of love and reconciliation,* both within and beyond your congregations.

## Fresh Insights Highlight the Enduring Identity
## of Religious Consecration and Mission

During the past two decades, there have also been profound insights into the meaning and value of Religious life. Many of these insights, conceived in the experience of prayer and penance and authenticated by the teaching charism of the Church, have contributed greatly to ecclesial life. These insights have borne witness to *the enduring identity of Religious consecration and mission* in the life of the Church. At the same time they have testified to the need for Religious to adapt their activity to the needs of the people of our times.

## Ecclesial Nature of Religious Vocation Calls for
## Cooperative Spirit Between Orders and Local Churches

4. Fundamental to the Council's teaching on Religious life is an emphasis on *the ecclesial nature of the vocation to observe the evangelical counsels.* Religious consecration "belongs inseparably to the life and holiness of the Church." "The counsels are a divine gift, which the Church has received from her Lord and which she ever preserves with the help of his grace" (*Lumen Gentium,* 44). It was precisely within this ecclesial context that in 1983 I asked the Bishops of the United States to render a pastoral service by offering to those of you whose Institutes are engaged in apostolic works special encouragement and support in living your ecclesial vocation to the full. I now wish to thank the Bishops and all of you for your very generous collaboration in this important endeavor. In particular I thank the Pontifical Commission headed by Archbishop John Quinn. By God's grace there now exists a fresh cooperative spirit between your Religious Institutes and the local Churches.

## Gratitude for Many Forms of Communion and
## Collaboration with the Local Churches

*Your continuing participation in the mission of the Church at the diocesan and parish levels is of inestimable value* to the well-being of the local Churches. Your communion with the local Bishops and collaboration with the pastoral ministry of the diocesan clergy contributes to a strong and effective spiritual growth among the faithful. Your creative initiatives in favor of the poor and all marginalized persons and groups, whose needs might otherwise be neglected, are deeply appreciated. Your evangelizing and missionary work both at home and in other parts of the world is one of the great strengths of the Church in the United States. Alongside your traditional apostolates—which are as important now as ever before and which I encourage you to appreciate in their full significance—you are engaged in almost every area of defending human rights and of building a more just and equitable society. *This is a record of unselfish response to the Gospel of Jesus Christ.* Yes, the entire Church in the United States benefits from the dedication of American Religious to their ecclesial mission.

### Decline of Vocations and Aging Membership Are Serious Challenges

5. At the same time you are concerned about certain weaknesses affecting the structure of your Institutes. The decline in vocations and the aging of your membership are serious challenges for each one of your Institutes and for the corporate reality of Religious life, and yet these are not new phenomena in the long experience of the Church. History teaches us that in ways generally unpredictable *the radical "newness" of the Gospel message is always able to inspire successive generations* to do what you have done, to renounce all for the sake of the Kingdom of God, in order to possess the pearl of great price (see Mt. 13:44–45).

### Joyful Witness to Consecrated Love Will Attract Vocations

You are called at this hour to fresh courage and trust. Your *joyful witness to consecrated love*—in chastity, poverty and obedience—will be the greatest human attraction for young people to Religious life in the future. When they sense the authenticity of renewal in you and your communities, they too will be disposed to come and see! The invitation is directly from Christ, but they will want to hear it from you too. Your own essential contribution to vocations will come *through fidelity, penance and prayer,* and through confidence in *the power of Christ's Paschal Mystery to make all things new.*

### Show Special Appreciation for Aged and Infirm Members

In the best traditions of Christian love, you will know how to show your special appreciation for the aged and infirm members of your communities, whose contribution of prayer and penance, suffering and faithful love is of immense value to your apostolates. May they always be comforted in knowing that they are respected and loved within their own Religious families.

### Religious Profession Directs Baptismal Consecration
### to the Perfection of Charity

6. Your vocation is, of its very nature, a radical response to the call which Jesus extends to all believers in their baptismal consecration: *"Seek first his kingship over you, his way of holiness"* (Mt. 6:33). Your response is expressed by your vowed commitment to embrace and live in community the evangelical counsels. Through chastity, poverty and obedience you live in expectation of an eschatological kingdom where "they neither marry nor are given in marriage" (Mt. 22:30). And so, even now, "where your treasure is there your heart is also" (Mt. 6:21).

Through your Religious profession, the consecration which the Holy Spirit worked in you at baptism is *powerfully directed anew to the perfection of charity.* By practicing the vows, you constantly die with Christ in order to rise to new life with him (see Rom. 6:8). In fidelity to your vow of *chastity* you are empowered to love with the love of Christ and to know that deep encounter with his love which inspires and sustains your apostolic love for your neighbor. Treading the path of *poverty* you find yourselves truly open to God and aligned with the poor and suffering, in whom you see the image of the poor and suffering Christ (see Mt. 25:31ff). And through *obedience* you are intimately united with Jesus in seeking always to fulfill the Father's will. Through such obedience there is unlocked in you *the full measure of Christian freedom* which enables you to serve God's people with selfless and unfailing devotion. The Catholic people, and indeed the vast majority of your fellow citizens, have the highest respect for your religious consecration, and they look to you for the "proof" of the transcendent Christian hope that is in you (see 1 Pt. 3:15).

7. The disciple, though, is not above the Master. It is only right for you to expect, as has always been the Church's understanding, that if you follow the laws of Christ's Kingdom—in essence, the new commandment of love and the new values proclaimed in the Beatitudes—*you will be in conflict with the "wisdom of this age"* (see 1 Cor. 2:6). In a particularly personal and courageous way, Religious have always been in the front line of this never-ending struggle.

### Discernment Needed in Encounter
### Between the Gospel and the Culture

Today, the encounter between the saving message of the Gospel and the forces that shape our human culture calls for *a profound and prayerful discernment* of Christ's will for his Church at this moment of her life. In this regard the Second Vatican Council remains the necessary point of reference and the guiding light. This discernment is the work of the whole Church. No person or group of people can claim to possess sufficient insights so as to monopolize it. All members of the Church, according to the ministry received for the good of the whole Body, must be humbly attuned to the Holy Spirit, who guides the Church into the fullness of truth (see Jn. 16:13; *Lumen Gentium,* 4) and produces in her the fruits of his action, which Saint Paul lists as "love, joy, peace, patient endurance, kindness, generosity, faith, mildness and chastity" (Gal. 5:22–23). And since the Holy Spirit has placed in the Church the special pastoral charism of the Magisterium, we know that *adherence to the Magisterium is an indispensable condition for a correct reading of "the signs of the times"* and hence a condition for the supernatural fruitfulness of all ministries in the Church.

### Important Place in the Church's Dialogue with Complex Culture

You indeed have an important role in the Church's dialogue with the complex and varied cultural environment of the United States. The first law of this dialogue is *fidelity to Christ and to his Church.* And in this fundamental act of faith and trust you already show the world the basis of your special position within the community of God's people. Also required for this dialogue is *a true understanding of the values involved in America's historical experience.* At the same time the Christian concepts of the common good, of virtue and conscience, of liberty and justice, must be distinguished from what is sometimes inadequately presented as the expression of these realities. As Religious, you are especially sensitive to the implications of this dialogue with the world in which you are called to live and work. As men and women consecrated to God, you are aware of having a special responsibility to be a sign—an authentic prophetic sign—that will speak to the Church and to the world, not in terms of easy condemnation, but humbly *showing forth the power of God's word to heal and uplift, to unite and bind with love.*

### Church Must Proclaim the Full Truth About God and the Human Condition

At this important moment of the history of the human family it is essential for the Church to proclaim the full truth about God—Father, Son and Holy Spirit—and the full truth about our human condition and destiny as revealed in Christ and authentically transmitted through the teaching of the Church. The faithful have the right to receive the true teaching of the Church in its purity and integrity, with all its demands and power. When people are looking for a sure point of reference for their own values and their ethical choices, they turn to the special witnesses of the Church's holiness and justice—to you Religious. They expect and want to be convinced by the example of your acceptance of God's word.

### Validity and Fruitfulness Depend upon Union with Jesus Christ

8. Dear sisters and brothers: *the life we now live is not our own; Christ is living in us.* We still live our human life, but it is a life of faith in the Son of God, who loved us and gave himself for us (see Gal. 2:20). In these words Saint Paul sums up the core of our Christian experience, and even more so *the heart of Religious life.* The validity and fruitfulness of Religious life depends upon *union with Jesus Christ.*

### Union with Christ Demands Life of Prayer and Life Based on Sacraments of Penance and Eucharist

Union with Christ demands *a true interior life of prayer,* a life of closeness to him. At the same time it enables you to be effective witnesses before the world of the healing and liberating power of the Paschal Mystery. It means that above all in your own lives and in your own communities the Paschal Mystery is first being celebrated and experienced through *the Eucharist and the Sacrament of Penance.* In this way your works of charity and justice, of mercy and compassion will be true signs of Christ's presence in the world.

### Be Examples of Faith and Charity, Hope and Joy, Obedience, Sacrifice, Service

9. The challenges which you faced yesterday you will face again tomorrow. The thousand tasks that now draw upon your courage and your energies will hardly disappear next week, next month, next year. What then is the meaning of our meeting? What "word of the Lord" is addressed to us here? As the one who for the time being has been given the place of the Fisherman from Galilee, as the one who occupies the Chair of Peter for this fleeting hour in the Church's life, allow me to make my own the sentiments of the reading from our Evening Prayer: *"Be examples to the flock"* (1 Pt. 5:3)—examples of faith and charity, of hope and joy, of obedience, sacrifice and humble service. And "when the Chief Shepherd appears, you will win for yourselves the unfading crown of glory" (v. 4).

### Contemplatives Witness to Primacy of Spiritual Values

To the *contemplative Religious* of the United States, whose lives are hidden with Christ in God, I wish to say a word of profound thanks for reminding us that "here we have no lasting city" (Heb. 13:14), and that all life must be lived in the heart of the living God. May the whole Church in this land recognize the primacy and efficacy of the spiritual values which you represent. The Second Vatican Council deliberately chose to call you "the glory of the Church" (*Perfectae Caritatis,* 7).

### Country Needs Witness of Spirituality and Commitment to Power of the Gospel

Brothers and Sisters, men and women Religious of the United States: your country needs the witness of your deep spirituality and your commitment to the life-giving power of the Gospel. America needs to see all the power of love in your hearts expressed in evangelizing zeal. The whole world needs to discover in you "the kindness and love of God our Savior" (Ti. 3:4). Go forward, therefore, in the mystery of the dying and rising of Jesus. *Go forward in faith, hope and charity, expending yourselves in the Church's mission of evangelization and service.* Always be examples to the flock.

And know that "when the Chief Shepherd appears, you will win for yourselves the unfading crown of glory" (1 Pt. 5:4).

In this Marian Year of grace may you find joy and strength in an ever-greater devotion to Mary, the Virgin Mother of the Redeemer. As "the model and protectress of all consecrated life" (can. 663, sec. 4) may she lead each one of you to perfect union with her Son, our Lord Jesus Christ, and to ever-closer collaboration in his redemptive mission. And may the example of Mary's discipleship confirm you all in generosity and love.

## SEPTEMBER 18, 1987

## 42. MEETING WITH MEMBERS OF THE LAITY FROM THROUGHOUT THE UNITED STATES

To him whose power now at work in us can do immeasurably more than we ask or imagine—to him be glory in the Church and in Christ Jesus through all generations. (Eph. 3:20–21)

Dear Brothers and Sisters,

Dear Catholic Lay People of America,

1. I am grateful to you for your kind welcome and pleased *to be with* you this morning in glorifying the Father, "in the Church and in Christ Jesus," through the working of the Holy Spirit. I also wish to thank you for the informative presentations which have been made in the name of the Catholic laity of the United States.

### Our Ultimate Vocation, to Glorify God and to Attain to the Fullness of God

The Letter of Saint Paul to the Ephesians has a deep meaning for the life of each one of us. The text movingly describes *our relationship with God* as he reveals himself to us in the mystery of the Most Holy Trinity. Saint Paul reminds us of two fundamental truths: first, that our ultimate vocation is to glorify the God who created and redeemed us; and secondly, that our eternal and highest good is to "attain to the fullness of God himself"—to participate in the loving communion of the Father and the Son and the Holy Spirit for all eternity. God's glory and our good are perfectly attained in the Kingdom of heaven.

### Salvation Comes to Us Through the Church, Communion with Christ and with One Another

The Apostle Paul also reminds us that *salvation,* which comes as a free gift of divine love in Christ, is not offered to us on a purely individual basis. It comes to us *through and in the Church.* Through our communion with Christ and with one another on earth, we are given a foretaste of that perfect communion reserved for heaven. Our communion is also meant to be *a sign or sacrament* which draws other people to Christ, so that all might be saved.

## Redemption Includes the Gifts of the Spirit at Work in the Church

This gift of the Redemption, which originates with the Father and is accomplished by the Son, is brought to fruition in our individual lives and in the life of the world by *the Holy Spirit.* Thus we speak of the gifts of the Spirit at work within the Church—gifts which include the hierarchical office of shepherding the flock, and gifts given to the laity so that they may live the Gospel and make their specific contribution to the Church's mission.

## Common Call to Sanctity, Common Dignity and Activity for Building Up the Body of Christ

The Council tells us that "everyone in the Church does not proceed by the same path, nevertheless all are called to sanctity and have received an equal privilege of faith through the justice of God" (see 2 Pt. 1:1). "And if by the will of Christ some are made teachers, dispensers of mysteries, and shepherds on behalf of others, yet all share a true equality with regard to the dignity and activity common to all the faithful for the building up of the Body of Christ" (*Lumen Gentium,* 32). *Through a great diversity of graces* and works, the children of God bear witness to that *wonderful unity* which is the work of one and the same Spirit.

## By Baptism and Confirmation Laity Are Commissioned to Share in the Church's Saving Mission

2. Dear brothers and sisters: it is in the context of these mysteries of faith that I wish to reflect with you on your role as laity in the Church today. What is most fundamental in your lives is that *by your Baptism and Confirmation you have been commissioned by our Lord Jesus Christ himself to share in the saving mission of his Church* (see *Lumen Gentium,* 33). To speak of the laity is to speak of hundreds of millions of people, like yourselves, of every race, nation and walk of life, who each day seek, with the help of God, to live a good Christian life. To speak of the laity is to speak of the many of you who draw from your *parish* the strength and inspiration to live your vocation in the world. It is to speak also of those of you who have become part of national and international *ecclesial associations and movements* that support you in your vocation and mission.

## You Cherish the Basic Hope of Faithfulness to Christ and to Living His Message

Your struggles and temptations may differ according to your various situations, but all of you cherish the same basic hope to be faithful to Christ and to put his message into practice. You all cherish the same basic hope for a decent life for your-selves and an even better life for your children. All of you must toil and work and bear the sufferings and disappointments common to humanity, but as believers you are endowed with faith, hope and charity. And often your charity reaches heroic dimensions within your families or among your neighbors and co-workers. To the extent that your resources and duties in life permit, you are called to support and actively to participate in Church activities.

### Specific Task of the Laity
### Is to Reorder Temporal Affairs According to the Mind of God

It is within the everyday world that you the laity must bear *witness to God's Kingdom;* through you the Church's mission is fulfilled by the power of the Holy Spirit. The Council taught that *the specific task of the laity* is precisely this: to "seek the Kingdom of God by engaging in temporal affairs and by ordering them according to the plan of God" (*Lumen Gentium,* 31).

You are called to live in the world, *to engage in secular professions and occupations,* to live in those ordinary circumstances of family life and life in society from which is woven the very web of your existence. You are called by God himself *to exercise your proper functions according to the spirit of the Gospel* and to work for the sanctification of the world from within, in the manner of leaven. In this way you can make Christ known to others, especially by the witness of your lives. It is for you as lay people *to direct all temporal affairs to the praise of the Creator and Redeemer* (*Lumen Gentium,* 31).

### Temporal Order Encompasses the Social, Cultural,
### Intellectual, Political, Economic Life

The temporal order of which the Council speaks is vast. It encompasses the social, cultural, intellectual, political and economic life in which all of you rightly participate. As lay men and women actively engaged in this temporal order, you are being called by Christ to sanctify the world and to transform it. This is true of *all work, however exalted or humble,* but it is especially urgent for those whom circumstances and special talent have placed in positions of leadership or influence: men and women in public service, education, business, science, social communications, and the arts. As Catholic lay people you have an important moral and cultural *contribution of service to make to the life of your country.* "Much will be required of the person entrusted with much" (Lk. 12:48). These words of Christ apply not only to the sharing of material wealth or personal talents, but also to the sharing of one's faith.

### Service to Christian Family
### Entails Service of Love and of Life

3. Of supreme importance in the mission of the Church is *the role that the laity fulfill in the Christian family.* This role is above all a *service of love* and a *service of life.*

The love of husband and wife, which is blessed and sealed in the Sacrament of Marriage, constitutes the first way that couples exercise their mission. They serve by being true to themselves, to their *vocation of married love*. This love, which embraces all the members of the family, is aimed at forming *a community of persons* united in heart and soul, an indissoluble communion where the love of spouses for each other is a sign of Christ's love for the Church.

*The service of life* rests on the fact that husband and wife cooperate with God in transmitting the gift of human life, in the procreation of children. In this most sacred responsibility, the service of life is intimately united to the service of love in the one conjugal act, which must always be open to bringing forth new life. In his encyclical *Humanae Vitae,* Pope Paul VI explained that in the task of transmitting life, husband and wife are called to "conform their activity to the creative intention of God, expressed in the very nature of marriage and of its acts, and manifested by the constant teaching of the Church" (no. 10).

### The Family Both Educates and Evangelizes

While "love and life constitute the nucleus of the saving mission of the Christian family in the Church and for the Church" (*Familiaris Consortio,* 50), the family performs *a service of education,* particularly within the home, where the parents have the original and primary role of educating their children. The family is likewise *an evangelizing community,* where the Gospel is received and put into practice, where prayer is learned and shared, where all the members, by word and deed and by the love they have for one another, bear witness to the Good News of salvation.

### Recognize Special Burdens of Single-Parent Families, of the Separated and Divorced

At the same time we must recognize the *difficult situation* of so many people with regard to family living. There are many with special burdens of one kind or another. There are the single-parent families and those who have no natural family; there are the elderly and the widowed. And there are those separated and divorced Catholics who, despite their loneliness and pain, are striving to preserve their fidelity and to face their responsibilities with loving generosity. All of these people share deeply in the Church's mission by faith, hope and charity, and by all their many efforts to be faithful to God's will. The Church assures them not only of her prayers and spiritual nourishment, but also of *her love, pastoral concern and practical help.*

### Church Cannot Admit Divorced and Remarried to Communion, But Loves Them

Although, in fidelity to Christ and to his teaching on Christian marriage, the Church reaffirms her practice of not admitting to Eucharistic Communion those divorced persons who have remarried outside the Church, nevertheless, she assures these Catholics too of her deep love. She prays for them and encourages them to persevere in prayer, to listen to the word of God and to attend the Eucharistic Sacrifice, hoping that they will "undertake a way of life that is no longer in contradiction to the indissolubility of marriage" (*Familiaris Consortio*, 84). At the same time *the Church remains their mother, and they are part of her life.*

## Appreciation of Women's Contributions

4. I wish to express the deep gratitude of the Church for *all the contributions made by women* over the centuries to the life of the Church and of society. In speaking of the role of women, special mention must of course be made of their contribution, in partnership with their husbands, in begetting life and in educating their children. "The true advancement of women requires that clear recognition be given to the value of their maternal and family role, by comparison with all other public roles and all other professions" (*Familiaris Consortio,* 23). The Church is convinced, however, that all the special gifts of women are needed in an ever-increasing measure in her life, and for this reason hopes for their fuller participation in her activities. Precisely because of their equal dignity and responsibility, the access of women to public functions must be ensured. Regardless of the role they perform, the Church proclaims *the dignity of women as women*—a dignity equal to men's dignity, and revealed as such in the account of creation contained in the word of God.

## Lay Participation in All Areas of Ecclesial Life
### Should Not Clericalize Laity

5. The renewal of the Church since the Council has also been an occasion for *increasing lay participation* in all areas of ecclesial life. More and more, people are joining with their pastors in collaboration and consultation for the good of their Diocese and parish. An increasing number of lay men and women are devoting their professional skills on a full-time basis to the Church's efforts in education, social services and other areas, or to the exercise of administrative responsibilities. Still others build up the Body of Christ by direct collaboration with the Church's pastoral ministry, especially in bringing Christ's love to those in the parish or community who have special needs. I rejoice with you at this great flowering of gifts in the service of the Church's mission.

At the same time we must ensure both in theory and in practice that these positive developments are always rooted in *the sound Catholic ecclesiology taught by the Council.* Otherwise we run the risk of "clericalizing" the laity or "laicizing" the clergy, and thus robbing both the clerical and lay states of their specific meaning and their complementarity. Both are indispensable to the "perfection of love," which is the common goal of all the faithful. We must therefore recognize and respect in these states of life a diversity that builds up the Body of Christ in unity.

## Union with God in Christ
## Is Realized Through Prayer and Worship

6. As lay men and women you can fulfill this great mission authentically and effectively only to the extent that you *hold fast to your faith,* in communion with the Body of Christ. You must therefore live in the conviction that there can be no separation between your faith and your life, and that apart from Christ you can do nothing (see Jn. 15:5). Since union with God in Christ is the goal of all Christian living, *the laity are called to prayer:* personal prayer, family prayer, liturgical prayer. Generations of devout lay people have found great strength and joy in invoking the Blessed Virgin Mary, especially through her rosary, and in invoking the Saints.

In particular, the laity must realize that they are a *people of worship called to service.* In the past I had occasion to emphasize this aspect of the life of the laity in the United States: "All the striving of the laity *to consecrate the secular field of activity to God* finds inspiration and magnificent confirmation in the Eucharistic Sacrifice. Participating in the Eucharist is only a small portion of the laity's week, but the total effectiveness of their lives and all Christian renewal depends on it: the primary and indispensable source of the true Christian spirit!" (*Ad Limina* Discourse, July 9, 1983).

## Live Beatitudes in the Face of Many Challenges:
## Secularism, Relativism, Consumerism, Hedonism

7. Every age poses *new challenges and new temptations* for the People of God on their pilgrimage, and our own is no exception. We face a growing *secularism* that tries to exclude God and religious truth from human affairs. We face an insidious *relativism* that undermines the absolute truth of Christ and the truths of faith, and tempts believers to think of them as merely one set of beliefs or opinions among others. We face a materialistic *consumerism* that offers superficially attractive but empty promises conferring material comfort at the price of inner emptiness. We face an alluring *hedonism* that offers a whole series of pleasures that will never satisfy the human heart. All these attitudes can influence our sense of good and evil at the very moment when social and scientific progress requires strong ethical guidance. Once alienated from Christian faith and practice by these and other deceptions, people often commit themselves to passing fads, or to bizarre beliefs that are either shallow or fanatical.

We have all seen how these attitudes have a profound influence on the way people think and act. It is precisely in this society that lay men and women like yourselves, all the Catholic laity, are called *to live the Beatitudes,* to become leaven, salt and light for the world, and sometimes a "sign of contradiction" that challenges and transforms that world according to the mind of Christ. No one is called to impose religious beliefs on others, but to give the strong example of a life of justice and service, resplendent with *the virtues of faith, hope and charity.*

## Laity Must Challenge Society's Conscience on Moral Issues

On moral issues of fundamental importance, however, it is at times necessary to challenge publicly *the conscience of society.* Through her moral teaching the Church seeks to defend—for the benefit of all people—those basic human values that uphold the good which humanity seeks for itself and that protect the most fundamental human rights and spiritual aspirations of every person.

### Laity Are Called to Incarnate the Gospel in Society

The greatest challenge to the conscience of society comes from your fidelity to your own Christian vocation. It is up to you the Catholic laity to *incarnate without ceasing the Gospel in society*—in American society. You are in the forefront of the struggle to protect authentic Christian values from the onslaught of secularization. Your great contribution to the evangelization of your own society is made through your lives. Christ's message must live in you and in the way you live and in the way you refuse to live. At the same time, because your nation plays a role in the world far beyond its borders, you must be conscious of the impact of your Christian lives on others. *Your lives must spread the fragrance of Christ's Gospel throughout the world.*

Saint Paul launched a great challenge to the Christians of his time, and today I repeat it to all the laity of America: "Conduct yourselves, then, in a way worthy of the Gospel of Christ, so that, whether I come and see you or am absent, I may hear news of you, that you are standing firm in one spirit, with one mind, struggling together for the faith of the Gospel, not intimidated in any way" (Phil. 1:27–28).

### Mary Represents the Perfection of Love We Aspire To

8. Dear brothers and sisters, representatives of the millions of faithful and dedicated Catholic laity of the United States: in bringing my reflections to a conclusion I cannot fail to mention the Blessed Virgin Mary, who reveals the Church's mission in an unparalleled manner. She, more than any other creature, shows us that *the perfection of love* is the only goal that matters, that it alone is the measure of holiness and the way to perfect communion with the Father, the Son and the Holy Spirit. Her state in life was that of *a laywoman,* and she is at the same time the Mother of God, the Mother of the Church and our Mother in the order of grace.

The Council concluded the *Dogmatic Constitution on the Church* with *an exhortation* on the Blessed Virgin. In doing so, the Council expressed the Church's ancient sentiments of love and devotion for Mary. Let us, especially during this Marian Year, make our own these sentiments, imploring her to intercede for us with her Son, for the glory of the Most Holy and Undivided Trinity (see *Lumen Gentium,* 69).

### 43. HOMILY AT MASS
### CELEBRATED AT CANDLESTICK PARK

Go . . . and make disciples of all nations. (Mt. 28:19)

It was in Antioch that the disciples were called Christians for the first time. (Acts 11:26)

Dear fellow Christians, dear Brothers and Sisters,

## Messianic Mission Continues in the Apostolic Mission

1. Today, here on the West Coast of America, *in San Francisco,* we hear once again the words with which *Jesus sends the Apostles* into the world after his Resurrection. He hands on to them a mission. He sends them forth as he himself had been sent by the Father.

These words of Christ come at the end of his earthly *messianic mission.* In his Cross and Resurrection are found the basis for his "authority both in heaven and on earth" (Mt. 28:18). This is *the authority of the Redeemer,* who through the blood of his Cross has ransomed the nations. In them he has established the beginning of a new creation, a new life in the Holy Spirit; in them he has planted *the seed of the Kingdom of God.* In the power of his authority, as he is leaving the earth and going to the Father, Christ says to his Apostles: "Go . . . and *make disciples of all nations.* Baptize them in the name of the Father, and of the Son, and of the Holy Spirit. Teach them to carry out everything I have commanded you. And know that I am with you always, until the end of time" (Mt. 28:19–20).

## From Jerusalem the Mission Moved to Antioch

2. The Acts of the Apostles describe *the beginning of this mission.* The point of departure was the Upper Room in Jerusalem. From *Jerusalem* the travels of the Apostles and of their first collaborators led them first to the neighboring countries and to the people who lived there. In today's second reading, we hear that the witnesses of the Crucified and Risen Christ reached *Phoenicia, Cyprus and Antioch* (see Acts 11:19).

This occurred also as a result of the dispersion which began with the death of the deacon Stephen and *with the persecution of the disciples of Jesus.* We know that, at the stoning of Stephen, Saul of Tarsus was present as a persecutor. But the Acts of the Apostles later present him as Paul, after his conversion on the road to Damascus. Together with Barnabas, Paul worked for a whole year in Antioch, and there "they instructed many people." And it was precisely "in Antioch that the disciples were *called Christians* for the first time" (Acts 11:26).

## In Baptism to Accept Christ Himself
## Who Works in the Power of the Spirit

3. *What does it mean to be a Christian?*

It means accepting the testimony of the Apostles concerning the Crucified and Risen Christ. Indeed, it means *accepting Christ himself, who works in the power of the Holy Spirit.* This acceptance is expressed in *Baptism,* the Sacrament in which we are born again of water and the Holy Spirit (see Jn. 3:5). In this Sacrament, *Christ comes to meet us spiritually.* As Saint Paul teaches, we are baptized into Christ's death. Together with him we die to sin, in order to rise with him, *to pass from the death of sin to life in God,* to the life of sanctifying grace. To new life!

### In Baptism Christ Comes with the
### Salvific Power of His Paschal Mystery

Christians then are those who have been baptized. We are *those to whom Christ has come with the salvific power of his Paschal Mystery,* those whose lives have been totally shaped by this salvific power. Indeed, Baptism gives us *an indelible sign*—called a character—with which we are marked throughout all our earthly life and beyond. This sign is with us when we die and when we find ourselves before the judgment of God. Even if in practice our lives are not Christian, this indelible sacramental sign of Baptism *remains with us for all eternity.*

### Christian Is One Who Climbs the Lord's Mountain
### to Learn the Ways of the Lord

4. The readings of today's liturgy permit us *to respond still more fully* to the question: What does it mean to be a Christian?

In the book of the Prophet Isaiah we read about "the mountain of the Lord's house" (Is. 2:2), raised above all things. The Prophet says: "All nations shall stream toward it; many peoples shall come and say: 'Come, *let us climb the Lord's mountain,* to the house of the God of Jacob, that he may instruct us in his ways, and we may walk in his paths.' For from Zion shall go forth instruction, and the word of the Lord from Jerusalem" (Is. 2:2–3). Yes, *the word of the Lord did go forth from Jerusalem.* This word is the word of the Gospel. The word of the Cross and Resurrection. Christ charged his Apostles to go forth with this word to all the nations—to proclaim it and to baptize.

*Through Baptism Christ comes to every person* with the power of his Paschal Mystery. To accept Christ through Baptism, to receive new life in the Holy Spirit—this is what it means to become a Christian. In this way, through the centuries, individuals and entire nations have become Christian.

### Christian Means to Enter the Temple of the
### Holy Spirit in Order to Follow Christ

*To be a Christian means to go up to the mountain to which Christ leads us.* To enter into the temple of the living God that is formed in us and in our midst by the Holy Spirit. To be Christian means to continue to become Christian, learning from Christ *the ways of the Lord* so as to be able "to walk in his paths" (see Is. 2:3). To be a Christian *means to become one every day,* ascending spiritually toward Christ and *following him.* In fact, as we recall, when Christ first called those who were to become his disciples, he said to them: "Follow me."

### From Antioch to San Francisco for Two Hundred Years
### Peoples of the Most Varied Cultures Follow Christ

5. "It was *in Antioch that the disciples* were called Christians for the first time." And it was more than two hundred years ago that *people in the San Francisco area*

were called Christians for the first time. Since the arrival of the first settlers and the missionary efforts of Father Palou and his companions, there have always been Christians in San Francisco—people of the most varied cultural backgrounds who have believed God's word, been baptized, and followed in the footsteps of the Lord.

### City Built on Hopes by Franciscan Missionaries, Pioneers and Even Statesmen Founding the U.N.

*Here is a city built on hopes:* the hopes of Father Serra's Franciscan missionaries who came to preach the Good News, the hopes of pioneers who came to make their fortunes, the hopes of people who came here to seek peace, the hopes of those who still come to find refuge from violence, persecution or dire poverty. It is the city in which, some forty years ago, statesmen met to establish the United Nations Organization, an expression of our common hopes for a world without war, a world committed to justice and governed by fair laws.

### City Built with Great Effort on the Three Things That Last

But this city was built also with hard work and effort. Here the Church advanced from the little Mission Dolores to the establishment of the Archdiocese of San Francisco in 1853. It took effort and determination for the city and the Church to recover from the devastating effects of the severe earthquake and terrible fire in the spring of 1906. Yes, it takes great effort to move from initial enthusiasm *to something that will really last.* "There are in the end," Saint Paul tells us, "*three things that last: faith, hope and love,* and the greatest of these is love" (1 Cor. 13:13). It is precisely these virtues— faith and hope and love—that have directed and sustained all the efforts of the Church in San Francisco in the past, and that will sustain her well into the future.

### To Deepen Communion with Christ a Systematic Catechesis Is Needed

6. "It was in Antioch that the disciples were *called Christians* for the first time." Here in San Francisco, and in every city and place, it is necessary for the followers of Jesus *to deepen their communion* with him so that they are not just Christians in name. The primary means the Church has always employed for this task is *a systematic catechesis.*

### Understanding of the Mystery of Faith Completes Baptism

When Jesus sent his disciples forth on mission, he told them *to baptize and to teach.* Baptism alone is not sufficient. The initial faith and the new life in the Holy Spirit, which are received in Baptism, need *to advance to fullness.* After having begun to experience the mystery of Christ, his followers must develop their understanding of it. They must come to know better Jesus himself and the Kingdom which he proclaimed; they must discover God's promises in the Scriptures, and learn the requirements and demands of the Gospel.

## The Apostolic Church Is a Model of a Church
## Enlivened by Systematic Cathechesis

In the Acts of the Apostles we are told that the members of the first Christian community in Jerusalem "devoted themselves to *the Apostles' instruction* and the *communal life,* to *the breaking of bread* and *the prayers*" (Acts 2:42). Here we have a model of the Church that can serve as a goal of all catechesis. For the Church needs continually to feed on God's word which comes to us from the Apostles, and she needs to celebrate the Eucharist, to be faithful to regular prayer and bear witness to Christ in the ordinary life of the community.

## Catechesis Must Be a Systematic Presentation
## of Essentials of Faith

The experience of history has proved the importance of a carefully programmed study of the whole of the Christian mystery. "*Teach them to carry out everything* I have commanded you," Jesus tells the Apostles (see Mt. 28:20). There is no substitute for a *systematic presentation of all the essentials* of our Catholic faith, a presentation which can provide the basis for sound judgments about the problems of life and society, and which can prepare people to stand up for what they believe with both humility and courage. As I stated in my Exhortation on Catechesis: "Firm and well-thought-out convictions lead to courageous and upright action. . . . Authentic catechesis is always an orderly and systematic initiation into the revelation that God has given of himself to humanity in Christ Jesus, a revelation stored in the depths of the Church's memory and in Sacred Scripture, and constantly communicated from one generation to the next by a living, active *traditio*" (*Catechesi Tradendae,* 22).

## Purpose of Catechesis Is to Achieve Close Identity
## with Christ in All the Activities of Life

7. What is the purpose of catechesis? What does it mean, not only to be called Christians, but truly to be Christians? It means *being identified with Christ,* not only at Mass on Sunday—which is extremely important—but also in all the other activities of life. In speaking about our relationship to him, Jesus himself said: "Remember what I told you: no slave is greater than his master. If they persecuted me, they will also persecute you. If they kept my word, they will also keep yours" (Jn. 15:20).

## Goal Is to Call Believers to Conversion of Mind and Heart

To be identified with Christ means that we must live according to God's word. As the Lord told his first disciples: "You will live in my love *if you keep my commandments,* even as I have kept my Father's commandments and live in his love"

(Jn. 15:10). For this reason the Church never ceases to proclaim the whole of the Gospel message, whether it is popular or unpopular, convenient or inconvenient. And the Church is ever mindful of her great task to call people to conversion of mind and heart, just as Jesus did. The first words spoken by Jesus in the Gospel are these: "This is the time of fulfillment. The reign of God is at hand! *Reform your lives and believe in the Gospel*" (Mk. 1:15).

## Grace of Conversion and of Living According to God's Word
## Means a Personal Willingness to Accept Opposition

8. Those who accept the grace of conversion and who live according to God's word find that, with God's grace, they begin to put on the mind and heart of Christ. They become increasingly identified with *Christ,* who is *a sign of contradiction.* It was Simeon who first foretold that the newborn Son of Mary would be for his own people a sign of contradiction. He tells the Virgin Mother: "This child is destined to be the downfall and the rise of many in Israel, *a sign that will be opposed*" (Lk. 2:34). And so it happened. Jesus met with opposition in the message that he preached, and in the all-embracing love that he offered to everyone. Almost from the beginning of his public ministry, he was in fact "a sign that people opposed."

## Church Shares in Being a Sign of Contradiction

Simeon's words hold *true for every generation.* Christ remains today a sign of contradiction—a sign of contradiction in his Body, the Church.

Therefore, it should not surprise us if, in our efforts to be faithful to Christ's teachings, we meet with criticism, ridicule or rejection. "*If you find that the world hates you,*" the Lord told the Twelve, "*know that it has hated me before you.* If you belonged to the world, it would love you as its own; the reason it hates you is that you do not belong to the world. But *I chose you out of the world*" (Jn. 15:18–19).

## Christian Community and Families
## Called to Give Gospel Witness

These words of our loving Savior are true for us not only as individuals but *also as a community.* In fact, the witness to Christ of the entire Christian community has a greater impact than that of a single individual. How important, then, is the Gospel witness of every Christian community, but especially that most fundamental of them all, *the Christian family.* In the face of many common evils, the Christian family that truly lives the truth of the Gospel in love is most certainly a sign of contradiction; and at the same time it is a source of great hope for those who are eager to do good. Parishes, too, and Dioceses, and all other Christian communities which "do not belong to the world," find themselves meeting opposition *precisely because they are faithful to Christ.* The mystery of the Cross of Christ is renewed in every generation of Christians.

## Church Proclaiming Gospel Message
## Proclaims a Message of Justice and Peace

9. When Jesus Christ sent his Apostles throughout all the world, he ordered them to *"teach all the nations"* (see Mt. 28:19–20).

The Gospel, and together with it the salvific power of Christ's Redemption, is addressed to every person in every nation. It is also addressed to *entire nations and peoples.* In his vision, the Prophet *Isaiah sees the peoples* who go up to the mountain of the house of the Lord, asking to be instructed in his ways and to walk in his paths (see Is. 2:2–3). We too ask to walk in the paths of the living God, the Creator and Redeemer, the one God who lives in inscrutable unity as Father, Son and Holy Spirit.

Continuing to describe his vision, Isaiah says:

*He shall judge between the nations,*
and impose terms on many peoples.
They shall beat their swords into plowshares
and their spears into pruning hooks;
*One nation shall not raise the sword against another,*
nor shall they train for war again. (Is. 2:4)

How greatly we desire to see the future of humanity in the light of these prophetic words! *How greatly we desire a world* in which justice and peace prevail! Can the Church, which has come forth from such a prophecy—the Church of the Gospel—ever cease to proclaim *the message of peace* on earth? Can she ever cease to work for the true progress of peoples? Can she ever cease to work for the true dignity of every human person?

To be Christian also means to proclaim *this message* untiringly in every generation, in our generation, at the end of the second millennium and at the threshold of the third!

"O house of Jacob, come, *let us walk in the light of the Lord!"* Amen.


## 44. VISIT TO BLESSED SACRAMENT CATHEDRAL

Praised be Jesus Christ!

Dear Archbishop Szoka,

Dear Cardinal Dearden,

My Brothers and Sisters,

### Celebrate the Deep Reality of the Eucharist,
### the Bishop and the Particular Church
### in the Oneness of the Universal Church

1. I have been looking forward to this happy moment when in this Cathedral, the Mother Church of the Archdiocese of Detroit, I would have the opportunity to

express *my love for all of you in Christ.* It is indeed fitting that we greet one another here in this place of worship, in *this church dedicated to the Most Blessed Sacrament,* since it is the Eucharist above all that expresses and brings about our unity with Christ and with one another (see *Lumen Gentium,* 3, 11). As Saint Paul writes, "Because the loaf of bread is one, we, many though we are, are one body, for we all partake of the one loaf" (1 Cor. 10:17). In accordance with the whole life and tradition of the Church, the Eucharist unites the People of God with their Bishop in the unity of the Church (see Saint Ignatius of Antioch, *Ad Phil.*).

This is the relationship that we are celebrating today: the deep reality of the Eucharist, the local Church and the Bishop in the oneness of the universal Church.

### Holy Spirit Realizes Our Communion with Christ and with One Another to Make of Us an Instrument of Redemption

2. The Second Vatican Council refers to the Church as a *mystery*—a mystery of communion. This means that the Church is more than just a community or tradition with shared beliefs and practices, more than an organization with moral influence. Using the imagery of Scripture, the Council also speaks of the Church as a sheepfold, a cultivated field, and a building. The Church is Christ's Body, his Bride, and our Mother (see *Lumen Gentium,* 6–7).

We believe that our communion with Christ and with one another comes into being through *the outpouring of the Holy Spirit.* We believe too that the Holy Spirit makes it fruitful. The Council says that it is he, the Holy Spirit, who bestows upon the Church both "hierarchic and charismatic gifts," and by special graces makes all the faithful "fit and ready to undertake various tasks and offices for the renewal and building up of the Church" (*Lumen Gentium,* 4, 12). Established by Christ as *an instrument of Redemption,* the People of God are "a communion of life, love and truth" and "a most sure seed of unity, hope and salvation for the whole human race." In this way believers become the light of the world and the salt of the earth (see Mt. 5:13–14; *Lumen Gentium,* 9).

### City, Its Suburbs and Rural Areas Offer Opportunities for Baptismal Mission

Dear Brothers and Sisters: what great opportunities *your city and its suburbs and rural areas* give to the mission that is yours by Baptism: to build up the Body of Christ in unity by means of the gifts you have received (see Eph. 4). Yours is a mission that unfolds amid the *social, cultural, political and economic forces* that shape the life of the great metropolis of Detroit—forces that also raise questions of fundamental importance for the future of humanity. By *personal conversion and holiness,* and by your daily witness to the Gospel in keeping with your state in life, each of you builds up the Body of Christ, and thus contributes to the further *humanization of the family of mankind,* without losing sight of *that Kingdom to come* which is not of this world and for which we yearn. As the Council also tells us, the Holy Spirit "constantly renews the Church and leads her to perfect union with her Spouse. For the Spirit and the Bride both say to Jesus, the Lord, "Come!" (see Rv. 22:17; *Lumen Gentium,* 4).

### Cathedral's Fiftieth Anniversary Marks Its Role in Great Events of Diocese

3. This year is the *fiftieth anniversary* of the designation of this building as your Cathedral. It has witnessed the great events and—more frequently—the great liturgical celebrations that mark your ecclesial life, as well as the daily worship of a parish community. I am very glad that it is so full this evening, *full of God's glory, full of God's praise.*

### Successor of Saint Peter Comes with Special Ministry to Confirm Your Faith

Within the context of the communion that we share, I come to you as *the Successor of Saint Peter,* and therefore, as the Council reaffirms, as the Vicar of Christ and pastor of the whole Church, as shepherd of all Christ's flock. This is because in Saint Peter the Lord set up *a lasting and visible source and foundation* of our unity in faith and in communion (see *Lumen Gentium,* 18, 22). Yet one has only to read about Saint Peter in the Gospels to know that this ministry of his is *a great gift of God's grace* and not the result of any human merit. It is precisely at a moment that reveals Saint Peter's human weakness, that is, the moment when Jesus foretells that Peter will deny him three times, that Jesus also adds: "I have prayed for you that your faith may never fail. You in turn must strengthen your brothers" (Lk. 22:31–34). And so, dear brothers and sisters, relying on the help of God, I come here today *with the desire to strengthen you,* as together we continue our pilgrimage of faith to our heavenly home.

### We Commend Ourselves to Mary, Spiritual Mother and Advocate of Grace

The Communion of Saints to which we belong embraces all those who have gone before us in faith on this pilgrimage. In particular, *Mary the Virgin Mother of God* is constantly with us on our journey. I commend all of you—the clergy, Religious and laity of Detroit—to her, the spiritual mother of humanity and the advocate of grace (see *Redemptoris Mater,* 35, 47). May she be for all of you "a sign of sure hope and solace" and "a model of faith, charity and perfect union with Christ" (*Lumen Gentium,* 63, 69).

To him, Jesus Christ, with the Father and the Holy Spirit, be glory forever. Amen.

### SEPTEMBER 19, 1987

### 45. MEETING WITH POLISH AMERICANS

You are to be my witnesses . . . to the ends of the earth. (Acts 1:8)

Dear Polish Brothers and Sisters of America,

## Detroit Is an Important Polish Community

1. In the course of my lengthy pilgrimage to the Church in the United States, God has led me to Detroit, the largest community of people of Polish origin after Chicago.

## Expresses Personal Solicitude and Manifests Natural Bonds of Blood Origin, Faith and Culture

Right from the beginning I wish to tell you two things: first, as Saint Paul would say, I have longed to come to you. I have greatly desired to be with you in this important moment, to give prominence to the solicitude of the Church, and my own personal apostolic solicitude for you, and to manifest publicly the natural bonds, the bonds of blood, origin, faith, culture and, to a certain extent also, of language and of love for our common mother, the homeland: your homeland or that of your parents or forebears.

## This Symbolizes a Meeting with the Entire American *Polonia*

And I wish also to extend our meeting today, which is necessarily limited by time and place, to all the United States, and in a certain sense to all of America. I see it as a meeting with the entire American *Polonia,* with every American man and woman whose origin is drawn from the old country on the Vistula, with every Pole whose destiny it is to live in this land.

## Meets with Those Whose Roots Are Set Here and with Recent Immigrants

I wish then to meet both those whose roots have been deeply set here for generations and those who, while their hearts are still filled with the scenery of the land of their birth, are seeking a new beginning, certainly not without difficulty. In saying this, I am well aware that I find myself before the largest part of the Polish emigration in the world, which constitutes a large part of the Church in the United States. Even today there are more than eight hundred Polish parishes.

"You are to be my witnesses . . . to the ends of the earth."

## Gratitude to Those Who Prepared This Meeting

How can we not thank God then for this meeting and for our prayer together? How can we not thank those who have made it possible and those who have prepared this encounter? The American authorities and those of the American *Polonia,* the Bishops, priests, sisters, lay people, the various organizations.

## Greetings to Cardinal Szoka, to All Present and to All Who Are Spiritually United

Together with the host of this encounter, Archbishop Edmund Szoka, I wish to greet most cordially and to welcome all of you who are gathered here and all the guests who honor us with their presence. I cordially greet all those who are spiritually united with us.

## Greetings to Those of Other Slavic Nations

I extend a word of cordial greetings to all our brothers and sisters from other Slavic nations, and in particular from the kindred Ukrainian community, who are present here in large number.

## Greetings to the Ukrainian Community of Detroit

I cordially greet the entire Ukrainian community of Detroit. You are close to my heart. As you solemnly celebrate the millennium of Christianity in the Rus of Kiev and in the Ukraine, from the depths of my Slavic heart I bless all the sons and daughters of Saint Vladimir and Saint Olga, as well as all the faithful of the Church in the Ukraine and in the diaspora.

## We Look at the Rich History of Polish Settlements in the U.S.A. and of the Faithful Dedication to the Church

2. Meanwhile, today, we wish to be closely united with the sons and daughters of Poland who live on this continent, with all who share or should share in the historical heritage of the same homeland and the same Church. In this way we find ourselves together before the homeland and the whole nation, before its history, its heritage, before its "yesterday" and its "today." And at the same time we find ourselves before all the heritage of *Polonia* in this vast and rich country which has received and continues to receive so many people from all continents, nations, races and languages; the country that became the homeland for your forebears is also yours.

If we recall the past, if we look attentively at our "today," we do so above all with thought and concern for the future. For, as it has been said, "the nation which lets itself be cut off from its tradition descends to the level of a tribe" (A. Slominski).

We recall briefly the first Poles who, according to the chronicles, came to North America in 1608 and settled in Jamestown, Virginia. And then those who in the second half of the eighteenth century gave the beginning to *Polonia* in Michigan.

## Economic Emigration in Last Century to Find Work

The greatest wave of emigration took place, as is known, at the end of the last century and at the beginning of the present century. It was an economic emigration. There were enterprising, hard-working people, worthy people who in the homeland were unable to find food. They left a Poland which had been torn apart by partitions and, as the latest arrivals, they were viewed in different ways. Most often they were uneducated. They brought with them no material riches, but they possessed two great values: an innate love of the faith and of the Polish spirit. Besides, many of them had left with the thought of returning after a time. They did not think that their descendants would put down stable roots in a new country and would collaborate fruitfully in its construction at the end of the second and beginning of the third millennium after Christ.

Their tears, sufferings, difficulties, humiliations, wanderings and nostalgia are known and described. Yet it was they who built all that is until now, and will remain in the future, the glory and the patrimony of *Polonia* in North America.

### They Created a Network of Churches, Schools, All Sorts of Works

First of all they created a whole network of parishes with monumental churches, schools, hospitals, houses of assistance, organizational structures, the press, publications. We recall here Father Leopold Moczygemba and his nearly one hundred parishioners who on Christmas Eve 1854 founded the first Polish parish and gave rise to the village of Panna Maria (the Virgin Mary) in Texas. And also those who in 1872 founded the first Polish parish in Detroit, dedicated to Saint Albertus. With great emotion I journey spiritually as a pilgrim to these two places.

### They Developed All Sorts of Religious Congregations

Moreover, these immigrants have produced a great number of priestly and religious vocations, and thousands of vocations of women Religious, both to Polish congregations and to others. There arose also the various new Polish congregations of women. All this served to make the contribution of the immigrants to the development of religious life and to ecclesiastical structures a great and irreplaceable treasure for the Church in America.

### They Organized Catholic Organizations

The same spirit was deepened and developed by the different Catholic organizations—both by the older ones which have been more than one hundred years in existence, as well as by those which were established more recently. It is not possible to mention all of them here. However, I came to know of them in the course of earlier visits to the United States as Archbishop of Cracow and through their letters to me in Rome on different occasions.

### They Contributed a Great Deal to Poland Itself

This faithful dedication to the Church is closely tied to a love for Poland and everything associated with it. One has only to think of the volunteers for General

Haller's army during the First World War; the financial support for independence activities before the year 1918, and in particular for the support of the Polish Committee in Paris; the enormous gifts and loans to Poland after it gained its independence and began to rise from destruction and ruin. Nor may we forget that this same generation of immigrants, by hard work and sacrifice, also secured a better life for their children and grandchildren.

### The Polish Seminary of Orchard Lake
### Disseminates an Awareness of Polish Culture

Another page in the history of *Polonia* was written by Saints Cyril and Methodius Seminary, established in Detroit and later transferred to Orchard Lake, which not long ago celebrated its centenary. This seminary grew out of a true love of the Church and out of an attachment to the Polish spirit. Using the language of the Second Vatican Council, we may say that it sought to read "the signs of the times" and to meet the needs of Polish immigration. It developed into a complete scientific and educational complex, from which more than three thousand priests for the service of Polish immigrants and approximately fifteen thousand immigrant leaders have come forth. It disseminates Polish culture and the liturgy in the Polish language, and contributes to the preservation of awareness concerning the Polish origins of so many Americans. To the representatives of Orchard Lake who are here today I express gratitude for all that has been accomplished in the past; my hope is for constant fidelity and a new responsiveness to the needs of today's Church and of *Polonia* as it exists in the world today.

Later history witnessed new events, new trials, and a new wave of emigrants.

### New Post-Second World War Immigrants
### Retain a Strong Solidarity with Homeland and Nation

As a result of the Second World War and its aftermath, many more Poles came to the United States. These emigrants were different than the first group in that they came with a higher level of culture, and with a different national and political consciousness that retained a strong solidarity with the homeland and the nation. A word of acknowledgment is due to the *Polish American Congress* for its many activities on behalf of the nation, and also to the *Catholic League,* which provided great material aid to the Church in Poland after the war and continues to provide that aid today. For this I wish to express the heartfelt gratitude of the Church in Poland as well as my own personal gratitude.

### Most Recent Contribution Has Been the Foundation
### in the Vatican and Its Various Works

The most recent great undertaking of *Polonia* throughout the world, but especially of *Polonia* in the United States and of some American friends, is the *Foundation in the Vatican* and the Pilgrim House, the Center for Polish Christian Culture and the Documentation Center in Rome which that Foundation operates.

I know that efforts continue; for example, the establishment of Associations of Friends of the Foundation to ensure the continued activity and development of these institutions. God will surely reward them.

### Present Tasks

And so, having touched only briefly on past history, we arrive at the present, and the tasks the present creates for *Polonia* and the Church.

### Each Immigration Brought Richness
### but also Harmful Divisions

The last wave of emigration, like those that preceded it, also becomes a "sign of the times" for today and a challenge. It calls us to reflection and action. Each emigration has brought with it a new richness as well as new problems. There have been and there continue to be cases of harmful divisions, even splits, which have impeded *Polonia* in the United States from playing the full role of which it is capable in both the religious and spiritual spheres and the social and political spheres.

### Need for Double Process of Integration—Awareness
### and Maturity in Polonia and Integration in U.S.A.

3. Thus there remains, always alive and very real, a process of integration that is twofold. It is integration in the sense of a growth in awareness and maturity in *Polonia* itself, and integration within the country which is now your home.

### The Greater the Awareness of Identity and Christian Culture
### the More You Will Serve Your Country

Dear brothers and sisters: the more you are aware of your identity, your spirituality, your history and the Christian culture out of which your ancestors and parents grew and you yourselves have grown, the more you will be able to serve your country, the more capable will you be of contributing to the common good of the United States.

### Ways of Integration Must Respect Full Personality
### of the Individual, the Community and the Nation

Precisely out of concern for the common good, this country—in the face of a diversity of peoples, races and cultures unknown elsewhere—has sought integration in various ways. Theories include "nativism," the "melting pot" and others that proved incapable of giving results. Today there is talk of the ethnic principle, of "roots," since from these roots the full personality of the individual, the community and the nation arises.

### Church Wishes to Be at the Service of
### Such Personal and Social Integration

The Church wishes to be at the service of such personal and social integration. I have spoken of this on numerous occasions, and many documents of the Church address this issue. It is necessary to study them and put them into practice.

### The Nation Has Many Strengths

Today I wish to repeat once again the words of the poet: "There are so many strengths in the nation," and I wish to pray with him: "Make us feel the strength" (S. Wyspianski, "Liberation").

### Strength of Faith, the Paschal Mystery,
### Love of Ideals, of Truth, Freedom, Love of Peace

Our strength comes from faith, from God himself, and from our millennary heritage, in which there resounds, in such a vibrant way, the Paschal Mystery of Christ: his Passion and Resurrection. This richness has been manifested and continues to be manifested in the love of ideals, of truth, of freedom—"ours and yours," in the love of peace, and in respect for the dignity of individuals and of nations.

### Value of Love Reflected in Saint Maximilian Kolbe

In our own day there have been moments when these values have shone before the whole world with special brightness. Who among us, and not only us, can forget first the beatification and then the canonization of that son of Polish soil and spiritual son of Saint Francis, the humble priest Saint Maximilian Mary Kolbe, who, in the midst of atrocities and the inhumanity of the concentration camp, exhibited once again before all of contemporary humanity that love unto the end!

### Recent Saints and Blessed Express Most Fully
### What Is Partially in Each of Us

These values, this richness, this inheritance were also manifested in a fuller way and acquired a new light during my three pilgrimages to the homeland. I dwell only on the saints and the blessed because they express most fully that which is partially in each of us individually and in all of us together. At the same time they are the most perfect models on our pilgrimage toward our final destiny in Christ.

There is Blessed Brother Albert Chmielowski, a patriot and artist, who wished to be all kindness in the face of Polish poverty and toward the needy; Blessed Raphael

Kalinowski; Blessed Ursula Ledochowska; Blessed Caroline Kozka, a simple country girl who gave her life in defense of her dignity; finally, the last in order of time, Blessed Michael Koza, Bishop and martyr of Dachau.

## Christian Inheritance Reflected When the Millennial Christian Nation Reclaimed Its Dignity and Rights

But this inheritance, as a testimony of the Polish soul, has also been manifested in recent years in another form, when the millennial Christian nation reclaimed its own dignity and legitimate rights.

## "Solidarity" Expresses a Multitude of Christian Social Values

Among other things, I spoke of this on the Polish seacoast, and much of what I said refers to the whole world, including the United States. There, on the Baltic, "the word 'solidarity' was spoken . . . in a new way that at the same time confirms its eternal content. . . . In the name of man's future and the future of humanity, it was necessary to say that word, 'solidarity.' Today it rolls like a wide wave over the face of the world, which realizes that we cannot live according to the principle of 'all against all,' but only according to another principle, 'all with all,' 'all for all.' Solidarity must take precedence over conflict. Only then can humanity survive, can each nation survive and develop within the great human family. . . . Solidarity means a way of existing, for example, of a nation, in its human variety, in unity, with respect for differences, for all the diversity that exists among people, and so, unity in variety, in plurality. All this is contained in the concept 'solidarity'" (Address in Gdynia, 11 June 1987).

## Poland's Great Musical, Literary and Spiritual Heroes Open New Ways to the Human Spirit

4. With justifiable pride and gratitude we may turn to the great authors of our culture: to writers, poets, artists, politicians, to religious and spiritual guides, to all those who also in this land have pointed out new ways to the human spirit.

Tadeusz Kosciuszko, Kazimierz Puławski, Włodzimierz Krzyżanowski, Ignacy Paderewski, Helena Modrzejewska, Artur Rubinstein, and the already mentioned Father Leopold Moczygemba, Father Jozef Dabrowski, founder of the Polish Seminary, and so many others, without forgetting the authors and leaders alive today.

## Recall Many Unknown Heroes, Parents of Families Who Handed on the Faith

But along with them we remember too the unknown multitudes of mothers and fathers of families who, guided by their force of temperament and sense of faith, living an authentic Christian life and in fidelity to God and their human ideals, were able to mold those lofty ideas into the values that model and determine everyday living. In their daily lives they themselves lived those values, forged down through the centuries, and they succeeded in transmitting them in their families to each new generation. How many priests are there today who bear witness that they owe their priestly vocation in the first place to their saintly mothers.

### Foster the Christian Vision of the Family, the Domestic Church

Perhaps the most threatened institution in today's world is precisely the family. For that reason, the Church "wishes to offer guidance and support to those Christians and others who are trying to keep sacred and to foster the natural dignity of the married state and its superlative value" (*Gaudium et Spes,* 47).

The fundamental task of the family is to serve life, "transmitting by procreation the divine image from person to person" (*Familiaris Consortio,* 28).

Faithfulness to the family extends also to education. The Second Vatican Council teaches that "since parents have conferred life on their children, they have a most solemn obligation to educate their offspring. Hence, parents must be acknowledged as the first and foremost educators of their children" (*Gravissimum Educationis,* 3).

Family—the domestic Church.

"You are to be my witnesses . . . "

### Call to Priests to Build Up the Christian Culture on the Bonds Between the Faithful and Poland, Bonds of Faith, Culture, Language

5. I now wish to address you, "servants of Christ and administrators of the mysteries of God" (1 Cor. 4:1); you the priests, the pastors of *Polonia*. I have spoken at length about the priesthood during this present visit to the United States. In the context of the present meeting I wish to thank you for all the good that the American *Polonia* has received and continues to receive from your ministry. Remember that the Polish emigration is important for Poland, just as Poland is important for the emigration. From your awareness of and relationship to our common Christian heritage will depend, in great part, the bonds between your faithful and the nation of which they are sons and daughters, bonds of faith, culture and language. Respect for and preservation of this heritage should constitute one of the fundamental principles of your pastoral care. How consoling it is that young people throughout the world are experiencing a growing interest in their past. Young people discover themselves as they search for the foundations of their own identity, its sources and roots, the first strata from which it proceeds.

### Help Young People to Know Their Roots

I know that our young people living here are very much a part of this process, and that more and more they are willing to learn the history, the language and all the richness of the homeland from which their forebears came. They gladly say: "I am proud to be American." But they are no less proud of their origins, especially when they know more about them, because then they feel no complex. Help them in this learning and liberation. Then too, meet the spiritual needs of the most recent emigration. Do not lose heart. Do not be enclosed in the golden tower of prejudice, routine, pastoral minimalism and ease.

## Do Not Diminish Whatever Serves
## the True Well-Being of the Faithful

Do not diminish, do not reduce, do not close whatever serves the true well-being of the faithful, strengthens their spiritual relationship with the Savior and leads to genuine growth of the spirit.

## The Power of the Spirit Enables You to Be Witnesses

6. Dear brothers and sisters: "You are to be my witnesses . . . to the ends of the earth." This announcement and call was addressed by Christ to the Apostles shortly before his Ascension. Before that, he said to them: "you will receive power when the Holy Spirit comes down on you" (Acts 1:8). That is, you are to be my witnesses when you receive the power of the Holy Spirit. We are witnesses of Christ in the power of the Holy Spirit.

The Holy Spirit is the beginning, the source, the foundation of Christian life in the new era of the history of salvation, in the time of the Church, in the time of mission, in the time of witness. May his power fill your hearts and minds and wills, to enable you to bear witness to Christ with your own witness and that of your forefathers, with the witness of the millennary Christian heritage of that land that has the right and wishes to call you her sons and daughters.

## May Mary Carry Your Soul to Everything That Is Good,
## Beautiful and Great

This heritage is marked in a special way by the presence of the Blessed Virgin, the Mother of God, Mary blessed by God. She who "defends bright Czestochowa, and shines in the morning Gate!" Our poet cried out to her: "carry there my soul full of nostalgia!" Your hearts do not feel nostalgia, because you are already sons and daughters of this land and citizens of this country. Still, may Mary carry your souls toward everything that is good, beautiful, great; toward those values that make life worth living. This we ask of her, especially today. This we ask of her in the Marian Year.

Now I wish to bless all of you present, your families and dear ones, the children and young people, the sick, the old, those who are alone. I bless the priests, the deacons, the Religious families of men and women, the seminarians, the parishes, the places of work and recreation. I bless the whole of *Polonia* in North America.

## 46. MEETING WITH DEACONS AND THEIR WIVES

Dear Brothers in the Service of Our Lord,

Dear Wives and Collaborators of these men ordained to the
permanent diaconate,

1. I greet you in the love of our Lord Jesus Christ, in whom, as Saint Paul tells
us, God has chosen us, redeemed us and adopted us as his children (see Eph. 1:3ff).
Together with Saint Paul, and together with you today, *I praise our heavenly Father* for
these wonderful gifts of grace.

### Progress of Permanent Diaconate Great and
### Visible Sign of the Working of the Spirit

It is a special joy for me to meet with you because you represent *a great and
visible sign of the working of the Holy Spirit* in the wake of the Second Vatican Council,
which provided for the restoration of the permanent diaconate in the Church. The
wisdom of that provision is evident in your presence in such numbers today and in
the fruitfulness of your ministries. *With the whole Church, I give thanks to God for the
call you have received and for your generous response.* For the majority of you who are
married, this response has been made possible by the love and support and collaboration of your wives. It is a great encouragement to know that in the United States
over the past two decades almost eight thousand permanent deacons have been
ordained for the service of the Gospel.

### Vatican Council, Paul VI,
### Ancient Tradition Emphasize Call to Service
### of the Mysteries of Christ and of Brothers and Sisters

It is above all *the call to service* that I wish to celebrate with you today. In
speaking of deacons, the *Vatican Council* said that "strengthened by sacramental grace,
in communion with the Bishop and his presbyterate, they serve the People of God in
the service of the liturgy, the word, and charity" (*Lumen Gentium,* 29). Reflecting
further on this description, my predecessor Paul VI was in agreement with the Council that "the permanent diaconate should be restored . . . as a driving force for the
Church's service (*diakonia*) toward the local Christian communities, and as a sign or
sacrament of the Lord Christ himself, who 'came not to be served but to serve'" (*Ad
Pascendum,* August 15, 1972, Introduction). These words recall *the ancient tradition
of the Church* as expressed by the early Fathers such as Ignatius of Antioch, who says
that deacons are "ministers of the mysteries of Jesus Christ . . . ministers of the
Church of God" (*Ad Trallianos,* II, 3). You, dear brothers, belong to the life of the
Church that goes back to saintly deacons, like Lawrence, and before him to Stephen
and his companions, whom the Acts of the Apostles consider "deeply spiritual and
prudent" (Acts 6:3).

This is at the very heart of the diaconate to which you have been called: *to be a servant of the mysteries of Christ and, at one and the same time, to be a servant of your brothers and sisters.* That these two dimensions are inseparably joined together in one reality shows the important nature of the ministry which is yours by ordination.

### Deacon's Service of the Word, Altar and Charity
### Is the Church's Service Sacramentalized

2. How are we to understand the mysteries of Christ of which you are ministers? A profound description is given to us by Saint Paul in the reading we heard a few moments ago. *The central mystery is this:* God the Father's plan of glory to bring *all things in the heavens and on earth into one under the headship of Christ,* his beloved Son. It is for this that all the baptized are predestined, chosen, redeemed and sealed with the Holy Spirit. This plan of God is at the center of our lives and the life of the world.

At the same time, if service to this redemptive plan is the mission of all the baptized, what is the specific dimension of your service as deacons? The Second Vatican Council explains that *a sacramental grace conferred through the imposition of hands* enables you to carry out your service of the word, the altar and charity with a special effectiveness (see *Ad Gentes,* 16). *The service of the deacon is the Church's service sacramentalized.* Yours is not just one ministry among others, but it is truly meant to be, as Paul VI described it, a "driving force" for the Church's *diakonia.* By your ordination you are configured to Christ in his servant role. You are also meant to be *living signs of the servanthood of his Church.*

### All Three Forms of Service Are Inseparably
### Joined Together in Service of God's Plan

3. If we keep in mind the deep spiritual nature of this *diakonia,* then we can better appreciate *the interrelation of the three areas of ministry* traditionally associated with the diaconate, that is, the ministry of the word, the ministry of the altar, and the ministry of charity. Depending on the circumstances, one or another of these may receive particular emphasis in an individual deacon's work, but these three ministries are *inseparably joined together as one in the service of God's redemptive plan.* This is so because the word of God inevitably leads us to the Eucharistic worship of God at the altar; in turn, this worship leads us to a new way of living which expresses itself in acts of charity.

### Ministry of Charity Flows from the Gospel and Worship
### in Order to Bear Lasting Fruit

This charity is both *love of God and love of neighbor.*

As the First Letter of John teaches us, "One who has no love for the brother he has seen cannot love the God he has not seen . . . whoever loves God must also love his brother" (1 Jn. 4:20–21). By the same token, acts of charity which are not rooted in the word of God and in worship cannot bear lasting fruit. *"Apart from me,"* Jesus says, *"you can do nothing"* (Jn. 15:5). The ministry of charity is confirmed on every page of the Gospel; it demands *a constant and radical conversion of heart.* We have a forceful example of this in the Gospel of Matthew proclaimed earlier. We are told: "offer no resistance to injury." We are commanded: "love your enemies and pray for your persecutors." All of this is an essential part of the ministry of charity.

### Needs of World—Spiritual, Material Poverty, Loss of Faith and Hope—Offer Opportunities

4. Certainly *today's world* is not lacking in opportunities for such a ministry, whether in the form of the simplest acts of charity or the most heroic witness to the radical demands of the Gospel. All around us many of our brothers and sisters live in either *spiritual or material poverty* or both. So many of the world's people are *oppressed by injustice* and the denial of their fundamental human rights. Still others are troubled or suffer from a *loss of faith* in God, or are tempted to give up hope.

### Appreciation of Direct Service of Deacons to the Needy

In the midst of the human condition it is a great source of satisfaction to learn that so many permanent deacons in the United States are involved in *direct service to the needy:* to the ill, the abused and battered, the young and old, the dying and bereaved, the deaf, blind and disabled, those who have known suffering in their marriages, the homeless, victims of substance abuse, prisoners, refugees, street people, the rural poor, the victims of racial and ethnic discrimination, and many others. As Christ tells us, "as often as you did it for one of my least brothers, you did it for me" (Mt. 25:40).

### Ministry of Charity Obliges Deacons to Be a Positive Force for Change

At the same time, the Second Vatican Council reminds us that the ministry of charity at the service of God's redemptive plan also obliges us to be *a positive influence for change* in the world in which we live, that is, to be a leaven—to be the soul of human society—so that society may be renewed by Christ and transformed into the family of God (see *Gaudium et Spes,* 40ff). The *"temporal order"* includes marriage and the family, the world of culture, economic and social life, the trades and professions, political institutions, the solidarity of peoples and issues of justice and peace (see *Apostolicam Actuositatem* 7; *Gaudium et Spes,* 46ff). The task is seldom an easy one. The truth about ourselves and the world, revealed in the Gospel, is not always what the world wants to hear. *Gospel truth often contradicts commonly accepted thinking,* as we see so clearly today with regard to evils such as racism, contraception, abortion, and euthanasia—to name just a few.

### Deacon Has a Special Witness to Give on Account of the
### Grace of Ordination and His Secular Occupation

5. Taking an active part in society belongs to the baptismal mission of every Christian in accordance with his or her state in life, but the permanent deacon has *a special witness to give*. The sacramental grace of his ordination is meant to strengthen him and to make his efforts fruitful, even as his *secular occupation* gives him entry into the temporal sphere in a way that is normally not appropriate for other members of the clergy. At the same time, the fact that he is an ordained minister of the Church brings a special dimension to his efforts in the eyes of those with whom he lives and works.

### Deacon and His Wife Are Automatically Involved
### in the Transformation of Family Life

Equally important is the contribution that a married deacon makes to *the transformation of family life*. He and his wife, having entered into a communion of life, are called to help and serve each other (see *Gaudium et Spes,* 48). So intimate is their partnership and unity in the Sacrament of Marriage that the Church fittingly requires the wife's consent before her husband can be ordained a permanent deacon (can. 1031, sec. 2). As the current guidelines for the permanent diaconate in the United States point out, the *nurturing and deepening of mutual, sacrificial love between husband and wife* constitute perhaps the most significant involvement of a deacon's wife in her husband's public ministry in the Church (Guidelines, NCCB, p. 110). Today especially, this is no small service.

### Deacon and His Wife Are to Exemplify
### Fidelity and Indissolubility

In particular, the deacon and his wife must be a living example of *fidelity and indissolubility in Christian marriage* before a world which is in dire need of such signs. By facing *in a spirit of faith* the challenges of married life and the demands of daily living, they strengthen the family life not only of the Church community but of the whole of society. They also show how the obligations of family, work and ministry can be harmonized in the *service of the Church's mission*. Deacons and their wives and children can be a great encouragement to all others who are working to promote family life.

### Parish Is the Ecclesial Context for Ministry

Mention must also be made of another kind of family, namely the *parish,* which is the usual setting in which the vast majority of deacons fulfill the mandate of their ordination "to help the Bishop and his presbyterate." The parish provides *an ecclesial context* for your ministry and serves as a reminder that your labors are not carried out in isolation, but in communion with the Bishop, his priests and all those who in varying degrees share in the public ministry of the Church. Permanent deacons have an obligation to respect the office of the priest and to cooperate conscientiously and generously with him and with the parish staff. The deacon also has a right to be accepted and fully recognized by them and by all for what he is: an ordained minister of the word, the altar and charity.

## Qualities Expected Are Fidelity to Christ, Moral Integrity, Obedience to the Bishops

6. Given the dignity and importance of the permanent diaconate, what is expected of you? As Christians we must not be ashamed to speak of *the qualities of a servant* to which all believers must aspire, and especially deacons, whose ordination rite describes them as "servants of all." A deacon must be known for *fidelity, integrity and obedience,* and so it is that fidelity to Christ, moral integrity and obedience to the Bishop must mark your lives, as the ordination rite makes clear (see also *Ad Pascendum,* Introduction). In that rite *the Church* also *expresses her hopes and expectations* for you when she prays:

"Lord, may they excel in every virtue: in love . . . concern . . . unassuming authority . . . self-discipline and in holiness of life. May their conduct exemplify your commandments and lead your people to imitate their purity of life. May they remain strong and steadfast in Christ, giving to the world the witness of a pure conscience. May they . . . imitate your Son, who came, not to be served but to serve."

## Ordination Prayer Commits Them to Lifelong Spiritual Formation

Dear brothers: this prayer commits you to *lifelong spiritual formation* so that you may grow and persevere in rendering a service that is truly edifying to the People of God. You who are wives of permanent deacons, being close collaborators in their ministry, are likewise challenged with them *to grow in the knowledge and love of Jesus Christ.* And this of course means growth in prayer—personal prayer, family prayer, liturgical prayer.

## Constant and Diligent Study of the Scriptures

Since deacons are ministers of the word, the Second Vatican Council invites you *to constant reading and diligent study of the Sacred Scriptures,* lest—if you are a preacher—you become an empty one for failing to hear the word in your own heart (see *Dei Verbum,* 25). In your lives as deacons you are called to *hear* and *guard* and *do* the word of God, in order to be able to proclaim it worthily. To preach to God's people is an honor that entails a serious preparation and a real commitment to holiness of life.

## Be Steeped in the Spirit of the Liturgy

As ministers of the altar you must be *steeped in the spirit of the liturgy,* and be convinced above all that it is "the summit toward which the activity of the Church is directed and at the same time the source from which all her power flows." You are called to discharge your office with the dignity and reverence befitting the liturgy, which the Council powerfully describes as being "above all the worship of the divine majesty" (see *Sacrosanctum Concilium,* 10, 33). I join you in thanking *all those who devote themselves to your training,* both before and after your ordination, through programs of spiritual, theological, and liturgical formation.

## Servanthood Is the Mystery
## Through Which Christ Redeems the World

7. "Sing a new song unto the Lord! Let your song be sung from mountains high!" *Sing to him as servants,* but *also* sing *as friends* of Christ, who has made known to you all that he has heard from the Father. It was not you who chose him, but he who *chose you, to go forth and bear fruit*—fruit that will last. This you do by loving one another (see Jn. 15:15ff.). By the standards of this world, servanthood is despised, but in the wisdom and providence of God it is *the mystery through which Christ redeems the world. And you are ministers of that mystery,* heralds of that Gospel. You can be sure that one day you will hear the Lord saying to each of you: "Well done, good and faithful servant, enter into the joy of your Lord" (see Mt. 25:21).

Dear brothers and sisters: as one who strives to be "the servant of the servants of God," I cannot take leave of you until, together, we turn to Mary, as she continues to proclaim: "I am the servant of the Lord" (Lk. 1:38). And in *the example of her servanthood* we see the perfect model of our own call to the discipleship of our Lord Jesus Christ and to the service of his Church.

## 47. ADDRESS ON SOCIAL JUSTICE ISSUES

Dear Friends,

1. I am happy that, almost at the end of my second pastoral visit to the United States, I am able to address such a large number of people in this well-known industrial city of Detroit. I greet all of you most cordially: Christian leaders and leaders of other religions; civic leaders from the federal, state and municipal governments; people of various races and ethnic backgrounds, fellow Catholics; Christian and non-Christian brothers and sisters; men and women of good will!

## Detroit Is a Special City of Workers and of Current Problems

I feel that I must *thank the Lord our God* for this wonderful occasion. Detroit is a place where work, hard daily work—that privileged duty and vocation of the human person (see *Laborem Exercens,* 9)—is a truly distinctive characteristic of urban life. This is indeed *a city of workers,* and very many of you here—men and women, younger people and older people, immigrants and native-born Americans—earn your living and that of your families in and around Detroit through the work of your hands, your mind, indeed your whole person. And many of you suffer from the problems that not infrequently characterize the work situation in an industrial urban setting.

### Theme of Social Progress and Human Development
### Close to Holy Father's Heart

This is why I would like to make reference to a subject which, as you are well aware, is close to my heart. This subject is *social progress and human development* in relation to the requirements of justice and to the building of a lasting peace, both in the United States and throughout the world.

### Incomparable Dignity of People of Detroit
### Faced with the Challenge to Provide for Livelihood

Of course, dear friends, dear people of Detroit and this whole area, it is *you* I have primarily in mind in dealing with such a subject—you who have been created in the image and likeness of God, you who have been redeemed by the blood of the Savior, you who are children of God and brothers and sisters of Christ, you who for all of these reasons possess an incomparable dignity. But in looking at you, assembled here in Hart Plaza, *I see beyond you all the people of this country and the peoples of the whole world.* I see all the men and women who, like you, are confronted every day anew with the obligation and the challenge to provide for their livelihood and for the livelihood of their family through their own work. Work means any activity, whether manual or intellectual, whatever its nature or whatever its circumstances, by which a human being earns his or her daily bread and contributes to science and progress, civilization and culture (see *Laborem Exercens,* 1). Human work is such a fundamental dimension of human existence, that one cannot speak about it without touching upon all its aspects.

### Christ's Teaching Makes Us Realize Our Partnership
### with God in Bringing Creation to Fulfillment

2. *Social progress and human development are the concern of all.* They are of particular concern to *the Church.* From the very beginning of her existence in time, the Church has endeavored to fathom the total richness of the message which Jesus Christ proclaimed both by his words and his actions. Sent by the Father to assume our humanity and bring salvation to all, the Lord Jesus provided us with the key to understanding our humanity. He taught us about our origin and destiny, which are in God. He taught us the transcendent value of all human life and the supreme

dignity of the human person, created in the image and likeness of God (see Gn. 1:27). He taught us that human life is fulfilled in knowing and loving God, and in loving our neighbor according to the measure of God's love for us. He invited us to follow him, to become his disciples. He summoned us to be converted in our hearts by entering into the mystery of his Passion, Death and Resurrection. He revealed that we are God's partners in bringing creation to fulfillment. And he now fashions us into a chosen people, a communion of faith with a commitment to his Kingdom.

### Church in Applying Christ's Gospel
### Has Gradually Developed Thought and Guidelines
### That Make Up Social Teaching

In fidelity to Christ, the Church has endeavored *to bring his message to bear on all aspects of life,* throughout the changing circumstances in the course of the centuries, bringing out from the heritage of the Gospel "both the new and the old" (Mt. 13:52). New challenges affecting the life of every person individually and of society as a whole have presented themselves at every turn on the path of humanity through history. In trying to meet those challenges, the People of God have always turned to the message of Jesus, in order to discover the principles and the values that would ensure solutions in consonance with the dignity and destiny of the human person. Throughout her history, the Church has listened to the words of Scripture and has sought to put them into practice, in the midst of different political, economic and social circumstances. This has been a truly common effort. Individual Christians have struggled to be faithful to the Gospel inspiration in their daily lives; centers of learning have contributed their specialized studies; groups and associations have addressed issues of particular concern; communities have developed practical initiatives; individual Bishops and Episcopal Conferences have provided guidance; and the Magisterium of the Church has made pronouncements and issued documents. In a continuous interaction the Church has thus developed a tradition of thought and practical guidelines that are called *the social teaching of the Church.* This social teaching has recently been expressed in documents of the Second Vatican Council and in writings of the Popes, who have systematically addressed the rapid changes in contemporary society.

Also today, the various categories of the People of God—according to their respective calling—continue to address the social problems in their various historical and cultural settings.

### Faith Offers a Deep Motivation for Personal Involvement and
### Social Participation in Building an Order of Justice in Peace

3. Today, dear friends, on this last day of my second extended visit to the United States of America, I would urge you to continue *your personal involvement in*

*that never-ending quest for justice and peace.* Under the guidance and inspiration of the Church's Magisterium—which is that of the Pope and of the Bishops in union with him—each one of you is called to make a contribution. Each one of you must be instrumental in promoting a social order that respects the dignity of the human person and serves the common good. Each one of you has an irreplaceable contribution to make to secure a social order of justice in peace. In your country today, participation at different levels of economic, social and political life has greatly intensified the awareness of the unique dignity of every human person and at the same time reinforced your sense of responsibility to yourselves and to others. As Christians you find in your faith *a deep motivation for* your *social responsibility and involvement.* Do not let this hour pass without renewing your commitment to action for social justice and peace. Turn to the Gospel of Jesus Christ to strengthen your resolve to become instruments for the common good! Learn from the Gospel that you have been entrusted with the justice and peace of God! We are not merely the builders of justice according to the standards of this world, but we are the bearers of the life of God, who is himself justice and peace! Let your endeavors to achieve justice and peace in all the spheres of your lives be a manifestation of God's love!

### The Parable of the Rich Man and Lazarus
### Challenges Believers

In a setting similar to this one some eight years ago in New York's Yankee Stadium, I proclaimed *the Gospel challenge contained in the parable of the rich man and Lazarus.* You are all familiar with this marvelous lesson in social responsibility which Jesus left us. Knowing your faith and your openness to challenge, I now ask you today: What have you done with that parable? How many times in the past eight years have you turned to that parable to find inspiration for your Christian lives? Or have you put it aside, thinking that it was no longer relevant to you or to the situations in your country?

### Discover the Poor in Your Midst—
### the Old, the Weak, the Unemployed

4. In any modern society, no matter how advanced, there will be situations, some old and some new, that summon your Christian sense of justice to action. Our Lord has said: "The poor you will always have with you" (Mt. 26:11). *You must therefore discover the poor in your midst.* There is poverty among you when the old and the weak are neglected and their standard of living constantly declines. There is poverty when illness takes away the wage earner from a family. There is material need and suffering in those areas or groups where unemployment risks becoming endemic. There is poverty in the future of those that cannot enjoy the benefits of basic education.

## Show Concern for the Unskilled
## Who Experience Hardship from Technological Change

*Some modern technological developments contain the potential for new hardships and injustice* and must therefore be part of our concern. The introduction of robotics, the rapid development of communications, the necessary adaptation of industrial plants, the need to introduce new skills in management—these are but some of the factors that, if not analyzed carefully or tested as to their social cost, may produce undue hardship for many, either temporarily or more permanently.

## A Sensitive Social Conscience
## Will Discover Other Areas of Concern

These are just a few *areas where our social responsibility is challenged.* Others include the situation of marriage and family life and the factors that threaten their underlying values; the respect for the sacredness of unborn human life; the situation of newly arrived immigrants; open or disguised expressions of discrimination based on "race, origin, color, culture, sex or religion" (*Octogesima Adveniens,* 16). To the degree that its social conscience is sensitive, every community will discover where instances of injustice or threats to peace still exist or are potentially present.

But the very attempt to look at some of the challenges in the domestic scene brings us to another important consideration regarding progress and human development. I am referring to *the international dimension.*

## Debates About Domestic or National Problems
## Are Affected by the Fact of Worldwide Interdependence

5. Without implying in any way that domestic or national problems do not exist any more—and they most certainly do—it becomes ever more evident that such local or national problems, and their solutions, are fundamentally linked with realities that transcend the boundaries of countries. Not only do decisions taken by one nation affect other regions of the world, but the solution to many domestic problems can no longer be found except on an international, and even a worldwide level. All major problems that concern the life of the human person in society have become world problems. Any decision that is envisaged in the political, economic or social sphere must be considered within the context of its worldwide repercussions. What now most deeply affects any debate on social progress and human development is the *fact of worldwide interdependence.*

## So Many Events Make Us Aware
## That the Social Question Has Become Worldwide

Already twenty years ago, in 1967, Pope Paul VI wrote, at the very beginning of his encyclical letter "On the Development of Peoples" (*Populorum Progressio*): "Today the principal fact that we must all recognize is that the social question has become worldwide" (no. 3). In following years, *this affirmation of Paul VI was further vindicated by a succession of events*. There was the emergence on the political scene of peoples who, after centuries of colonial domination and dependence, demanded ever more forcefully their rightful place among the nations and in international decision making. A worldwide economic crisis brought home the fact that there exists an increasingly interdependent economy. The continuing existence of millions of people who suffer hunger or malnutrition and the growing realization that the natural resources are limited make clear that humanity forms a single whole. Pollution of air and water threatens more and more the delicate balance of the biosphere on which present and future generations depend and makes us realize that we all share a common ecological environment. Instant communication has linked finance and trade in worldwide dependence.

### Interdependence Changes the Perspective
### for Relations Between Nations

The poorer nations of the world are inclined to view this interdependence as a continuing pattern of economic domination by the more developed countries, while the latter sometimes view interdependence as the opening up of new opportunities for commerce and export. Interdependence clearly demands that relations between nations be seen in this new context and that *the social question needs an appropriate ethic*. Nobody can say anymore: "Let others be concerned with the rest of the world!" The world is each one of us!

### Needed Are New Ethical Choices,
### a New World Conscience, New Solidarity Beyond Frontiers

6. When I addressed the participants of the sixty-eighth session of the International Labor Organization on June 15, 1982, I was able to state: "There is a common good which can no longer be confined to a more or less satisfactory compromise between sectional demands or between purely economic requirements. New ethical choices are necessary; *a new world conscience must be created;* each of us without denying his origin and the roots of his family, his people and his nation, or the obligations arising therefrom, must regard himself as a member of this great family, the world community. . . . This means that the worldwide common good requires *a new solidarity without frontiers*" (no. 10).

### This New Solidarity Is a Conscience of Faith
### in the Equal Dignity of Each Person

*The Church's social teaching sees this new solidarity as a consequence of our faith*. It is the attitude, in the international reality, of those who heed the Lord's commandment: "Love one another as I have loved you" (Jn. 15:12). It is the consequence of our faith in the mystery of Creation: that God has created every human person in his own image and likeness. Every human being is endowed with the same fundamental and inalienable dignity. Every individual is called to acknowledge this fundamental equality within the unity of the human family. Everyone is invited to respect the common destiny of everyone else in God. Everyone is asked to accept that the goods of the earth are given by God to all for the benefit of all.

## Solidarity Is a Moral Duty
## Stemming from the Spiritual Union of All Human Beings

For the disciple of Christ, *solidarity is a moral duty stemming from the spiritual union of all human beings,* who share a common origin, a common dignity and a common destiny. In creating us to live in society, in a close network of relations with each other, and in calling us through Redemption to share the life of the Savior not merely as individuals but as members of a pilgrim people, *God himself has created our basic interdependence and called us to solidarity with all.* This teaching is formulated in an incomparably effective manner in *the parable of the Good Samaritan,* who took care of the man who was left half dead along the road from Jerusalem to Jericho. We all travel that road and are tempted to pass by on the other side. Referring to the Samaritan, who was moved by compassion, Jesus told his listeners: "Go, and do the same." Today, Jesus repeats to all of us when we travel the road of our common humanity: "Go, and do the same" (see Lk. 10:37).

## The Catholic Church's Interest in the U.N. Is Due to the
## Issues It Treats and the Reasons for Its Foundation

7. In speaking to you about social progress and human development, I feel impelled to stress the international dimension because of the objective need to promote *a new worldwide solidarity.*

There is also another reason why I am especially mindful today of the larger international scene. You know well that the Bishop of Rome and the Holy See follow closely *international activities* and therefore have *a special interest in the work of the United Nations Organization* in New York. I would have liked very much to visit once again its headquarters, as I did in 1979, and as Pope Paul VI did in 1965. I regret that I am not able to accept at this time the kind invitation which the secretary-general of the United Nations has extended to me for a new visit. The interest of the Catholic Church in this international organization is linked to the importance of the issues that it treats and to the reasons for which it was founded. To work for *the establishment and maintenance of a just and lasting peace is a goal that deserves support and collaboration.* This is in fact why the United Nations Organization was created in the first place, in that bright daylight which followed the long drawn-out night of the Second World War. I pray that despite its inevitable shortcomings it will be able *to fulfill ever more effectively its unique role of service to the world,* a service that the world truly needs.

## U.N. Deals with Disarmament and Arms Control

The United Nations deals with *disarmament and arms control*—the control of nuclear weapons in the first place, but also biological, chemical and conventional weapons. Its patient, painstaking and sometimes even frustrating dedication to this cause of paramount importance for the world and all its people is recognized and appreciated as being an incentive and support for the bilateral negotiations by the superpowers for arms reduction. Here it is indeed a question that must be addressed with an unfailing commitment, extreme lucidity and a clear sense of the value of human life and the integrity of creation.

## U.N. Is Concerned with Other Conditions for True Peace

The United Nations is also concerned with many of the *other conditions for true peace*. It is fitting here to reflect on some of them in relation to the international dimension of the social question.

## Concern for Human Rights as Shown in the Impact of the Universal Declaration of Human Rights

In the first place, I would like to single out the concern for *human rights*. You remember, I am sure, that the United Nations adopted, more than forty years ago, the Universal Declaration of Human Rights. The basic inspiration of this important document was the recognition that the way toward a peaceful and just world must necessarily pass through the respect for each human being, through the definition and recognition of the basic human rights, and through the respect for the inalienable rights of individuals and of the communities of peoples. The adoption of the Universal Declaration was followed over the years by many declarations and conventions on extremely important aspects of human rights, in favor of women, of children, of handicapped persons, of equality between races, and especially the two international covenants on economic, social and cultural rights and on civil and political rights, together with an optional protocol. In 1981, the General Assembly also adopted a solemn declaration against every form of religious intolerance. The United Nations must also be given proper credit for having set up the Commission for Human Rights as a monitoring organ to follow carefully the positive and negative developments in this important field. The *commitment* of the United Nations *to human rights* goes hand in hand with its commitment *to peace*. Experience has taught that disrespect or lack of respect for human rights, oppression of the weak, discrimination because of sex, color, origin, race or religion create conflict and jeopardize peace. Here again, what concerns human beings in any one place affects all human beings everywhere.

## Concern for a More Just and Equitable International Society

Through the different specialized institutions and programs, the United Nations develops its *commitment to a more just and equitable international society*. This work and commitment include the struggle against diseases and illiteracy; action undertaken for the advancement of women; protecting the rights of children and the handicapped; the development of international law; the peaceful use of atomic energy; the protection and preservation of famous monuments which belong to the cultural patrimony of humanity; the defense of the environment; the struggle against hunger, malnutrition and underdevelopment; and the defense of the homeless.

### The History of the U.N. Shows the Need to Reinforce International Authority for Global Common Good

8. The existence and activities of the United Nations Organization, its achievements and also its failures, underline in a dramatic way *the need for reinforcing international authority* at the service of the global common good. It is already a sign of great progress that the importance of global social issues and the need for effectively promoting peace are becoming more universally recognized. It is also *a sign of hope* that an international organization, formed by the great majority of states, tries, within the limited means at its disposal, and notwithstanding internal and external difficulties, to increase the awareness of worldwide problems and their appropriate solutions.

### Challenge to Make a Decisive Contribution to the Building Up of a True World Community

It is also a marvelous challenge for all the peoples and nations of the world—now that every day we become more aware of our interdependence—to be called upon by the urgent demands of a new solidarity that knows no frontiers. Now that we move toward the threshold of the third millennium of Christianity, we are given the unique chance, for the first time in human history, *to make a decisive contribution to the building up of a true world community*. The awareness that we are linked in common destiny is becoming stronger; the efforts to reach that goal are being multiplied by men and women of good will in a diversity of activities—political as well as economic, cultural as well as social. People in all walks of life and nations and governments alike are being challenged in the name of our common humanity, in the name of the rights of every human being and in the name of the rights of every nation.

### Nations Must Respect Human Rights of All Citizens and the Full Rights of Fellow Nations

In order to succeed and give the correct answer to the many demands that the *de facto* interdependence of all nations makes upon the sense of solidarity of all, we must create a just balance between the constraints put by interdependence upon the nations and the call for effective solidarity addressed to all the nations. In the life of every nation, social progress and human development are ensured by the respect given to the rights of the human person. The human person's very existence in dignity and his or her rightful participation in the life of the community are safe-guarded by the deep respect that every person entertains for the dignity and the rights of every fellow human being. In the same way, respect for the rights of peoples and nations must safeguard the existence in liberty of every nation and thus make possible its rightful and effective participation in all aspects of international life. Without this, it would be impossible to speak about solidarity. In order to be capable of global solidarity, *nations must* first of all *respect the human rights of their citizens* and in turn be recognized by their people as the expression of their sovereignty; secondly, *nations must respect the full rights of their fellow nations* and know also that their rights as a nation will not be disavowed.

### America's National Vocation Is to Be Aware of Gifts, Capacity to Serve and to Live Up to Responsibilities

9. Dear friends: America is a very powerful country. The amount and quality of your achievements are staggering. By virtue of your unique position as citizens of this nation, *you are placed before a choice and you must choose.* You may choose to close in on yourselves, to enjoy the fruits of your own form of progress and to try to forget about the rest of the world. Or, as you become more and more aware of your gifts and your capacity to serve, you may choose to live up to the responsibilities that your own history and accomplishments place on your shoulders. By choosing this latter course, you acknowledge *interdependence* and opt for *solidarity.* This, dear friends, is truly *a human vocation, a Christian vocation,* and for you as Americans it is *a worthy national vocation.*

### Prayer Is the Deepest Inspiration and Dynamism of All Social Consciousness

10. In drawing attention to the need for an ever-greater social consciousness in our day, I also wish to draw attention to *the need for prayer.* Prayer is the deepest inspiration and dynamism of all social consciousness. In speaking to the Bishops of America in 1983 I stated: "It is indeed in prayer that a social consciousness is nurtured and at the same time evaluated. It is in prayer that the bishop, together with his people, ponders *the need and exigencies of Christian service. . . .* Through prayer the Church realizes the full import of Christ's words: 'This is how all will know you for my disciples: your love for one another' (Jn. 13:35). It is in prayer that the Church understands the many implications of the fact that justice and mercy are among 'the weightier matters of the law' (Mt. 23:23). Through prayer, the struggle for justice finds its proper motivation and encouragement, and dis-covers and maintains truly effective means" (*ad Limina* Address, December 3, 1983).

## Ask God's Help to Be Ever More Aware of Global Interdependence and Sensitive to Human Solidarity

Finally, to you the Catholic people of Detroit and all this area I repeat the words with which Paul VI concluded his message to the Call to Action Conference that was held eleven years ago in this very city of Detroit: "In the tradition of the Church, any call to action is first of all a call to prayer. And so you are summoned to prayer, and above all to a greater sharing in Christ's Eucharistic Sacrifice. . . . It is in the Eucharist that you find the true Christian spirit that will enable you to go out and act in Christ's name." And for all of you dear friends, people of every religion, race and ethnic group, I ask God's help so that you may be *ever more aware of global interdependence and ever more sensitive to human solidarity.*

## 48. HOMILY AT MASS CELEBRATED IN THE SILVERDOME

Conduct yourselves in a way worthy of the Gospel of Christ. (Phil. 1:27)

Dear Brothers and Sisters in Christ,

1. The Apostle Paul addresses this appeal to the Christians of Philippi. And today *the Church's liturgy repeats this appeal* to all who believe in Christ. As my visit to your country comes to an end, it is my special joy this evening to reflect on those words with you, the people of the Church in Detroit, as well as visitors from elsewhere in Michigan, from nearby Canada and from other areas.

### Maturity and Fruitfulness of Continuous Proclamation of God's Word in the Detroit Area

From the humble beginnings of the foundation of Detroit in the year 1701, *the proclamation of God's word* in this region has continued unbroken, despite hardships and setbacks, and has reached a level of maturity and a fruitfulness unimagined by the early missionaries. Many years separate us from the first celebration of the Eucharist by the priests who accompanied Cadillac, the founder of Detroit, and yet we know that our communion this evening in the Body and Blood of Christ also links us with them and with *all who have gone before us in faith.*

### Appreciation of the Hard Work and Sacrifices of Those Who Handed on the Faith

With you, I give thanks to God for the courage, dedication and perseverance of the many clergy, Religious and laity who worked so hard during all these years, first to share their faith with the Native Americans of this area, and then *to preserve and spread the faith* among those of almost every race and nation who settled here. I also give thanks with you for the intrepid Catholic faith of so many of your parents and grandparents who came to Michigan in order to find liberty and in order to build a better life for themselves and especially for you, their children and grandchildren. Whatever may be the path by which you have received the gift of your Catholic faith, it is due in some measure to those who have gone before you here. *Their voices are joined to that of Saint Paul* when he says to us: "Conduct yourselves in a way worthy of the Gospel of Christ."

## The Vineyard of the Parable of the Workers
## Is an Image of God's Kingdom

2. We read this exhortation this evening in the light of the Gospel *parable of the workers* sent by the owner of an estate into his vineyard, after he has agreed with them on the daily wage. Our Lord often taught through parables like this one. By using images from daily life, he led his hearers to insights about the Kingdom or Reign of God. Using parables, he was able to raise their minds and hearts *from what is seen to what is unseen.* When we remember that the things of this world already bear *the imprint of God's Kingdom,* it is not surprising that the imagery of the parables is so well suited to the Gospel message.

On the one hand, the vineyard of which Jesus speaks is an earthly reality, as is the work to be done in it. On the other hand, *the vineyard is an image of the Kingdom of God.* This Kingdom is described in the Gospels as "the vineyard of the Lord."

## In the Earthly Vineyard the Church Focuses Attention
## on the Dignity and Rights of Workers

3. Let us reflect for a moment on the first of these realities —*the earthly vineyard*—as a workplace, as the place where you and I must *earn our daily bread.* As I said in the encyclical *Laborem Exercens:* "Man must work, both because the Creator has commanded it and because of his own humanity, which requires work in order to be maintained and developed. Man must work out of regard for others, especially his own family, but also for the society he belongs to, the country of which he is a child, and the whole human family of which he is a member, since he is the heir to the work of generations and at the same time a sharer in building the future of those who will come after him in the succession of history" (*Laborem Exercens,* 16).

Accordingly, *the Church considers it her task to focus attention on the dignity and rights of workers,* to condemn violations of that dignity and those rights, and to provide guidance for authentic human progress (see *Laborem Exercens,* 1). The Church's goal is to uplift ever more the family of mankind in the light of Christ's word and by its power.

## Central Tenet of Social Teaching
## Is Superiority of People over Things

Central to the Church's teaching is the conviction that *people are more important than things;* that work is "for man" and not man "for work"; that the person is both the subject and purpose of all work and cannot be reduced to a mere instrument of production; that *the person is to be valued for what he or she is* rather than for what he or she owns (see *Laborem Exercens,* 6, 12; *Gaudium et Spes,* 35). This last truth in particular reminds us that the only gift we can offer God that is truly worthy of him is the gift of ourselves, as we discover in the message of today's Gospel parable.

## In the Vineyard as Kingdom of God, Generosity to the
## Latecomers Differs from Recompense for Just Human Work

4. That message, as I mentioned, has to do with *a spiritual reality,* the Kingdom of God, toward which Jesus seeks to raise the minds and hearts of his listeners. He begins today's parable with the words: "The reign of God is like the case of the owner of an estate who went out at dawn to hire workmen for his vineyard" (Mt. 20:1). That our Lord is speaking about *more than just human work and wages* should be clear from the owner's actions and the ensuing conflict between him and some of the workers. It is not that the owner refuses to honor the agreement about wages. The dispute arises because he gives the same pay to everybody, whether the person worked all day or only part of the day. Each receives the sum which had been agreed upon. Thus the owner of the estate shows *generosity to the latecomers,* to the indignation of those who had worked all day. To them this generosity seems to be an injustice. And what response does the owner give? "I am free," he says, "to do as I please with my money, am I not? Or are you envious because I am generous?" (Mt. 20:15).

## Gospel Paradox Arises from the Kingdom's Standard—
## the Giving of the Gift of Self

In this parable we find one of those seeming contradictions, those *paradoxes,* that appear in the Gospel. It arises from the fact that the parable is describing *two different standards.* One is the standard by which justice is measured by things. The other standard belongs to the Kingdom of God, in which the way of measuring is not the just distribution of things but *the giving of a gift* and, ultimately, the greatest gift of all—*the gift of self.*

## The Undeserved Generosity of God's Gift of Himself
## Cannot Be Measured in Material Terms

5. The owner of the estate pays the workers according to the value of their work, that is, the sum of one denarius. But in the Kingdom of God the pay or wages is *God himself.* This is what Jesus is trying to teach. When it comes to salvation in the

Kingdom of God, it is not a question of just wages but of *the undeserved generosity of God,* who gives himself as the supreme gift to each and every person who shares in divine life through Sanctifying Grace.

### The Gift of Self Cannot Be Measured in Quantity

Such a recompense or reward *cannot be measured in material terms.* When a person gives the gift of self, even in human relations, the gift cannot be measured in quantity. The gift is one and undivided because the giver is one and undivided.

### How Do We Respond to Such a Gift?

*How can we receive such a gift?* We look to Saint Paul for an answer. His words in the Letter to the Philippians are fascinating: "I firmly trust and anticipate that I shall never be put to shame for my hopes . . . Christ will be exalted through me, whether I live or die. For, to me, 'life' means Christ; hence dying is so much gain" (Phil. 1:20–21).

### We Must Respond with the Gift of Self
### Which Cannot Be Measured by Hours of Work

With these words of Saint Paul we find ourselves at the very heart of that standard of measurement which belongs to the Kingdom of heaven. When we receive a gift, *we must respond with a gift.* We can only respond to the gift of God in Jesus Christ—his Cross and Resurrection—in the way that Paul responded—with the *gift of ourselves.* All that Paul is is contained in this gift of self: both his life and his death. The gift of a person's life cannot be valued merely in terms of the number of hours spent in an earthly vineyard.

### The Measure of Love Is to Love Without Measure

Saint Paul, and everyone like him, realizes that one can *never match or equal the value of God's gift of himself to us.* The only measure that applies is the measure of love. And love's measure, as Saint Bernard says, is *to love without measure* (*De Diligendo Deo,* I, 1). This makes it possible for the last to be first, and the first last (see Mt. 20:16).

### Exchange of Self-Giving
### in Luke's Account of the Sinful Woman's Generosity

6. There is another episode, in the Gospel of Luke, when Jesus says to one of the Pharisees who is scandalized at *the behavior of a woman known to be a sinner:* "her many sins are forgiven—because of her great love" (Lk. 7:47). We do well to reflect upon the love in the heart of this woman, who washed the Lord's feet with her tears and wiped them with her hair. We can imagine the bitter sorrow that led her to such an extravagant gesture. Yet *by giving herself humbly to God,* she discovered the far greater and undeserved

gift of which we have spoken, namely, *God's gift of himself to her.* Through this exchange of gifts, the woman found herself once again, only now she was healed and restored. "Your sins are forgiven," Jesus says to her, "go in peace" (v. 48).

### Through Faith and Repentance
### We Can Experience the Power of Love to Transform

For us too, sinners that we are, it is all too easy to squander our love, to use it in the wrong way. And like the Pharisee, we do not easily understand *the power of love to transform.* Only in the Life, Death and Resurrection of Christ do we come to see that love is the measure of all things in the Kingdom of God, because "God is love" (1 Jn. 4:8). We can fully experience love in this life *only through faith and repentance.*

### How Do We Work Both in This World
### and in the Lord's Vineyard?

7. "Conduct yourselves in a way worthy of the Gospel of Christ." As Christians we *live and work in this world,* which is symbolized by the vineyard, but at the same time we are *called to work in the vineyard of the Lord.* We live this visible earthly life and at the same time the life of the Kingdom of God, which is the ultimate destiny and vocation of every person. How then are we to conduct ourselves worthily in regard to these two realities?

### The Growth of the Kingdom of God
### Consists in Deeper Knowledge of Christ,
### Greater Hope and Love, and Love for Others

In the *Credo of the People of God* proclaimed by my predecessor Paul VI, we find an answer to that question—an answer that reflects *the faith of the Church* in the light of the Second Vatican Council, particularly the *Pastoral Constitution on the Church in the Modern World:*

"We confess that the Kingdom of God . . . is not of this world . . . and that its growth cannot be confused with the progress of civilization, science or technology. The true growth of the Kingdom of God consists in an ever deeper knowledge of the unfathomable riches of Christ; in an ever stronger hope in eternal blessings, in an ever more fervent response to the love of God. . . . But this same love also leads the Church to show constant concern for the true temporal welfare of people. . . . Although the Church does not cease to remind her children that here they have no lasting city, she also urges them to contribute—according to their vocation and means—to the welfare of this their earthly home . . . and to devote themselves to helping the poorest and neediest of their brothers and sisters. This intense solicitude of the Church . . . for the needs of people, their joys and hopes, their griefs and labors, is nothing other than her great desire to be present with them in order to illuminate them with the light of Christ and gather them into one in him who alone is their Savior" (*Credo of the People of God,* June 30, 1968).

### Conduct Worthy of the Gospel of Christ
### Is to Offer the Gift of Ourselves to the Father

Dear brothers and sisters: these words tell us what is meant by *conduct worthy of the Gospel of Christ*—that Gospel which we have heard and believed, and are called to live every day. And today *in this Eucharistic Sacrifice we offer our work, our activities, our whole lives to the Father* through his Son, Jesus Christ. We call upon God to accept the gift of ourselves.

### Measure the Things of This World
### by the Standard of the Kingdom of God

8. The Lord is just in all his ways
and holy in all his works.
The Lord is near to all who call upon him,
to all who call upon him in truth. (Ps. 144/145:17–18)

In the first reading, the prophet Isaiah speaks in the name of the Lord, who in the Gospel parable is symbolized by the owner of the vineyard. The Lord says: "my thoughts are not your thoughts, nor are your ways my ways. . . . As high as the heavens are above the earth, so high are my ways above your ways and my thoughts above your thoughts" (Is. 55:8–9).

And so, my brothers and sisters, "Conduct yourselves in a way worthy of the Gospel of Christ," that is to say, *measure the things of this world by the standard of the Kingdom of God.*

*Not the other way around!*
Not the other way around!
"Seek the Lord while he may be found,
call to him while he is near." (Is. 55:6)
*He is near!* The Lord is near!
The Kingdom of God is within us. Amen.

### 49. DEPARTURE FROM DETROIT
### METROPOLITAN AIRPORT

Mr. Vice President,

Dear Friends, dear People of America,

### Thanks to Vice-President Bush for His Presence
### and Thanks to All for Warm Welcome

1. Once again God has given me the joy of making a pastoral visit to your country—the United States of America. I am filled with *gratitude to him and to you.* I

thank the vice president for his presence here today, and I thank all of you from my heart for the kindness and warm hospitality that I have received everywhere.

### Thanks to Bishops, All Their Collaborators, Police and All

I cannot leave without expressing my thanks *to all those who worked so hard* to make this visit possible. In particular I thank my brother Bishops and all their collaborators, who for many months have planned and organized all the details of the last ten days. My gratitude goes to all those who provided *security* and ensured such excellent *public order.* I thank all those who have worked to make this visit above all a time of *fruitful evangelization and prayerful celebration of our unity in faith and love.*

### Grateful to Persons of Other Churches, Creeds, to News Media, to All Americans, to Those Who Prayed

I am also grateful to the people of *other Churches and creeds* and to *all Americans* of good will who have accompanied me, in person or through the media, as I traveled from city to city. A particular word of thanks goes to *the men and women of the media* for their constant and diligent assistance in bringing my message to the people, and in helping me to reach millions of those with whom otherwise I would have had no contact. Most importantly, I am grateful to *all those who supported me by their prayers,* especially the elderly and the sick, who are so dear to the heart of Jesus Christ.

### Gratitude to God and Hope That America Will Be Conscious of Her Responsibility for Justice and Peace

As I leave, I express my gratitude to God also for what he is accomplishing in your midst. With the words of Saint Paul, I too can say with confident assurance "that *he who has begun the good work in you will carry it through to completion,* right up to the day of Christ Jesus" (Phil. 1:67). And so I am confident too that America will be ever more conscious of her responsibility for justice and peace in the world. As a nation that has received so much, she is called to continued generosity and service toward others.

### Admiration for Blessing of Blend of Cultural Traditions, Ecumenical Spirit, Enthusiasm of Young, Aspirations of Immigrants

2. As I go, I take with me vivid memories of a dynamic nation, a warm and welcoming people, a Church abundantly blessed with a rich blend of cultural traditions. I depart with admiration for the ecumenical spirit that breathes strongly throughout this land, for the genuine enthusiasm of your young people, and for the hopeful aspirations of your most recent immigrants. I take with me an unforgettable memory of *a country that God has richly blessed from the beginning until now.*

## America Is Blessed in So Many Ways

*America the beautiful!* So you sing in one of your national songs. Yes, America, you are beautiful indeed, and blessed in so many ways:

—In your majestic mountains and fertile plains;

—In the goodness and sacrifice hidden in your teeming cities and expanding suburbs;

—In your genius for invention and for splendid progress;

—In the power that you use for service and in the wealth that you share with others;

—In what you give to your own, and in what you do for others beyond your borders;

—In how you serve, and in how you keep alive the flame of hope in many hearts;

—In your quest for excellence and in your desire to right all wrongs.

## Your Greatest Beauty and Blessing Is the Human Person

Yes, America, all this belongs to you. But *your greatest beauty and your richest blessing is found in the human person:* in each man, woman and child, in every immigrant, in every native-born son and daughter.

## The Ultimate Test of Your Greatness Is the Way You Treat Every Human Being, but Especially the Weakest

3. For this reason, America, your deepest identity and truest character as a nation is revealed in the position you take toward the human person. *The ultimate test of your greatness is the way you treat every human being, but especially the weakest and most defenseless ones.*

## Great Causes Have Meaning Only to the Extent That You Guarantee Right to Life and Protect the Human Person

The best traditions of your land presume respect for those who cannot defend themselves. If you want equal justice for all, and true freedom and lasting peace, then, America, defend life! All the great causes that are yours today will have meaning only *to the extent that you guarantee the right to life and protect the human person.*

—Feeding the poor and welcoming refugees;

—Reinforcing the social fabric of this nation;

—Promoting the true advancement of women;

—Securing the rights of minorities;

—Pursuing disarmament, while guaranteeing legitimate defense:

all this will succeed only if respect for life and its protection by the law is granted to every human being *from conception until natural death.*

### Every Human Person Is a Being of Inestimable Worth
### Created in the Image of God

Every human person—no matter how vulnerable or helpless, no matter how young or how old, no matter how healthy, handicapped or sick, no matter how useful or productive for society—is a being of inestimable worth created in the image and likeness of God. This is the dignity of America, the reason she exists, the condition for her survival—yes, the ultimate test of her greatness: to respect every human person, especially the weakest and most defenseless ones, those as yet unborn.

### May God Bless America so That She May Become One Nation
### Under God with Liberty and Justice for All

With these sentiments of love and hope for America, I now say good-bye in words that I spoke once before: "Today, therefore, my final prayer is this: that God will bless America, so that she may increasingly become—and truly be—and long remain—'One Nation, *under God,* indivisible, with liberty and justice for all'" (October 7, 1979).

May God bless you all.

God bless America!

### SEPTEMBER 20, 1987

### 50. ADDRESS TO NATIVE PEOPLES

Grace and peace to you from God our Father and the Lord Jesus Christ. (Rom. 1:7)

Dear Aboriginal Brothers and Sisters,

1. I wish to tell you how happy I am to be with you, *the native peoples of Canada,* in this beautiful land of Denendeh. I have come first from across the ocean and now from the United States to be with you. And I know that many of you have also come

from far away—from the frozen Arctic, from the prairies, from the forests, from all parts of this vast and beautiful country of Canada.

### Successor of the Apostle Peter—Source and Foundation of Unity—Comes to Proclaim the Gospel

Three years ago I was not able to complete my visit to you, and I have looked forward to the day when I could return to do so. Today is that day. I come now, as I did then, as *the Successor of the Apostle Peter,* whom the Lord chose to care for his Church as "a permanent and visible source and foundation of unity of faith and fellowship" (*Lumen Gentium,* 18). It is my task to preside over the whole assembly of charity and protect legitimate variety while at the same time seeing that differences do not hinder unity but rather contribute toward it (see *Lumen Gentium,* 13). To use Saint Paul's words, I am "a servant of Christ Jesus, called to be an apostle and set apart to proclaim the Gospel of God" (Rom. 1:1). Like Saint Paul, I wish to proclaim to you and to the entire Church in Canada: *"I am not ashamed of the Gospel. It is the power of God leading everyone who believes in it to salvation"* (Rom. 1:16).

### Joins Missionaries Whose Efforts Contributed to Rebirth of Your Culture

2. I come to you, then, like so many missionaries before me who have *proclaimed the name of Jesus among the native peoples of Canada*—the Indians, Inuit and Metis— and have learned to love you and the spiritual and cultural treasures of your way of life. They have shown respect for your patrimony, your languages and your customs (see *Ad Gentes,* 26). As I remarked on the occasion of my previous visit, the "rebirth of your culture and traditions which you are experiencing today owes much to the pioneering and continuing efforts of missionaries." Indeed, the missionaries "remain among your best friends, devoting their lives to your service, as they preach the word of God" (Address at Yellow Knife, September 18, 1984, no. 2). I too come to you as a friend.

### The Gospel So Purifies Culture That We Can Now Say That Christ, in the Members of His Body, Is Indian

3. Such constructive service is *what Jesus wants of his disciples.* That has always been the Church's intention in making herself present in each place, in each people's history. When the faith was first preached among the native inhabitants of this land, "the worthy traditions of the Indian tribes were strengthened and enriched by the Gospel message. [Your forefathers] knew by instinct that the Gospel, far from destroying their authentic values and customs, had the power to purify and uplift the cultural heritage which they had received. . . . Thus not only is Christianity relevant to the Indian peoples, but Christ, in the members of his Body, is himself Indian" (Address at Shrine Field, Huronia, Ontario, September 15, 1984, no. 5).

## Comes to Proclaim Dignity and Support
## Right to Their Own Culture

In that spirit of respect and missionary service, I repeat what I said on the occasion of my previous visit, that my coming among you looks back to your past in order *to proclaim your dignity and support your destiny.* Today I repeat those words to you, and to all the aboriginal peoples of Canada and of the world. The Church extols the equal human dignity of all peoples and defends their right to uphold their own cultural character with its distinct traditions and customs.

## Affirms Right of Aboriginal Peoples to a Just Measure
## of Self-Governing Along with a Land Base
## and Adequate Resources for a Viable Economy

4. I am aware that the major aboriginal organizations—the Assembly of First Nations, the Inuit Tapirisat of Canada, the Metis National Council, and the Native Council of Canada—have been engaged in high-level talks with the prime minister and premiers regarding ways of protecting and enhancing the rights of the aboriginal peoples of Canada in the Constitution of this great country. Once again, I affirm your right to a "just and equitable measure of self-governing," along with a land base and adequate resources necessary for developing a viable economy for present and future generations (Address at Yellow Knife, September 18, 1984). I pray with you that a new round of conferences will be beneficial and that, with God's guidance and help, a path to a *just agreement* will be found to crown all the efforts being made.

## Catholic Bishops and Christian Leaders
## Have Called for a "New Covenant" to Ensure Rights

These endeavors, in turn, were supported by the Catholic Bishops of Canada and the leaders of the major Christian Churches and communities. Together, they have called for a "new covenant" *to ensure your basic aboriginal rights,* including your rights to self-government. Today, I pray that the Holy Spirit will help you all to find the just way so that Canada may be a model for the world in upholding the dignity of the aboriginal peoples.

## Recalls Pope Paul III, Who in 1537
## Proclaimed Rights of Native Peoples in *Pastorale Officium*

Let me recall that, at the dawn of the Church's presence in the New World, my predecessor *Pope Paul III* proclaimed in 1537 *the rights of the native peoples of those times.* He affirmed their dignity, defended their freedom and asserted that they could not be enslaved or deprived of their goods or ownership. That has always been the Church's position (see *Pastorale Officium,* 29 May 1537: DS 1495). My presence among you today marks my reaffirmation and reassertion of that teaching.

## Close Links Exist Between Teaching of the Gospel
## and Human Advancements

5. *There are very close links between the teaching of the Gospel of Jesus Christ and human advancement.* In his famous encyclical on the Development of Peoples, Pope Paul VI reflected on this reality against the background of the deep aspirations of peoples all over the world toward freedom and development. In his words, the fundamental desire of peoples everywhere is "to seek to do more, know more and have more in order to be more" (*Populorum Progressio,* 6). Is that not the deepest hope of the Indian, Metis and Inuit peoples of Canada? *To be more.* That is your destiny and that is the challenge that faces you. And today I have come in order to assure you that the Church stands with you as you strive to enhance your development as native peoples. Her missionary personnel and her institutions seek to work for that cause with you.

## Human Progress Is Not Just a Material Well-Being
## but Entails Religious and Spiritual Growth

6. At the same time, instructed by the teachings of Christ and enlightened by history, the Church appeals to all developing peoples everywhere not to limit the notion of *human progress* to the search for material well-being, at the cost of *religious and spiritual growth.* Paul VI wisely wrote that "personal and communal development would be threatened if the true scale of values were undermined. The desire for necessities is legitimate, and work undertaken to obtain them is a duty. . . . But . . . increased possession is not the ultimate goal of nations or of individuals" (*Populorum Progressio,* 18–19).

## True Values of Cultural and Religious Patrimony
## Must Not Be Sacrificed to Material Considerations

There are other values which are essential to life and society. Each people possesses a civilization handed down from its ancestors, involving institutions called for by its way of life, with its artistic, cultural and religious manifestations. *The true values contained in these realities must not be sacrificed to material considerations.* "A people that would act in this way would thereby lose the best of its patrimony; in order to live, it would be sacrificing its reasons for living" (*Populorum Progressio,* 40).

What Christ said about individuals applies also to peoples: "For what will it profit a man, if he gains the whole world and forfeits his life?" (Mt. 16:26). What would become of the "life" of the Indian, Inuit and Metis peoples if they cease to promote the values of the human spirit which have sustained them for generations? If they no longer see the earth and its benefits as given to them in trust by the Creator? If the bonds of family life are weakened, and instability undermines their societies? If they were to adopt an alien way of thinking, in which people are considered according to what they *have* and not according to what they *are?*

## Hunger for Justice, Peace, Love, Fortitude,
### Responsibility, Dignity Demands Spiritual Strength

The soul of the native peoples of Canada is *hungry for the Spirit of God*—because it is hungry for justice, peace, love, goodness, fortitude, responsibility and human dignity (see *Redemptor Hominis,* 18). This is indeed a decisive time in your history. It is essential that you be *spiritually strong and clear-sighted* as you build the future of your tribes and nations. Be assured that the Church will walk that path with you.

## Wish to Underline Dignity of Native Peoples
### and Show Concern for Their Future

7. By coming among you I have wished to underline your dignity as native peoples. With heartfelt concern for your future, I invite you to *renew your trust in God, who guides the destinies of all peoples.* The eternal Father has sent his Son to reveal to us the mystery of our living in this world and of our journeying to the everlasting life that is to come. In the Paschal Mystery of the Death and Resurrection of Jesus Christ, we have been reconciled with God and with each other. *Jesus Christ is our peace* (see Eph. 2:14).

"May the God of our Lord Jesus Christ, the Father of glory, grant you"—the aboriginal peoples of Canada—"*a spirit of wisdom and insight to know him clearly.* May he enlighten your innermost vision that you may know *the great hope to which he has called you*" (Eph. 1:17–18).

In the love of our Lord and Savior Jesus Christ, I bless each one of you and pray for the peace and happiness of your families, your bands and your nations. God be with you all!

## 51. HOMILY AT MASS CELEBRATED AT FORT SIMPSON

Seek the Lord while he may be found,
call him while he is near. (Is. 55:6)

Dear Brothers and Sisters,

## At Last, After Three Years,
### We Can Celebrate the Eucharist Together

1. We have waited a long time for this moment. Almost exactly three years ago my visit to Denendeh was prevented by weather conditions. Now, at last, God has brought us together and gives us the privilege of *celebrating the Eucharist of the Twenty-fifth Sunday of the Year.*

## Greetings to Authorities of Church, State,
## and of Tribes and First Nations

I greet my brother Bishops, especially Bishop Croteau of this Diocese of Mackenzie-Fort Smith, the priests, Religious and laity. I am grateful for the presence of Her Excellency the governor-general, and the representatives of Canadian public life. I am especially pleased to meet *the members of the tribes and nations,* descendants of the first inhabitants of these lands, who have repeatedly expressed the hope that I would come, and who have now gathered in large numbers for this festive occasion. I express my appreciation to the Assembly of First Nations, the Inuit Tapirisat of Canada, the Metis National Council and the Native Council of Canada for their collaboration in arranging this visit. I greet you all in the love of our Lord Jesus Christ. Once more I proclaim your human and Christian dignity and support you as you strive to attain your temporal and eternal destiny.

## Invitation to a Relationship of Trust with Creator
## as You Work to Consolidate Rights and Preserve Culture

2. *"Seek the Lord while he may be found, call him while he is near"* (Is. 55:6). These words from the first reading are a pressing invitation to raise your thoughts to the Father, from whom all good gifts come, that he may continue to guide your destiny as aboriginal peoples along the path of peace, in reconciliation with all others, in the experience of an effective solidarity on the part of the Church and of society in attaining your legitimate rights.

For untold generations, you the native peoples have lived in *a relationship of trust with the Creator,* seeing the beauty and the richness of the land as coming from his bountiful hand and as deserving wise use and conservation. Today you are working to preserve your traditions and consolidate your rights as aboriginal peoples. In this circumstance today's liturgy has a deep application.

## Isaiah Speaks to a People
## Yearning for Rebirth of Culture and Spiritual Renewal

3. The Prophet Isaiah is speaking to a people experiencing the sufferings of exile and *yearning for rebirth,* especially a renewal of the spirit through the rebirth of their culture and traditions. He seeks to console them and strengthen them in their task by reminding them that the Lord is not far from them (see Is. 55:6–9).

## Three Steps for Unveiling God's Presence
## in Personal/Collective Experience

But where is he to be found? How can we live in God's presence? The Prophet indicates three steps for unveiling the presence of God in our personal and collective experience.

### Call on Him in Prayer

First, he says: *"call him."* Yes, *in prayer we will find the Lord.* By calling upon him with trust you will discover that he is near.

### Conversion Leads to Pure Heart

But *prayer must come from a pure heart.* Consequently, the Prophet launches a call to *conversion:* "turn to the Lord for mercy . . . to our God, who is generous in forgiving" (Is. 55:7).

### Learn to Walk in the Ways of the Lord

And finally, we are called to *transform our lives* by learning to walk in the ways of the Lord: "As high as the heavens are above the earth, so high are my ways above your ways and my thoughts above your thoughts" (v. 9). *The covenant between God and his people* is constantly renewed when they invoke his merciful forgiveness and keep his commandments. God is our God and we are more and more his people.

### Unlimited Generosity of God Who Pays His Workers According to Each One's Needs

4. In the Gospel reading, Jesus speaks of the owner of an estate who goes out at different hours to hire workers for his land (see Mt. 20:1–16). The parable portrays *the unlimited generosity of God,* who is concerned about providing for the needs of all people. It is the landowner's compassion for the poor—in this case, the unemployed—that compels him to pay all the workers a wage that is calculated not only according to the laws of the marketplace, but according to the real needs of each one.

### Solidarity, Sharing and Community Mark Life in God's Kingdom

Life in God's kingdom is based on a true sense of solidarity, sharing and community. His is *a kingdom of justice, peace and love.* It is our task to build a society in which these Gospel values will be applied to every concrete situation and relationship.

### Parable of Cultivating the Lord's Vineyard Corresponds to Desire to Promote Religious, Cultural, Social Values

5. Today, this parable of cultivating the Lord's vineyard presents *a real challenge to aboriginal nations and communities.* As native peoples you are faced with a supreme test: that of promoting the religious, cultural and social values that will uphold your human dignity and ensure your future well-being. Your sense of sharing, your understanding of human community rooted in the family, the highly valued relationships

between your elders and your young people, your spiritual view of creation, which calls for responsible care and protection of the environment—all of these traditional aspects of your way of life need to be preserved and cherished.

### Your Concern Includes Openness to Wider Community in Respect and Collaboration

This concern with your own native life in no way excludes your *openness to the wider community*. It is a time for reconciliation, for new relationships of mutual respect and collaboration in reaching a truly just solution to unresolved issues.

### Visit Should Comfort and Encourage Catholic Communities in Process of Revitalization

6. Above all, I pray that my visit may be a time of comfort and encouragement for *the Catholic communities* among you. The pioneering efforts of the missionaries— to whom once again the Church expresses her profound and lasting gratitude—have given rise among you to living communities of faith and Christian life. The challenge is for you to become more active in the life of the Church. I understand that Bishop Croteau and the other Bishops of the North are seeking ways of *revitalizing the local Churches* so that you may become ever more effective witnesses of God's Kingdom of love, justice, peace, forgiveness and human solidarity.

### Young People Should Accept Rules of Ecclesial Responsibility in Priesthood and Religious Life

My dear Indian, Inuit and Metis friends, I appeal to all of you, especially the young people, to accept roles of responsibility and to contribute your talents to *building up the Church among your peoples*. I ask all the elders, leaders and parents to encourage and support vocations to the priesthood and religious life. In this way the Church will become ever more at home in your own cultures, evangelizing and strengthening your traditional values and customs.

### Proclaim Christ Your Friend and Your Savior

7. I have come today, dear brothers and sisters, *to proclaim to you Jesus Christ* and *to proclaim that he is your friend and your Savior*. In his name, with the love of the Good Shepherd, I repeat the words of the second reading: "Conduct yourselves in a way worthy of the Gospel of Christ" (Phil. 1:27). By doing this, Christ will be exalted in all your actions (see v. 20), and his peace will reign in your hearts.

### Renew Our Baptismal Promises to Renew Our Covenant with God

We are about to renew our *baptismal promises*. This is a solemn moment. By rejecting sin and evil, and by renewing our trust in the power of Christ's saving mysteries, we are, in fact, *reaffirming our covenant with God.* He is our God, and we are his people.

As we commit ourselves further to God's ways, may we be filled with the spiritual joy of Mary, the Mother of the Redeemer and our Mother in the faith. May her words express the deepest sentiments of our own hearts:

> My being proclaims the greatness of the Lord,
> *my spirit finds joy in God my savior . . .*
> *God who is mighty has done great things for me,*
> *holy is his name.* (Lk. 1:46–47, 49)

Amen.

Part II

## *Ad Limina* Addresses
## to the Bishops of
## the United States

Dear Brothers in our Lord Jesus Christ,

One of the greatest consolations of the new Pope is to know that he has the love and support of all the People of God. Like the Apostle Peter in the Acts of the Apostles, the Pope is powerfully sustained by the fervent prayers of the faithful. And so it is a special joy for me today to be with you, my brothers in the Episcopate, the pastors of local Churches in the United States of America. I know that you bring with you the deep faith of your people, their profound respect for the mystery of Peter's role in God's design for the universal Church, and their love for Christ and his brethren. In the providence of God I have been able to visit your land and to know some of your people personally. Thus our being together is itself a celebration of the unity of the Church. It is also an attestation of our acceptance of Jesus Christ in the totality of his mystery of salvation.

As Servant and Pastor and Father of the universal Church, I wish at this moment to express my love for all those who are specially called to work for the Gospel, all those who actively collaborate with you in your Dioceses to build up the Kingdom of God. Like yourselves, I learned as a Bishop to understand firsthand the ministry of priests, the problems affecting their lives, the splendid efforts they are making, the sacrifices that are an integral part of their service to God's people. Like yourselves, I am fully aware of how much Christ depends on his priests in order to fulfill in time his mission of Redemption. And like yourselves I have worked with the Religious, endeavoring to give witness to the esteem that the Church has for them in their vocation of consecrated love, and urging them always to full generous collaboration in the corporate life of the ecclesial community. All of us have seen abundant examples of authentic *evangelica testificatio.* Now I ask you all to take my greetings to the clergy and Religious, to assure them all of my understanding, my solidarity, my love in Christ Jesus and in the Church.

I am aware also that my pastoral obligations extend to the whole community of the faithful. During this audience I would like to offer a few basic reflections that I am firmly convinced are relevant for each local Church in its entirety. In establishing priorities, my predecessors Paul VI and John Paul I chose topics of extreme importance, and all of their exhortations and directives to the American Bishops I ratify with full knowledge and personal conviction. The very last *ad Limina* address (and the only one given by my immediate predecessor) was on the Christian family. Already during the first weeks of my Pontificate I too have had occasion to speak on this theme and to extol its importance. Yes, may all the wonderful Christian families in God's Church know that the Pope is with them, united in prayer, in hope, in confidence. The Pope confirms them in their mission given them by Christ himself, proclaims their dignity, and blesses all their efforts.

## Role of Doctrine

I am thoroughly convinced that families everywhere and the great family of the Catholic Church will be greatly served—a real pastoral service will be rendered to them—if a renewed emphasis is placed on the role of doctrine in the life of the Church. In God's plan a new Pontificate is always a new beginning, evoking fresh hopes and giving new opportunities for reflection, for conversion, for prayer and for resolves.

## Purity of Doctrine

Under the care of Mary, Mother of God and Mother of the Church, I wish to commit my Pontificate to the continued genuine application of the Second Vatican Council, under the action of the Holy Spirit. And in this regard, nothing is more enlightening than to recall the exact words with which, on the opening day, John XXIII wished to spell out the orientation of this great ecclesial event: "The greatest concern of the Ecumenical Council is this: that the sacred deposit of Christian doctrine should be more effectively guarded and taught." This far-seeing vision of Pope John is valid today. It was the only sound basis for an Ecumenical Council aimed at pastoral renewal; it is the only sound basis for all our pastoral endeavors as Bishops of the Church of God. This then is my own deepest hope today for the pastors of the Church in America, as well as for all the pastors of the universal Church: "that the sacred deposit of Christian doctrine should be more effectively guarded and taught." The sacred deposit of God's word, handed on by the Church, is the joy and strength of our people's lives. It is the only pastoral solution to the many problems of our day. To present this sacred deposit of Christian doctrine in all its purity and integrity, with all its exigencies and in all its power, is a holy pastoral responsibility; it is, moreover, the most sublime service we can render.

## Sound Discipline

And the second hope that I would express today is a hope for the preservation of the great discipline of the Church—a hope eloquently formulated by John Paul I on the day after his election: "We wish to maintain intact the great discipline of the Church in the life of priests and of the faithful, as the history of the Church, enriched by experience has presented it throughout the centuries, with examples of holiness and heroic perfection, both in the exercise of the evangelical virtues and in service to the poor, the humble, the defenseless."

## Collegiality and Unity

These two hopes do not exhaust our aspirations or our prayers, but they are worthy of intense pastoral efforts and apostolic diligence. These efforts and diligence on our part are in turn an expression of real love and concern for the flock entrusted to our care by Jesus Christ, the chief Shepherd—a pastoral charge to be exercised within the unity of the universal Church and in the context of the collegiality of the Episcopate.

These hopes for the life of the Church—purity of doctrine and sound discipline—intimately depend on every new generation of priests, who with the generosity of love continue the Church's commitment to the Gospel. For this reason, Paul VI showed great wisdom in asking the American Bishops "to fulfill with loving personal attention your great pastoral responsibility to your seminarians: know the content of their courses, encourage them to love the word of God and never to be ashamed of the seeming folly of the Cross" (Address of June 20, 1977). And this is my ardent desire today, that a new emphasis on the importance of doctrine and discipline will be the postconciliar contribution of your seminaries, so that "the word of the Lord may speed on and triumph" (2 Thes. 3:1).

And in all your pastoral labors you can be sure that the Pope is united with you and close to you in the love of Jesus Christ. All of us have a single goal: to prove faithful to the pastoral trust committed to us, to lead the People of God "in right paths for his name's sake" (Ps. 23:3), so that, with pastoral accountability, we can say with Jesus to the Father: "As long as I was with them, I guarded them with your name which you gave me. I kept careful watch, and not one of them was lost" (Jn. 17:12).

In the name of Jesus, peace to you and to all your people. With my Apostolic Blessing.

## FIRST *AD LIMINA* ADDRESS TO THE BISHOPS OF THE UNITED STATES

### APRIL 15, 1983

Dear Brothers in our Lord Jesus Christ,

1. It is a great joy for me to welcome you as the first group of American Bishops making your *ad Limina* visit in this Holy Year of the Redemption. I wish to tell you immediately how close I feel to the faithful of the New York region and of the Military Ordinariate and to all the faithful of the United States, who are very much in my thoughts and prayers. But I wish to emphasize, above all, my spiritual union with you, my brother Bishops. I am sure that all of you, like me, find special strength in our meeting today, because, in the power of the Holy Spirit, we are actuating the episcopal collegiality of the Church. For you, moreover, it is right and just to know that *you do not work and toil alone*. You are supported by the Successor of Peter and the entire College of Bishops.

### Jesus Christ, Redeemer and Reconciler

2. Today, I wish to reflect with you on our common mission as Bishops: *to proclaim Jesus Christ, the Redeemer and Reconciler of humanity*. I wish to do so within

the double context of the Holy Year of the Redemption and the forthcoming Synod of Bishops that has as its theme "Reconciliation and Penance in the Mission of the Church." In my letter of January 25 last to the Bishops of the Church, I endeavored to point out how these two events are intimately linked: "Reconciliation," I wrote, "is nothing other than the Redemption which the Father has offered to every person in the Death and Resurrection of his Son, and which he continues still today to offer to every sinner, waiting, like the Father in the parable of the prodigal son, for the repentant return of his son through conversion" (no. 2).

### Bishops' Ministry of Reconciliation

The Synod, linked to the Holy Year, will seek ways of more effectively proclaiming the reconciliation of the Redemption and of eliciting from the faithful a response of conversion and penance to God's call; and we can be sure that the Synod will bring immense insights to its collegial task. But already as Bishops we have the task every day of proclaiming reconciliation according to the rich apostolic patrimony of the Church. Ours is truly, in the expression of Saint Paul, "the ministry of reconciliation" (2 Cor. 5:18).

### Implications of Proclaiming Reconciliation

3. And today I would propose for your consideration this *ministry of reconciliation in all its implications*. We are truly called to proclaim the reconciliation of humanity with God. This means reviving a sense of God, of his word, of his commandments—of the need for accepting his will as the real criterion for human action. Proclaiming reconciliation means reviving a sense of sin among our people; this in turn can lead us to recognize the roots of human responsibility in the varied fields of economic, social, historical, cultural and political ills. When man understands his alienation from God, he can begin to perceive how he is in opposition with his brothers and sisters and with creation itself. The proclamation can then become an effective call to peace. Proclaiming reconciliation means insisting on the greatness of God's pardon and on his compassionate love. To offer the response of the Redemption to a world made conscious of sin is to proclaim the revelation of mercy and the message of hope which is in "Christ Jesus our hope" (1 Tm. 1:1).

### Promote the Sacrament of Penance

4. To proclaim reconciliation means, in a particular way, *promoting the Sacrament of Penance*. It means stressing the importance of the Sacrament as it relates to conversion, to Christian growth, to the very renewal of society that cannot be healed without the forgiveness of sins.

## The Importance of Personal Conversion

It is our role as Bishops to point out that both original and personal sin are at the basis of the evils that affect society and that there is a constant conflict between good and evil, between Christ and Satan. It is salutary for our people to realize that they are involved in the continuation of the paschal conflict—*Mors et vita duello conflixere mirando*—but that they are fortified by the strength of the Risen Christ. Only when the faithful recognize sin in their own lives are they ready to understand reconciliation and to open their hearts to penance and personal conversion. Only then are they able to contribute to the renewal of society, since personal conversion is also the only way that leads to the lasting renewal of society. *This personal conversion, by divine precept, is intimately linked to the Sacrament of Penance.*

## Personal Conversion Linked to the Sacrament of Penance

Just five years ago this month, Paul VI spoke to the New York Bishops during the last *ad Limina* visit. With prophetic insistence he emphasized both the importance of conversion and its relationship to the Sacrament of Penance. He stated at that time: "conversion constitutes the goal to be achieved by our apostolic ministry: to awaken a consciousness of sin in its perennial and tragic reality, a consciousness of its personal and social dimensions, together with a realization that 'grace has far surpassed sin'" (Rom. 5:20). His solicitude for conversion and its various sacramental aspects is my own today. His words retain their total relevance for the Church in the United States and throughout the world, and *I propose them once again to your pastoral zeal and responsibility.*

## The Special Priority of the Confessional

In particular he requested that priests be encouraged by the Bishops *to give special priority to the ministry of the Sacrament of Penance.* He wrote: "if priests deeply understand how closely they collaborate, through the Sacrament of Penance, with the Savior in the work of conversion, they will give themselves with ever greater zeal to this ministry. More Confessors will readily be available to the faithful. Other works, for lack of time, may have to be postponed or even abandoned, but not the Confessional." Our ministry as priests and Bishops certainly means that we are called upon to go in search of those who have sinned, so as to invite them to return to the fullness of the Father's love. In doing so, let us hold up hope and proclaim mercy. Let us, together with our priests, concentrate the attention of the faithful on the person of Jesus Christ the Redeemer, who personally forgives and reconciles each individual. For the glory of the Father let us encourage our people to understand the great truth that "the blood of Jesus his Son cleanses us from all sin" (1 Jn. 1:7). Yes, dear brothers, let us emphasize over and over again the immense value of a personal encounter with the God of mercy *through individual confession.* Let us, with our people, raise a hymn of praise to "the blood of Christ, who through the eternal Spirit offered himself without blemish to God" (Heb. 9:14).

## The Exceptional Nature of General Absolution

5. In speaking to the group of New York Bishops, Paul VI also dealt *with the question of general absolution* and its proper application. The experience of the universal Church confirms the need on the part of all the Bishops for further pastoral vigilance. The new Code of Canon Law points out again the exceptional character of this practice, repeating that general absolution is not envisioned solely because of large numbers of penitents assembled for a great celebration or pilgrimage: *ratione solius magni concursus paenitentium, qualis haberi potest in magna aliqua festivitate aut peregrinatione* (can. 961, 1, 2).

## The Importance of First Confession

I would ask once again for your zealous pastoral and collegial solicitude to help ensure that these norms, as well as *the norms regulating the First Confession of children,* are understood and properly applied. The treasures of Christ's love in the Sacrament of Penance are so great that children too must be initiated into them. The patient effort of parents, teachers and priests needed to prepare children for this Sacrament are of great value for the whole Church.

## Need to Promote the Sacrament of Penance

6. In this Holy Year of the Redemption I would ask that *a whole pastoral program be developed around the Sacrament of Penance and be* effected by practical means. This will include a renewed effort at catechesis, so that the Sacrament can be made a dynamic part of the lives of young and old alike. Frequent penitential celebrations, including the individual confession and absolution of sins, will be a great help to the faithful in grasping better the realities of sin and grace, and in experiencing the great joy of meeting Christ in an encounter of love, mercy and pardon. The availability of Confessors, emphasized and publicized in different ways, such as Church bulletins, can give a great impetus to the faithful to go to Confession, since God's grace has already awakened a desire or a need for the Sacrament in the hearts of many. Something totally consonant with our priestly and apostolic ministry is for us to invite the faithful repeatedly to reconciliation with God and with the ecclesial community. As pastors, we must be humbly conscious of our weaknesses and our sins, and yet, in God's plan of mercy, we have been given the charism and obligation to call the faithful to repentance and conversion, and to lead the way.

## Lenten Celebration of the Sacrament

As mentioned in the *Ordo Paenitentiae,* the celebration of the Sacrament of Penance is always permitted during any season or on any day (see no. 12). Yet it is *particularly appropriate during Lent,* so as to prepare the faithful for a fitting celebration of the Paschal Mystery, the grace of which is so effectively presented to them during the liturgy of the Sacred Triduum. The faithful are certainly to be encouraged to confess their sins before these last days of Holy Week as a spiritual preparation for them; at the same time this will help to diminish the heavy pressure on Confessors. Nevertheless, I would ask that Bishops urge their priests to do everything possible in their pastoral generosity and zeal to make Confessions available also during the last days of Holy Week. There will inevitably be people who, in spite of everything, will need this opportunity of grace. This generous sacrifice on the part of priests will allow them to share even more deeply in the Paschal Mystery and will be amply rewarded by Christ.

The Holy Year is also an excellent time to help our people reflect on the rich content of the "Our Father" as a prayer of reconciliation: "Forgive us our trespasses as we forgive those who trespass against us." By the grace of God and through your apostolic ministry may the Holy Year find the Church ever more as a reconciling and reconciled community, attentive *to the word of God as the criteria according to which the whole "ministry of reconciliation" is applied.*

## Criteria of Ministry Is in the Word of God

7. As we pursue our ministry of reconciliation, let us always look to both aspects of the person's return to God: the reconciling action of God and the response of the individual through penance and conversion. There is no doubt that penance and conversion involve great effort, and are sometimes extremely painful. There is no doubt that the word of God is demanding, and sometimes the human being is confused in concrete situations which call for much more than human effort and which require humble and persevering prayer. And yet as pastors *we must not underestimate the limitless power of Christ's grace,* nor can we attempt to alter the requirements of the Gospel. We are accountable to Jesus Christ the Good Shepherd for exercising true pastoral compassion, and we must not be surprised if the world falsely equates fidelity to the eternal word of God with insensitivity to human weakness. On the contrary, the Redemption touches hearts precisely through the revelation of God's word. What we must do is to give the prophetic example of reconciliation, conversion and penance in our own lives, proclaiming by word and example that Jesus Christ is the only Redeemer and Reconciler of humanity.

## Collegial Unity: Guarantee of Effectiveness

Let us, dear brothers, walk this path together, united with Mary the Mother of Jesus and united among ourselves and with the worldwide Episcopate. In this great bond of collegiality between all the Bishops and the Successor of Peter there is strength for your pastoral initiatives and the important guarantee of their supernatural effectiveness. In the ministry of reconciliation, in the dispensation of the mystery of the Redemption through the Sacrament of Penance, supernatural effectiveness is of supreme importance. Be convinced, dear brothers, that *if we walk together,* the Lord

Jesus will reveal himself to us; he will convert us ever further to his love; *he will use us as servant pastors to bring his Redemption to the world.*

## SECOND *AD LIMINA* ADDRESS TO THE BISHOPS OF THE UNITED STATES

### JULY 9, 1983

Dear Brothers in our Lord Jesus Christ,

1. It is a very great joy for me to be with you today during this collegial meeting. You come from Dioceses stretching across your country: from Baltimore, the primatial See of the United States, to Fairbanks in Alaska. You bring with you the hopes and aspirations, the joys and the sorrows of a great number of the Catholic faithful of America. Sharing, as we do, a common pastoral responsibility for these local Churches of yours, we have at the same time the opportunity to offer them to Jesus Christ, the Chief Pastor of the universal Church. I ask him, by the power of his Resurrection, to sustain you all in the hope of your calling: to strengthen your priests, Religious and laity—the whole People of God whom you serve with dedication, sacrifice and love.

In examining the many relevant topics which the Episcopal Conference offered to my consideration, and for which I thank you, I have noted one that concerns *the celebration of Sunday*—the strengthening of the Lord's Day. And I am pleased to reflect briefly with you on this issue of such capital importance, and in particular on the Sunday *Eucharistic celebration.* I pray that you in turn may confirm your people in a matter that profoundly touches their lives as individuals and as a community. Throughout the United States there has been a superb history of Eucharistic participation by the people, and for this we must all thank God.

### Sunday Celebrates Christ's Resurrection

2. In the whole tradition of the Church, the Sunday Eucharist is a special expression of *the Church's faith in the Resurrection of Jesus Christ.* It is by virtue of the Holy Spirit that the Church calls the faithful together to proclaim their faith in this mystery, as well as in the mystery of their "birth unto hope which draws its life from the Resurrection of Jesus Christ from the dead" (1 Pt. 1:13). The liturgical assembly built up around the Eucharist has always been, from its apostolic origin, the special mark of the Church's celebration of the Lord's Day, and the Second Vatican Council has reiterated the importance of Sunday Mass (see *Sacrosanctum Concilium,* 106). It is in fact the whole Paschal Mystery that the People of God are called to celebrate and to participate in each Sunday: The Passion and the Resurrection and the glorification of the Lord Jesus.

## Sunday Eucharist Builds Up Church Community

3. *The vitality of the Church* depends to a great extent on the Sunday Eucharistic celebration, in which *the mystery of salvation* is made present to God's people and enters into their lives. In the expression of *Lumen Gentium,* God wills to save and sanctify us as a people (see no. 9), and there is no moment in which we are more intimately united as a community than during Sunday Mass.

It is at this moment that *the Eucharist builds the Church* and is, at one and the same time, the "sign of community and the cause of its growth"—as you yourselves pointed out some time ago in your pastoral message *To Teach as Jesus Did* (no. 24).

## Worship Renews the Liturgical Dignity of the People of God

The *whole life of the ecclesial community* is linked to the Sunday Eucharist. It is here that Jesus Christ prays with his people, who become with him a people of worship, adoring the Father "in spirit and in truth" (Jn. 4:23). *The aspect of worship is central to an understanding of the full dignity of the People of God.* Jesus Christ presents his brothers and sisters to his Father as a worshiping people, a liturgical community. And in this role they fulfill the purpose of all liturgy, which the Second Vatican Council powerfully describes as being "above all the worship of the divine majesty" (*Sacrosanctum Concilium,* 33).

I am convinced, venerable and dear brothers, that we can render a great pastoral service to the people by emphasizing their liturgical dignity and by directing their thoughts to the purposes of worship. When our people, through the grace of the Holy Spirit, realize that they are called to be "a chosen race, a royal priesthood, a holy nation" (1 Pt. 2:9), and that they are called to adore and thank the Father in union with Jesus Christ, *an immense power is unleashed* in their Christian lives. When they realize that they actually have a Sacrifice of praise and expiation to offer together with Jesus Christ, when they realize that all their prayers of petition are united to an infinite act of the praying Christ, then there is fresh hope and new encouragement for the Christian people. Young people have shown themselves particularly sensitive to this truth.

## Participation: Source of the Christian Spirit

4. Essential to the whole liturgical renewal of this century, and confirmed by its experience, is the principle that the *full and active participation* by all the people in the liturgy is the "primary and indispensable source from which the faithful are to derive the true Christian spirit" (*Sacrosanctum Concilium,* 14). And from our own experiences—yours and mine—we know how much our people are capable of doing, how great their Christian contribution to the world is, when the Lord Jesus touches their lives, when they themselves enter into his Sacrifice. Let us continue, dear brothers, to strengthen the understanding of the faithful and their appreciation of their role in Eucharistic worship. And let us continue to work to bring about that full and

active participation which the Church wills for everyone, but always according to the differing roles of the various members of the one Body of Christ.

### The Power of the Eucharist Reinforces Christian Service

5. In these differing roles of Eucharistic participation, the unity of the whole Body is ensured and the dignity of each one respected. For the laity it is a question of *actuating the call to worship inherent in their Baptism and Confirmation*. For priests, it is also a question of performing the irreplaceable service of making Christ's Sacrifice present in the Church. For all the members of the Church, the Eucharist, and especially the Sunday Eucharist, is the source and summit of all Christian living. All the activities of our people—all their efforts to live the Gospel, to bear witness to Christ, to put his word into practice in their family life and in society—all of these efforts are ennobled and supported by the power of the Eucharist, in particular at the Sunday celebration.

All the striving of the laity *to consecrate the secular field of activity to God* finds inspiration and magnificent confirmation in the Eucharistic Sacrifice. Participating in the Eucharist is only a small portion of the laity's week, but the total effectiveness of their lives and all Christian renewal depends on it: the primary and indispensable source of the true Christian spirit!

### Eucharistic Worship Reinforces
### Every Form of Ecclesial Service

6. In promoting the participation of the faithful in the liturgy of the word and of the Eucharist, we are rendering *an eminently pastoral service* and contributing to so many aspects of the Church's life: marriage and the family are fortified; evangelization is fostered; human rights find their confirmation in the liberating message of Jesus, which is fully proclaimed in the sacramental renewal of the Paschal Mystery. Through the proclamation of God's word, zeal for catechesis is nurtured in the Christian people; vocations are offered by Christ; and light and strength are given to the faithful to meet human problems, even the most vexing and difficult ones. And all of this spells out the relevance of the Eucharistic mystery and its celebration for God's people. All of this confirms the importance of the Sunday liturgy in the life of the community.

7. It is also extremely useful to recall that the Second Vatican Council, in its treatment of Christian education, emphasizes as one of the purposes of Christian education that the baptized may learn to adore God the Father "in spirit and in truth" (see *Gravissimum Educationis*, 2). *Education,* too, like other Christian activity, *is oriented to the worship of God.*

### Sacredness of the Lord's Day

8. I wish at this time to support you in all your efforts to help the faithful celebrate worthily their Christian dignity in the sacred liturgy. May the People of

God in America be led to an ever greater conviction of *the sacredness of the Lord's Day*. Despite changes in society and different types of pressures, as well as various difficulties, may they continue to the full extent of their power to maintain that great tradition fostered in your land of sanctifying the Sunday and the Holy Days of Obligation. May each of the faithful realize the privilege that is his or hers to be part of the praying Church: to be able to say to God: "By your gift I will utter praise in the vast assembly" (Ps. 22:26). Besides the Eucharistic liturgy, the other aspects of the Sunday celebration—the Liturgy of the Hours, rest and freedom from work, the performance of charitable works and the broadcasting of religious radio and television programs where possible—contribute to the Christian dimension of society and help lift up people's hearts to God the Creator and Redeemer of all.

Dear brothers, be assured that, in the charity of Christ, I am close to you and to all your brothers in the priesthood, who share with you the pastoral service of making God's people *ever more conscious of their dignity as a people of worship*.

United with each other, and with the other Bishops of America, and together with the universal Church, let us work with all our energy to encourage our people in their generous efforts to maintain unaltered the apostolic tradition of participating in the Sunday Eucharist. There are many other considerations that could complete these reflections. Let us, however, as pastors united with our people, proclaim without ceasing *the faith of the Church* that is at the basis of every Sunday Eucharist: the Resurrection of our Lord and Savior Jesus Christ from the dead. It is he whom we await in joyful hope; and it is in the name of the Risen Jesus that all our episcopal, pastoral and collegial ministry is exercised. Praised be Jesus Christ!

## THIRD *AD LIMINA* ADDRESS TO THE
## BISHOPS OF THE UNITED STATES

### SEPTEMBER 5, 1983

Venerable and dear Brothers in our Lord Jesus Christ,

The experience of the whole postconciliar life of the Church confirms *just how much the renewal willed by the Second Vatican Council depends on the ministry of the Bishops*: on the way this ministry is conceived, on the way it is exercised. As Bishops gathered collegially in the Holy Spirit, let us reflect together on certain aspects of this ministry of ours.

### Bishops' Holiness: Credible Witness to the Living Lord

1. It is clear that *the incarnational economy of salvation* is continued through us as servant pastors chosen to lead God's people to the fullness of life that exists in Jesus Christ the Incarnate Word of God. To understand the Church of the Incarnate Word, in which all grace is dispensed through the sacred humanity of the

Son of God, is to understand how important it is for every Bishop in his own humanity to be *a living sign of Jesus Christ* (see *Lumen Gentium,* 21). We who are invested with the mission of the Good Shepherd have to make him visible to our people. We must respond in a specific way to the cry that comes from every corner of the world: "We wish to see Jesus" (Jn. 12:21). And the world wants to see him in us.

Our effectiveness in showing Jesus to the world—the final effectiveness of all our pastoral leadership—depends to a great extent on the authenticity of our discipleship. Our own *union with Jesus Christ* determines *the credibility of our witness.* Precisely for this reason we are called to exercise prophetically the role of holiness: to anticipate in our own lives that state of holiness to which we are striving to lead our people.

## Personal Conversion Needed

In order to be a living sign of Jesus Christ in holiness of life, we Bishops experience *the need for personal conversion*—deep personal conversion, sustained conversion, renewed conversion. And I, John Paul II, your fellow apostle and your brother Bishop in the See of Rome, in order to be faithful to the fullness of my mandate, to confirm my brothers (see Lk. 22:32), while being conscious of my own weaknesses and sins, feel the need to speak to you about conversion—the conversion to which Jesus invites you and me. And you, on your part, in the name of Jesus, while still desiring ever greater personal conversion, must call your people to conversion, especially in this Holy Year of the Redemption. I emphasized this in my address last April to the Bishops of New York, and I pointed out its special relevance for Religious in the letter that I wrote to all the Bishops of the United States at Easter. No one of us is exempt from this call, this invitation, this summons to conversion that comes from the Lord Jesus. Only through conversion and the holiness of our lives can we succeed in being living signs of Jesus Christ. Our whole humanity will communicate Christ only if we live in union with him, only if, through conversion, we "put on the Lord Jesus Christ" (Rom. 13:14).

## Bishops Express Christ's Universal Charity

2. In particular, the Bishop is *a sign of the love of Jesus Christ*: he expresses to all individuals and groups of whatever tendency—with a universal charity—the love of the Good Shepherd. His love embraces sinners with an easiness and naturalness that mirrors the redeeming love of the Savior. To those in need, in trouble and in pain he offers the love of understanding and consolation. In a special way the Bishop is the sign of Christ's love *for his priests.* He manifests to them *the love of friendship*—just as he once liked to experience it from his Bishop—a friendship that knows how to communicate esteem, and through warm human exchange can help a brother priest even rise from moments of discouragement, sadness or dejection.

## Bishops Witness to the Unity
## Between Christ's Love and Truth

3. As a sign of Christ's love, the Bishop is also *a sign of Christ's compassion,* since he represents Jesus the high priest who is able to sympathize with human weakness, the one who was tempted in every way we are and yet never sinned (see Heb. 4:15). The consciousness on the part of the Bishop of personal sin, coupled with repentance and with the forgiveness received from the Lord, makes his human expression of compassion ever more authentic and credible. But the compassion that he signifies and lives in the name of Jesus can *never be a pretext* for him to equate God's merciful understanding of sin and love for sinners with a denial of the full liberating truth that Jesus proclaimed. Hence there can be no dichotomy between the Bishop as a sign of Christ's compassion and as a sign of Christ's truth.

The Bishop, precisely because he is compassionate and understands the weakness of humanity and the fact that its needs and aspirations can only be satisfied by the full truth of creation and Redemption, *will proclaim without fear or ambiguity the many controverted truths* of our age. He will proclaim them with pastoral love, in terms that will never unnecessarily offend or alienate his hearers, but he will proclaim them *clearly,* because he knows the liberating quality of truth.

## The Indissolubility of Marriage
## and Other Points of Sexual Ethics

Hence the compassionate Bishop proclaims *the indissolubility of marriage,* as did the Bishops of the United States when in their splendid pastoral letter *To Live in Christ Jesus* they wrote: "The covenant between a man and a woman in Christian marriage is as indissoluble and irrevocable as God's love for his people and Christ's love for his Church." The compassionate Bishop will proclaim the incompatibility of premarital sex and homosexual activity with God's plan for human love; at the same time, with all his strength he will try to assist those who are faced with difficult moral choices. With equal compassion he will proclaim the doctrine of *Humanae Vitae* and *Familiaris Consortio* in its full beauty, not passing over in silence the unpopular truth that artificial birth control is against God's law. He will speak out for the rights of the unborn, the weak, the handicapped, the poor and the aged, no matter how current popular opinion views these issues. With personal humility and pastoral zeal the Bishop will strive to discern, not alone but in union with the universal Episcopate, the signs of the times and their true application to the modern world. With his brother Bishops he will work to ensure the participation of every category of people in the life and mission of the Church, in accordance with the truth of their calling.

## Promote the Dignity of Women, Not Their Ordination

This zeal will be manifested in supporting *the dignity of women,* and every legitimate freedom that is consonant with their human nature and their womanhood. The

Bishop is called upon to oppose any and all discrimination of women by reason of sex. In this regard he must likewise endeavor to explain as cogently as he can that the Church's teaching on the exclusion of women from priestly ordination is extraneous to the issue of discrimination and that it is linked rather to Christ's own design for his priesthood. The Bishop must give proof of his pastoral ability and leadership by withdrawing all support from individuals or groups who in the name of progress, justice or compassion, or for any other alleged reason, promote the ordination of women to the priesthood.

In so doing, such individuals or groups are in effect damaging the very dignity of women that they profess to promote and advance. All efforts made against the truth are destined to produce not only failure but also acute personal frustration. Whatever the Bishop can do to prevent this failure and frustration by explaining the truth is an act not only of *pastoral charity* but of *prophetic leadership*.

### Fidelity to Church Teaching

4. In a word, the Bishop as a sign of compassion is at the same time *a sign of fidelity to the doctrine of the Church*. The Bishop stands with his brother Bishops and the Roman Pontiff as a teacher of the Catholic faith, whose purity and integrity is guaranteed by the presence of the Holy Spirit in the Church.

### Proclaims the Gospel as Truly the Word of God

Like Jesus, the Bishop proclaims the Gospel of salvation *not as a human consensus but as a divine revelation*. The whole framework of his preaching is centered on Jesus, who states: "I say only what the Father has taught me" (Jn. 8:28). Hence the Bishop becomes a sign of fidelity because of his sharing in the special pastoral and apostolic charism with which the Spirit of Truth endows the College of Bishops. When this charism is exercised by the Bishops within the unity of that College, Christ's promise to the Apostles is actuated: "He who hears you hears me, and he who rejects you rejects me, and he who rejects me rejects him who sent me" (Lk. 10:16). Christ's promise, by guaranteeing the authority of the Bishops' teachings and imposing on the faithful the obligation of obedience, makes it crystal clear why the individual Bishop has to be a sign of fidelity to the doctrine of the Church.

And in this important task of proclaiming the Gospel in all its purity and power, with all its demands, the Bishop accepts willingly the apostolic challenge that Paul put to Timothy: "I charge you to preach the word, to stay with the task whether convenient or inconvenient—correcting, reproving, appealing—constantly teaching and never losing patience" (2 Tm. 4:2).

### Witnesses to the Certainty of Faith

5. And because episcopal teaching, guaranteed by a charism, must be nothing else than the word of God in its application to human life, the Bishop becomes for

his people *a sign of the certainty of faith*. Called to proclaim salvation in Jesus Christ and to lead the flock effectively to this goal, the Bishop inculcates certainty in the people of God, who know that he will listen to them, accept their numerous insights into the truth of the faith, and impose no unnecessary burdens on their lives. And yet they know that the Church's teaching which he announces is much more than human wisdom. The Church, through her Bishops, rejects all triumphalism; she publicly denies that she has ready-made solutions to all particular problems, but she definitely claims to possess the light of revealed truth—which transcends all human consensus—and she works with all her strength so that this light of faith will illumine the experiences of humanity (see *Gaudium et Spes*, 33).

### Teacher of Prayer

6. In communicating to the People of God the certainty of faith and the tranquillity that flows therefrom, the Bishop has a special role to play as *a teacher of prayer*. How closely the Bishop's role is linked here to that of Jesus the teacher, who so zealously responded to the needs of the disciples to learn how to pray. Surely there are millions of voices rising up from every corner of your combined Dioceses, directed to you and pleading: "Teach us to pray" (Lk. 11:1). In giving the same response that Jesus gave, you open up to your people the immense treasures of the "Our Father," initiating them into *the dialogue of salvation,* catechizing them in the mystery of their divine adoption, and bearing witness to the exquisite humanity of the Son of God, who knows more than anyone else the needs and aspirations of his brothers and sisters.

And through his personal prayer the Bishop will convincingly communicate the value of prayer and he himself become more and more *a living sign of the praying Christ,* who submits all his pastoral initiatives to his Father, including the very choice of his Apostles (see Lk. 6:12–13).

### Choose Able Teachers of Faith

7. *The choice of Bishops,* successors of the Apostles, is as important today for the Church as was the choice of the Twelve for Jesus. The recommendation and selection of every new Bishop deserves the greatest prayerful reflection on the part of all those associated with the process of the selection of candidates. In this regard, the Bishops themselves have a special role in proposing those whom they judge the most suitable, with God's help, to be living signs of Jesus Christ—priests who have already proven themselves as *teachers of the faith as it is proclaimed by the Magisterium of the Church* and who, in the words of Paul's pastoral advice to Titus, "hold fast to the authentic message" (Ti. 1:9). As so many Bishops in this postconciliar period lay down their pastoral charge and render account for their flocks, it is a great consolation of conscience for them to know that they have proposed to the Roman Pontiff as candidates for the episcopal office only those priests who will be true shepherds in each aspect of the one pastoral mission of Jesus to teach, govern and sanctify God's people.

## Sign of Unity of the Universal Church

8. It is important for the episcopal candidate, as for the Bishop himself, to be *a sign of the unity of the universal Church*. The unity of the College of Bishops through *collegialitas affectiva* and *collegialitas effectiva* is an apt instrument to serve the unity of Christ's Church. Never is the unity of the local Church stronger and more secure, never is the ministry of the local Bishop more effective than when the local Church under the pastoral leadership of the local Bishop proclaims in word and deed the universal faith, when it is open in charity to all the needs of the universal Church, and when it embraces faithfully the Church's universal discipline.

The Bishop is thus called to be *a sign of Catholic solidarity* in the local Church, which is the miniature reflection of the one, holy, Catholic and apostolic Church, which really and truly does subsist in the local Church.

## Sign of Contradiction

Finally, it is evident in all of this that the Bishop, a living sign of Jesus Christ, must vindicate to himself the title and accept the consequences of the fact that he is, with Jesus Christ, *a sign of contradiction*. Despite every dutiful effort to pursue the dialogue of salvation, the Bishop must announce to the young and old, to the rich and poor, to the powerful and weak the fullness of truth, which sometimes irritates and offends, even if it always liberates. The justice and holiness that he proclaims are born of this truth (see Eph. 4:24). The Bishop is aware that he must preach "Jesus Christ and him crucified" (1 Cor. 2:2), the same Jesus who said: "If anyone would come after me, let him deny himself and take up his cross and follow me" (Mt. 16:24).

Precisely because he cannot renounce the preaching of the Cross, the Bishop will be called upon over and over again *to accept criticism,* and to admit failure in obtaining a consensus of doctrine acceptable to everyone. As a living sign of Christ, he must be with Christ a sign of fidelity and therefore a sign of contradiction.

## Signs of Hope in the Living Christ

10. Venerable and dear brothers, these reflections, partial though they may be, speak to us of the reality of the Episcopate of our Lord Jesus Christ in which we share. I offer them to you as *the expression of our common strivings,* and perhaps to some extent of our common failings. As your brother in the See of Peter, humbled and repentant, I offer them as *a challenge of grace* in a moment of grace, a moment of collegiality, and a moment of fraternal love. I offer them to your apostolic responsibility and to your pastoral accountability to Jesus Christ, "the Chief Shepherd" (1 Pt. 5:4), and to me, his servant Vicar. I offer them as a manifestation of *deep gratitude* for what you are and intend, with God's grace, ever more to become: in Christ *a sign of hope* for the People of God, as strong and unbreakable as *the sign of the Cross,* becoming *a living sign of the Risen Christ.* It is the Risen Jesus, the Incarnate Word, who communicates through his humanity and ours the mystery of salvation in his name.

As I take leave of you today, my thoughts turn once again to one who is a close friend of many of us, your brother Bishop and mine, *Cardinal Cooke.* In his hour of suffering I have spoken to him and written to him to thank him for what he has been in the Church of God—a living sign of Jesus Christ, a faithful pastor and servant of his people, living and willing to die for the Church. A special friend, yes; an illustrious member of the Hierarchy of the United States, yes; a faithful collaborator of the Holy See, yes. And yet, simply one of so many holy American Bishops who live and die so that Jesus Christ, the Good Shepherd, may continue to lead his people to the newness of life and the fullness of salvation.

Dear brothers, there is no deeper meaning in our lives as Bishops than to be *living signs of Jesus Christ!* May Mary the Mother of Jesus help us to realize fully this vocation.

## FOURTH *AD LIMINA* ADDRESS TO THE BISHOPS OF THE UNITED STATES

### SEPTEMBER 9, 1983

Dear Brothers in our Lord Jesus Christ,

A few days ago I had the joy of being with another group of American Bishops. At that time we reflected *on the Episcopal Office,* which, like the Church herself, is a *mystery* rooted in Jesus Christ and in his saving love for humanity. We reflected on the Bishop's calling to be a living sign of the Incarnate Word, a living sign of Jesus Christ. Today we may well emphasize again the Bishop's personal role in teaching, governing and sanctifying the People of God; his altogether particular responsibility for the transmission of the Gospel, and the unique task that is his as the builder of community within the Church. For the love and zeal with which you fulfill your special ministry in the Church, I thank you in the name of Christ our Lord.

### Priestly Unity, Fraternity and Shared Responsibility

1. And yet there is another great ecclesial reality that complements our consideration of the episcopacy, and it is *the unity of the priesthood of Christ,* which we share with our brother priests. It is to them that our thoughts turn today—to our esteemed and loved co-workers, who participate with us in a ministry and mission that comes from Christ, belongs to Christ and leads to Christ.

And if the Bishop's role is unique, so too is that great witness in the Church of *a united priesthood.* Unique also is that wonderful *fraternity* of the presbyterate which is gathered about the Bishop and works with him and under his leadership to build up the unity of the Church, but which already expresses this oneness in the powerful and dynamic unity of priestly consecration and mission. Unique too is that depth of *shared responsibility* between the Bishop and his priests. For the Bishop, the priests are brothers, sons, friends, counselors and needed helpers in the vast task of effectively proclaiming Jesus Christ and salvation in his name. Not only as individuals do priests perform these roles, but the priests' councils providentially assist the Bishop in the pastoral government of the Diocese and are to be promoted according to the norms of the new Code of Canon Law (see can. 495–502).

## Eucharistic Faith Deepened by Daily Mass

2. In addressing ourselves to the reality of the priesthood, we have a special personal apostolic challenge to fulfill. We are above all called upon *to live the mystery of the priesthood* as worthy examples to our brother priests. In this regard, our celebration of the Eucharist tells our priests, as well as the whole world, so much about *our own Eucharistic faith*. Even after years of experiencing the joys attached to a vast number of apostolic activities, we can look back and say that our greatest strength and the deepest source of gladness for our hearts has been *the daily celebration of Mass,* beginning with those early days after our priestly ordination. And we have always been convinced that the Eucharist is our most outstanding contribution to the Church, our greatest priestly service to the people, the deepest meaning of that splendid vocation which we share with our brother priests.

## Priestly Identity Is Rooted
## in the Celebration of the Eucharist

3. Just yesterday, with my approval, the Sacred Congregation for the Doctrine of the Faith, in a letter to the Bishops of the Church, reiterated *the vital role of the priest as the minister of the Eucharist.* Only the priesthood can furnish the Eucharist to God's people. And only priests have the wonderful opportunity to serve God's people by supplying them with the bread of life. Already, on the day of its publication, this document of the Holy See received the supportive commentary of a pastoral letter of a brother Bishop of yours. He expressed so much of the Church's understanding of the priesthood in the following terms: "The priestly ministry requires us to do many things: to preach the Word of God, to minister the other Sacraments, to encourage, to console, to serve human need, to serve the Church in administration, which the New Testament numbers among the charisms, and to do a variety of other things in virtue of the mission we receive from the Church. This means, of course, that the Priesthood does not consist exclusively in the celebration of the Eucharist. And yet, if we reflect carefully on the Church's faith about the essential link between the Sacrament of Holy Orders and Eucharist, it does mean that the celebration of the Eucharist is at the heart of what it means to be a priest. It means that somehow and in an ultimate way the priest finds his identity in this link between the Priesthood and the Eucharist" (Pastoral Letter of Archbishop John Quinn, p. 4).

Hence as we strive to live this mystery of the priesthood, we have the task of *extolling the importance of the priesthood* to the Christian people. In explaining the relationship between the Eucharist and the priesthood, we are in effect proclaiming the mystery of the Church's life.

### Priestly Priorities Are Prayer and the Service of the Word

4. Another aspect of our apostolic charge is *to confirm our brother priests in their identity* as ministers of the Eucharist, and therefore ministers of the Church. Before the people and before our priests, in moments of calm and in times of crisis, we must assert the priorities of the priesthood. Each brother priest is meant to be, with us, in the words of Saint Paul, "a servant of Christ, called to be an apostle and set apart to proclaim the Gospel of God" (Rom. 1:1). It is in the very act of "proclamation" that we assert our common identity and confirm our brothers. Even back to the earliest times, the choice made by the Twelve was very clear. The apostolic priorities for the priesthood, as expressed in the Acts of the Apostles, are "to concentrate on prayer and the ministry of the word" (Acts 6:4).

### The Eucharist Builds Up Community

5. The Second Vatican Council did not fail to emphasize both elements for the priests of today. For example, it clearly states: "The ministry of priests takes its start from the Gospel message" (*Presbyterorum Ordinis,* 2). At the same time the Council points out that *the ministry of the word terminates in the Eucharist,* which is itself "the source and summit of the whole work of evangelization" (*Presbyterorum Ordinis,* 5). Yes, if we read carefully the signs of the times as they relate to the priesthood, we will discern that the Eucharist determines the meaning of the priesthood and the identity of our priests. The Council is clear and concise. Its testimony means so much to clarify the meaning of our priesthood, to shed light on postconciliar questionings and theological reflections. Let us all listen again, together with our presbyterates. It is the Holy Spirit speaking through the Council and saying: "Priests fulfill their chief duty in the mystery of the Eucharistic Sacrifice. In it the work of our redemption continues to be carried out" (*Presbyterorum Ordinis,* 13). It is crystal clear today and for the future: *the priesthood is forever linked to the Eucharistic Sacrifice* and to the actuation of the Redemption.

But the Eucharist is also linked to the building of community. Here too all our priests can fulfill their divine vocation and their human aspirations. Through our priests, each local community is built up in faith and charity, and in an openness to the universal Church of which it is a miniature expression.

### The Eucharist: Source of Pastoral Charity
### Confirms Celibacy Promise

6. In the Eucharistic Sacrifice the priest finds *the source of all his pastoral charity* (see *Presbyterorum Ordinis,* 14). The spirituality of all diocesan and Religious priests is linked to the Eucharist. Here they obtain the strength to make the offering of their

lives together with Jesus, High Priest and Victim of salvation. Through the Eucharistic Sacrifice, *celibacy is confirmed and strengthened.* From his Cross the Lord Jesus speaks to all his priests, inviting them to be, with him, signs of contradiction before the world. Jesus' plea has entered into the apostolic tradition: "Do not conform yourselves to this age" (Rom. 12:2).

### The Ministry of Reconciliation

7. In every age of the Church there are many meaningful actuations of the priestly ministry. But after the Eucharist what could be more important than *the "ministry of reconciliation"* (2 Cor. 5:18) *as exercised in the Sacrament of Penance?* What greater human fulfillment is there than touching human hearts through the power of the Holy Spirit and in the name of the merciful and compassionate Redeemer of the world? Like the laity, our priests must strive to serve in many relevant ways every day, but they alone can forgive sins in the name of the Lord Jesus. And connected with the forgiveness of sins is new life and hope and joy for the People of God.

### Union with Christ in the Liturgy of the Hours

With fidelity to Christ, in whose "person" he acts, the priest realizes his identity and mission also through the Liturgy of the Hours, through different forms of prayer, through the reading of the word of God and through the oblation of his will, made in union with that of Christ. The priest's special love will always be with the sick and dying, with those in pain and sorrow, and with those in sin. For every Bishop and priest there is but one ideal—the person who says: "I am the good shepherd . . . and I lay down my life for the sheep" (Jn. 10:14–15).

### Priestly Identity and Mission Exclude
### Secular and Political Activity by Priests

8. In the light of this principle, so many other aspects of the priesthood are clarified: the value of celibacy is proclaimed, not so much as a practical exigency, but as an expression of a perfect offering and of a configuration to Jesus Christ. An understanding of the need for priests to perform, with full human commitment and deep compassion, *those activities which only ordained priests can do,* confirms the wisdom of the Bishops' Synod of 1971, in regard to that *general exclusion of priests from secular and political activity.* It is more than ever necessary that "as a general rule the priestly ministry shall be a full-time occupation" (Part Two, 2, a).

### Pray and Work for Vocations

9. Dear brother Bishops, since so much of the Church's life depends on the ministry of priests, let us mobilize the People of God *to pray and work for vocations.* And let us encourage our brother priests to do everything possible to help young

men respond to the call of Jesus Christ, no matter what the cost. The Lord of the harvest will not desert his Church.

## Collegial Approach to Seminary Visitation

10. Before concluding, let me thank you for the zeal with which you have welcomed and supported the *Seminary Visitation Program* headed by Bishop John Marshall, now being conducted in America. It is being done by my authority but in the spirit of full *collegial responsibility*. For this reason I invite you to open your seminaries willingly to this visitation, and to do everything possible for its success. What is at stake is the effective training of the present and future generations of priests, so that they may be able to transmit the message of salvation in all its purity and integrity, in accordance with Christ's command: "Teach them to carry out everything I have commanded you" (Mt. 28:20).

Dear brother Bishops, in building up the priesthood of Jesus Christ, one of our greatest instruments is *fraternal love*—fraternal love among ourselves and for our priests. But this love must be clearly manifested, so that our priests will know, beyond all doubt, of the esteem and solidarity that love begets in us. In the attitude of our daily pastoral contacts with them, let us repeat convincingly in word and action: For you I am a Bishop, with you I am a priest.

Praised be Jesus Christ, the one High Priest of our salvation. And may his Mother Mary be a Mother to us all!

## FIFTH *AD LIMINA* ADDRESS TO THE BISHOPS OF THE UNITED STATES

### SEPTEMBER 19, 1983

Dear Brothers in our Lord Jesus Christ,

1. I have recently spoken to other groups of American Bishops about two important aspects of the great mystery of the Church: the Episcopate and the Priesthood. I would now like to reflect with you on yet another special gift of God to his Church, and this gift is *the religious life*.

## Religious Life: Integral Part of Pastoral Responsibility

So much is religious life a part of the Church, so intimately does it touch her constitution and her holiness, that it must form an integral part of the pastoral solicitude of the Pope and the Bishops, who have a unique responsibility for the entire life of the Church and are meant to be signs of her holiness. In speaking about religious life we are speaking about an ecclesial reality which concerns the Bishops *by reason of their very office*.

### Call to Conversion to Witness to Redemption

2. At every moment, but especially during the Holy Year of the Redemption, the Church offers *the call to conversion* to all her members, particularly to Religious. This call to conversion goes out to Religious so that they may acquire the full benefits of the Redemption and be ever more faithful witnesses of that Redemption; so that they may be ever more authentic channels of the Redemption for the People of God through their own spiritual vitality, which, in the Communion of Saints, is a supernaturally effective contact with the Redemption; and so that through conversion they may live more faithfully the unity of the Church, which is itself the effect of the Redemption and a participation in it.

### Special Pastoral Service to the Religious of the United States

For this reason I wrote to all the Bishops asking for their *special pastoral service to the Religious of the United States in the context of the Holy Year of the Redemption*. In my letter I stated: "It is my earnest hope that the Holy Year of the Redemption will truly be for religious life a year of fruitful renewal in Christ's love. If all the faithful have a right—as they do—to the treasures of grace that a call to renewal in love offers, then the Religious have a special title to that right."

### Invitation to Holy Year Renewal

The whole thrust of my initiative was formulated as an invitation, a call to be extended to the Religious to open wide the doors of their hearts to the Redeemer. In this regard I wrote: "*I ask you to invite all the Religious* throughout your land, in my name, and in your own name as Bishops, in the name of the Church and in the name of Jesus, to seize this opportunity of the Holy Year to walk in newness of life, in solidarity with all the pastors and faithful, along the path necessary for us all—the way of penance and conversion."

### Special Papal Commission and Essential Elements of Religious Life

3. This pastoral endeavor is of such importance that it could be fulfilled only by *a full collegial commitment* on the part of all the Bishops of the United States. At that time I promised you my fraternal and prayerful support. I also named a Commission headed by Archbishop John Quinn, whose task it would be to assist you in the exercise of collegiality and to facilitate your pastoral work of "helping the Religious of your country whose Institutes are engaged in apostolic works to live their ecclesial vocation to the full." I am deeply grateful to the Commission for the generosity and zeal with which they are striving to formulate a suitable program that will effectively assist the body of Bishops who have the main responsibility in this matter. As guidelines for both the Commission and yourselves in this important work, I approved a

summary of the salient points of the Church's teaching on religious life prepared by the Sacred Congregation for Religious and Secular Institutes.

### Collegial Responsibility for the Progress of Religious Life

Since then I have also had the opportunity, as I had hoped, to speak personally with so many Bishops about religious life, hearing their viewpoints and learning about their own devoted pastoral service to Religious. I am deeply grateful to our Lord Jesus Christ that this initiative has been so zealously undertaken by the Commission and by individual Bishops, and that it is seen for what it is, *an application—* an extremely important application—*of the principle of collegiality,* a principle so forcefully enunciated by the Second Vatican Council. In proposing this initiative to your pastoral zeal, my first intention has been to affirm collegial responsibility for the state of religious life, which is intimately linked to the mystery of the Church and to the mystery of the Episcopate. Religious need the support and assistance of the Bishops in their lives of consecrated witness to the holiness of Christ and to the primacy of God. Your collegial collaboration is not only a means of giving *general support* to Religious and of assisting them in solving *particular problems* that inevitably touch their lives; it also signifies an *authentic functioning of collegiality,* an authentic and vital relationship between the Episcopate and the Religious.

### The Aim of This Aspect of Conversion of Heart: Full Acceptance of the Person of Christ

4. The collegial service that you, as Bishops, are asked to render to Religious in the precise area of episcopal competence is, above all, to proclaim a call to holiness, a call to renewal and a call to penance and conversion. In other words, *in the name of the Redeemer to extend the call of the Holy Year,* asking for the greatest possible response of love. In my letter to you I mentioned that "this call is linked in a particular way with the life and mission of Religious . . . it affects them in a special way; it makes special demands on their love, reminding them how much they are loved by Christ and his Church."

This initiative of pastoral care for Religious is one aspect of *the great dialogue of salvation,* which begins with an awareness of God's love, made visible in the Incarnation, and leads to the fullness of salvation effected by this love. The whole dialogue of salvation is directed *to the full acceptance, through* metanoia, *of the person of Jesus Christ.* In the case of the Religious, as in the case of the faithful, the process is the same: in the very moment in which we Bishops recognize our own need for conversion, the Lord asks us to go out to others—humble and repentant, yet courageous and without fear—to communicate with our brothers and sisters. Christ wants to appeal through us, to invite and call his people, especially his Religious, to conversion. *The aim of all dialogue is conversion of heart.*

### Proclaim Nature and the Charism of Religious Life

5. It is not my intention on this occasion to speak about all the essential elements of the Church's teaching on religious life, as described in my letter and in the document of the Sacred Congregation. I am convinced that you will continue to reflect on all of these points, which are taken from authentic sources, so as to be able to explain and promote them all. At this time I would like *to emphasize only a few points* intimately linked to the theme of conversion and holiness of life in the context of religious life and of the pastoral responsibility of the Bishops, who are "entrusted with the duty of caring for religious charisms, all the more so because the very indivisibility of their pastoral ministry makes them responsible for perfecting the entire flock" (*Mutuae Relationes,* 9, c). Bishops must proclaim the nature of religious life as teachers of the faith and representatives of the Church that guarantees the charism of Religious. This proclamation is both an instruction for the People of God and an encouragement for the Religious.

## First Duty of Religious: Contemplation and Union with God

In selecting certain aspects of religious life for special reflection, the notion of *prayer* stands out immediately. The new Code of Canon Law states that *the first and principal duty of all Religious* is the contemplation of things divine and constant union with God in prayer (see can. 663, 1). The question of Religious being united with God in prayer precedes the question of what activity they will perform. The idea of prayer is again underlined as it touches the apostolate. The Code insists that the apostolate of all Religious *consists primarily in the witness of their consecrated life,* which they are bound to foster *through prayer and penance* (see can. 673).

## The Dignity and Beauty of Religious Consecration

6. All of this tells us something very profound about religious life. It speaks to us about the value of living for God alone, of witnessing to his Kingdom, and of being consecrated to Jesus Christ. Through the vows of chastity, poverty and obedience, Religious consecrate themselves to God, personally ratifying and confirming all the commitments of their Baptism. But even more important is the divine action, the fact that *God consecrates them* to the glory of his Son; and he does this *through the mediation of his Church,* acting in the power of his Spirit.

## Special Contribution of Religious Life

All of this emphasizes the esteem that we Bishops must have for the Religious and for the immense contribution that they have made to the Church in the United States. And yet this contribution is more a contribution of *what they are* than of what they have done and are doing. In speaking of Religious, we must say that their greatest dignity consists in this: that they are persons individually called by God and consecrated by God through the mediation of his Church. The value of their activity is great, but the value of their *being* religious is greater still.

Hence one of the Bishop's contributions is *to remind the Religious of their dignity and to proclaim their identity before the People of God.* This enables the laity to understand more clearly the mystery of the Church, to which the Religious offer so much.

## The Essential Ecclesial Dimension of Religious Life

7. *The ecclesial dimension* is absolutely essential for a proper understanding of religious life. The Religious are who they are because the Church mediates their consecration and guarantees their charism to be religious. Although their primary apostolate is to witness, their other apostolates involve a multiplicity of works and activities performed for the Church and coordinated by the Bishops (see can. 680).

Since *the value of the consecration of Religious and the supernatural efficacy of their apostolates depend on their being in union with the Church*—the entirety of which has been entrusted to the Bishops' pastoral care for governing (see Acts 20:28)—it follows that Bishops perform a great service to the Religious by helping them to maintain and deepen their union with the Church, and by assisting them to harmonize all their activities with the life of the Church. The fruitful living of the religious charism presupposes the faithful acceptance of the Church's Magisterium, which in fact is an acceptance of the very reality and identity of the Episcopal College united with the Pope. The College of Bishops, as the successor of the Apostolic College, continues to enjoy the guidance of the Holy Spirit; the words of Jesus apply still today: "He who hears you hears me, and he who rejects you rejects me, and he who rejects me rejects him who sent me" (Lk. 10:16).

## Religious Make Visible the Spousal Aspect of the Church's Love for Christ

8. Venerable and dear brothers, in the dialogue of salvation I would ask you to speak to the Religious about their *ecclesial identity* and to explain to the whole People of God how the Religious are who they are only because the Church is what she is in her sacramental reality. And I would ask you to emphasize the special feminine role of women Religious: in the Church and personifying the Church as the Spouse of Christ, they are called to live for Christ, faithfully, exclusively and permanently, in the consciousness of being able to make visible the spousal aspect of the Church's love for Christ.

## Ecclesial Identity: Necessary Condition
## for the Success of Any Apostolic Activity

And may everyone realize that *the greatest misunderstanding* of the charism of Religious, indeed the greatest offense to their dignity and their persons, would come from those who might try *to situate their life or mission outside its ecclesial context.* Religious are betrayed by anyone who would attempt to have them embrace teaching against the Magisterium of the Church, who conceived them by her love and gave them birth in her liberating truth. The acceptance of the reality of the Church by Religious and their vital union—through her and in her—with Christ is *an essential condition for the vitality of their prayer,* the effectiveness of their service to the poor, the validity of their social witness, the well-being of their community relationships, the measure of the success of their renewal and the guarantee of the authenticity of their poverty and simplicity of life. And only in total union with the Church does their chastity become the full and acceptable gift which will satisfy the craving of their hearts to give themselves to Christ and to receive from him, and to be fruitful in his love.

## Pastoral Leadership by Example of Love and Sacrifice

9. Dear brothers, through our collegial action, especially in the Holy Year of the Redemption, *let us manifest our pastoral love* in a special way to the Religious of the United States. And *let us lead the way in the sacrifice and love demanded by conversion.* As Bishops we must help ensure for this generation and for those to come that the magnificent contribution made by the Religious of the United States to the mission of the Church will continue.

But, above all, what is at stake in the collegial service of our pastoral love is to confirm the Religious of America in their charism *to be* religious, and *to be* ever more *the expression of Christ's holiness* in the mystery of the Church. May they live for Christ, as Mary lived for Christ, in renunciation, sacrifice and co-redemptive love, filling up "what is lacking in the sufferings of Christ for his body, the Church" (Col. 1:24). The first and principal duty that springs from their being religious will always be "the contemplation of things divine and constant union with Christ in prayer" (can. 663, 1).

Finally, for the benefit of all, let us recall those memorable words of Paul VI that apply to every age of the Church's life: "Do not forget, moreover, the witness of history: faithfulness to prayer or its abandonment is the test of the vitality or decadence of the religious life" (*Evangelica Testificatio,* 42).

All of this is part of the ministry whereby we, as Bishops, live the mystery of the Church, encouraging the Religious, whom we love and for whom we live and are willing to die, to strive to become ever more "the very holiness of God" (2 Cor. 5:21).

## SIXTH *AD LIMINA* ADDRESS TO THE
## BISHOPS OF THE UNITED STATES

### SEPTEMBER 24, 1983

Dear Brothers in our Lord Jesus Christ,

### Christian Marriage and Family Life

1. It is a real joy for me to welcome you to this collegial gathering in which we come together in the name of Christ, who is "the Chief Shepherd" (1 Pt. 5:4) of the Church and the Lord and Savior of us all. And as we assemble here on the occasion of your *ad Limina* visit, I wish to reflect with you on one of the most important areas of our common pastoral responsibility: *Christian marriage and family life*.

### The Health of Society Depends on the
### Well-being of Marriage and Family Life

In the Pastoral Constitution *Gaudium et Spes,* the Bishops of the Second Vatican Council stated that "the well-being of the individual person and of human and Christian society is intimately linked with the healthy condition of the community set up by marriage and the family" (no. 47). We are all aware of *certain contemporary trends* that seem to threaten the stability, if not the very existence, of the family: a shift of emphasis toward the comfort of the individual over the well-being of the family as society's basic social unit, increasing divorce rates, attitudes of sexual permissiveness and the suggestion that other types of relationships can replace marriage and the family.

### Bishops Called to Particular Support
### for the Family Life Apostolate

In the face of these attitudes we have *the important mission of proclaiming Christ's Good News about Christian married love,* the identity and worth of the family, and the importance of its mission in the Church and in the world. Accordingly, in *Familiaris Consortio,* I noted that the Bishop should exercise particular solicitude for the family, "devoting to it personal interest, care, time, personnel and resources, but above all personal support for the families and for all those who, in the various diocesan structures, assist him in the pastoral care of the family" (no.73).

### The Richness of Church Teaching
### on the Sacrament of Marriage

2. This pastoral responsibility is based on the fact that *Christian family life is founded on the Sacrament of Marriage,* which is "the specific source and original means

of sanctification for Christian couples and families" (*Familiaris Consortio,* no. 56). It is up to us, together with our priests, to offer to the faithful the richness of the Church's teaching on the Sacrament of Marriage. This teaching, when explained well, is so very powerful, presenting as it does the covenant of God's relationship with his people and of *Christ's relationship with the Church.* It is of extreme importance for Christian couples to be aware of the divine truth that, in their human love elevated and sanctified by sacramental marriage, they actually "signify and partake in that fruitful love between Christ and his Church" (*Lumen Gentium,* 11).

### Christian Conjugal Covenant Irrevocable and Fruitful

Because Christian marriage expresses the relationship of Christ and the Church, it possesses the qualities of *unity, permanence or indissolubility, fidelity and fruitfulness.* In the words of the Second Vatican Council we proclaim: "The intimate partnership of married life and love has been established by the Creator and qualified by his laws, and is rooted in the conjugal covenant of irrevocable personal consent. Hence by that human act whereby spouses mutually bestow and accept each other, a relationship arises which by divine will and in the eyes of society too is a lasting one" (*Gaudium et Spes,* 48).

### Primary Responsibilities:
### Develop Conjugal Love and Pursue Responsible Parenthood

3. *The primary responsibilities* of married couples are described in both *Gaudium et Spes* and *Humanae Vitae* in terms of *developing conjugal love* and *pursuing responsible parenthood.* Basic to the marriage relationship is that special interpersonal love which the spouses give to one another. The Church proclaims this conjugal love as eminently human, involving the good of the whole person and enriching and ennobling both husband and wife in their Christian life. This love creates a special unity between a man and a woman, resembling the unity between Christ and his Church. *Gaudium et Spes* assures us that married love is caught up in God's love and is affected by Christ's redemptive power and the saving activity of the Church. As a result, the spouses are led to God and assisted and strengthened in the sublime role of being a father or a mother (see no. 48).

### Creative Love Builds Family Life

*Marriage is also directed toward building a family.* The spouses share with God in the continuing work of creation. Conjugal love is rooted in divine love, and is meant to be creative and life-sustaining. It is through spiritual union and the union of their bodies that the couple fulfill their procreative role by giving life, love and a sense of security to their children.

## Primary Responsibilities of Married Couples:
## Give Life and Education

*Giving life* and helping their children to reach maturity through *education* are among *the primary privileges and responsibilities* of married couples. We know that married couples usually look forward to parenthood but are sometimes impeded from achieving their hopes and desires by social conditions, by personal circumstances or even by inability to beget life. But the Church encourages couples to be generous and hopeful, to realize that parenthood is a privilege and that each child bears witness to the couple's own love for each other, to their generosity and to their openness to God. They must be encouraged to see the child as an enrichment of their marriage and a gift of God to themselves and to their other children.

## Conscientious Decisions Must Respect Inherent Connection
## Between Unitive and Procreative Aspects

4. Couples should thoughtfully and prayerfully make their decisions regarding the spacing of births and the size of their family. In pursuing these decisions they need to be attentive to the teaching of the Church regarding *the inherent connection between the unitive and procreative dimensions of the marriage act* (see Humanae Vitae, 12). Couples must be urged to avoid any action that threatens a life already conceived, that denies or frustrates their procreative power, or violates the integrity of the marriage act.

## Show How the Church's Teachings
## Uphold the Vocation to Love

5. As Bishops, together with your priests and others in the family apostolate, you are called upon to help couples know and understand the reasons for *the Church's teaching on human sexuality*. This teaching can only be understood in the light of God's plan for human love and marriage as they relate to creation and Redemption. Let us often present to our people the uplifting and exhilarating affirmation of human love, telling them that "God inscribed in the humanity of man and woman the vocation, and thus the capacity and responsibility, of love and communion. Love is therefore the fundamental and innate vocation of every human being" (Familiaris Consortio, 11).

## Sexuality Transcends the Biological Sphere;
## Concerns the Innermost Personal Being

Thus, in order to avoid any trivialization or desecration of sexuality, we must teach that sexuality transcends the purely biological sphere and concerns the innermost being of the human person as such. Sexual love is truly human only if it is an integral part of the love by which a man and a woman commit themselves totally to one another until death. *This full self-giving is possible only in marriage.*

It is this teaching, based on the Church's understanding of the dignity of the human person and the fact that *sex is a gift of God,* that must be communicated to both married and engaged couples, and indeed to the whole Church. This teaching must be at the basis of all education in sexuality and chastity. It must be communicated to parents, who have the primary responsibility for the education of their children, and also to pastors and religious teachers who collaborate with parents in the fulfillment of their responsibility.

### Support Education in Natural Family Planning

6. A special and important part of your ministry to families has to do with *natural family planning.* The number of couples successfully using the natural methods is constantly growing. But much more concerted effort is needed. As stated in *Familiaris Consortio,* "the ecclesial community at the present time must take on the task of instilling conviction and offering practical help to those who wish to live out their parenthood in a truly responsible way. . . . This implies a broader, more decisive and more systematic effort to make the natural methods of regulating fertility known, respected and applied" (no. 35).

### Support Couples Who Practice Natural Family Planning

Those couples who choose the natural methods perceive the profound difference—both anthropological and moral—between contraception and natural family planning. Yet they may experience difficulties; indeed, they often go through a certain conversion in becoming committed to the use of the natural methods, and they stand in need of competent instruction, encouragement and pastoral counseling and support. We must be sensitive to their struggles and have a feeling for the needs that they experience. We must encourage them to continue their efforts with generosity, confidence and hope. As Bishops we have the charism and the pastoral responsibility to make our people aware of *the unique influence that the grace of the Sacrament of Marriage has on every aspect of married life, including sexuality* (see *Familiaris Consortio,* 33). The teaching of Christ's Church is not only light and strength for God's people, but it uplifts their hearts in gladness and hope.

Your Episcopal Conference has established a special program to expand and coordinate efforts in the various Dioceses. But the success of such an effort requires the abiding pastoral interest and support of each Bishop in his own Diocese, and I am deeply grateful to you for what you do in this most important apostolate.

### The Domestic Church Hands on the Faith
### to Successive Generations

7. The family is rightly described as *the domestic Church.* As such, it transmits the faith and the Christian value system from one generation to the next. Parents are called to be involved in the education of their children, precisely as young Christians.

The family is also the center of sacramental catechesis. Increasingly, parents are called upon to take an active role in preparing their children for Baptism, First Confession and First Communion. Married couples are also active in programs of marriage preparation. All of this touches *the role of the family in sharing in the life and mission of the Church*. With all our hearts we should encourage family prayer and a family sacramental life centered around the Eucharist. For the vitality of the Christian family derives from its union with Christ in the life of grace, which is nourished by the liturgy and by family prayer.

## The Social Role of Families

8. The Christian family also has a responsibility to participate in *the development of society*. As Bishops in the United States you have *a long history of devoted service to families with special needs,* particularly through your Catholic social service agencies. Your diocesan agencies have also shown a special concern for the poor, for racial, ethnic and cultural minorities, as well as for the disadvantaged. But as the 1980 Synod of Bishops urged, and as was pointed out in *Familiaris Consortio,* "the social role of families is called upon to find expression also in the form of *political intervention:* families should be the first to take steps to see that the laws and institutions of the State not only do not offend but support and positively defend the rights and duties of the family" (no. 44). Your Episcopal Conference has been diligent in fostering this role through its pro-life activity, and especially the annual *Respect Life Program,* which begins next week for the current year.

## Prepare a Directory for the Pastoral Care of the Family

9. The pastoral challenge is great, and it requires your personal and constant leadership, the collaboration of priests and Religious and the generous and dedicated efforts of the Catholic laity, especially families. In a country as vast as yours, the task is very complex. But again I commend to you the recommendations of *Familiaris Consortio,* that is, that the Episcopal Conferences should formulate a *Directory for the Pastoral Care for the Family,* which will include the content of the preparation for marriage, and that priests and seminarians be given special preparation for pastoral work with families. Specifically for this reason a special institute has been established for the study of marriage and family life at the Pontifical Lateran University.

I am aware of your many other pastoral responsibilities and concerns, but from my pastoral journeys I am very much convinced of the vitality of Christian family life even in the face of so many tensions and pressures. I urge you to show the family special love and concern, to collaborate with others in supporting family life, and to proclaim constantly to your people that "the future of humanity passes by way of the family" (*Familiaris Consortio,* 86).

## Conjugal Love:
## Sacramental Expression of Christ's Love for the Church

10. We simply cannot accept the contemporary pursuit of exaggerated convenience and comfort, for as Christians we must heed the vigorous exhortation of Saint Paul: "Do not conform yourselves to this age" (Rom. 12:2). We must realize that in our struggles to overcome the negative influences of modern society, we are identified with Christ the Lord, who by his suffering and death has redeemed the world. Thus we can better impart to our people the message of the Second Vatican Council that in following Christ, who is the principle of life, "by the sacrifices and joys of their vocation and through their faithful love, married people will become witnesses of the mystery of love which the Lord revealed to the world by his death and Resurrection" (*Gaudium et Spes*, 52). Yes, dear brothers, *marriage and the family are closely linked to the Paschal Mystery* of the Lord Jesus. And human conjugal love remains forever a great sacramental expression of the fact that "Christ loved the Church and gave himself up for her" (Eph. 5:25). In the power of the Holy Spirit let us communicate this gift of God's truth to the world.

*The proclamation of this truth is our contribution* to married couples; it is the proof of our pastoral love for families; and it will be the source of immense vitality for the Church of God in this generation and for generations yet to come. With determination, confidence and hope let us proclaim Christ's Good News for married love and family life. And may Mary, the Mother of Jesus, be with us in this apostolic task.

# SEVENTH *AD LIMINA* ADDRESS TO THE
# BISHOPS OF THE UNITED STATES

## OCTOBER 22, 1983

Dear Brothers in our Lord Jesus Christ,

### The Bishop's Role as Minister of God's Word

1. Some weeks ago, during another *ad Limina* visit, I spoke about various aspects of *the Bishops' identity as a living sign of Jesus Christ,* within the context of the sacramentality of the Church. I would now like to pursue that general theme, reflecting with you on the Bishop's role as *a minister of God's word,* "a minister of the Gospel" (Eph. 3:7). For indeed, it is as a minister of God's word, acting in the power of the Holy Spirit and through the charism of his episcopal office, that the Bishop manifests Christ to the world, makes Christ present in the community and effectively communicates Christ to all who open wide their hearts.

### Special Charism for Specific Mission
### of Preaching and Teaching

As a minister of the Gospel, the Bishop is a living expression of Christ, who, as the Incarnate Word, is himself the supreme revelation and communication of God.

The ministry of the word clearly defines our identity as servants of Jesus Christ, called to be apostles and "set apart to proclaim the Gospel of God" (Rom. 1:1). *By preaching and teaching we fulfill our specific mission.* Each of us thus actuates his special charism to be a living sign of the Christ who says: "I must proclaim the Good News of the Kingdom of God . . . because that is what I was sent to do" (Lk. 4:43).

### Preaching and Teaching with the Authority of Christ

2. The Second Vatican Council captures the notion of our identity when it states: "Among the principal duties of Bishops, the preaching of the Gospel occupies an eminent place. For Bishops are heralds of the faith who lead new disciples to Christ. They are authentic teachers, that is teachers endowed with the authority of Christ, who preach to the people committed to them the faith they must believe in and put into practice" (*Lumen Gentium,* 25). As preachers and teachers, the Bishops have a vital role to fulfill, a vital message to communicate. *Bishops exist in order to proclaim God's free gift of salvation* offered to humanity in Jesus Christ and effected through his Paschal Mystery.

### Need to Help the People of God
### Realize the Obedience of Faith

All the activities of Bishops must be directed to proclaiming the Gospel, precisely because the Gospel is "the power of God leading everyone who believes in it to salvation" (Rom. 1:16). Salvation is found in the Gospel, and the Gospel is received in faith. Hence everything the Bishop does should be directed toward helping people to give "the obedience of faith" (Rom. 1:5) to God's word, helping them to embrace the full content of Christ's teaching. The role of the Bishop as minister of the Gospel is profoundly pastoral, and precisely *as the proclamation of God's word, it reaches its apex in the Eucharist,* in which the work of our salvation is sacramentally actuated.

### Episcopal Charism to Continue the Mission
### and Mandate of the Apostles

3. The Council emphasized that God wills that *everything he has revealed* for the salvation of the world *should be preserved in its full integrity and handed on to future generations.* For this reason Christ commissioned his Apostles to proclaim the Gospel, and his Apostles transmitted their own teaching role to their successors, the Bishops (see *Dei Verbum,* 7). The Council also declares that *the episcopal office of teaching in the Church is conferred by episcopal consecration and can be exercised only in hierarchical communion* with the head and the members of the College of Bishops (see *Lumen Gentium,* 21). I mention these truths to indicate just how much the ministry of the word is linked to our own sacramental identity and to our whole episcopal mission. Our lives as Bishops revolve around the mandate of Christ to teach everything that he commanded the Apostles. What is more, our apostolic

ministry is endowed with a sharing in that full authority given to Jesus, which he himself evoked before he sent his disciples forth to make disciples of all nations, to baptize and to teach. Our ministry is likewise strengthened by that special abiding presence of the Lord with us until the end of the world (see Mt. 28:18–20). All of this constitutes the episcopal charism, sacramentally transmitted, sacramentally received, sacramentally exercised.

Our response as Bishops to Christ's mandate must be expressed in *a vital proclamation,* through preaching and teaching, *of all the truths of faith:* the truths that lead our people to salvation, the truths that invite our people to give the obedience of faith. The Bishops exercise the teaching role of the Apostles precisely in order "to keep the Gospel forever whole and alive within the Church" (*Dei Verbum,* 7). For this reason, the Council's Decree on the Bishops' Pastoral Office encourages Bishops explicitly to expound, in the power of the Holy Spirit, "the whole mystery of Christ" (*Christus Dominus,* 12).

### Pastoral Love Means Fidelity in Safeguarding the Deposit of Faith

4. It is easy to see how the Bishop's role of vital preaching, faithful custody of the deposit of faith, and authoritative teaching exercised in union with the Pope and the whole College of Bishops also involves *the duty to defend the word of God against whatever would compromise its purity and integrity.* If we understand the nature of the Church, in which the Paschal Mystery is lived out, we will not be surprised to find, in every generation of the Church's life, including our own, not only sin but also some measure of error and falsehood. A serene sense of realism and Church history will, however, help us to exercise our role as authentic teachers of God's word without either exaggerating or minimizing the existence of error and falsehood, which our pastoral responsibility obliges us to identify and to reject. Our fidelity to the word of God also requires us to understand and put into practice that great reality proclaimed by the Council: "The task of authentically interpreting the word of God, whether written or handed on, has been entrusted exclusively to the living teaching office of the Church, whose authority is exercised in the name of Jesus Christ" (*Dei Verbum,* 10).

In studying and listening to the word of God, in guarding and explaining the deposit of faith, in preaching and teaching the mystery of Christ, *vigilance and fidelity on the part of Bishops are synonyms of pastoral love.* The words Paul spoke to Timothy are relevant for each one of us: "I charge you to preach the word, to stay with this task whether convenient or inconvenient—correcting, reproving, appealing—constantly teaching and never losing patience. . . . Be steady and self-possessed; put up with hardship, perform your work as an evangelist, fulfill your ministry" (2 Tm. 4:2,5). We find immense consolation and strength in the realization that we exercise our special service to the word of God through a divine mandate, with the help of the Holy Spirit and in virtue of a sacramentally conferred charism.

## Single Authentic Magisterium
## Requires Collegial Communion

5. The fruitful exercise of the Magisterium requires us to reflect on various aspects of the mystery of God's word and its transmission in the Church. We know that *the authentic Magisterium of the Church is characterized by unity.* It makes no claim to be above the word of God; rather, it seeks humbly to serve that word, through its specific charism, exercised in the name of Christ and by his authority. As such, the Magisterium has no parallel in the Church. *There is only one ecclesial Magisterium,* and it belongs to the Bishops. On the part of individual Bishops, the communion of teaching with the Pope and the whole college is of extreme importance, because it is the guarantee of authentic doctrine and of the supernatural effectiveness of every pastoral initiative.

The teaching charism of the Bishop is *unique in its responsibility.* As such it must be exercised personally and cannot be delegated. By episcopal consecration the Bishop has a unique relationship to Jesus Christ the Teacher; by Christ's authority he is enabled to teach with particular effectiveness. In a unique way he is a living sign of Jesus Christ, proclaiming God's word with special power.

## Priests Exercise Responsibility

*The priests are intimately related to the sacramental ministry of the Bishop,* and with the Bishop, *as co-workers of the episcopal order,* they exercise their own proper responsibility for the word of God. This relationship of ours to our priests in the word of God gives us a special motive for a deep pastoral and fraternal love for them, as well as an opportunity to thank God for their partnership in the Gospel.

## Sound Doctrinal Development Lies in the
## Growth of Understanding of God's Word

6. At the same time the Bishops are servant pastors in their local Church, where *the whole ecclesial community*—priests, deacons, Religious and laity—collaborate with them, in accordance with the constitution of the Church, to proclaim and live the word of God. The Bishops' sacramental service to the word of God is ordered to the well-being of the entire community of the faithful. The Bishops guide the faithful to understanding the word of God. The very proclamation of the word of God by the Bishops has a power that leads to the assent of faith. And after this assent of faith has been given, the faithful themselves contribute to the further growth of the Church's understanding of God's word (see *Dei Verbum,* 8), and, in this sense, faith develops in each succeeding generation of the Church. But, in the words of Saint Vincent of Lerins, "it must truly be development of the faith, not alteration of the faith. . . . The understanding . . . of individuals as well as of the whole Church ought then to make great and vigorous progress with the passing of the ages and the centuries, but only along its own line of development, that is, with the same doctrine, the same meaning

and the same import" (*First Instruction,* Ch. 23). Understanding the development of doctrine in this way, we know that the present or "current" teaching of the Church does not admit of a development that is either a reversal or a contradiction.

## Growth of *Sensus Fidelium* Depends Both on Cooperation with the Magisterium and the Spirit

7. Through the exercise of their own charism, the Bishops provide a great service to the faithful and assist them to carry out *their own role of contributing to the growth of the faith.* In this regard I would repeat once again what I said in Chicago to all the Bishops of the United States: "In the community of the faithful—which must always maintain Catholic unity with the Bishops and the Apostolic See—there are great insights of faith. The Holy Spirit is active in enlightening the minds of the faithful with his truth, and in inflaming their hearts with his love. But these insights of faith and this *sensus fidelium* are not independent of the Magisterium of the Church, which is an instrument of the same Holy Spirit and is assisted by him. It is only when the faithful have been nourished by the word of God, faithfully transmitted in its purity and integrity, that their own charisms are fully operative and fruitful. Once the word of God is faithfully proclaimed to the community and is accepted, it brings forth fruits of justice and holiness of life in abundance. But the dynamism of the community in understanding and living the word of God depends on its receiving intact the *depositum fidei;* and for this precise purpose a special apostolic and pastoral charism has been given to the Church. It is one and the same Spirit of truth who directs the hearts of the faithful and guarantees the Magisterium of the pastors of the flock" (AAS, 71, 1979, p. 1226).

## Theologians' Special Ecclesial Role

8. I wish at this time, as I did during my visit to The Catholic University of America, to say *a special word of appreciation for the role of the theologians* in the Church, and in particular for the assistance that they give to the Bishops and the service that they render to the faith. Since theology receives its object from faith, and since it is vitally concerned with the sacred deposit of revelation, there are many elements that are common to the role of Bishops and to that of theologians. Although in different ways, both Bishops and theologians are called upon to guard the word of God, to study it more deeply, to explain it, to teach it, to defend it. Both Bishops and theologians are called to live and work and pray for the same great cause: "that the word of the Lord may speed on and triumph" (2 Thes. 3:1).

Theologians have special qualifications for studying and elucidating the reasons for the doctrinal and moral teaching of the Church. By their training and scholarship, and following their specific method, theologians are in a position to probe and illustrate the data of faith and the interpretation that the Magisterium gives of these data in doctrine and morals.

## Bishops and Theologians:
## Responsibilities Within the Body of Christ

In their role of teaching theology, theologians are called upon to open the treasure of faith ever wider and *to inculcate respect for the Magisterium,* which in turn guarantees the interpretation of God's word. It is this respect for the Magisterium that is indeed *"a constituent element of the theological method"* (see Paul VI, *ad Limina* Discourse, June 20, 1977). On their part the Bishops know that the exercise of their own sacramental charism is linked to reading, study, consultation and, above all, prayer. But it remains a charism at the service of the faith of the whole Church.

Venerable and dear brothers, in inviting you to reflect with me on our configuration to Jesus Christ in our ministry of the word, I desire with all my heart *to confirm you in your deepest identity as Bishops of the Church of God.* The word of God is our life and ministry, our joy and our strength, our wisdom and our hope. But even more, it is the salvation of our people, their vital contact with the Lord. Our proclamation of God's word is linked to a special sacramental power, and our teaching of God's word is guaranteed by the authority of Christ the Teacher. As ministers of the Gospel we are indeed living signs of Jesus Christ. The Council assures us: "In the Bishops . . . our Lord Jesus Christ, the supreme High Priest, is present in the midst of all those who believe" (*Lumen Gentium,* 21).

And may Mary, the Mother of Jesus the Incarnate Word, be with us as we endeavor to communicate to the world the Gospel of her Son.

## EIGHTH *AD LIMINA* ADDRESS TO THE
## BISHOPS OF THE UNITED STATES

### OCTOBER 28, 1983

Dear Brothers in our Lord Jesus Christ,

### Catholic Education

1. Once again I am very happy to share an intense experience of ecclesial communion with another group of American Bishops. You come from different regions of the United States, and the pastoral situations of your individual local Churches vary greatly. And yet I am sure that in all your Dioceses there is a deep common interest in the topic that I would like to touch on today: *Catholic education.*

### Called to Communicate Christ

The very notion of Catholic education is closely related to the essential mission of the Church, *to communicate Christ.* It is linked to our own episcopal mandate *to teach*—to teach everything that Jesus commanded to be taught (see Mt. 28:20). And as teachers, we are called to bear witness by word and example to the Christ whom the Church is endeavoring to communicate. Simply put, the aim of Catholic education is to help people "to arrive at the fullness of Christian life" (can. 794, 1). It is identified with the great ideal of Saint Paul, who is not satisfied "until Christ is formed" (Gal. 4:19) in the Galatians; he yearns to see this process completed.

## Various Goals of Catholic Education

2. The Second Vatican Council presented the aim of all Christian education *in various aspects,* which include "ensuring that the baptized . . . may grow ever more conscious of the gift of faith which they have received; that they may learn to adore God the Father in spirit and in truth (see Jn. 4:23), especially through liturgical worship; and that they may be prepared to lead their personal lives according to a new nature, in justice and holiness of truth (Eph. 4:22–24); so that they may reach perfect maturity . . . and make their contribution to the increase of the Mystical Body" (*Gravissimum Educationis,* 2).

## Concern for the Whole Person

These are elements with far-reaching implications; they take into account the fact that *Catholic education is indeed concerned with the whole person,* with his or her eternal destiny and with the common good of society, which the Church herself strives to promote. In practice this requires that the physical, moral and intellectual talents of children and young people should be cared for, so that they may attain a sense of responsibility and the right use of freedom and take an active part in the life of society (see can. 795).

## The Evangelizing Role and Impact on the Formation of the Believing Laity

3. All of these elements have been promoted by Catholic education in your country. Indeed, Catholic education constitutes a *privileged chapter in the history of the Church in America.* Catholic education has been a very effective dimension of evangelization, bringing the Gospel to bear on all facets of life. It has involved different individuals and groups in the educational process, and it has succeeded in making generations of people feel part of the ecclesial and social community. Despite limitations and imperfections, Catholic education in America can, under God's grace, be credited to a high degree with forming the splendid Catholic laity of America. Catholic education was itself the foundation for understanding and accepting the teaching of the Second Vatican Council, which was a consistent development of principles that the Church has held and taught throughout the centuries. The blessings of the Council were effectively brought to bear on the lives of many because years of generous Catholic education had prepared the way.

Catholic education in your land has also fostered *numerous vocations* over the years. You yourselves owe a great debt of gratitude to that Catholic education which enabled you to understand and to accept the call of the Lord. Among other contributions of Catholic education is the quality of citizens that you were able to produce: upright men and women who contributed to the well-being of America, and through Christian charity worked to serve all their brothers and sisters. Catholic education has furnished *an excellent witness to the Church's perennial commitment to culture* of every kind. It has exercised a prophetic role—perhaps modestly in individual cases, but overall most effectively—to assist faith to permeate culture. The achievements of Catholic education in America merit our great respect and admiration.

### Gratitude to Parents, Parishes, Dioceses, Women Religious and Generous Laity

4. There is still, however, a debt of gratitude to be paid, before the witness of history, *to the parents* who have supported a whole system of Catholic education; *to the parishes* that have coordinated and sustained these efforts; *to the Dioceses* that have promoted programs of education and supplemented means of support, especially in poor areas; *to the teachers*—who always included a certain number of generous lay men and women—who through dedication and sacrifice championed the cause of helping young people to reach maturity in Christ. But, above all, gratitude is due *to the Religious* for their contribution to Catholic education. In writing last Easter to the Bishops of the United States about Religious life, I stated: "Religious were among your pioneers. They blazed a trail in Catholic education at all levels, helping to create a magnificent educational system from elementary school to university" (Letter of April 3, 1983, no. 2).

*To women Religious* is due a very special debt of gratitude for their particular contribution to the field of education. Their authentic educational apostolate was, and is, worthy of the greatest praise. It is an apostolate that requires much self-sacrifice; it is thoroughly human as an expression of religious service: an apostolate that follows closely human and spiritual growth, and accompanies children and young people patiently and lovingly through the problems of youth and the insecurity of adolescence toward Christian maturity. How many married couples of your generation could—and did—point to women Religious who influenced their lives and helped them to reach that stage of personal development in which their vocation to married love and parenthood could be realized? And how many priests, brothers and sisters found edification in the witness of sacrificial love exemplified in Religious life, and the encouragement necessary for them to embark on the preparation for their own vocation?

5. Major factors in the Catholic education about which we have been speaking include *the Catholic teacher, Catholic doctrine* and *the Catholic school.*

### Primary Role of the Parents and the Contribution of Teachers

While the entire mission of Catholic education is essentially linked to the Church's life of faith and as such forms part of the Bishop's ministry, *the first educators* of individual children are *the parents*. In the new Code of Canon Law the whole treatment of education begins with the word "parents." In the eyes of the Church, and before God, their obligations and rights are unique, as are the sustaining graces they receive in the Sacrament of Marriage. It is this Sacrament that "gives to the educational role the dignity and vocation of being really and truly a 'ministry' of the Church" (*Familiaris Consortio*, 38). But *all Catholic teachers are invested with a great dignity* and are called to be "outstanding in true doctrine and uprightness of life" (can. 803, 2). The whole structural system of Catholic education will have value to the extent that the formation and education given by the teachers conform to the principles of Catholic doctrine.

### New Urgency to Explain Christ's Teaching

In religious education there is *a new urgency to explain Catholic doctrine*. Many young people of today look to Catholic educators, rightly saying: "You do not have to convince us; just explain well." And we know that, in whatever forum God's word is communicated, it has power to illuminate minds and to touch hearts: "Indeed, God's word is living and effective, sharper than any two-edged sword" (Heb. 4:12).

### Enormous Contribution of the Catholic Schools

6. In the history of your country an extremely effective instrument of Catholic education has been *the Catholic school*. It has contributed immensely to the spreading of God's word and has enabled the faithful "to relate human affairs and activities with religious values in a single living synthesis" (*Sapientia Christiana*, 1). In the community formed by the Catholic school, the power of the Gospel has been brought to bear on thought patterns, standards of judgment and norms of behavior. As an institution the Catholic school has to be judged extremely favorably if we apply the sound criterion "You will know them by their deeds" (Mt. 7:16), and again, "You can tell a tree by its fruit" (Mt. 7:20). It is easy therefore in the cultural environment of the United States to explain the wise exhortation contained in the new Code: "The faithful are to promote Catholic schools, doing everything possible to help in establishing and maintaining them" (can. 800, 2).

### Expressions of Esteem from Recent Popes

Your Catholic school system has long enjoyed *the esteem of the Holy See*. Pius XII at the very beginning of his pontificate wrote to the American Bishops at that time, saying: "It is with good reason then that visitors from other lands admire the organization and system under which your schools of various levels are conducted" (*Sertum Laetitiae*, 8, November 1, 1939). Years later, Paul VI, in canonizing Mother Seton, felt the need to praise the providence of God who raised up this woman to inaugurate in your country the work of the Catholic school (see *Address to American Bishops*, September 15, 1975). And two years later, in canonizing John Neumann, Paul VI spoke of the "relentless energy" with which he promoted the Catholic school system in the United States (Address of June 19, 1977).

## Maintain Institutional Identity

At every level of Catholic education the importance of the Catholic teacher and of Catholic doctrine is felt. At every level, up to and including the university level, there is the need for *an institutional commitment* of the Catholic school to the word of God as proclaimed by the Catholic Church.

And this institutional commitment is an expression of the Catholic identity of each Catholic school.

## Pastoral Leadership of the Bishop Takes a Variety of Forms

7. *Pastoral leadership of the Bishop is pivotal* in lending support and guidance to the whole cause of Catholic education. It is up to the Bishop, together with his priests, to encourage all Catholic educators to be inspired by the great ideal of communicating Christ. Only the Bishop can set the tone, ensure the priority and effectively present the importance of the cause to the Catholic people.

At the same time, the Bishop's zeal finds an endless challenge in providing *pastoral care for students*, realizing the special spiritual needs of students engaged in higher studies, inside and outside Catholic institutions, whose progress is very closely linked to the future of society and of the Church herself (see *Gravissimum Educationis*, 10).

## Maintain Pride of Place for
## an Organic and Systematic Catechesis

8. A particular dimension of Catholic education, which is at the same time a stage of evangelization, is *the question of catechesis* as it relates to Catholic institutions, as it is performed outside of Catholic schools, and as it is exercised directly by parents. From every viewpoint, catechesis involves "educating the true disciple of Christ by means of a deeper and more systematic knowledge of the person and message of our Lord Jesus Christ" (*Catechesi Tradendae*, 19). Especially under this catechetical aspect of imparting Catholic doctrine in an organized and systematic way, the Catholic school remains a truly relevant instrument at the service of faith, assisting the young to enter into the mystery of Christ. For this reason and for the other reasons already given, I renew *that prophetic appeal of Paul VI* to the American Bishops: "Brethren, we know the difficulties involved in preserving Catholic schools, and the uncertainties of the future. And yet we rely on the help of God and on your own zealous collaboration and untiring efforts, so that the Catholic schools can continue, despite grave obstacles, to fulfill their providential role at the service of genuine Catholic education, and at the service of your country" (Address of September 15, 1975).

### The Presence and Action of the Holy Spirit

9. In all of these things our own ministry at the service of the word depends on *the outpouring of the Holy Spirit.* It is he, venerable and dear brothers, whom we invoke today, asking him to assist you in your pastoral initiatives and to bring to fruition the efforts of so many dedicated priests, deacons, Religious and lay people in the local Churches that you represent.

He alone can actually enable us to communicate Christ; indeed, "no one can say: 'Jesus is Lord,' except in the Holy Spirit" (1 Cor. 12:3). Only through his action can Christian maturity be ensured and, hence, the aim of all Catholic education attained. As we proclaim the sovereignty of the sanctifying action of the Holy Spirit, let us ask him to submit our ministry totally to his will. And let us ask this grace of docility through the intercession of Mary, beneath whose heart the Word of God became man and was first communicated to the world.

*Veni Sancte Spiritus!*

# NINTH *AD LIMINA* ADDRESS TO THE BISHOPS OF THE UNITED STATES

## DECEMBER 3, 1983

Dear Brothers in our Lord Jesus Christ,

With deep fraternal affection I extend to you a cordial welcome to the See of Peter and willingly share with you this special hour of collegial unity and ecclesial communion. Through you I send my greetings of love and peace to the local Churches that you represent and serve: to all the priests, deacons, Religious, seminarians and lay people, who under your pastoral leadership are striving to live to the full the mystery of Christ and his Church. And in your persons I desire to honor Jesus Christ, the Shepherd and Bishop of our souls (see 1 Pt. 2:25).

### Sacred Liturgy and Prayer

1. I have already had the occasion to speak to another group of American Bishops about the Church's celebration of Sunday, and hence in particular about the Sunday Eucharistic celebration. Today I would like to make reference in a wider context to *the sacred liturgy and prayer* as they relate to the ministry of Bishops and to the life of the Church.

### Continue Apostolic Activity of Praising and Thanking God

Immediately before his Ascension, Jesus assured his Apostles that they would receive the Holy Spirit and be clothed with power. As they awaited the fulfillment of Christ's promise, "they were to be found in the temple constantly, speaking the praises of God" (Lk. 24:53). As Successors of the Apostles, the Bishops are called upon to continue through the liturgy of the Church the great apostolic activity of praising God. Especially in the liturgy *each Bishop is a sign of the praying Christ,* a sign of the Christ who speaks to his Father, saying: "I offer you praise, O Father, Lord of heaven and earth" (Lk. 10:21). The liturgy is the greatest instrument of praise, petition, intercession and reparation that the Church possesses. At no other moment in the ministry of the Bishop is his activity more relevant or useful to God's people than when he offers the Church's sacrifice of praise.

## Offer the Church's sacrifice of Thanksgiving
## for Manifold Graces

As a pastor of Christ's flock, the Bishop experiences personally *the need to thank God for the mystery of Christ's Cross and Resurrection* as it is actually lived each day in the pilgrim Church over which he presides and which he serves. The Bishop praises and blesses "the God and Father of our Lord Jesus Christ" (1 Pt. 1:3) for the marvels of grace that have been accomplished in the Christian people through the blood of Christ: for the fidelity to Christ that is lived by so many priests and Religious and by countless families in the world; for the splendid efforts made by young people to follow Christ's teaching; for the gift of conversion constantly given to the faithful in the Sacrament of Penance; for every vocation to the priesthood and Religious life; for the paschal combat and for the victory over evil that the Lord continually effects in his Body, the Church; for the good that is accomplished every day in the name of Jesus; for the gift of eternal life that is given to all who eat Christ's flesh and drink his blood, and for everything that God has given to his people in giving them his Son.

## The Worship of Divine Majesty
## Requires Profound Reverence and Faith

2. The liturgy occupies *a place of capital importance in the life of the Church.* The full and active participation in the liturgy has so rightly been pointed out by the Second Vatican Council as "the primary and indispensable source from which the faithful are to derive the true Christian spirit" (*Sacrosanctum Concilium,* 14). This principle is vital for a proper understanding of conciliar renewal, and deserves repeated emphasis. Equally vital is an understanding of the liturgy as being "above all the worship of the divine majesty" (*Sacrosanctum Concilium,* 33). As such, it must be approached by our priests and people with that sense of profound reverence which corresponds to the deepest instincts of their Catholic faith. The liturgy in itself contains a special power to bring about renewal and holiness, and the people's awareness of this power—its contemplation in faith—actuates it even more. I recently expressed this to the Bishops of America in this way: "When our people, through the grace of the Holy Spirit, realize that they are called to be 'a chosen race, a royal priesthood, a holy nation' (1 Pt. 2:9), and that they are called to adore and thank the Father in union with Jesus Christ, *an immense power is unleashed* in their Christian lives. When

they realize that they actually have a sacrifice of praise and expiation to offer together with Jesus Christ, when they realize that all their prayers of petition are united to an infinite act of the praying Christ, then there is fresh hope and encouragement for the Christian people" (July 9, 1983).

### The Community of Worship Prays Both Liturgically as the Body of Christ and Through Individuals

3. *The true Christian spirit* that the faithful derive from the liturgy ensures the building up of the Church in many ways. Through the acquisition by her members of this Christian spirit, the Church becomes ever more *a community of worship and prayer,* conscious of "the necessity of praying always and not losing heart" (Lk. 18:1). This characteristic of constant prayer, as befits the Body of Christ, is manifested in the official prayer of the liturgy: in the Eucharist, in the celebration of the other sacraments and in the Liturgy of the Hours. In all these actions, the mediation of Christ the Head continues, and the whole Church is offered to the Father: the entire Body of Christ intercedes for the salvation of the world.

### Christ Asks for Private Prayer

At the same time the Church realizes that her vital activity and hence her duty to pray is not restricted to liturgical prayer. The Council has explicitly stated: "The spiritual life however is not confined to participation in the liturgy" (*Sacrosanctum Concilium,* 12). Christ still asks *individual prayer* from all of us his members, repeating his injunction: "Pray to your Father in private" (Mt. 6:6). Among nonliturgical forms of prayer, one that is worthy of special esteem is the Rosary of the Blessed Virgin Mary. In addition, every effort to make the Christian family a place of prayer deserves our full encouragement and support.

### The Liturgy Proclaims the Truth and Helps to Make It Living

4. The liturgy is eminently effective in rendering the Church an ever more dynamic *community of truth.* In the liturgy, the truth of God is celebrated and his word becomes the sustenance of the people that glories in his name. By its power, the liturgy helps us to assimilate what is proclaimed and celebrated in our midst. In the words of the prophet Jeremiah: "When I found your words, I devoured them; they became my joy and the happiness of my heart, because I bore your name, O Lord, God of hosts" (Jer. 15:16). Through the sacred liturgy the People of God received the strength to live God's word in their lives: to be doers of that word and not hearers only (see Jas. 1:23).

### The Eucharist Is the Source of the Church's Internal Unity

5. The sacred liturgy, and in particular the Eucharistic Sacrifice, is *the source of the Church's internal unity*—"that unity which is tarnished on the human face of the

Church by every form of sin, but which subsists indestructibly in the Catholic Church" (see *Lumen Gentium,* 8; *Unitatis Redintegratio,* 2, 3; *AAS* 71, 1979, p. 1226). And while the celebration of the Sacrifice of the Mass and participation in the Supper of the Lord already require this Catholic unity, it is through them that we pour out to God our earnest desire for that complete unity in faith and love that Christ desires for all his followers. In the Eucharist the Church declares her perfect conformity to Christ's will for ever-greater purification, conversion and renewal.

### Unity Between Worship and Ecclesial and Social Service

6. *The relationship of worship and prayer to service and action* has a deep meaning for the Church. The Church considers herself called from worship into service; at the same time she looks upon her service as related to her prayer. She attaches extreme importance to the example of Christ, whose actions were all accompanied by prayer and accomplished in the Holy Spirit. For all Christ's disciples the principle is the same and, as Bishops, we must help our people never to forget this essential aspect of their service; it is *a specifically Christian and ecclesial dimension of action.*

It is indeed in prayer that a social consciousness is nurtured and at the same time evaluated. It is in prayer that the Bishop, together with his people, ponders *the need and exigencies of Christian service.* Seven years ago, in his message to the Call to Action Conference in Detroit, Paul VI formulated important principles, stating: "The Lord Jesus does not want us ever to forget that the mark of our discipleship is concern for the brethren. . . . Yes, the cause of human dignity and of human rights is the cause of Christ and his Gospel. Jesus of Nazareth is forever identified with his brethren." Through prayer the Church realizes the full import of Christ's words: "This is how all will know you for my disciples: your love for one another" (Jn. 13:35). It is in prayer that the Church understands the many implications of the fact that justice and mercy are among "the weightier matters of the law" (Mt. 23:23). Through prayer, the struggle for justice finds its proper motivation and encouragement, and discovers and maintains truly effective means.

### A Prayerful Church Should Be a Natural Community of Service

Only a worshiping and praying Church can show herself sufficiently sensitive to the needs of the sick, the suffering, the lonely—especially in the great urban centers—and the poor everywhere. The Church as a *community of service* has first to feel the weight of the burden carried by so many individuals and families, and then strive to help alleviate these burdens. The discipleship that the Church discovers in prayer she expresses in deep interest for Christ's brethren in the modern world and for their many different needs. Her concern, manifested in various ways, embraces—among others—the areas of housing, education, health care, unemployment, the administration of justice, the special needs of the aged and the handicapped. In prayer, the

Church is confirmed in her solidarity with the weak who are oppressed, the vulnerable who are manipulated, the children who are exploited, and everyone who is in any way discriminated against.

The Church's service in all these fields must take on specific and concrete forms, and this requires understanding and competence on the part of the various members of the ecclesial community. But *the whole program of diakonia must be sustained by prayer,* by vital contact with Christ, who insists on linking discipleship with service. For this reason Paul VI concluded his message to the Detroit Conference with these insights: "In the tradition of the Church, any call to action is first of all a call to prayer. And so you are summoned to prayer, and above all to a greater sharing in Christ's Eucharistic Sacrifice. . . . It is in the Eucharist that you find the true Christian spirit that will enable you to go out and act in Christ's name."

### The Link Between Eucharistic Peace
### and Concrete Peacemaking

7. There is moreover a real relationship between the peace that is proclaimed and actuated in the Eucharist and all the initiatives of the Church to bring Christ's peace to the world. Your own dedicated efforts to promote peace and to help establish in the world those conditions that favor peace are, like peace itself, totally dependent on God's grace. And this grace, this strength, this help is God's gift to us, given freely, but given also because it is sought in the name of Jesus, through prayer, through the Eucharist. Your local Churches are called to be *communities promoting peace, living peace, invoking peace.*

### The Practice of Collegiality Entails Promoting Unity
### Between the Local and Universal Churches

8. In every other sector, too, of Christian life, the Church lives out her nature and reaches her aims by prayer and worship. Indeed, it is in this way that she becomes ever more *a communion of love.* And we, as Bishops in the Church of God, are called to make our specific contribution to the building up of the communion of love by our own *practice of collegiality,* by every personal effort that we expend to promote, defend and consolidate the unity of faith and discipline between the local Churches and the universal Church. And all of these efforts are conceived in prayer and effected through union with the praying Christ. It is supremely significant that in the very act—the offering of the Eucharistic Sacrifice—in which your local Churches attain their deepest identity as a community of worship and a communion of love, you and I are mentioned by name. The identity of our Catholic people and the authenticity of their worship are forever linked to our own ministry, which is none other than the ministry of Jesus Christ, through whom and with whom and in whom all glory and honor is given to the Father and every prayer attains its efficacy.

The worship that animates your local Churches, the inspiration for *diakonia* and the whole true Christian spirit that derives from the Church's liturgy are by their essence Christocentric, and directed to the Father in the unity of the Holy Spirit. Indeed, every prayer we offer for our people is made with Christ the Lord and High Priest of our salvation. And because our prayer as Bishops is also apostolic, we make it together with Mary the Mother of Jesus (see Acts 1:14).

Dear brother Bishops, in praying with Mary we shall discover ever more clearly *the meaning of our pastoral ministry of worship, of prayer and of service* to Christ's Church and to the modern world.

## FIRST *AD LIMINA* ADDRESS TO THE BISHOPS OF THE UNITED STATES

## REGION IX: PROVINCES OF DUBUQUE, KANSAS CITY, OMAHA AND ST. LOUIS

## MARCH 5, 1988

Dear Brothers in our Lord Jesus Christ,

1. With this visit there begins the 1988 series of the *ad Limina* visits of the American Bishops. Today I am very pleased to welcome all of you who make up the first group and who come from the ecclesiastical provinces of Dubuque, Kansas City, Omaha and Saint Louis. You represent a great cross section of the Catholic people of the United States, bringing with you, as you do, *the hopes and aspirations, the joys and difficulties of so many people*—individuals, families and entire particular Churches within the states of Iowa, Kansas, Nebraska and Missouri.

### Continuity Between *ad Limina* Visits and Papal Trips

For all of us this is *an hour of ecclesial communion* that follows closely upon my second visit to the United States and especially our important meeting in Los Angeles. There is, moreover, a continuity between this present series of *ad Limina* visits and that of 1983, which in turn was in continuity with my first visit to America in 1979. All of these encounters are likewise linked to the future of the Church in the United States, which I hope to be able to reflect on again next year in a meeting with American Bishops.

### The Mystery of Communion—Our Salvation in Faith

2. Because this present hour is one of ecclesial communion, it is linked to *our own salvation*. The Church began her Lenten celebration proclaiming with Saint Paul: "Now is the acceptable time! Now is the day of salvation!" (2 Cor. 6:2). Like all the other members of the Church *we ourselves must approach our salvation in faith*—faith in the mystery of Jesus Christ and his Church. As Bishops we put this faith into practice by actuating the mystery of our own hierarchical communion in the Church.

*By living this mystery of communion today, we are giving the response of faith to Christ* as he holds up before us his design of unity for his Church and for all who make up the College of Bishops.

On this occasion, you and I, united in ecclesial communion as pastors of individual Dioceses in America and as the Pastor of the universal Church, respectively, have *the task of offering to Jesus Christ,* the Supreme Shepherd of the entire flock, *the Church in the United States.* This Church belongs to Jesus Christ by right. He loves her intensely and intends to possess her ever more fully and to purify her ever more deeply in every aspect of her ecclesial reality.

### Gratitude to Christ for the Ecclesial Reality

3. I wish to express once again sentiments of *profound gratitude and satisfaction* at having been able *to visit for a second time the Church in the United States* and to have experienced so many aspects of her life. Coupled with these sentiments are also those of *admiration* for everything that the grace of Christ has accomplished in the lives of God's people in your land. *The ecclesial reality in the United States is an expression of the power of Christ's Paschal Mystery at work* in the lives of countless individuals and numerous communities. Over and over again this ecclesial reality deserves our prayerful reflection.

### Liturgical Celebrations and Expressions of the Faith Life

During the course of my September visit to nine Dioceses I was able to experience *the life of faith* which is lived in all 186 Dioceses throughout the United States, which include twelve Eastern Rite Dioceses and the Military Ordinariate. What was especially gratifying was to meet all *the various categories* that make up the one People of God: Bishops, priests, deacons, Religious, seminarians and Religious in formation, and the Catholic laity. All of these categories were present not only in special encounters arranged for me but in the large liturgical celebrations held in each Diocese. Repeatedly I *witnessed the faith* of a Church that could address herself to God in the words of the Psalm: "I will give you thanks in the vast assembly; in the mighty throng I will praise you" (Ps. 35:18). And again: "I will give thanks to the Lord with all my heart in the company and assembly of the just. Great are the works of the Lord, exquisite in all their delights" (Ps 111:1–2).

### The Experience of the Church as Incarnate in Many Contexts

In every event in which I took part, the local Bishop was at my side. *Together we experienced the Church* as she is incarnate in the historical, geographical, social, economic, political and religious context of the United States of America. I saw. I listened. I was addressed. I spoke. And the Church prayed—Christ prayed in his Body, in us, the Church. And all of us entered into closer communion with each other and with him, the Supreme Shepherd.

## The Papal Message:
## Proclaim Christ and Ask for the Response of Faith

4. My particular role throughout the whole visit was *to proclaim Jesus Christ* as the Son of God and the Redeemer of man—every man, woman and child. At the same time I came to America in order *to ask everyone to meet Jesus Christ* and *to give him the response of faith:* to believe in his name, to accept his word, to be open to his love and the love of his Father and the Holy Spirit.

## The Incarnation as the New Foundation
## of Human Dignity for Everyone

At the basis of all my exhortations to *fraternal solidarity and love* was that *pivotal truth* proclaimed by the Second Vatican Council: "By his Incarnation the Son of God united himself in a certain way with each human being" (*Gaudium et Spes,* 22). The Incarnation as the expression of God's love is *the new foundation of human dignity for everyone.* Hence I could not speak of God's love without speaking of human dignity and what it requires. And so at the very beginning of my visit in Miami I stated: "I come *to proclaim the Gospel of Jesus Christ* to all who freely choose to listen to me; to tell again the story of God's love in the world, to spell out once more the message of human dignity with its inalienable human rights and its inevitable human duties" (September 10, 1987).

## The Response of Faith Took Many Forms
## During the Papal Visit

5. All of us were in fact able to perceive *a great response of faith,* in so many ways, on the part of the people—everything being accomplished by the Lord, in accordance with the words of the psalm: "Come! behold the deeds of the Lord, the astounding things he has wrought" (Ps. 46:9). This response of faith was evident in the wonderful collaboration and hard work of preparation for my visit, in the understanding and acceptance of my role as the Successor of the Apostle Peter, in an openness to the proclamation of the Gospel message, and in our common worship. In so many ways the people expressed their faith in the Church as she exists by the will of Christ: both particular and universal.

## The Mystery of the Universal Church
## Realized in Particular Churches

One of the great riches of the Church in the United States is *the way in which she herself incarnates universality or catholicity* in her ethnic makeup, taken as she is "from every nation and race, people and tongue" (Rv. 7:9). The Church in the United States has the advantage of being naturally disposed to live catholicity and to show solidarity with all those particular Churches where her people came from originally. The ethnic contributions to the various liturgies celebrated during my visit were not mere folkloric expressions; they were rather keys opening the door to a fuller understanding of the ecclesial reality of the Church in the United States.

In witnessing aspect after aspect of the Church in your land, I was conscious in each Diocese of the mystery of the universal Church as she subsists in particular Churches that *joyfully make their pilgrimage of faith,* amidst obstacles and opposition, to the Father of our Lord Jesus Christ.

The ecclesial reality presented to me in each diocesan community was a portion of Christ's flock, invested with his Spirit—as poured out through the Paschal Mystery—and living by that same Spirit. It was *the Church of Christ living the mystery of Redemption* in the modern world, being herself continually purified after her immersion into the bath of regeneration (see Eph. 5:26).

## The Church in U.S.A.: Open to Pastoral Challenges

6. As the Church in the United States works to be faithful to her task of actuating the Kingdom of God in its initial stage, she strives earnestly *to meet pastoral challenges* all around her, the fundamental one of which is *to be constantly converted or renewed in God's love.* Being convinced of the openness of the Church in the United States to challenge, of her good will, and, above all, of Christ's grace active within her, I too challenged her in various ways, including setting before her the need to be open to renewal by God himself.

## The Chief Challenge:
## Call to Conversion, Call to Pursue Holiness

In effect, being renewed in God's love has *very concrete requirements* for the whole Church, and hence for the Church in the United States. It means that she must live to the full *her vocation to holiness.* In the world she must be herself; she must always be what she is meant to be: the holy Body of Christ. In chapter 5 of *Lumen Gentium* the Church has given to all her sons and daughters a great gift in clearly enunciating the universal call to holiness: "All Christ's followers therefore are invited and bound to pursue holiness and the perfect fulfillment of their proper state" (no. 42). The application of this principle to married couples, Christian parents, widowed and single people is of extreme importance. The Church is truly *the Sacrament of holiness for everyone.* The Council insisted "that all the faithful of Christ of whatever rank or status are called to the fullness of Christian life and to the perfection of charity" (*Lumen Gentium,* 40).

## The Universal Call to Holiness Affects the Laity

How important it was for the whole Church that the Council should so strongly present this challenge to the laity! Without this principle the full participation of the laity in the life and mission of the Church could never have been ensured. The universal call to holiness was also at the basis of the recent Synod of Bishops on the Laity.

Specific consequences of this principle have been spelled out in the Pastoral Constitution *Gaudium et Spes,* which does not admit "false opposition between professional and social activities on the one part, and religious life on the other" and which tells us that the "split between the faith which many profess and their daily lives deserves to be counted among the more serious errors of our age" (no. 43).

## The Challenge of Evangelization:
## To Discover the Meaning of Life in Christ's Redemption

7. As the Church in all her own members endeavors to live her vocation of holiness, she is also mindful of her obligation *to help all people to discover in Christ's Redemption the full meaning of life* in this world. This is another great challenge for the Church. At the beginning of my Pontificate, I expressed it in my first encyclical, saying: "The Church's fundamental action in every age and particularly in ours is to direct man's gaze, to point the awareness and experience of the whole of humanity towards the mystery of Christ, to help all people to be familiar with the profundity of the Redemption taking place in Christ Jesus" (*Redemptor Hominis,* 10).

## The Challenge Flows from the
## Missionary Nature of the Church

This challenge to help all people to be open to the Redemption is linked with *the Church's missionary activity* and therefore with her own *missionary nature.* The Church in the United States—like the universal Church—must be committed to this cause today and forever. During my visit to Phoenix I had the opportunity to touch upon this vital aspect of the Church's life, citing also the American Bishops' 1986 Pastoral Statement on World Mission. The question that I asked in Phoenix still requires further answers from the Church both in the United States and throughout the world: "Who will respond to God's missionary call at the end of the twentieth century?"

## Evangelization Requires Programs
## Designed to Meet Human Needs

8. To bring the fullness of God's word to people, to point their gaze to the mystery of Christ, to help them to understand human dignity and the meaning of life through the key of the Redemption is *the supreme service of the Church to humanity.* The Church renders this service in the name of Christ and through the power of his Spirit. At the same time she knows that, in consequence of the principle of the Incarnation—Christ's union with every human being—she must constantly link with her missionary activity and all her work of evangelization *a vast program to help meet*

*other human needs.* She is vitally interested in making her specific contribution to uplifting humanity to the level that corresponds to the rightful dignity already granted to it in the mystery of the Word made flesh.

## The Gospel Inspires Ecclesial Solicitude for Human Need

*The Church finds in Jesus Christ,* the Incarnate Word, *the principle of her solicitude for humanity,* for the future of humanity on earth and for the whole of development and progress (see *Redemptor Hominis,* 15). All of the Church's motives are inspired by the Gospel of Christ (see *Sollicitudo Rei Socialis,* 47).

## Mission of Solidarity:
## Serious Responsibility for the Church Today

The *mission of solidarity,* to which I have dedicated my latest encyclical and on which there will be further opportunities for reflection, represents *a specially grave responsibility* for the Church today. During my visit to the United States I was able to see with what *seriousness* the local Churches have responded to the needs of their brothers and sisters, with what *generosity* they have striven to alleviate suffering and pain, with what *alacrity* they have shown their solidarity with humanity. Not only do I recall the panorama of charitable works and health care that was presented to me in San Antonio and Phoenix, and also efforts of many of your local Churches to respond to the farm crisis, but I know the *commitment of all the People of God in America to carry out their vocation of Christian service.*

## God Wants Us to Take Up the Challenge of Service

This challenge of service, with its motivation in Christ and his Gospel, must accompany the Church in the United States during the whole length of her pilgrimage of faith. Acceptance of this challenge is *extremely pleasing to God;* failure to do so is fatal. The Second Vatican Council reminds us: "The Christian who neglects his temporal duties neglects his duties toward his neighbor and even God, and jeopardizes his eternal salvation" (*Gaudium et Spes,* 43).

## Support of the Prayers of the Virgin Mary

These and other challenges, dear brothers, stand before the Church of God in the United States—a beloved Church living in the power of Christ's Spirit and called to ever greater holiness of life, especially during this Marian Year of grace. As you rise up humbly with your people to meet these challenges, you have every reason to be filled with *hope.* In all your efforts to live worthily the mystery of the Church, you are supported by the prayers of the Blessed Virgin Mary, who, "as a sign of sure hope and solace" (*Lumen Gentium,* 68), accompanies you on your pilgrimage of faith toward the final goal of eternal life in Christ Jesus. As you make your pilgrim way along this path, I ask you to take *deep encouragement from the words of the Prophet:* "The Lord God is in your midst, a mighty savior; he will rejoice over you with gladness and renew you in his love" (Zep. 3:17).

In this love I send my Apostolic Blessing to all your local Churches, being especially mindful of all those who bear the Cross of Christ in pain and suffering.

## SECOND *AD LIMINA* ADDRESS TO THE BISHOPS OF THE UNITED STATES

### REGION X: TEXAS, OKLAHOMA AND ARKANSAS

### APRIL 17, 1988

Dear Brothers in our Lord Jesus Christ,

1. It is a great pleasure for me to welcome all of you, the Bishops of Texas, Oklahoma and Arkansas. In you I greet all your beloved faithful and each of your local Churches with all its priests, deacons, Religious, seminarians and laity. I recall with special joy my recent visit to San Antonio, the wonderful welcome given me and the impressive faith of the people. I assure you that I remain close to you in your ministry of faith, as does the Mother of Jesus, la Virgen de Guadalupe.

### Pastoral Events of Visits Related to Goals of Holiness, Evangelization and Service

In my recent talk to your brother Bishops of Region IX, I mentioned a series of related pastoral events that are, in effect, inspired by a single vision of faith and directed to the goals of deep personal renewal and ever more effective evangelical service in the United States. These events include the present *ad Limina* visits and those of 1983, the papal visits of 1979 and 1987, as well as the meeting with American Bishops foreseen for 1989.

### Serious Preparation for the Jubilee of the Second Millennium

Today I would like to view in this context still another event—one which concerns the universal Church and therefore the Church in the United States. It is *the great Jubilee of the year 2000,* marking the close of the Second Millennium of Christianity and the inauguration of the Third. This anniversary requires of the whole Church a period of serious preparation at both the universal and local levels. From the beginning of my Pontificate, and in particular in the encyclical *Redemptor Hominis,* I have attempted to direct the attention of the Church to the season of "a new Advent" (no. 1), which precedes all the grace-filled opportunities and activities which we ardently hope for in the year 2000.

## Elicit the Response of Faith to the Incarnate Word

2. The *aim of the Jubilee and of its preparation* is to "recall and reawaken in us in a special way our awareness of the key truth of faith which Saint John expressed at the beginning of his Gospel: 'The Word became flesh and dwelt among us' (Jn. 1:14)" (*Redemptor Hominis,* no. 1). The whole celebration of the Millennium is meaningful only in the light of the mystery of the Incarnation and of its divine motivation and purpose, which are also explained to us by Saint John, when he says: "God so loved the world that he gave his only Son, that whoever believes in him may not die but may have eternal life" (Jn. 3:16). Emphasizing these truths, the Church strives to provide *a framework of principles* from which she will continue to draw out from her life "the new and the old" (Mt. 13:52) in order to elicit the response of faith to the Father's love and to his Incarnate Word, and to lead us all to eternal life.

## This Mystery Explains the Mystery of the Church and Gives Perspective to Human Life

*By reflecting on the Incarnation,* the Church of the year 2000 will be able to understand herself ever more fully in her twofold nature—human and divine. She will also understand the sublime union of these two elements in the everyday reality of her life as the Body of the Word made flesh. The Church is convinced that, by placing the Incarnation before the People of God with all the power of her being, mankind will rediscover in this mystery of God's revealed love the truth that explains and directs all human activity. Only in the light of the Incarnation does all human living take on its proper perspective, or as I stated in that first encyclical: "Through the Incarnation God gave human life the dimension that he intended man to have from his first beginning" (no. 1).

## Dynamic Vision: Church Faithful to Christ and Looking to the Full Realization of the Kingdom

3. Our present pastoral effort as Bishops, those envisioned for 1989 and those beyond should be directed to creating that *profound and dynamic vision which must characterize the Church in the year 2000.* The Church of the Millennium must have an increased consciousness of being the Kingdom of God in its initial stage. She must show that she is *vitally concerned with being faithful to Christ;* hence she must strive mightily to respond to the great challenges of holiness, evangelization and service. At the same time the Church of the Millennium must emerge as *a clear sign of her own eschatological state,* living by faith the mystery that is yet to be fully revealed. As she does this the Church must proclaim with Saint Paul that "eye has not seen nor has ear heard what God has prepared for those who love him" (1 Cor. 2:9).

### Purification Through Suffering Elicits Hope
### in the Eschatological Glory to Be Revealed

The Church of the Millennium will still be *the Church undergoing purification through suffering*—the salvific value of which she fully knows. Yet in her purifying experiences the Church will still be able to cry out that the sufferings of this time are "as nothing compared with the glory to be revealed in us" (Rom. 8:18). As a Church living in expectation of glory to be revealed she will find ever greater strength to *proclaim the value of celibacy* that is lived for the Kingdom of God, the final state of which is in preparation: "Thy Kingdom come!"

### Readiness to Meet Christ in Glory

At such an important juncture of her life, the Church of the Millennium must declare that she is ready at any moment to meet the Lord, just as she is ready to go on faithfully in joyful hope awaiting his Coming. But in both her waiting and her expectation she is reinforced in hope because *she knows that Christ her Head has gone before her* in his Ascension to prepare a place for her. And as she waits, she remembers what he once said to the disciples: "If I go and prepare a place for you, I will come back again and take you to myself, so that where I am you also may be" (Jn. 14:3).

### Hope of Sharing in the Triumph of the Head of the Body

The Church is convinced of her right to be with Jesus, who, seated at the right hand of the Father, has already united her to himself in glory. *The triumph of the Head already belongs to the members* of the Body. This makes it easy for the Church as she lives the new Advent to accept with keen conviction the words of her victorious Redeemer: "Remember, I am coming soon" (Rv. 22:12). During the Millennium the Church is called upon to remember. It is also the special hour for the Church to respond with fidelity and confidence, proclaiming by her actions and by her whole life: "Come Lord Jesus!" (v. 20).

### Prepare for the Millennium
### by Total Concentration of Christ Redeemer

4. *The Church's program* for the Millennium and its preparation must be *a total concentration of Jesus Christ*. She must proclaim Jesus Christ as victorious in the Redemption that he brought about in his blood; she must proclaim Jesus Christ, crucified and glorified, the One wearing "a cloak dipped in blood" and bearing the name "the Word of God" (Rv. 19:13). The Church is called upon to proclaim the supreme effectiveness of Christ's death; to proclaim that the triumph of the Lamb is already operative in the Church for two millennia, and that it belongs to all his chosen and faithful followers (see Rv. 17:14). The Church's proclamation in the Millennium must be the proclamation of her own victory over sin and death accomplished by

him who is "the first-born from the dead" (Rv. 1:5) and who communicates this victory to all his members throughout the ages.

### Proclaim the Word Made Flesh
### and in Him the Exaltation of Human Life

*The Christ of the Millennium* is this first-born from the dead, "the King of kings and Lord of lords" (Rv. 19:16), the Eternal Son, *Word of God made flesh,* the person who identifies himself as "the One who lives" (Rv. 1:18) and who tells his Church: "There is nothing to fear!" (v. 17). It is precisely this Christ, *divine and incarnate,* that the Church presents to the world as the supreme exemplar of all human life. In this sense the Church makes her own the presentation of Pontius Pilate: *"Ecce homo"* (Jn. 19:5). *The proclamation of the Millenium* will be the proclamation of *this man Jesus Christ* and in him the exaltation of all humanity. The Word, who remains forever with his Father and as such is the truth and life of humanity, in taking human flesh becomes *the way for humanity* (see Saint Augustine, *Tract. in Ioannem* 34, 9).

### Christ as Man Is the Power and Wisdom of God
### for Transforming History and Culture

The Christ of the Millennium is *the divine Christ of the Gospels* who has entered into his glory and who is forever alive in his word and in his Church. He is not a weak and ineffective Christ but a Christ who has triumphed throughout twenty centuries and who remains "the power of God and the wisdom of God" (1 Cor. 1:24). To those who accept him, moreover, he gives the power to become the children of God, to become by adoption what he is by nature—the Son of God. The Christ of the Millennium is *the Man* who has entered into the history of nations, has uplifted cultures by his message, transformed the destinies of peoples and who, in revealing God to man, has revealed all humanity to itself (see *Gaudium et Spes,* 22).

### The Millennium Is the Hour of Christian Identity
### in Its Catholic Universality

5. The Millennium becomes therefore *the hour of our Christian identity in all its Catholic universality.* In order to celebrate the Millennium effectively, the Church must recall her *origin* and reflect deeply on her *mission.* To do this she must retrace the path she has taken up till now, bearing her apostolic message down the centuries, beginning "in Jerusalem, throughout Judea and Samaria, yes, even to the ends of the earth" (Acts 1:8). It is truly the appropriate hour to foster a consciousness of our Christian tradition and culture. These elements have found expression in the art, architecture, music, literature and other expressions of genius which each generation and all generations together in the Church have created throughout the centuries in the name of Christ. There are many ways to foster this consciousness, but certainly the means of social communications at our disposal must be utilized to the full.

## A New Pentecost of Vast Internal Renewal
## Through New Attitudes

6. Living in the Spirit sent to her by Christ, the Church looks forward to the Millennium as *a time of vast internal renewal*. By his power the Holy Spirit is truly able to effect in the Church a *new Pentecost*. On the part of all of us, however, this requires *new attitudes* of humility, generosity and openness to the purifying action of the Spirit.

## Special Place of Private Confession
## and the Celebration of the Eucharist

The whole concept of renewal must be seen in its relationship to *Penance and the Eucharist*. In *Redemptor Hominis* I emphasized "that the Church of the new Advent . . . must be the Church of the Eucharist and of Penance" (no. 20). Only with these means will the Church be herself and have the strength to fulfill her mission. The Millennium is the supreme moment for the glorification of the Cross of Christ and for the proclamation of forgiveness through his blood. I ask all the Bishops of the Church—and today in a special way the Bishops of the United States—to do everything possible, in preparing for the Millennium, to promote the faithful observance of the centuries-old practice of individual Confession, guaranteeing thereby the individual's right to a personal encounter with the crucified and merciful Christ, and the right of Christ to meet each one of us in the key moment of conversion and pardon (see *Redemptor Hominis*).

Presiding over every celebration of the Millennium will be *the Eucharistic Lord,* himself renewing his Church and presenting her to the Father in union with himself. It is mainly through the Eucharist that the Millennium will actuate the power of the Redemption. In the Eucharist the Church will find the sure source and guarantee of her commitment to the service of humanity.

## The Special Role of the Laity in the Church and the World

From the Eucharist *the Catholic laity* will derive the strength to perform with joy and perseverance their specific role in the Church and in the world. During the Millennium there must be an ever more generous actuation of everything that the Post-Synodal document on the laity will propose for the life and mission of the laity.

## Bring Christ to the World
## by Proclaiming the Church's Teaching on
## Truth, Justice, Chastity, Evangelical Peacemaking

7. In all her activities the Church of the Millennium must be totally absorbed with *the task of bringing Christ to the world*. This will require her to understand the world ever more deeply and to dialogue ever more intensely with all people of good

will. As the Church does this with *love* and *respect,* and as she reinforces her own *meekness—after* the example of the meek and humble Christ—she must at the same time shed any remnant of fear at the prospect of displeasing the world when she presents to it her Founder's message in all its purity and with all its exigencies. She must also divest herself of any trace of defensiveness as she acknowledges Christ to be forever "a sign of contradiction," and proclaims his teaching on issues such as *truth, justice, evangelical peacemaking* and *chastity.*

The Pastoral Statement of the Bishops of Texas on Human Sexuality represents a much-appreciated pastoral effort to present the Church's teaching on chastity without fear or reticence, with trust in the power of truth and the grace of God.

The whole event of the Millennium is the hour for the apostolic Church to bear witness to the Christ who sent her to the nations, telling her: "Teach them to carry out everything I have commanded you and know that I am with you always" (Mt. 28:20).

### Vision of the Millennium as Pastoral Initiative, Ecclesial Event, Response of Faith

8. Dear brothers, what I wish to do today is leave with you and with the whole Church in America a vision of the Millennium as a pastoral *initiative, an ecclesial event, a response of faith* to the God who "so loved the world that he gave his only Son" (Jn. 3:16). This vision must be captured by the whole Church in the United States and expressed in each Diocese, each parish, each community. All the institutions in the Church must be challenged by this spiritual event. The Church's fidelity to Christ is at stake in the way she will proclaim the Incarnation and the Redemption, in the way she will celebrate, interiorly and publicly, the most important anniversary that humanity has ever known.

### Theological Reflection Will Reinforce Faith

Whereas the year 2000 still seems somewhat distant, *the period of "the new Advent" is already a reality for the Church.* Long-range preparations are needed now. *Theological reflections* must help to reinforce the faith of God's people, so that they may mightily proclaim their Redeemer by word and deed in the great Jubilee. Your own pastoral zeal and creativity will help you to prepare worthily your local Churches for this event and to adopt means commensurate with the goals to be attained. All the faithful of the Church must understand the spirit of the Millennium so that they can all contribute to its preparation and celebration.

### Priests and Seminarians Join Bishops in Bringing Forth a New Christian Humanism

By their very nature *the seminaries* in your country must fulfill a key role in the renewal required by the Millennium. Together with their Bishops, *the priests* of the new Advent must be able to unite their communities around the person of the Redeemer and to give spiritual leadership in bringing forth *a new Christian humanism*.

## Diverse Contributions of Contemplatives, of the Sick and Suffering, and of Intellectual Circles

The special support of *prayer and penance* must be sought from *contemplative Religious* and that of *salvific suffering* from all *the sick*. *Catholic institutions of higher learning* must contribute with faith by enunciating ever more clearly the Gospel heritage in its relationship to all human learning. All the categories of God's people must be invited to unite in a great hymn of praise: "To him who loves us and freed us from our sins by his blood . . . to him be glory and power forever and ever" (Rv. 1:5).

May this hymn of praise to the Redeemer, dear brothers, truly resound throughout Texas, Oklahoma, Arkansas and the whole United States during the new Advent and in preparation for the Jubilee celebration itself.

## THIRD *AD LIMINA* ADDRESS TO THE BISHOPS OF THE UNITED STATES

## REGION V: PROVINCES OF LOUISVILLE, MOBILE AND NEW ORLEANS

## MAY 31, 1988

Dear Brothers in our Lord Jesus Christ,

1. Once again it is a great joy for me to welcome a group of American Bishops. In you I greet all the priests, deacons, Religious and laity of the Provinces of Louisville, Mobile and New Orleans. Memories of New Orleans encourage me to send special greetings to those groups that I met there: the youth of America, the apostles of Catholic education, the beloved black community throughout your land, and all those striving to meet the challenge of greatness in higher Catholic education. At the same time I remember in my thoughts and cherish in my heart all the faithful of America, for whom we are striving to provide true pastoral service in the name of "the Chief Shepherd of the flock" (1 Pt. 5:4), our Lord and Savior Jesus Christ.

## Call for Organic Pastoral Planning to Restore the Sacrament of Penance to Its Rightful Place

In all the pastoral events that I experience with you, the Bishops of the United States—each event in continuity with the preceding ones—it is my intention to reflect with you on *an organic pastoral view* of our episcopal ministry. This organic view must take into account the perennial exigencies of the Gospel; it must also express the indisputable priorities of the life of the Church today, both in her universal needs and in the special requirements of the Church in the United States. At the same time it must faithfully reflect *the call of the Second Vatican Council to reform and renewal* as reiterated by the Bishop of Rome and the worldwide Episcopate in communion with him. This communion is especially evident in the different sessions of the Synod of Bishops, the conclusions of which are of special urgency for all pastoral planning in the Church.

### Conversion as Proclaimed by Christ
### Is the Basis for Organic Pastoral Plan

2. One of the essential themes of the Gospel that has been emphasized by both the Second Vatican Council and the Synod of Bishops is *the call to penance or conversion*—and consequently to reconciliation—incumbent on all members of the Church, and particularly relevant to our own lives and ministry as Bishops. *Conversion as proclaimed by Christ is a whole program of life and pastoral action.* It is the basis for an organic view of pastoral ministry, because it is linked to all the great aspects of God's revelation.

### Acknowledge Primacy of God
### and Reality of Sin Through Christ

Conversion speaks to us about the need to acknowledge the primacy of God in the world and in our individual lives. It presupposes the reality of sin and the need to respond to God in and through Christ the Savior, who frees us from our sins. Christ's command of conversion imposes on us "the obedience of faith" (Rom 1:5) in all its implications.

### Conversion: Inmost Change of Heart
### That Passes to Deed and Life

Conversion becomes for us a *synthesis of the Gospel,* and repeated conversions throughout the ages reflect the unceasing action of the Risen Christ on the life of the Church. Jesus himself introduces us to the meaning of penance or conversion when he says: "Repent and believe in the Gospel" (Mk. 1:15). Conversion signifies *an internal change* of attitude and of approach to God and to the world. This is the way the Church has always understood this reality. The synod of 1983 described it as "the inmost change of heart under the influence of the word of God and in the perspective of the Kingdom," and again as "*a conversion that passes from the heart to deeds,* and then to the Christian's whole life" (*Reconciliatio et Paenitentia,* 4).

### Apostolic Call Continues Jesus' Call to Conversion

3. Our conversion is understood as *a response to the call of Jesus* to embrace his Gospel and enter his Kingdom. His call had been anticipated by the Precursor of his

Kingdom, John the Baptist: "Repent, for the Kingdom of heaven is at hand" (Mt. 3:2). Jesus himself entrusted this call to his Apostles and through them to us. On the day of Pentecost it was taken up by Peter, who encouraged the people to proclaim Jesus Christ as Lord and Messiah, saying: "Repent and be baptized, every one of you in the name of Jesus Christ for the forgiveness of your sins; and you will receive the gift of the Holy Spirit" (Acts 2:38). The Apostle Paul bore public testimony to the fact that he "preached the need to repent and turn to God, and to do works giving evidence of repentance" (Acts 26:20).

### Call to Conversion Entails Conformity with God's Truth About the Human Creature

In imitating the Apostles Peter and Paul, by striving to embrace the reality of conversion and by preaching it, we are in effect proclaiming the full content of the truth that Jesus revealed about repentance. In speaking of conversion or penance we direct people's attention to God himself and to the need to live in conformity with the truth that God has expressed regarding human nature. To call to conversion means to proclaim God's dominion over all creation, especially over all humanity. It means extolling God's law and acknowledging all the practical effects of creation. In the act of conversion the human person proclaims his or her dependence on God and acknowledges the *need to obey God's law in order to live in freedom.*

### Conversion Includes Superiority of Grace Over Human Rebellion and Failure

Conversion presupposes *an acknowledgment of the reality of human rebellion* against the majesty of God. In each person's heart, conversion signifies the vast superiority of grace over sin, so much so that "where sin increased, grace overflowed all the more" (Rom. 5:20). Conversion is made possible and actually brought about in human hearts by the victory of Jesus in his Paschal Mystery. Every individual conversion is an expression of the divine plan whereby human beings must consent to God's salvific action. Hence every conversion expresses the nobility of human effort and at the same time its total insufficiency. *Every conversion proclaims the supremacy of grace.*

### Revelation of Mercy and Grace Opens Human Beings to New World

4. By reflecting on Jesus' words to be converted, to repent, to open our hearts to life and grace, to renounce sin, we discover *the relationship between conversion and God's love,* the relationship between conversion and God's power. As we reflect on the call of Jesus to do penance we discover *the new world of mercy,* which is revealed in the Cross. The Cross of Jesus Christ is indeed, as I have stated before, "a radical revelation of mercy, or rather of the love that goes against what constitutes the very

root of evil in the history of man: against sin and death . . . the Cross of Christ, in fact, makes us understand the deepest roots of evil" (*Dives in Misericordia*, 8).

### Conversion Means Acquiescence in Truth and Openness to God's Law

*Mercy in turn presumes conversion* on the part of all of us, and the notion of conversion forces us to reflect on the *truth* which we must live. It often happens that when the Church speaks of the requirements of truth in relation to conversion and mercy the world reacts negatively. But the Church cannot proclaim the reality of God's infinite mercy without pointing out how *the acceptance of mercy requires an openness to God's law*. It requires the personal observance of God's law as a response to his covenant of mercy. In demonstrating his fidelity to his fatherly love, God cannot contradict his own truth. Hence true conversion, which consists *in discovering God's mercy*, includes repentance from whatever negates the truth of God expressed in human nature.

### Conversion Brings with It the Gift of Reconciliation

5. At the same time, conversion brings with it *reconciliation*. Reconciliation is *the result of conversion*. It is the gift of the heavenly Father given through Christ and in the Holy Spirit to those who are converted. In the words of Saint Paul, God "has reconciled us to himself through Christ and given us the ministry of reconciliation" (2 Cor. 5:18).

### Personal and Interior Conversion Will Contribute to the Reform of Social Structures

Conversion remains *the key to all reconciliation* and to the Church's ministry of reconciliation. *All individual and collective reconciliation springs from the conversion of hearts*. The social fabric of the Church and the world will be reformed and renewed only when conversion is interior and personal. The needed reform of oppressive economic and political structures in the world cannot be effected without the conversion of hearts. The reconciliation of humanity at the level of individuals, communities, peoples and blocs of nations presumes the conversion of individual hearts and must be based on truth. The Synod on Reconciliation and Penance fully proclaimed this truth, showing how *at the basis of all divisions there is personal sin,* the ultimate essence and darkness of which is "disobedience to God" (*Reconciliatio et Paenitentia*, 14; see no. 16).

### The Church as Sacrament of Reconciliation

6. In being called to be a sign of reconciliation in the world, the Church is therefore called to be a sign of conversion from sin and of obedience to God's law. In

her very nature *the Church is the great Sacrament of Reconciliation.* To live this truth fully she must at all times be both a reconciled and reconciling community that proclaims *the divisive power of every personal sin* but above all *the reconciling and unifying power of Christ's Paschal Mystery,* in which love is stronger than sin and death.

### Restore Proper Sense of Human Sin

In fidelity to her mission, the Church must preach the existence of evil and sin. With great insight the Synod of Bishops acknowledged with Pope Pius XII that "the sin of the century is the loss of the sense of sin" (see *Reconciliatio et Paenitentia,* 18). In the Post-Synodal Apostolic Exhortation I noted that the "restoration of a proper sense of sin is the first way of facing the grave spiritual crisis looming over man today" (*Reconciliatio et Paenitentia*). Already the early Church had reacted vigorously to *the illusion of sinlessness* on the part of some, as stated in the First Letter of Saint John: "If we say we have no sin, we deceive ourselves and the truth is not in us" (1 Jn. 1:8).

### Holy Spirit Convicts Us of Sin
### and Opens Us to Ecclesial Renewal

When we take to heart this statement, we open ourselves to the action of the Holy Spirit who reveals to us our limitations and defects and "convicts" us of our sins of act and omission. At the same time, both as individuals and as communities in the Church, we know that we have not yet reached our goal, we do not yet fully live the Gospel, we have not yet perfectly applied the Council. The more we have a sense of our limitations and personal sins, the more *we will divest ourselves of any sentiments of neotriumphalism* and take to heart all pertinent observations and suggestions about our life and ministry.

### Organic Pastoral Plan for Restoring the Sacrament of Penance
### as the Heart of Pastoral Life

7. Humbled before God and reconciled with him and within herself, the Church is able to pursue with interior freedom her *specific mission,* which is "to evoke conversion and penance in man's heart and to offer him the gift of reconciliation" (*Reconciliatio et Paenitentia,* 23). This she does in different ways, particularly through catechesis and the sacraments entrusted to her by Christ. At this moment in the Church's life, both in the United States and throughout the world, it is opportune to reflect on *the Sacrament of Penance* with a view to reinforcing, in communion with the whole Church, *an organic pastoral approach* to a matter of such supreme importance for the conversion and reconciliation of the world.

### Pastoral Realism Alerts to the Depth of the Crisis to Be Faced

The general experience of the Bishops participating at the Synod and of many others throughout the Church in regard to the use of this Sacrament was summarized in this way: "The Sacrament of Penance is in crisis. . . . For the Sacrament of Confession is indeed being undermined" (*Reconciliatio et Paenitentia*, 28). These statements are neither negative expressions of pessimism nor causes for alarm; they are rather expressions of *a pastoral realism* that require positive pastoral reflection, planning and action. By the power of Christ's Paschal Mystery that is active within her, the Church is capable of responding to all the crises that she ever faces, including this one. But she must make sure that she acknowledges the crisis, and that she adequately faces it with the supernatural means at her disposal.

### Need of Organic Pastoral Plan in Each Diocese

8. In this crisis, which becomes *a challenge to the Church's fidelity,* the Bishops have a particular responsibility, which they can meet with a unique effectiveness. In something as sacred as this Sacrament, *sporadic efforts are not enough to overcome the crisis.* For this reason I appeal today to you and through you to all the Bishops of the United States for organic pastoral planning in each Diocese to restore the Sacrament of Penance to its rightful place in the Church and to renew its use in full accordance with the intention of Christ.

### Need of Correct View on the *Gravis Necessitas* Required for General Absolution

A key point in this renewal process is "the obligation of pastors to facilitate for the faithful the practice of integral and individual confession of sins, which constitutes for them not only a duty but also an inviolable and inalienable right, besides being something needed for the soul" (*Reconciliatio et Paenitentia*, 33). In this task the Bishops need the support and fraternal collaboration of all concerned. Of special importance are the concerted efforts of all the members of the Conference of Bishops in insisting that the *gravis necessitas* required for general absolution be truly understood in the sense explained in Canon 961. In various regions of the world, the crisis facing the Sacrament of Penance is due in part to unwarranted interpretations of what constitutes the conditions of the *gravis necessitas* envisioned by the Church. The Bishops, not only of the United States but of all countries, can make a great pastoral contribution to the true renewal of the Sacrament of Penance by their sustained efforts to do everything possible to promote the proper interpretation of Canon 961. At stake is the whole question of *the personal relationship that Christ wills to have with each penitent* and which the Church must unceasingly defend. In the encyclical *Redemptor Hominis* I spoke of this relationship as involving rights on the part of each individual and of Christ himself (see no. 20).

### Encourage Priests to Persevere in the Ministry of Hearing Individual Confessions

9. As Bishops we also contribute to true renewal *by fraternally encouraging our priests to persevere in their incomparable ministry as confessors.* This means that they

must first travel this path of conversion and reconciliation themselves (see *Reconciliatio et Paenitentia,* 29). In this too we must give them an example. Priests are meant by Christ to find immense spiritual fulfillment in accomplishing the Church's "ministry of reconciliation" (2 Cor. 5:18) in a unique and supremely effective manner.

## Sacrament of Penance Needed
## for Complete Renewal Intended by Vatican II

Reflection on the Sacrament of Penance as the Sacrament of Conversion and Reconciliation will truly help individuals and communities within the Church to understand the real nature of the renewal called for by the Second Vatican Council. *The Sacrament of Penance is the actuation of Christ's pastoral victory,* because it is the personal application of his reconciling action to individual hearts. Without the proper use of the Sacrament of Penance, all other forms of renewal will be incomplete, and at the same time the very reform and renewal of structures will be limited. For this reason the Sacrament of Reconciliation will prove to be *a true key to social progress* and a sure measure of the authenticity of all renewal in the Church in the United States and throughout the world.

## Collegial Cooperation: Way to Success

10. As we move closer toward the year 2000, *we must ever more effectively proclaim the fullness of Christ's mercy* and offer to the world the hope that is found only in a loving and forgiving Savior. In order to accomplish this, we are called to do everything possible *to promote the Sacrament of Mercy and Forgiveness* in accordance with the Second Vatican Council, the pertinent liturgical norms of the Church, the Code of Canon Law and the conclusions of the Synod of 1983 as formulated in *Reconciliatio et Paenitentia.* A goal of this magnitude cannot be attained without *the constantly renewed collegial commitment of the worldwide Episcopate.* Today, in particular, I ask this commitment of you and all your brother Bishops in the United States. To each of you and to all your local Churches: "Grace, mercy, and peace from God the Father and Christ Jesus our Lord" (1 Tm. 1:2).

## FOURTH *AD LIMINA* ADDRESS TO THE
## BISHOPS OF THE UNITED STATES

### REGION IV: PROVINCES OF BALTIMORE,
### WASHINGTON, ATLANTA AND MIAMI

### JUNE 10, 1988

Dear Brothers in our Lord Jesus Christ,

1. I extend a warm and fraternal greeting to all of you, Pastors of the local Churches in the Provinces of Baltimore, Washington, Atlanta and Miami.

It is a pleasure to note the presence of Archbishop Hickey in anticipation of the Consistory in which he will be created a Cardinal. In Archbishop Borders I greet the first See of Baltimore as it prepares to celebrate next year its bicentennial, with profound significance for the whole Church in the United States. With particular fraternal affection I send greetings to Archbishop Marino of Atlanta, the first black Archbishop in the United States, who will be arriving soon to receive the Pallium. With great gratitude I reciprocate the cordial welcome given me by Archbishop McCarthy on my arrival in Miami. And to all of you, dear brothers in the Episcopate, I express my esteem and solidarity in Christ Jesus.

### Call to Prayer

I recently spoke to the Bishops of Region V about the call to conversion, and on this occasion I would like to speak to you about *the call to prayer.*

### Precept of the Lord Jesus to Pray Always

We have all meditated on the words of Jesus: "Pray constantly for the strength . . . to stand secure before the Son of Man" (Lk. 21:36). And today we accept once again the call to prayer as it comes to each of us and to the whole Church from Christ himself. *The call to prayer places all the Church's activity in perspective.* In 1976, in addressing the Call to Action meeting in Detroit, Paul VI stated that "in the tradition of the Church any call to action is first of all a call to prayer." These words are indeed more relevant today than ever before. They are a challenge to the Church in the United States and throughout the world.

### Prayer Offers to the Church
### the Way to Full Trinitarian Communion

2. The universal Church of Christ, and therefore each particular Church, *exists in order to pray.* In prayer the human person expresses his or her nature; the community expresses its vocation; the Church reaches out to God. In prayer the Church attains fellowship with the Father and with his Son, Jesus Christ (see 1 Jn. 1:3). *In prayer the Church expresses her Trinitarian life,* because she directs herself to the Father, undergoes the action of the Holy Spirit and lives fully her relationship with Christ. Indeed, *she experiences herself* as the Body of Christ, as the mystical Christ.

### Prayer Fosters Interpersonal Relationship with Christ

The Church meets Christ in prayer at the core of her being. It is in this way that she finds the complete relevance of his teaching and takes on his mentality. By fostering *an interpersonal relationship with Christ,* the Church actuates to the full the personal dignity of her members. In prayer the Church concentrates on Christ; she possesses him, savors his friendship and is therefore in a position to communicate him. Without prayer all this would be lacking, and she would have nothing to offer to the world. But by exercising faith, hope and charity in prayer, her power *to communicate Christ* is reinforced.

## The Goal of Catechesis
## and the Way to Humanize Human Activity

3. Prayer is *the goal of all catechesis* in the Church, because it is a means of union with God. Through prayer the Church expresses the supremacy of God and fulfills the first and greatest commandment of love.

Everything human is profoundly affected by prayer. *Human work is revolutionized by prayer,* uplifted to its highest level. Prayer is the source of the full humanization of work. In prayer the value of work is understood, for we grasp the fact that we are truly collaborators of God in the transformation and elevation of the world. Prayer is the consecration of this collaboration. At the same time it is the means through which we face the problems of life and in which all pastoral endeavors are conceived and nurtured.

## Prayer Summons Us to Christian Sensitivity
## to the Needs of Our Brothers and Sisters

The call to prayer must precede the call to action, but the call to action must truly accompany the call to prayer. *The Church finds in prayer the root of all her social action*—the power to motivate it and the power to sustain it. In prayer we discover the needs of our brothers and sisters and make them our own, because in prayer we discover that their needs are the needs of Christ. *All social consciousness is nurtured and evaluated in prayer.* In the words of Jesus, justice and mercy are among "the weightier matters of the law" (Mt. 23:23). The Church's struggle for justice and her pursuit of mercy will succeed only if the Holy Spirit gives her the gift of perseverance in attaining them. This gift must be sought in prayer.

## Prayer Fosters Evangelical Awareness of
## Human Development and the Urgency of Action

4. In prayer we come *to understand the Beatitudes* and the reasons why we must live them. Only through prayer can we begin to see all the aspirations of humanity from the perspective of Christ. Without the intuitions of prayer we would never grasp *all the dimensions of human development* and the urgency for the Christian community to commit itself to this work.

## Prayer Calls for an Examination
## of Personal and Collective Responsibility

Prayer calls us to examine our consciences on all the issues that affect humanity. It calls us to ponder our personal and collective responsibility before the judgment of

God and in the light of human solidarity. Hence prayer is able to transform the world. Everything is new with prayer, both for individuals and communities. *New goals and new ideals emerge.* Christian dignity and action are reaffirmed. The commitments of our Baptism, Confirmation and Holy Orders take on new urgency. The horizons of conjugal love and of the mission of the family are vastly extended in prayer.

### Prayer: The Condition for the Correct Discernment

Christian sensitivity depends on prayer. *Prayer is an essential condition*—even if not the only one—*for a correct reading of the "signs of the times."* Without prayer, deception is inevitable in a matter of such importance.

### Prayer Gives Courage to Sustain Decisions

5. *Decisions require prayer;* decisions of magnitude require sustained prayer. Jesus himself gives us the example. Before calling his disciples and selecting the Twelve, Jesus passed the night, on the mountain, in communion with his Father (see Lk. 6:12). For Jesus, prayer to his Father meant not only light and strength. It also meant confidence, trust and joy. His human nature exulted in the joy that came to him in prayer. The measure of the Church's joy in any age is in proportion to her prayer.

The gauge of her strength and the condition for her confidence are fidelity to prayer. The mysteries of Christ are disclosed to those who approach him in prayer. The full application of the Second Vatican Council will forever be conditioned by perseverance in prayer. The great strides made by the laity of the Church in realizing how much they belong to the Church—how much they are the Church—can only be explained in the last analysis by grace and its acceptance in prayer.

### Discovery of the Word of God in Scripture
### Generates and Sustains Prayer

6. In the life of the Church today we frequently perceive that the gift of prayer is linked to the word of God. A renewal in discovering the Sacred Scriptures has brought forth the fruits of prayer. God's word, embraced and meditated on, has the power to bring human hearts into ever greater communion with the Most Holy Trinity. Over and over again this has taken place in the Church in our day. The benefits received through prayer linked to the word of God call forth in all of us a further response of prayer—the prayer of praise and thanksgiving.

### Prayer Generates and Sustains
### the Pastoral Work of Evangelization

The word of God generates prayer in the whole community. At the same time it is in prayer that the word of God is understood, applied and lived. For all of us who are ministers of the Gospel, with the pastoral responsibility of announcing the message in season and out of season and of scrutinizing the reality of daily life in the light of God's holy word, prayer is the context in which we prepare the proclamation of faith. All evangelization is *prepared in prayer;* in prayer it is first applied to ourselves; in prayer it is then offered to the world.

### Prayer Helps the Local Church to Preserve Proper Identity

7. Each local Church is true to itself to the extent that it is *a praying community* with all the consequent dynamism that prayer stirs up within it. The universal Church is never more herself than when she faithfully reflects the image of the praying Christ: the Son who in prayer directs his whole being to his Father and consecrates himself for the sake of his brethren "that they may be consecrated in truth" (Jn. 17:19).

### Collegial Solidarity in Teaching and Living the Call to Prayer

For this reason, dear brothers in the Episcopate, I wish to encourage you in all your efforts *to teach people to pray.* It is part of the apostolic Church to transmit the teaching of Jesus to each generation, to offer faithfully to each local Church the response of Jesus to the request: "Teach us to pray" (Lk. 11:1). I assure you of my solidarity and of the solidarity of the whole Church in your efforts *to preach the importance of daily prayer* and *to give the example of prayer.* From the words of Jesus we know that where two or three are gathered in his name, there he is in their midst (see Mt. 18:20). And we know that in every local Church gathered in prayer around a Bishop there dwells the incomparable beauty of the whole Catholic Church as the faithful image of the praying Christ.

### Encourage Pastoral Initiative That Supports Growth in Prayer

8. In his role as Pastor of the universal Church, the Successor of Peter is called to live *a communion of prayer* with his brother Bishops and their Dioceses. Hence all your pastoral initiatives to promote prayer have my full support. In fraternal and pastoral charity I am close to you as you call your people to daily prayer, as you invite them to discover in prayer their dignity as Christians. *Every diocesan and parish initiative aimed at furthering individual and family prayer is a blessing for the universal Church.* Every group that gathers together to pray the rosary is a gift to the cause of God's Kingdom. Yes, wherever two or three are gathered in Christ's name, there he is. *Contemplative communities are a special gift of Christ's love to his people.* They need and deserve the full measure of our pastoral love and support. Their particular role in the world is to bear witness to the supremacy of God and the primacy of Christ's love "which surpasses all knowledge" (Eph. 3:19).

## Pastoral Responsibility Is Reinforced
## by Hope of Renewal to Be Worked by the Holy Spirit

When, as Bishops, we exercise *our apostolic responsibility to call our people to prayer,* we also deeply fulfill our own pastoral ministry. Not everyone is waiting to be called to prayer; not everyone is willing to respond, but millions of people are. And the Holy Spirit is willing to use the Bishops of the Church as instruments in a work that by reason of its supreme delicateness belongs to him alone as the *Dextrae Dei Digitus.* The outpouring of the Holy Spirit can totally renew the Church today through the gift of prayer. We must aspire to possess this gift—so much linked to God's love; we must invoke it for the Church here and now, and see it also as *the hallmark of the Church of the Millennium.* This is the vital context in which, as pastors, we must call the Church to prayer. Here, too, we touch upon *the identity of the Bishop as a sign of Christ,* "a sign of the praying Christ, a sign of the Christ who speaks to his Father, saying: 'I offer you praise, O Father, Lord of heaven and earth' (Lk. 10:21)" (*ad Limina* Address of December 3, 1983).

## The Efficacy of Eucharistic Worship and the Sacred Liturgy
## for Consecration of Secular Activity

9. Prayer reaches a level of special dignity and efficacy for the community *in the Sacred Liturgy of the Church* and particularly *in Eucharistic worship,* which is the source and summit of Christian living. In this regard the Eucharistic celebration of the Sunday is of immense importance for your local Churches and for their vitality. Five years ago, in speaking at some length about this matter, I mentioned that "Throughout the United States there has been a superb history of Eucharistic participation by the people, and for this we must all thank God." The time is ripe to renew gratitude to God for this great gift and *to reinforce this splendid tradition of American Catholics.* On that occasion I also mentioned: "All the striving of the laity *to consecrate the secular field of activity to God* finds inspiration and magnificent confirmation in the Eucharistic Sacrifice. Participating in the Eucharist is only a small portion of the laity's week, but the total effectiveness of their lives and all Christian renewal depends on it: the primary and indispensable source of the true Christian spirit!" (*ad Limina* Address of July 9, 1983).

## The Sunday Eucharist
## Renews the Church's Sense of Destiny in Christ

In the Sunday Eucharistic assembly the Father repeatedly glorifies the Resurrection of his Son Jesus Christ by accepting his Sacrifice offered for the whole Church. He confirms *the paschal character of the Church.*

The hour of Sunday Eucharistic worship is a powerful expression of the Christocentric nature of the community, which Christ offers to his Father as a gift. And as he offers his Church to his Father, *Christ himself convokes his Church for her mission:* her mission, above all of love and praise, to be able to say: "By your gift I will utter praise in the vast assembly" (Ps. 22:26).

## Convokes the Church to Service of
## Evangelization and Human Advancement

At the same time that the Church is summoned to praise, she is summoned to service in fraternal charity and in justice, mercy and peace. In the very act of convoking his Church to service, Christ consecrates this service, renders it fruitful and offers it in the Spirit to his Father. This service to which the Church is called is the service of evangelization and human advancement in all their vital aspects. It is *service in the name of Christ* and of his mercy, in the name of him who said: "My heart is moved with pity for the crowd" (Mt. 15:32).

## Prayer Helps the Church Face Suffering and Sin

10. There are many other aspects of prayer, both private and liturgical, that deserve reflection. There are many other dimensions of the call to prayer that the Church would like to emphasize. I wish at this time, however, to allude only to *two realities* which the Church must constantly face and which she can face adequately only in prayer. They are *suffering* and *sin*.

## Prayer Helps the Church Cope with Suffering

It is in her prayer that the Church understands and copes with suffering; she reacts to it as Jesus did in the Garden: "In his anguish he prayed with all the greater intensity" (Lk. 22:44). Before the mystery of suffering, the Church is still unable to modify the advice of Saint James or to improve on it: "Is anyone among you suffering? He should pray" (Jas. 15:13). Combined with all her efforts to alleviate human suffering—which she must multiply until the end of time—*the Church's definitive response to suffering is found only in prayer.*

## Prayer Renews Ecclesial Courage to Tackle Human Sin

The other reality to which the Church responds in prayer is *sin.* In prayer the Church braces herself to engage in paschal conflict with sin and with the devil. In prayer she asks *pardon for sin;* in prayer she implores *mercy for sinners;* and in prayer she extols *the power of the Lamb of God* who takes away the sins of the world. The Church's response to sin is to praise salvation and the superabundance of the grace of Jesus Christ, the Savior of the world. "To him who loves us and freed us from our sins by his own blood . . . be glory and power forever and ever!" (Rv. 1:5–6).

## Proclaim the Call to Prayer

Profoundly convinced of the power of prayer and humbly committed to it in our own lives, let us, dear brothers, confidently *proclaim throughout the Church the call to prayer.* At stake is the Church's need to be herself, the Church of prayer, for the glory of the Father. The Holy Spirit will assist us and the merits of Christ's Paschal Mystery will supply for our human weaknesses.

## Mary, the Model of Prayer

The example of Mary, the Mother of Jesus, as a *model of prayer,* is a source of confidence and trust for all of us. As we ourselves look to her, we know that her example sustains our clergy, Religious and laity. We know that her generosity is a legacy for the whole Church to proclaim and imitate.

Finally, in the words of Paul, I ask you all: "Pray for me that God may put his word on my lips, that I may courageously make known the mystery of the Gospel. . . . Pray that I may have courage to proclaim it as I ought. . . . Grace be with all who love our Lord Jesus Christ with unfailing love" (Eph. 6:19–20,24).

## FIFTH *AD LIMINA* ADDRESS TO THE BISHOPS OF THE UNITED STATES

### REGION XI: PROVINCES OF LOS ANGELES AND SAN FRANCISCO

### JULY 8, 1988

Dear Brothers in our Lord Jesus Christ,

1. Your welcome presence here today evokes the remembrance of all those events that we celebrated together in the provinces of Los Angeles and San Francisco during my pastoral visit last September.

## Grateful Recollection of Visit to California

Each event not only concerned the local Church but involved the participation of many other people. Besides, there was the extensive spiritual presence of millions of the faithful. In this way, for example, I could address from San Francisco the whole Catholic laity and all the Religious of the United States. The previous events in Los Angeles and Monterey likewise had a great significance for the direction that the Catholic Church must take in her own life and in her service to humanity, as she moves, under the action of the Holy Spirit, toward the purification so necessary for a proper celebration of the Millennium. It would take a great deal of time to recall in detail all the events that we lived together in California. Although it is not possible to do so at this moment, I would request the Church in the United States to relive the commitment of those days and also renew her openness to the word of God as proclaimed by the Successor of Peter in those situations. This attitude is necessary to ensure the success of *an overall pastoral plan* that must wisely guide the Church in your country in the years ahead.

### The Pressing Need for Initial and Continuing Evangelization

2. One event of those days has a very special relevance now. It is the visit that I made to the Basilica of Carmel and to *the tomb of Fray Junípero Serra*. In less than three months from now, some of us will gather again here as the Church beatifies him, officially proclaiming him worthy of honor and imitation by all. In venerating "the Apostle of California" at his tomb I spoke of his contribution, which was "to proclaim the Gospel of Jesus Christ at the dawn of a new age" (September 17, 1987). I also endeavored to present his essential message, which is *the constant need to evangelize*. In that context I stated: "Like Father Serra and his Franciscan brethren, we too are *called to be evangelizers,* to share actively in the Church's mission of making disciples of all people."

### In the Mystery of Christ the Mystery of God and the
### Mystery of the Human Person Become Comprehensible

Initial evangelization and continuing evangelization are pressing needs in the world today. As the Church pursues this task of hers—striving to relate the mystery of man to the mystery of God—she needs to have very clear ideas of her goal and the means by which she proposes to attain it. Of great help in all of this are the guiding principles and succinctly formulated intuitions of the Second Vatican Council. One of these truths so forcefully expressed by the Council is "that only in the mystery of the Incarnate Word does the mystery of man take on light" (*Gaudium et Spes,* 22). To understand humanity fully, including its dignity and its destiny, the world must understand Christ. Christ not only reveals God to man but he also reveals man to himself. *The mystery of humanity becomes comprehensible in the Incarnate Word.* This principle becomes a guiding force for the Church in all her activities which are directed to clarifying the mystery of humanity in the mystery of Christ.

### An Organic Plan of Catechesis
### in Christ's Impact on Our View of the Human Person

3. Above all, this is true in *catechesis,* where the Church endeavors to lead the individual to a greater self-understanding through, in, and with Christ. To reach God, man must understand himself, and to do this he must look to Christ. The human being is created in *the image and likeness of God.* The full image of God is eternally found in Christ, whom Saint Paul calls the "image of the invisible God" (Col. 1:15).

## As the Image and Likeness of God
## Destined for Community with the Trinity

As a creature, man is also *a social being* called to live in community with others. The highest form of community and interpersonal relation is that lived by Christ in the communion of the Most Holy Trinity.

## Unity of Body and Soul,
## Able to Share in Christ's Divine Nature

The human being further understands himself as made up of *body and soul* intimately united in one person. In Christ there are hypostatically united in the one divine person both the human and the divine natures. Man's wonderful destiny is to share, through Christ's humanity, in his divine nature (see Pt. 1:4). Man is called to glorify God in his *body* and treat his body in a way worthy of its dignity. In Jesus himself there dwells, bodily, the fullness of divinity (see Col. 2:9). Through his *intellect* man surpasses the whole of the material universe and comes into contact with the divine truth. Jesus as the Incarnate Word claimed in all exactness to be identified with that truth when he said: "I am the way, and the truth, and the life" (Jn. 14:6).

## The Human Person Can Know the Plan of God

By the action of the Holy Spirit man is in a position to know *the plan of God,* as regards both creation and Redemption. Jesus himself is that plan of God: "Through him all things came into being, and apart from him nothing came to be" (Jn. 1:3). Moreover, we know that God has made him "our wisdom and also our justice, our sanctification and our redemption" (1 Cor. 1:30).

## The Human Person Can Detect in Himself
## the Inner Law of Love

In coming to know himself, man detects in the depth of his *conscience* a law which he does not impose upon himself, but which holds him in obedience (see *Gaudium et Spes,* 16). Jesus himself reveals the fullness and essence of all law, which is summarized in the love of God and the love of neighbor (see Mt. 22:37–40). To love in the way which Jesus commands is the only way to satisfy fully the human heart.

## Christ Redeems Human Freedom

Authentic *freedom* is a special sign of God's image in man. Jesus the man embodies the highest form of human freedom, by which he consecrates his life and his death to his Father and lives totally according to his will. He declares that his freedom is for his Father when he says: "I always do what pleases him" (Jn. 8:29). At the same time Jesus destroys what is opposed to freedom in the human person. His mission is to cast out the one who holds man's conscience in bondage.

### Christ Conquers Human Death

The final riddle for human beings is *death*. In looking to Christ, man learns that he himself is destined to live. Christ's Eucharist is the pledge of life. The one who eats Christ's flesh and drinks his blood already has eternal life (see Jn. 6:54). Finally, in conquering death by his Resurrection, Christ reveals the resurrection of all; he proclaims life and reveals man to himself in his final destiny, which is *life*.

### Key Themes of Christocentric Catechesis Offer Central Focus

4. Of supreme relevance for the Church today is the presentation of *the person of the Incarnate Word as the center of all catechesis*. Some years ago, in 1971, in accord with the Council's Decree *Christus Dominus,* the Congregation for the Clergy issued the *General Catechetical Directory* for the Church. Its aim was to promote a Christocentric catechesis for all the People of God. In doing this it stated: "Catechesis must proclaim Jesus in his concrete existence and in his message, that is, it must open the way for man to the wonderful perfection of his humanity" (no. 53).

Eight years later I endeavored to give impetus to this *Christocentric* approach to catechesis by the publication of *Catechesi Tradendae*. In this document I said: "At the heart of catechesis we find, in essence, a Person, the Person of Jesus of Nazareth. . . . The primary and essential object of catechesis is . . . 'the mystery of Christ.' Catechizing is a way to lead a person to study this Mystery in all its dimensions. . . . It is therefore to reveal in the Person of Christ the whole of God's eternal design reaching fulfillment in that Person. . . . Accordingly, the definitive aim of catechesis is to put people not only in touch but in communion, in intimacy, with Jesus Christ" (no. 5).

This important effort toward Christocentric catechesis, so fully dealt with in the Synod of 1977 and in the Apostolic Exhortation to which I have alluded, has also become the guiding principle in the preparation of *a universal catechism* for serving the common needs of the Church. This document is meant to be a point of reference for all the catechetical efforts at the national and diocesan levels, and also for catechisms of a general and special nature which the Bishops may subsequently draft with the purpose of imparting proper knowledge of the content of the Catholic faith. At the center of this effort is the profound conviction that the mystery of the Incarnate Word sheds light on all life and human experience and that he himself is in a position personally to communicate the truth that he is. Once again, in the words of *Catechesi Tradendae:* "We must therefore say that in catechesis it is Christ the Incarnate Word and Son of God who is taught—everything else is taught with reference to him— and it is Christ alone who teaches—anyone else teaches to the extent that he is Christ's spokesman, enabling Christ to speak with his lips" (no. 6).

## In Sum, the Mystery of the Incarnate Word Is the
## Revelation of the Father and the Unity and Goal of Creation

What Christ teaches is *the truth that he is,* in himself and for us. He reminds us: "My teaching is not mine, but his who sent me" (Jn. 7:16). He speaks as the revelation of the Father, the blueprint of all creation, the creating Word of God. In revealing the Father to humanity, Jesus reveals in himself how the Father looks upon humanity. He reveals God's plan for human nature in all its expressions and applications. Human love and human work participate in the divine model of uncreated and creating love. Procreation is a special participation in that divine prerogative. The authenticity and finality of human sexuality, justice and freedom are found in *the eternal plan of God expressed in Christ.*

## The Aspiration for Liberation
## and the Quest for Freedom Flow from a Christian Heritage

5. As pastors of the Church you are daily experiencing, especially in the case of migrants and immigrants, the tragic and pressing *problems of poverty.* You have repeatedly called your people to a sense of solidarity with those in need. You have stood by all those who are struggling to live in a way consonant with their human dignity. You are able to affirm from personal knowledge that "the powerful and almost irresistible aspiration that people have for *liberation* constitutes one of the principal *signs of the times* which the Church has to examine and interpret in the light of the Gospel" (*Instruction on Certain Aspects of the "Theology of Liberation,"* August 6, 1984, I, 1). At the same time you have experienced how the quest for freedom and the aspiration to liberation, which are universal and yet differ in form and degree among peoples, have their source and impetus in the Christian heritage. In 1979, in the context of Puebla, I proposed three basic truths to orient all the efforts of the Church aimed at liberating and uplifting those in need. These are the truth about Jesus Christ, the truth about the Church, the truth about humanity. In effect, however, the truth about the Church and humanity is to be pondered *in the light of the mystery of Jesus Christ the Incarnate Word.*

## Providence and the Incarnate Word
## Explain the Progress of History

The same can be said of *all dimensions of the human and Christian life.* God's providence is understood only in conjunction with the eternal destiny of the human person as revealed by the Incarnate Word. The full meaning of *human progress* or development must take into account Christ's teaching: "Not on bread alone is man to live but on every utterance that comes from the mouth of God" (Mt. 4:4; see Dt. 8:3). The *imperfections of human justice* and the inadequacy of all earthly fulfillment are ultimately linked to God's design revealed in Christ that "here we have no lasting city, but seek one that is to come" (Heb. 13:14). The question of *physical and spiritual suffering* on the part of the innocent requires an explanation that only the Incarnate Word could give. And in order to give it as effectively as possible, he gave it from the Cross.

### The Phenomena of Agnosticism and Atheism Provoke Believers to Give Reasons for the Hope That Is in Us

6. In your ministry as Bishops you constantly come across the complicated phenomena of *agnosticism and atheism*. You are rightly convinced of the need for sustained dialogue and fraternal collaboration in projects of service to humanity. You and your local Churches are committed to giving an explanation for the hope that is in Christianity every time you are asked. You rightly count on the power of example and prayer; you know the need for patience and persevering trust. The great illuminating force, however, for all doubting and denying consciences is only the light of the Incarnate Word which is for them too like "a lamp shining in a dark place until the first streaks of dawn appear and the morning star rises" (2 Pt. 1:19).

In facing atheism, which the Council says is "among the most serious problems of this age" and which is manifested in phenomena which are quite distinct from one another, the Church must also accept the judgment of the Council that "believers can have more than a little to do with the birth of atheism" (*Gaudium et Spes,* 19). This is so to the extent that they fail to reveal the authentic face of God and religion—which is found in the Incarnate Word.

### The Christian Mystery Can Inspire the Birth of a New Humanism

7. In directing the minds and the hearts of the faithful to the mystery of the Incarnate Word, the Church ardently desires to bring this mystery to bear on *all human activity, all human culture.* The Church in effect desires *the birth of a new humanism,* profoundly Christian in its inspiration, in which earthly reality in its totality will be elevated by the revelation of Christ. One of the first characteristics of this new humanism is that it marks the community by a sense of interdependence expressed in solidarity. This is in accordance with Christ's intention to save humanity not merely as individuals, without mutual bonds, but to gather them into a single people (see *Lumen Gentium,* 9; *Gaudium et Spes,* 32). The Second Vatican Council already perceived the existence of this reality when it stated: "Thus we are witnesses of the birth of a new humanism, one in which man is defined first of all by his responsibility towards his brothers and sisters and towards history" (*Gaudium et Spes,* 55). Only with a consciousness of interdependence—pushed to a worldwide dimension—will communities unite to cultivate those natural goods and values that foster the well-being of humanity and constitute its basic culture.

## True Christian Humanism Must Deal
## with the Problems of Peace and Development

The response of every community, including those in the Church, to a consciousness of interdependence is the exercise of solidarity, which is "a firm and persevering determination to commit oneself to the common good" (*Sollicitudo Rei Socialis,* 38). In turn, this solidarity or determination is expressed in a new moral concern for all the problems faced by humanity. Two extremely relevant problems faced by millions of our brothers and sisters throughout the world are *development* and *peace* (see *Sollicitudo Rei Socialis,* 26). The outcome of these issues is profoundly affected by the way these realities are conceived in the context of a true Christian humanism.

The specific contribution of the Church—of her members and of her individual communities—to the cause of a new humanism, of true human culture, is *the full truth of Christ about humanity*: the meaning of humanity, its origin, its destiny, and, therefore, its incomparable dignity.

## The Principal Catechists of People Are the
## Principal Heralds of the Mystery of the Incarnate Word

8. Dear brother Bishops: yours is a great task to guide, in union with the universal Church, your local Churches in the way of salvation and with fraternal and paternal love to help the different categories of the faithful to fulfill their duty and privilege of bearing witness to Christ in the world. But you must also remember—and this will bring you great joy—that you are the principal communicators of Christ, the principal catechists of your people, *the principal heralds of the mystery of the Incarnate Word*. To you and to all your brothers in the College of Bishops, united with the Successor of Peter, there has been entrusted, in a unique way, for faithful custody and effective transmission, the truth of the Gospel. This truth we proclaim not only as salvation and deliverance from evil, but also as the basis of that new humanism which will speak to the whole world about universal solidarity and loving concern for all human beings.

## Evangelize in the Footsteps of Previous Missionaries

All of this stems, dear brothers, from that profound conviction and principle enunciated by the Second Vatican Council: "The truth is that only in the light of the Incarnate Word does the mystery of man take on light." In the footsteps of your own Apostle of California, and in solidarity with all your evangelizing predecessors, may you continue to proclaim confidently up and down El Camino Real, and beyond, the mystery of the Incarnate Word. In his love I send my blessing to all the priests, deacons, Religious, seminarians and laity of California, Hawaii and Nevada. "Peace to all of you who are in Christ" (1 Pt. 5:14).

## SIXTH *AD LIMINA* ADDRESS TO THE
## BISHOPS OF THE UNITED STATES

### REGIONS XII AND XIII: PROVINCES OF ANCHORAGE, PORTLAND, SEATTLE, DENVER AND SANTA FE

### SEPTEMBER 2, 1988

Dear Brothers in our Lord Jesus Christ,

1. With deep fraternal affection I welcome all of you, the Bishops of Regions XII and XIII. Our meeting today is meant to be not only an experience in ecclesial communion for us as Pastors of God's people, but also *a renewed commitment* on the part of all the Dioceses in the provinces of Anchorage, Portland, Seattle, Denver and Santa Fe to that unity which Christ wills between the particular Churches and the universal Church.

### Organic Link Between Anthropocentrism and Theocentrism

At this moment our program calls us to reflect together on our ministry and on the profound pastoral solicitude that we as Bishops must have for humanity and for every human being. To be authentic, our episcopal ministry must truly be *centered on man.* At the same time it must be centered *on God,* whose absolute primacy and supremacy we must constantly proclaim and urge our people to recognize in their lives.

### Source of Pastoral Effectiveness

The Vatican Council has invited us to adopt both of these approaches—*anthropocentrism and theocentrism*—and to emphasize them together, linking them in the only satisfactory way possible, that is, in the divine Person of Christ, true God and true man. This task for us is both formidable and exhilarating. The effect it can have on the local Churches is profound. In my encyclical on God's mercy I stated that the deep and organic linking of anthropocentrism and theocentrism in Jesus Christ is perhaps *the most important principle of the Second Vatican Council (Dives in Misericordia,* 1). The basic reason for this is the pastoral effectiveness of this principle.

### Christ Is the Key to the Link
### Between Anthropocentrism and Theocentrism

2. In concentrating on Christ, the Church is able to exalt human nature and human dignity, *for Jesus Christ is the ultimate confirmation of all human dignity.* The Church is also able to concentrate on humanity and on the well-being of each human

being because of the fact that in the Incarnation Jesus Christ united all humanity to himself.

In Christ, God the Father has placed the blueprint of humanity. At the same time, in concentrating on Christ, the Church emphasizes the centrality of God in the world, for in Christ—through the hypostatic union—God has taken possession of man to the greatest possible degree.

### To Proclaim Christ Is to Exalt God Supremely
### and to Exalt Man Supremely

To proclaim Christ to the full extent willed by the Second Vatican Council is to exalt man supremely and to exalt God supremely. To proclaim Christ fully is to proclaim him in the Father's plan of the Incarnation, which expresses man's greatest glory and God's greatest accomplishment in the world. *Anthropocentrism and theo-centrism truly linked in Christ* open the way for the Church to a proper understanding of her pastoral service to humanity, for the glory of God.

### Christ Linked the Two Commandments
### of Love of God and Love of Neighbor

3. As the Lawgiver of the New Testament, Christ links in his own person the two commandments of love of God and love of neighbor. While maintaining for the Church the priority of love of God, Saint Augustine clarifies its order of fulfillment: "Loving God comes first as a commandment, but loving one's neighbor comes first as a deed. (*Dei dilectio prior est ordine praecipiendi, proximi autem dilectio prior est ordine faciendi)*" (In *Joann. Tract.*, 17). In this sense Saint John's words remain a lasting challenge to the Church: "One who has no love for the brother he has seen cannot love the God he has not seen" (1 Jn. 4:20).

### Jesus Christ Is the Chief Way for the Church,
### the Human Person is the Primary Route

In Christ—in his person and in his word—the Church discovers *the principle of her solicitude for humanity* (see *Redemptor Hominis,* 15). Her inspiration and her strength in all dimensions of her pastoral service are found in Christ. With a view to serving man, the Church will always reflect on him in relationship to Christ, and she will endeavor to approach God only through Christ. From this viewpoint it is possible to hold that "man is the primary route that the Church must reveal in fulfilling her mission; he is the primary and fundamental way for the Church" (*Redemptor Hominis,* 14). At the same time, without contradiction we proclaim that "Jesus Christ is the chief way for the Church" (*Redemptor Hominis,* 13). This is so because Christ is the fullness of humanity. Christ is God's expression of what humanity is meant to be, how humanity is meant to be transformed, how humanity is meant to be introduced into communion of the Blessed Trinity, namely: "through him, and with him, and in him."

## Creation in Image and Likeness of God
## Is the Immutable Basis of Christian Anthropology

4. In speaking here of anthropocentrism, that is, in emphasizing the dignity of humanity in relation to Christ and to the Church's mission, it is necessary to make reference to *the immutable basis of all Christian anthropology,* which is creation in the image and likeness of God (see Gn. 1:26–27). This God is the God who reveals himself as a communion of persons, a saving God, a God of love and mercy.

## Human Dignity Is Based on Creation,
## Redemption and Baptism

In the Church's solicitude for man and for human dignity, which finds expression in every *social program* initiated by her, the Church must proclaim the reality of creation as it is renewed by the Redemption and by the uplifting—effected in Baptism—of each individual person. In her inner being the Church feels *impelled to proclaim human dignity:* the dignity of man raised to the level of Christ, to the level of divine adoption. Hence, with the proclamation of natural human dignity, the Church also proclaims *full Christian dignity:* the dignity of the children of God called to a supernatural dignity, called to worship the Father with Christ.

## Consciousness of Dignity as People of Worship

In speaking to the American Bishops five years ago, I made reference to "the pastoral service of making God's people ever more conscious of their dignity as a people of worship." In particular I noted "that we can render a great pastoral service to the people by emphasizing their liturgical dignity and by directing their thoughts to the purposes of worship. When our people . . . realize that they are called . . . to adore and thank the Father in union with Jesus Christ, *an immense power is unleashed in their Christian lives*" (Address of July 9, 1983, no. 8, no. 3).

## The Church: Defender of Christian and Human Rights

With regard to rights within the Church, Pope John Paul I, ten years ago, on the occasion of one of the two *ad Limina* visits of his short Pontificate—on the very day he died—spoke in these terms: "Among the rights of the faithful, one of the greatest is the right to receive God's word in all its entirety and purity, with all its exigencies and power" (September 28, 1978). Under every aspect the Church is irrevocably committed to *the vigorous defense of all human and Christian rights,* both in themselves and especially when these rights are threatened. With the realization that she lives in anticipation of the fullness of the Kingdom of God, she must pursue constantly the work of the Messiah, of whom the Psalmist says: "He shall have pity on the lowly and the poor; the lives of the poor he shall save. From fraud and violence he shall redeem them" (Ps. 72:13–14). The Church must then always be at home among the poor, vigilant in the defense of all their rights.

### Defense of Human Rights
### Entails Structure of Human Relationships

5. In giving us the basis for the defense of human rights, Christ proclaims *a whole structure of human relationships*. He teaches us that to save our life we must lose it (see Lk. 17:33). Indeed, the human being cannot fully find himself without first making a sincere gift of self (see *Gaudium et Spes,* 24). This is so because to be a person in the image and likeness of God is to exist in relation to another and to others. What Christ and his Church advocate is not the mere external defense of human rights, nor the mere defense of human rights by the organisms and structures at the disposal of the community—however providential and useful these may be— but *the total commitment of giving on the part of each individual in the community* so that the rights of all may be ensured through the great structure of proper human Christian relationships in which the charity of Christ reigns supreme and in which justice is "corrected" by love (see *Dives in Misericordia,* 14). This structure of personal relationships—the only one conducive to the full defense of human and Christian rights—must view the human being as created in the image and likeness of God as God exists: a communion of persons.

### Pastoral Challenge: Need to Face Crisis of Family Values,
### Women's Dignity and Vocation and the Crisis of Truth

6. *A phenomenon which militates against this whole structure* of personal relationships and therefore against human rights, a phenomenon which I have brought to the attention of the whole Church, is "the decline of many fundamental values, values which constitute an unquestionable good not only for Christian morality but simply for human morality, for moral culture: these values include respect for human life from the moment of conception, respect for marriage in its indissoluble unity, and respect for the stability of the family. . . . Hand in hand with this go the crisis of truth in human relationships, lack of responsibility for what one says, the purely utilitarian relationship between individual and individual, the loss of a sense of the authentic common good and the ease with which this good is alienated" (*Dives in Misericordia,* 12). Each one of these areas would merit to be developed at length. In the past I have spoken to you in some detail on some of these topics. I am profoundly grateful to you for your persevering efforts in so many pastoral challenges, one of the greatest being the defense and support of human life.

7. A major area of human rights in need of constant defense is that concerned with *the family* and its members, both parents and children. The Charter of the Rights of the Family presented five years ago by the Holy See has spelled out these rights

and deserves renewed attention at this time. One of the fundamental principles enunciated in this document is "the original, primary and inalienable right" of parents to educate their children (Art. 5) according to their moral and religious convictions, and to supervise closely and to control their sex education. The Church must continue to present human sexuality as linked to God's plan of creation and constantly proclaim *the finality and dignity of sex.*

Ways by which the human family is greatly wounded included the unsolved problems of immensely lucrative *drug trafficking and pornography.* Both of these plague society, debase human life and human love and violate human rights.

8. In dealing with *the specific rights of women as women,* it is necessary to return again and again to the immutable basis of Christian anthropology as it is foreshadowed in the Scriptural account of the creation of man—as male and female—in the image and likeness of God. Both man and woman are created in the image of *the personhood of God,* with inalienable personal dignity, and in complementarity one with the other. Whatever violates the complementarity of women and men, whatever impedes the true communion of persons according to the complementarity of the sexes offends the dignity of both women and men.

Through the first draft of your proposed document on the concerns of women for the Church and society, I know that you are making real efforts to respond with sensitivity to these greatly varying concerns, by presenting women as partners in the mystery of the Redemption as this mystery is lived out in our day. You are rightly striving *to help eliminate discrimination based on sex.* You are also rightly presenting *Mary the Mother of God as a model of discipleship* and a sign of hope to all, and at the same time as a special symbol and model for women in their partnership with God in the ministry of the Church.

Throughout the whole Church a great prayerful reflection still remains to be made on *the teaching of the Church* about women and about their dignity and vocation. I have already announced my own intention to publish a document on this subject, and this document will come out shortly. The Church is determined to place her full teaching, with all the power with which divine truth is invested, at the service of the cause of women in the modern world—to help clarify their correlative rights and duties, while defending *their feminine dignity and vocation.* The importance of true Christian feminism is so great that every effort must be made to present the principles on which this cause is based, and according to which it can be effectively defended and promoted for the good of all humanity. The seriousness of this commitment requires the collaboration not only of the entire College of Bishops but also of the whole Church.

### The Christocentric Church Can Link Human Rights and Dignity to God in Christ

9. The status of all human dignity and all human rights is immeasurably enhanced by the supernatural condition and destiny of humanity, which are found only in relation to God, only in relation to Christ. Paul VI, in his powerful social encyclical *Populorum*

*Progressio,* wanted to present these elements together. He wanted the Church to follow a course of social action that would be solidly secure. In other words, he wanted *to link human rights and dignity*—indeed the whole of humanism—*to God, in Christ.* In a word, he wanted to insist that the Church can and must be both *anthropocentric and theocentric at the same time, by being Christocentric,* by concentrating on Christ, the Redeemer of man, the Redeemer of all humanity. This message of his is more important now than ever before for our people, namely, that "by union with Christ man attains to new fulfillment of himself, to a transcendent humanism that gives him his greatest possible perfection" (no. 16). And again: "There is no true humanism but that which is open to the Absolute and is conscious of a vocation which gives human life its true meaning" (no. 42). For all of us this vocation is the Christian vocation—essentially linked to the Incarnation and to the cause of human dignity and human rights as they are incomparably spelled out by the Incarnate Word.

### Charity of Christ Extends the Horizons of Service and "Corrects" the Practice of Justice

And when human justice is not only practiced but "corrected" by love, the cause of all humanity is immeasurably enriched. *Through the charity of Christ* the Incarnate, *the horizons of service*—exercised in the name of the Gospel and of the mission of the Church—*are vastly extended.*

As pastors of God's people, dear brothers, we have known from experience how relevant all these principles are at every level of the Church, in every community of the faithful, no matter how small or how large. There is no other path to take than man and human dignity. There is no other direction in which to point him than to God. There is no other way to arrive than through *Christ.* In building up the Kingdom of God, there is no other cause than *the cause of humanity understood in the light of Christ,* who says: "As often as you did it for one of my least brothers, you did it for me" (Mt. 25:40).

With these reflections, dear brothers, I assure you of my prayers that all your local Churches will ever increasingly find in Christ the everlasting link between the cause of humanity and the Kingdom of God, and that in Christ they will experience inspiration and strength for their lives. May God reward you for your own zeal and generosity and for all the pastoral love with which you serve his holy people. With my Apostolic Blessing.

### SEVENTH *AD LIMINA* ADDRESS TO THE BISHOPS OF THE UNITED STATES

### REGIONS I AND VIII: NEW ENGLAND STATES, MINNESOTA, NORTH DAKOTA AND SOUTH DAKOTA

### SEPTEMBER 9, 1988

1. For the seventh time this year I have the joy of welcoming to the See of Peter my brother Bishops from the United States on their *ad Limina* visit. In you, the

Bishops of Regions I and VIII, I greet all the beloved Catholic people who make up the Church in New England and in the states of Minnesota, North Dakota and South Dakota. I realize that there are great differences between your regions and in the makeup of your local Churches, but I know that you all experience *common challenges* in living the one, holy, Catholic and apostolic faith.

### The Church's Mission of Solidarity with All Humanity

During the previous visits I had the occasion to reflect with the Bishops on the pastoral mission of the Church. All my discourses were aimed at helping them to lead their ecclesial communities to live *the life of faith* as fully as possible. In this way I was able to treat a series of topics which are relevant for all the Dioceses in America: the mystery of the Church as it exists in the United States—the wonderful reality of God's grace that I was able to witness personally and that must constantly be called to ever-greater heights of holiness; the preparation required for the Millennium, as a period of special renewal of the Church in her identity and mission; the call to penance and reconciliation; the call to prayer; reflection on Jesus Christ as the One who communicates the mystery of God and reveals man to himself; and, finally, the organic linking in Christ of all the anthropocentric and theocentric efforts of the Church, including her role of proclaiming human dignity and human rights. Today, dear brothers, I would like to add to this series by reflecting on the consciousness that the Church in the United States must have of *her mission of solidarity with all humanity.*

### Solidarity Is the Expression of the Church's Life

2. The Church, like the individual human beings who are her members, is strong in the act of giving (see *Gaudium et Spes,* 24). Like the human person, the ecclesial community finds itself in reaching out and in sharing the gift of itself. *Solidarity is the expression of the Church's life* and of her dynamism in Christ. Such solidarity involves *a practical awareness of the great network of interdependence that exists among God's people.* It consists in a firm and persevering commitment to the good of all (see *Sollicitudo Rei Socialis,* 38).

### Solidarity at the Levels of Divine Mystery; at Every Level of Catholicity

As the Body of Christ, the Church discovers and puts into practice solidarity at the level of divine mystery, at every level of her catholicity and at every level of human need. All the particular Churches that make up the one Catholic Church are called to live the same universal solidarity with their sister Churches, in an awareness of the one Catholic communion that unites them in the mission of Christ. Each local Church expresses this interdependence in faith and love and in whatever touches the lives of human beings. Each *local Church* perceives its interdependence in the need to be open to others and learn from them, as well as by helping them to bear their burdens according to the expression of Saint Paul: "Help carry one another's burdens; in that way you will fulfill the law of Christ" (Gal. 6:2). Wherever, throughout the universal Church, the faithful experience need, there the response of solidarity is called for. For the Church, solidarity is *the expression of catholicity* of her being as she reaches out to all her sons and daughters in need.

### Solidarity at the Level of Human Need

3. *Precisely because she is the Church,* she is called to embrace *all humanity in need,* to respond to the needs of all people. The Church clearly acknowledges and proclaims *universal interdependence and the interrelation of human needs.* In your Pastoral Letters on Peace and on Economic Justice, you as a Conference expressed these points well when you said: "Since we profess to be members of a 'catholic' or universal Church, we all must raise our sights to a concern for the well-being of everyone in the world. . . . We commit ourselves to this global vision" (*Economic Justice for All,* 363). And again: "The interdependence of the world means a set of interrelated human questions. Important as keeping the peace in the nuclear age is, it does not solve or dissolve the other major problems of the day" (*The Challenge of Peace,* III, B, 3).

### Solidarity Is a Moral and Social Attitude, a Virtue, a Duty

For the Church, solidarity is a moral and social attitude to be cultivated, a virtue to be practiced, a duty to be expressed in many forms of fraternal assistance and collaboration. As far as *solidarity in social progress* is concerned, the Church has seen the need in recent decades to emphasize *the worldwide dimension.* It is this worldwide dimension or universal character of the Church's social teaching that characterized *Mater et Magistra, Gaudium et Spes,* and *Populorum Progressio,* and now it has been further explored in my own encyclical *Sollicitudo Rei Socialis.* To cite Paul VI in this regard, "Today the principal fact that we must all recognize is that the social question has become worldwide" (*Populorum Progressio,* 3).

### Solidarity Has a Worldwide Dimension: an Ecclesial, an Ecumenical, an Interreligious Dimension

4. Solidarity is relevant in itself as *a human and Christian virtue,* but it is further relevant in its relationship to *peace.* It is indeed a factor of peace in the modern world, and when it includes solidarity in truth, freedom, justice and love, it becomes the firm basis for a new world order. Solidarity is a factor of peace because it is crucial for development: "There can be no progress towards the complete development of man without the simultaneous development of all humanity in the spirit of solidarity" (*Populorum Progressio,* 43).

It is important for the Church to realize that she exercises solidarity with the whole world as *an expression of her own ecclesial life.* Her social concern, like her evangelizing zeal, knows no barriers, precisely because she is the Church, "a kind of sacrament of intimate union with God, and of the unity of all mankind, that is, she is a sign and an instrument of such union and unity" (*Lumen Gentium,* 1).

At the same time, the Church willingly exercises solidarity with *an ecumenical and interreligious dimension,* which she considers extremely important. She lives to serve—like Christ—the cause of humanity: "The Son of Man has not come to be served but to serve—to give his life in ransom for many" (Mk. 10:45). The Church also knows that she must imitate the sensitivity of Christ for humanity; she frequently recalls his words: "My heart is moved with pity for the crowd" (Mt. 15:32).

### Solidarity Can Impel the Church to Face a Multiplicity of Needs

5. With this sensitivity the Church is called to understand and face *a multiplicity of needs* that differ among themselves, demonstrating her solidarity and offering her help according to her means and her specific nature. This great openness to others has been *characteristic of the Church in the United States.* It is a gift of God implanted in the hearts of your people; it must be nurtured, maintained, reflected upon and acted upon. During my first visit to the United States in 1979, I spoke to the Bishops at Chicago in these terms: "An evident concern for others has been a real part of American Catholicism, and today I thank the American Catholics for their generosity. . . . For me this is an hour of solemn gratitude" (October 5, 1979, no. 1). I express these sentiments once more.

### Solidarity Includes a Spirit of Sharing, Real Human Feeling, Supernatural Charity

The solidarity about which we speak is that genuine solidarity which is expressed in *a spirit of sharing,* accompanied by real *human feeling,* and motivated by *supernatural charity.* It is a social concern that embraces all men, women and children in the totality of their personhood, which comprises their human rights, their condition in this world and their eternal destiny. We cannot prescind from any of these elements. It is a solidarity that accepts and emphasizes the equality of basic human dignity and translates itself into Christian prayer, according to the formula of Jesus: "Our Father. . . . Give us this day our daily bread."

### Solidarity Defends Human Right to Life

*All human needs enter into the Church's concern* and call for involvement on the part of her members. As I have stated, *collaboration is the act proper to solidarity* (see *Sollicitudo Rei Socialis,* 39), and both solidarity and collaboration are means of defending human rights and serving the truth and freedom of humanity. How wonderful is the solidarity that has grown up in the United States today among so many men and women of good will who are pledged to the defense and service of human life!

How effectively they contribute to that great American ideal of "liberty and justice for all"!

Solidarity is the response to Christ's challenge, and while it is carried out *in the name of Christ and his Church,* it is done without distinction of creed, sex, race, nationality or political affiliation. The final aim can only be *the human being in need.*

## A New Moral Concern Based on the Interdependence of Humanity and the Indivisibility of Peace

6. Among the positive signs of *a new moral concern* in the world, a concern which is increasing among the Catholic people in the United States, are not only a renewed awareness of human dignity but also a conviction of the basic interdependence of all humanity, especially in facing poverty and underdevelopment. Consequently, there is a growing consciousness that peace is indivisible and that true development is either shared by all or it is not true development (see *Sollicitudo Rei Socialis,* 17). From this point of view we see how important economic and commercial relations are among the countries and peoples of the world, and how important it is that justice be observed in this sector.

As pastors of God's people, you have asked them to reflect on both the indivisibility of peace and on the consequences of economic interdependence. You have stated that "all of us must confront this reality of such economic bonding and its consequences and see it as a moment of grace . . . that can unite all of us in a common community of the human family" (*Economic Justice for All,* 363).

## True Human Development Includes the Integral, Interior and Transcendent Dimensions

7. The twentieth anniversary of *Populorum Progressio* offered the whole Church the opportunity to reflect further on *the meaning and content of true human development* as it affects individuals and all people. This reflection will continue in the Church because of the importance of this theme as it relates to her mission of service in the name of Christ. The integral, interior and transcendent dimensions of human progress merit attention, as do the economic, social and cultural indices of underdevelopment and poverty.

## Transcendent Aspect of Genuine Progress

My latest encyclical attempted to place renewed emphasis on the transcendent reality of the human being and thus to spell out again the meaning of authentic development in terms of *the specific nature of man.* Many conclusions supporting human dignity flow from these principles. Underdevelopment in all its forms is more easily identified and combated when the true nature of development is known. The distinction between "being" and "having" is still essential in understanding *genuine progress.* For this reason Paul VI pointed out that the exclusive pursuit of possessions is a real obstacle to development and that "avarice is the most evident form of moral underdevelopment" (*Populorum Progressio,* 19). Considering how important *human rights* are to the human person, it is clear that they must be vigorously defended in every program of development. To this end all the resources of human solidarity must be mobilized. It is evident that individual efforts are insufficient. *Concentrated efforts must be made to identify true progress and to ensure its attainment by all through universal solidarity.*

## Special Areas of Social Concern Are Poverty, Underdevelopment, Hunger, Homelessness

8. Areas of special social concern are *poverty and underdevelopment.* On the international level the underdevelopment of peoples is accompanied and aggravated by the immense problem of their countries' debts. The individual issues of *hunger, homelessness, unemployment and underemployment* are formidable and call for the creative collaboration of each ecclesial community.

## CRS Is an Example of Creative Solidarity

One *extraordinary example* of the creative solidarity of American Catholics is *Catholic Relief Services,* founded by the American Bishops in 1943 to help meet urgent needs in Europe and North Africa. Subsequently, and with equal creativity, the organization responded on behalf of the Catholic Church in the United States to other needs throughout the world, and it is still known today as "the official overseas aid and development agency of American Catholics." This organization, which has done so much in the past and which is still so needed for real service in the world today, exists as a result of the application of the principles on which we have been reflecting.

In the case of Catholic Relief Services, the American Bishops conceived and constituted a whole ecclesial program on the basis of the principles of interdependence, solidarity and collaboration, to be carried out with keen *human sensitivity* and the full power of *Christian charity.* The supreme motivation for solidarity—for the Church and all her institutions—will remain the love that God has in Christ for all humanity: "God so loved the world that he gave his only Son" (Jn. 3:16).

## The Church Must Respond to the Higher Needs of Humanity

9. Side by side with all her social concerns there is and always must be the response of the Church to the even *higher needs* of humanity. Her religious mission impels the Church, in season and out of season, to repeat with Jesus: "Not on bread alone is man to live but on every utterance that comes from the mouth of God" (Jn. 4:4; see Dt. 8:3). Like the Incarnate Word—and until he comes again in glory—the Church must continue to show her solidarity with all humanity, being conscious of the central fact of history that "the Word became flesh" (Jn. 1:14).

Dear brothers: in the love of Christ I send my greetings and blessing to all your local Churches as they find strength and practice solidarity in his name.

## EIGHTH *AD LIMINA* ADDRESS TO THE BISHOPS OF THE UNITED STATES

### REGION III: NEW JERSEY AND PENNSYLVANIA

### OCTOBER 7, 1988

Dear Brothers in our Lord Jesus Christ,

1. In you, the Bishops of Region III, I greet with deep pastoral love all the People of God in the states of New Jersey and Pennsylvania. During your *ad Limina* visit the bonds of hierarchical communion are being strengthened between the Bishop of Rome and his brothers in the Episcopate, together with their local Churches. At the same time, the horizon of our pastoral service opens wide to view the Church as "a sign and instrument of intimate union with God and of the unity of the whole human race" (*Lumen Gentium,* 1).

### Zeal for Christian Unity

In this context we are called *to renew our zeal for the unity of all Christians,* as well as our openness to those who profess other religions and indeed to all people of good will. This is the reflection that I would now like to make with you.

### Incarnate Word Is the Source and Model of Ecclesial Communion

Our faith in the Church is inseparable from our profession that Jesus is "the Christ, the Son of the living God" (Mt. 16:16). The mysterious communion between God and man in Christ is prolonged in the Church. The Church is the fruit of that hypostatic union which achieved its full redeeming efficacy in the Paschal Mystery. And the Church is the means that the Holy Spirit uses to incorporate all people into Christ by incorporating them into the Church. Indeed, the Church belongs to the work of Redemption. In Christ she is throughout all history *the instrument of saving communion* which is open to all humanity.

### Links Between the Eternal Communion of the Trinity and Ecclesial Communion

There is a close relationship between the temporal and visible ecclesial communion and the eternal and invisible communion of the Most Holy Trinity. They are not parallel realities. As the Second Vatican Council says, citing Saint Cyprian, the

Church is "made one with the unity of the Father and the Son and the Holy Spirit" (*Lumen Gentium,* 4). *The communion of the Blessed Trinity is the source from which is derived the communion of the pilgrim Church,* that earthly sphere of saving union with God. With deep faith the Second Vatican Council teaches that "this pilgrim Church is necessary for salvation" (*Lumen Gentium,* 14).

## Sense of Mission Based on God's Plan of Salvation in Christ and the Necessity of the Church

2. A great *love of God's plan of salvation in Christ* and the conviction of the necessity of the Church are at the root of that zealous sense of mission which should animate all Catholics. Opposed to this zeal is the relativism which would deny the unique value of Christ's Gospel and his Church. To offer Christ and his message to the world will always be a challenge to Christian fidelity and pastoral wisdom.

## Dialogue of Salvation

If we are convinced—and we are—that Christ is the fullness of Truth; if we profess—and we do—that the Church has been instituted by Christ for the salvation of all, then to be consistent we will want to engage constantly in *the dialogue of salvation,* so that as many as possible may find joy in the Good News of God's merciful love revealed in his Son Jesus Christ.

## Charity Expresses Itself in Genuine Respect for Others' Beliefs

Since it is charity that spurs us on in our task, we will carry out this mission with prayer, good example and sacrifice—with a charity *that expresses itself in genuine respect for the beliefs of others.* Zeal for the Gospel of Christ, which should characterize all of the faithful, leads us to understand, to forgive and to respect the action of God's grace, which works through human freedom. We do not subject people to pressure or offend anyone when we follow in Christ's footsteps and travel the path of self-denial and service that began in Bethlehem, was consummated on the Cross and reaches us in the Eucharist.

## Foster the Inner Unity and Love Among Catholics

3. It is also necessary *to increase unity and fraternal love among Catholics.* This is essential if our ecumenical zeal is to be credible: "This is how all will know that you are my disciples, if you have love for one another" (Jn. 13:35). As my Predecessor Paul VI so clearly said at the time of the Council: "The unity of the Church must be received and recognized by each and every member of the Church. It is not enough to call oneself a Catholic. We must be truly united." And he continued: "Today people speak a great deal about reestablishing unity with our separated brethren, and this

is good. This is a very worthwhile endeavor, and we all ought to cooperate in it with humility, tenacity and confidence. But we must not forget our duty to work even more for the Church's internal unity, which is so necessary for her spiritual and apostolic vitality" (General Audience, March 31, 1965).

## Affective and Effective *Communio* Includes the Pope's Special Role

On the occasion of our meeting today, dear brothers, when there is manifest a *communio* which is both affective and effective, I cannot but repeat what the Council said about our role in this regard: "The Roman Pontiff, as the Successor of Peter, is the perpetual and visible principle and foundation of unity of both the Bishops and of the faithful. The individual Bishops, however, are the visible principle and foundation of unity in their particular Churches" (*Lumen Gentium,* 23). May all of us work together to foster the inner unity of the Church, which is the will of Christ and which also guarantees the effectiveness of our ecumenical efforts.

## Ecclesial Unity Has Room for Legitimate Diversity and Climate of Freedom

4. Within the Catholic Church herself we have to live the well-known maxim: *in necessariis unitas, in dubiis libertas, in omnibus caritas.* In this way we can properly combine unity with diversity and ensure the necessary climate of freedom within the ecclesial community. This principle sustains the common patrimony of faith and moral teaching while leaving options in theological studies, spirituality, means of evangelization, and ways of infusing the Christian spirit into the temporal order. In the one Body of Christ there will always be room for a variety of ministries and for the development of associations, groups and movements of different types.

As pastors of God's people we must love *legitimate diversity in the Catholic Church,* and loyally respect and help direct to the common good all authentic charisms wherever they are found among the faithful. It is a part of our own charism to authenticate the discernment of these gifts. The diversity of ministries and institutions allows individuals and communities, under the leadership of the Bishops in effective communion with the Bishop of Rome, to find their proper way within the universal pilgrimage of the Church.

## Catechesis on Ecumenism Will Explain How the One Church of Christ Subsists in the Catholic Church

5. The climate of freedom in the Church should be accompanied by a truly *adequate catechesis on ecumenism.* Among all the Catholic faithful there should be an open and committed attitude with respect to the ecumenical movement, particularly where there is frequent contact with other Christians. There is a great tradition of

pastoral activity in this area on the part of the Bishops of the United States. Without treating the subject at length, I would just like to emphasize several related points.

It is necessary to continue *to explain the Council's teaching* that the one Church of Christ "subsists in the Catholic Church" (*Lumen Gentium,* 8), and to show how much the Catholic Church desires to see realized within the one Church the unity of all Christ's followers, "so that the world may believe" (Jn. 17:21).

### Organic Development of Doctrine Is the Standard of Progress

Any progress which the Catholic Church makes along the path of ecumenism must always be in keeping with *the organic development of doctrine.* Although the patrimony of faith and moral teaching can be better explained and understood, the essential content of salvation which the Catholic Church has always proclaimed must remain intact. When new doctrinal and moral questions arise, the Church must resolve them with the same principles and with the same logic of faith with which she has acted from her origins under the inspiration of the Holy Spirit.

### Catechesis on Principles Governing Common Worship

All the faithful should know *the Church's principles governing common worship* or *communicatio in sacris.* These principles were succinctly outlined by the Council (see *Unitatis Redintegratio,* 8). Their proper application, which has been the constant solicitude of the Holy See, is indeed an effective contribution to authentic ecumenism. Canon 844 is particularly relevant to the question as it concerns the Sacraments of Penance, the Eucharist and the Anointing of the Sick. When the reasons regulating the discipline of intercommunion are explained, the Eucharistic assembly can more easily understand that there is *an indissoluble link between the mystery of the Church and the mystery of the Eucharist,* between ecclesial and Eucharistic communion.

There are many practical opportunities for priests in parishes to explain these principles, such as weddings and funerals. Every effort made to encourage Christians to pray for full Christian unity and to promote it by proper means helps ecumenism. Explaining the conditions for receiving Holy Communion and the reasons for these conditions fosters the cause of both truth and fraternal love.

### Much Has Been Done to Implement the Ecumenical Impulse of the Council

6. *Much has been done in the United States to bring Christians closer together.* The strong desire for full communion has been expressed in ways that amply show the impulse given by the Second Vatican Council, an impulse which the Holy See has constantly upheld in its efforts to implement the Council. Catholics have come to acknowledge and esteem the truly Christian endowments from our common heritage which are found among other Christians. An excellent climate has been created for the continuation of a fruitful dialogue between competent experts. Their efforts to

find what is held in common and to formulate the controversial points in terms which render them more exact and more intelligible even to those who do not agree upon them are highly commendable.

*The Week of Prayer for Christian Unity* has continued to emphasize the importance of prayer and other spiritual means to bring about the full communion in faith and charity that is our goal. We are convinced that the union of Christians can only be the fruit of grace, a sign of that forgiveness of God which we must first humbly implore from him.

*Prayer in common* has greatly strengthened our ties and advanced the cause of true Christian unity. I myself cherish the memory of the Service of Christian Witness at the University of South Carolina a little more than a year ago.

To be applauded also is *the whole network of cooperation among fellow Christians* in activities which have a social dimension and which ultimately serve to promote the welfare of all the citizens of your country. I would encourage you, as I also mentioned on my first pastoral visit to the United States, to undertake in common a creative ecumenical action especially as regards the sacred value of marriage, family life and the unborn (see Ecumenical Prayer Service, October 7, 1979).

In all this, it is essential for us to live a more intense Christian life. The Council placed ecumenism in the context of the *renovatio Ecclesiae* (*Unitatis Redintegratio,* 6), and saw its immediate source in *interior conversion* and in *holiness of life.* This profound conviction continues to be valid.

Special emphasis has to be placed on *the dynamic Christocentrism of the ecumenical movement:* union with Christ and love for him is the key to union and love in the Church. From this source we draw the strength to pursue the evangelizing mission with all its demands.

### Respect for Different Religions, Reaching the Unchurched

7. *The Church must make herself available to all people.* She comes forth from the redeeming love of Christ, who died for all. An important part of this attitude is *the Church's respect for different religions.* In them there can frequently be found the *semina Verbi,* the presence of a truth which, although hidden in shadow, leads people toward the complete encounter with God in Christ. The Church will always strive to defend these values.

The many *"unchurched"* people of our cities and towns deserve our special attention and fraternal love. It is necessary that Catholics become closer to them and help them discover their true vocation in Christ. This is the best service we can render to them and the best expression of solidarity and friendship.

Dear brothers: by God's grace the Catholic Church in the United States of America has been very fruitful in holiness and love. This has happened in a society which from its origins has been pluralistic and open to all men and women. An important aspect of this vigor of Catholicism is found *in the union of truth and freedom.* Upon you, pastors of the Church in the United States, rests this great heritage, with its immense challenges. I ask Saints Peter and Paul to support you in your arduous apostolic labors and I commend you all to Mary, Queen of the Apostles and Mother of Christ's Church.

## NINTH *AD LIMINA* ADDRESS TO THE
## BISHOPS OF THE UNITED STATES

### REGION II: NEW YORK STATE

### OCTOBER 15, 1988

Dear Brothers in our Lord Jesus Christ,

1. It is a special joy for me to welcome all of you, my brother Bishops from New York. On this occasion there come before my mind so many remembrances of my pastoral visit in 1979. At the same time I wish to honor in your persons the pilgrimage of faith and love that the millions of Catholic people living in your state are making, in union with Christ, to the Father, in the Holy Spirit.

### Proclamation of the Gospel Is Urgent Task

Today we are gathered together as pastors, conscious of the words of Jesus to his Apostles: "Go therefore and make disciples of all nations . . . teaching them to observe all that I have commanded you" (Mt. 28:19–20). These words must find a constant echo in our minds and hearts. As successors of the Twelve, we have as our preeminent duty *the proclamation of the Gospel* to all people (see *Christus Dominus,* 12). This is a task that is always necessary, but it is even more urgent wherever there is ignorance, error or indifference to the truth.

After commanding us to teach, Jesus assures us of his presence and support: "Behold I am with you always, to the end of the age" (Mt. 28:20). This promise fills us with peace; it challenges us to confidence and hope. The Lord Jesus Christ sends us forth and remains with us! He wants us to do our part, to carry out our mission, to be vigilant. He wants us ourselves to walk in the light of Christ and to offer this light to the Church and to the world. Today I wish to refer to a concrete means of offering this light to humanity. It is the *Catholic college and university,* with its institutional commitment to the word of God as proclaimed by the Catholic Church.

### Lofty Mission of the Catholic University and College:
### Prepare the Reevangelization of Society

2. As the Second Vatican Council states: "The destiny of society and of the Church herself is intimately linked with the progress of young people pursuing higher studies" (*Gravissimum Educationis,* 10). Accordingly, the same Council exhorts Bishops to pay careful pastoral attention to university students. They need this care if they are to sanctify themselves in the exercise of their obligations and "inform

culture with the Gospel" (*Sapientia Christiana,* Prologue, 1). The reevangelization of society depends in great part on today's university students. While pursuing their higher studies, they have *the right to receive a Catholic formation*—both doctrinal and moral—at a level that corresponds to their scholastic endeavors.

## Catholic Identity Offers Fundamental Direction for Teaching and Studies

The lofty mission of Catholic colleges and universities is to provide a public, enduring and pervasive influence of the Christian mind in the whole enterprise of advancing higher culture, and to equip students to bear the burdens of society and to witness to their faith before the world (see *Gravissimum Educationis,* 10). Catholic institutions of higher learning, which educate a large number of young people in the United States of America, have a great importance for the future of society and of the Church in your country. But the degree of their influence depends entirely on preserving *their Catholic identity.* This Catholic identity has to be present in the fundamental direction given to both teaching and studies. And it must be present in the life of these institutions which are characterized by a special bond with the Church—a bond that springs from their institutional connection with the Catholic message. The adjective "Catholic" must always be the real expression of a profound reality.

## Faith Protects and Guarantees Freedom

3. We are convinced that it is necessary to respect the legitimate autonomy of human sciences. But we are also convinced that when Christians, *with reason enlightened by faith,* know the fundamental truths about God, man and the world, they are in a position to have their intellectual efforts produce more abundant fruits of authentic human progress. Faith does not limit freedom in the pursuit of knowledge. On the contrary, it is its greatest guarantee. This leads us once again to focus our attention on the true significance of freedom in the service of and the search for truth.

"If you remain in my word," Jesus tells us, "you will truly be my disciples, and you will know the truth, and the truth will set you free" (Jn. 8:31–32). These words of our Lord proclaim *the liberating power of truth.* Their profound meaning is easier to grasp when we realize that Christ himself is the Truth. It is he, Christ, who contains in himself the complete truth about man; it is he who is the highest revelation of God.

## Freedom Is Ordered to Truth

*The profound connection between truth and freedom* affects the order of all knowledge. In this order there exists in fact a bond between faith and human knowledge. Truth does not limit freedom. On the contrary, freedom is ordered to truth. Furthermore, the truth of faith does not limit human knowledge. Rather, human knowledge opens up the way that leads to Christian faith, and Christian faith guides human knowledge. While faith does not offer solutions for investigation by reason—which follows its own principles and methodologies in different fields and enjoys a legitimate autonomy—nevertheless, faith assists reason in achieving the full good of the human person and of society.

## Philosophy, Human Sciences and Culture
## Are Incomplete Without Man's Transcendent Dimension

When Catholic colleges and universities promote true freedom in the intellectual sphere, they provide a singular service for the good of all society. Today's culture, influenced by methods and ways of thinking characteristic of the natural sciences, would be incomplete without *the recognition of man's transcendent dimension.* Hence any philosophical current proclaiming the exclusive validity of the principle of empirical verification could never do justice to the individual or to society.

The findings of all study can be fully utilized only *in consonance with the fundamental truths concerning man,* his origin, destiny and dignity. For this reason the university by its nature is called to be ever more open to the sense of the absolute and the transcendent, in order to facilitate the search for truth at the service of humanity.

## Foundation and Fundamental Disposition
## of All Theology Is Faith

4. In reflecting on theological knowledge, we turn immediately to faith, *since faith is the indispensable foundation and fundamental disposition of all theology.* Faith constitutes its starting point and its constant intrinsic point of reference. Saint Anselm of Canterbury has given us that well-known definition of the work of theology: *faith seeking understanding.* Theology springs from faith, from the desire of the believer to understand the faith.

## Faith Teaches Divine Revelation,
## Which Grows in Understanding

What faith teaches is not the result of human investigation but comes from *divine revelation.* Faith has not been transmitted to the human mind as a philosophical invention to be perfected; rather, it has been entrusted to the Spouse of Christ as a divine deposit to be faithfully guarded and infallibly interpreted (see First Vatican Council: *Dei Filius,* ch. IV: *DS* 3020). In the area of strictly human knowledge, there is room not only for progress toward the truth but also, and not infrequently, for the rectification of substantial error. Revealed truth, however, has been entrusted to the Church once and for all. It has reached its completion in Christ. Hence the profound significance of the Pauline expression *"deposit"* of faith (see 1 Tm. 6:20). At the same time, this deposit allows for a further explanation and for a growing understanding as long as the Church is on this earth.

## The Magisterium, Thanks to Its *Charisma Veritatis Certum*, Has a Special Role

This task of achieving an ever-deeper understanding of the content of faith belongs to every member of the Church. But the Second Vatican Council assures us that "the task of authentically interpreting the word of God, whether written or handed down, has been entrusted exclusively to the living teaching office of the Church" (*Dei Verbum*, 10). This *Magisterium* is not above the divine word but serves it with a specific *carisma veritatis certum* (*Dei Verbum*, 8), which includes the charism of infallibility, present not only in the solemn definitions of the Roman Pontiff and of Ecumenical Councils but also in the universal and ordinary Magisterium (*Lumen Gentium*, 25), which can truly be considered as the usual expression of the Church's infallibility.

## The Church Fosters a Legitimate Pluralism of Theology Within the Unity of Faith

5. This does not, however, prevent the Church from recognizing and fostering *a legitimate pluralism in theology*. Right after the Council, Paul VI stated that "a moderate diversity of opinions is compatible with the unity of the faith and with fidelity toward the teachings and norms of the magisterium" (Address to the International Congress on the Theology of the Council, October 1, 1966). The extent of this pluralism is limited by the unity of faith and the teachings of the Church's authentic Magisterium. But within its scope, the plurality of theologies should have a certain conceptual common ground. Not every philosophy is capable of providing that solid and coherent understanding of the human person, of the world, and of God which is necessary for any theological system that strives to place its knowledge in continuity with the knowledge of faith.

In order to understand the limits of theological pluralism, it is necessary to distinguish it clearly from *the unity of faith,* which depends totally on revealed truth. With respect to the noninfallible expressions of the authentic Magisterium of the Church, these should be received with religious submission of mind and will (see *Lumen Gentium*, 25).

## Conscience Is an Instrument for the Detection of Moral Truth; It Is Not Free to Establish What Is Right or Wrong

6. With the passing of time it is ever more evident how certain positions on the so-called "right to dissent" have had harmful repercussions on the moral conduct of a number of the faithful. "It has been noted"—I mentioned in my address last year to the Bishops gathered in Los Angeles—"that there is a tendency on the part of some Catholics to be selective in their adherence to the Church's moral teachings" (September 16, 1987). Some people appeal to "freedom of conscience" to justify this way of acting. Therefore, it is necessary to clarify that it is not conscience that "freely" establishes what is right and wrong. Using a concise expression of John Henry Newman's Oxford University Sermons, we can say that conscience is "an instrument for detecting

moral truth." *Conscience detects moral truth:* it interprets a norm which it does not create (see *Gaudium et Spes,* 16; Paul VI, General Audience, February 12, 1969).

## Collaboration of Bishops with Theologians and Ecclesiastical Faculties

7. Dear brothers: to carry out the prophetic mission that falls to us as pastors of the Church, it is of great importance to have *the collaboration of Catholic theologians and ecclesiastical faculties.* As a reflection on the faith, made in faith, theology is an ecclesial science that constantly develops within the Church and is directed to the service of the Church. This is at the root of the theologian's grave responsibility, particularly if he has received the *missio canonica* (see *CIC* 812) to teach in an ecclesiastical faculty. The authentic faith of theologians nourished by prayer and constantly purified through conversion is a great gift of God to his Church. On it depends the well-being of theology in our day. As I mentioned at The Catholic University in Washington: "It behooves the theologian to be free but with the freedom that is openness to the truth and the light that comes from faith and from fidelity to the Church" (October 7, 1979).

## The Catholic University of America Marks Its Centenary

The Catholic institution in which the Bishops of the United States have placed great hope and which they have loyally supported—The Catholic University of America—last year celebrated the one hundredth anniversary of its founding. Next year will mark the centenary of the granting of its papal charter. All the achievements of the past are due to God's grace, on which is well founded the hope for a future that will see ever-greater academic achievements, including those in theological scholarship. In particular, it is to be hoped that this university and all the other Catholic universities and colleges will contribute even more to the enrichment of the Church in the United States and elsewhere, that they will constantly meet their calling to prepare students who are *heralds of culture, servants of humanity and witnesses of faith.*

May the Blessed Virgin Mary, *Sedes Sapientiae,* obtain for all of you the light of her Son, our Lord Jesus Christ. May she sustain you in pastoral wisdom, and bring joy and peace to the hearts of your people.

## TENTH *AD LIMINA* ADDRESS TO THE BISHOPS OF THE UNITED STATES

### REGION VI: PROVINCES OF CINCINNATI AND DETROIT

### OCTOBER 24, 1988

Dear Brothers in our Lord Jesus Christ,

1. My fraternal welcome goes to all of you, the Bishops of the Ecclesiastical Provinces of Cincinnati and Detroit; at the same time I extend cordial greetings to all

the faithful throughout the states of Michigan and Ohio, who are spiritually present here with you today.

### Christ Reveals the Greatness of the Father's Love

The Second Vatican Council reminds us that only Christ has taught the whole truth about man, and he has done so "by the revelation of the Father and his love" (*Gaudium et Spes,* 22). Christ has revealed the greatness of the Father's love not only with words but above all through the total giving of himself in sacrifice. To see Christ is to see the Father (see Jn. 14:9). Christ also shows that the Father's love is more powerful than any kind of evil which is in man, in humanity or in the world (see *Dives in Misericordia,* 7). This love is present in the personal history of each human being. *To understand the Church of the Incarnate Word it is necessary to understand God's love.*

### The Love of Christian Couples
### Is Interpersonal and Self-Giving

2. One of the most important expressions of this love is *the love of Christian couples.* Since "God is love" (1 Jn. 4:8), and since man is created in the image and likeness of God, there is inscribed in the humanity of man and woman the "capacity and responsibility of love" (*Familiaris Consortio,* 11). Love in its deepest and richest meaning involves self-giving. Christ, the Son of God and perfect Image of the Father (see Col. 1:15), gave himself totally in the very fullness of love through his redeeming Sacrifice. In the case of husband and wife, genuine love is expressed in the gift of self to each other, which includes giving the power to beget life. In the words of *Gaudium et Spes:* "This love is an eminently human one since it is directed from one person to another through an affection of the will. It involves the good of the whole person. . . . Such love, merging the human with the divine, leads the spouses to a free and mutual gift of themselves" (no. 49). "From one person to another" (*a persona in personam*): these few words express a profound truth about conjugal love, a love which is eminently interpersonal. It is a love which involves the gift of the whole person. Included in this gift is their whole sexuality with its openness to the transmission of life.

### Positive Teaching of *Humanae Vitae* Sheds Light
### on Sexual Dimension of the Marital Relationship

3. As we commemorate the twentieth anniversary of the teaching of the "prophetic" encyclical *Humanae Vitae* of Paul VI, we see ever more clearly today how relevant and positive it is. In this anniversary year I wish to make special mention of our pastoral concerns for marriage and family life. I note with interest and gratitude the Statement of the National Conference of Catholic Bishops' Committee for Pro-Life Activities commemorating the encyclical. As we all know, marriage is much more

than a social institution; it is truly, in Paul VI's words, "the wise institution of the Creator to realize in mankind his design of love" (*Humanae Vitae,* 8). The Church's teaching on marriage is fundamental to understanding the many dimensions of the marriage relationship, especially the sexual dimension. For sexuality is not just a biological reality, but concerns the innermost being of the human person as such (see *Familiaris Consortio,* 11). It allows spouses to express in a specific way that interpersonal love that binds them together *in permanent, faithful and exclusive covenant* and that leads them to parenthood.

## Special Mission to Understand Sex
## in the Context of Conjugal Love

Marriage is a unique type of relationship, and all the actions whereby spouses manifest their love for each other are part of God's plan and signs of his love. In the sexual act the married couple have the opportunity to grow in grace, in intimacy, in generosity and in their willingness to cooperate with God in bringing into being new human persons. But in order to strengthen their love and deepen their unity, married couples must be led to appreciate ever more fully "the inseparable connection, willed by God and unable to be broken by man on his own initiative, between the two meanings of the conjugal act: the unitive meaning and the procreative meaning" (*Humanae Vitae,* 12). In a world that often reduces sex to the pursuit of pleasure, and in some cases to domination, the Church has a special mission *to place sex in the context of conjugal love* and of generous and responsible openness to parenthood.

## Need to Affirm the Positive Value of Children

4. As pastors we must encourage couples to maintain an openness to life and a spirit of joyful sharing in regard to children. As the Council has taught us, children are really *the supreme gift of marriage* and contribute in their own way to making their parents holy (see *Gaudium et Spes,* 50, 48). But materialistic and selfish attitudes often deny *the value of the child.* Each child, however, is a new revelation of God's love and of the fidelity of the spouses. "Each child is also a test of our respect for the mystery of life, upon which, from the very first moment of conception, the Creator places the imprint of his image and likeness" (*Christmas Message,* 1979).

## Pastoral Programs and Advocacy
## to Respect Unborn Human Life

I deeply appreciate the efforts of your Episcopal Conference to proclaim the sanctity of human life from conception onward. Throughout the world we have seen an increase in the number of abortions and a decline in the protection of unborn human life. The Bishops of the United States have steadfastly opposed this destruction of human life by programs of education and pastoral care and by advocating laws and public policies that protect and sustain human life, before and after birth.

Your annual "Respect Life Program" continues the effort *to create respect for human* life at every stage and in every circumstance.

## Christian Marriage as Vocation to Holiness

This twentieth anniversary of *Humanae Vitae* challenges us once again as Pastors to intensify our efforts to present Christian marriage as *a vocation to holiness,* and to help couples understand the role of the Christian family in the life and mission of the Church. We are called to provide engaged and married couples with the fullness of the Church's teaching on human sexuality, conjugal love and responsible parenthood. We must emphasize the sanctity of human life as a precious gift from God that needs to be protected and fostered, while making greater and more systematic efforts to offer instruction in the natural methods of family planning. Natural family planning enables couples to understand God's design for sex, and invites them to dialogue, mutual respect, shared responsibility and self-control (see *Familiaris Consortio,* 32). Our people need to have prayerful confidence that God will bless and sustain them in their efforts to lead lives of holiness and to be witnesses to his love in the modern world.

## Religious Consecration Offers Special Witness to Love

5. Another indispensable form of witness to God's love for humanity is *the practice of the evangelical counsels in consecrated life.* The Church profoundly esteems consecrated persons. She rejoices in their consecration and their special witness to love. Chastity, poverty and obedience are manifestations of love not only because they are at the root of innumerable and sublime apostolic works which serve the needs of humanity, but above all because they express the power of Christ's Paschal Mystery, which conquers everything that is opposed to the love of God. To understand love fully, the world needs the sign of the authentic "contradiction" provided by religious consecration. This religious consecration will be authentically actuated in the true love of self-giving when consecrated persons act in union with the Church, in conformity with the teaching and directives of the Magisterium of Peter and of the pastors in communion with him (see *Redemptionis Donum,* 14–15).

## Priestly Celibacy, God's Gift to the Church and Sign of the Church's Charity

6. The Church offers to the world a witness of singular importance to Christ's love through the *celibacy* of her priests. Celibacy involves the total gift of self to the Lord for lifelong service in his Church, with the renunciation of marriage for the sake of the Kingdom of God. It is a gift that God gives to his Church and that manifests the charity which inspires her. The Council showed the courage of faith when it reaffirmed the traditional discipline of celibacy with full confidence that God would not fail to continue to bestow the graces which support this charism.

### The Priest Is a True Witness of God's Love for His People

Priestly celibacy signifies that the priest is not a delegate of the people or even a "functionary" of God, but *a true witness to God's love for his people*. The rule of celibacy for the Latin Church is more than an ecclesiastical law. It has deep theological and doctrinal roots that confirm its value and show its desirability for those who are chosen to act *in persona Christi capitis* (see *Presbyterorum Ordinis*, 2,6). Last year marked the twentieth anniversary of the encyclical *Sacerdotalis Caelibatus*. May all of us, together with our priests, continue to find inspiration in this teaching as we strive to proclaim the love of Christ in all its fullness.

## Different Forms of Witness Linked
## to the Pastoral Love of Bishops

7. The different forms of witness to God's love for humanity are linked in no small way *to the pastoral love of Bishops*, who teach, govern and sanctify the People of God. We all know the profound reality to which Jesus himself made reference when he cited the prophetic words: "I will strike the shepherd and the sheep of the flock will be scattered" (Mt. 26:31; see Zec. 13:7). We should never lose sight of the fact that to a great extent the eternal happiness and even the temporal well-being of innumerable people depend on our own faithfulness to Christ's grace.

### Love Casts Out Fear When Proclaiming the Word of Truth

Certainly we face difficulties in exercising our mission as shepherds. *Fear may beset our hearts*. Will we be understood? Will our message be accepted? How will the world react? How will public opinion judge us? Will our human weakness impede our mission? It is in these moments that we recognize that our love, our pastoral charity, still needs to grow. With Saint John we must confess: "Love has no room for fear; rather perfect love casts out all fear . . . love is not yet perfect in one who is afraid" (1 Jn. 4:18). And because love is a victory over fear, it is a triumph in our ministry.

It is necessary now more than ever to proclaim to the world the truth in love, including "the fullness of truth which sometimes irritates and offends even if it always liberates" (Address of September 5, 1983). In the faithful, persevering and courageous *proclamation of God's word,* we Pastors must fulfill our mission and our destiny as witnesses of divine love.

The *Bishop's love for his priests* will be a particularly effective expression and sign of the love of Christ. With his deep fraternal and paternal interest in them, with his understanding, human affection and concern for whatever weighs upon them—while encouraging them to strive for holiness in spite of human weakness—the Bishop must help his priests to be witnesses before the people to that love which is at the root of every apostolate. Through the Bishop, priests should be able to experience once again the power of Christ's love for all humanity, so that with the Beloved

Disciple they will be able to say: "We have come to know and to believe in the love God has for us" (1 Jn. 4:16).

As heralds of Christ's love we turn to his Mother Mary, *Mater pulchrae dilectionis,* to continue in prayer our reflection on that great mystery of love which comes forth from, and returns to, the Most Holy Trinity—to whom be glory forever and ever.

## ELEVENTH *AD LIMINA* ADDRESS TO THE BISHOPS OF THE BYZANTINE RITE OF THE PROVINCE OF PITTSBURGH

### NOVEMBER 26, 1988

Dear Brothers in our Lord Jesus Christ,

### Faithful Witnesses to Apostolic Tradition

1. Through you I would like to extend warm greetings today to all the Byzantine Catholics of the Province of Pittsburgh, and at the same time to express my love and esteem for all the other Eastern-Rite Catholics in the United States. In your particular Churches there shines forth "that tradition which was handed down from the Apostles through the Fathers and which forms part of the divinely revealed and undivided heritage of the universal Church" (*Orientalium Ecclesiarum,* 1). Indeed, you bear *faithful witness to the catholicity of the Church* and to her ability to sustain and develop in the present—in continuity with the past—diverse religious traditions which derive from the one Gospel of our Lord and Savior Jesus Christ.

In your own history, acceptance of the Gospel has exercised a profound influence on your people. The Christian culture which was generated over centuries in your lands of origin and which you have inherited is *a great treasure to be preserved, shared and developed organically* in the present situation of your lives in the United States. Acceptance of Christ never fails to produce fruit in all sectors of human activity (see *Euntes in Mundum,* 21).

### Profound Contribution

2. The celebration of the recent Marian year has provided the Church with a special opportunity of appreciating more fully *the contribution of the East to the common patrimony of the Church's worship.* Here in Rome, on a number of memorable occasions we have offered the liturgy according to various rites, and in our prayer we have experienced a profound communion with all the Eastern Churches. These celebrations vividly expressed the lofty aspirations of the whole Church to adore the majesty of God and to be joined in communion with the Most High Trinity. The divine plan, according to which the Eternal Word took on human nature in the womb of the Virgin Mary, continually makes possible the fulfillment of his longing.

Together we have honored the All-holy Mother of God, the archetype of the human creature's supernatural elevation to union with God in Jesus Christ. Mary,

Daughter of God the Father, Mother of God the Son, Spouse and Temple of God the Holy Spirit, is at the very heart of the mystery of salvation (see *Mulieris Dignitatem,* 3–4). The special place that *Marian piety* holds in the Eastern Churches leads us to a deeper understanding of Christ, and through him, of the Father and the Holy Spirit.

## Mary: Model of Total Service

3. From the very beginning of her divine motherhood, Mary takes up *her role in relation to the messianic service of Christ,* the Son of Man, who came not to be served but to serve (see Mk. 10–45), and this service constitutes the foundation of that kingdom in which "to serve" means "to reign." She who is "full of grace" expresses her joy at the gift she has received by saying: "Behold, I am the handmaid of the Lord" (Lk. 1:38). As pastors of the Church, we too find joy in our life of service as we recall the challenge of the Second Vatican Council: "In exercising their office of father and pastor, bishops should stand in the midst of their people as those who serve" (*Christus Dominus,* 16). In this our apostolic ministry, we look to Mary as our model of total service.

Among the many tasks incumbent upon Bishops, the Second Vatican Council speaks of the obligation "to promote every activity that is of interest to the whole Church, especially that the faith may increase and the light of full truth appear to all people" (*Christus Dominus*). The service that the laity render in this area is of immense importance and requires a persevering commitment on their part. As they pursue their specific role of consecrating from within all temporal reality, they can be greatly strengthened and inspired by the example of Mary. Thus in their daily occupations, in their work and family life, they need to be invited to respond to the universal call to holiness by identifying themselves with Christ, by carrying out all their activities as perfectly as possible, and by bearing genuine witness to the Lord and his Gospel. With God's grace the laity can make their ordinary work *a great act of generous and sanctifying service in union with Mary.*

The Queen of Apostles is the perfect example of the union of the spiritual and apostolic life in the midst of everyday concerns (see *Apostolicam Actuositatem,* 4). She is an incomparable source of *inspiration, particularly for lay women* in today's world, which, along with the scientific and technological development that produces material progress for some people and degradation for others, risks becoming steadily more inhuman. The family, the Church and society need that feminine "genius" which guarantees human sensitivity (see *Mulieris Dignitatem,* 30). Through the teaching of the Church and with the help of the Holy Spirit, women can increasingly discover in Mary the full meaning of their femininity and offer the gift of its untarnished beauty to a world in need of being humanized.

## The Cost of Religious Liberty

4. Dear brothers: We are all heirs of a spiritual and civil freedom which has been won at a great price. Many of your people have personally experienced *how costly*

*liberty is,* especially *religious liberty.* When we speak about this topic we are motivated by the truth about man and by concern for the well-being of each nation. Indeed, we have the best interests of all humanity at heart, for religious freedom supports and guarantees all other freedoms. As I said in this year's message for the World Day of Peace, the freedom of individuals and communities to profess and practice their own beliefs is an essential element for peace in the world.

Freedom is hampered in many ways, one of them being the pressures of a secularized cultural environment. You are faithful to your pastoral and prophetic mission when you alert your people, who so prize their religious liberty, *not to let the pleasures and allurements of the world deprive them of that inner freedom* which not even persecution itself could destroy in them or their forebears.

### Protect and Advance Ecclesial Traditions

5. The presence of Eastern-Rite Catholics in America has come about both as a result of religious persecution in their homelands and through other variously motivated emigrations. Taking their situation into account, the Holy See over the years has fostered *the protection and advancement of their ecclesial traditions* by establishing parishes and special hierarchies in accordance with their spiritual needs (see *Orientalium Ecclesiarum,* 4).

Today, many difficult situations of economic, political and social unrest have forced millions of people to leave their homes and seek a better life elsewhere. As pastors we must continually invite the faithful to be sensitive to the needs of the poor and of all who suffer. The "logic of the Gospel" does not permit us to remain passive in regard to anyone in need. The love of Christ impels us therefore *to defend and support the just cause of migrants, immigrants, and refugees* (Message for World Migrants' Day, October 4, 1988).

### The Church Is Missionary

6. By the will of her divine Founder, the Church is forever and essentially *missionary.* On the ecclesial level, your particular Churches contribute to the fulfillment of Christ's command to go forth and make disciples of all nations (see Mt. 28:19) by displaying to the world the universality of Christ's salvation and by passing on your cherished traditions to successive generations.

*Culturally,* you bring the heritage of the East to a society which owes much of its foundation to Western Christianity. *Eastern and Western traditions* in Christianity *have complemented each other* and produced in the fields of music, literature, the visual arts and architecture, as well as in modes of thought, the inculturation of the one and undivided deposit of faith entrusted by Christ to his Church (see *Euntes in Mundum,* 12).

The desire for unity, which is an outstanding sign of our times, is particularly strong at the level of *ecumenism.* The Fathers of the Second Vatican Council expressly thanked God for the communion of the Eastern Churches with the See of Peter, the visible foundation of the unity of the Spouse of Christ (*Unitatis Redintegratio,* 17). By helping our Orthodox brethren to reflect on the character of the relations that existed between their Churches and the Roman See before separation, your Churches contribute greatly to a constructive ecumenical dialogue. Now more than ever, you are called upon to pray and work for building up the visible unity of the Church.

## Mary: Embodiment of Our Vocation to Holiness

7. Dear brother Bishops: from your exceedingly rich liturgical and spiritual tradition, with your long experience of faithfulness to Christ in the midst of changes and adversity, you draw the necessary spiritual strength to help the faithful entrusted to your care to correspond to their *vocation to holiness and service* in the context of the Church in the United States.

As we look forward to the Third Christian Millennium, let us entrust all our concerns and hopes to the Virgin Mother of God, to whom we owe the birth of Christ and who was present at the birth of the Church, which is one and universal from the beginning. The Marian year has ended, but the period now opening up before us is a Marian event, *a Marian path leading to the year 2000.* As we travel this path together, with our eyes raised to her who is indeed the Star of the East, let us constantly present her to our people as a model of service, an incentive to holiness, our Mother of Perpetual Help. Upon you, dear brothers, and upon all the Ruthenian Byzantine Catholics of the Metropolitan See of Pittsburgh and the Eparchies of Passaic, Parma and Van Nuys—as well as the faithful of all the other Eastern Churches in the United States—I invoke the grace and peace of our Lord Jesus Christ, and I impart to all my Apostolic Blessing.

## TWELFTH *AD LIMINA* ADDRESS TO THE BISHOPS OF THE UNITED STATES

### REGION VII: PROVINCES OF CHICAGO, INDIANAPOLIS AND MILWAUKEE

### DECEMBER 10, 1988

Dear Brothers in our Lord Jesus Christ,

1. We are coming to the end of the 1988 *ad Limina* visits, and I am happy that I can mark this occasion with such a large group of American Bishops. To all of you who make up the Ecclesiastical Provinces of Chicago, Indianapolis and Milwaukee I extend a welcome of fraternal love.

## Profound Call to Holiness Through a Life of Faith

During this year I have spoken to your brother Bishops on a variety of topics, but always endeavoring to emphasize that *the Church in the United States is called to holiness* through a life of faith in Jesus Christ the Son of God and Savior of the world. This emphasis is the consequence of a profound conviction that only through living faith can the Church give a valid pastoral response to all the situations in which she finds herself in the modern world.

In my first talk of the present *ad Limina* series I stressed that the Church in the United States "belongs to Jesus Christ by right. He loves her intensely and intends to possess her more fully and to purify her ever more deeply in every aspect of her ecclesial reality" (March 5, 1988). And today I would suggest that together we turn our thoughts and hearts once more to Jesus Christ, so that in him we can better understand this ecclesial reality. In the words of the Letter to the Hebrews: "Let us keep our eyes fixed on Jesus, who inspires and perfects our faith" (Heb. 12:2). And because "he has taken his seat at the right of the throne of God" (Heb. 12:2), it is by looking to Christ in the reality of his heavenly Kingdom that we will understand his Church on earth.

### The Eschatological Nature Is an Essential Part of Her Mystery

2. Since *the Church is already the Kingdom of God in its initial stage,* it is fitting, at the conclusion of the *ad Limina* visits, that our attention should be directed to the final consummation of the Church. *Her eschatological nature* is an essential part of her mystery, and it is of great importance for our pastoral leadership in the Church.

### The Eschatological Dimension Is the Dynamic of Her Evangelizing Activities

We have been placed by the Holy Spirit as Pastors to guide the Church in accomplishing her mission. To do so adequately, we must always keep in mind that there is a specific dynamic at work at the center of *the Church's evangelizing activities.* It is her eschatological dimension. Everything that brings about her final fulfillment promotes her vitality. But if eschatology were to remain devoid of consequences, the Church's progress would be halted and her course misdirected. In this case, her activities would be irrelevant to authentic evangelization.

### Ecclesial Communion Is Eschatological

*Ecclesial communion,* too, is profoundly eschatological. Founded on communion through Christ with the Father in the Holy Spirit, the Church knows she is imbued with a life that transcends death. Her life is the life of the Risen Christ, the life that through the Cross conquered death by the power of loving obedience to the Father's will. By the exercise of his saving power, Christ communicates his own glorious life to the Church. The Church begins to exist as a consequence of this act of the Risen Jesus. She already lives this life of her Lord and Savior while longing for her definitive fulfillment.

## Pastoral Office Exists to Foster Holiness,
## Which Anticipates the Realization of the Kingdom

3. By his life-giving act the Lord brings his Church into union with himself and thus fills her with *holiness*. But this holiness must be sustained and increased. In all the dimensions of their human existence the members of the Church must open themselves ever more to the Lord's sanctifying power. In this way, the Kingdom gradually takes shape in each Christian and in the Church, and grows indefinitely.

It is precisely in holiness that the Church anticipates and actually inaugurates the Kingdom of God. *The pastoral office in the Church exists to foster holiness.* To understand fully the pastoral office we must look to the holiness of the Church in her eschatological form: the holiness that Christ wills for his Church, the holiness that consummates the union of Christ and his Bride in heaven. In presenting an American Bishop to the whole world as a model of pastoral charity, Paul VI called the canonization of John Neumann both a "celebration of holiness" and a "prophetic anticipation . . . for the United States . . . of a renewal in love" (June 19, 1977).

## The Full Coming of the Kingdom
## Requires the Gift of Self to God and to Others

The full coming of Christ's Kingdom requires from all the faithful the gift of themselves to God and to others. Inseparable from this gift is *prayer*. We see this in Christ Jesus. Our Lord goes to the Cross in the very context of that prayer which he began in Gethsemane and which was consummated when he gave up his spirit into the hands of the Father (see Lk. 23:46). By virtue of our divine filiation we are called to follow in this path. Authentic prayer is possible only when we are ready to carry out the saving plan of the Father. We must try, therefore, to help God's people achieve a clear understanding of what prayer means: dialogue with God involving personal commitment. As pastors, we ourselves must bear witness to prayer, being convinced that through it the saving power of God transforms the ecclesial community.

## Our Hope in Certain Victory
## Calls Us to Live in Peace and Serenity

4. The Church proclaims that her members are to be "children of the resurrection" (Lk. 20:36), and she waits *"in joyful hope* for the coming of our Savior Jesus Christ." She looks forward to the hour when her glory will be revealed in the fullness of communion with the Most Holy Trinity. It is Christ's coming that in turn will definitively inaugurate "new heavens and a new earth" (2 Pt. 3:13). As we await these realities we are called to live in deep peace and serenity. Victory is certain, evil will not prevail: Jesus Christ has overcome the world (see Jn. 16:33).

For this reason, Christians must seek to use temporal goods without the anxiety and hyperactivity of those whose only hope is in this life. Certainly, faith does not permit us to remain passive in the face of suffering and injustice. Our hope spurs us on to work actively for the coming of the universal Kingdom of God (see *Gaudium et Spes,* 39). But we can never do this with the uncertainty of those who place their ultimate happiness in earthly history. A Christian's struggle breathes *serenity* and communicates *peace,* not only as the goal it seeks but as the very style with which it promotes justice. A basic security and optimism inspires the whole life of the Church. We know beforehand the goal to which we aspire with God's help. We may experience hesitation with regard to certain means, but the objective is clear and unchanging. In its light we can discern the path to be followed and we correct any course that may have been taken by mistake.

The Church can never succumb to the temptation to "remake" herself. Her essential identity is guaranteed by the assurance that Jesus Christ will return in glory.

### Expectation of Christ's Glorious Return
### Gives Perspective to the Church's Temporal Concerns

5. This expectation of Christ's return in glory gives meaning to all the Church's activities and places *all temporal concerns in proper perspective.* In all she does, the Church looks to a horizon far beyond human history, where everything will be subjected to Christ and by him offered to the Father. At the moment foreordained, everything in heaven and on earth will definitively be placed under the headship of Christ (see 1 Cor. 15:24–28).

Meanwhile, by God's design, the life of the Church is interwoven in the fabric of human history but always directed to eternal life.

The Church can never be a community at the service of merely temporal objectives. *Her end is the Kingdom of God,* which she must unceasingly extend until its completion in eternity (see *Lumen Gentium,* 9). Hence her initiatives and efforts cannot be motivated by merely temporal values. The Church lives in the midst of human beings—she herself being the new humanity in Christ—and she shares the experience of the whole human family. She lives in solidarity with all people, and nothing human is foreign to her. The concerns of the ecclesial community embrace those of the civil community in such areas as peace, culture, the family and human rights. Yet the perspective from which the Church approaches all these issues has as its characteristic originality a relationship with the Kingdom of God. If the Church were to lose this transcendent perspective, she could not make her distinctive contribution to humanity.

### The Eucharist Is the Banquet of the Kingdom and, with the
### Sacrament of Penance, Is the Center of Pastoral Renewal

6. Any consideration of the eschatological dimension of the Church must necessarily include *the Holy Eucharist.* The Church constantly finds her nourishment in the Sacrament of the Body and Blood of the glorified Christ. At the end of time, the saving power of the Eucharist will attain its full effect when the holiness of the Church

will be complete and the entire universe will be perfectly restored in Christ. Meanwhile, we "proclaim the death of the Lord until he comes" (1 Cor. 11:26).

The renewal of the Sacrifice of Christ on Calvary is at the same time the banquet of the Kingdom. As such it is the object of the Church's *profound solicitude* and of her legislation. Recently, there was a clarification of the supplementary character of the faculty granted to lay persons to distribute Holy Communion as extraordinary Eucharistic ministers. The conditions established in the Code of Canon Law were authentically interpreted last year, at which time I directed the Congregation for the Sacraments to communicate the decision to the Episcopal Conferences throughout the world. In some cases there may still be a need to revise diocesan policies in this matter, not only to ensure the faithful application of the law but also to foster the true notion and genuine character of the participation of the laity in the life and mission of the Church.

As we prepare for the Jubilee of the year 2000, let us place the Sacraments of *Penance and the Eucharist at the center of pastoral renewal.* This is in accord with the consistent teaching of the Second Vatican Council, which sees the Eucharist as the culmination of the proclamation of the word and the call to Penance. The Christ who calls us to the Eucharistic banquet is the same merciful Christ who calls us to conversion (see *Redemptor Hominis,* 20). It is my earnest hope that in every Diocese of the United States, under the pastoral leadership of the Bishops, there will be *effective plans for the genuine renewal of the Sacrament of Penance,* with the promotion of the individual Confession. The Church is convinced and proclaims that the implementation of *aggiornamento* as envisioned by the Second Vatican Council is closely linked to the renewal of the Sacrament of Penance. Individual conversion is at the heart of all reform and renewal.

### Mary Is the Perfect Realization of the Church's Life of Faith and Model of Lay Apostolic Activity

7. Mary the Mother of Jesus is *the perfect realization of the Church's life of faith and goal of happiness.* In her we have a great sign that sums up and completely expresses the holiness that we sinners strive to attain through conversion. She who is now body and soul in heaven is the first of the redeemed and the totally sanctified one.

In the Decree on the Apostolate of the Laity, the Council presents a synthesis, applicable to Mary, of living in the temporal order without ever losing sight of the spiritual order in its eschatological fullness. The Council says that "while leading the life common to all here on earth, one filled with family concerns and labors, she was always intimately united with her Son and in an entirely unique way cooperated in the world of the Savior (*Apostolicam Actuositatem,* 4). In her femininity as Virgin, Wife and Mother, Mary stands in and before the Church as *the Woman of all salvation history.* Having now been assumed into heaven, she lives her spiritual motherhood interceding on our behalf, helping us in the midst of our earthly pilgrimage not to forget the goal which inspires all the Church's activities.

### The Church of the Bishops' Activity Is the
### Apostolic Structure of Unassailable Unity

8. It is our role as Bishops to offer to the Father, in union with Christ the High Priest, the Church and all her activities. We offer her as Christ desires her to be: his Body and his Spouse, the Church of his divinity and his humanity, the Church that reflects his generosity and lives his Sacrifice, the Church of truth and merciful love, the Church of prayer and service, the Church of conversion, holiness and eternal life.

The Church that we offer to the Father and work daily to build up in charity is by no means a so-called monolithic structure, but rather *the apostolic structure of unassailable unity,* in which, as Bishops, all of us are called, in the expression of Saint Paul, to "be united in the same mind and in the same purpose" (1 Cor. 1:10). Strengthened by this unity, our ministry becomes ever more effective in all its dimensions.

The present hour in the life of the Church calls for great hope, based on the eschatological promises of God and expressed in renewed confidence in the power of Christ's Paschal Mystery. This is the hour for renewed effort in inviting young people to the priesthood and religious life, the hour for renewed serenity in proclaiming the most difficult demands of Christianity and the loftiest challenges of the Cross. It is the hour for *a new commitment to holiness* on the part of the Church, as she prepares for the great Jubilee of the year 2000 and invokes the coming of the Lord Jesus.

As we conclude this series of *ad Limina* visits, in continuity with those of 1978 and 1983 and with my two pastoral visits to the United States, I wish to renew my deep gratitude to all of you, my brother Bishops, for your partnership in the Gospel. In this same spirit I look forward to the special meeting of Bishops planned for next year, so that by *continued pastoral collaboration* we may assist the Church in the United States to live her vocation of holiness through a life of dynamic faith. Meanwhile, I entrust to Mary, Mother of the Church and Queen of Heaven, the beloved faithful of your land and bless them all in the name of the Lord Jesus.

# Part III

---

# Letters to the Bishops of the United States

# EASTER MESSAGE TO THE
# BISHOPS OF THE UNITED STATES

## APRIL 3, 1983

To my dear brother Bishops in the United States of America,

1. In this Extraordinary Holy Year which has just begun, *the whole Church is seeking to live more intensely the mystery of the Redemption.* She is seeking to respond ever more faithfully to the immense love of Jesus Christ, the Redeemer of the world.

In the Bull of Indiction of the Jubilee, I pointed out that "the profound meaning and hidden beauty of this Year . . . is to be seen in the rediscovery and lived practice of the sacramental economy of the Church, through which the grace of God in Christ reaches individuals and communities" (*Aperite Portas Redemptori,* 3). While these words have a personal meaning for everyone, they are *particularly relevant to individual men and women Religious and to each Religious community.* It is my profound hope and ardent prayer that the grace of the Redemption will reach Religious in great abundance, that it will take possession of their hearts, and become a source of Easter joy and hope for them—that the Holy Year will be a fresh beginning for them to "walk in newness of life" (Rom. 6:4).

By their very vocation, *Religious are intimately linked to the Redemption.* In their consecration to Jesus Christ they are a sign of the Redemption that he accomplished. In the sacramental economy of the Church they are instruments for bringing this Redemption to the People of God. They do so by the vitality that radiates from the lives they live in union with Jesus, who continues to repeat to all his disciples: "I am the vine, you are the branches" (Jn. 15:5). Religious bring the People of God into contact with the Redemption by the evangelical and ecclesial witness they bear by word and example to the message of Jesus. Their communion with their local Churches and with the universal Church has a supernatural effectiveness by reason of the Redemption. The important collaboration they give to the ecclesial community helps it to live and perpetuate the mystery of the Redemption, especially through the Eucharistic Sacrifice, in which the work of the Redemption is repeatedly actuated.

The Church presents the Year of the Redemption to all the People of God as *a call to holiness, a call to renewal and a call to penance and conversion,* because "there is no spiritual renewal that does not pass through penance and conversion" (*Aperite Portas Redemptori,* 4). But this call is linked in a particular way with the life and mission of Religious. Thus the Jubilee Year has a special value for Religious; it affects them in a special way; it makes special demands on their love, reminding them how much they are loved by the Redeemer and by his Church. Especially relevant to

Religious are these words of the Apostolic Bull: "The specific grace of the Year of the Redemption is therefore a renewed discovery of the love of God" (no. 8). In this regard, as pastors of the Church, we must proclaim over and over again that the vocation to Religious life that God gives is linked to his personal love for each and every Religious. It is my earnest hope that the Holy Year of Redemption will truly be for Religious life a year of fruitful renewal in Christ's love. If all the faithful have a right—as they do—to the treasures of grace that a call to renewal in love offers, then the Religious have a special title to that right.

2. During this Jubilee of the Redemption you will be coming to Rome for your *ad Limina* visits, and I shall have an opportunity to consider with you some of the aspects of Religious life as you see them. This makes my thoughts turn at this time in a special way to *the Religious of the United States*. In reflecting on their history, their splendid contribution to the Church in your country, the great missionary activity that they have performed over the years, the influence they have exerted on Religious life throughout the world, as well as on the particular needs which they experience at the present time, I am convinced that, as Bishops, we must offer them encouragement and the support of our pastoral love.

The Religious life in the United States has indeed been *a great gift of God to the Church and to your country*. From the early colonial days, by the grace of God, the evangelizing zeal of outstanding men and women Religious, encouraged and sustained by the persevering efforts of the Bishops, have helped the Church to bring the fruits of the Redemption to your land. Religious were among your pioneers. They blazed a trail in Catholic education at all levels, helping to create a magnificent educational system from elementary school to university. They brought into being health care facilities remarkable both for their numbers and quality. They made a valuable contribution to the provision of social services. Working toward the establishment of justice, love and peace, they helped to build a social order rooted in the Gospel, striving to bring generation after generation to the maturity of Christ. Their witness to the primacy of Christ's love has been expressed through lives of prayer and dedicated service to others. Contemplative Religious have contributed immensely to the vitality of the ecclesial community. At every stage in its growth, the Church in your nation, marked by a conspicuous fidelity to the See of Peter, has been deeply indebted to its Religious: priests, sisters, brothers. The Religious of America have also been a gift to the universal Church, for they have given generously to the Church in other countries; they have helped throughout the world to evangelize the poor and to spread Christ's Gospel of peace. This generosity has given evidence of a strong and vital religious life, ensured by a steady flow of vocations.

3. And because I have stressed the pastoral character and the full participation of the local Churches in the celebration of the Holy Year, I now turn to you, the Bishops of the United States, *asking you during this Holy Year to render special pastoral service to the Religious* of your Dioceses and your country. I ask you to assist them in every way possible to open wide the doors of their hearts to the Redeemer. I ask that, through the exercise of your pastoral office, as individual Bishops and united as an Episcopal Conference, you encourage the Religious, their Institutes and associations

to live fully the mystery of the Redemption, in union with the whole Church and according to the specific charism of their Religious life. This pastoral service can be given in different ways, but it certainly includes the personal proclamation of the Gospel message to them and the celebration of the Eucharistic Sacrifice with them.

It will likewise mean *proclaiming anew to all the People of God the Church's teaching on consecrated life.* This teaching has been set forth in the great documents of the Second Vatican Council, particularly in *Lumen Gentium* and *Perfectae Caritatis.* It has been further developed in *Evangelica Testificatio,* in the addresses of my predecessor Paul VI and in those which I myself have given on many occasions. More recently still, much of this doctrinal richness has been distilled and reflected in the revised Code of Canon Law promulgated earlier this year. The essential elements are lived in different ways from one Institute to another. You yourselves deal with this rich variety in the context of the American reality. Nevertheless, there are elements which are common to all forms of Religious life and which the Church regards as essential. These include a vocation given by God, an ecclesial consecration to Jesus Christ through the profession of the evangelical counsels of public vows, a stable form of community life approved by the Church, fidelity to a specific founding gift and sound traditions, a sharing in Christ's mission by a corporate apostolate, personal and liturgical prayer, especially Eucharistic worship, public witness, a lifelong formation, a form of government calling for religious authority based on faith, a specific relation to the Church. Fidelity to these basic elements, laid down in the constitutions approved by the Church, guarantees the strength of religious life and grounds our hope for its future growth.

I ask you, moreover, my brother Bishops, to show the Church's profound love and esteem for the Religious life, directed as it is to the faithful and generous imitation of Christ and to union with God. *I ask you to invite all the Religious* throughout the land, in my name, and in your own name as Bishops, in the name of the Church and in the name of Jesus, to seize this opportunity of the Holy Year to walk in newness of life, in solidarity with all the pastors and faithful, along the path necessary for us all—the way of penance and conversion.

In their lives of *poverty,* Religious will discover that they are truly relevant to the poor. Through *chastity* they are able to love with the love of Christ and to experience his love for themselves. And through *obedience* they find their deepest configuration to Christ in the most fundamental expression of his union with the Father—in fulfilling his Father's will: "I always do what pleases him" (Jn. 8:29). It is especially through obedience that Christ himself offers to Religious the experience of full Christian freedom. Possessing peace in their hearts and the justice of God from which that peace flows, they can be authentic ministers of Christ's peace and justice to a world in need.

In those cases, too, where individuals or groups, for whatever reason, have departed from the indispensable norms of Religious life, or have even, to the scandal of the faithful, adopted positions at variance with the Church's teaching, I ask you my brother Bishops, sustained by hope in the power of Christ's grace and performing an act of authentic pastoral service, to proclaim once again the Church's universal call to conversion, spiritual renewal and holiness. And be sure that the same Holy Spirit who has placed you as Bishops to shepherd the Church (see Acts 20:28) is ready to utilize your ministry to help those who were called by him to a life of perfect charity, who were repeatedly sustained by his grace and who have given evidence of a desire—which must be rekindled—to live totally for Christ and his Church in accordance with their proper ecclesial charism. In the local Churches the discernment of the exercise of these charisms is authenticated by the Bishops in union with the Successor of Peter. This work is a truly important aspect of your episcopal ministry, an aspect to which the universal Church, through me, asks you to attach special priority in this Jubilee Year.

4. As an expression of my solidarity with you in this area of your pastoral service, acknowledging the special links between Religious life and the Holy See, I am hereby appointing Archbishop John R. Quinn of San Francisco as Pontifical Delegate to head a special Commission of three Bishops *whose task it will be to facilitate the pastoral work of their brother Bishops in the United States* in helping the Religious of your country whose Institutes are engaged in apostolic works to live their ecclesial vocation to the full. Associated with him in the Commission are Archbishop Thomas C. Kelly of Louisville and Bishop Raymond W. Lessard of Savannah. Working in union with the Sacred Congregation for Religious and Secular Institutes and following a document of guidelines which the Congregation is making available to them and to you, the Commission has authority to set up a suitable program of work which, it is hoped, will be of valuable help to the individual Bishops and to the Episcopal Conference. I would further ask the Commission to consult with a number of Religious, to profit from the insights that come from the experience of religious life lived in union with the Church. I am confident that the Religious of contemplative life will accompany this work with their prayers.

In asking the Commission to be of assistance to you in your pastoral ministry and responsibility, I know that it will be *very sensitive to the marked decline in recent years in the numbers of young people seeking to enter Religious life,* particularly in the case of Institutes of apostolic life. This decline in numbers is a matter of grave concern to me—a concern which I know that you and the Religious also share. As a result of this decline, the median age of Religious is rising and their ability to serve the needs of the Church is becoming increasingly more limited. I am concerned that, in a generous effort to continue manifold services without adequate numbers, many Religious are overburdened, with a consequent risk to their health and spiritual vitality. In the face of this shared concern, I would ask the Commission, in collaboration with Religious, utilizing the prayerful insights of individual Religious and major superiors, to analyze the reasons for this decline in vocations. I ask them to do this with a view to encouraging a new growth and a fresh move forward in this most important sector of the Church's life.

And in addressing the many issues affecting the consecrated life and ecclesial mission of Religious, these Bishops will work closely with you, their brother Bishops. Besides having as an aid the document on the salient points of the Church's teaching on Religious life prepared by the Sacred Congregation for Religious and Secular

Institutes, *you and they will have my full fraternal and prayerful support.* The *ad Limina* visits of the American Bishops will truly offer an excellent opportunity for you and me to speak personally about the pastoral service that we wish to render together in the name of Jesus, Chief Shepherd of the Church and Redeemer of the world.

By requesting that this call to holiness, to spiritual renewal and to conversion and penance be initiated during the Jubilee Year of the Redemption, I am trusting that the Lord Jesus, who always sends laborers into his vineyard, will bless the project with his redeeming love. The power of the Holy Spirit can make this call a vital experience for all who respond to it, and *a sign of hope for the future of religious life in your country.* May Mary the Patroness of the United States, the first of the Redeemed and the model of all Religious, support your episcopal ministry with her motherly prayer, so that it may come to fruition, bringing renewed joy and peace to all the Religious of America, and offering ever greater glory to the Most Holy Trinity.

From the Vatican, the Solemnity of the Resurrection, April 3, 1983.

## LETTER TO THE BISHOPS OF THE UNITED STATES
### NOVEMBER 4, 1986

To my dear brother Bishops in the United States of America,

1. As you are gathering in Washington for your annual Meeting, I wish to be spiritually present with you in order to support you in your pastoral ministry. I wish to assure you of my fraternal solidarity with you as you work and toil, day in and day out, to bring the Gospel to your people. At the same time I wish to encourage you, in the midst of the challenges and difficulties, to place all your trust in our Lord Jesus Christ, "the chief Shepherd" (1 Pt. 5:4), who is always with his Church. My desire in addressing you is motivated by my own ministry as Successor of Peter and therefore as the first servant of *the Church's unity and universality.*

I would like at this time to reflect with you, the pastors of the particular Churches in the United States, on some aspects of this Petrine ministry. Although it is indeed burdensome, it is made lighter by God's grace and by your fraternal collaboration and your prayers, and for all of this I am deeply grateful.

The very *mystery of the Church* impels us to recognize that the one, holy, Catholic and apostolic Church is present in each particular Church throughout the world. And since the Successor of Peter has been constituted for the whole Church as Pastor and as Vicar of Christ (see *Lumen Gentium,* 22), all the particular Churches—precisely because they are Catholic, precisely because they embody in themselves the mystery of the universal Church—are called to live in communion with him.

*Our own relationship of ecclesial communion—collegialitas effectiva et affectiva—*is discovered in the same mystery of the Church. It is precisely because you are Pastors of particular Churches in which there subsists the fullness of the universal Church that you are, and must always be, in full communion with the Successor of Peter.

To recognize your ministry as "vicars and delegates of Christ" for your particular Churches (see *Lumen Gentium,* 27) is to understand all the more clearly the ministry of the Chair of Peter, which "presides over the whole assembly of charity, protects legitimate variety, and at the same time sees to it that differences do not hinder unity but rather contribute to it" (*Lumen Gentium,* 13).

To promote the universality of the Church, to protect her legitimate variety, to guarantee her Catholic unity, to confirm the Bishops in their apostolic faith and ministry, to preside in love—all this is what the Successor of Peter is called by Christ to do. This *Petrine service* by the will of Christ is directed to the good of the universal Church and all the ecclesial communities that compose her.

For this reason I endeavor to be of service to all the Bishops of the Church, so that together as one College, each of us having a different role, we can all serve the Church of Christ in the distinctive ministry assigned to us as Bishops.

It is an awareness of my own role in the Church, and especially in regard to her unity and universality, that has prompted me to do everything possible *to confirm my brother Bishops* throughout the world in their own collegial ministry. In several specific ways I have tried to be of service to you, my brother Bishops in the United States, placing my full trust in you and counting on your collaboration.

2. Because of the great importance of seminary training, and with the intention of assisting you in one of your greatest responsibilities for the Church, I called for an *Apostolic Visitation to the Seminaries* in your country. This project was entrusted to Bishop John Marshall of Burlington. He in turn shared the responsibility with many competent collaborators, who visited seminaries throughout the country, consulting at length with the Rector, the staff and the students of each institution. The aim of the entire project was to do everything possible to ensure the ever more faithful application of the Second Vatican Council to seminary training. The Visitation met with splendid cooperation and interest, beginning with the Bishops of the seminaries visited. Bishop Marshall has conferred with the Holy See on a number of occasions, and I wish to thank him again for all his dedicated work. My thanks go also to the different teams that worked so generously with him, and to the seminaries themselves.

Already the first phase of the Visitation his been completed. The Congregation for Catholic Education has made its suggestions and comments, and has expressed great satisfaction for all the good that has been accomplished in the process. Cardinal Baum has informed you and myself of all the positive results and of the recommendations made. There are still other phases to be completed, and further implementation to be made, but the manner in which the Visitation was conducted *renders honor to the Church in the United States and gives great hope for the future.* I am convinced that many people were open to the grace of the Holy Spirit and that our collegial enterprise has been blessed by the Lord.

3. Another way in which I endeavored to be of service to the Church in the United States was through the *Pontifical Commission for Religious Life* that I established in 1983, naming Archbishop John Quinn as Pontifical Delegate and Archbishop Thomas Kelly and Bishop Raymond Lessard as members. The task of these Bishops, as I explained in my letter entitled *In This Extraordinary Holy Year* was "to facilitate

the pastoral work of their brother Bishops in the United States in helping the Religious of your country whose Institutes are engaged in apostolic works to live their ecclesial vocation to the full." I asked "the Commission to consult with a number of Religious, to profit from the insights that come from the experience of Religious life lived in union with the Church." I likewise asked the Commission to be concerned for the decline of Religious vocations and "in collaboration with Religious, utilizing the prayerful insights of individual Religious and major superiors, to analyze the reason for this decline in vocations." All of this was requested "with the view to encouraging a new growth and fresh move forward in this most important sector of the Church's life." Although it was my decision to undertake this work, it had also been suggested to me by American Bishops who had foreseen its usefulness.

This Commission worked very hard to help you *to render special pastoral service to the Religious of your Dioceses and your country,"* as I had requested. As it worked closely with you, the Commission reported to me on various occasions. I am very grateful to Archbishop Quinn, Archbishop Kelly and Bishop Lessard for their protracted and devoted collaboration. I am likewise deeply thankful to all of you, the Bishops of the United States, for your own response. It was indeed a wonderful response of personal generosity and collegial collaboration toward the pastoral goal of encouraging "the Religious, their Institutes and associations to live fully the mystery of the Redemption, in union with the whole Church and according to the specific charism of their religious life." My deep appreciation goes also to the Religious themselves, who have so generously worked with you in response to the Church's call.

After over three years of constant work by the Pontifical Commission, I have now received its final report. I have likewise received the many letters that you the Bishops wrote me as *testes fidei,* concerning religious life in your Dioceses. This report and these letters shall continue to be studied, and I shall be subsequently in a position to give you a response.

Although the work of the Pontifical Commission has been completed, *the pastoral ministry and responsibility of the Bishops for religious life remain,* and I would ask all of you to exercise this mission of yours in accordance with the above-mentioned letter of mine and the document attached to that letter, *Essential Elements,* which is a summary of the Church's teaching on religious life. In thanking you for your solidarity and collaboration in this question of immense importance for the Church in the United States and for the universal Church, I also thank our Lord Jesus Christ who has permitted us, working together in the pastoral ministry, to be of service to his Church.

4. With great joy I am now looking forward to *my Pastoral Visit to the United States,* which is to take place September 10 to 18, 1987, and which will include Miami, Columbia in South Carolina, New Orleans, San Antonio, Phoenix, Los Angeles, Monterey and San Francisco. I regret that I am not able to accept at this time the many other invitations that I received. I shall however be deeply united spiritually with all your particular Churches at the time of my coming.

The aim of my Pastoral Visit is *to celebrate with you our unity in Jesus Christ and in his Church,* to proclaim Jesus Christ and his Gospel, and to confirm you all in faith and love. I look forward to being with all the priests, deacons, Religious, seminarians and laity, and I shall rejoice in seeing once again firsthand "your work of faith and labor of love and steadfastness of hope in our Lord Jesus Christ" (1 Thes. 1:3). I look forward to visiting your fellow Christians, your fellow believers and all Americans of good will.

Meanwhile, dear brothers in the Episcopate, let us continue to reflect on the great mystery of the universal Church and all the particular Churches that share her life and unity. It will be for all of us a source of joy and strength, of courage and confidence. Let us thank the Lord Jesus who has called us to shepherd his people in his name, and with him "to gather into one all the scattered children of God" (Jn. 11:52).

Once again I commend you and all your people to the Immaculate Virgin Mother of God, Patroness of the United States, and in the love of Christ Jesus I send you my Apostolic Blessing.

From the Vatican, November 4, 1986.

# Index

Abortion: From the moment of conception life is sacred, 76, 114, 473–74; Defined by Second Vatican Council as "abominable crime." Spawns other social injustices, 265

Civilization, Effect of Abortion on: Disregard for the sacred character of life in the womb weakens the very fabric of civilization, 276. *See also* Euthanasia; Family, Christian; Genetic Engineering

Ecumenism and: United stand for human life, 277

International Increase of: and decline in the protection of unborn human life, 473

Afro-Americans: Black Catholic community in the United States is a sign of hope for society and of the Church's catholicity, 173, 175

Evangelization and: Black Catholic cultural gifts as tools for evangelizing, 172, 173, 175–76; The family is the first setting of evangelization, 173; Catholic schools contribute profoundly to evangelization of Afro-Americans, 174–75; Laity and the mass media, evangelize, 175; Black cultural heritage as an instrument of the Holy Spirit to, 175

Vocations Among: Black community must support vocations to the Religious life and priesthood, 172; Black Religious give witness to the Church and society, 172

Anti-Semitism: Collaborative Catholic-Jewish studies help to understand roots of anti-Semitism, 147–48. *See also* Ecumenism, Jewish-Catholic Dialogue.

Art, Media Influence: Media helps citizens profit from culture, 175, 255. *See also* Culture, Media's Effects on; Journalism.

Atheism: To those who have lost faith in God, know that there is hope and peace in Jesus Christ, 5; Can be caused by believers who fail to reveal the Incarnate Word, 449

Birth Control. *See* Family.

Bishops: The bishop calls to the priesthood, 49; Support human rights and human dignity, 75–76; Bishops support marriage and family life, 275; and seminary training, 280, 375; The bishop and ecclesial unity, 292, 388, 499; The common mission of bishops, 375, 377; The bishop is the sign of the love of Jesus Christ, the Good Shepherd, 384; the bishop is the sign of Christ's compassion, 385; and the charism of the People of God, 385, 418; Bishops proclaim salvation and are signs of prayer and submission to the Father's will, 387; The choice of bishops is as important today as was the choice of the Twelve by Jesus, 387; The bishop, like Christ, is a sign of contradiction, 388; The bishop is a living expression of Christ, the Incarnate Word, supreme revealer of the Father, 404; Lives of bishops revolve around Christ's mandate to the Apostles—to teach everything He commanded, 405–6; The bishop thanks God for the mystery of Christ's Cross and Resurrection as it is lived in the Church, 415; Bishops, pastors united in ecclesial communion, offer to Jesus, the Supreme Shepherd, the entire Church in the United States, 420; and individual confession, 429, 435. *See also* Family.

Abortion, Euthanasia and. *See* Abortion; Civilization, Effects of Abortion on; Euthanasia; Family, Christian.

Catholic Truth and: Holiness of Truth, speaking clearly but in love, 73–79; Bishops and Catholic universities, 108, 195, 197, 272, 409–10, 413; Bishops are assisted by the responsible scholarship of Catholic theologians, 108, 471; Bishops monitor and safeguard the Christian authenticity and unity of faith and moral teachings, 128; Bishops are witnesses to Christ's Cross and Resurrection, 265; One loyalty, to the Word of God, entrusted to the College of Bishops, 267–68; Bishops as authentic teachers of the faith, 271, 374; Unite generations in the faith, 272; Must explain vision of marriage to the laity, 274–76, 399, 401; Duty to proclaim moral life and practice, 281–82, 385; Signs of fidelity to Church teaching, 386; Principal catechists, 450

Evangelization and. *See* Evangelization

Family and. *See* Family